Autocracy, Capitalism, and Revolution in Russia

Autocracy, Capitalism, and Revolution in Russia

Tim McDaniel

UNIVERSITY OF CALIFORNIA PRESS

Berkeley • Los Angeles • London

University of California Press
Berkeley and Los Angeles, California

University of California Press, Ltd.
London, England

Copyright © 1988 by The Regents of the University of California

Library of Congress Cataloging-in-Publication Data
McDaniel, Tim.
   Autocracy, capitalism, and revolution in Russia.
   Bibliography: p.
   1. Labor and laboring classes—Soviet Union—History.   2. Soviet Union—
Economic conditions—1861–1917.   3. Labor policy—Soviet Union—History.
I. Title.
HD8526.M385   1987   322.4'2'0947   86-30790
ISBN 0-520-05532-2 (alk. paper)
ISBN 0-520-06071-7 (pbk.)

Printed in the United States of America

1   2   3   4   5   6   7   8   9

To my mother

Contents

Acknowledgments

It is a pleasure to be able to acknowledge the help of the many people, organizations, and institutions that were indispensable for the completion of this work. Most important to me has been the continuing intellectual and psychological support of Victoria Bonnell, who read and tolerated the first inadequate formulations of these ideas and encouraged their development in countless ways. It would have been a much poorer work without the benefit of her knowledge and judgment. Reginald Zelnik's encouragement has been more important than he probably realizes. William Kornhauser provided crucial intellectual guidance in the early stages of this project and served as the chair of my dissertation committee. Elbaki Hermassi, Neil Smelser, and Harold Wilensky all contributed to this work in numerous ways while I was at Berkeley. Various incarnations of the ideas and the book have been discussed and evaluated by Daniel Chirot, Peter Gordon, Jeff Haydu, Henry Landsberger, Daniel Levy, Lars Lih, Andrew Scull, Gerald Surh, Carlos Waisman, and Jeff Weintraub. Elise Kimerling, David Mandel, and Gerald Surh were kind enough to share their then unpublished work with me, and I appreciate their generosity. I am grateful to Ruth Carr, Elizabeth Otero, and Kevin Walsh for research assistance, and to Stanley Holwitz, my editor at the University of California Press, for his support and wisdom. (I hope he is wrong, though, in his belief that "fat books have no legs.") Lois Smith did a skillful job of copy editing.

IREX supported an academic year of research in the Soviet Union in 1980–1981, an enormously enjoyable and profitable experience for me intellectually and personally. Various institutions in the Soviet Union provided me with help far beyond what I would have expected. Most important was the assistance I received at the Central State Historical Archive in Leningrad. The staff there could not have been more cooperative. Also of great help were the Central Government Archive of the October Revolution in Moscow; the Public Library and Library of the

Academy of Sciences in Leningrad; and the Historical Library and the Lenin Library in Moscow. In the United States I want to acknowledge the aid of the Hoover Library, in particular of Hilja Kuk, who was always kind and helpful. The Russian Institute of Columbia University granted me the privileges of a visiting scholar in the summer of 1980.

The generous help and encouragement of all these people and institutions demonstrate once again that scholarship is a collective enterprise.

Notes on Dates and Transliteration

All dates are given according to the Julian calendar, which is thirteen days behind the Gregorian calendar in the twentieth century. The Russian calendar was changed to the Gregorian (Western) system in February 1918.

I have used the Library of Congress system of transliteration, except in cases of well-known names and places with a familiar Western form (for example, Axelrod, Chernyshevsky).

CHAPTER
1

Introduction: The Proletarian Revolution in Russia

The political revolution in France and the Industrial Revolution in England mark the beginning of the modern age—the age of revolution. In no other period of human history have so many societies undergone violent and dramatic alterations in their social structures, cultures, and political systems; and never before has the myth of revolution become so widely accepted. The underlying sources of revolutionary change are multifarious, including the rise of centralized states, the cultural influence of the West, colonialism, the rise of market economies, and industrialization. Similarly, the range of revolutionary actors has been virtually universal, embracing both traditional and modern social groups: displaced religious elites, various sectors of the middle class, peasants, craftsmen, and industrial workers.

Marxism, the most politically consequential theory seeking to explain the sources of modern revolutions and identify their main actors, paid special attention to one process, industrialization, and one revolutionary group, the industrial proletariat. In most great twentieth-century revolutions, however—including the Mexican, Chinese, Vietnamese, Cuban, and Iranian cases—industrialization had either negligible or secondary significance. Correlatively, in none of these countries was the industrial proletariat even remotely the most vital revolutionary force. Workers have, of course, played a prominent part in a number of revolutionary situations, including 1905 and 1917 Russia; Germany, Hungary, Italy after World War I; republican Spain; and Allende's Chile. Except for 1917 Russia, however, all of these revolutions failed, partly because of divisions within the labor movement and insufficient worker radicalism.

The reasons the Marxist model were unable to identify the main revolutionary processes and actors in the modern world have been well explored in numerous theoretical and historical works. In advanced Western countries the processes of social and political integration have softened the class cleavages that Marx argued would be fatal for capitalist societies. By contrast, in a great many Third World countries industrialization has not been profound enough to restructure society, and industrial workers have formed part of the relatively privileged modern sector, courted by governments even before they could press their claims as an independent force.

Only for Russia can it be plausibly maintained that an industrial labor movement was the pivotal revolutionary actor and that the process of industrialization was the wellspring of the revolution. This is not to say that the Russian revolution was in any uncomplicated sense a proletarian revolution. Indeed, the identification of any great revolution with a single social class is an unwarranted, though common, oversimplification.[1] Rather, the Russian revolution, like other revolutions, was a concatenation of overlapping revolutionary processes, to some degree independent of but all feeding upon and influencing one another. If the events of 1917 were partly a proletarian revolution against capitalism and private property, they also constituted a peasant revolution against the landed elite (but not against private property in land as such), a soldiers' rebellion against their officers, a number of national rebellions against Russian dominance, and even a "bourgeois" revolution against the autocratic state. The rhythm of the revolution, from February to October to victory in the Civil War, would undoubtedly have been different if any one of these processes had been absent.

Yet despite the multilayered character of the Russian revolution, the thesis of the hegemony of the proletariat has much to recommend it in the Russian case. Stripped of a certain metaphysical element, that the proletariat in some deep sense stood for the exploited classes as a whole, Lenin's and Trotsky's arguments on this point essentially ring true. Though dwarfed in population by the vastness of rural Russia, the urban centers—particularly the capital—occupied a preponderant place in the politics of the empire. As embodiments of, in Trotsky's words, "the fundamental tendencies of the new society,"[2] they were the focus of political life, industry, trade, and modern communications. Modern industry, though still lagging far behind the advanced European countries and the United States, had made great strides in the 1890s and in the years before the outbreak of World War I. Russia was by no means a modern industrial country, and its per capita income remained much lower than that of its European rivals, but in gross output it still ranked among the major industrial producers of the world.[3]

Industrialization gave rise to an important core of modern factory workers in the main cities, particularly St. Petersburg and Moscow. (In 1913, the capital had roughly 230,000 factory workers, an increase of 44 percent since 1908. Moscow's industrial proletariat numbered approximately 160,000, a 31 percent increase over the same period. The main category in the capital was metal and machine industry workers [95,000], whereas in Moscow the textile industry was the main employer [66,000 workers]).[4] These urban industrial workers, often of peasant origin, had economic and political significance far beyond what their mere quantitative weight in the society as a whole would have given them. On various occasions mass strikes and, in 1905, a radical proletarian revolutionary wave shook the regime and exposed its rotting foundations.

The industrialists, by contrast, historically had been economically and politically thwarted and so were incapable of leading the "bourgeois" revolution against the autocracy in order to establish their own social and political dominance. The peasants, though potentially revolutionary, were without political initiative or independent leadership. Finally, the soldiers lacked revolutionary traditions, experience, and ideas; and although, as Trotsky was willing to admit, "the heavyweight peasant garrison decided the outcome of the struggle,"[5] he is surely right to insist that it did not lead or shape the revolution.

The workers constituted the main social base of the Bolsheviks in October, and far from being led in any simple sense by the party, they often accelerated the tempo of events beyond the party's wishes. Further, the party frequently had to take account of the independently expressed wishes of workers and their organizations in its deliberations. For these reasons it makes sense to conclude, with Smith, that "it was the organized working class, not the Bolshevik party, which was the great power in society."[6] Only the October insurrection itself was primarily the action of the party leadership, and even then the overriding concern was the mood of the Moscow and Petrograd workers. In early September Lenin referred to the planned action as "an insurrection by the Peter and Moscow workers," and on that basis claimed—erroneously—that "the majority of the people support us."[7] Similarly, the main argument advanced by his more cautious opponents within the party leadership was that the workers were not sufficiently mobilized or organized. Much more remains to be said about the interaction between political parties and workers, a complex theme that rules out any simple formulas. Of the significance of a partially independent revolutionary labor movement before and during 1917, however, there can be no doubt.

The aim of the following chapters is to describe and explain the genesis and nature of this very rare historical phenomenon, a victorious revolutionary labor movement. To assert the existence of an authentic workers' movement in the revolution is perhaps even more controversial than to insist upon the significance of workers as a social category in the revolution, for it endows Russian worker protest with a degree of continuity and organization that is often denied it. It is often assumed, because of the severity of tsarist repression, that no coherent movement was ever able to emerge among the workers, and, as a consequence, for many scholars the history of socialism in 1917 is equivalent to the history of the revolutionary parties.

It is undeniably true that with respect to established organizations and a shared proletarian culture, the Russian labor movement suffered greatly by comparison with the more established Western European movements. As will be discussed in part III of this study, however, in the last three decades of tsarist rule the hallmarks of a distinct social movement were plainly present. There were patterned roles, established leaders, an accumulation of organizational experience, models and traditions of collective action, elements of a shared political culture, and a mounting sense of affiliation to a movement. After the 1905 revolution all of these were buttressed by a profound sense of the political significance of the labor movement. Discontinuities in all of these traits also became part of the pattern of the movement, which expressed itself in extreme ebbs and flows rather than through established organizational channels.

Many of the traits that made the Russian labor movement look less like its counterparts in Europe also made it more revolutionary. It was revolutionary not primarily in the sense that Russian workers consciously willed revolution more than did workers in France or Germany, but rather in the basic assumptions of its mass base (many of these formed by the autocratic state and essentially traditional), in its organizational structure, in its characteristic patterns of collective action, and in the nature of its leadership. Consciously willed or not by the majority of workers themselves, worker protest had an internal dynamic that led it to challenge the social and political power structure. Conversely, the structural bases for moderation were extremely weak. Often reduced to silence by the tsarist state, the Russian labor movement made up for its absence of voice by tremendous outbursts of militancy at uneven intervals.

If worker protest before the October revolution should be interpreted within the context of an identifiable social movement, it follows that the role of workers in 1917 was rooted in the prior development of the labor movement. The political assumptions, patterns of action, and forms of organization of the labor movement in 1917 were all connected to the movement's past history and social characteristics. For this reason the proletarian revolution of 1917 is interpretable partly in terms of the pattern of industrialization in Russia that had shaped the prerevolutionary labor movement. It was not the war alone or the dynamics of the revolutionary situation that accounted for the radicalization of industrial conflict during the revolution; it was also in a deeper sense the pattern of Russian industrialization as a whole as it had shaped the interrelations of urban social groups and the state.

The preceding statements imply the utility of a classical logic for the analysis of the urban revolution in Russia: to link industrialization, the rise of movements of social protest, and the process of revolution; or, more generally, to analyze revolution in terms of the social movements engendered by the contradictions of the old regime. Despite obvious differences in theoretical perspective, this is the logic followed by Tocqueville, Marx, and structural functionalism. In recent years it has come under attack from two different directions in sociology. First, Charles Tilly and his followers have questioned the value of approaches centered on the model of structural contradictions, preferring to emphasize the relative resources of the contending actors, including the state. A revolution occurs when the balance of forces shifts away from the state so that a major contender can establish a situation of dual power. Tensions, contradictions, and disequilibria exist in all modern societies; what distinguishes revolutionary situations is the differential opportunity for collective action.[8]

By contrast, Barrington Moore (in *Social Origins of Dictatorship and Democracy* but not in *Injustice*) and Theda Skocpol downplay the importance of social movements in revolution, focusing on variables such as elite coalitions, the breakdown of the state, and the impact of international relations. They do not deny that social forces become mobilized during revolution, Moore stressing the peasantry and Skocpol, both the workers and the peasants.[9] Their highly structural approaches, however, lead them to deemphasize the independent impact of lower-class social movements, and indeed to pay little attention to the revolutionary process itself. Skocpol goes furthest in this respect, summarizing the lessons of her book with the formula: "Revolutions are not made. They come."[10]

In following the classical logic the present study analyzes revolution in a different way from either structural theories or Tilly's collective mobilization approach, for it aims to integrate structure and action by showing how fundamental contradictions shape social movements and how social movements both emerge from and exacerbate old regime crises. An analytical model of the contradictory combination of autocracy and capitalism in Russia will be developed to illuminate the relation between the state and the industrial elite, as well as the interaction of both of these with the working class and the labor movement (the latter including nonworkers, primarily the intelligentsia, as well.) The ambiguities born of the autocratic state's sponsorship of capitalist development, and the correlative weakness of both political and economic elites, help explain the state's repressive labor policy, which almost completely prohibited the development of mass worker organizations. Thus one of Tilly's crucial variables—organization—can itself be explained in terms of a model of structural contradictions as these shape the actions of the state and social elites. Similarly, this model illuminates the sources of both the state's and the capitalist class's increasingly weak legitimacy, a crucial variable—even, it might be argued, a resource—that shapes the propensities for and the goals of protest. In this sense a short-term analysis of the revolutionary situation in terms of contenders and their resources can be integrated with an appreciation of the historical and structural determination of these resources. It is misleading, in my view, to analyze organized action apart from the "structures" that shape it.

Just as structural contradictions help determine the resources and goals of social movements, so social movements help define class and political relations. Structural explanations that fail to take account of the impact of collective action on "structures" run the risk of reification and miss important dimensions of the role of social movements in social change. Aside from their obvious significance as mass bases for parties and elites, a role that allows them to alter the balance of forces, sometimes decisively, social movements have a number of other social and political effects. For example, they help to define the image of the social base they represent both for the mass base itself and in the eyes of other groups, including opponents. Thus in Russia there was a "working class" partly because there was a labor movement, and the perceptions of this working class on the part of government officials and employers were in large part shaped by the movement. Given that concepts and perceptions are constitutive of social life and not appendages that can be detached from "harder" realities such as institutions or structures, social movements help to crystallize class and political relations.

These perceptions and relations in turn shape elite policy, that of both the state and employers. For example, because of the role of the labor movement in the 1905 revolution and the elite perceptions of the working class that emerged from (or were reinforced by) it, elites were unwilling to permit trade unions to develop freely despite the potential for moderation they showed.[11] This policy had a decisive impact on the radicalization of the labor movement and the position of the working class in Russian society. In the same way, the nature of the labor movement shaped the perspectives of the intelligentsia and, correlatively, the relationship between party and class. The rival Menshevik and Bolshevik interpretations of the role of the labor movement in the 1905 revolution deepened their rift and conditioned the relations between both factions and the workers.

To insist on the decisive role of social movements in revolutions, then, is not to commit the fallacy of voluntarism; it is to stress that "structural" relations cannot be understood apart from collective action and perceptions. The role of the state, the relation between the state and the indus-

trialists, class relations, and party-worker relations were partly determined by the nature of the labor movement, which was also shaped by its
position in this set of relations. It is difficult, then, to speak of the independent role of the labor movement, for it was defined only through its
relations with other groups. Correspondingly, it is misleading to analyze
the urban revolution without an appreciation of the labor movement as a
constituent part of this complex set of relations, which was the social
matrix for the various possible outcomes of the revolution.[12]

The urban revolution in 1917 Russia has inspired an enormous number of debates and interpretations. The great majority of these have been
less sociological than historical: whether the revolution would have
taken place without the war; the significance of Lenin's leadership; the
errors of the Provisional Government; the nature of the Bolsheviks' man-
date, and so on. The major sociological interpretations tend to cluster
around two central poles, one rooted in Marxist class theory and the
other in mass society theory. According to the first, Russian industrialization, whatever its historical peculiarities as compared with the Western
European model, gave rise to a revolutionary class movement led by the
advanced sectors of the working class (particularly the metalworkers in
large-scale industry) and the Bolshevik party. This view found its classic
expression in Trotsky's *History of the Russian Revolution*, and in broad
outlines it continues to be the foundation of Soviet historical orthodoxy.
In the West it has found sophisticated elaboration in the recent work of a
number of social historians of labor.[13]

Whereas this first perspective emphasizes capitalism and class, the rival
interpretation centers on the importance of autocracy and the immature
worker masses. From this second standpoint, originally developed by
Mensheviks and embraced by a great many Western historians and
sociologists, capitalism in Russia was too young and the autocracy too
repressive to allow a mature working-class movement to emerge.
Bolshevism drew its strength from uprooted peasants and angry young
workers who were susceptible to the most irresponsible slogans. The
Bolsheviks seduced the worker masses, who were too callow to have
any firm political values and assumptions of their own.

In the following chapters I develop an alternative interpretation of
worker radicalism based on a synthesis of elements of class and mass
radicalism. This highly explosive combination can be traced to the combined effects of capitalism and autocracy and also to the interaction
between them, which hindered reform. It is this contradictory pattern of
development that provides the key to the emergence of a revolutionary
labor movement and therefore helps to explain the distinctiveness of the
urban revolution in 1917.

The logic of this book is essentially sociological, although it presents a great deal more historical detail than is usual in sociological studies of revolution. It is sociological in that it presents and illustrates a general way of looking at revolution, and also a theoretical explanation for key features of the Russian revolution. Further, along with the detailed analysis of a particular case, it suggests and makes use of relevant comparisons with other countries in order to buttress the argument. Indeed, the preoccupation with what Weber called the "historical individual" did not preclude but rather has necessitated a comparative perspective. Thus a comparative thread—or, rather, various comparative threads—can be found to run through this study, as the Russian experience is contrasted with those of European and Third World industrializing countries. At the same time, the systematic development of these comparative themes would have led to an entirely different kind of study with a different purpose.

The overall sociological interpretation has inevitably shaped the selection of topics and questions. Some issues that would have been more central in a chronological and descriptive account have thereby been slighted. For example, in the section on labor policy I mention the many insurance projects discussed by elites after the 1905 revolution only in passing, for they are not germane to my comparative question: why was the tsarist government so singularly unable to permit the development of worker organizations? Similarly, my analyses of the "mass" and "conscious" workers are intended to be ideal-typical: I am less interested in, say, changes after the 1905 revolution or during the 1912–1914 period than in how the continuing exclusion of Russian workers created a labor movement defined by these types and their interaction with each other and the intelligentsia, as compared to the roles and types characteristic of, for example, England or Germany. A final example: in the chapter on worker organizations my goal is less an exhaustive description of forms of organization and changes in them over time than an ideal-typical analysis of the distinctive pattern of revolutionary organization in Russia. In all of these examples I trace the peculiar features of the Russian context to the larger structural traits of autocratic capitalism. The survival of this system ensured a large degree of continuity in government policy and basic traits of the labor movement, and if I have not always attempted to describe nuances within the basic patterns, I hope to have given at least a synoptic view of the patterns themselves—these, I deem, give the Russian revolution its general sociological interest.

The study is divided into four parts, not according to chronology but by virtue of the logic informing the work as a whole. Part I includes a general overview of the chief traits of the model of autocratic capitalist industrialization and a theoretical analysis of the implications of this pattern for the Russian labor movement. Part II demonstrates how the failure of tsarist labor policy can be understood in terms of the model of autocratic capitalist industrialization, thus linking structural contradictions and policy. Part III describes the structure and basic traits of the Russian labor movement as these were shaped by government policy and the contradictions of the system. My aim is to describe and explain the uniquely revolutionary character of the Russian movement. Finally, part IV illustrates how the historical patterns of political and class relations illuminate the process and outcome of the 1917 revolution, not rigidly determining it but nonetheless providing the matrix of likely possibilities. From this perspective the Bolshevik victory was by no means inevitable, but it was not simply a putsch without deep social roots. To understand these social foundations of the revolution through an analysis of the distinctive comparative traits of Russian development: this has been my central aim.

PART I

THEORETICAL AND COMPARATIVE PERSPECTIVES

CHAPTER
2
Autocratic Capitalism as a Model of Industrialization

In the past few decades enormous scholarly interest has been shown in the comparative study of industrialization and its social and political correlates. Sociologists, historians, and political scientists have recognized the limited generalizability of the Western European experience and the theories built upon it and have proposed a number of alternative paths and outcomes of development. Among the most important of these efforts are Gerschenkron's analysis of "backwardness," Kerr and his colleagues' typology of modernizing elites, Moore's study of class coalitions and their implications for social change, and the efforts of dependency theorists to uncover the consequences of structural dependency in the world economy.

A number of these typologies were obviously constructed with the Russian experience in mind and have illuminated a great deal about social change in Tsarist Russia. For the purpose of explaining Russian development and the nature of Russia's urban revolution, however, none of these models or theories seems satisfactory. For example, the explanation of social movements and revolutions is only marginally within the purview of Gerschenkron's analysis of backwardness; Moore underestimates the significance of the urban revolution in Russia and concentrates on the failure to modernize agriculture and the weight of agrarian class relations; and dependency theory, in its focus on international structures and exploitation, has not yet been fruitful for understanding internal processes of social change.

In the following pages I propose a model of Russian industrialization based upon the contradictions between capitalist economic institutions and autocracy in the political realm. These contradictions shaped the relationship between the state and the capitalist elite, created conflicts and ambiguities within both the state bureaucracy and the capitalist class, and thus hindered efforts to develop and apply new principles and policies to deal with the working class and the labor movement. In addition, it was within this context of autocracy, capitalism, and the paralysis of elites that there emerged a revolutionary labor movement that threatened both economic and political stability and thereby made reform all the more difficult. In numerous ways—in its structure, organization, patterns of leadership, and political orientation—this movement bore the imprint of its origins in this contradictory system. Further, this whole complex of contradictory institutions, paralyzed elites, and a revolutionary social movement decisively shaped the 1917 revolution, which must be partly interpreted in the light of this previous pattern of development.

Thus the model of autocratic capitalism will permeate the analysis throughout, applicable alike to questions of large-scale social organization and to aspects of intergroup relations and even individual lives. The assumption behind this method is that the meaning and import of the various parts of society, and the processes of social change, can be understood only in relation to the fundamental traits of society as a whole.

Although based on the Russian case, this model employs abstract sociological ideas about capitalism and autocracy, and so is fundamentally comparative. In practice, the combination of these two sets of institutions is extremely rare, for very few truly autocratic regimes have survived into the modern world and even more exceptionally have they permitted or sponsored capitalist industrialization. Weber was convinced that Russia was a doomed species, for the powerful penetration of Western ideas was decomposing the "patriarchal Communist conservatism."[1] The only similar case that comes to mind is Iran under the Pahlavis, but an analysis of the Iranian experience would also have to take account of a much higher degree of foreign influence than in Russia.[2] Nonetheless, despite the dearth of relevant cases, the model can still be used analytically in order to make comparisons with contrasting patterns of development, and, in Louis Dumont's sense, it is universal without being general.[3]

The contradiction between autocracy and capitalism was one aspect of the more general contradiction between tradition and modernization in Russia. Since the time of Peter the Great the Russian state, under pressure from the West, had been promoting social and economic modernization while seeking to maintain the stability of autocratic power. Western ideas, modern education, the rise of new social classes, and economic development had all widened the breach between state and society and also augmented pressures for political change. Social elites, at first mainly disaffected members of the nobility and later various middle sectors (many of whom would come to constitute a socially heterogeneous "intelligentsia"), spearheaded these demands for change, which took a variety of forms. The rapid capitalist industrialization of the late nineteenth century gave birth to two new social classes with new demands and sources of power, and further accelerated this long-term corrosion of the autocratic political model. Thus in one sense capitalist industrialization was part of the broader conflict between state and society in Russia, but it was also distinct. Modernization and the emergence of civil society posed the question of the general struggle against autocracy and advanced social elites to the leading oppositional roles. Industrialization and its social consequences certainly fueled this conflict, but they also raised the issue of class struggle within civil society and how this latter process in turn was shaped by the autocratic state.

The connection between these two master processes, modernization and industrialization, and their interrelations with Russian autocratic traditions was one of the main themes of social thought in the last decades of tsarist rule. Conservatives, liberals, and radicals addressed these issues, sometimes with surprising results. For example, many reactionary thinkers rejected the combination of modernization (including Westernization and political reform) and industrialization as interrelated corrosive processes, but others, such as the arch-conservative Pobedonostev, were convinced that industrialization could strengthen the country's economy without entailing political reforms. He thus felt that there was no contradiction between capitalist industrialization and autocracy.

Many populist opponents of both the absolutist state and modernization also saw autocracy and industrialization as mutually reinforcing; but unlike Pobedonostev, they rejected both and dreamed of the pre-Petrine Russian community. By contrast, the important "legal populist" thinker Vorontsov embraced autocracy and industrialization but rejected capitalism, advocating instead state-sponsored industrialization that would ensure social equality. The autocratic state might thus pave the way for socialism. "Let us hope," he said in a memorable phrase, "that it will be Russia's destiny to bring about equality and fraternity, though she is not destined to fight for liberty."[4]

No Marxist opposed industrialization or celebrated the advantages of the autocratic state, but Mensheviks and Bolsheviks came to very different conclusions about the desirability of modernization and the emergence of civil society. Orthodox Menshevism accepted the revolutionary role of the capitalist class and foresaw a long process of deepening of the bourgeois revolution. The struggle of society against the state took temporary precedence over the class struggle. By contrast, Lenin was extremely hostile toward liberalism and feared that the consolidation of a modern liberal system would prevent the triumph of socialism. Modernization and the bourgeois revolution were antagonistic to class conflict and the socialist revolution, a manifest rejection of the relationship posited by Marx.

With the benefit of hindsight, a number of conclusions may be drawn about these various viewpoints. First, conservatives who, like Pobedonostev, believed that capitalist industrialization did not threaten the foundations of autocracy were clearly mistaken. Second, those who hoped that the contradiction would be resolved through the suppression of only one of the two poles—capitalism for Vorontsov, autocracy for the Mensheviks—also miscalculated. The revolution, when it came, would eliminate both at virtually the same time, for they had severely weakened each other despite their mutual dependence. In this respect, it was Lenin who foresaw that the movement based on class conflict would be more politically decisive than the movement based on modernization and opposition to the autocratic state, and that the urban revolution would be socialist, not "bourgeois," in essence.

In order to understand the ascendancy of the proletarian over the liberal dimension of the urban revolution, the special contradictions of the process of Russian industrialization, which exacerbated class conflict, must be separated from the more general tensions inherent in modernization, which pitted society against the state. Precisely this is the aim of the following model of autocratic capitalist industrialization, the purpose of which is to analyze how autocracy and capitalism, in their fateful interdependence, undermined each other and thus prepared the ground for a revolution against both.

AUTOCRACY VERSUS CAPITALISM

The moral, religious, sociological, and political underpinnings of capitalism, in the sense of both the forces that made possible its rise and those that must be present to sustain it, have been classic themes of social theory. The presence of certain kinds of religious ethos; the political independence of city-states; an orientation toward time as historical rather than cyclical; the opportunities opened up by the discovery of the New World; a deep-seated rationalistic approach to the world; secularization, including the separation of church and state—all these and more have been adduced as causes of and sometimes prerequisites to capitalist industrialization. In the study of such large and complex and ultimately perhaps unanswerable questions, cause and effect become mingled in discouragingly intricate patterns. It is difficult to separate the essential from the accidental. Particular historical causes are hypostatized as general patterns or laws.

Subtle critiques have been made of the logic and assumptions of many such studies.[5] And yet there is danger in going to the opposite extreme, in which structure is dissolved into strategy. Not all social and political institutions are equally propitious for capitalist industrialization, and some may even prevent it altogether. It is legitimate to inquire into the interrelations between a capitalist economy and different social institutions, as did such classic nineteenth-century sociologists as Marx and Weber.

To minimize the risks involved in this kind of analysis, its scope will be limited here in two respects. First, I will deduce certain minimal implications of capitalist relations, ones that are tied to vital aspects of capitalism in a rather clear-cut way. Undoubtedly there are other conditions that nurture capitalism, some of them perhaps more important than those I have chosen. Yet the traits I will single out are particularly relevant because of their tensions with an autocratic political regime. Second, I will not argue that the absence of these conditions makes capitalist industrialization impossible. After all, capitalist industrialization did take root in Russia and, had it not been for the war, might possibly have overcome the obstacles inherent in Russian politics and society. Rather, my aim is to point out tensions whose political consequences for labor policy and the development of the labor movement will be described in the following chapters. This analysis helps illuminate the fate of capitalism in Russia; it does not imply that its destruction was inevitable.

The strength and legitimacy of capitalism depend upon a triad of institutions that were poorly developed in Russia because of its autocratic political structure: private property, law, and contract. Without these there were no firm bases for entrepreneurial initiative and authority, without which capitalists were hesitant to take risks and workers reluctant to obey without compulsion. The fear and timidity of employers interacted with the challenges of workers to turn a political context already highly unfavorable for reform into an intractable one.

THE LEGITIMACY OF PRIVATE PROPERTY

Modern capitalism, like all other types of economies, depends upon a stable system of property, but, as compared with other economic systems, the institutional context of capitalism gives rise to new challenges because of the greater differentiation of the economic and political realms. The medieval European manor or the traditional Indian estate was both a political and an economic unit, and "private property" was part of a whole political and economic system. There was no separate ownership as a purely economic phenomenon, and property rights were linked to social and political status.[6] In pre-Petrine Russia property was especially strongly connected to the political realm, for it was granted by the tsar in order to enable loyal elites to serve him. In theory, control over landed property could be revoked at the tsar's discretion, for he was the judge of service.

European feudalism provided a much firmer foundation for the development of private property than did Russian patrimonialism, for the elite in Western Europe had always enjoyed a measure of economic and political independence denied to the Russian nobility after consolidation of the Muscovite state.[7] It is true that in Russia Peter and his successors enacted a number of reforms to buttress private property and make landholding more secure for the nobility, no longer linking it to state service. For example, Peter made estates hereditary and indivisible; further, by the end of the eighteenth century the tsars had granted the nobility full property rights, at the same time eliminating their compulsory service obligation to the state. Thus the tsars attempted to achieve a degree of separation between political and economic power and also to legitimate private property in the economic realm. Despite this series of measures, however, in some respects private property was even more tenuous than the older service-linked property, for there was no longer any legal basis for it and its legitimacy was never accepted by the peasantry.[8] In addition, whatever the law, the nobility was still subject to the arbitrary will of the autocrat. Thus according to the great statesman and theorist Speransky, as late as the early nineteenth century "property itself has no firm basis in any respect whatsoever."[9]

By the late nineteenth century part of this heritage had been overcome, but much of the traditional popular and governmental hostility toward private property had survived. In addition, the property rights of the industrial capitalist were weakened from a number of new directions. From the virtual beginnings of modern industry in Russia, the state had played a key role in creating and subsidizing factories. Industry was thus frequently seen as an artificial creation of the state, but even those who rejected this judgment had to admit that Russian industry depended upon state subsidies of many kinds.[10] On what basis, then, was the Russian capitalist's property legitimate? Few in Russia could accept the liberal myth of appropriation (that the possession of property was the result of individual efforts, either by oneself or by one's ancestors) or the belief that the economic mechanism apportions rewards according to relative contributions. Marx may have had to struggle against such ideas among workers in Western Europe, but in Russia the workers, intelligentsia, and much of the state bureaucracy had already been converted.

Capitalist private property was also undermined because of the nonelite or foreign origin of so many of the industrialists and because of the crucial role of foreign capital in Russian industrialization. (In 1900, roughly 28.5 percent of the capital of private companies was foreign-owned, a figure that had risen to 33 percent by 1913.)[11] Broad sectors of Russian society saw the factory owners as parasitic outsiders who had no legitimate claim to the favors they received. Hostility toward the industrialists as an upstart class was particularly widespread among the traditional elites. Similarly, all social groups, including native capitalists, felt enmity toward the foreign entrepreneurs. Even native entrepreneurs could not escape the suspicion that they were somehow foreign to the true Russia, that they undermined basic Russian traditions in fundamental ways.[12]

In autocratic Russia the capitalist's property was thus quite tenuous, threatened from above and below. It could only have been legitimate in the context of a civil society that was beginning to emerge and of beliefs that had not yet congealed. He was still a capitalist, though, and there was no traditional basis for the legitimacy of his property. The practices of the Russian state did not help: we will see threats coming from the government to expropriate factories because of charges of exploitation of workers or poor management. These were seldom carried out, but they caught the popular imagination because of their resonance with traditional standards of justice. Anticapitalism among workers would thus come to have both conservative and radical dimensions, rejecting private property in the name of the implicit ideal of the service state as well as for the sake of socialism. This fusion of ideals was a logical counterpart of what Weber, as early as 1906, called the "patriarchal Communist conservatism."

THE WEAKNESS OF LAW

Dominated by the patrimonial authority of the autocratic ruler, and without traditions of either feudal contract or independent ecclesiastical law, medieval Russia lacked crucial antecedents for the emergence of a modern legal system. The changes introduced by Peter and the demands for a more coherent administrative structure created pressures for more explicit legal norms to regulate relations between state and society and among different government bodies. Similarly, the rise of the Russian gentry in the eighteenth century led some nobles to demand the guaranteed rights of a true aristocracy. Would-be reformers such as Nikita Panin (in his *Discourse*) or, a few decades later, Speransky, appealed to their rulers to protect the aristocracy through laws safeguarding its freedom and property. Such measures would have entailed the replacement of the autocratic system by a monarchical regime.[13]

The modernization of Russia in the last half of the nineteenth century led many government officials to recognize the essential role of law and a modern legal system in regulating social relations as well as relations between the state and the increasingly complex society. Officials could see that changes in European societies and the United States had been accompanied by significant innovations in areas such as property law and the law of contracts. Many realized that if Russian society were to equal the dynamism of its competitors, social groups would have to be able to act on the basis of expectations grounded in legal guarantees. Despite serious reverses, pressure for legal reform was thus a significant current both within and outside government from the time of the great reforms (the 1860s) onward.

Because all of these pressures and tendencies for legal reform conflicted with the fundamental nature of autocratic rule, the rule of law made only limited headway in late Tsarist Russia. Whole areas of law crucial to capitalist development, such as contract law, remained undeveloped pending innumerable discussions in the various organs of state. Further, no matter how many formal concessions the last tsars may have made, even when these were enacted as law, the government often failed to respect them. Civil judicial procedures were adopted in the reform era, but the government never really accepted them, relying on administrative procedure whenever convenient. The distinction between law and administration, so crucial in a liberal political system, remained vague in practice, and the autocratic state refused to recognize the judicial norms that it had itself enacted.[14] The autocracy's violations of the law were neither accidental nor restricted to marginal issues, as evidenced by its violation of the October Manifesto, the constitution wrenched from Nicholas II in the last months of the 1905 revolution. The resulting hybrid was described by the Almanach de Gotha as "a constitutional monarchy with an autocratic Tsar."[15]

Paradoxically, it seemed that any formal gains won against autocratic power only encouraged the state to be more arbitrary in the assertion of its challenged authority. As Wortman remarks, "it was difficult for the ruler to maintain his former image as champion of the law. Shedding the guise of absolute ruler, guardian of the rights and welfare of the population, the last two tsars tried instead to resume the role of patriarch, personal and religious leader of the nation."[16] Prerevolutionary Russia thus embodied a contradictory synthesis of an incipient modern legal system and traditional autocratic arbitrariness. The former did little to buttress the position of the elites or to further the development of civil society as a relatively independent sphere. The latter increasingly undermined itself and the integrity of the social structure that it ultimately wanted to safeguard.

THE FRAILTY OF CONTRACT

The strength and legitimacy of capitalism also depend upon acceptance of the institution of contract. For if the labor contract is truly acknowledged as morally binding, the result of free agency, the acceptance of authority is based upon exchange. From Durkheim we know that the validity of contract depends upon noncontractual assumptions that make it sociologically real as an agreement. Without these, contract will not be seen as an act of will committing both sides to honor it, not just out of advantage but also out of conviction.

Contract in this sense depends upon trust.[17] Trust, in turn, is rooted in familiarity and predictability.[18] Beyond these general prerequisites the institution of contract can have either individualistic or hierarchical foundations. In the former case, individuals regard themselves as free agents, and submission to authority through contract is linked to an ideology of merit justifying unequal power and rewards. One of the best examples of these connections is the Puritan idea of calling.[19] Men and women were called upon to be active instruments of God's will, to be "serviceable," making use of their skills and initiative. Work became the "self-affirming activity of the godly," a matter of conscience, not just necessity. According to Walzer, this new view of work "opened the way to responsible and impersonal commitments among men. Obligation in the work-a-day world formed the basis for a wide network of contractual arrangements."[20] These included social hierarchy, for God "organized men as he organized angels: through a division of labor in a chain of command."[21] Later, during England's Industrial Revolution, a secular ideology of equal opportunity and achievement through merit took root among the English working class and provided the moral basis for entrepreneurial authority.[22] Inequality of outcomes in the liberal model of contract is thus founded on an activist conception of the individual and presumed opportunity for the meritorious.

Contract can also be grounded in hierarchical assumptions that dispense with the idea of equality of opportunity and individual initiative. Inequality is equitable because elites are regarded as inherently superior, and by virtue of their special resources and capacities, their solicitude and protection benefit the lower orders. These were the traditional principles underlying social relations in premodern Europe and other hierarchical social orders, and in some societies, such as Germany and particularly Japan, they survived into the period of rapid industrialization, thereby buttressing modern class relations. In such cases a contract embodying inequalities of power and reward was legitimate not mainly because it signified an act of free will in the interests of both parties but because inequality itself was presumed to benefit the weaker party. Nowhere did such hierarchical assumptions go completely unchallenged even before rapid industrialization, and certainly once this process began they were further weakened, in part because of their repudiation by elites. Further, they did not necessarily ensure social peace, for the violation of traditional expectations could be the most potent source of discontent and protest.[23] Yet these assumptions could also strengthen the consensual basis of contract when individualistic assumptions were weakly developed.

In autocratic Russia the enforced passivity of social groups and state-imposed barriers to interaction ruled out trust, having diminished familiarity and predictability. There was a gulf between classes and between classes and the state, a gulf made insurmountable by the restrictions on participation, open contact, and free activity. With little ability to calculate or rely upon the actions of the other side, both parties were denied the experience of the mutual fulfillment of expectations.

Further, potential individualistic or hierarchical underpinnings of contract were unsubstantial in capitalist Russia. Neither religious nor political traditions had inculcated the ideas of free agency and responsibility as norms of conduct, stressing instead the duty of unconditional submission. Merit in the explicit form of service to the state was an important basis of traditional elite legitimacy, but it was not easily transferrable to the modern Russia of social classes and private property, and in any case it had less to do with relations between social groups than with relations between social groups and the state. Similarly, social hierarchy as a principle penetrating social relations had always been more delimited in Russia than in feudal or postfeudal societies, for there was an egalitarian premise inherent in the basic concept of universal submission to the state. Just as the autocracy continually undermined the peasant's loyalty to the nobility, so it excluded strong hierarchical ties between worker and employer. The state, aware of the potential explosive consequences of this disjunction for its own position, preached that there was a continuous, ordained line of subordination from tsar through social elites to the lower orders, but the legitimacy of both rural and urban elites nonetheless remained tenuous.[24] Contract based on hierarchical principles could not take root in this barren soil.

These three deep-rooted institutional features of Russian society gravely weakened the legitimacy of capitalism and the position of the industrialists. Their effect was reinforced by considerable hostility from the state, the nobility, and public opinion (including even liberal public opinion, which might conceivably have been the industrialists' main source of support). Although many high government officials of various persuasions recognized the need for industrialization and accepted the indispensability of private entrepreneurs, the basic values of the governing elite were rooted in the vision of a stable, predictable society that could be controlled by the state. Contract and the market were "spontaneous" and so even they were distrusted, just as the typical official distrusted private action in the pursuit of personal interest in general. The ideal of a self-regulating society generating elites according to its own logic was beyond the officials' political imagination and was inconsistent with their basic political vision, which always stressed the primacy of state interests.

Like government officials, the Russian nobility also had contempt for the industrialists, just as they had traditionally despised merchants. In Western Europe the conflict between nobility and capitalist merchant-industrialist was stronger the more the nobility's status depended upon its relationship to the state. Germany was the classic case of noble-bourgeois rivalry—there it even had a regional basis. By contrast, in England the nobility had long been open to commercial pursuits and status was much more dependent on wealth. The new class of industrialists certainly met social resistance in nineteenth-century England, but it was relatively mild. According to Schumpeter, this relative tolerance allowed the bourgeoisie to benefit enormously from the continued rule of preindustrial elites: they ruled in the bourgeoisie's favor and accorded the state a kind of sanctity and stability that the bourgeoisie alone would have been unable to provide.[25] In late Tsarist Russia the economic position of the nobility had been so undermined that its only real buttress was its connection with the state, and there was continuous rivalry between the two social elites—landowning nobility and industrialists—for state favor. After 1905 the nobility waged a successful campaign to exercise greater political power, reversing the proindustry stance of previous governments and restricting the political participation of their rival elite.[26] These economic and political rivalries combined with traditional cultural prejudices to create a climate of condenscension and hostility toward the industrialists.

Enterpreneurs in many industrializing societies have been excoriated by public opinion for the sins of a single-minded pursuit of profit and insensitivity to the misery of their workers. To these virtually universal themes public sentiment in Russia added several additional indictments connected with the relative backwardness and dependency of Russian industry: that the industrialists were not dynamic enough, that they were an artificial creation of the state, and that they were in league with foreigners and betraying the interests of Russia for their own gain. On some combination of these themes traditionalist could agree with modernizer, conservative with radical. As a consequence throughout the last decades of tsarist rule, and particularly in times of revolutionary crisis, the industrialists felt isolated from and abandoned by society as a whole. Russian industry, they would lament in 1917, had no home.

In the context of these various sources of weakness, decisive government influence over the affairs of industry was virtually inevitable, and although this may sometimes have helped the industrialists in the short run, it also robbed them of independence and legitimacy and created uncertainty in the overall social, political, and economic climate surrounding them. Indeed, government policy often contradicted the interests and desires of the industrialists. The withdrawal of many government subsidies and favors to industry after 1905 has already been mentioned. Similarly, government officials frequently criticized the industrialists for insensitivity to the workers' misery and threatened to intervene in labor disputes on the side of the workers. The state also did much to inhibit the organization of the industrialists as an interest group, fearing that they might become too independent of government control. Such considerations are at the heart of Weber's analysis of the lack of fit between patrimonialism and modern industrial capitalism:

> Material and personal innovations, new classes that are not sanctified by tradition, new kinds of acquisition and enterprise that run counter to tradition, are in a very precarious situation and at the least exposed to the arbitrariness of the ruler and his officials. Both traditionalism and arbitrariness affect very deeply the developmental opportunities of capitalism.[27]

Weber emphasizes the economic consequences of patrimonial rule upon the action of the industrialists: hesitancy to take risks, inability to make calculations, and thus disincentives to investment. Just as important were the social and political implications of a capitalist system deprived of its main potential sources of legitimacy. The Russian industrialists, correspondingly weakened in their legitimacy and fearful of the future, had too little confidence in themselves to take risks or extend trust. In these circumstances important sectors of them became powerful opponents of reform in labor relations, supplementing the profound obstacles to change inherent in the autocratic political structure.

CAPITALISM VERSUS AUTOCRACY

For Montesquieu, despotic governments were distinct from either republics or monarchies because of their lack of connection with society. State and society were completely split apart, and despotic princes "have nothing to regulate either their own or their subjects' hearts."[28] Around despotic power "there is an absolute vacuum."[29] This made despotism less stable than other forms of government, for it could not count upon an elite with an interest in preserving stability. Civil wars were more likely under monarchies, for there were potential sources of rival power, but revolutions were much more common in despotic governments, where change had to be complete: "Thus all our histories are full of civil wars without revolutions, while the histories of despotic government abound with revolutions without civil wars."[30] Nothing kept a despotic government in power other than its subjects' fear. No principles commanded the loyalty of the population, and so despotic governments by nature were corrupt.

By contrast, Weber argues that the very absence of a feudal (or independent aristocratic) elite in pure patrimonialism forces it to develop ties with broader sections of society. Without an elite to support him, the ruler is more vulnerable to unrest (Montesquieu agrees) and must take other measures to shore himself up (Montesquieu denies this possibility).[31]

Weber, then, affirms what Montesquieu denies: that autocracy does have a social logic. Let us draw together the elements of this logic in order to show how capitalism corrupted them.

Montesquieu, like Hobbes, held that fear was at the root of despotism. For Montesquieu, however, this was primarily the subjects' fear of the ruler, whereas for Hobbes it was mainly the subjects' fear of one another. Hobbes's ideas suggest that one source of the stability of absolute rulers is the subjects' fear of chaos. For Hobbes, chaos and internal war were the natural state of society. Perhaps it is more appropriate to argue that autocracy, by isolating social groups from one another and limiting free association, is itself a source of the friction that social groups fear.[32] As Tocqueville writes, "the segregation of classes, which was the crime of the late monarchy [in France], became at a late stage a justification for it. . . . [The country was] incapable of administering itself, and it was needful that a master should step in."[33] As we will see, this fear of chaos in general and the masses in particular was one of the abiding sentiments of the middle and upper sectors in Russia and helped cement them to the regime despite considerable distaste for it.

The atomization of society well suited the tsarist state because it hindered the initiative and internal solidarity of social groups. Ideally, society was composed of isolated groups of petitioners incapable of generalizing their specific demands to create the basis for broad oppositional movements.[34] These social demands should be purely economic rather than political, and they should not be ideologically formulated. Given these conditions, each atom could be directly linked to the center. The nature of the tie is supplied by the ideology of above-class protectionism: the idea that the government is better able to protect the true interests of social groups than they themselves are through their own actions. In such a context, political rights are unnecessary because the tsar directly satisfies the just aspirations of the population.[35] Thus the open struggle of social forces will be reduced to a minimum and replaced by a protectionist relation of each of them to the higher authorities.[36] To fulfill this logic, the state must oppose the assertion of independence even by the elites.

The state must eliminate elite autonomy for another reason as well. We have seen that one of the main traits of an autocracy is fear of an independent elite. In order to minimize this danger, autocracy has a populist side: "Against the dangerous aspirations of the privileged status groups patriarchalism plays out the masses, who everywhere have been its natural following. . . . The 'welfare state' is the legend of patrimonialism."[37] The elite is kept in check by the autocrat's hold over the people's loyalty through such popular images as the "good tsar." The tsarist government itself preached to the common people that it protected their interests through curbing the greed of the nobility and bourgeoisie. This paternalistic ideology particularly flourished during the nineteenth and early twentieth centuries, when the tsars recognized the danger that they would lose the loyalty of their people. With such fears and concerns, Nicholas I formed his Third Deparment, the elite corps of secret police, whose purpose was expressed in the following instructions to his staff officers by Count Benckendorff, the first great *eminence grise* of the department: "Every man will see in you an official who through my agency can bring the voice of suffering mankind to the throne of the Tsars, who can instantly place the defenseless and voiceless citizen under the protection of the Sovereign Emperor."[38] The theme of the state, and especially the person of the tsar, as patron of the exploited and suffering lower classes was also one of the most popular motifs of Zubatovism (see the following chapter). Nor was it confined simply to government officials. It took a long time to die among workers and peasants. And it was even an ideological strain among revolutionary populist intellectuals. The young Chernyshevsky wrote of the monarchy as follows:

> [It] must stand above all classes, and is specially created to protect the oppressed, i.e., the lower classes, the peasants and the workmen. The monarchy must be sincerely on their side, must be at their head and protect their interests. Its duty is to use all its energies to work for future equality—not a formal equality but real equality. . . . To my way of thinking this is what Peter the Great did.[39]

Thus many populist revolutionaries saw capitalism as a greater danger than tsarist absolutism, not understanding that the project of capitalist industrialization made the realization of this autocratic utopia quite out of the question. Just as autocracy undermined capitalism, so, in two major ways, capitalism subverted the logic of autocracy and sapped its legitimacy. First, it created the potential for class formation, in the sense of both class identity and class action in the pursuit of shared interests. It did this through the processes described by Marx and many other thinkers: the aggregation of large numbers of people in factories, the growth in literacy, urbanization, the exposure to socialist ideas, and so on. Workers and industrialists were no longer content to have their interests represented and defended by the government, and in response to government attempts to keep them atomized, they themselves insisted on asserting them. Such a transformation forced the government to respond according to its nature: the independent, collective action of the workers, and often of the industrialists too, was repressed. Gradually the workers became disabused of the idea that the government cared for their welfare, despite all its pronouncements to the contrary.[40] Paradoxically, the assertion of autocratic norms and the use of repression actually helped group formation by affirming the identity and increasing the solidarity of the classes being formed by industrialization. The more the government tried to curtail group formation in the name of its tutelary principles, the more it reinforced group identity and undercut its own ideology. In the new circumstances of modernizing Russia, the autocracy weakened itself the more it remained true to its own principles.

The government came into conflict with the workers for another reason. No matter how hostile it may have been toward capitalism and particularly the capitalists, it was still committed to the capitalist industrialization of the country. It simply could not follow through on the populist promises that it made. This is one of the major lessons of the failure of the Zubatov experiment. No government committed to industrialization can sacrifice its industrializing elite, and this is all the more true when this elite is weak and beleaguered from all sides. As much as the government reviled the capitalists for their egoism, it could do little to defend the workers from it. The arbitrary will of the autocrat was limited by the impersonal purpose of industrialization, a project that nullified patriarchal norms and robbed them of their vitality.

Not only capitalist industrialization undermined the integrity of the autocratic model of rule. All the changes that took place in nineteenth-century Russia—the influx of new ideas from the West, the introduction of truncated reforms, the emergence of whole new social categories—had similarly corrosive effects. Capitalist industrialization played a particularly large role in undercutting the autocratic model as it was applied to the labor question and so is of particular significance for this study.

AUTOCRATIC CAPITALISM AND THE LABOR QUESTION

Late Tsarist Russia was thus an uneasy combination of capitalism without a suitable political framework and autocracy without the kind of social policy that might have given it legitimacy. As will be seen in part III, this combination was decisive in shaping the nature and course of the Russian labor movement. In addition, it created intractable problems for tsarist policy toward the labor question. The government was paralyzed by contradictions, and its inability to act in a matter that it knew was of critical political significance created many of the conditions that fostered a radical labor movement. In the following pages I present a general argument linking autocratic capitalism to the government's failure to cope with the labor question. In part II I make use of these ideas to analyze government policy and its dilemmas in detail. Thus the model of autocratic capitalism will be used to illuminate actual government policy-making.

A few qualifications are necessary at the beginning. First, I am not proposing an all-encompassing explanation for government inaction. Partly this can be traced to autocratic political institutions alone, apart from the program of capitalist industrialization. Because of the inadequate development of administrative law, tsarist governments were composed of rival satrapies, each ministry uncoordinated with the others and often pursuing contrary aims.[41] The situation became even more serious in periods of pressure for change, and particularly when change was as dangerous as in the reform of the court system or in the labor question. Yet beyond these obstacles stemming from a poorly organized and ineffective bureaucracy, the special dilemmas arising from the project of autocratic capitalism were of great significance.

Second, in pointing to the implications of these political contradictions for labor policy, I do not thereby mean to suggest that failure was inevitable. Rather, the model serves to identify certain persistent dilemmas that greatly complicated the adoption of any effective labor policy. In the absence of commitment perhaps commensurate with Alexander II's dedication to the emancipation of the serfs, there was little chance of success. The government's repeated failures even when the need for decisive measures was obvious testify to the profound systemic constraints on reform.

By the turn of the century many important government officials were aware of the need to develop new policies toward the working class. There had already been a few decades' experience with strikes, and socialist ideas were making more inroads among the workers, particularly in St. Petersburg, politically the most vital area. The urgency of reform was recognized at the highest government levels—for example, at the Special Conference held in March 1902.[42] It unanimously recognized the necessity of the development of factory legislation "as soon as possible," a conclusion that had also recently been reached by the Ministry of Interior. It was widely assumed that the tsarist state would be able to act expeditiously to protect the workers' interests because of its greater autonomy from social forces. Sipiagin, a high official later to become Minister of Interior, referred to the "complete independence of our government," and Witte alluded to the "single Will above the struggle of parties and private interests."[43] In fact the tsarist state proved to be virtually impotent.

GOVERNMENT INCOHERENCE

One of the main sources of the government's impotence was administrative incoherence aggravated by the project of autocratic capitalism. Governmental disarray was evident on the ideological as well as organizational levels. Throughout the last decades of tsarist rule everything was in flux. Western ideas and institutions had been imported but not assimilated. The traditional models had decayed but not entirely so, and many conservatives hoped to revive them. These conflicting views of the future of Russia could be seen not just in the labor question but also in the debate over the peasant commune. On one hand conservatives favored traditional institutions because they were presumed to maintain patriarchal relations and prevented the emergence of a landless peasantry. Reformers criticized their economic inefficiency and wanted to stimulate the creation of a prosperous peasantry as a bulwark for the autocracy.[44]

In labor policy the debates were parallel. Some officials favored a basically liberal model, with considerable leeway for the two classes to struggle on the basis of their own interests. This point of view was persuasively argued in the Federor Commission's report on revising labor legislation (mid-1906):

> Factory life is extremely complicated, and the regulation of it in no case can be accomplished only through government interference by means of factory inspection and police. In this matter it is essential to place both sides in such a situation so that neither of them can outweigh the other. From this flowed the necessity to allow the workers themselves to organize with the goal of self-defense and the improvement of their situation.[45]

It is interesting to note that it was the government that was to ensure an equilibrium of forces, even if this violated their relative social weight. The paternalistic tone of this passage suggests that bureaucratic liberalism included a significant admixture of traditionalism as well, and that the conflict between rival sets of principles was pervasive, dividing ministries internally as well as against each other, and even making individual officials somewhat schizophrenic.

Such relatively liberal ideas had many enemies. Appealing to themes deeply rooted in the autocratic tradition, skeptical opponents distrusted independent action by social groups and urged the state to take responsibility for superintending class relations. They opposed trade unions and strikes in favor of government regulations and police interference. And they rejected any suggestion that industrial relations could take shape partly on the basis of a social logic internal to them, without the overriding control of the state.

Such conflicts were not confined to government officials. The industrialists, too, were deeply split over the desirable degree of worker independence, and even many workers continued to be attracted by a paternalistic model of state protection. Further, the tension and uncertainty were within individuals just as much as among them. In a context of such rapid change, who could be certain of the best path? Witte himself is a good example of such ambivalence. He was devoted to autocracy yet equally committed to the rapid capitalist industrialization of Russia. In 1885 he could write in a Slavophile publication of the degrading effects of Western capitalism, urging that Russian workers be allowed to maintain their rural ties and advocating labor legislation and attention to the spiritual needs of the workers.[46] Yet in a famous secret circular of December 1895 he defended capitalism from a traditionalist standpoint, asserting that "in our industry a patriarchal cast of relations between masters and workers predominates. This patriarchal quality is expressed in many cases by the concern of the factory owner for the needs of his workers and employees in the factory, in care for the maintenance of harmony and agreement, in the simplicity and justice of their interrelations."[47] A few years later, in 1902, he adopted the opposite viewpoint, arguing that strikes were a "completely natural phenomenon, organically tied to contemporary economic conditions of industrial life."[48] Perhaps the best example of his divided mind was his ambivalence over the 1905 political reforms for which he had argued so forcefully and which would be politically fatal for him.[49]

The most famous and significant organizational expression of this ambivalence was the long dispute between the two major ministries—Finance and Internal Affairs—over a whole range of issues connected with labor policy. Basically the Ministry of Finance took a liberal view, whereas Internal Affairs was committed to continued government regulation, although such a broad generalization does not do justice to the significant ambiguities and debates within each ministry. (These will be discussed at length in part II.) Concrete disputes arose over such issues as the proper sphere of activity of the factory inspectorate, the role of the police, and the desirability of legalizing strikes. Beginning in the late 1890s, the disputes led to charges and countercharges, to inconclusive agreements, and to authoritative conferences whose decisions, when there were any, were seldom obeyed. One of the best examples of the difference in principle was the conflicting attitude toward the Zubatov experiment, which will be described in chapter 4.

As the two competing views took shape they became more ideological. The importation and influence of liberal ideas made the old autocratic model more extreme. Its adherents turned it into an ideology, which more and more lost touch with social reality. Liberal ideas, too, came to be rigidly defined through the process of conflict, whereas in England, their original home, they had emerged gradually as part of a whole process of change. Consequently, the government was all but paralyzed in the resolution of an issue crucial for its survival. It had no firm principles or ideas with which to face the modern world, one source of the "terrifying spiritual poverty" of the regime of which Max Weber wrote after the 1905 revolution.[50]

THE WEAKNESS OF THE STATE AND INDUSTRIALISTS

The process of autocratic capitalist industrialization weakened both the state and the industrialists. The state truly became, like Montesquieu's despotism, suspended in a void, with virtually no social base outside of an ambivalent and decaying nobility. Enough has already been said of the congenital weakness of the Russian industrialists.

In such circumstances elites are loath to take risks. Reform is more acceptable to strong states and classes, for they are more confident that they can weather both the changes and the aspirations for more change to which reform gives birth. In Russia government officials and the industrialists insisted that the salutary changes that reform might have brought about should precede the reforms themselves. Thus before legalizing unions they wanted worker organizations to be nonpolitical. Before recognizing worker leaders in strikes they wanted the leaders to be moderate. They were unwilling to take the risk that such characteristics would develop only after reform, and so they made reform all the more difficult.

Their weakness had other consequences for labor policy as well. Because the industrialists' economic and social position was so fragile and yet at the same time crucial for the goals of the regime, the state was severely compromised in its independence. It could not adopt many protective measures to benefit the workers because, as the Ministry of Finance pointed out tirelessly, this would more deeply undermine the position of the factory owners. Further, the government was frequently forced to intervene in industrial conflicts on the side of the employers, who could count on neither their own strength nor the workers' acceptance of an elementary set of rules of controlled conflict. Paradoxically, then, the state was wedded to the industrialists in large part because it undermined their position. Autocratic claims made protective measures all the more difficult to enact in practice. This was the paradox of autocratic capitalism: the state was even less independent than in other types of capitalist systems precisely because it claimed to be autonomous. In no other pattern of industrialization was the promise of labor reform broken so completely and dramatically.

Because of their own weakness, the factory owners had to depend upon the state to maintain order—a dependence that debilitated them further. Much as they might proclaim the need for political reform during times of ferment, ultimately they felt themselves to be wedded to the autocratic state.[51] For there was nothing beyond this to bind the workers to them, just as the state could count on little voluntary loyalty. Thus starting in late 1905, when the revolutionary threat was at its height, most factory owners openly cooperated with the government in its program of repression of the labor movement. Voices for reform continued to be heard, but they were in the minority. In the factories the behavior of management mirrored that of the state. No more than the tsarist officials could the industrialists conceive of the worker as a citizen with rights. In Russia, noted one observer, "the entrepreneur sees the worker as a rightless subject," and "the very thought about the equality of rights of the sides in any sense horrifies not only the honorable estate of factory owners, but also the governmental sphere."[52] It need only be added that these sentiments stemmed from their weakness at least as much as from their presumption of superiority.

The complex relations between the tsarist state and the industrialists in the area of labor policy will be discussed in greater detail and with more nuances in part II. Behind this complex interplay of forces and opinions a common theme can nonetheless be discerned: how the weakness of both sides narrowed their perceived options and tied them to each other in preserving the contradictory system that continued to debilitate them. For this reason, despite important signs of a tendency toward moderation and accommodation among organized workers in 1906 and 1907, neither the state nor the factory owners could act on the basis of their long-term interest in a stable institutional structure.

COMPARATIVE PERSPECTIVES

The logic of this analysis of autocratic capitalism suggests a general approach to the comparative study of industrialization. Instead of beginning with a typology of elites, as Kerr and his colleagues have done, in order to explain numerous variations in industrializing societies,[53] the first step is to develop a model of the interrelations between political and economic institutions. From such a model inferences can be made about the interrelations of social and political elites (including the agrarian elite) and the strategies they will adopt to confront the challenges of industrialization. All of the previous factors largely determine the response of the working class to industrialization, which depends more upon the action of elites and the constraints they impose than upon any inherent characteristics of their own, although it is also true that the pattern of working-class action helps to shape elite responses. An analytical model of the interrelations of state and economy thus makes it possible to order and interrelate a range of variables and so can be the basis for a typology. Each type would have an associated elite structure and strategy and a correlative working-class response, all of which help explain basic patterns of social change.

From this perspective the Russian model of industrialization approximates a type that may be contrasted with other types in terms of structural contradictions, configurations of elites, working-class responses, and patterns of social change. The two basic elements of the typology are the form of the state and the nature of the industrial elite. For capitalist societies three major types other than autocratic capitalism may be discerned. The first of these corresponds to what might be called *liberal industrialization*, a type best represented by England. The state is relatively differentiated from society and not the motive force of industrialization. The industrialists are dynamic and self-confident, with considerable authority and legitimacy. The agrarian elite does not depend wholly upon the state for its status and therefore is relatively open to the claims of the emerging industrialists. In this overall context political leaders and social elites are receptive to reform, and the outcome is what Waisman calls accommodation of the working class, a key component of liberal democracy.[54] The labor movement develops in a reformist direction, with only relatively minor periods of challenge to the overall political and economic structure of the society.

The second type is best represented by Germany and Japan. Here state authority is much more paramount than in the liberal model, but in contrast to Russia, social elites are not so thoroughly undermined. Hierarchy pervades the social structure instead of being debased, as in Russia. In Germany the complex interweaving of princely and aristocratic authority through the bureaucracy in the period of enlightened despotism made possible the coexistence of both state and elite authority.[55] Later, in the nineteenth century, the industrialists entered the state-noble alliance as a weaker partner but still one with considerable leverage. Barraclough even argues that by the late nineteenth century the industrialists were really the dominant power in the country, although other scholars, such as Gerschenkron, still see the Junkers as predominant.[56] In any case, the German industrialists were strong enough to be the envy of their Russian counterparts.[57] Moore makes this contrast a central aspect of his explanation of fascism: in future fascist countries, "even if the commercial and industrial element is weak, it must be strong enough (or soon become strong enough) to be a worthwhile political ally. Otherwise a peasant revolution leading to communism may intervene. This happened in both Russia and China after unsuccessful efforts to establish such a coalition."[58] Moore maintains that in Germany and Japan feudal traditions survived together with a strong element of bureaucratic hierarchy. Russia and China were agrarian bureaucracies rather than feudal polities.[59]

Scholars of Japanese industrialization emphasize the close connection, even more than in Germany, between political authority and industrializing elites in the Meiji period.[60] Further, there was less conflict between agrarian and industrial elites.[61] Because of this greater coherence, there was not the threat to capitalist elites along Russian lines, nor was the state so compromised in its sponsorship of capitalism. As Moore suggests, feudal traditions are much more propitious for the legitimacy of capitalism than are autocratic ones.

Both Germany and Japan represent a type that may be called *feudal capitalism*. Both state and elites are relatively strong and legitimate. Because of authoritarian traditions, there is less willingness to accommodate the working class than in England, but the elites' strength gives them more flexibility than in Russia. The result is a complex pattern of repression combined with conciliation. The latter can take the form of protective government legislation as well as the toleration of some form of worker organization. In contrast to Russia, "feudal capitalist" regimes are able to make some response to the labor question, even if it is made up of contradictory elements. In addition, in the context of more pervasive hierarchical norms, industrialists in feudal capitalism are more likely to extend protection to their workers in exchange for loyalty than in Russia. Thus the working class does not remain so utterly outcast and rightless and the labor movement tends to be more quiescent (as in Japan) or reformist and divided (as in Germany).[62]

The third type may be called *dependent capitalist development*. In such societies the major economic actor is not an indigenous industrial bourgeoisie, because of the importance of foreign-linked commercial and industrial sectors. The national capitalist class is correspondingly weakened in its internal power and legitimacy, particularly because it is internally divided between national and foreign-linked sectors. This weakness does not stem from autocratic state power, however, for the state itself, though pervasive, is not capable of determining social relations. Instead, it acts as a power broker among highly fragmented elites and derives much of its centrality from this role. The state in dependent societies acts to conciliate the interests of the different sectors of the dominant economic elites—the traditional agrarian groups, the exporters, and the new industrialists—and to make up for its own political weakness it sometimes seeks the working class as an ally.[63] Dependent societies are "broken societies, 'dualized' and disarticulated, where the State is at the same time freer than elsewhere with respect to social forces and more fragile."[64]

In such societies elite strategies toward the working class vacillate. With the fragmentation of classes and the instability of state power, episodes of populist cooptation and unstable democracy alternate with periods of authoritarian corporatism. The state and the elites are too weak for more than isolated experiments with complete accommodation, but the state rarely has the wherewithal to engage in systematic repression. Attempts at cooptation are the most typical elite strategies, but policies shift toward repression when mobilization becomes too dangerous. The labor movement is relatively unstructured, neither accepting the dependent capitalist system nor becoming fully radicalized. These societies are characterized by social flux more than by social change, for their fragmentation and incoherence almost exclude real change just as much as real stability.

In none of these three types of industrialization was the state so unsuccessful in coming to terms with the labor question as in Russia, where the combination of a powerful state and a weak industrialist class hampered the development of even moderately successful concessions, particularly in the area of worker organization. In part II the tsarist state's vain attempts to fashion a coherent labor policy will be examined in light of this model of autocratic capitalism, keeping in view the comparative framework outlined earlier. This analysis in turn provides a critical point of departure for understanding the special character of the Russian labor movement and the 1917 revolution. Before turning to this detailed analysis of the tsarist state's labor policy, however, some consideration must be given to the social movement to which it vainly tried to respond.

CHAPTER
3

Theoretical Perspectives on the Russian Labor Movement

INTRODUCTORY REMARKS

Revolutionary labor movements have been very rare phenomena historically. Appearances and rhetoric to the contrary, revolutionary ideology and action have been only undercurrents in major European countries, at times of crisis appearing more significant than they really were. Even when it was outlawed and outcast (1878 to 1890) the German Social Democratic Party as a whole rejected uncompromising radicalism and instead embraced parliamentarianism. It is true that the left wing of mainstream Social Democracy (with Bebel as leader) saw no contradiction between moderate tactics and the victory of the immanent revolution. Yet the fact remains that whatever its rationale, the party did not act in a revolutionary way.[1] Similarly, in contemporary developing countries labor also has not been a revolutionary force, even when, as in Chile, on the surface it appeared to be so. This may not validate Huntington's claim that industrial workers in present-day industrializing countries play a more conservative role than they did during the industrialization of Europe, but nowhere have they displayed the kind of militancy and solidarity characteristic of Russian workers.[2]

Many good explanations have been advanced to interpret this departure from Marxist predictions. Scholars such as Marshall and Bendix trace worker moderation to the political incorporation of workers as citizens of the nation-state, with shared rights and responsibilities. Others, such as Michels and, more recently, Huntington (for Third World countries) and Shorter and Tilly (for France) emphasize how large-scale organization has transformed labor protest, making the labor movement a significant participant in national politics with commitments to the status quo. Finally, radicalism has been seen as basically foreign to the workers' mentality and so characteristic of labor movements only under special circumstances. Perlman, for example, posits a separation between the concrete goals of the workers for economic improvement and the abstract ideals of the intellectuals for political change. Unless hindered by political repression, the trade union mentality of the workers will eventually triumph over the imported ideas of the intellectuals.[3] Martin Malia expresses this view concisely:

> The protest of the workers (and indeed of the peasants or the bourgeoisie) is always specific, and ultimately reformist in nature. It is a protest which remains near to concrete grievances and precise remedies. . . . The masses want primarily to live, to achieve security, and ultimately to advance in terms of the situation in which they find themselves.[4]

The Russian labor movement was a major exception to the general tendency toward reformism, in practice if not in ideology, among labor movements. By the early years of the twentieth century it was the most class conscious and explosive labor movement in Europe, an inspiration to radicals outside Russia who were dissatisfied with the complacency visible in labor movements in their own countries. Russian labor militancy arose not from any peculiar psychological makeup of the Russian workers or of the revolutionary intelligentsia but from the structure, organization, and culture of the labor movement as shaped by government policy and the class and political structure of Russian society.

My approach to explaining the Russian labor movement is controversial in at least two respects. First, some deny the uniqueness of the Russian case by arguing that all labor movements are radical in the early stage of capitalism. The distinctiveness of Russia, they maintain, was that World War I interrupted the transition to mature industrialism and the workers' latent reformism could never express itself. It is as if the evolution of English labor history had been interrupted in the 1820s or as if German history had stopped in the 1880s, although even in these relatively militant periods I doubt that worker radicalism was comparable in any sense to the Russian case. In this view radicalism appears everywhere in the early stages of industrialization because the old patterns of hierarchy and subordination have disappeared without a new mode of integration to take their place. In much of Western Europe this temporary crisis was ameliorated through the development of a new complex of expectations and institutions: formal equality, citizenship, the democratization of the state and the extension of its role in softening class conflict, and ideologies of merit.[5] A new form of social contract between classes and between the state and social groups gradually emerged to replace the outmoded institutions of traditional society. If logically the argument seems teleological, it nonetheless illuminates much of the process of social transition in nineteenth-century Europe. By contrast, I maintain that the nature of the transition in Russia—the combination of autocracy and capitalism—gave a special character to the Russian labor movement that was not found in Europe in a comparable stage of economic development.

The second point of controversy is that not all scholars accept that there was a labor movement in Russia in any real sense, much less that it could be termed revolutionary. The concept of a social movement implies shared traditions and goals, a collective identity, historical continuity, patterned leadership, and a degree of organization. A social movement is not merely an aggregate of collective behavior but structured action with purpose and coherence. Seldom outside the Soviet Union has it been maintained that Russian labor protest displayed any of these traits to a significant degree. Contemporaries, too, were skeptical of the coherence and continuity of Russian worker protest. Government officials tended to ascribe strikes to economic discontent played upon by outside agitators, with little attention given to shared political perspectives or collective identities among the workers. Likewise, Russian socialists repeatedly lamented the spontaneity, unpredictability, and irrationality of Russian worker protest, identifying the revolutionary movement only with themselves and a small group of conscious workers. In the same vein, numerous scholars have traced Russian labor militancy to social breakdown, to hunger and war—that is, to immediate events that called forth incoherent, angry responses—rather than to the influence of a social movement. Thus in accounts such as Ulam's *The Bolsheviks* or Schapiro's *The Russian Revolutions of 1917*, words such as "crowd" and "mass" rather than class are used, and there is not the slightest suggestion of the existence of a social movement among the workers. By contrast, my contention is that there was an authentic labor movement, with continuity and pattern, in prerevolutionary Russia and that the nature of this movement helps to explain the course and outcome of the 1917 revolution. By European standards it was indeed a rather peculiar pattern, with a vulnerable foundation and more discontinuities. It was precisely these idiosyncracies, however, that made it more revolutionary. In fact, weak institutionalization and unevenness formed part of a distinctive pattern with its own established modes of action and continuity.

To insist upon the social movement dimensions of Russian labor protest and to trace the revolutionary traits of the labor movement to the structural context of autocratic capitalism is in no sense to deny the significance of specific economic and political events. Military catastrophe and its political implications without doubt set the stage for the 1905 and 1917 revolutions; and the downturn of labor militancy after the defeat of the 1905 revolution, as well as its resumption after 1910, were intimately bound up with changes in the labor market and the overall pace of industrialization. Such events clearly helped to determine the outbreak and timing of labor protest; but it is equally true that the overall pattern of Russian development and the structure of the labor movement decisively conditioned the process and outcome of the revolutions, their potentialities and limits. It was the institutional setting of the Russian labor movement, not economic crisis or war, that distinguished it from its European counterparts and explains the uniqueness of the 1917 revolution. And it is to this institutional context and its consequences that special attention will be devoted in this book.

What does it mean to say that a social movement is revolutionary? Perhaps most commonly it means that a group of people seeks to overthrow a political regime and make radical alterations in the social system. In this sense Puritans, Spanish anarchists, and Bolsheviks were revolutionaries. And it is in these terms that Moore concluded of post-World War I Germany that "the mass of the workers was not revolutionary. They did not want to overturn the existing social order and replace it with something else."[6] Such a definition is too restrictive for my purposes. It probably excludes all broad popular movements, for among worker or peasant participants in revolution the level of ideological clarity and intention is generally weak, and only a small minority are committed members of a revolutionary organization. Should a revolutionary movement be understood, then, as simply a group of people who participate in the revolution, regardless of their social and political awareness? Are peasants fighting on the side of the revolution to protect their plots of land revolutionary? Surely this meaning is too broad, for there must be some commitment to basic social change in the movement.

When I maintain that the Russian labor movement was revolutionary, I mean two things. First, a great many workers participated in activities aimed at threatening the foundations of the old regime. As individuals, their purposes may not always have been subversive, but a movement is not simply an aggregation of individual wills. Because collective action was given its meaning by the leadership and also the government's responses to it, its significance was an "emergent reality" not reducible to individual purposes. It did not matter whether workers participated in demonstrations out of a sense that traditional expectations had been violated or because they accepted socialist ideals. Under the system of autocratic capitalism, traditional values could be as explosive as modern ones; and with the lack of moderate organizations or fixed leadership, episodes of major protest acquired a revolutionary dynamic whatever their origins.

Second, the Russian labor movement was revolutionary not merely in its emergent purposes but also in its capacity to threaten the regime and, when the regime was overthrown in 1917, to apply pressure for further radical change. Part of the potency of the labor movement stemmed from its participants' willingness to use violent tactics and create illegal organizations, a willingness not at all shared by, for example, the German Social Democrats even in the period of their most intense persecution. Its strength was also rooted in the internal weakness of moderation: no established reformist tradition could survive tsarist repression. The movement's subversive potential was strongest in times of war, but it also posed serious political threats in 1903 and 1912–1914. Without World War I ultimately it may not have been successful (scholars still debate this point), but there is no doubt of the grave challenge it could pose even in times of peace. Social movements without this political capacity (such as isolated sects) may still legitimately be considered revolutionary, but the Russian labor movement was revolutionary in this added sense as well. Of course, the strength of the labor movement's threat was the other side of the regime's weakness, but power is relative in any political situation.

The special revolutionary character of the Russian labor movement was occasionally recognized at the time. Rosa Luxemburg counterposed the energy of the young Russian movement, with its emphasis on the mass strike and its combination of economic and political demands, with the sclerotic German Social Democratic movement. If only the German party would lead the movement and not restrain it, she urged, German workers would be just as revolutionary as the Russians.[7] For labor protest in Russia was exceptional compared with other European countries. France was known for its revolutionary tradition, and French workers certainly took a leading part in the great nineteenth-century revolutionary events, including 1848 and the Commune. By the last decades of the nineteenth century, however, the French labor movement had been significantly transformed by the growth of large-scale organization. Even though labor militancy and mass strikes reached new heights in the 1880s with the growth of unions, these strikes were aimed not so much at revolutionary transformation as at state intervention in the workers' favor, and they were basically economic in inspiration.[8] In Russia huge strikes took place in the virtual absence of organization, and workers could almost always rely on a harsh government response—if not immediately, at least eventually. Whereas French industrial conflict became gradually (though never completely) institutionalized as part of the political system, even if militancy remained an important aspect of the pattern, in Russia labor unrest had much more unsettling implications: it was understood as a direct challenge to the political regime and the social framework of capitalism.

Russian labor militancy was impressive in its quantitative as well as qualitative dimensions. Even before the 1905 revolution, and in the context of the autocratic state, Russia was comparable to other European countries (except England, where the level was higher) in terms of the average size of strikes, the number of workers participating, and the number of work days lost (although because of repression strikes tended to be shorter).[9] With the 1905 revolution Russia easily took the lead: in that year there were more than three million strikers. Previously the highest intensity of any strike movement worldwide had been in the United States in 1894, when more than 500,000 workers struck.[10]

Strikes—even mass strikes—are not necessarily a good measure of radicalism, although in Russia they were probably a better indicator of this than in other countries. Russia was distinctive in other ways as well: in the labor movement's special relationship to revolutionary parties; in the fact that militancy provoked no splits among the workers themselves, as it had in countries such as England and Germany (although it did exacerbate splits among the parties); and in the relative centrality of a revolutionary tradition in establishing the continuity of the movement. All of these traits made the Russian labor movement revolutionary in a sense not true of movements in other European countries, at either earlier or later stages of development.

AUTOCRATIC CAPITALISM AND THE RUSSIAN LABOR MOVEMENT

Thus the key question becomes, how, within sixty years, did the Russian workers become transformed "from a small segment of a caste of peasant-serfs into Europe's most class-conscious and revolutionary proletariat"?[11] One hypothesis can be ruled out. Revolutionary labor movements do not develop simply as a consequence of revolutionary situations in capitalist societies, as Rosa Luxemburg argued. For her the dynamics of political ferment and the mass strike would radicalize any labor movement through a dialectic of deepening economic and political demands. In fact, in other revolutionary situations with significant labor unrest the labor movement has become more fragmented, even to the point of rival worker factions struggling against one another. This was the case in 1918 Germany and to a lesser extent in 1972–1973 Chile[12]—decisive evidence that the labor movements had not been shaped historically to act in a unified way. As we shall see, the role of the Russian workers in 1917 was different: the revolutionary situation increased rather than lessened crucial dimensions of solidarity and radicalism.

The distinctiveness of Russian labor protest was rooted in the unusual combination of autocracy and capitalism. This outcome was somewhat paradoxical, for in many ways both autocracy and capitalism impede radical and solidary collective action.

In a traditional autocratic system social protest can have little organization because of social atomization and political repression. When protest does emerge, it is relatively unpredictable and uncontrollable, for it has little leadership or strategy. It may be more violent and perhaps more dangerous, but usually it is also more ineffective. Demands will be fragmented and poorly articulated. Action will be spontaneous and often irrational. In addition, autocracy diminishes contact and trust and so undercuts the possibility for joint action among and within social groups. In prerevolutionary France, writes Tocqueville, the bourgeois was severed from the noble, the peasant from both, and "a similar differentiation had taken place within each of these three classes, with the result that each was split up into a number of small groups almost completely shut off from each other."[13] In Russia, too, the autocracy spawned petitioning status groups jealous of their distinctions. The diverse horizontal ties that make up a complex civil society develop only with difficulty under such a regime. Thus scholars of prerevolutionary Russia have often noted how little capacity there was for cohesive action among all social groups.[14]

Capitalism, too, often impedes solidary and radical class action. As Weber has pointed out, it entails an endless differentiation of market positions, and this differentiation is compounded by a diversity of organizational resources. Metalworkers have often enunciated the exclusive demands of their own category through their own organizations, and miners or textile workers have done the same. Intelligent government policy during the crisis of industrialization accentuated these differences through legislation granting discriminatory rights and privileges. The resulting "aristocracies of labor" have been the despair of revolutionaries in England and Germany as well as in Brazil and Mexico.

Autocracy and capitalism in their separate effects clearly did fragment the Russian labor movement in many of these ways. The overall pattern of autocratic capitalism, however, also hindered the emergence of some of the most important cleavages found in Western European labor movements. The resulting pattern was both complex and distinctive: solidarity and radicalism were unparalleled in periods of ferment but, more than in Europe, strikingly absent in years of the movement's decline; and even in revolutionary periods severe fissures were temporarily obscured though fated to be revealed again.

Autocratic capitalism created the conditions for a revolutionary labor movement in four main ways. *First, it ruled out any significant differentiation between economic and political issues,* so that discontent in one sphere reinforced resentment in the other. Ultimately the whole social order was questioned and put to the test. This lack of differentiation was partly the consequence of autocratic claims to omnipotence. The tsarist state inevitably suffered from what Tocqueville described as "a malady which is the natural and incurable disease of powers that undertake to regulate, to foresee, to do everything. It had become responsible for everything."[15] This idea was echoed in the report of the 1906 Fedorov Commission, convoked by the government to reform labor policy in a time of revolutionary threat. By interfering in class relations, the report said, the purely economic relations of workers and employers took on a political cast, and the workers began to believe that the authorities were their enemy, that the authorities supported the capitalists and opposed workers' efforts to improve their lives. "Such a situation naturally turned the workers away from the industrialists and against the existing order."[16]

Similarly, by a process of reciprocal subversion, autocracy and capitalism created the context for an uneasy alliance between the state and the industrialists, who resented but still depended on each other. This cooperation facilitated the fusion of economic and political discontent, reinforcing the effects of the autocratic state's claims to omnipotence. Both main actors increasingly lost their legitimacy, and each became tainted with the sins of the other. Just as autocratic interference in class relations led to their politicization, so this alliance of challenged elites encouraged class consciousness.[17] Opposition to tsarism and opposition to capitalism were increasingly linked, much to the chagrin of the industrialists in 1917, who tried desperately but unsuccessfully to dissociate themselves from the old regime. It was not simply that the industrialists were weak; even more devastating was their former symbiotic relationship with the state. This connection between economic and political protest made the classic Marxist separation between the bourgeois and socialist revolutions almost irrelevant during the political events of 1917.

Second, in Russia autocratic capitalism generated both traditional and modern opposition to capitalism and so created the conditions for a synthetic social movement. Russian tradition, we have seen, was much more hostile to private property, contract, and authority in the civil realm than was the case in Germany or Japan. And whereas in Germany splits occurred between workers adhering to traditional authority patterns and those seeking to transform capitalism,[18] in Russia worker traditionalism dovetailed in important respects with worker socialism. For example, consider the factory inspector Gvozdev's description of his own provincial region, cut off from the urban hotbeds of class conflict. Workers, he observed, had little understanding of political and economic relations and the law. They thought that the factory owner had no right to close the factory and that if he managed his affairs poorly the state would take over his property. The workers were also mistakenly convinced that the employer was obliged to give work to all of the local population and to build housing for his workers. Further, they assumed that the authorities could make the factory owner raise the workers' wages and that if he made a great deal of money the government would compel him to build another factory. "In a word, the workers in these questions turned out to be real children and completely unconsciously were preaching state socialism." These views were not, he added, the result of outside agitation, and even the most conservative workers espoused them.[19]

Evidence for the "unconscious radicalism" of the masses schooled by the autocracy is not difficult to detect in prerevolutionary labor history. For example, worker unrest was especially prevalent before major holidays because of traditional expectations of government protection and benevolence. Indeed, not until the 1890s, wrote Social Democrat Akimov, did revolutionary groups begin to expect arrests of workers on the first of May; previously Christmas and Easter had been the great days for discontent and repression.[20] Many of the greatest events of labor history, notably the Zubatov and Gapon experiments in what the revolutionaries called "police socialism," gave ample proof of the depth of many workers' belief that the state had a duty to protect them—although its inclination to do so was increasingly called into question. The same events also gave all too palpable testimony of the workers' weak commitment to the expectations and laws necessary for capitalist relationships to flourish.

It is also true that worker traditionalism could be a barrier to collective action and to solidarity. Those who await succor from above are not inclined to act independently. The revolutionaries who urged the workers to rise up and defend their interests attacked the tsar-protector, for many the only source of hope in their cheerless world. Such pleas could arouse great hostility among those workers who conceived themselves not as outcast proletarians but as the tsar's loyal subjects.

Especially during times of ferment, however, these traditional expectations proved to be vital for the development of a more general worker radicalism and solidarity in two senses. First, they were bound to be betrayed in the context of a state committed to capitalist industrialization, and so unconscious radicalism could easily be made conscious.[21] Second, they obviously corresponded closely with many socialist ideas, just as, in an analogous way, Islam and socialism were often interpreted as congruent in Iran. No more than a small minority of workers ever became committed socialists or even had much insight into socialist teaching; but a much larger number were receptive to many socialist ideas, particularly in periods of unrest. What seemed, therefore, to be dramatic changes in consciousness were often much less puzzling when considered in the light of this inner connection. Thus in the Zubatov societies former worker radicals could be recruited to an updated traditional ideology, and when the experiment failed, "backward" Zubatov workers could participate in trade union and socialist activities. The same blend of traditionalist and modern radicalism was evident in the Gapon movement, in which traditional religious ideas gave legitimacy to new social and political demands that challenged the framework of state and society. Indeed, the victory of Bolshevism among virtually all categories of urban workers in 1917 must be traced partly to its correspondence with traditionalist conceptions of the state and its relationship to social elites and the masses.

Autocratic capitalism created the preconditions for a revolutionary labor movement in a third way: it diminished the importance of the potential sources of fragmentation and moderation within the movement. Autocracy clearly has the potential to atomize social groups, but this potential was significantly counterbalanced by capitalist industrialization, which generated the potential for shared identity and organized action even in the absence of political rights. The growth of capitalism created a nucleus of common interests and purposes, a new shared status for all as industrial workers in a society that treated them without exception as outcasts. This new status never completely nullified the more particular statuses deriving from regional, occupational, or gender differences, but when combined with the opportunities for increased contact in cities and factories, it was central enough to provide a basis for impressive joint action when conditions were ripe. Collective action was also the consequence of urbanization and increased literacy, which facilitated the emergence of worker leaders who could bring more organization to industrial protest. Permanent class organizations could not yet take shape, but at least some planning and strategy could be introduced. Demands became more rational and standardized, and some discipline and control could be exercised. Under a traditional autocracy protest takes the form of "collective behavior"; in an autocracy undergoing capitalist development it acquired some "social movement" traits as well. Organized strikes, recognized worker leaders, underground organizations, the emergence of more coherent political ideas, and the growth of traditions of protest indicated that protest now had more structure and direction.

In many European countries the "social movement" dimension came to dominate over the "collective behavior" dimension. Capitalism and democratization nurtured reformist social movements in which radical intellectuals were increasingly marginalized and social cleavages led to organizational and political divisions. Social movements came to be represented by political organizations, and with the extension of rights these became less like sects and more like modern parties integrated into the political system. This transformation made notable progress in Germany even in the 1880s, when the antisocialist laws were still in effect and the Reichstag was politically marginal.[22] Leaders became cautious, partly out of concern for their organizational interests. Militant action became subordinate to rational strategy. These are all classic themes in the history of the German Social Democrats, particularly after 1890. Perrot has described a similar transformation in French strikes in the late nineteenth century: they became more rational in the sense that leaders took account of economic and political circumstances, although she also emphasizes that "the echo of some movements, their character as an epidemic wave, surpasses calculation and correlation."[23] The strike is still partly "a cry, a festival, a project or dream," although now it becomes part of a larger pattern of institutionalized conflict in which the act gives way to the word.

These transformations could not be recapitulated in Russia. Spontaneous mass action, undisciplined and uncontrollable, could never be displaced by organization and strategy because the tsarist state never permitted the development of stable organizations that could have real authority and control. Thus worker protest in Russia continued to display spontaneity, often apart from all regard for consequences. This militancy became more effective through the rudiments of factory-level organization and the influence of the revolutionary parties, both facilitated by capitalist development. Although these parties could not organize the mass of workers or inculcate their own values to any appreciable degree, in periods of unrest their influence was immense for lack of an alternative. Thus although autocracy isolated the masses from the intelligentsia, autocratic capitalism guaranteed their interdependence by depriving the workers of autonomy and rights.

Similarly, internal differences within the working class, even more pronounced than in Western Europe because of the isolation imposed by the autocracy and the rapid pace of industrialization, had less significance for the labor movement. Social differences could not resurface as organizational or political cleavages. For this reason class solidarity could be based on a shared political status, which transcended the multitude of distinct class positions inherent in capitalism. The organizations that embodied this underlying lack of differentiation were industrial unions—always more significant in Russia than craft unions in the brief periods in which unions were permitted—and soviets, the clearest expression of the distinctiveness of the Russian labor movement. The weakness of civil society in Russia thus worked in favor of class solidarity, but it had little effect in counteracting the vast social and cultural disparities that accompanied this solidarity, which was not rooted in a deep correspondence of life experiences or values.

Fourth, the very internal cultural and organizational differentiation imposed upon the Russian labor movement by the autocratic regime facilitated, within the context of increasing industrial protest, a high degree of

interdependence. Mass workers, conscious workers, and the revolutionary intelligentsia were severed from one another and became incapable of
establishing routine relations based on mutual interest and knowledge.
As compared to Western Europe, where all three of these categories
could also be discerned, each group in Russia was closer to the ideal type.
Mass workers, more deprived of rights, were less integrated into capitalist social relations, less ideologically sophisticated, more oriented toward
the state, and more volatile. Conscious workers possessed a more distinctive identity and numerous traits of an isolated sect. And the intelligentsia
was more quintessentially ideological and deprived of sustained contact
with a mass base.

This differentiation helps to explain the spasmodic character of the
Russian labor movement. In periods of quiescence each group was cut off
from the others and regarded them with suspicion. Protest was localized
and episodic. Once a certain threshold was reached, however, their relationships were temporarily transformed, isolation and hostility giving
way to mutual sympathy and interdependence. Sympathy was rooted in
the links between unconscious and conscious radicalism; interdependence stemmed from the helplessness of each category when isolated from
the others, a helplessness engendered by the autocratic regime. The pattern of action that emerged during these periods of ferment embodied a
revolutionary synthesis without parallel in the history of industrial labor
movements.

TOCQUEVILLE AND TROTSKY: A SYNTHESIS

The special traits of autocratic capitalism require theoretical synthesis
in order to clarify the roots and nature of the Russian labor movement.
Such a synthesis provides an alternative to the more exclusive perspectives centered on either autocracy or capitalism in isolation. Mass society
theory, inspired by Tocqueville, draws attention to how autocracy creates the potential for an unstructured mass movement susceptible to
ideological guidance from outside. Marxism, especially in Trotsky's
adaptation of it to backward countries, makes intelligible the rise of an
organized class movement in the context of capitalist development.
Under autocratic capitalism, neither theoretical tradition is sufficient, nor
are they contradictory. Instead, they can correct and complement each
other in order to explain the distinctiveness of the Russian labor movement, a movement in which "mass" and "class" traits combined in a
revolutionary way. Theoretical synthesis is necessary because Russian
industrialization and the Russian labor movement were themselves
synthetic.

In *The Old Regime and the French Revolution* Tocqueville offers an unrivaled account of the ways in which despotic regimes prepare the way for revolutionary mass movements. Despotism breaks down hierarchy and reciprocity among social groups and deprives them of the practical experience necessary to temper judgment. They are internally fragmented and isolated from one another and have tenuous bonds to the political regime. In thus atomizing society and undermining the implicit or explicit social and political contracts, such regimes become more vulnerable to breakdown and the revolutionary crisis will embrace both state and society.

More recent writers have built upon some of these ideas in the theory of mass society, which sees social stability threatened under conditions of atomization and low political participation.[24] Without participation in intermediate organizations, such as trade unions, people lack "multiple proximate concerns" and become available for mass movements. Perlman has made use of related ideas explicitly to interpret the radicalism of Russian workers. Prevented from organizing trade unions, they were unable to pursue their immediate interests and so never developed the pragmatic orientation of workers in other countries. They had no independent commitments and perspectives born of their own experience. "Thus the Revolution's chief instrument was a laboring mass with minds like 'virgin soil', open to whatever seeds the intellectuals of the revolutionary parties might choose to sow."[25] It was primarily the workers' immaturity as a class that explains their revolutionary role—a role in which they are manipulated and betray their own authentic interests. And the most revolutionary workers are likely to be the least integrated into urban industrial society: young workers, uprooted peasants, and the unskilled.

When applied to the Russian labor movement, these ideas have much to recommend them. A vast number of workers, unintegrated into the emerging industrial society, were clearly in a "mass situation." Social relations, developing without reciprocity or trust, were fragmented and fragile, ready, as Tocqueville suggests, to collapse when seriously challenged. Actors and groups, unable and unwilling to judge and calculate on the basis of knowledge and contact, were primed for action. And when they acted, the combination of emotion and ideology tended to outweigh considerations of long-term rational strategy.

One serious flaw with the mass society perspective as applied to Russia is its underestimation of the importance of traditional cultural expectations among the masses—the very notion of a "virgin mind" is impossible to accept. Autocracy nurtured worker radicalism not only through excluding participation and integration but also by fostering a definite set of attitudes toward the state and social elite. Just as crucially, this tradition underestimates or misses the extent to which capitalist industrialization in Russia had engendered class consciousness, organization, and socialist ideology. Russian labor protest had its mass dimensions, but these were entirely intertwined with elements of a class movement. In terms of leadership, modes of action, and organization, it was precisely this interpenetration of mass and class action that made the labor movement so explosive.

In its attention to the dynamics of backward capitalism under an autocratic political system, Trotsky's Marxist analysis of the Russian labor movement corrects many of the insufficiencies of mass society theory. For Trotsky the rapid pace of industrialization and the ferocity of tsarist political repression created unusually fertile ground for class formation and revolutionary action. The lack of institutionalization of the movement created not a mass situation but an especially explosive class movement led by conscious workers and the Bolshevik party. Worker protest was not without organization, but it lacked the conservatism born of deep-seated traditions and bureaucratic leadership. Trotsky believed that a movement roughly of the kind that Marx predicted emerged in Russia because Russian economic development and political institutions departed from the European model. The Marxist model of a revolutionary social movement emerges without major alteration while its sociological underpinnings are thoroughly revised.

It was, I believe, Trotsky's error not to draw the necessary conclusions from his own model of backward capitalism in Russia. His economic determinism does not allow him to give sufficient weight to the consequences of autocracy, and so he largely ignores the revolutionary significance of traditionalism in the labor movement. In addition, although he acknowledges certain "mass" traits of the labor movement—for example, lack of ideological sophistication, poor organizational habits, and diverse levels of worker consciousness[26]—there is little attempt to link these to fragmentation within the working class or to cleavages between the workers and the Bolshevik party, which is treated as relatively unproblematic. Trotsky did not assimilate these insights in order to lay bare the synthetic nature of the Russian labor movement. Throughout he underemphasizes (though hardly ignores) the decisive imprint of the tsarist state on all aspects of social relations in Russia. For these reasons the themes developed in Tocqueville and mass society theory can supplement Trotsky's own analyses of the labor movement, bringing it more into line with his theory of the combined character of Russian development. For the labor movement, too, was more "combined" than he was willing to admit, with weighty consequences for both his own theoretical analysis and the political practice of the Bolshevik party.

Trotsky's tendency to underemphasize the role of the state in shaping working-class culture and the labor movement is shared by other theorists who give primary importance to the process of industrialization itself. For them industrialization marks the great divide between "primitive" and "modern" social movements, a dichotomy that dominates their thought. Culture and politics are clearly less significant than variables linked to economic development such as urbanization, literacy, and class consciousness. For example, according to George Rudé,

> in industrial society the disturbances most prone to be historically significant take the shape of strikes and other labor disputes, or of public mass meetings and demonstrations conducted by political organizations; their objects tend (though by no means always) to be well defined, forward looking, and rational enough . . . and participants tend to be wage earners or industrial workers.[27]

In other words, collective behavior tends to become transformed into a social movement.

Rudé would probably recognize that all movements of social protest include elements of diffuse collective action as well as ideologically and organizationally guided action. And I have no quarrel with his contention that the balance toward the latter shifts with industrialization, even if this can be understood without reference to a Marxist vision of history. Yet it is important to note that as regards the Russian labor movement, shaped by autocracy and capitalism, there was no such transition. As opposed to preindustrial struggles, the typical form of protest was the strike or political demonstration, not the food riot, and it was spearheaded by industrial workers rather than a mixed population of the lower orders. Neither is Rudé's description of industrial protest very relevant to Russia, however; tsarist repression did not allow for the kind of control and strategy that his scheme implies. Indeed, it was precisely the combination of preindustrial and industrial elements in the Russian labor movement that made it a formidable opponent of the regime. Rudé's linear model suffers from a schematization based on European experience and a developmentalism that undervalues the independent significance of politics and the state.

The Russian labor movement thus achieved much of its coherence through the unintended effects of tsarist politics and policy. Enough shared goals and common identity existed to warrant the use of the concept "social movement." It would be a mistake, however, to overemphasize the shared culture, sense of membership, and common goals of Russian workers. Critics such as Charles Tilly have rightly censured "social movement" approaches to collective action for their tendency to exaggerate integration and value consensus. The concept of social movement need not be wedded to these assumptions of excessive integration, however. Indeed, I seek to show that it was partly the immense differentiation within the Russian labor movement that held its parts together through mutual interdependence. Tsarist absolutism, coupled with traditional incompatibilities of outlook between intellectuals and workers and the barriers to common understanding among various kinds of workers, created a fragmented social movement, united by each segment's hostility to the old regime and lack of self-sufficiency. This ultimately gave the movement the ability violently to overthrow the old order but not the capacity to construct a democratic alternative to it.

Without an appreciation of the coherence of the labor movement, its resilience and vigor disappear from sight. Equally, inattention to internal conflict and cleavage makes the outcome of the revolution incomprehensible. More generally, both consensus and internal conflict, as these are rooted in the overall society and in the structure and culture of the movement itself, must be incorporated into our understanding of social movements.

In sum, the combination of autocracy and capitalism gave rise to a revolutionary labor movement of exceptional, though uneven, militancy and solidarity. A theoretical synthesis of mass society theory with ideas from the Marxist tradition (especially Trotsky) is most appropriate for understanding the effects of this combined pattern of Russian development. Such a synthesis also calls into question the general applicability (especially outside the advanced West) of the primitive-modern theoretical scheme for understanding social movements, as this perspective fails to take adequate account of the impact of differing political regimes. Similarly, neither the consensual nor the strategic model of collective action, the first centered on the concept of "social movements" and the second on the differing interests and resources of "collective actors," seems theoretically compelling. Instead, attention should be directed to the interplay between solidarity and fragmentation, value consensus and ideological conflict, alliance and schism, all understood within the context of the overall social and political structure.

PART II

AUTOCRATIC CAPITALISM AND TSARIST LABOR POLICY

INTRODUCTION

The decisive force in shaping the development of the Russian labor movement was government policy. Certainly variables such as economic cycles, technological innovations, or changes in managerial strategies had important effects as well, but the basic distinguishing trait of the Russian experience was the government's failure permanently to legalize strikes or to permit the development of a trade union movement either independent or closely regulated by the government (as in corporatist experiments). This lack of legality and institutionalization in turn shaped the movement's patterns of leadership, modes of struggle, internal group structure, and forms of organization—all conducive to revolutionary action. In addition, the lack of reform ensured the survival of the contradictory system of autocratic capitalism, which weakened autocracy and capitalism as well as the elites, who in the short term benefited from the system. Thus to understand the uniqueness of the Russian labor movement and its role in the revolution, we must begin with an analysis of the failures of tsarist labor policy—its nature, causes, and consequences. These are the questions addressed in the following three chapters.

To put such analytic priority on government policy assumes that the initiative lay with the government, not with the labor movement, an assumption that is fully justified by the evidence. It is true that beginning about the turn of the twentieth century, the labor movement presented the state with a formidable challenge: how to deal with an uneven and relatively amorphous but increasingly militant and politicized movement. At least until the 1905 revolution, however, and probably even after this crucial watershed,[1] the tsarist state could almost certainly have directed the labor movement along a reformist path had it undertaken the appropriate policy. The threat of inevitable revolution does not, therefore, explain the impotence of the tsarist state. Nor is the mere existence of an irrationally perceived threat on the part of elites a convincing explanation. Talk of outside agitators and senseless crowds was certainly pervasive, and the fear of revolution often paralyzed the will of elites. Government inefficacy began well before the real or perceived threat of revolution, however, and it continued in periods of quiescence imposed by force.

In the following chapters I analyze the futility of government policy in terms of the general model of autocratic capitalism. Thus I seek to link structural contradictions with policy and, given that policy largely molded the labor movement, with an analysis of social movements and social change. The key points of my argument were outlined in chapter 2: to summarize, autocratic capitalism weakened political and economic elites and made them hesitant to undertake reform; and it disarticulated the state apparatus both ideologically and organizationally, thus making any change problematic. These themes will be illustrated, explicated, and expanded in the following chapters through a detailed analysis of many of the most important government initiatives in labor reform. My goal is not an exhaustive description of government labor policy in the late tsarist period. In line with my overall purposes, special attention will be given to the question of the legalization of organizations, the lynchpin of all efforts toward reform and the most delicate of all political issues. Several other policy areas, especially relatively peripheral questions such as mutual aid funds or various types of insurance, receive only the briefest mention, although they occupied a disproportionately large share of the bureaucracy's time and efforts. Such initiatives, even had they been more far-reaching than they turned out to be, had virtually no potential to reshape class relations or change the nature of the labor movement absent the emergence of broad, legal, class organizations.

The organization of the following three chapters is chronological. Chapter 4 deals with government labor policy in the years preceding the 1905 revolution. In many respects this could have been the most fruitful period for reform. The threat of labor militancy had been clearly perceived, but the problem had not yet taken on overwhelming proportions. The two most important reform initiatives, the Zubatov societies and the law to elect factory representatives, were stillborn for reasons linked to the contradictions of the system.

Chapter 5 analyzes government labor policy in the revolutionary period, concentrating on the various government conferences and the temporary law legalizing organizations (passed in March 1906). Proposals for change cut most deeply during these years, but the revolution also aroused resentment and fear, reinforcing the divisions and cleavages that prevented effective action. In the end counterrevolution triumphed over reform, and even those measures that were enacted were systematically violated.

Chapter 6 describes the sterility of government labor policy in the period between the end of the revolutionary threat and the outbreak of war. This period was marked by a striking indifference toward the most crucial issues in labor policy, especially the question of labor organization. The profound political contradictions of the tsarist system now hampered not only action but even serious debate.

Chapter 6 ends with an analysis of the dilemmas of government action (for despite its inability to confront and resolve basic issues, the government did have to act) in the absence of fixed rules. Without meaningful laws or even reliable guidelines, tsarist officials were victims of the contradictions that they succeeded only in exacerbating. The government's handling of labor unrest, together with its incapacity to enact reforms, became crucial determinants of the radicalization of the Russian labor movement.

CHAPTER
4
Government Labor Policy before 1905

THE LABOR QUESTION IN RUSSIA

The emergence of a labor question in nineteenth-century industrializing countries was rooted in the rise of a new class of industrial workers without a fixed place in the social order and in the decay of old models of traditional rule and hierarchical social relations. The appearance of a large and concentrated category of urban workers would by itself have constituted a significant challenge to preindustrial elites, but because of the atrophy of hierarchical social relations and increasing demands for greater political participation, the question was posed for them in an extremely explosive way. Elite responses to this highly threatening new social issue were one of the crucial determinants of different countries' political evolution.

The decline of traditional relationships based upon what J. S. Mill called the "theory of dependence"[1] and the correlative rise of contractual relationships created new sources of insecurity even as they diminished the personal dependence of the worker on his or her master. The great instability of capitalist production, unmitigated by government efforts to soften the consequences of periods of economic decline, increased the workers' vulnerability and created fertile soil for discontent. At the same time, industrialization and urbanization gave the workers new possibilities for understanding their situation and new ways to act upon it. Contact with other social classes and also dissident political movements, education and literacy, and close contact with other workers in large factories helped turn discontent into protest. And it was active protest, not any prior abstract or theoretical insight into the sociological dimensions of industrialization, that made social and political elites aware of the new dangers they faced.

In one sense Russian elites in the late nineteenth century were in a favored position, for being able to take account of the previous experiences of Western European countries, with the aid of hindsight they could foresee many of the issues they might be forced to confront. Indeed, in the period of the great reforms (especially 1857–1864) various governmental commissions deliberated measures that might have resolved some of the most crucial issues even before they had fully appeared. Most important were the Shtakel'berg Commission's recommendations, which advocated freedom of contract, the creation of a corps of factory inspectors, the development of urban industrial courts (including workers' participation in the election of members), and the legalization of various types of worker associations. Also in the 1860s a small but prominent group of St. Petersburg industrialists and technical specialists were sympathetic to the workers' plight and favored progressive measures to improve their situation.[2]

Ironically, the very immaturity and docility of the Russian industrial proletariat in these years hindered efforts to take immediate action on what was not yet a pressing problem. Over the next couple of decades industrial unrest increased dramatically and together with it the awareness that measures must be taken to maintain order. Particularly worrisome were the dangerous connections between workers and revolutionary populists (Marxism did not become prominent until the 1890s). It was in these years (the 1870s and 1880s) that the Russian government enacted its first significant laws on the labor question, particularly the 1886 law regulating the labor contract to a slight degree. The late 1890s marked another significant turning point in governmental awareness of the labor question, as worker unrest reached new dimensions with the great 1896–1897 textile strikes in the capital. After these momentous strikes, officials showed unprecedented awareness of the insecurity and harshness of the workers' lives and made numerous proposals to improve their conditions.

In the last decades of the century Russian officials perceived the potential danger of worker unrest,[3] but they also tended to be optimistic that its pernicious effects could be avoided because of what Sipiagin, soon to be minister of Internal Affairs, called "the complete independence of our government."[4] They assumed that the autocracy, standing above social groups, had both the power and the moral right to dictate the shape of the employer-worker relationship so that the workers would see in the state "their steadfast defender, the just and merciful protector which our rural population see in it." The factory owners had no right to complain about any concessions they would be forced to make, for with the help of the state they made enormous profits.[5] With such a powerful state role, Russia would be able to avoid class conflict.

It is remarkable how little trust government officials evinced in the paternalistic goodwill of the employers. They occasionally referred approvingly to, in Witte's phrase, the "patriarchal cast of relations between masters and workers," but such statements tended to be for public consumption. Far more common was the charge that worker unrest stemmed from the factory owners' exploitation and the workers' subjugation to an impersonal market. Some officials even explicitly concluded that the interests of the two sides were directly contradictory, a state of affairs, they warned, that was bound to lead to disorders.[6] Nor were many observers blinded by the myth that the Russian workers' close ties to the land would protect them from the proletarianization characteristic of Western Europe. Such ideas might have been convincing (though not really accurate) in the 1860s, but by the 1890s it was widely accepted that, as Sipiagin reported, "here there has already been formed, and is growing rather rapidly, a class of workers cut off from the land and living exclusively by factory labor."[7]

In their efforts to explain the accelerating class conflict and labor unrest that they found so foreign to Russian conditions, government officials fixed on two basic causes. First, as noted earlier, many traced worker discontent to inadequate wages and intolerable working conditions, consequences of the factory owners' selfish concern for profits above justice and public order. Sometimes their denunciations sounded much like Marxist propaganda, as in the March 1898 report of Ministry of Internal Affairs official Panteleev. Employers, he declared, take advantage of the workers' helplessness to "exploit their labor for their own benefit." They receive "enormous profits" but they pay the workers poorly and "with few exceptions they do almost nothing for the improvement of the living conditions of the workers and their families." Panteleev regarded the conduct of factory owners as especially unjust because the worker "gives to the factory all his vital forces," and this alone makes the factory's prosperity possible,[8] a police version of the labor theory of value. Such charges did not go unanswered by the industrialists' defenders, particularly conspicuous in the Ministry of Finance, who explained the workers' low wages by their low productivity and meager needs.[9]

A far less controversial explanation for worker unrest was the insidious influence of outside agitators acting on the basis of ideas imported from the West. According to this view the workers were loyal to the tsar but also ignorant and susceptible to outside manipulation. Thus for Pobedonostev, the powerful reactionary advisor to the last two tsars, "our workers are in large part an ignorant mass, capable of taking in any kind of false teaching, be it of a religious or purely economic nature. It is enough to point to the multitude of our people's sects and the extreme stupidity of the contents of their teaching." Despite the inapplicability of Western ideas to Russian conditions, these uncultivated souls could easily be convinced to embrace subversive ideas.[10] For some observers the employers' economic exploitation acted together with outside agitators to make the workers all the more susceptible to these absurd Western teachings. Ministry of Finance officials tended to single out the influence of outside agitation for special attention, thus deflecting the blame from the industrialists.[11]

Both of these analyses, by far the most frequent explanations of worker unrest before the turn of the century, presumed that industrial protest was somehow artificial or unnatural in Russian conditions, a symptom of moral turpitude on the part of outside agitators or of government ineffectiveness in controlling employers. Occasionally, however, another note was sounded: the acceptance of worker protest as a natural consequence of basic traits of capitalist industrialization, especially the emergence of a more urban, literate, and sophisticated cadre of permanent industrial workers exposed to the risks and uncertainties of market relations. Various reports referred to the political unreliability of the fully urbanized and proletarianized workers, who were seen as much more inclined to embrace subversive ideas.[12] A great many officials deplored the consequences of these changes, hoping to combat them with stronger police measures, but some also came to adopt the view that conflict was inevitable in a capitalist society. Witte, for example, argued that factory disorders were of two kinds: one arising naturally on the basis of contractual relations and the other instigated by criminal propaganda. Conflicts of the first type should be resolved by the factory inspectorate without police intervention; by contrast, those caused by political agitation should be combatted with the most forceful measures.[13] Although the division between economic and political conflict was already somewhat artificial in 1897 Russia, Witte's basic insight that disorder was inevitable in capitalist societies constituted a profound challenge to the time-worn governmental assumption that all social protest—indeed, virtually all concerted group action—infringed upon social order and should be prohibited. Several years would have to pass before this insight could be deepened and translated into significant new directions in labor policy.

CONSERVATIVE TUTELAGE

Until the turn of the century the basic political assumptions of the ruling elites and the most widespread diagnosis of the causes of worker protest did not permit anything more than a cautious, traditional approach to industrial conflict, one that might appropriately be labeled "conservative tutelage." According to this view, which found expression in numerous reports and diagnoses of the labor question, all initiative must remain in the hands of the state, which was responsible for the protection of all subordinate groups, particularly the weak. In a declaration made famous by socialist propaganda, Witte appealed to the capital's textile strikers in 1896 in flowery paternalistic phrases to recognize that the "law defends the workers and indicates the path by which they can discover the truth if they feel themselves to be injured. . . . The government will occupy itself with the improvement of their situation and the lightening of their work insofar as this is beneficial for the workers themselves."[14] In advocating legal remedies, officials were not espousing an autonomous legal order empowering individuals and social groups. Rather, the model was a "type of bureaucratic positive law"[15] that explicitly defined the obligations, privileges, and benefits of each party and their relations to the state. Virtually all forms of independent activity and organization were frowned upon, for they would infringe upon the state's capacity to define social relations according to its higher criteria.[16] In this context law was barely distinguishable from orderly administration.

Conservative tutelage was clearly rooted in the fundamental traits of the Russian state, but it was not strictly a traditional policy. Rather, it was a relatively recent response to the widening breach between state and society created by incipient modernization. Beginning especially with Nicholas I, Russian rulers could not fail to perceive the tenuous nature of their legitimacy even within the most favored strata of society. Rejecting the policy of granting more rights and independence to social groups, they sought to gain loyalty through paternalistic protection. Nicholas I, for example, saw in the secret police "the essential link between himself and his people—observing all that went on, righting wrongs and averting evils."[17] This broadening of state tutelage was also part of modernization in the sense that it was facilitated by the extension of bureaucratic rule, a relatively recent phenomenon that gave new resources to rulers seeking to extend the scope of their authority.

Conservative tutelage was hardly confined to Russia. Indeed, in this regard Russian rulers were once again following a path earlier traced by several other European regimes, which continued to rely upon it late into the nineteenth century. Thus in an 1884 circular that might well have been written by a Russian minister of Internal Affairs, Waldeck-Rousseau ordered local police prefects to supervise labor relations carefully.[18] When it is recalled that this same Waldeck-Rousseau was also responsible for the legalization of trade unions in France, however, the essential difference becomes apparent: in Russia this policy was meant to substitute for—not accompany—more profound changes in the relationship between state and society.

Numerous concrete measures to cure labor relations were proposed by officials operating in accordance with the general logic of conservative tutelage. In general, the recommendations fell under two categories and corresponded to the officials' diagnosis of the dual causes of worker unrest. First, virtually all observers insisted on the need for more effective police measures to isolate workers from outside agitators, to take the latter from circulation "like rats infected by the plague," in the words of Odessa governor general Shuvalov.[19] In addition, the government was urged to undertake what the same official called "the management of labor." Police officials, provincial governors, and important St. Petersburg bureaucrats repeatedly stressed the workers' defenselessness and exhorted the government to enact more rules and laws regulating contractual relations, working conditions, and other aspects of the workers' daily lives. Some of these proposals were extremely ambitious, far outstripping the scope of labor legislation in the most advanced European countries. Sipiagin, for example, wanted to establish criminal punishment for employers who violated the labor contract; sought to guarantee minimum wages for certain categories of workers; and favored obligatory old-age, sickness, and accident insurance. In short, he sought "to carefully regulate all conditions of life and work in the factory." With the aid of such measures he hoped to foster the emergence of "solid and sober elements" who would support the status quo, and to this end he advocated measures to facilitate property ownership among the workers.[20] Panteleev's report also proposed an impressive array of remedial steps: wages should be increased and working conditions improved, and various types of new institutions and facilities—including hospitals, bathhouses, pension funds, shops, recreational facilities, reading rooms, and factory schools—should be formed.[21] Often these improvements were to be obligatory for the factory owners, who in turn would be guaranteed industrial peace. There was frequent disagreement over details—for example, some accepted that the market, not the state, governed wages, whereas others wanted government control over this, too—but the same basic spirit pervaded these reports.

Officials unanimously recognized the inadequacy of existing governmental institutions for both of the tasks just mentioned, and they invariably ended their reports with lengthy lists of suggestions on the proper organization of police surveillance and the optimal relationship between the police and factory inspectors. Kleigel's, for example, complained that there was insufficient information on factory life, the mood of the workers, and similar issues. Factory personnel lists were often incomplete, he said, and police had little acquaintance with the work force in local factories. The aid of guards, doorkeepers, factory owners, and local shopkeepers should be enlisted to find out nicknames, apartment addresses, industrial specialties, educational backgrounds, and life-styles.[22] Other officials criticized the factory inspectors, either for their poor relations with the police or for their inattention to the workers' needs. Criticism was accompanied by detailed plans of reorganization to ensure greater coordination and efficiency. With their formidable resources so mobilized, officials hoped to achieve a police utopia in which no one could fail to honor his or her carefully defined rights and responsibilities.

It is not difficult to understand the appeal of conservative tutelage to bureaucratic minds confident of their own superior wisdom and equally contemptuous of the ignorant masses, especially when these minds had been shaped by the ethos of autocracy. And it is no doubt true that the vision of paternal benevolence had significant resonance among the workers, especially when it was combined with expressions of hostility toward the factory owners, which was frequently the case.[23] In several basic senses, however, it was absolutely utopian in the context of Russian politics and industrial relations at the turn of the century.

First, conservative tutelage was bound to be ineffective because of the impossibility of careful attention to so many possible sources of discontent in so large a population. Government resources would have been inadequate in any case, but the task was made even more difficult because of the workers' lack of rights, which made them afraid to speak out against abuses. Shuvalov and Sviatopolk-Mirskii both recognized this dilemma in their reports and proposed, respectively, conciliation chambers and permanent worker representatives.[24] These procedures were never effectively institutionalized, however,[25] and workers remained fearful of denouncing violations of their rights. Further, as the Ministry of Finance never tired of pointing out, modern capitalist class relations were highly complex and involved numerous issues beyond the understanding or control of government officials, who lacked the technical expertise to make satisfactory rules.[26] For all of these reasons, no pre-established set of rules or administrative arrangements could possibly have satisfied either the workers or the employers.

Conservative tutelage, even when practiced, also had its drawbacks. As the Ministry of Finance complained, government intervention in industry undercut the authority of the employers and so was itself a source of worker discontent.[27] The ministry also attacked the police's reliance on arbitrary administrative methods and espoused reliance on the slow and careful development of law. This conflict mirrored the more general tension between commitment to fixed rules and insistence on the autonomous will of the tsar and his officials that so crippled Russian administration throughout the nineteenth century. Disagreement on all of these counts created deep conflicts between the Ministries of Finance and Internal Affairs, and although the Ministry of Finance was not able to impose its will completely, its influence was sufficient to impede progress toward the fulfillment of the conservative police utopia it combatted.

Finally, some mention should be made of two shortcomings of conservative tutelage from the workers' own perspective, an issue seldom addressed by tsarist officials. First, if these ideas and projects had been capable of realization, they might well have satisfied the aspirations of the great mass of workers, but they most definitely fell short of the demands of a significant stratum of skilled, educated, and politically aware proletarians. This latter group demanded not only benefits but rights, not only tutelage but participation. To the extent that the appeasement of this sector was crucial for the resolution of the labor question, the vision of conservative tutelage was already outmoded by the 1870s.[28] Second, the model entailed an unforeseen consequence highly undesirable from the standpoint of governmental legitimacy: by making claims to be able to protect the workers in lieu of granting rights of self-protection, the government assumed responsibility for all their felt discontent. It would thus be the government to which the workers appealed for justice, and so the government, ultimately up to the person of the tsar, was held responsible for their distress.

This last consequence was only dimly, if at all, perceived by tsarist officials by the turn of the century. Many of them, however, in both the Ministry of Internal Affairs and the Ministry of Finance, had clearly begun to perceive the inadequacy of conservative tutelage. In different ways, sometimes cautiously and sometimes with great daring, a small number of officials before 1905 began to consider the feasibility of a pathbreaking direction in labor policy: the organization and even mobilization of the working class in the interest of public order, a strategy that had never before been attempted. The remainder of this chapter will be devoted to an analysis of the two major efforts along these lines, the Zubatov experiment and the law on factory elders, as well as to the causes of their respective failures, which largely stem from the contradictions of autocratic capitalism.

THE ZUBATOV EXPERIMENT IN POLICE SOCIALISM

By far the most ambitious and interesting attempt in prerevolutionary Russia to transcend the limits of conservative tutelage and yet remain within the general framework of conservative values was the Zubatov experiment in controlled mobilization. It was also the most daring example of what the revolutionaries contemptuously called "police socialism"—so named because Zubatov was chief of the Moscow secret police. The novelty of Zubatov's approach can be appreciated if it is recalled that the great majority of Russian officials were hostile to lower-class (or, indeed, any) organization and participation. State initiative and obedience, not active support, were their ideals. Zubatov, by contrast, clearly perceived the inability of the tsarist government effectively to satisfy the workers by such a policy: for example, reliance on labor legislation he dismissed as a "fairy-tale for grown-up children. Everyone feared the workers: the bosses, both ministries, and diverse sectors of society."[29] Further, he believed that even if enacted, legislation alone could not fulfill the workers' aspirations. More far-reaching measures were necessary, and it was in this light that he initiated his program of police-controlled worker organizations to give the workers much greater voice, within limits set by the police, in industrial relations.

The failure of the Zubatov societies is interesting on a theoretical basis because of the insights it provides into the tsarist government's impotence in labor policy. The Zubatov experiment was the closest the Russian state ever came to a corporatist policy of creating and coopting dependent organizations, a strategy that achieved notable successes from the standpoint of the authorities in numerous other countries. In Russia, however, the industrialists' weak legitimacy, stemming from challenges to their authority by the autocratic regime, provided a shaky foundation for corporatism, which requires a substantial acceptance of social hierarchy. In Russia, lacking a strong tradition of hierarchy in civil relations, the societies quickly became anticapitalist, demonstrating the explosive character of Russian traditionalism. They thus gave an early foretaste of the subsequent fusion of traditional and modern radicalism and so prefigured later developments in the labor movement. In this sense autocracy showed itself to be incompatible with a corporatist solution to the labor question.

The Zubatov societies, founded in early 1901 in Moscow and later, on a smaller scale, in several other cities, at first enjoyed phenomenal success. The first society was conceived and founded in early 1901 by machine workers as a mutual aid society, and with the help of the police it rapidly expanded its functions and gave rise to a network of similar societies. Within six months a lecture series with the participation of prominent liberal intellectuals had been initiated, a consumers' cooperative was in the works, and a newspaper, library, labor exchanges, mutual aid fund, housing construction, and courts of arbitration were being planned. In addition, at the suggestion of the Moscow police a central Council of Workers of Machine-Building Factories was established to coordinate the activities of the district assemblies of various parts of the city. The workers' satisfaction with these new societies was fully matched by that of the police, who thought they saw Zubatov's ambitious goals being realized before their eyes. The police could be complacent in the knowledge of their great influence over the society's leaders, whom Zubatov had previously indoctrinated with his views in special educational circles. Officers of the societies also received a monthly stipend from the Moscow police to help ensure continued close ties. More formal means of control were not lacking either, as the police carefully supervised the membership and activities of the council and prescribed the societies' permissible activities. In September 1901 Zubatov could boast with some truth that "we [the police] are in possession of the Council and have available the forces of the entire laboring masses, and thanks to this lever we can twist the whole thing."[30]

Never did more than a small number of workers actually become members of the Zubatov societies (perhaps 1,800 in Moscow at the beginning of 1902),[31] but thousands of others attended the public lectures and were infected by the enthusiasm the whole experiment engendered.[32] A letter from September 1901 intercepted by the Okhrana (secret police) from Anna Pogozheva to her husband communicates a sense of the ferment in Moscow.

> In Moscow for the time being there is only one thing of interest. . . . From newspapers you can judge how the movement, or more exactly, organization, grows. . . . You know from newspapers what interesting questions are put up for discussion. I ascribe enormous significance to this movement and consider that in the history of the labor question it plays the same immense role as the liberation of the serfs in the history of the peasant question.[33]

Indeed, as Bonnell remarks, Zubatov's "audacious and imaginative project had no precedent, either in Russia or in Western Europe."[34]

Although the Zubatov societies were highly original in some ways, they can also be understood in terms of comparable efforts in other countries to come to terms with the labor question by reconciling traditional institutions and modern pressures for participation. The linchpin of these programs, wherever they have been undertaken, has been the formation of conservative organizations to guide the workers in acceptable directions and control their activities. Such organizations have flourished in many countries and have often had a major effect on the development of labor movements. Where the industrialist class has been relatively weak, as in Argentina and Brazil, the state has taken the initiative in creating government-controlled organizations. In cases in which factory owners have had more legitimacy and independence, as in Germany and Japan, they themselves formed paternalistic organizations to buttress their authority, often, as in Japan, to great effect.[35] Sometimes conservative worker organizations were created before significant independent mobilization of the workers, as in Brazil and Japan, and sometimes afterward, as in Germany and Argentina. Despite parallels in purpose and design between the Russian experiment and these other cases, however, a crucial difference stands out. In other countries employer-sponsored unions or state corporatism either neutralized independent labor activism entirely or, at the very least, created major internal divisions within the movement. By contrast, in Russia the Zubatov societies were an unqualified failure from the point of view of the government, accomplishing nothing toward the end of deradicalizing the labor movement. What underlying conditions explain the government's inefficacy in this regard, and how can they be related to the basic pattern of Russian industrialization? Zubatov's experiment, its logic and also its contradictions in the context of autocratic capitalism, goes far to illuminate the distinctive obstacles to labor reform in Tsarist Russia.

ZUBATOV'S PROGRAM

Zubatov's political career began when, as a gymnasium student in his native Moscow, he participated in revolutionary populist groups. By his early 20s he was informing for the Moscow Okhrana, whose service he would soon enter and in whose ranks he would rapidly prosper. The causes of Zubatov's political transformation cannot be discovered from the surviving documents, but it is clear that his experiences with revolutionaries led him to take their threat to the monarchy very seriously, thus stimulating him to rethink the ideal role of the monarchy in social and political life.[36]

Zubatov's analysis of the causes of worker discontent was virtually the same as the diagnosis found in conservative tutelage. He shared the hostility of men such as Panteleev, Shuvalov, and Kleigel's toward both the industrialists and the revolutionary intelligentsia. Like them, he believed that exploitation was artificially driving the workers into the arms of the revolutionaries, for the latter's influence was not based upon any real coincidence of interests or long-term goals. Because of their selfishness, he declared to a meeting of factory owners, the industrialist "estate" is isolated from all other estates, including the working class, the intelligentsia, and the clergy, all of whom look upon industrialists as swindlers.[37] This judgment was justified, said Zubatov, for the factory owners commited "all kinds of actions known under the name of the exploitation of working people. At the time when this estate [the factory owners] was concerned only with its own awakening, it did nothing about the improvement of the workers' living condition."[38]

Also like conservative officials but with the fervor of a convert, Zubatov was convinced that only the monarchy could ensure tranquillity and justice among social groups. What was novel in his approach was the strategy of mobilization with which he proposed to counteract the "arrogance" of the factory owners and so reestablish a community of loyal subjects in which "all the oppressed and insulted will find in the Okhrana Department paternal attention, advice, support, and help in word and in deed."[39] Through the creation of worker societies, balance in the community of subjects would be restored, not purely through control but now by countermobilization. The workers would be able to defend their economic interests and also fulfill their cultural needs for education and self-respect, all within limits strictly defined by the police. The realm of activity was to exclude politics in the larger sense, but within this circumscribed sphere the workers were to have considerable opportunities for independent action and self-expression. In such a context they would come to understand that their aspirations were directly contrary to those of the revolutionary intelligentsia. In Zubatov's view factory owners themselves should be grateful for these innovations, for they would establish a solid foundation for private property and the development of capitalism. Accordingly he explained to the factory owners, who were probably startled by the idea, that the only refuge for their "estate"—the only place where it could find true sympathy and firm defense of its legal rights—was the Okhrana itself. Unfortunately, he chided them, not only did they fail to understand this but, not acting like true subjects, they were subverting the authorities' will by opposing the project.[40]

Zubatov, very much a theorist,[41] went on to draw out the general implications: the revolutionary labor movement was the antithesis of trade union organization. Where one flourished the other withered, for their goals and methods were completely different. The revolutionary labor movement sought to take power; for it, the government was an enemy, and its ultimate goal was socialism. The trade union movement aimed to improve workers' concrete situation; it trusted the government, accepting its tutelage and avoiding conspiracy, and this movement was not based on any ultimate aim. Until the present time, Zubatov claimed, only the revolutionary labor movement existed, but "the future belongs to the trade union movement and the government."[42] With a reversal of values, much of this could have been written by Lenin.

Zubatov recognized that his ideas were inconsistent with the prevailing political assumptions of the Russian state, and he also knew that similar ideas had emerged in Europe, only to fail (from his point of view) in practice. Yet, for a number of reasons, he was convinced that his ideas were viable for Russia and that their application would strengthen the monarchy. First, he believed that the traditional autocratic strategy of "divide and rule," applied by the tsars to elites for many years, could also be effective with respect to the industrialists and workers, who would be allowed to mobilize against each other. It was still explicitly a strategy of divide and rule, but it was to be rule over real actors, not just jealous petitioners.[43] Zubatov wrote,

> For the above-class autocracy, "divida et impera" is necessary. As a form of antidote to the bourgeoisie, who feel proud and act impudently, and to create a balance of forces, we must pamper [literally, give additional food] to the workers, thus killing two rabbits: taming the bourgeoisie and ideologists, and winning over the workers and peasants. . . . The struggle of social forces unties the hands of the just autocracy unconditionally and guarantees its long life.[44]

Zubatov assumed, as his frequent use of the term "estate" suggests, that this struggle of social forces would always be controlled and manipulated by the government, which would still be responsible for defining the respective rights of the two sides in accord with its own interests. In many ways the whole model was similar to European corporatist ideas, particularly that version Philippe Schmitter calls "state corporatism."[45]

Zubatov premised the success of his ideas not only on the benefits they would bring to the state but also on the advantages for both contenders. Workers would no longer be exploited, and at the same time they would be permitted a real measure of participation. Factory owners would have to sacrifice some of their profits, but ultimately their position in society would be strengthened through their greater legitimacy, in the eyes of the state as well as the workers. Consequently, both sides would have much cause to be grateful to the state, and also in this sense the autocracy would be strengthened. Rather than being undermined by the class struggle, as had previously been the case, the state could thus soften class conflict and so ensure its own survival.

Student as he was of the social question in Europe, Zubatov was acquainted with similar ideas in Europe, in Napoleon III's France and Bismarck's and Wilhelm II's Germany,[46] and he knew that they had not been able to resolve the labor question there. The socialist movement had continued to grow and threaten the foundations of social and political life. Russia, he believed, did not suffer from the vacillation of European governments, and it also had the advantage of weaker classes and parties unable to press their egoistic claims on the government. There was thus every reason to hope for success in Nicholas II's Russia.[47]

Zubatov's project was an amalgam of elements from three separate traditions: monarchism, populism, and Western liberalism. The vast chasm separating these ideas was bridged in Zubatov's system by the majesty and authority of the tsarist state, which could reconcile hierarchy and participation, traditional and modern relations. As if to symbolize the synthesis of these three components and to reaffirm their basic compatibility, Zubatov gathered around him three key figures to help his project prosper: Moscow police chief Trepov; former populist revolutionary-turned-monarchist Lev Tikhomirov; and professor of financial law at Moscow University Ozerov. The combination of the diverse ideas and purposes represented by these men demonstrates the syncretic nature of the Zubatov experiment, from which stemmed many of its contradictions and dilemmas.

D. F. Trepov, appointed chief of police for Moscow in 1896 and a man whom Zubatov later called "my political pupil, my alter ego,"[48] was the first high official to come under the sway of Zubatov's ideas. It was probably because of Trepov's influence that Zubatov gained another, even more important, ally, the Grand Duke Sergei Aleksandrovich, governor-general of Moscow and an arch-conservative anti-Semite. Trepov's support for Zubatov underlines the kinship of Zubatov's project with many traditional police goals, although Trepov also went beyond the usual police assumptions. For example, he welcomed the Zubatov Council's direct mediation in labor disputes, arguing that it was more beneficial for the employers than intervention by the factory inspector;[49] and he came to believe that a certain amount of ferment in industrial life was beneficial for the ultimate protection of industrial and political order.[50] Such views clearly marked a departure from the usual bureaucratic suspicion of interest representation and collective action. Nonetheless, it is clear from his reports that Trepov looked upon the Zubatov societies primarily as a means of achieving order in the factories. He praised the "not only useful, but absolutely necessary" contributions of the Zubatov leaders in counteracting the developing revolutionary labor movement.[51] Similarly, in his suspicion of "formal juridical legality" and his elevation of state interest over law, Trepov echoed a central principle of autocracy.[52] Despite these limitations, Trepov's views exemplify the kinds of conclusions that might possibly have been drawn by conservative elites if the Zubatov experiment had been successful.

Professor Ozerov was passionately convinced of the potential for development inherent in the experiment, although he looked upon it with some misgivings. His views on the labor question, much more than Zubatov's or Trepov's, were shaped by a positive evaluation of the experience of Western Europe, and he hoped that government labor policy in Russia would gradually evolve in that direction. He believed that contractual rather than patriarchal relations already predominated in Russian industry, but because of the workers' lack of organization they were defenseless before the factory owners. He favored freedom of strike and the legalization of worker organizations.[53] As he wrote later, "Among us, in Russia, the air of the West had begun to blow and I wanted to work. . . . I hoped that if only in the narrow sphere of the trade union movement it would be possible to foster somewhat the habits of thinking and acting in common."[54] Despite its limitations, the experiment would usher in a new era, for once begun, the process was irreversible.[55]

Zubatov recruited Ozerov to the Moscow societies as a lecturer, and apart from Ozerov's intellectual contributions, he hoped that the professor would give his project legitimacy in the eyes of the liberal intelligentsia. Ozerov clearly had qualms about police participation in the movement, but he also believed that, as he said, "all roads lead to Rome": any organization would be beneficial, for "developing life will fill such organizations with a new content,"[56] no matter what the will of its founders. In this sense Ozerov clearly recognized the liberal dimensions of Zubatov's ideas and hoped that the experiment might soon lead to the Europeanization of Russian labor relations. He predicted that once these measures were adopted, the labor movement would evolve in a moderate direction, for workers could satisfy their demands through collective action and organizations would also have a restraining effect on workers' claims.[57]

Europeanization was not at all the goal of Lev Tikhomirov, Zubatov's third key associate in the movement. In the 1880s he had been the chief theorist of "the People's Will," the most intransigent wing of the populist movement, which, in its pursuit of a distinctive Russian peasant socialism, embraced both the "social" struggle (working among the people) and the "political" struggle against the state. At this time much of Tikhomirov's opposition to the tsarist government was based upon its sponsorship of capitalist industrialization. He later became a devout monarchist,[58] but despite grudging recognition of some positive features of capitalism, he remained deeply critical of Western European institutions.

Tikhomirov authored a number of interesting reports expounding his interpretation of the meaning and goals of the Zubatov experiment.[59] His ideas can be seen as the germs of an ideology interpreting traditional values in a modern, activist way, paralleling in this respect the ideas of Latin American liberation theology or Iranian Ali Shariati's Islamic socialism. Tikhomirov's vision was far from revolutionary, however: he advocated modern activism for the lower classes, but within the context of the traditional autocracy. This unsolved contradiction helps to explain the practical irrelevance of Tikhomorov's ideas within the movement.

Tikhomirov excoriated the modern West and its ideological servants in Russia, the intelligentsia, for their materialism and overemphasis on the future. The freedom they offered was illusory, for it had nothing in common with popular welfare, which depended on a benevolent state and a communal organization of society. As opposed to purely traditional ideas, however, for Tikhomirov the communal organization of the workers required their independence and active, in contrast to the traditional passive, loyalty. Independence had two major advantages. First, it would allow the workers to defend their own interests, for some degree of struggle was necessary in any society. Second, and more important, the workers could develop an autonomous moral vision opposed to that of the revolutionary intelligentsia. Tikhomirov was convinced that he knew what this independent moral vision would be: conscious and willed loyalty to the benevolent monarch and active acceptance of social institutions. Thus he was convinced that this "mental independence," this "worker thought," would coincide with his own ideals—an ever-recurring error of the Russian intelligentsia, with its gnosticism and desire to reunite with the people.

Tikhomirov set forth two methods to stimulate worker independence: the development of worker organizations and popular education based upon religious and moral teachings. Both goals could be accomplished in the Zubatov societies, in whose bosom could develop a "popular intelligentsia" made up of the workers themselves. Fortunately, said Tikhomirov, the Russian people have a special abundance of very capable people from which to recruit these future leaders, whose task would be to advise and lead their fellow workers and also defend their own point of view against the intelligentsia.[60] Like Sipiagin's stable element of property owners, this popular intelligentsia would shape the labor movement according to its own values of loyalty and stability. The training and cultivation of this, new core of leadership would be left to the Church and right-thinking members of the intelligentsia: a perfect expression of the coexistence of two rival values—independence and paternalism—in Tikhomirov's ideas and, indeed, in the Zubatov experiment as a whole.

At the end of his reflections on the significance of the grandiose march of tens of thousands of workers to the tsar on 19 February 1902, Tikhomorov captured perfectly the opposing tendencies in his ideological synthesis. The Moscow workers, he said, had shown the path of subsequent Russian development

> With God
> With the Autocratic Tsar
> Consciously
> Independently
> With united forces.[61]

Tikhomirov introduced some distinctive notes into the ideology of Zubatovism.[62] He stressed the need for police control and, in general, government regulation much less than Trepov or Zubatov. Similarly, his emphasis on the integral Russian community and the significance of popular enthusiasm clearly stemmed from his revolutionary past, a past most unlike that of Trepov or even Zubatov. Many of these ideas must have disturbed his more cautious counterparts, who could only be suspicious of too much enthusiasm. In one sense Tikhomirov was a prophetic guide to the development of the societies: the ideal of the mobilized worker community had enormous appeal to many Moscow workers. In another sense, however, he was profoundly mistaken: this ideal posed a serious threat to the status quo, not as he envisioned it but as it really was. The nature of this threat was clearly perceived by many other groups and actors whose opposition to the whole experiment definitively sealed its fate.

Zubatov's ideas thus had a number of different strands, not always consistent with one another and sometimes even contradictory. At first it was not at all clear which current would become predominant, or even what their interrelations were. This issue would be settled, however, not only by the elites' ideas but also by their acceptance and interpretation by the workers themselves. The latter, too, participated in the making of Zubatovism, transforming it into something significantly different from the ideals of its theorists.

THE WORKERS' RESPONSE

Worker Leaders

For both Zubatov and Tikhomirov the realization of their ideals was bound up with the emergence of a core of committed worker leaders who could shape the workers' aspirations and struggle against intelligentsia domination. It was the responsibility of the Okhrana, sympathetic members of the liberal intelligentsia, and the clergy to cultivate such an authoritative elite so that the workers might better understand their own interests, which at heart coincided with those of the rest of society. Zubatov had exacting standards regarding the background and traits of his "worker-initiators." They were to be well read, cultivated, and of wide experience. In particular he valued prior experience in the revolutionary movement, for only workers who had felt the strength of its appeal personally could combat it effectively. Amazingly, he even preferred workers who had run afoul of the law, an indication of his boundless confidence in the rightness of his ideas and his own powers of persuasion, which were indeed considerable.[63] For these reasons Zubatov had no qualms about recruiting his cadre of leaders from worker activists arrested by the police. His interrogations became at the same time confessionals and indoctrination sessions.

Unfortunately, there is limited material on the views, goals, and activities of these worker leaders. Although the names of a few of them—Afanas'ev, Slepov, Zhilkin, Krasivskii—are known, only sketchy information is available on their backgrounds and beliefs. Contemporary analysts have to make what they can of the few available speeches, articles, and reports that have survived.

Most of the Zubatov worker leaders in Moscow seem to have approached the Okhrana chief's ideals. They tended to be skilled, experienced factory workers who had participated in Marxist study circles and become involved in the Social Democratic movement as militant agitators. For example, Mikhail Afanas'ev, a patternmaker and chairman of the council, had been arrested as a Social Democratic activist in 1896; Nikifor Krasivskii, leader of the Zubatov textile workers, had also been arrested and imprisoned for his revolutionary activities. Such workers had demonstrated special leadership qualities even before Zubatov recruited them (Krasivskii, in particular, was known as a compelling orator), and their selection by Zubatov seemed only to reinforce their view of themselves as a "conscious" elite somehow superior to their fellows. In his 1903 "Essay on the Emergence of the Moscow Society of Mutual Aid for Workers in Mechanical Production," Afanas'ev described himself as "developed and well-read," a man who reflected on his situation in order to make possible a brighter future for the workers. He immodestly declared that it required great efforts on his part to convince the workers to form a mutual aid society—much tact and eloquence.[64] Afanas'ev and other worker leaders celebrated their new insights and knowledge, convinced that this was the path to a better life and that rival ideas were deeply mistaken, the errors of youth or the perfidious teachings of traitors.[65]

> Where consciousness reigns in people
> There's no place for poverty.
> Long live reason and knowledge,
> Long live the light of truth.[66]

Like the Zubatov project itself, this new consciousness which the worker leaders celebrated was a synthesis of different elements. On one hand, they admired the successes of Western European trade unions, which had clearly gained a much better life for the workers. In creating their original mutual aid society they turned to Ozerov and Den'', both liberal professors deeply influenced by the model of Western trade unions, to draft the statutes and later to deliver lectures on the labor question. These men did not emphasize government tutelage and the need for loyalty so much as the need for worker organization for self-defense in the class struggle. Similarly, Afanas'ev referred to an important meeting of the society as the equivalent of a German or English trade union congress.[67] Many hoped, like Ozerov, that adjusting for Russian conditions, these organizations would soon achieve the influence and independence of trade unions in Europe.[68] They accepted Zubatov's idea that the revolutionary movement was hostile toward the emergence of trade unions, and thus they branded the revolutionaries as their enemies. The workers' true task was to defeat ignorance and poverty, not to overthrow the government, and for this they needed organization and unity, not "revolutionary ideas fanatically preaching the almost complete destruction of the existing order."[69]

Conversely, admiration for European trade unions and hostility toward the revolutionaries on the basis of Western-type reformism was only one strand in the ideas of the Zubatov worker leaders. An entirely different orientation is evident from the speeches and writings of Fedor Slepov, secretary of the council and one of the original worker leaders of the movement. It is difficult to determine how widespread Slepov's views were or the degree to which his writings influenced either the leadership or the mass base of the societies. Schneiderman considers Slepov's xenophobia and anti-Semitism to be "unique among the council's leaders,"[70] but the truth seems to be that Slepov's ideas found at least some support among his colleagues. The remarkable speech that will be analyzed now was given again, this time by Afanas'ev, at another meeting and was also to be given at twelve more district meetings.[71] Clearly, these were more than the idiosyncratic ideas of an isolated crackpot.

Consistent with the general ideology of Zubatovism, Slepov expressed in his speech a deep hostility toward the revolutionary intelligentsia. Even in this respect, however, his tone is set apart by an especially strong dose of venom. The revolutionaries, he said, are worse than thieves or murderers, for the latter could rob or kill by chance, but the revolutionaries had consciously chosen to become enemies of mankind. It was too great an honor for them to be locked up with common criminals, for behind the revolutionary idea all kinds of crimes are hidden: mass murder, lies, calumny. They would return Russia to the Time of Troubles or kill thousands of people, as was done in the French Revolution (40,000 in a single night, he said). Slepov's hatred clearly distinguishes his tone from that of another important Zubatovite document, the "Letter of Sixty-Five Workers." The idea of socialism, said this letter, "is good in itself, but the means to reach it are not," for violence will call forth violence. "All roads lead to Rome, but the one that is closer and more peaceful is better."[72]

Even more revealing are Slepov's attitudes toward the factory owners. Zubatov and Tikhomirov wished for cooperation and mutual support between workers and employers. Similarly, Afanas'ev explicitly stated that the goal of the Zubatov societies was to further the shared interests of workers and factory owners.[73] By contrast, to the probable astonishment of all of his listeners, Slepov announced that contrary to what the revolutionaries said, no factory owners remained in Russia.

> All the former factory owners and capitalists (as the revolutionaries like to say) have now disappeared. The government changed them into mere directors and employees. The government did this with the goal of smashing the contemporary magnate-kings more successfully. They were in large part foreigners who, having enriched their pockets with Russian capital, left for their native countries.[74]

Russian industry, he claimed, had always been in the hands of foreigners, for Peter the Great had needed their specialized talents, and the "abnormal conditions" they created in the factories had always been the cause of worker discontent. The government, however, had been trying to rectify this injustice since the time of Alexander III, who advocated "Russia for Russians."[75] Indeed, for Slepov the revolutionaries and factory owners were almost equally objectionable. Both sought to break apart the solidary Russian community and drive a wedge between tsar and people; the factory owners were foreigners, the revolutionaries inspired by foreign ideas; and they both were a source of chaos for eternal "Rus'."

Workers, by contrast, were "Russian people" and not mere proletarians, as the revolutionaries asserted. And as true Russians they were "the descendants of those glorious ancestors who in the square in Nizhnii Novgorod, in a great surge of spirit which only Russian people are capable of, exclaimed as one man: we will sell our property, give our women and children as hostages, in order to save our dear fatherland from ruin."[76] The government, Slepov believed, was aware of the workers' loyalty and was taking all possible measures to help them, for the workers had a special claim to government solicitude. This, he suggested, was the significance of the Zubatov experiment, which would ultimately lead to the reconstruction of the community fractured by foreign influence and revolutionary ideas.

It followed rather directly from these ideas that all the workers' deprivations were both unjustified and traceable to the factory owners. They were the result of usurped privilege and not of the blind laws of the market or rewards for relative merit. No better illustration could be found of how autocratic principles undermined the authority of the factory owners. And Slepov's conclusion to this line of reasoning was also widely shared; he expected the government not merely to protect the workers' interests but to take their side. Or, rather, he saw no distinction between these two, because the other side had no moral claims. In this context the doctrine of political mediation by the state, espoused by Zubatov, made no sense. The tsar, to act as a true tsar, would right wrongs, not reconcile claims.

It is not surprising that these ideas bore some resemblance to the goals of the revolutionaries, who also saw the capitalists as illegitimate. The partial coincidence of perspectives indicates that the autocratic traditions discussed in the previous chapter helped prepare the way for socialism, for both were hostile toward private authority and privilege. Slepov's ideas, however, had a very traditional cast, and in fact had their roots in the old Russian ideal of the service society. The fusion of traditional and modern forms of anticapitalism in the labor movement would have explosive consequences for the fate of the Zubatov experiment and, in a larger sense, for the development of the labor movement as a whole. Indeed, appeals and arguments very much like Slepov's, dismissing the factory owners and political mediation by the state alike, were frequently heard in 1917.

Although the views expressed in Slepov's speech were quite distinct from the more trade unionist ideals of other worker leaders, there were also some elements shared by all the activists. First, all leaders expected the workers to derive immediate benefits from the activities of the societies, and even leaders who at first tried to moderate the workers' demands rather quickly began to inflame them. Whether because of their Social Democratic backgrounds or (like Slepov) more traditional autocratic values, their speeches frequently attacked the capitalists. According to a 1901 November 8 letter from "M" to Professor Aleksandr Chuprov intercepted by the police, "the whole meaning of their speeches is that the government will give the workers all they want, including the eight-hour day, but to achieve this the workers must obey the police and avoid relations with the 'petty intelligentsia.'"[77] Second, those such as Afanas'ev or Krasivskii with a Marxist past could agree with Slepov that the workers were entitled to special protection: for the former, they were members of an exploited class; for Slepov, they were the tsar's truest and most loyal subjects. Both versions had practical implications far removed from Tikhomirov's vision of a communally based estate society. The divergence will become especially clear when the rank-and-file workers' response to these ideas is examined.

Rank-and-File Workers and Zubatovism

As noted earlier, the Zubatov movement embraced many more workers than its formal membership figures, which never surpassed a few thousand, might have indicated. Thousands of workers heard the public lectures sponsored by the societies and thousands more participated in the labor ferment that it stimulated. Further, at the height of its influence, under the movement's auspices approximately 50,000 Moscow workers participated in a march to the tsar to show their loyalty on the anniversary of the emancipation of the serfs. Clearly this was a major event in Russian working-class history.

Unfortunately, little is known either about the social composition of the society's membership or about the larger number of workers who came under its influence. A few scattered names with references to social origin appear in the archives, but these are useless for the purposes of generalization. Martov hypothesized that part of the social base consisted of workers who, because of their more privileged positions, older age, or more conservative views, were repelled by Social Democracy yet still yearned for organization and independent activity.[78] Similarly, in his essay on the emergence of the societies, Afanas'ev also singled out the importance of the more literate and developed workers, who had in many cases come into contact with foreign workers and were aware of the advantages of organization.[79] Certainly these observations seem reasonable with respect to the original recruits, but as the movement developed it embraced very broad sectors of the working class, not only in Moscow but also in the surrounding areas. Thus Martov also noted that the movement appealed to the most impoverished and exploited categories of workers, and both the Moscow governor and factory inspector Astaf'ev referred to substantial ferment among workers in factories and villages never before touched by labor unrest.[80] It also included workers of all levels of skill and both artisanal and factory workers.[81]

It is not difficult to understand the breadth and depth of this appeal. Sophisticated workers such as Afanas'ev had to be courted and ideologically won over to the Okhrana chief's views (with the help, in some cases, of Okhrana salaries), but the average worker—particularly in isolated factories out of touch with socialist ideas—had every reason to respond to these unexpected overtures. Factory conditions were unbearable, and there were no prudent and effective ways either to express discontent or to bring about changes. Further, the Okhrana connections were far less ominous for rank-and-file workers than for the intelligentsia or the more politicized worker elite. In this regard the printer trade union activist Sher, after interviewing numerous Moscow printers, concluded that only a small number of them were repelled by Okhrana sponsorship of the societies, for they were accustomed to police interference in factory affairs, occasionally against the factory owners and to the workers' benefit. Thus they could still be convinced that the organizations served their own interests even after the police connection was widely publicized. According to Sher, the Marxists' contention that only "dark," "unconscious" workers were willing to participate in the movement was simply false, another rhetorical skirmish in the worker-intelligentsia conflict.[82]

Thus just as Ozerov, Tikhomirov, Afanas'ev, and Slepov could find a place, even if temporary, within the Zubatov experiment, so could workers with European-style trade unionist aspirations and workers with more traditional perspectives and goals. Workers of the first type could listen to Professor Den" lecture on the vulnerabilities of workers under capitalism and acquire organizational experience that would later be invaluable in the formation of trade unions. Rural or less sophisticated urban workers could see in the societies the fulfillment of traditional promises of state tutelage.

Indeed, the traditionalist expectations nurtured in the workers by the societies far surpassed what the authorities had in mind, for these expectations became linked with images of justice deeply rooted in popular culture, as this had been shaped by idealized autocratic values. Zhilkin and Krasivskii were widely rumored to be tsarist emissaries, and Krasivskii was seen as none other than the illegitimate son of Emperor Alexander II, sent to help the workers.[83] These beliefs bore a close resemblance to the traditional peasant images of the true tsar that had been employed in the eighteenth century by the peasant rebel Pugachev to win legitimacy. Rumors of similar content had also been widespread in the decades after the emancipation of the serfs and had given rise to peasant discontent.[84] Other rumors of imminent government measures to improve the workers' lives were also rampant: the government was about to decree a minimum wage, legislation limiting the length of the workday was forthcoming, and the workers believed that employer resistance would lead the government to expropriate the factories.[85] Again, rumors of this type antedated the formation of the Zubatov societies, stemming from the traditional conviction that the government was truly committed to protect the workers. For example, they had also appeared at the time of the 1896 textile strikes in St. Petersburg and were even noted in a report from Moscow province in April 1901, well before the Zubatov project could have had any influence there.[86] Thus they had an independent existence in popular culture, for they were rooted in a traditional rejection of the market and private authority as determinants of popular welfare. They only needed to be called forth by some new indication of government solicitude in order to give rise to dangerous new aspirations.

Despite these significant differences in worker consciousness, workers with modern and traditional aspirations in the Zubatov movement could also find much to unite them, for concerted action benefited them all.

Further, as will be described shortly, a sense of emotional solidarity began to develop among the workers and, correlatively, a conviction of their own superiority over other groups, particularly the factory owners and the intelligentsia.

With this diverse social base and distinctive admixture of aspirations, the Zubatov movement soon began to display a number of dangerous traits. Most obvious was an increase in labor unrest observable, according to factory inspector reports, throughout the Moscow region.[87] Clearly, many workers were highly receptive to the militant ideas now being promoted by leaders of the societies. The most notorious and significant case of worker militancy occurred at the Guzhon and Mussi silk mills, which began with a dispute over the discharge of two workers in early February 1902. The Zubatov council, the police, directors of the Association of Silk Mills, and the Ministry of Finance all quickly became involved in issues that transcended the original dispute: the scope of police authority, relations between the police and the Ministry of Finance, the rights of the Zubatov council, and overall relations between the government and the factory owners. The Moscow administration, in Zubatov's words, "was compelled to place itself on the side of the workers for the maintenance of its reputation,"[88] but the Ministry of Finance felt equally compelled to support Guzhon. For its part, the Zubatov weavers' organization was responsible for a work stoppage involving 1,500 Moscow-area weavers, during which demands surfaced for the recognition of worker collective bargaining agents and a closed shop, both quite rare in labor disputes before 1905.[89]

The causes of this emerging militancy are not difficult to detect. The promises of the Moscow administration and the open activities of the societies had given the workers enormous self-confidence and a sense of their own power. They believed that the government was fully behind them, and thus against the factory owners, and the council came to be regarded as a "governmental organ created especially for the defense of their class interests."[90] Just as important, the workers came to believe in the efficacy of their own efforts and the strength of their new organizations. In the Guzhon strike, for example, they assumed that the striking weavers would be supported by donations collected by the council from employed workers. Some maintained that "there are a million of us; if each donates fifty kopeks, then we'll have half a million rubles, and with this money it will be possible to live for a very, very long time."[91] When the factory inspector warned the workers that the employers might simply close the factory, they retorted that they would compel him to reopen it. The factory inspector responded that there might be no money available for this, and the workers assured him that in that case the factory would be taken over by the state. Under no conditions, they said, would they remain without work: the council had assured them of this.[92] In this case as well a traditional faith in state tutelage is explosively combined with a modern conviction of workers' growing strength as an organized class. Both instilled in workers the conviction that "our time, the time of struggle" had arrived and that soon they would be freed from the "yoke of the factory owners."[93]

A sense of citizenship was beginning to dawn among the workers, and as a natural consequence they began to evince a heightened awareness of their own dignity. One indication of this momentous change was a precipitate increase in workers' complaints of coarse treatment and beatings in the Moscow region: in 1901, only 161 were registered by the factory inspectors; in 1902 there were 2,146 recorded cases. According to the factory inspector report, this difference was directly attributable to the influence of the Zubatov movement.[94] At the same time, the workers began to look upon both the intelligentsia (whom they called "petty" [*melkii*]) and the factory owners with condescension. For them, it may be conjectured, both of these groups belonged to the middle sectors of Russian society, a stratum that had historically been the object of much ill will. The workers, by contrast, could associate themselves with the state, to which they pledged their loyalty, thus investing themselves with some of its sanctity. Resentment turned to contempt for these insolent outsiders.

The other side of this contempt was a growing sense of solidarity as members of the workers' estate among Zubatov members. Although the strength of this sentiment is impossible to measure with any precision, it emerges in expressions such as the following, which opened an appeal to workers by the worker Il'ia Sokolov to celebrate 19 February: "Brothers in blood, friends by labor, and all the Russian orthodox people."[95] Similarly, Zubatov workers in three district meetings took up a collection to help five arrested workers, and in sending it to Trepov they declared that "we donate to them not because we sympathize with their harmful idea, by which, unfortunately, they were carried away, but only because we take pity on them as our prodigal brother workers, who may change their minds for the better after this."[96] As further evidence, twenty foremen of the Bromlei plant in Moscow, pleading that they too were workers, complained of the local Zubatov society's refusal to admit them to meetings. "The interests of the workers are already too egoistical, one-sided and extremely short-sighted," they charged. "With very few exceptions they do not want to see anything beyond their noses, beyond their own private interests." The Bromlei foremen proceeded to express considerable jealousy over the special privileges enjoyed by the workers and appealed to the need for greater understanding between workers and foremen.[97] The evidence is scant but suggestive, and in any case it corresponds to what might be anticipated in such circumstances, particularly as the idea of solidarity was frequently promoted by leaders of the movement— including, for example, Tikhomirov and Slepov.

Thus in essential respects Zubatov and his colleagues' teachings changed significantly as they became interpreted by rank-and-file workers. Zubatov hoped that government protection and the formation of the societies would allow workers to defend themselves against the power of their employers and create the basis for a harmonious community regulated by the state. The workers came to see themselves as a specially protected caste entitled to immediate benefits as compensation for and alleviation of their sufferings. The societies, it is true, did seem to be a highly effective mechanism for winning over workers to the regime, as was clearly demonstrated by the massive public celebration on the anniversary of the emancipation, perhaps the largest officially sanctioned mass demonstration in Russian history until that time.[98] This policy, however, had the unintended effect of sharpening conflicts with the factory owners to an unmanageable degree. If Zubatov's hopes for a loyal, solidary estate began to be realized, so did the revolutionaries' commitments to class isolation and enmity. This outcome was paradoxical from the standpoints of both Zubatov and the revolutionaries, who were equally convinced that social and political hierarchies were linked. The contradictions between the two hierarchies, however, and those between autocracy and capitalism sealed the fate of the Zubatov experiment and thus helped prepare the way for the fulfillment of the revolutionaries' expectations, which were still premature in 1902.

THE FATE OF ZUBATOVISM

As a result of the workers' heightened mobilization, the Zubatov experiment frightened a great many industrialists of the Moscow region and aroused them to protest openly against the societies.[99] The disturbances of the early months of 1902—especially the Guzhon conflict— encouraged concerted industrialist action, with which they, like the workers, had had little experience. They sent declarations and complaints to Witte and Grand Duke Sergei, warning them of the danger of permitting "anticapitalist activity, which undoubtedly has equally [sic] political significance, especially as coping with masses who have been attracted by any success in this regard can consequently appear extremely difficult, if not impossible."[100] In pointing to the threat to public order, the factory owners made a particularly telling point, for many conservatives in the government were already opposed to the experiment on this basis.

In addition, the industrialists had an extremely able spokesman in Witte, who, together with various other officials in his ministry, had been opposing police interference in the factories for a number of years.[101] Factory inspector Astaf'ev and Witte's assistant Kokovtsov (later to be minister himself) had filed highly critical reports on Trepov's interference in Moscow factory affairs in early 1898.[102] They charged that police involvement in industrial relations undermined the employers and factory inspectors (the latter under the jurisdiction of the Ministry of Finance) and also stimulated workers to make further claims. To these complaints they added the allegation that the police often went beyond the law, either out of contempt for it or through ignorance. They advocated a stricter delimitation of police functions; the factory inspectors were to play the key role in internal factory affairs. Only the Ministry of Finance, its officials claimed, had the expertise to protect workers without raising their demands to an unacceptable level and sacrificing the interests of industry.[103] Reports and rebuttals to reports were exchanged, interministerial conferences convened, and administrative directives issued,[104] but the conflict, rooted in basic differences connected with the contradictory project of autocratic capitalism, continued to simmer.

These conflicting perspectives and commitments became sharper with the initiation of the Zubatov societies.[105] Witte was outraged at what he regarded as the illegal meddling of the police in factory affairs, and Trepov and Zubatov were equally disturbed by what they saw as the egoism of employers and the Ministry of Finance. Their respective commitments were strengthened by the pressures of their constituencies—the industrialists and Zubatov workers, respectively. Witte took his case to Minister of Internal Affairs Sipiagin and then reported his concerns directly to the tsar. Zubatov and Trepov also appealed to powerful figures for help, succeeding, through the mediation of Grand Duke Sergei, in winning over Grand Duke Vladimir. The conflict appeared to be at a stalemate.

The justifications of the societies by Trepov and Zubatov are of particular interest.[106] Trepov took great pains to counter the charge that the societies were undermining public order, arguing that they had been extremely useful because they allowed workers to formulate complaints and make the authorities aware of these complaints. The scope of worker unrest, he added, had been greatly exaggerated for political purposes, and in any case the factory owners—particularly Guzhon himself—were responsible for the problems that did exist. The truth, Trepov reported, was that the factory owners rejected any form of worker organization on principle, for it would harm them economically. He also accused them of opposing the very principle of government mediation in factory life, for they believed that this would weaken their control over the workers.

In making this allegation Trepov in essence accused them of violating the basic principle of autocracy, the right of the state to mediate among social interests. By contrast, in Trepov's view, police interference in factory affairs was both traditional and just. It was the factory owners who were appealing to a logic foreign to Russian political traditions.[107] Although Trepov did not formulate his critique in this way, he surely would have rejected the idea that police interference undermined the factory owners' authority, which, in his view, could only have stemmed from the factory owners' submission to the authority of the state. Unfortunately, both the factory owners and Trepov were right, for in a capitalist system the industrialists needed independent authority but under autocracy independent authority had no substantial roots. In any case, in line with these views Trepov cast the blame on the industrialists, urging that Guzhon in particular be prohibited from economic activities in Russia as a "harmful foreign citizen."

Zubatov advanced many of the same arguments, including allusions to the harm done by factory owners to the authority of the autocratic state, but he added some fascinating observations and judgments that would have been completely foreign to the mentality of a man like Trepov. He was exhilarated by the monarchist enthusiasm aroused in the workers by the societies' activities. In particular, rumors circulating in the Moscow region that Zhilkin and Krasivskii were state emissaries sent to help the workers convinced him that his strategy was valid. His reaction, expressed in a 3 April 1902 report to L. A. Rataev, is worth citing at length:

> In the tales of popular talk our purely national world view stands out sharply: evidently the policy of impartiality and justice in the labor question and the struggle with the dark sides of national industry, reflected in a whole number of external phenomena, deeply touched the heart and mind of the people, and the latter, trying to understand, give it a poetical and ideal monarchist interpretation. On the one hand, this gives me great spiritual delight, since it gives clear proof that I truly grasped and mastered the meaning of our national state ideal, and, on the other, it perfectly depicts those goals to which the legalization of the labor movement undoubtedly leads—that is, to the strengthening and flowering of the monarchical, and not liberal democratic, ideal. From this you can comprehend the rumors you have heard about the transfer of the Mussi [Guzhon] factory to the state, about monetary help from the government and the Okhrana department, and the like.[108]

Zubatov's reaction contrasts with that of Witte, who, in a letter to Minister of Internal Affairs Plehve, had a much keener appreciation of the dangers of monarchist enthusiasm in modern Russia: "It is hardly possible to doubt that the completely arbitrary and supralegal actions of the local administration in the regulation of the labor question can only aid the spread of rumors about hidden laws, about factory expropriations to benefit the workers, and the like, and in conclusion they will lead to disorders."[109] Although Zubatov may well have been right that worker discontent was not based on socialist ideas and had no roots in political or philosophical principles, he did not want to recognize that unprincipled anticapitalism was, after all, still anticapitalism. Nor did he perceive how deeply autocracy undermined the basic relations and institutions of capitalism.

The Guzhon affair and the complaints of the factory inspectors, Ministry of Finance, and industrialists eroded the Zubatov societies' support in high government circles, including in the Ministry of Internal Affairs. Minister Sipiagin had reportedly issued an order to abolish the council before his death, but its enactment was opposed by Grand Duke Sergei.[110] On 2 April 1902, Sipiagin was assassinated, to be replaced by Viacheslav Plehve, a hard-line conservative known for his part in the repression of the populist movement in the 1880s. The tenor of his attitudes may be inferred from his reply to Zubatov's attempt to defend his program: "In Russia there are no social forces, but only groups and circles," and the latter need only be controlled by arrests.[111]

By late summer all these developments had sealed the fate of the Zubatov experiment as an attempt at countermobilization.[112] Zubatov was transferred to St. Petersburg (a personal promotion, but one probably applauded by his enemies), and the societies' activities were more carefully controlled by the police. The lectures became much more conservative—often religious—in orientation, and the council attempted to contain worker demands and discourage strikes. The Moscow workers began to lose interest, and there were factional struggles among the worker leaders.

Another turning point occurred after the massive summer 1903 strikes in the south of Russia, which had developed partly through the influence of Zubatov-inspired organizations. Zubatov was forced to retire in August 1903, and Trepov began to count on the old methods of repression to deal with labor unrest. The societies continued to exist, with some traces still surviving as late as 1914, but they clearly no longer constituted a bold experiment to reorient the Russian labor movement. If anything, they were now at the end of events, responding to more important developments elsewhere and without effective leadership. For example, the Zubatov organizations appear to have become politically radicalized during 1905 and their leaders discredited. According to an *Iskra* correspondent's report on a meeting from early 1905, the Zubatov workers wanted to allow students to speak at the meetings so they could discuss politics and economics. Some openly called for representative government, criticized the war with Japan, and advocated civil and political freedom. Afanas'ev was shouted down when he read government statutes imposing controls over the organizations with cries of "Be quiet, provocateur."[113] Shortly afterward, in early March 1905, several leaders of the society sent a petition in the name of the society to the Minister of Finance with a number of demands that had already become common currency in the political ferment of the time: the legalization of trade unions and strikes; establishment of industrial courts; reform of factory legislation; a shorter workday; government accident, sickness, and old-age insurance; and broader educational programs for workers.[114] These demands indicate both the strength of the pressures upon the leadership and the basically reactive character of its posture.

The failure of the Zubatov societies was of crucial significance in Russian labor history, for never again did the tsarist regime come so close to adopting a cooptive strategy toward the working class. There were related efforts after the decline of Zubatovism—principally the Gapon societies, to be discussed in a later chapter, and the Ushakov organizations, both in the capital—but these were never intended as ambitious new undertakings with the potential of resolving the labor question as a whole. Their leaders had little of the daring or intelligence of Zubatov, and although the Gapon societies arguably constitute an even more significant episode in Russian history, their importance was not primarily rooted in their implications for labor policy.

In his preface to a 1902 illegal publication of a government project on strikes, Peter Struve, a leading revolutionary intellectual previously a Marxist but by then a liberal, remarked that the "Zubatovshchina" was the only method available to the police for satisfying the aspirations of the working class. At the same time, he predicted that the experiment would fail, first because it was based upon administrative arbitrariness and a capricious attitude toward law and, second, because the Russian factory owners would never tolerate its extralegal protection of the workers.[115] Even earlier, in his 1896 book *Contemporary Russia*, Martov, later the great leader of the Mensheviks, referred to the inflexibility of the tsarist state and predicted that there was no danger "that the politically immature working class may find in some Witte a charmer who might put to sleep its political consciousness with the charlatan Utopias of state socialism."[116] These thinkers, among the most astute in Russia, thus pointed to traits of the state and also the influence of the factory owners as factors ruling out some kind of Bismarckian solution.

How, with the benefit of hindsight, can the miscarriage of Zubatov's project be explained? Three basic obstacles stand out, all related to the contradictory combination of autocracy and capitalism, as these were discussed in chapter 2. First, there were serious reservations and divisions within the government, not just between Finance and Internal Affairs but also within Internal Affairs itself, as the skepticism of both Sipiagin and

Plehve demonstrates. These reservations stemmed partly from the experiment's challenge to the basic assumptions of autocracy but also from the Ministry of Finance's perceived need to protect the industrialists in a context of rapid state-sponsored industrialization.

The second factor was the very weakness of the industrialists. Without any significant independent basis of legitimacy, they depended upon the state to maintain their positions in the factories. When the state undertook measures that inadvertently undermined their authority, the outbreak of a crisis was not difficult to predict. An experiment of this nature would have had much greater success in a society in which social hierarchy had deeper roots. Thus even though the factory owners had only limited real political power, their vulnerability forced the government to defend them. Ironically, the autocratic state was in this sense less independent and more closely tied to its weak elites than more liberal governments.

The third decisive factor in the failure of the Zubatov experiment was the character of the workers' responses, which were very different from Zubatov's ideals. The two elements of Zubatov's synthesis, monarchism and trade unionism, were carried far beyond tolerable limits.[117] The workers' aspirations were both too traditional and too modern, a conclusion that underlines the essential fragility of the regime's political model. As a consequence worker mobilization in the form of trade unionism arose to challenge traditional autocratic assumptions, and an updated version of monarchism opposed the logic of liberal capitalism. The Zubatov movement thus displayed, in embryo, the two aspects of the "combined development" of the Russian labor movement: the synthesis of traditional and modern anticapitalism, and the interweaving of economic and political aspirations. Both pairs would be more fully expressed in the years to come and further exacerbate the internal conflicts within the government. In Martov's prescient words (in 1896), "the entire future history of the Russian labour movement will be at the same time a history of the disintegration of those foundations on which tsarism rests."[118]

The significance of the Zubatov experiment lay partly in its prefiguration of basic future trends of the labor movement, but it also had a number of other direct consequences, albeit these are difficult to pinpoint. For the government, it marked the high point of a conservative mobilizational strategy and confirmed the conviction of many officials, particularly in the Ministry of Finance, that a more liberal approach to labor policy, one based more on the independent action of the two conflicting sides and less on government intervention, was indispensable. At the same time, the Zubatov experiment accelerated the decomposition of the tsarist bureaucracy as a coherent policymaking agent—this, wrote Martov, was the fate of any outdated governmental organ in its encounter with life.[119] Like Ministry of Finance officials, many important factory owners had als~ been repelled by the administrative arbitrariness displayed in the Zubatov affair, and many of them also became more receptive to a liberal solution to the labor question. Correlatively, the experiment may have facilitated the adoption of more democratic political ideas as well, a transition that few bureaucrats could make openly.

Finally, the Zubatov experiment had a number of implications for the development of the labor movement. Most obviously, it involved masses of ordinary workers in organized activities that had never been permitted before. They became acquainted with all kinds of issues, both practical and abstract, hitherto unfamiliar to them. Of special importance were the lectures on the Western labor movement, emphasizing the necessity of independence and unity and describing the beneficial effects of trade unions. Even Slepov's speeches against the revolutionaries would have served to acquaint them with what was for most an exotic phenomenon.

On a more subtle level, the failure of Zubatovism taught workers a lesson encountered numerous times in Russian labor history: that their welfare depended upon the state, but the state, despite its promises, was not willing to protect them. Espousal of the monarchical ideal thus inevitably led to disillusionment with it, for worker monarchism, as we have seen, was never unconditional—it was premised on concrete benefits. As Ozerov, referring to the government's promise of protection, concluded, "here our system itself tried to destroy the workers' faith."[120] Similarly, the whole experience must surely have undermined even further the workers' tenuous commitment to law, which already had few previous roots in the autocratic system. As a factory owner report of 1905 from the central industrial region pointed out, the very authorities who had recently persecuted strikes and organizations now encouraged them, and the government did this while the punitive laws against collective action were still officially in force.[121]

Just as the experiment discredited traditional ideals, it gave impetus to the emergence of new goals in the labor movement. If the workers could not rely on the government, they had to rely on themselves, and the Zubatov societies helped them develop the new skills necessary for independent trade union activity. Many future trade union leaders underwent their apprenticeship in the societies, and in 1905–1907 they would put their knowledge to good use. The societies also provided organizational models later utilized by the trade unions.[122] Many of these innovations would have met with Zubatov's approval, except that they took place in an overall political context repugnant to him. Of course, worker leaders were often more sanguine in their judgments. F. Bulkin, later an important leader in the Petersburg metalworkers' union, evaluated the experiment as follows: "The Zubatovshchina played . . . a great role in the

workers' movement, facilitating the unification of workers, the development of class consciousness among them, giving [them] the possibility for
organized struggle with employers and demonstrating to workers their
strength."[123]

THE 1903 STAROSTA LAW

The second major government attempt before 1905 to resolve the
labor question and redirect the labor movement along a less threatening
path was the effort to legalize the workers' election of factory representatives, an effort that culminated in the passage of the *starosta* (elder) law
of June 1903. Although very modest in its ambitions and even more so in
its accomplishments, the law absorbed a great deal of government time
and effort for more than two years and aroused considerable debate,
which often extended to profound questions of social and political principles. In its final form a compromise measure that achieved the ends of
no one, the law and the process by which it acquired its final form are
highly instructive for the additional light they shed on the obstacles to
labor reform in Russia.

Under existing laws workers were prohibited from holding meetings or
engaging in any kind of collective action, including the election of representatives. Those workers who did emerge as leaders in illegal collective
action, particularly strikes, were subject to arrest and prosecution by the
authorities. The authorization of elections and the legalization of delegates chosen by the workers themselves might thus have been a significant advance in the direction of the institutionalization of labor conflict.
And, as compared to the Zubatov project, these measures had a number
of notable advantages. First, their inspiration, the need for order in
factory affairs, was extremely traditional, and in fact in some factories
the election of worker delegates had already been permitted (although
illegally) for this purpose.[124]

Second, although the election of elders was conceptualized from the
beginning as part of the overall issue of worker organization, it was certainly a primitive form of association and explicitly regarded as only a
partial measure. Similarly, it did not necessarily imply the need for large-
scale political changes that would have been obviously unacceptable.
Thus as opposed to the Zubatov experiment, the proposal to permit the
election of starostas was neither overwhelmingly ambitious nor closely
connected to a broad ideological vision of the labor question and the
future of Russian society. For these reasons the starosta project never
aroused the passions or debates created by the Zubatov societies.
Indeed—and this was another of its advantages—the starosta project

gained the support of a surprising array of government officials in both of the warring Ministries of Finance and Internal Affairs.

Despite its modesty, the project might well have had enormous consequences for the Russian labor movement, for though limited in its initial form it was clearly, though subtly, related to many of the largest issues. If the workers showed themselves capable of electing responsible representatives, would this not undermine the opposition to the legalization of trade unions? And if workers could conduct themselves responsibly in the workplace, would not arguments for greater participation in social and political affairs outside the workplace be strengthened? In this sense the starosta project was a perfect example of what Hirschman calls "forward linkage": once established, it may well have had consequences far beyond the original intentions that inspired it.[125] In particular it might have initiated a gradual process of reform before worker unrest posed the same issues in much starker terms. Whatever the law's abstract potential, however, the tsarist system proved too fragile and inflexible to breathe any life into it.

The starosta law was basically initiated and developed within the Ministry of Finance, which promoted the project for two different reasons. First, the ministry saw it as an effective way to ensure order within the factories and lessen the sway of agitators and irresponsible elements in industrial life. Every discussion of the project, whether by Ministry of Finance or by Ministry of Internal Affairs officials, declared order to be the primary goal and benefit of the law. Order, they held, would be strengthened in a variety of ways: (1) The workers could make known their needs and desires and thus appropriate measures could be adopted before the outbreak of unrest. (2) The worker leaders, whose election would be supervised by the authorities and whose activities would be circumscribed by them, would be more moderate than those who emerged illegally. (3) Once disturbances had begun, it would be easier to negotiate with established leaders than with a crowd. And (4) in open rather than secret meetings the influence of revolutionaries would be reduced.[126] In sum, the authorities were confident that they could create such a law that would further, not threaten, the goals of both government officials and the industrialists while at the same time granting the workers new rights. As in the case of Zubatov's project, the proposal was couched in terms of its contribution to peace and harmony as defined and regulated by the government.

The Ministry of Finance's second motive was considerably more pedestrian: it wanted to reduce the role of the police in the factories as much as possible. The law had its origin in the request of factory inspectors that they be allowed "to summon [*vyzyvat'*] worker deputies and talk with them" before the police intervened. The Ministry of Internal

Affairs, they claimed, did not sufficiently recognize this duty of the factory inspectorate, and unfortunately all disorders were dealt with by the police.[127] Such grass-roots complaints were fully consonant with the views of higher officials in the ministry—including Witte—who were equally disturbed by police interference in factory affairs and particularly by the Zubatov experiment.[128] Many in the ministry hoped that a moderate degree of worker autonomy combined with supervision by the factory inspectorate would tranquillize the workers and make police supervision, so dangerous for the authority of the factory owners, superfluous. It was for this reason that there was considerable sentiment in favor of the legalization of some forms of strikes as early as 1897, and the ministry's bureaucracy began to grind out draft proposals,[129] although strikes were not actually legalized until late 1905.

Clearly the Ministry of Finance's position suffered from a rather obvious internal contradiction. On the one hand, in order to undercut the police's tutelary vision, it frequently advocated considerable autonomy for the two contending classes: "Our legislation," it replied to Ministry of Internal Affairs official Panteleev, "grants a broad sphere of freedom to contractual agreements, [and] government supervision has the task precisely of safeguarding this freedom from outside infringements. The interference of the authorities can take place only when this freedom of agreement is infringed by arbitrariness, deception, or coercion."[130] On the other hand, many in the ministry were extremely suspicious about any significant worker autonomy: the factory inspector was to "summon" worker representatives but was himself to play the dominant role; truly independent worker organizations were scarcely envisioned before 1905. Witte, like Trepov or Plehve, was primarily concerned with social order, in his case so that rapid industrialization could proceed smoothly.[131] Just as the monarchist vision of Zubatov or Tikhomirov could also embrace the goal of some degree of worker independence, so the "Western" Ministry of Finance was deeply imbued with the ethos of autocracy. In their different ways both viewpoints reflected the ambiguities and contradictions of a state apparatus attempting to renew itself while maintaining its cardinal assumptions intact.

The dual origin of the starosta proposal corresponded to two broader visions of labor relations, for both of which the project was seen as an essential part. Thus although the project was modest in itself, it raised significant issues. And its essential compatibility with both of these two competing visions gained it widespread support from officials and institutions with conflicting overall orientations.

First, the starosta project was completely compatible with the goals of those who valued order above all else and saw the government as the source of all order. For these officials the worker deputies would serve to aid the authorities in their tasks. For this reason police officials such as Trepov and high Ministry of Internal Affairs bureaucrats such as Sviatopolk-Mirskii proposed legalizing worker representatives quite independently of the Ministry of Finance.[132] Perhaps the most interesting case was Plehve, who most fully expressed the conservative interpretation of the law. In his defense of the project before the State Council, he argued that both the causes of and solutions to worker unrest were straightforward. Rooted in local economic conditions, which are played upon by outside agitators, labor protest would disappear with the satisfaction of basic economic needs. In order to improve the workers' position, he continued, some form of worker organization was essential. What kind? Plehve's answer derives from his conservative bureaucratic view of social groups, which, as we saw, he refused to regard as social forces. The art of government, he declared, is essentially the official's capacity to manage the different social groups through intermediaries. "The power of the strong military leader completely depends on the organization of his soldiers. . . . Thus, in essence, I cannot react negatively to the thought of representation."[133] For Plehve the idea of representation did not imply autonomy; indeed, it was a more effective means of control through which social groups could be subject to quasi-military discipline. It did not occur to Plehve that such a form of organization might be anathema to the workers.

Second, others saw in the law the first step toward the realization of a completely different vision, one centered on the ideal of a factory community based on mutual rights and obligations. They affirmed that industrial relations had a logic and balance partly independent of state control and that the two contending sides, if properly regulated, could establish a harmonious relationship. This rival vision was most completely expressed in the Ministry of Finance's "clarifying article" attached to the legal project, which set forth the rationale for worker representation.[134]

The article begins with an almost Burkean analysis of a community based upon tacit understandings and implicit consent. Echoing a standard European conservative theme, it affirms that not all vital issues can be spelled out by contract. Together with written provisions, there also exist conditions hallowed by custom, which the workers' interests and needs have helped shape. "In the creation of these conditions, the personality of the worker, his interests and his need to satisfy them play a far from insignificant role." Further, the realization and promotion of these implicit standards depend upon the active participation of the workers: "Relations between management and workers are always changed through the demands of both sides and a peaceful resolution of the questions that arise is one of the most essential needs of factory life." The model of the factory autocrat violates the mutuality of the worker-management relationship, and so the factory owner "must sensitively pay attention to the workers' expressed opinions and determine the level of their reasonableness and soundness. Otherwise, it will not be able to avoid the unjust and economically unprofitable use of the workers' labor." This support for paternalistic authority—it was the factory own-er who was to determine the "soundness" of worker aspirations—is bal-anced by the belief that this mutuality implies new rights: "The present law and its established interpretation evidently did not correspond to the complex conditions of industrial life which have arisen, and they re-quired changes in the form of permitting some forms of factory worker organization." The starosta law was thus called forth "by life itself. It is possible to expect with assurance that it only answers to an essential and mature need."

This vision of a community in which actual reciprocity was to be ful-filled through formal law was exceptional. It departed from standard tsarist assumptions by insisting upon the partial autonomy of civil socie-ty, and it appealed to social relations built on trust and consent. Law was only to formalize a relationship that already existed. Its task was not to determine relationships but to institutionalize them by granting rights protected by the state. Such a view of law and the state might, in other contexts, have conservative implications—it was far from a vision of legal activism. In Tsarist Russia, however, where the state was accus-tomed to attempt to freeze social relationships in the past or else to re-define them without regard to custom, it had revolutionary implications.

The vision outlined in the Ministry of Finance's article was far from an accurate reflection of industrial relations in autocratic Russia. Like reform-ers in the Shtakel'burg Commission, the Ministry of Finance officials who composed this document confronted a formidable dilemma: the model they wished to promote presumed conditions that could be brought about only by the policies they advocated. It followed that their ideas challenged established viewpoints and practices and so remained marginal in their impact. Indeed, this vision of an incipient industrial community played virtually no part in the debates on the 1903 law, which were overwhelmingly concerned with the problem of social order. In its final form the starosta law turned out to be much more closely connected to Plehve's principles than to these more liberal conceptions.

An analysis of the origins and evolution of the legal project clearly demonstrates the forces at work to bring about this result. The 1903 law, as noted earlier, had inauspicious beginnings as a proposal designed to counter police intervention in factory affairs. Since the 1897 circulars that authorized police administrative action in times of labor unrest, the factory inspectors had been complaining that the police did not allow them to mediate conflicts. In the 9 April 1901 Ministry of Finance conference called to discuss measures to guarantee order for the upcoming 1 May, various factory inspectors made this complaint, arguing that the rapid resort to police force cut off the possibility of peaceful agreement between the two sides. They proposed that special instructions from the Ministry of Finance should be sent to factory inspectors and factory owners authorizing the workers to choose permanent deputies to negotiate for them. The inspectors maintained that these representatives would be useful in maintaining order, as the factory inspector could gather information about the workers' needs and aspirations and also explain to them through the deputy when their demands were groundless. The senior factory inspector of Vladimir province even urged that these worker representatives should be specifically protected from retaliation by the factory owners.[135]

This proposal had some promising traits. First, it was not part of a broad liberal vision but was seen solely as a mechanism to safeguard social order. It was not connected with political demands for greater freedom but pertained solely to representation in industrial relations. Most interestingly, the proposal arose as a purely administrative measure within the Ministry of Finance: the ministry was simply urged to send out new instructions authorizing the change. In this form the proposal made excellent sense and should have had a good chance of being adopted. It met many of Hirschman's descriptions of an effective reform strategy, being low-key and yet at the same time providing a basis for further change. For it would indeed have been a significant departure from previous practice: the proposal recognized not only that worker complaints could be well founded (this was traditional) but that they were truly a collective concern and should be resolved through group representation.

These proposals were first made in April 1901. The law legalizing factory representatives was finally approved in June 1903. Between these two dates, what might have been an uncomplicated administrative measure became a formal legal project, then a law, finally modified in fundamental ways after months of debate. By the time it had been examined in numerous conferences and governmental organs, the law placed so many restrictions on worker representation that the workers met it with silence. Nor had the factory owners become reconciled to it, despite the major role they played in shaping it to their own interests.

The factory inspectors' original proposal had been extremely simple: they wanted the Ministry of Finance to authorize them to negotiate with recognized worker representatives in order to mediate labor conflict. Shortly thereafter, the Ministry of Finance worked out a set of guidelines sent to factory inspectors that already foreshadowed the fate of the project.[136] The ministry clearly recognized the drawbacks of the workers' lack of representation: they were forced to act as a crowd, with the disorder this entailed, because individual workers were afraid to present demands out of fear of reprisals. To remove this "abnormal situation," the ministry, with the agreement of the Ministry of Interior, found it desirable that the workers have the right to elect elders. In order that this measure not undermine the authority of the factory owner, however, he should be authorized to work out the concrete rules of operation, including detailed definition of the rights and obligations of the elders and the means of their selection. Further, the factory owner should have the right to confirm the elected candidates. All of this was to be with the approval of the senior factory inspector and the governor, and it was subject to certain general rules. It was always to be introduced with "circumspection," however, and in no case could it be made obligatory for the factory owner.

Here was the fatal flaw, the source of the law's irrelevance. A project that was meant to encourage negotiation and conciliation through the granting of rights to workers was twisted to favor the factory owners in an extraordinarily blatant way, for they were given the right to define the starosta's role and the mode of his selection. No consideration was given to the question of how a representative so circumscribed in his rights might still gain the workers' trust, particularly when, as was widely admitted, patriarchal relations were so weak. All this before the factory owners even had a chance to make their fears known! This, too, would happen soon enough, however, and the various government bodies proved to be highly receptive to the owners' pleas.

For reasons that are not completely clear, the proposals were never enacted administratively—perhaps because of a cool reception from the Ministry of Internal Affairs, which never responded to the Ministry of Finance's circular to the factory inspectors.[137] In any case, the proposals were sent to a new Ministry of Finance commission, formed on 14 March 1902, whose task was to evaluate various proposals to deal with the labor question. A year later the Ministry of Finance's legal project, based partly on this commission's work, was ready to be submitted to several conferences and various sessions of the State Council for further debate and modification. It was finally approved by the tsar in June 1903, in radically changed form. In the following discussion I will outline the major positions of the various actors in these different forums without presenting a chronological account. Such an analytical summary should serve as an adequate basis for explaining the failure of this initiative, which might have been the stepping-stone for further reform if the risk had been taken.

Poorly organized though they were, the factory owners played a significant part in reshaping the ministry's legislative project. The organized

St. Petersburg industrialists, accustomed for several previous years to participating in legislative deliberations, prepared a critical report on the project on their own initiative. Further, St. Petersburg and Moscow entrepreneurs were invited to participate in a Ministry of Finance conference to discuss the measure, and, through industrialist members in the State Council, they also influenced that important body's discussions.[138] As in other matters, the factory owners were far from speaking with a single voice. The old split between St. Petersburg industrialists, with their ties to the government and foreign capital and their emphasis on lobbying, and the Moscow enterpreneurs, more independent and nationalistic and more accustomed to self-assertion through the press and public activities, was acutely felt throughout the deliberations. In general, the organized St. Petersburg industrialists opposed the project whereas their Moscow counterparts tended to favor it, though often with considerable skepticism.[139] Much of this difference can be explained by the Muscovites' bitter experiences with police intervention, which made them more ready to experiment with a different approach, and also, perhaps, by the stronger paternalistic ties between the more traditional Moscow employers and their workers.[140]

The leading opponent of the starosta project was the head of the St. Petersburg Society of Factory Owners, the influential S. P. Glezmer. He wrote a report to the Ministry of Finance, signed by thirty-six St. Petersburg industrialists, attacking the project after it was introduced in the State Council.[141] The report claimed that organization would only increase workers' demands and eventually lead to a recapitulation of the European experience, with isolated and organized "worker masses artificially fused into one whole" and subject to the influence of the "international organization of workers." For Glezmer, the proposed government and management supervision over the selection and actions of the starostas would be ineffective; and if the starostas did manage to control them, the workers would never invest confidence in their representatives—so far was Glezmer from any patriarchal illusions about class relations.

Glezmer's mistrust of the workers and his insistence on the maintenance of traditional Russian patterns were echoed again and again throughout discussions of the project. The specter of the German unions, committed to Social Democracy, was dragged out as a warning against "artificial" interference by the state in labor affairs. It was claimed that the factory owners already knew the needs of the workers, and in any case their mutual rights and obligations were already defined by law. And, as M. A. Ogranovich, the manager of the Pipe Factory in St. Petersburg remarked, "to give the worker the right to speak with the boss whenever it enters his mind—this will only lead to undermining the boss' authority."[142]

The industrialist supporters of the starosta project were often no less skeptical about the theoretical desirability of worker organization, but they were more realistic about the alternatives, either police-run unions or underground revolutionary organizations. In a moment of candor, Moscow factory owner V. V. Iakunchikov exclaimed that "like any factory owner I consider that the idea of worker unions in itself is very terrible. Therefore in principle I cannot be a supporter of them. But I know from my own experience that to conduct affairs with a crowd is absolutely impossible."[143] Further, accepting the fact that Russia did indeed have a labor question, proponents of worker representation drew an entirely different conclusion from the European experience than Glezmer—that the European governments had not intervened effectively before industrial discontent became unmanageable. The Russian state should seize the opportunity to act before underground socialist teachings had developed deep roots among the workers.

The differences between these two viewpoints seemed very wide on the interpretation of the character of Russian industrialization and the kind of industrial society that should emerge, as well as in their evaluation of Western European experience. Undoubtedly rival spokesmen exaggerated their claims in order to present ideal models in accord with their own policy prescriptions. Perhaps what was most fundamental in the differences between the two sides was not so much their actual positions—overstated as these were—but their willingness to take risks. Glezmer and his allies, believing that their future security lay with the tsarist state and not an organized civil society, preferred always to assume the worst and act upon their fears. Such insecurity was of course rooted in the tenuous status of the capitalists in autocratic Russia, who were caught between a contemptuous nobility and condescending state bureaucracy on one side and, on the other, a working class that looked to the state, not to the laws of the market, for protection. Not surprisingly, the willingness to take risks, so crucial for reform, was in short supply. Few were those who could, like Iakunchikov, express uncertainty about what the starostas would become—either terrible or optimistic predictions could be made, he said—and yet be willing to gamble.[144] Most preferred short-term security to any larger vision. In such circumstances reform depended almost wholly on the state bureaucracy.

Within this context of a divided industrialist class, the Russian bureaucracy had, in principle, considerable leeway for action. There was also firm support within the government for the enactment of some version of the starosta project. Only a minority in the government shared Glezmer's outright opposition to the proposal. For example, in the 31 May 1903 general meeting of the State Council, eleven members opposed the project, whereas forty-seven supported it. Equally few had much faith in the trustworthiness of the workers to act responsibly on their own. Just as there was general agreement that worker representation was essential, so was there a virtual consensus that the representatives should be carefully supervised by both the factory owners and government officials. The law that finally emerged was the product of these assumptions and so, from the workers' point of view, was completely inappropriate as a channel for worker representation.

The most formidable proponent of a restrictive version of factory representation was Minister of Interior Plehve, some of whose views have already been discussed. One additional point should be mentioned. Following the logic of the disciplined army, Plehve might have concluded that all supervision should be under the control of the government—after all, only revolutionary armies have dual command. Instead, in a revealing line of argument he advocated extensive factory owner supervision. Worker representation, he declared, must not conflict with the central task of the state, which is to oversee all social groups and their interrelations in order to preserve social tranquillity. This task, in turn, links the state to the factory owners, "the class of society most of all interested in the maintenance of governmental order. This circumstance necessarily compels us to lean precisely on this class in various measures."[145] The worker army, then, would have two sets of officers. Plehve believed that such joint command would strengthen subordination, but, as has been suggested throughout, it actually created insoluble contradictions.

Witte's views on the starosta project were not very different from Plehve's.[146] He saw worker representation as primarily a means to ensure social order and was worried that socialists might be elected by the workers. This fear was Witte's only strong basis for objection to the project, and he queried Iakunchikov if he had any misgivings in this regard.[147] More than Plehve, Witte was impressed with the growing danger of worker unrest, which had increased precipitously in recent years.[148] The disorders must be stopped, but it was no longer possible simply to rely upon police methods—bayonets and bullets, he said, were a "terrible path," and, as we know, he was also preoccupied with police subversion of the industrialists' authority. The only alternative was organization, which was already emerging among the workers as a natural result of industrialization, although in a dangerous form. If organization was recognized by the government, it could be channeled according to the latter's purposes and would prove to be no threat to the factory owners or to the state. In place of disorder and chaos, discipline and harmony would reign. In sum, "It is necessary to regulate the labor question. It is the holy obligation of the state and government to be at the head of the movement. This will save the workers from underground influences, and from this the government, the factory owners, and the workers themselves will all gain."[149] Witte's vision was similar in many ways to Zubatov's or Tikhomirov's, except that the factory inspectors and industrialists were to replace the police and worker representation was to substitute for worker mobilization.

Thus both Witte and Plehve were primarily committed to the goal of maintaining social order, and for this reason they advocated strong government interference in the election and activities of the starostas. Both also favored substantial industrialist control over the whole process and so were willing to violate the principle of reciprocity implicit in the Ministry of Finance's clarifying article. The Ministry of Finance was afraid of the factory owners' weak legitimacy; the Ministry of Internal Affairs saw factory owners as a bulwark of order in a hierarchical social system. The one argument stemmed from the weakness of capitalism under an autocracy; the other, from the logic of the autocratic system itself. Together they point to the inescapable conclusion that the worker representatives could have no real autonomy.

The law as finally enacted embodied all these fears and had a deeply conservative tone. The establishment of elders was to be optional for the factory owner, and not obligatory, as was originally proposed. The factory owner had the right to choose the representative from a list chosen by the workers, and he also determined the time and place of meetings. Workers were to be subdivided into groups for the elections, thus avoiding the potential for disorder of a general worker meeting. The minimum age for elders was raised to twenty-five, and factory owners were given the right to raise it further. The starosta was formally made responsible for appropriate order in workers' discussions, and, among other duties, he was charged with transmission of the factory administration's regulations to the workers.[150] In all these senses Struve was surely correct that the main contradiction of the law was that one of the two contracting parties was completely subjected to the other.[151]

The impact of the 1903 law, after so much hard work, was negligible. Factory owners were extremely hesitant to appy it: before 1905 starostas were permitted in only thirty to forty enterprises throughout Russia, many of them small.[152] Bonnell asserts that most workers were probably unaware of the law's existence;[153] Ozerov claimed that of those who knew, many were indifferent.[154] At the same time, the law probably had two more long-range effects, both unintended by its proponents: first, it legitimated the workers' demands for organization; second, it reinforced the sense of many workers that the state and factory owners were allied against them. Perhaps for both reasons, in their 1903 congress the Social Democrats, though well aware of its shortcomings, called upon activists

to make use of the law for organizational and agitational purposes.[155] A flawed law was in many respects more advantageous to them than one that would have granted much fuller rights.

CONCLUDING REMARKS

The five years preceding the 1905 revolution in many ways offered the most propitious circumstances for the development of new government policies toward the working class. The threat of labor protest had become apparent, but it did not yet appear to menace the whole social and political order. Some, like Glezmer, could downplay the significance of the signs of worker revolt (perhaps for their own political ends), but the vast majority seemed to accept the conclusion that the time was ripe for government initiative. There was, however, a noteworthy paradox here. Many officials and factory owners preferred to act when the atmosphere was tranquil—to wait, when necessary, for "the quieting of minds and the reestablishment of the normal course of factory work."[156] Yet such an atmosphere also implied less incentive to act, an irony that will be crucial during and immediately after the 1905 revolution.

Nonetheless, there was a widespread sense of urgency among many officials. The two major efforts to initiate a new policy—the Zubatov experiment and the starosta law—had much in common. Both accepted the notion that some form of organization was essential to reorient the workers and ensure harmony among the state, factory owners, and workers. They held in common the assumption that opportune government action could shape social relations and lessen the need for autonomous action on the part of the two rival classes. Neither embraced to any great extent the potentially explosive idea that the state should remain aloof from the autonomous interaction of social classes and reduce its role in social life. In all these ways both initiatives were in tune with many traditional Russian political assumptions, particularly in the case of the starosta law. Nevertheless, both projects also would have introduced novel practices and assumptions into Russian industrial life. For no matter what the legislators' intentions, organization implies some degree of collective action, mediation, and independence if it is to be rooted in its social base. It cannot be purely an instrument of the elites if it is to be connected to its constituency. The legitimacy of collective action and mediation, though somewhat controversial,[157] was generally accepted by factory owners and officials alike, but they were extremely suspicious of any significant increase in autonomy. None of the founders, for example, favored Zubatov societies without police control; and none of the government advocates of the starosta project wanted anything resembling

trade unions. The very different reasons for the failure of the two projects clearly demonstrate the dilemma: on one hand the Zubatov movement went far beyond what the authorities would countenance; on the other, the law was essentially stillborn because of excessive restrictions. Probably a middle way existed, but it was narrow and difficult to follow.

The narrowness of this path becomes more apparent when contrasted with the very different conjunctures in the other patterns of development described in chapter 2. The most clear-cut context in which states will permit the relatively free development of organizations is the pattern of liberal industrialization, as in England or France. Differences between these two countries are, of course, important. The French class structure was more rigid, the factory owners less tolerant of worker independence, and the labor movement more politicized, although in none of these traits was it comparable to Russia. In both France and England industrial elites were relatively strong and self-confident. They were basically legitimate, both because of their strength and because they were part of a developed civil society based upon independent social groups. They did not need so much state protection; in fact, in France the state actually helped balance the inequality of power in favor of the workers.[158] In such a pattern of development the state may stimulate industry, but rapid industrialization is not a state project in the sense that it would later be for less advanced countries. For these reasons the state is not forced to be vitally concerned with the welfare of the industrialists. Further, the industrialists are not so fearful of reform. Although many French employers objected to unions because they infringed upon their ideal of the factory as a family and introduced outsiders into factory life,[159] the French factory owners viewed the Waldeck-Rousseau law legalizing unions with indifference, confident in their ability to fight the workers on their own.

Japan and Germany represent two variants of responses to the labor question in feudal capitalist countries. Faced with the challenge of justifying their supremacy, industrial elites in both countries could appeal both to their economic success and to traditional patterns of hierarchy. In Japan private elites took the initiative in developing company unions to institutionalize these claims. In Germany, where traditional hierarchy was weaker than in Japan, the efforts of the industrialists in this direction were supplemented by a more elaborate program of state tutelage. In Germany there was also considerable repression of rival claimants to represent and organize the workers, particularly in 1878–1890. In both cases, however, collective action, mediation, and a measure of independence were permitted because the elites were relatively confident that they could exercise a certain amount of control over worker organizations. Germany, with its strong socialist movement and more developed class conflict, is less pure an example, but even so there were undoubtedly many more industrialists resembling Iakunchikov than in Russia. In both cases, too, all of these efforts were in line with the traditional political culture, which emphasized social hierarchy.

In the case of dependent capitalist industrialization, there are two distinct patterns that share some underlying traits. In Chile, which represents the first type, a relatively liberal labor policy was initiated in the 1920s (although not without serious infringements) as a result of inter-elite competition for lower-class support after considerable worker mobilization had already taken place. Argentina in the 1920s also approximates this pattern. By contrast, in Brazil, Vargas initiated the corporatist experiment of the Estado Novo in order to forestall independent worker mobilization and strengthen his social base. Argentina under Perón came to resemble this second pattern, as did, to a lesser extent, Chile under Ibañez, although their prior histories of limited liberalism and worker mobilization also left an important imprint, which distinguished them from Brazil.

Despite these differences among dependent capitalist countries, certain common characteristics stand out: the state's repressive capacity is relatively weak, social and political elites are divided, and the working class, not yet a truly threatening force, can become a crucial base of support for rival elites. Elites are wary of too much worker independence, for the social and political order is relatively fragile, but for their own purposes they favor controlled organizations. Hierarchy between factory owners and workers is not so well developed as in feudal capitalism, but the factory owners do not feel overly menaced by state-regulated organizations. In any case, the industrialists were not a significant force in the formulation of government policy, partly because no project for rapid industrialization existed and, particularly in Chile, there was so much reliance on foreign capital. In Chile state regulation was less pronounced than in the other two countries, but it was significant enough to keep the labor movement weak and fragmented. In all three cases this policy was consistent with many Catholic teachings, which opposed both liberalism and statism.

In Russia, by contrast, the whole issue of organization is more complicated than in any of these patterns for a number of reasons. First, any form of lower-class organization was inconsistent with the traditional political culture, and so attempts to introduce it automatically created conflicts and ambiguities within the government, as was clear from the interministerial squabbles with respect to the police role in the factories. Second, because of their own weakness, the industrial elites were highly skeptical of worker organization, and even those who favored it could accept only limited forms. Finally, many government officials were highly ambivalent, either from a basic distrust of "social forces" or because they sought to protect the fragile position of the industrialists in order to further the state's policy of rapid industrialization. Ozerov criticized the government because "it courted industrialist spheres too much," but this was not so much because, as he suggested, it wanted them as a social base, as because it hoped the industrialists could thus promote the state's own goals.[160] For these three reasons—intergovernmental divisions, the fragility of the capitalists, and the strength of autocratic traditions—the hopes of many that the Russian autocracy would be better able to resolve the labor question because of the strength of autonomous state power turned out to be groundless. Rather, its very inconsistency with modern industrial capitalism based on an independent entrepreneurial class rendered it impotent. Only a revolutionary threat could temporarily shake the regime's lethargy, although revolution created dilemmas for labor policy never previously faced by an industrializing society. During and after this upheaval, too, the Russian state turned out to be incapable of boldness and initiative.

CHAPTER
5
Labor Policy in 1905–1907

The 1905 revolution, which began with the massacre of hundreds of St. Petersburg workers on 9 January 1905, dramatically altered the whole political atmosphere of Tsarist Russia. Precipitated by this unprovoked slaughter, which came to be known as Bloody Sunday, the ultimately unsuccessful revolution was deeply rooted in Russian society and politics. Ultimately its cause was the obsolescence of the Russian state, whose repressive social policy, attempts to curtail the growing independence of civil society, and inability to deal with the agrarian and labor questions had alienated virtually all sectors of Russian society. This long-term crisis was accentuated by (and also linked to) the regime's incompetence, particularly evident in its humiliating conduct of the war with Japan. Confronted throughout 1905 by massive social unrest, including peasant rebellions, student demonstrations, and strikes among all categories of workers, employees, and professionals, the regime attempted to quell the disturbances through concessions. The most significant of these was the famous October Manifesto, which, in response to the great strikes of September and October, promised a constitutional monarchy.

The mood of Russian elites can be gleaned from a report of 9 October 1905 from the usually self-possessed Witte: "The Russian revolt, senseless and merciless, will sweep away everything, reduce everything to dust. How Russia will escape from this unprecedented experience is unimaginable; the horrors of the Russian revolt can exceed anything that has occurred in History."[1] Even the promise of a constitution, which was far from universally trusted, was not enough to pacify the workers, however. November and December witnessed more strikes, which culminated in the December uprising in Moscow and another bloody response from the tsarist state now supported by much of the middle stratum of Russian society, especially the industrialists. The Moscow uprising marked the final outburst of violent labor militancy, but ferment continued throughout the following year.

These startling events, unprecedented in Russian history, dramatically altered the political context of the labor question. Many more government officials than ever before expressed the conviction that labor unrest threatened the foundations of the empire and demanded urgent measures. Yet labor unrest was only one part of a global crisis that complicated an effective response in any one area and left political elites disoriented and terrified. The array of challenges facing the regime was indeed formidable: demands for political democracy, agrarian and national revolt, and massive industrial strikes.

In the desperate search for palliatives, measures were contemplated that previously would have been anathema to the majority of political elites. The revolution thus brought to the fore tendencies that, though present in embryonic form in the prerevolutionary period, had never been take seriously before. Therein lay the dilemma: forced by the crisis to make concessions that they deeply hated, and now even more suspicious of social forces once they had expressed themselves so powerfully, many elites rejected the possibility of reform. In this sense the 1905 revolution was dangerous for both the regime and its opponents, for to many it seemed to offer no compromise. Consequently, forced to consider innovations that it could never sincerely embrace, the regime in its conduct from 1905 to 1907 offered dramatic examples of shifts in policy, contradictions between word and deed, and deception. In the end the autocracy triumphed and imposed its will on its helpless enemy with little concern for long-term consequences. The resolution of the labor question was now impeded by the victorious counterrevolution, which forged an alliance of fear between the outraged autocracy and the shaken factory owners. Thus an analysis of the bold new ideas introduced into public debate and the groping efforts made to realize them in these years of ferment must be prefaced by the observation that their very boldness conditioned their failure.

Before 1905 the dominant paradigm for resolving the labor question was, as we have seen, government regulation and protection. The regime's basic premise was that the independent political action of social groups would harm the social equilibrium over which it was to preside. In Russia rights were seen as "objective" benefits and privileges granted directly by the state, and not "subjective" political freedoms through which social groups could express and protect their interests. These objective rights might include the right of representation, but this representation could not conflict with the unlimited power of the sovereign.[2] The crisis of 1905 gave new prominence to the rival model of a liberal approach to the labor question. Many elements of a liberal vision had surfaced before 1905, particularly within the Ministry of Finance and among Moscow industrialists, but never before had they been set forth so consistently or boldly.

The heart of a liberal policy is the granting of rights of representation and organization to the workers and factory owners so that they can defend their own interests. Such a policy is embedded in a set of ideas utterly foreign to Russian political traditions. The ideological basis of a liberal policy is the conviction that state and society and, correlatively, politics and economics are distinguishable, if not completely separate, spheres. Society has rules of its own that ensure basic stability: in the economy the laws of the market; in social relations the balance of opposing forces, whether they be classes or interest groups. In this view social conflict arises naturally, and it can be resolved to some degree independently of the state through the organized action of both sides. Further, its free expression will lead to harmony, for each group will benefit as much as is feasible given the balance of forces. The government is no longer held responsible for defense of the interests of its subordinate groups and social conflicts become partially depoliticized.

Even before 1905 liberal ideas had some champions within the government, and, as opposed to the later period, these people could promote their ideas for reform without directly linking them to the overall problem of autocracy. After all, it was unclear at the time how far liberal reforms in industrial relations would challenge the foundations of the autocratic regime. If Western Europe were taken as a model, it might seem that changes in industrial relations implied political change, that the right to organize was bound up with the rights of free speech, assembly, and suffrage—for in the West these processes went together. For Russian statesmen such as Witte and Kokovtsov, however, it was not certain that reforms such as the right of workers to select representatives for negotiations would lead to political changes as well. Even in Western Europe the relation between changes in class relations and political reform was far from uniform. In England workers had the right to organize long before they had the right to vote, whereas in France the opposite was the case. Perhaps in Russia, thought high officials such as Witte or, in his own special way, Zubatov, reforms in industrial relations could even forestall broader political demands by removing the bases of economic discontent. Thus to many there appeared to be no insurmountable political obstacles to a liberal model of industrial relations. Rights of organization could be "objective"—clearly defined, delimited, operating within a space determined by the state, and not "subjective," which entails the group's ability to make claims vis-à-vis the state.[3]

Their presumed isolation from political reform made liberal ideas conceivable in government circles before 1905. In addition, a number of pressures in Russian social and political life gave them a certain degree of prominence. First there was the example of the West, which could be interpreted in a variety of ways. Some conservatives, such as Shuvalov, saw it as a warning against too much social independence and hoped that the Russian state could undertake measures to forestall social and political mobilization. Others, especially in the Ministry of Finance, seized on the ideas of contract, market, and social equilibrium in order to argue that industrial life was subject to its own logic and laws. Worker or employer violations of the labor contract, and even strikes, were seen to be civil matters unconnected with the general issue of social order.[4] In the view of these conservatives the Western example proved that the development of capitalism depended upon some degree of autonomy of civil society. At the same time, it must be emphasized that the ministry's views tended to have a narrow focus—the prosperity of industry and the authority of the factory owners. It had no serious intention, in Ozerov's phrase, "to regulate it [the labor question] according to the spirit of the new time,"[5] as the fate of the starosta project clearly showed.

A second factor encouraging liberalism was more prosaic: simply the high cost to the government of tutelage and repression, in terms of both material resources lost and legitimacy undermined. If some degree of social ferment was healthy, as Trepov claimed, and if the government did not have to be responsible for the welfare of the workers, as the Ministry of Finance tirelessly argued, the government could safely distance itself from factory affairs. Growing awareness on the part of the police that coercion was inadequate and that the workers must be allowed to defend themselves was one important source of their support for measures such as the Zubatov societies or the starosta law. Thus in his report during debates on the starosta law, head of the Department of Police Lopukhin explicitly declared that police measures alone were not sufficient and that coercion was taxing the police's energies. Precisely for this reason, he said, the starosta project had been developed.[6] Recall as well that Trepov ultimately hoped that the Zubatov council could negotiate with the factory owners largely independently of government intervention. The views of Ministry of Finance and police officials were thus similar in many ways despite the different motivations behind them. Before 1905 neither envisioned a laissez-faire economy or an autonomous class struggle, but both thought that some degree of controlled conflict was necessary and desirable.

Finally, the very vigor of autocratic practices before 1905 was bound to call forth a liberal reaction in a system that aimed to place new responsibilities on economic elites. For this reason among some officials and factory owners liberalism was at least as intense as it had been in England, where the forces of aristocratic privilege could hardly compare with Russian state centralism as a challenge to the rise of the new elites. Thus liberalism in Russia, as in England, was bound up with new claims to power and social position. One of the best examples of this process was the emergence of liberal ideas as a counterweight to police intervention and Zubatovism. Many Moscow industrialists and Ministry of Finance officials saw these intrusions as upsetting the harmony established by the market and the social balance of forces. Sometimes they even advocated the legalization of strikes and organizations in order that each side might be able to protect itself in the struggle of forces. Thus Guzhon wrote to Ministry of Finance official Kovalevskii that "personally not having anything against the right of workers to strike or the principle of worker association when it acts according to legally recognized statutes, we cannot submit to the demands of the Okhrana department, which pressures the factory owners through workers' associations."[7] Police tutelage was thus one of the best arguments for a liberal approach, even, if need be, one giving the workers important new rights. Trepov accused Guzhon of insincerity, but if he was right, Guzhon's unwilling espousal of the right of association demonstrates even more clearly the pressures for liberalism.

Despite all these favorable conditions, for reasons described in the previous chapter almost nothing was done before 1905 to promote these liberal ideas. Much had been discussed. The important March 1902 interministerial conference that was called to debate the labor question had endorsed changes in the law prohibiting strikes and also passage of the starosta project. Even more impressively, it appeared that Plehve had endorsed the suggestions of Ianzhul, a former factory inspector and advocate of Western labor policies, that strikes and labor unions should be legalized.[8] Projects had been drawn up and ideas clarified, and key elements of an identifiable liberal approach had emerged. It took the shock of 9 January and its aftermath of massive strikes, however, to channel these ideas into a powerful new set of policies that might win broad social and political support.

THE FAILURE TO DEVELOP A COMPREHENSIVE POLICY: THE MINISTERIAL COMMISSIONS OF 1905–1907

Bloody Sunday had been preceded in January by serious strikes in St. Petersburg led by an organization reminiscent of the Zubatov societies, the Gapon Assembly, which was named after the priest and dubious Okhrana collaborator Father Gapon. The Assembly, whose first meeting was held with the permission of the police in August 1903, originally concentrated its efforts on religious, educational, and cultural matters. Throughout 1904, however, there occurred a radicalization of the leadership, including Gapon himself, a crucial antecedent of the January conflicts over the firing from the Putilov factory of several workers for their participation in the organization. These disputes eventually led to a strike in Putilov itself, which set the stage for activation of the assembly's organizations throughout St. Petersburg and also supporting strikes that by 7 January involved about 105,000 St. Petersburg workers from 382 enterprises.[9]

The Ministry of Finance took a position antagonistic to the workers' demands in these strikes. On 7 January, Minister Kokovtsov wrote to Minister of Internal Affairs Sviatopolk-Mirskii that he and the factory owners had agreed that the workers' demands were impossible to fulfill. If the workers were permitted to determine their own wages, "they would become the bosses of the establishment, and the factory owners, who had borne the risks of production, would be deprived of their legal right to control their own affairs."[10] Gapon, he continued, was a dangerous man and his societies should be closed, for otherwise the workers would become convinced that they were acting with the support of the government.

After 9 January, Kokovtsov's tone changed—partly, no doubt, out of sympathy and partly because he saw the opportunity to establish definitive Ministry of Finance control over labor policy. On 11 January he composed an appeal to the tsar, begging his forgiveness for disturbing him during "the sorrowful moment experienced by You, during serious disturbances which embrace Your capital."[11] He then made bold to offer his suggestions for the pacification of the workers. Police influence and armed force were not enough. The first imperative measure was simply "the Sovereign word of YOUR IMPERIAL HIGHNESS," which could explain to the workers the error of their ways and how they had been used by unscrupulous conspirators. "The workers will believe YOUR word that they will find true benefit and protection only in YOUR mercy, and not in the deceptive promises of their leaders."

Such a paternalistic appeal was not all that Kokovtsov had in mind. In reports to the tsar on 14 January, 16 January, and especially 19 January,[12] he urged that the Ministry of Finance be given full authority to resolve the labor question without vacillation, satisfying those demands of the workers that were acceptable and demonstrating to them the government's solicitude.[13] He subjected the past policies of the Ministry of Internal Affairs to harsh criticism, arguing that they had created administrative chaos and paralysis and had also deepened worker discontent. He reserved his sharpest barbs for the Zubatov experiment, which he blamed for exacerbating class conflict, undermining the workers' respect for the law, and convincing them that they were "the predominant class in the state, that for them neither courts, nor factory inspectorate, nor police were necessary."[14] If only the Ministry of Finance had been free to pursue its own program of legislation on the workday, medical care, strikes, and worker organization the labor question would have been resolved. He concluded by advocating an ambitious program of reform to be undertaken entirely by the Ministry of Finance. It consisted of four basic proposals:

1. the legalization of worker organizations—in particular the obligatory organization of sick funds and the creation of conciliatory bodies composed of representatives of both sides to discuss and resolve their differences;

2. shortening of the workday;

3. the legalization of some forms of strikes; and

4. obligatory factory owner construction or sponsorship of hospitals.

Some of these proposals had already been broached in years past, but their grouping into an overall program of reform was novel. It is also noteworthy that Kokovtsov advocated both liberal and protective measures, and the combination was sure to arouse the opposition of many factory owners.

On the basis of these proposals in meetings of the Council of Ministers on 28 January and 31 January, the Ministry of Finance was authorized to pursue these proposals and develop appropriate legislation. The meetings, which included Minister of Internal Affairs Bulygin, also fully endorsed Kokovtsov's request that Finance be granted virtually full powers on these questions. The Council of Ministers authorized the formation of the Kokovtsov Commission to pursue these ends in the interest of social peace.[15]

The Kokovtsov Commission was the first of three government commissions (the others were the Fedorov Commission of mid-April 1906 and the Filosofov Commission, convened in December 1906) charged to initiate a new program of labor legislation. Factory owner obstructionism, ambivalence within the government, and the waning threat of labor unrest, however, all worked to reduce their accomplishments to two potentially notable achievements: the December 1905 rules legalizing some categories of strikes and the March 1906 temporary law permitting some types of worker organization. No coherent program of labor reform ever emerged, and even these two measures, potentially highly significant in their implications for the labor movement, were systematically violated by the government after the Stolypin coup d'état in June 1907.

There were noteworthy differences among the three commissions. The Kokovtsov Commission convened in the midst of the revolutionary crisis and military defeat in the Japanese War, and its work attracted little attention. It provides a lesson in how crisis stimulated debate but impeded results. The Fedorov Commission, under the auspices of the newly formed Ministry of Trade and Industry, never really emerged into public view and left few records of its deliberations. It is primarily important for the most consistent proclamation of liberal principles to come forth from any government commission or conference. The Filosofov Commission was accompanied by great public fanfare and broad press coverage. The revolution had died down and there was great hope for a comprehensive solution to the vexing problem of labor unrest. European laws and organizations were scrutinized and an avalanche of speeches and reports were made, but little of substance materialized. Deep divisions among the factory owners and lack of commitment to change on the part of government officials frustrated the hopes of the public. The challenged autocracy, unwilling to surrender its prerogatives or depart from its bureaucratic style of politics, temporarily postponed change; and many industrialists, painfully aware of their weakness and deeply ambivalent about reform, once again took refuge in the autocratic state.

No attempt will be made here to review all the deliberations and legal projects of the three commissions, nor is there space to discuss in detail their various similarities and differences in approach. Rather, a few basic themes closely connected to the dilemmas of autocratic capitalism will be discussed in order to highlight the impediments to reform.

Diagnoses in the commissions of the causes of labor protest ranged from the traditional explanations to perceptive and wide-ranging critiques of government policy as a whole. In his opening speech, for example, Minister Kokovtsov echoed a time-worn theme: worker unrest was not basically political in orientation but stemmed from workers' bad socioeconomic conditions, which could be ameliorated by factory owners without major sacrifice. And, as noted earlier, he singled out police interference and the unreasonable promises of tutelage for special condemnation.

The insights of the Fedorov Commission penetrated much more deeply, indicting the authorities for their politicization of the labor movement. The government was culpable for its departure from what the Fedorov report regarded as the "natural" solution to the labor question: "From the numerous reports composed by our industrialists on the events we have lived through, and equally from the demands put forth by the workers, it is evident that our industrial structure needs, above all, the greatest possible freedom from excessive administrative tutelage."[16] This involved a complete reexamination and revision of government policy; partial changes would not return the "industrial structure" to health. The report is striking for its "naturalistic" approach to the whole question. It was "natural" that with the rise of modern industry, the workers sought to improve their living conditions. The solution to the labor question, the freeing of the two sides, was also natural. Traditionally, of course, Russian officials had not taken such a positive view of the autonomy of social groups; as for Hobbes, so for them, freedom (and nature) were indissolubly linked to chaos. For the Fedorov Commission liberalization was the very foundation of industrial order.

The commission by no means expounded a simple laissez-faire approach to labor relations, however. Even in its advocacy of freedom of association it introduced the important qualification that the government must "place both sides in such a situation so that neither of them can outweigh the other." In addition, it explicitly distinguished among individualist, socialist, and reformist perspectives, preferring the reformist strategy for its avoidance of the two extremes of complete government nonintervention or total government control. Government and society, it declared, "are obligated to remove or, at least, soften the defects in the situation of the non-possessing classes of the population." The joint efforts of government, society, the industrialists, and the workers themselves were required to reach an equitable solution.

Unfortunately, the insights and recommendations of the Fedorov Commission had little impact. With hindsight it is apparent that a truly liberal labor policy depended upon corresponding political reforms that the government was not willing to countenance. The government never sufficiently trusted civil society, particularly the workers, to let class relations take their "natural" course. The Fedorov Commission's recommendations deeply violated the surviving autocratic assumptions of the regime.

This basic lack of trust in the wisdom and responsibility of social groups was painfully evident in both the Kokovtsov and Filosofov commissions. For example, characteristic of the Kokovtsov Commission from the very beginning was a strong insistence that all initiative should remain with the government. The factory owners were invited as informants; the workers were not invited at all. Speaking to the factory owners at the 16 May session, Kokovtsov explained his view of their role in the deliberations: "Appealing to your experience and knowledge, I invite you, dear sirs, to help the Ministry of Finance by illuminating all questions designated for our discussion by order of the Tsar, and I am completely certain that you came here in order to give this help." This help, he continued, would be useful not for the actual drawing up of the laws but only in order to clarify "the conditions of everyday life."[17] The commission, then, would listen to the factory owners' views according to its discretion.[18] Also instructive is the minister's response to a deputation of four workers from a Moscow mutual aid society. He counseled the workers to wait and trust in the superior wisdom and judgment of the government.

The impossible must not be demanded: laws cannot be worked out with such haste as to sacrifice their quality. Therefore the workers must peacefully await the results of the Commission's work and completely rely on the fact that, from its side, all measures will be undertaken for the immediate publication of laws. . . . In view of this, I propose to the workers to continue work peacefully in their industrial establishments and calmly to await the laws designated by the supreme power."[19]

The minister, then, still adhered to the hallowed conviction that the government alone should determine policy, for it alone could be disinterested and just. Social groups were still too lacking in judgment and maturity to have the right of real representation. Such a bureaucratic ethos may have been appropriate for a static Russia, but as Karl Mannheim remarks, by itself it is impotent to develop new laws and truly come to terms with explosive social forces.[20] This ethos prefers social tranquillity and predictable results. It collects information, considers all possibilities, and attempts to routinize crises that it does not understand, hoping for a "quieting of minds." It cannot act. Thus Kokovtsov justified delays by an appeal to the need to gather masses of material about the historical experience of the West, so that Russia's special needs could be considered broadly. He added that workers were not mature enough for some reforms—they lacked culture and education. This disturbed him because it meant that the outcome of the reforms could not be predicted beforehand and controlled properly. And in general he noted that if it were not for the overall situation of ferment, the ministry would be able to act with more dispatch in resolving these matters.[21] Later, in his memoirs he remarked that "given the state of mind of that time [1905], no liberal innovations could have had any effect upon the unchained passions which raged until the suppression of the Moscow riot [December]."[22]

The Filosofov Commission, held one and a half years later, suffered from the same failing. One hundred and one factory owners were invited to participate in the discussions, but the workers were once again excluded. "Of course, it would have been desirable," said Filosofov, "to have invited worker representatives here. But it was necessary to reject this given the complete absence of such organizations which could be real representatives of the working class, and not chance individual people."[23] This decision provoked some criticism. Ivan Ianzhul, former factory inspector and adviser to Plehve, argued that the workers could make positive contributions to the commission's work and, in addition, that participation would teach them to listen to opposing views and moderate their demands. His final argument was that the left-wing members of the Duma would be more inclined to accept the projects if the workers had

had a hand in them.[24] For the bureaucracy, however, participation was not a right but a privilege to be earned on the basis of proper behavior. It is interesting to note, too, that the factory owner organizations were hardly a model of coherent organization: as will be seen shortly, they were racked with internal dissension, and their representativeness might well have been questioned.

These autocratic assumptions doomed the Kokovtsov and Filosofov commissions to irrelevance and impotence. First, it was impossible to build an atmosphere of public pressure for reform—and even in Tsarist Russia public sentiment could be a weighty incentive to action. Even sincere and committed reformers, of which there was no lack, were forced to operate in a vacuum. Thus what was said of the Kokovtsov Commission was also true of the Filosofov Commission: they remained "in a void, deprived of any sympathetic surrounding atmosphere and real social support."[25]

Second, and equally important, the excessive caution born of a penchant for bureaucratic control led to an unwillingness to deal with the cornerstone of labor reform: the question of worker organization. Kokovtsov recognized the centrality of this issue. So crucial was it, he said in the 16 May session, that it could not be addressed right away:

> This question is completely new not only for us, but also for other governments, and if in some Western European countries it has received a certain development, there it is posed under completely different conditions from those which exist in our life, and therefore for us this new matter demands great attention and great caution and great preparation.[26]

By the time of the Filosofov Commission enough had been studied and learned to allow the publication in March 1906 of temporary rules permitting organization. The commission was unwilling, however, to make the rules permanent or to free worker organizations from administrative arbitrariness. A number of factory owners pointed out the crucial importance of this issue, among them Von Ditmar, a prominent industrialist from the south, but the question of organization was never formally broached. Filosofov had his reasons: freedom of strikes and union organization had been granted, but because of the influence of revolutionaries they had not yet yielded the desired results and it was necessary to continue the state of martial law in many places. "Time is necessary for the trade union organizations to be free from alien revolutionary aspirations. Then labor unions here, as everywhere, will guide the labor movement in a more peaceful channel."[27]

Thus to the traditional autocratic emphasis on the state's autonomy and the irresponsibility of social forces was added a new argument born of revolutionary ferment, the product of a challenged autocracy: reform must await the quieting of minds, a tranquil social atmosphere in which the bureaucracy could work without prejudice and in peace. The history of post-1906 labor policy—whose results added up almost to nothing— proves that without the pressure of protest the bureaucracy simply returned to its old ways, so incapable was the outmoded state apparatus of anticipating and preparing to meet social change.

If the government bears much responsibility for the lack of labor reform, so do the industrialists. The most clear-cut example was the behavior of the majority of factory owner representatives to the Kokovtsov Commission. Fifty-five of the sixty-two representatives challenged Kokovtsov's explanation of the causes of worker unrest, arguing that "the causes of these strikes are not so much the economic conditions of life of the workers as circumstances outside of industrial life"—namely, in the general political atmosphere of the country.[28] As the prominent Moscow industrialist Krestovnikov wrote to Glezmer, however, they could not risk appearing to the workers and the public as unyielding opponents of Kokovtsov's proposed reforms.[29] The solution to their dilemma appeared as a *deus ex machina*: the defeat of the Russian fleet by the Japanese at Tsushima in mid-May 1905. In the 18 May session Krestovnikov read a statement announcing that because of Russia's catastrophic defeat, the industrialists could no longer discuss these issues—the situation was too "nervous."[30] He added that nothing would be lost by delay, for if the great misfortune that had struck Russia failed to quiet the workers, new laws also would not help. Kokovtsov asked the industrialist representatives to reconsider their decision, but they were adamant. Kokovtsov ended by assuring them that government officials would stay at their posts—with what results we already know.

The factory owners' role in the Filosofov Commision was much more complex. More factory owners (101) were invited to participate, and as a result of the revolutionary ferment they were much better organized, though far from united either ideologically or organizationally. Some important representatives warned against precipitous action, for, as Glezmer stated, the minds of the workers were not yet in a state of equilibrium.[31] In contrast, V. I. Timiriazev, president of the Council of the Congress of the Association of Trade and Industry,[32] espoused the need for immediate reform and assured the officials that his organization wanted to cooperate fully with the government's efforts.[33]

Such complete cooperation on the part of the industrialists was not to be. First, there was widespread hostility toward any material concessions to the workers, especially on the length of the workday and the obligatory fourteen-day notice prior to dismissal (which the factory owners wanted to shorten or abolish). The debates over these and other issues provided the occasion for bitter condemnations of the workers that aroused the concern of Minister Filosofov, who felt it necessary to remind the factory owners that "we are concerned to soothe, and not aggravate [class relations]."[34] There was also more than a touch of hypocrisy to the industrialists' argument: they made countless references to the workers' capacity to defend themselves without government legislation, but they were well aware of the fragile nature of the nascent trade union movement and thus of the vacuity of their argument. Some factory owners recognized this contradiction and supported stronger worker organizations in place of legislation, but such voices were clearly in the minority.[35]

Because of these conflicts no new legislation emerged out of the Filosofov Commission. The most that can be said is that some of its work provided the foundation for the insurance law to be passed several years later. Its results were well summarized by a contemporary journalist, who, in considering the previous thirty years' efforts to resolve the labor question, lamented, "So many people, so many efforts, so many words. . . . So much waste of both time and, if you will, money and . . . a minimum of results."[36] None of the central issues had been resolved, and according to the Council of the Congress of the Association of Trade and Industry, industrial life still had not been given a firm foundation. It is true that temporary legislation had previously been passed in two crucial areas, the legalization of strikes and of unions. As will be discussed shortly, and as the council itself recognized, these temporary laws really resolved nothing. A detailed examination of the origins and limitations of these measures will allow us to understand the regime's paltry achievements from another angle.

TEMPORARY RULES ON STRIKES AND UNIONS AND THE BRIEF FLOWERING OF TRADE UNIONS

The 1905 revolution did succeed in stimulating the enactment of two liberal labor laws: the December 1905 temporary rules legalizing some categories of strikes and the March 1906 temporary rules permitting worker organizations. Together these measures might have constituted the foundation of a new labor policy, the beginnings of a transition parallel to the change to constitutional monarchy in the political sphere. In both cases the government appeared to have inaugurated significant changes while still maintaining substantial power and control within its own hands. The pace of change could thus be regulated in order to avoid excessive threat and to encourage a gradual transition. Reform from above was thus a conceivable outcome of the 1905 revolution, but the government never reconciled itself to any significant devolution of control. Trade unionism in the 1906–1907 period gave many indications that reform might have the moderating effects envisioned by so many liberals. The government destroyed its own venture after the June 1907 Stolypin coup d'état, however, which demonstrated how deeply hostile many officials had been to the reforms forced on the state.

As noted earlier, the Ministry of Finance had been advocating a law legalizing certain categories of strikes for many years. By late 1905 the time finally seemed ripe for the enactment of this measure, particularly as the government was well aware that it lacked the means to repress the strike movement by force. Similarly, many industrialist groups called for their legalization, as long as adequate provision was made for the protection of their property and they were allowed to break their legal obligations to striking workers. The Ministry of Finance's rationale for permitting strikes was spelled out in its project, "On Changes in the Punitive Articles of the Law on Strikes and Illegal Violation of the Wage Contract."[37] Its authors made use of familiar arguments from the ministry's arsenal. They pointed to the beneficial effects of the legalization of strikes in Western Europe and the futility of the Russian government's efforts to counteract them by force. Police methods, they declared, were counterproductive. Punitive measures such as dismissal, arrest, and exile did not remove the causes of the workers' discontent and embittered them against the regime. Forcing employers to make concessions gave workers the harmful idea that a strike is the surest means of satisfying their demands, independent of the justice or legality of those demands. It would be far better to recognize that strikes were a natural phenomenon of industrial life and should be punished only when, as was rarely the case, they threatened social order. The authors of the project also declared that the legalization of worker organizations would further reduce the danger of strikes by encouraging "the proper restraint appropriate for their own interests."

The ministry's project was discussed in a special subcommittee of the Kokovtsov Commission, with participation by the Ministry of Justice, after the factory owners had withdrawn from the commission's deliberations.[38] Representatives of the two ministries disagreed on important details, such as whether incitement to strike should still be a criminal offense, but there was general consensus on the desirability of the measure as long as proper guidelines were established. The rules approved in December permitted strikes when not accompanied by violence and damage to property and outside of state enterprises or those having social and political significance. Officials recognized that in a practical sense not all participants in illegal strikes could be punished, and so they favored action against instigators and especially guilty participants.[39] The government thus attempted to discriminate among different categories of strikes and participants, punishing only those in the most harmful categories.[40] Subsequent experience would show how arbitrary such judgments could become.

Recall that the Kokovtsov Commission had given central importance to a new law permitting worker organizations; but even before the industrialists' withdrawal, Kokovtsov had appealed to the need for more time for study and preparation. Meanwhile a project was being prepared within the Ministry of Finance under the direction of F. V. Fomin, an official at the Central Bureau of Factory Affairs. The draft proposal that emerged sometime in May, the Fomin project, was an exemplary piece of liberal legislation.[41] It took as its model Belgian and English laws and sought to equalize the rights and responsiblities of the factory owners and workers. It authorized the organizations to defend the members' interests, including—implicitly—by way of strikes. Organizations were to be relatively free of administrative interference and were to be closed only by order of the courts. Registration of organizations was to be unencumbered by complex regulations or prior investigation. Organizations could have paid attorneys and were given the right to form federations. In November 1905 Minister of Trade and Industry Timiriazev sent a slightly revised version of this project to the Council of Ministers with an appeal that, in view of the urgency of the issue, it be enacted immediately on a temporary basis until a more finished project could be devised. It was in the Council of Ministers that the first major objections to the project were voiced.[42] Some of the ministers believed that unions with approved bylaws should be subject to closing only by court order but that in other cases this should be the responsibility of the head police official of the province. Further, in accord with a Ministry of Justice project on societies and unions in general, the Council of Ministers unanimously recommended that the governor or head official of a province be able to close unions before a court decision if they threatened social peace and security or if their activities were immoral.[43]

These doubts and recommendations were then taken up by the State Council, which had the right to make final modifications of legal projects and whose approval was crucial for a project to become law, although the tsar could side with the minority.[44] By a majority of thirty-two to twenty-nine the State Council decided that the Ministry of Internal Affairs, and not the courts, should be given the right to close unions. In a special opinion twenty members of the State Council defended their decisions with most interesting arguments.[45] The courts, they said, would be faced with a dilemma: either they obey the letter of the law, in which case the interests of social order would suffer because not all infringements can possibly be covered by the law; or be freer in their interpretation, but then they would lower the law's prestige: "Adherence to politics always and everywhere brought the court down from that height upon which it must stand." These members further elaborated their argument with reflections on the conflict between law and politics: law must operate on stable norms, but state policy must vary by time and place, as risks will so vary. Thus it would be better to give to the organs of administrative justice authority for opening, registering, and closing societies.

This argument highlights one of the essential impediments to the emergence of a liberal policy in Russia: the widely shared official distrust of an autonomous legal system with its own rules and procedures independent of the sovereign will or the purposes of the administration. This distrust was connected to the traditional suspicion of even partially unfettered social forces, a sentiment that not only did not disappear but was in some circles even strengthened by the revolution.

The decision to delegate the power to regulate unions to the minister of Internal Affairs was far from trivial in its practical implications, and this was clearly understood by the members of the State Council. The twenty-nine members of the minority who favored judicial regulation explicitly pointed to the dangers of Ministry of Internal Affairs control. They foresaw what it would later lead to in practice: a revival of the old police arbitrariness in a regime that had pledged to renew itself. The forces of suspicion and skepticism, however—which, significantly, included Witte and Kokovtsov—were victorious. It would be interesting to know why these erstwhile defenders of the Ministry of Finance's prerogatives were willing to support a modification to the law that could easily lead to the intensification of police control over factory affairs.

The State Council modified the law in yet another crucial direction. In addition to illegal acts, the Council of Ministers had favored the prohibition of immoral activities and those threatening social peace and security. Thirty-eight members (again including Witte and Kokovtsov!) shared this opinion, once again supporting the introduction of an imprecise and arbitrary modification into the law. A minority of thirty-one favored the prohibition only of immoral or illegal activities. The decision of the majority was incorporated into the temporary rules on unions of March 1906. It was sufficiently vague to justify the ferocious repression of the union movement in the postrevolutionary period, for, particularly when left to the police, there was plenty of room for interpretation of exactly what constituted a threat to social peace.

A vague law to be administered by the police: a perfect formula for repression. Yet legislators seem to have thought—at the very least, they said—that they were creating the basis for an entirely new direction in labor policy. By this new law, it was stated in the State Council, "the workers are given a legal way to the satisfaction, by their joint efforts, of their material and spiritual needs, and in addition the temptation for them to engage in politics will be weakened."[46] Witte even argued that the conditions for such a transition were mature: the workers were disillusioned with their revolutionary leaders and were ready to embark on a purely economic struggle.[47] It was thought, therefore, that the new rules should be published immediately, even before the convocation of the Duma, so that the revolutionaries would have no more time to infect the workers with politics.

It was liberalism, perhaps, but liberalism interpreted within the framework of an autocratic regime, which still claimed the right to define the limits of the permissible purely from its own point of view. Like Zubatov, many Russian bureaucratic liberals made a sharp distinction between economic and political struggle and considered only the former to be legitimate. Thus the practical implications of their perspective were not so different from those that emerged from more conservative viewpoints. In attempting to enforce this distinction between economic and political action, they created the conditions under which it made no sense at all. As more consistent liberals such as Von Ditmar recognized,[48] it was not through police tutelage that the labor movement could become depoliticized. As we will see, in attempting to root politics out of the organized labor movement, the government temporarily all but destroyed it, once again preparing the conditions for the recurrent alliance of an uninstitutionalized labor movement and the revolutionary parties.

With all of their restrictions, the temporary rules did permit the formation of worker organizations at the initiative of the workers and so constituted an enormous advance over the starosta law. The opportunities opened for worker initiative created dilemmas for both the government and the labor movement. On the part of some government officials there was still considerable ambivalence about the series of measures promulgated against their will, and, as always, the requirements of social order were paramount. The dilemma of these officials was clearly expressed in a November 1905 report of the head of the political section of the police, Rachkovskii. After giving brief descriptions of the revolutionary parties and their goals, he recommended a series of strict measures that he recognized as inconsistent with the spirit of the October Manifesto. His justification follows:

A regime of true civil freedom can and must be established in the country only when the law-abiding majority can tranquilly be sure that a strong government will guarantee its human rights. The weary and frightened population will be grateful for a consistent government policy to introduce strict legality as the basis of freedom, and its first freedom will be freedom from the arbitrary will of rebels.[49]

After the defeat of the revolution, police officials used the same logic, often omitting, however, any reference to the ultimate desirability of full civil freedom. Thus in response to Witte's early 1906 appeal to reopen the Gapon societies, the governor general of St. Petersburg bluntly declared to Minister of Internal Affairs Durnovo that

> in order to avoid the always possible conflicts with the organized worker mass as a hostile force, the Governor General considered it positively necessary, in the interests of the maintenance of order and social security in the capital, that no organization among the workers should be permitted.[50]

In this same spirit, on 10 May 1907 the Ministry of Internal Affairs sent out a circular to the governors instructing them to permit unions only when there were "definite facts about the absence of ties with Social Democratic groups."[51] Such statements indicate that if it had been in their power, many police officials would have prohibited all worker organizations.

But until the June 1907 coup d'état, the state did not have the power to embark on a consistent policy of repression, for its coercive capacity remained weak. In addition, there were many officials, even within Durnovo's ministry, who still regarded some form of legal worker organizations as desirable, as long as they confined themselves to purely economic goals. This trend was even more pronounced within the Ministry of Trade and Industry, formed in November 1905, which continued to support liberal tendencies in labor policy, a position that created considerable friction in the administration of the rules.[52] Although the government did close many unions and certainly did not permit freedom of action for those which survived, there remained substantial scope for the development of a legal trade union movement. Repression before June 1907 was often fierce, but it was also arbitrary and unsystematic. Sometimes the police authorized unions without even inspecting their statutes, but sometimes unions were closed without any reasons given.[53]

Workers were also ambivalent about the desirability of cooperation with the March rules, but ultimately a majority of labor activists became convinced that "trade unions can use the temporary laws for the development of the proletarian struggle."[54] Until the political changes of June 1907, activists succeeded in creating a dynamic trade union movement with astonishing speed. In Moscow and St. Petersburg approximately ten percent of the total labor force joined unions, and in some industries and occupations the proportion reached two-thirds.[55] The unions also embraced an impressive variety of branches of the labor force, encompassing workers in the service sector as well as the standard industrial occupations. Skilled workers responded to the opportunity for organization with special élan, but some categories of unskilled workers also made impressive progress in organization.

There was much in the practice of trade unionism in these years to confirm the government's fears as well as those of the industrialists. As throughout 1905, the unions maintained close ties with the socialist parties, particularly the Mensheviks. Although few unions explicitly embraced party programs or developed formal ties with the parties, the great majority considered themselves to be socialist in orientation and so ultimately committed to the goal of revolution.[56] In addition, party activists, again primarily Mensheviks, played a key role in union activities, although they were far from controlling them. Skeptics within the government and among the industrialists could also point to the unions' far-reaching demands for workers' control as evidence of the perils they presented for the regime. As opposed to management's insistence on its traditional prerogatives, trade unions demanded participation in such sensitive matters as hiring, firing, and wage rates. For the unions, then, the economic and political spheres continued to be interrelated, and their orientation in each area certainly gave grounds for concern.

Nonetheless, as Bonnell demonstrates, there was another side to the trade unions' activities before June 1907, one that could give encouragement to those who believed in the "Western" future of the Russian labor movement. As in Germany in the last decades before the war, formal adherence to revolutionary ideas seems to have coincided with reformism in the class struggle. This tendency was never allowed to go very far in Russia, but its first signs were clearly visible in the practice of trade unionism in this period. First, activists did agree to work within the framework of the law and even took great pains to maintain the unions' legal status.[57] Similarly, a great part of the unions' activity was directed toward improvements in the workers' material situation, especially through mutual aid funds, which frequently absorbed up to half of the typical union budget.[58] They also sought to institutionalize, in Von Ditmar's phrase, "a customary law of war" through collective bargaining and participation in boards of conciliation.[59]

These practices allowed activists to rationalize their demands according to economic circumstances and their relative power and so to make their demands more realistic. Trade union leaders were also willing to impose their agreements on the workers, who were instructed in the virtues of calculation and disciplined struggle. They committed rank-and-file workers to the observance of the employers' rules as part of their negotiated agreements. As one trade union activist declared, "autonomy demands discipline from the workers themselves."[60]

Thus the goals of the more liberal government officials overlapped the aspirations of an important sector of the labor movement, although the conflicts and ambiguities within both sides continued to trigger struggles between them. At the extremes, those within the government who advocated order and feared worker autonomy confronted those aspects of the labor movement directed toward revolutionary goals. Some officials and labor activists, however, sought to create a context of controlled struggle ruled by a degree of trust and agreement. The contradictions of autocratic capitalism, which were a crucial source of the ambiguities within each side, thus also opened up an arena of convergence between the government and the labor movement in which the labor question might conceivably have been resolved. The example of the West could have fortified the convictions of those on both sides who favored the development of more autonomous civil relations, and initial successes might have weakened the position of their more intransigent opponents. At the same time, however, the traditional dialectic between political and economic elite intransigence and labor radicalism continued to reinforce the old patterns and assumptions, and key government officials never shed their belief that liberal reforms were neither desirable nor feasible. It was these voices that triumphed with the Stolypin coup d'état of June 1907, which put an end to the most dramatic period of efforts at labor reform in the history of Tsarist Russia.

The situation by late spring 1907 was aptly characterized by the Council of the Congress of the Association of Trade and Industry, which had consistently supported the general tenor of the Ministry of Trade and Industry's proposals for reform. In its May 1907 report, the Council observed that for the past several years the labor question had been discussed by the government and by society, yet to that date basic laws had not been enacted. It was reasonable to expect that after the October Manifesto laws on the labor question would be passed quickly, but there were still only legislative proposals. As a result relations between the workers and the factory owners, as well as other aspects of the workers' lives, were in an extremely indefinite situation. The old laws had lost their force, but new ones had not been created. The temporary rules, they said, did not resolve matters or regulate relations. All of this gave rise to administrative discretion, which the council regarded as extremely harmful. At the end of 1906 the minister of Trade and Industry had introduced various projects, but they still had not become law. It was necessary to enact these laws. Although they may not have been completely satisfactory, they were good enough, and their enactment would put industrial life on a firmer foundation.[61] The council's conclusions, which represented the viewpoint of a significant minority within the government and the industrialists, were simultaneously penetrating and yet completely out of tune with the regime's resurgent conservatism.

FACTORY OWNERS AND REFORM

Before 1905 the factory owners had made a number of critical contributions to government discussions of labor policy. In all cases they had been either consulted as knowledgeable (and interested) informants or they had stood forth, like Guzhon in the Zubatov affair, as impassioned petitioners, working especially through the Ministry of Finance. Neither of these roles had prepared them well for the catastrophe they would have to confront in 1905. The only reasonably influential industrialist organization was the St. Petersburg Society of Factory Owners, the weight of which depended more upon the cultivation of personal ties in the government than real power based upon independent resources. Nor was there anything like a unified perspective among factory owners, or even much of a sense that throughout the empire they had shared interests. Nothing, in short, had given them any opportunity to play an important role in national politics.

Inconsistencies, floundering, and internal divisions thus characterized the political debut of the factory owners in 1905; and no simple formulas can do justice to the delicacy of their situation or the complexity of their response. Nonetheless, one important conclusion suggests itself: their very weakness and divisions made them at best inconsistent advocates of reform; and on crucial points, such as the acceptance of trade unions, many of them clearly opposed their own long-term interest in a moderate and organized labor movement. Despite some courageous industrialist demands for social and political change, on balance factory owners' contribution to the resolution of the labor question must be judged as negative.

As noted in chapter 2, the lack of confidence and fragmentation of the Russian industrialists had deep historical roots. Because much of Russian industry had been called forth by the state for reasons of state, industry was widely regarded as "artificial"—a charge that Tugan-Baranovsky, in his classic study, *The Russian Factory*, took pains to refute. Scholarly argument could not put popular conceptions to rest, however, even though well before the turn of the century there clearly existed a large contingent of independent entrepreneurs, mainly centered in Moscow and linked to the consumer market. These native entrepreneurs, predominantly textile manufacturers, were not so economically dependent on the state, but like all other Russian subjects, their social and political autonomy was severely limited. In this sense, too, the Russian factory owners were no match for the Western industrial bourgeoisie; compared to Westerners' superior social and political standing, Russian industrialists became even more aware of their relative deprivation.

Seen not only as an artificial creature of the state, Russian industry had also been widely regarded as foreign, a noxious corruption of Russian traditions. This prejudice, not entirely without foundation, was reinforced during the rapid industrialization of the late nineteenth century, with the huge infusions of foreign capital. Many must have shared Zubatov leader Slepov's conviction that the "contemporary magnate-kings" were "in large part foreigners," who had created "abnormal conditions" in the factories. Foreign capital had the ancillary effect of increasing the regional and technological diversity of Russian industry and so furnished further obstacles to class formation.

Until the 1905 revolution, then, the Russian industrialists, whether economically dependent or relatively autonomous, whether native or foreign, had constituted a basically passive and conservative social category.[62] Russian industry was concentrated in three main regions, each with its distinctive traits. (A fourth industrial center, the old Urals mining and metallurgy industry, was in a state of severe decline.) Moscow had historically been the heartland of indigenous Russian industry, and its concentration on textile and other consumer products, as well as its sheer distance, had made it less dependent on the St. Petersburg bureaucracy. In addition, many Moscow industrialist families had humble social origins, particularly in the case of large numbers of Old Believer sectarians, whose heterodox religious beliefs were the source of considerable friction with the regime. Nonetheless, the Moscow industrialists, closely connected in origins to the traditional merchantry, were also deeply conservative socially and extremely nationalistic, and their ambivalent attitude toward secular authority rarely took the form of overt political opposition. This deviant background does help explain why a minority of Moscow industrialists were the leading advocates of political liberalism in 1905.

The second major industrial region, the South, centered on the Ukrainian metallurgical industry, gave birth to an entrepreneurial group different from that in Moscow. Industrialization in the South was relatively recent, the product of Witte's promotion of rapid economic growth in the 1890s. State subsidies and guarantees lured a great deal of foreign capital, and the advanced technology of the region ensured that the industrialist class would be much less traditional than in Moscow. Engineers and foreigners combined to create what was for Russia a highly distinctive business culture, one that harbored considerable skepticism about the competence of the tsarist bureaucracy and admired technical training and Western industry. Not surprisingly, these more modern entrepreneurs were able to create the professional society that became "the best organized and most permanent industrial interest group in the empire,"[63] the Association of Southern Coal and Steel Producers. Although political liberalism was not as marked as among some Moscow enterpreneurs, the southern industrialists tended toward a basically Western view of industrial relations, treating their workers as contractual employees and favoring worker organizations. Von Ditmar, whose unqualified advocacy of worker organizations in the Filosofov Commission has already been described, and Belov, whose penetrating critique of tsarist policy will be presented in the following pages, are prominent representatives of this reformist tendency.

The third sector of Russian industry during this period, consisting of the St. Petersburg industrialists, was distinctive for its political conservatism and its hostility toward labor reform. The first trait derived from this group's close ties to the tsarist bureaucracy and its dependency on government orders. Lobbying rather than agitation or public campaigns was the preferred mode of influence among St. Petersburg industrialists. Their hostility toward workers' demands stemmed partly from their early confrontation with a militant labor movement. Their conservatism was visible in the debates on the starosta law and also in their animosity toward the Kokovtsov Commission. During the 1905 revolution they demonstrated much less political independence and initiative than the other groups,[64] although they came into their own once again as the government and industrialists united to quell the strike movement.

Within this very diverse social group there were, then, some historical conditions favoring political independence, particularly in Moscow. Almost no one was prepared for "the most remarkable political phenomenon of the revolution of 1905,"[65] however: the advocacy of liberal political ideas by Russian industrialists and merchants on an unprecedented scale. Until the October Manifesto, which promised a constitutional regime, many industrialists openly expressed their disillusionment with the tsarist state, which could not ensure social peace or defend the country, through a broad range of oppositional activities. The causes and nature of this phenomenon bear closer examination because of their implications for labor policy and class relations.

The massacre of Bloody Sunday outraged a great many industrialists throughout the empire, just as it had shaken public opinion in general. The massacre itself and the strikes that followed forced the government and the industrialists to clarify their perspectives on the labor question. Recall that the Ministry of Finance announced its intention to embark on an ambitious program of labor legislation in the hope of improving the workers' material conditions. Despite many differences in nuance, the industrialists overwhelmingly rejected the implication that they were to blame for labor unrest.[66]

Four different declarations reveal the variety of the factory owners' responses: one from a group of liberal young Muscovites, the second from the Advisory Office of Iron Industrialists (from the industrial

South), the third from the much more conservative St. Petersburg Society, and the final one from the backward Urals. According to the Moscow liberals, the problems of Russian industry were rooted in the political system, particularly in the weakness of law, the lack of individual freedom, and the obstacles to scientific inquiry.[67] Worker unrest reflected these deep political inadequacies, and it was further inflamed by episodes such as the Zubatov experiment or the "shooting of peaceful unarmed residents." Not economic reforms but freedom of strikes, association, and organization were necessary to allow the two sides to regulate their own affairs. Although these ideas were obviously liberal in inspiration, the manifesto also included a heavy admixture of Slavophile and populist ideas: "the common people," it complained, "are cut off from the Supreme Bearer of true authority." The evident tension between traditional and modern ideas expresses the complex situation of a very conservative social group seeking to adapt itself to the world of modern capitalism.

The report from the Advisory Office of Iron Industrialists, dated 28 January, adopts a more consistently liberal position.[68] It admitted that the workers' economic situation was deplorable but denied that the industrialists had any control over the workers' welfare. They could presumably renounce profits and turn industry into a charity, but no one would ultimately gain by this. The workers' welfare depended, rather, on the overall economic level of the country and the general political structure. Until now private initiative had been smothered by government control in Russia, and so industry had not prospered as it should have. The labor movement was an inevitable response to this sad state of affairs: it had been prepared "by life itself and by the natural necessity, part of man's very nature, whether he be a commoner or noble, to seek freedom or the open expression of his oral and written thoughts in meetings and gatherings." Only the provision of political rights and free institutions for all of Russian society could remove the causes of the workers' discontent.

The St. Petersburg factory owners also affirmed that they could do nothing to help the workers: again, Russian industry was simply too weak.[69] In addition, as by now had become customary, they added some sterner notes of their own. Labor unrest, they said, attracted such great attention only because of the workers' coarse demonstrations and violence. The workers knew that such actions would achieve results and so they were encouraged to struggle, particularly when government interference convinced them that the government would force the factory owners to make concessions. It would be much better, the report declared, if the workers knew that they could depend only upon legal action and the law. It underplayed the issue of political change, referring vaguely to the need for "deeper reforms of a general governmental character."

The report from the Council of the Association of Urals Mining Industrialists is instructive for the light it sheds on the labor question in more backward industrial regions.[70] Unlike the St. Petersburg industrialists, Urals employers declared that there were serious and well-founded causes for the dissatisfaction of the Urals population, but they also stated that satisfaction of the workers' needs was beyond their capacity. The Urals, they declared, was a depressed area, and there was simply insufficient work for the population, both within and outside the factories. They espoused freedom of strike and organization not so much as a critique of previous government policy but in the hope that stronger organizations would moderate the labor movement. For example, if worker organizations had their own funds, they would strike only for serious reasons, for they would not risk their time and capital unless out of extreme necessity. This hope was probably rooted in desperation more than in any realistic appraisal of the situation.

The crisis in industrial relations sometimes also led to a *crise de conscience* among some factory owners, the most sensitive of whom were forced to evaluate their own position from a disturbing new perspective. One of the most impressive examples of such a searching reexamination of industrial relations was a speech by V. Belov, an industrialist from the southern industrial region.[71] Belov began in the traditional way by casting full blame on the government for labor unrest, mainly for its inability to enact reforms, thereby creating a broad oppositional front composed partly of revolutionary groups. Revolutionaries could find a warm reception among the workers because of government repression of strikes and organization, which turned all economic struggle into political conflict. Occasional concessions only worsened the situation, for the workers became even more convinced that political action was indispensable. One of the worst aspects of government policy, continued Belov, was that government repression and control extended to the factory owners as well and transformed class relations in a harmful way. His words could almost be taken from the pages of Tocqueville's analysis of how the centralized state isolates social groups from each other and makes their relations harsh and brittle:

> The previous patriarchal relations were replaced by a business-like formal order, in part natural because of the changing structure of industrial life, but partly—and to a greater extent—under the pressure of petty government regulation; between factory owners and workers there grew up a wall. Given such an estrangement, could the intelligentsia in general, and the industrialists in particular, have any influence over the workers? Where is the basis for that cordial feeling, the voice of which could in the necessary moment sway the crowd and exercise its moral influence? All of us intelligentsia, industrialists

and non-industrialists, feel every minute that we are under surveillance [*pod sekretom*] . . . Can I, for example, allow myself to read a proclamation, posted in my own factory or in the countryside, to my own workers in order to explain to them its senselessness and criminality? Of course not; but this would be necessary, for only in this way is the desired influence created. I repeat: between the industrialists and the workers there is a wall.

He continued by recounting his words to Minister of Internal Affairs Plehve, in which he concluded, "It seems that our government is like the merchant who brings goods into the store and is so afraid to open them for fear that a piece will be stolen. So it is with us, with the intelligentsia: because of the fear that somebody will take a proclamation into the countryside, it is better not to permit anyone there and not to believe any of us." So when disorders come, the government cannot blame us, the factory owners, for "we stand to the side, without any influence on the crowd; we do not have access to the stage."

Given this acute sense of their own weakness and isolation with repect to their workers, it is understandable that many factory owners feared reform. Indeed, the period before the October Manifesto was characterized by a widening rift between liberals and conservatives among the industrialists. Moscow, the cradle of entrepreneurial liberalism, was also the scene of violent conflicts between a minority of young reformers and the traditional old guard, who were more cautious about political demands or changes in labor relations. In March there was deep disagreement on the issues of legal workers' organizations and political reform. Numerous efforts were made to develop a consensus and also to create more organizational unity, but all such attempts merely showed how hopeless were the efforts to bridge the gaps. The reformers, for example, favored a bicameral legislative duma, with the lower chamber to be elected by universal, direct, and secret manhood suffrage, whereas the Moscow Exchange Committee decided in July to support the government's program of a consultative duma.[72] To these splits over principle were added regional rivalries, and as a consequence the industrialists never achieved organizational unity either politically or professionally. Numerous parties arose to represent them in the 1906 duma elections, and instead of professional consolidation a variety of new organizations were founded to represent different specialties and regions. The umbrella organization, the Association of Industry and Trade, was never able to achieve its impressive ambitions for unity.

Despite these profound differences, the factory owners did agree on the need to resist the workers' claims, and this agreement provided the basis for a degree of unified action, at least in matters of self-defense. The Moscow Exchange Committee took the initiative in February by forming a labor commission, one of whose tasks was to work out a coordinated strategy to deal with the workers' demands.[73] It attempted to define strikes and determine the rights and responsibilities of workers and industrialists with respect to them—whether, for example, workers should be liable for property damage or whether the industrialist had the right to fire striking workers. It also drew up a draft agreement on seven issues that was meant to serve as a model convention to be ratified by other factory owner organizations. These provisions included the following:

1. No concessions should be made on the length of the workday pending further government action.

2. No wage payments were permissible for time lost during strikes.

3. Workers could not be allowed to help determine wages and rules of work.

4. Workers should have no say in hiring or firing.

5. Fines were necessary to ensure work of adequate quality and demands for their elimination should be refused.

6. No minimum rate should be established for either piecework or daily wages.

7. No regulations on the use of overtime work should be made, and overtime work should be paid at one and a half times the standard rate.

The meeting concluded by advocating the legalization of worker organizations, for not to accept this, they said, would be unjust and would make a bad impression on the workers. These seven proposals were distributed to other industrialist organizations and provided the basis for a united strategy. For example, on 15 March a conference of St. Petersburg factory owners discussed the Moscow proposals and accepted all but the last. On 17 March a circular was sent out asking for adherence to these six points; ninety-two factory owners returned it with their signatures. The same circular was reissued on 25 May, collecting thirty-four more signatures.[74]

After the massive strikes of fall 1905 and the proclamation of the October Manifesto the factory owners closed ranks against the labor movement even more solidly. Reformist impulses among the factory owners, always prevalent only among a minority, were further weakened. With a small minority of exceptions, both liberal and conservative industrialists embraced the newly announced promise of a constitutional monarchy. Strikes, the industrialists now felt, no longer stemmed from essential needs of the workers but were the result of the criminal action of an organized minority of instigators. Before 17 October, political strikes may still have made sense, but with the granting of freedom of speech and association they were now harmful.[75] "Abandon your foolish demands," threatened one industrialist group. "Everything necessary has already been given to the people; it is called to the State Duma, and on its own it will forge its destiny."[76]

The strike movement did not abate, however, and continuing labor unrest turned the great majority of industrialists into ardent supporters of the throne. Erstwhile liberals supported stringent measures against the workers and in December even urged the government to use armed repression against them. The St. Petersburg Society was probably expressing the views of the vast majority of industrialists when it declared that "the use of military protection against violence can in no way be considered blameworthy, but it is only a sad necessity."[77] From here it was only a short distance to Mayor Guchkov's[78] rejection of a Kadet proposal to condemn the army and police for the murder of innocent civilians during the Moscow uprising, on the following grounds: this "would only pour oil on the fire. It would appear to the workers as a new call to violence."[79]

At the same time, many industrialist organizations succeeded in refining their own weapons against the strike movement. Retaliatory lockouts and blacklists made their appearance. Special committees were formed to work out a coordinated strategy. For example, in mid-November 1905 the St. Petersburg Society formed a committee on strikes, the goal of which was to collect and disseminate relevant information and issue directives. By mid-February twenty bulletins had been issued from the committee, with detailed suggestions on how best to respond to the workers' demands.[80] The Moscow Exchange Committee formed its Labor Commission at about the same time, and by 16 November the retaliatory lockout it had organized included twenty-six enterprises employing 58,634 workers.[81] Again, however, unity for such purposes was far removed from the much more distant goal of the creation of a unified class movement. And it did little to further—if it did not hinder—the industrialists' hope to gain greater respect for themselves at the court of public opinion. Industry and commerce, they knew, were regarded as "some kind of parasites on the Russian national economy, created according to the fantasy of minister-favorites."[82] "Russia must become," declared another organization, "an industrial country not only by order of the government, but also by popular wish, and this process demands enormous organizational efforts."[83] Both because of long-standing prejudices and because of their support for the autocracy by the end of 1905, the industrialists emerged from the year of revolution with little alteration of their status as a pariah class, rejected not only by the socialist left but also by engineers, lawyers, and other elements of the technical and liberal intelligentsia.[84] This isolation was both cause and consequence of its fateful inability to contribute significantly to the "bourgeois revolution."

After the December Moscow massacre, government violence drastically reduced labor militancy. Until June 1907, however, workers still had considerable scope to engage in strikes and organizational activities. The period before the Stolypin coup d'état witnessed the zenith of Russian trade unionism. The industrialists thus could not afford to ignore the question of organization, which, in any case, many of them had so recently promoted as the solution to the labor question.

It should be recalled that there was considerable ambivalence and disagreement among the industrialists about worker organizations even before the explosion of labor militancy in late 1905. Glezmer, for example, had rejected them on principle, arguing that the right of organization will "always and necessarily lead to one inevitable result": the unification of workers based on common demands which they will attempt to satisfy "by all means," including through association with the "international organization of workers."[85] Other industrialists opposed them more conditionally, supporting them in theory but declaring that the workers were not yet "developed" enough to form responsible organizations.[86] Many other industrialist groups supported the legalization of worker organizations, however, on the grounds that they were a fundamental prerequisite for industrial harmony.

These divisions continued to be felt after the passage of the temporary rules legalizing worker organizations in March 1906. On one hand, some industrialists believed that although trade unions might not lead to industrial peace and might indeed encourage militancy, their long-term effects would nonetheless be highly beneficial. For example, Von Ditmar observed that the English, French, and German trade unions engaged in political activities and increased the level of industrial ferment.[87] But he also listed several positive contributions: for example, they "ennoble the forms of this war, giving rise to a peculiar 'customary law of war'" in times of strike; and they lessen the number of strikes, discouraging those based on insignificant causes. He thus welcomed the transformation of the Russian labor movement according to the Western European model of moderate trade unionism. Accordingly, he criticized numerous provisions of the temporary rules that he felt impeded this transition. Various other industrialist groups also insisted that industrial life could never be stable or private property secure until authoritative worker organizations emerged.[88]

Conversely, the St. Petersburg Society represented an opposing current of opinion, one bluntly developed in the following August 1906 report to the Ministry of Internal Affairs:[89]

For the time being anarchy reigns in the government, and before the eyes of armed authorities, workers, united in unions, destroy factory property and beat up workers not wishing to submit to the dictatorship of the union; there can be no question of a professional movement among workers in the West European meaning of this term. No acts of agreement with such unions are conceivable by the industrialists. The demands announced by the unions pursue revolutionary goals, and not the evolution of the position of the working class. They are not compatible with the situation of industry not only in Russia, but even in the most economically powerful countries. Therefore, any act of agreement with the unions would have to be bought with such sacrifices as would in any case lead the factory to ruin in the shortest time. At the same time, such agreements would only lead to the professional revolutionary organizations' having enormous popularity among the worker masses. They would unite the masses and move them not against individual industrial establishments, but against industry as a whole. The process of the dying out of the country's industrial life and mobilization of a huge army of unemployed would be brought about in the shortest time.

As will be seen, this view corresponded much more closely to that of the Ministry of Internal Affairs than with Von Ditmar's. And it was this logic, based on a short-term perspective and a fundamental lack of trust, that shaped government policy toward the labor movement, particularly after mid-1907.

What, then, can be concluded regarding the factory owners' role in labor policy during the revolutionary period? With respect to matters of principle, the industrialists were deeply divided both before and after the October Manifesto. Before the manifesto some supported and some opposed a legislative duma; some advocated and some feared the legalization of worker organizations. After the tsar's political concessions, they became more united on general political principles and came to the government's support against worker militancy. They continued to disagree, however, on the optimal policy toward worker organizations and, in general, on the desirability of a liberal solution to the labor question. Along with these fundamental differences of principle, there was also overriding agreement on the need for struggle against the workers' concrete demands, a struggle that was conducted on two levels: through the creation of stronger class organizations to combat worker militancy and through a war of attrition against government labor projects in the Kokovtsov, and expecially in the Filosofov Commissions. In many respects, then, the industrialists impeded the emergence of a new approach to labor relations. Even though there was considerable sentiment in favor of legal worker organizations and a liberal model of class relations, these positions aroused enough opposition to forestall the expression of any strong pressure for a liberal policy. Disunited, fearful of risks, and generally unwilling to act upon their own long-term interests, the industrialists at times were simply no help, at other times a definite hindrance to policy innovation, a position comprehensible in terms of their weakness and incoherence within the context of the autocratic system.

The chapter on pre-1905 labor policy analyzed how the divided and threatened Russian political and economic elites were unable to initiate a new course in labor policy before the revolutionary outburst. Examination of the government commissions, legal projects, and factory owner positions in the 1905–1907 period sheds light on their failure to respond to the reality of revolution in a constructive way. Autocratic assumptions and practices were still too prevalent within the bureaucracy to permit a system of organized class struggle. To the elite's long-term weaknesses rooted in the systemic contradictions were added the fears born of revolution. And within the government and among industrialists alike a paralysis of will was compounded by accentuated differences of philosophy and purpose. Despite the lack of policy innovation that resulted, the need for reform continued to be almost universally admitted. But conditions were not yet ripe. Tranquillity remained the first priority. What sorry prospects tranquillity brought forth for a resolution—at last—of the labor question will become evident in the following chapter.

CHAPTER
6

Labor Policy at a Dead End

The Stolypin coup d'état of 3 June 1907[1] set the stage for a harsh government offensive against the developing trade unions and the labor movement as a whole. Although the basic causes of Stolypin's action were both political (the conflict between the duma majority and the government) and largely centered on differences over the land question, its effects on the labor movement were calamitous. Stolypin's efforts of the previous year to rely on more moderate elements, and even to come to terms with the Kadets (the party of the liberals) had failed, and although after the coup he continued to fight for major reforms in local government and land tenure, he no longer had any social or political base against the resurgent right wing. His rule (until his assassination in 1911) was marked by political paralysis in virtually all spheres of government activity, but it was particularly sterile in the area of labor policy, concerning which there were no new ideas or any sense of urgency. His administration's major attention was devoted to agrarian affairs, and even there virtually all of its initiatives were blocked by conservative forces, particularly in the State Council. Little was even attempted in the area of labor reform, and when massive worker unrest broke out again in 1912, the government was as impotent as before.

Even though labor unrest was not the primary cause of the dissolution of the Second Duma, those who opposed what they regarded as the government's (particularly the Ministry of Trade and Industry's) capitulative policy had been gathering strength for some time. With the restoration of the country's tranquillity, conditions were ripe for a return to Ministry of Internal Affairs dominance in the labor question. This most powerful of ministries continued to be skeptical of independent social forces, particularly in light of the fact that they had already revealed themselves as a threat to social peace. In addition, the government was well aware of the intimate connections between political reform and the reform of industrial relations, and when it sought to curtail the former, it was only natural simultaneously to undertake a repressive strategy toward labor as well.

We have seen that the contradictory synthesis of autocracy and capitalism induced at least a truncated form of liberalism in politics and labor policy. It would be too much to conclude that the failure of this social and governmental current was inevitable, but the severe systemic impediments to the realization of liberal ideas must also be stressed. The government, weakened in its legitimacy by the emerging new Russia and with a declining social base, was divided and fearful of risk, and at the same time hesitant to reform itself in principle. Could any prominent Russian statesman have echoed Gladstone in his defense of working-class franchise?

> Now sir, I maintain that there is no proof whatever that the working classes, if enfranchised, would act together as a class. Perhaps you ask for proofs to the contrary. It is exceedingly difficult to give a direct proof of that which has not happened: although in my opinion ample proof, substantial, even if indirect, of the correctness of my statement does exist.[2]

The industrialists, weakened by the autocracy just as they and industrial capitalism had weakened it, also lacked the flexibility born of strength. No outburst of opposition accompanied the government's repression of the organized labor movement—indeed, there was widespread employer cooperation with it. Only when their own positions were once again threatened beginning in 1912 did industrialists raise their voices against government policy to any significant degree. The quieting of minds for which Witte and Kokovtsov had appealed had certainly come to Russia, even though by force. It proved no more propitious for labor reform than the chaos of revolution, however.

The basic orientation of the Ministry of Internal Affairs is evident in a significant report prepared in early 1908 by Blazhchuk, a ministry official whose task was to review the implementation of the March 1906 law on worker organizations.[3] The first thing to note about Blazhchuk's report is that it is marked by a fundamental contradiction; he recognized the desirability of worker organizations in principle, yet he found them unacceptable in practice. Even Ministry of Interior officials, then, were still partly under the sway of liberal ideas, although they were uncertain about how to apply them to Russia. Blazhchuk had a surprisingly positive evaluation of the role of trade unions in "all European countries." Although he admitted that they arose as the result of workers' struggles against both capital and the government, he accepted that their antagonism toward the government quickly subsided as soon as the contending sides were given the right to regulate their own affairs. As a result, he concluded, a more or less acceptable relationship between employers and employees emerged everywhere in Europe, especially in England and even in Germany.

But in Russia, he argued, trade unions arose in troubled circumstances and thus gave rise to distinctive problems demanding a different policy. Emerging in 1904–1906, a time of great ferment, they began as illegal organizations posing serious threats to social tranquillity. The 4 March 1906 rules were published in response to their illegal existence, but they included insufficent provisions to guarantee public order. As a result of the rules, he declared, Russia became covered with a network of all manner of legal and illegal unions and societies. The administrative authorities turned out to be powerless to struggle against efforts for unification, even though these were prohibited in the law. Thus these organizations, far from fulfilling the purposes ascribed to them, once more posed a threat to political order.

Blazhchuk rejected the tempting vision of outright repression of worker organizations. He accepted the conclusion that the government alone could not satisfy the workers' needs through legislation, and consequently that the workers' desires for association were rooted in the very nature of capitalist class relations. In addition, citing the 1907 Congress of the Association of Trade and Industry, he argued that the industrialists also favored worker organizations (we know that this was only partly true). Finally, he recognized that the Russian government itself had clearly perceived the necessity for legal recognition of worker organizations, as was evident from the State Council's approval of the temporary rules. The issue, then, was how best to channel organized labor in the proper direction.

Blazhchuk had a simple analysis of the defects of Russian workers' organizations, and consequently a straightforward solution for their ills. The blame, naturally, lay with the revolutionary parties, which had taken advantage of the legal opportunities to infiltrate the unions and turn them against the government. This strategy, he said, stemmed from the revolutionaries' analysis of the failures of the revolutionary movement, whose flaw was that it had not involved the popular masses. For because of the absence of a law permitting organizations, there was no possibility of fusing and arming the proletariat against the government.[4] By a rather unconvincing logic, then, Blazhchuk saw organization as undermining revolution in Europe but as an essential revolutionary weapon in Russia. His reasoning becomes no more persuasive when he discusses the especially dangerous activities of the capital's printers' union, in fact a Menshevik stronghold willing to make use of moderate methods. He revealed another inconsistency in his argument when he blamed the high level of development of its members (what happened to the outside revolutionary agitators?) that allowed it to exercise leadership over other unions and professions. Clearly, much more was necessary than an attack upon the revolutionary parties, and Blazhchuk approvingly cited the closure of the St. Petersburg printers' organization on 17 October 1907.

Despite his efforts to blame the revolutionaries, then, Blazhchuk seemed to perceive that the problems were really much deeper. So much can be inferred from the series of modifications he suggested for the 1906 rules, which would have drastically curtailed the unions' growth even along purely professional lines. The development of trade unions along the Western pattern was, despite his pronouncements, not Blazhchuk's goal, however. He wanted to create "normal conditions," which meant the following: "Being free from outside influence, they would have the chance to develop and strengthen themselves properly, without any loss for the government, having as their final and only goal the full and most just agreement of the workers and employers."

There followed a lengthy discussion of the inadequacies of the temporary rules, which allegedly left the government powerless to struggle against harmful tendencies in the labor movement. Some of his suggestions resembled the provisions of the starosta law. For example, he criticized the election of union boards in general meetings without government confirmation of the candidates or prior investigation of their reliability. It is striking throughout how narrow was Blazhchuk's understanding of the proper tasks of trade unions. Thus in an addendum to the report, unions in Archangel province were rebuked for their subversive activities:

> The statutes of some societies, especially the societies of the metalworkers, have a militant tendency close to the Social Democratic program: the goals of the society are to seek the improvement of the legal conditions of the members' lives; the shortening of the workday; the elimination of overtime work; the end of fines for absenteeism and wage reductions for breaking or damaging tools; the construction of consumers' stores; proper fulfillment by the employer of his obligations; the mental and moral development of the members by means of the publication of newspapers, brochures and books and through the establishment of libraries, reading rooms, public lectures, readings, courses, evening events, trips, shows and discussions for general educational goals for the clarification of contemporary questions of life.[5]

These were the goals so heavily shaped by the Marxist revolutionaries!

From this point of view, virtually all trade union activities were subversive. And it was this judgment, rather than the theoretical desirability of an organized labor movement, that decided the fate of the union movement after 3 June. Police repression, previously inconsistent and unpredictable, now became systematic. The union movement was also damaged by a severe economic recession and the coordinated strategy of industrialist organizations. The cumulative effect of these three factors was disastrous.[6] In St. Petersburg only the metalworkers' union was able to maintain a significant membership. In Moscow the situation was even worse: by June 1909 the eight largest unions (of a total of sixteen) had a combined dues-paying membership of 1,231. Comprehensive data on the rest of the empire are lacking but the decline was similar, if not more pronounced. Some unions, of course, did manage to survive, but their activities were mainly oriented toward survival and mutual aid, with little opportunity to protect the workers' class interests.[7]

There is little evidence of significant opposition to the Ministry of Internal Affairs' policy within the government; the attackers of police interference in industrial life seemed to have vanished. Indeed, as noted earlier, the minister of Trade and Industry was in fundamental agreement that the trade union movement was politically dangerous and should not be given independence until it was purely economic.

The government's repression of the trade union movement enjoyed superficial success until 1912, when the labor movement revived once again in its old threatening forms. With the pacification of the workers, there was a theoretical possibility that a new labor policy might be designed by a government at last free from the pressure of the masses. As we shall see, nothing of the sort happened, however, showing once again the tsarist regime's incoherence and inability to deal with the pressing problems facing it.

GOVERNMENT INITIATIVES, 1907–1914

BEFORE 1912

Until mid-1912 the prospects for a major overhaul of government labor policy were at their bleakest since the turn of the century. No high official, whether in the Ministries of Internal Affairs, Finance, or Trade and Industry, espoused any ambitious new projects either to protect or to free workers. The extremes, it seemed, had played themselves out and had left almost a vacuum in the center. No new Trepov or Fedorov appeared even to challenge the orthodoxy. The government's only significant proposals were in the area of insurance legislation, and these were not particularly far-reaching even within their own narrow range.[8] The issue that for several years had been recognized as the linchpin of labor policy—the question of organization—was hardly even addressed.

Added to the government's conservatism was the lack of impetus from

within the duma, which was dominated by a moderate right-wing majority with little commitment to fundamental changes. Many within this
majority, spurred on by some groups of industrialists, attacked a number
of initiatives that the government had finally resolved to introduce after
substantial industrialist participation in the Ostrogradskii Commission,
the task of which was to study and initiate insurance legislation. Debates
were particularly heated over employer responsibility for medical care.
The government's proposal envisioned a series of obligations for the factory owners, including the provision of medical care and compensation
for accidents from the employers' insurance associations. The industrialist members of the duma committee wished to relieve the factory owners
of many of these responsibilities and transfer them to factory sick funds
made up of worker and employer contributions. Although on this issue
the duma as a whole sided with the government's project, the debates
showed the ability of duma opponents to obstruct legislation.[9] When
asked what the Third Duma had accomplished in the area of labor reform, the Kadet labor specialist Stepanov himself replied: "Almost
nothing."[10]

A third factor must be mentioned in evaluating the regime's failure to
undertake basic changes in labor relations. Despite the energy of the
forceful Stolypin and the government's willingness to take extreme measures to neutralize the lower classes, the Stolypin regime was still largely
politically impotent. The duma was deeply divided, and the moderate
party upon which Stolypin hoped to rely, the Octobrists, was internally
fragmented and often hostile to his programs. Outside the duma Stolypin
had to confront the intransigent opposition of reactionaries within the
government connected with a newly mobilized right-wing outside of it.
The 3 June system was characterized by social and political atomization
with no firm leadership by the tsar that might have broken the stalemate.
The new prominence of society in Russian politics seemed only to have
sharpened the contradictions inside and outside the government. Without a will to undertake dramatic new initiatives, the government probably also lacked the power to enact them if it had so wished.[11]

The government's repression of the trade unions and its passivity in
labor policy did not go entirely unopposed. In February 1909 the duma
approved a Social Democratic interpellation of the ministers of Justice
and Internal Affairs for their illegal closings of unions. Although such an
act could have little practical effect—in fact, the Ministry of Justice refused to provide any justification—it did succeed in exposing the issue. It
also foreshadowed future splits within the Octobrists, some of whom
supported the interpellation; others defended the government. The
Ministry of Internal Affairs, through its representative P. G. Kurlov, stood
behind the government's course of action by conventional references to
the subversive activities of the revolutionary parties and the threat of an

armed uprising. Moderate supporters of the interpellation appealed to the beneficial effects of trade unionism for social order, once more citing the example of Western Europe, whereas the socialist parties, for political reasons, attempted to downplay their own influence within the trade unions.[12]

The Social Democrats were, of course, the most vocal opponents of the government's labor policy and were regarded as the main spokesmen for the workers and defenders of their interests. Some subdued criticism emerged from other groups and institutions as well, however, including from within the government. The Department of Labor of the Society for the Assistance to Russian Industry and Trade published a thirty-three-page pamphlet in the fall of 1908 recommending various changes in the temporary rules to allow unions to function more freely.[13] More significantly, the Congress of the Association of Trade and Industry turned to the Ministry of Trade and Industry in July 1907 with a request for the immediate enactment of laws on strikes and unions to replace the temporary rules. The ministry considered these issues in late 1907, and in January 1908 a commission was formed under A. D. Arbuzov to work out a new legal project on unions. The Council of the Association criticized this commission because it was composed exclusively of government officials, and the ministry responded by appointing an industrialist representative, the only representative of "society."[14] The deliberations of this commission became grist for the mill of subsequent conferences and commissions.

The Ministry of Trade and Industry was not entirely inactive in these matters, sending a project to the duma in 1909 to eliminate criminal penalties for strikes and to change certain provisions in the rules on the labor contract. It also reviewed various European laws on strikes and unions but did not include a project to make the temporary rules permanent.[15] There were even occasionally minor splits between Internal Affairs and Trade and Industry. Internal Affairs, for example, favored strict police supervision over the projected health insurance funds, whereas Trade and Industry and some factory owners, referring to the Zubatov and Gapon societies, favored Trade and Industry control and more independence for the organizations.[16] None of these projects, debates, or commissions had any great significance in the post-1907 political climate, however. They are interesting mainly as evidence that the amnesia of the elites was not absolute.

1912–1914

The period from spring 1912 to the outbreak of war in early summer 1914 witnessed an impressive revival of the labor movement, although it never reached the level of the 1905–1907 period in scope or intensity. Strikes increased dramatically, the trade union movement gained strength, and the socialists, particularly the Bolsheviks, extended their influence among workers. These changes had several sources, some of which began to be felt before 1912. Of great significance were the economic revival beginning in late 1909, which gave workers greater leverage with employers, and the rebirth of oppositional sentiments within "society," a significant part of which began to oppose the lawlessness and heavyhandedness of Stolypin's administration. Stolypin's assassination in September 1911 and especially the massacre of workers in the Lena gold mines in April 1912 further encouraged opposition and forced the government to draw back from its policy of relentless repression. Popular outrage and governmental uncertainty combined to create a new opening for labor protest. Labor protest, in turn, stimulated a new series of reports, conferences, and debates on how to resolve the labor question. After so many years of fruitless controversy over the same issues, this new round of discussion was more than a little ridiculous. And in addition to the banality of these reports and debates, they had the same outcome as earlier periods of activity: nothing of real significance.

Governmental discussions ran along two basic tracks: how to deal with the resurgent strike movement in the short term and, *a la longue*, what kind of worker organizations to legalize. Neither of these was uncharted territory, but it is interesting to note how little reference was made to earlier debates or, in general, how little cumulation of experience had taken place. Indeed, the discussions of this period displayed much less penetration and imagination than the debates of earlier years, a telling indication that government policy had reached a dead end.

It is unnecessary to chronicle here the different meetings called to propose prophylactic measures against strikes.[17] A great many suggestions were made, almost all of which had often been heard before. Ministry of Internal Affairs officials advocated strict police vigilance over factory affairs and the consistent application of criminal penalties to strikers. Minister of Trade and Industry Timashev declared that he had no principled objections to these measures, but he warned that the government must be careful to prosecute only when it was certain of success.[18] And once again factory owners were condemned for their unwillingness to satisfy workers' demands. Minister of Internal Affairs Maklakov referred to "well-known cases" when the factory owners instigated strikes either to curtail production, or as an excuse to fire workers in order to replace them with new recruits on more favorable terms, or in order to be able to justify the tardy fulfillment of government orders.[19] In addition, some officials suggested changes in the rules on wage contracts, giving employers more freedom to fire workers without restrictions or liability.

Two proposals deserve special attention. On 31 August 1913 the director of the Department of Police, S. P. Beletskii, delivered a report urging the creation of conciliatory chambers composed of worker, employer, and government representatives, with the latter having the decisive voice. This proposal was later modified by Minister Maklakov, who, in the 24 October meeting of the Council of Ministers, also advocated the formation of conciliatory chambers—but with an important difference: they should consist of factory inspectors, provincial officials, police, gendarmes, and representatives of the Ministry of Justice, who would then have the right to invite representatives of the rival classes to their hearings. In addition to their conciliatory functions, these chambers would have the duty of discussing the situation of the workers and taking measures, within the framework of existing law, to ameliorate working conditions—all of this, said Maklakov, independent of the declarations of the two interested parties.[20]

This was a far cry from the Fedorov Commission's proposals on conciliatory chambers, and Maklakov's suggestions clearly demonstrated the unshakable hold of the time-worn political assumption of tsarist officials: that interrelations of social groups must be defined by a government endowed with greater impartiality and wisdom. Maklakov showed no awareness of the dilemmas involved in applying these ideas to the modern Russia of industry and social classes, even though some degree of historical awareness or acquaintance with past governmental deliberations would surely have given him pause to reflect. The council's reactions to Maklakov's proposal are also interesting: it was noted that the chambers might have greater authority if they included worker and industrialist representatives. At the same time, it was held that the participation of government officials would have the advantage of demonstrating the government's tutelary concerns for the workers and teaching them to seek their just requests not by strikes but by government protection.[21] Concerning the extraordinary naïveté of this declaration by October 1913 no further comments seem necessary.

A second recommendation of Ministry of Internal Affairs officials on the means to combat strikes is also highly instructive. Along with its criticisms of the factory owners, the ministry had traditionally tried to enlist employers' aid in keeping track of the workers and identifying potentially dangerous elements. Relying on the new strength of employer associations, however, some officials wanted to carry this logic even further in the 1912–1914 period. For example, in a November 1912 meeting St. Petersburg police officials met to discuss measures to deal with the revived strike movement. In addition to the usual appeals for arrest and exile, they expressed the hope that participants in political strikes would "not remain unfined, and in any case would not receive wages for time lost."[22] In a Moscow Okhrana report, it was explicitly argued that the factory owners could handle strikes much more effectively than the government if they would overcome their lack of coordination.

> Employer lockouts, immediately throwing enormous masses of workers onto the street, would then turn out to be a much more terrifying measure than the most severe government repression. And the role of the government in the struggle with economic strikes would be reduced at the present time to assistance for the planned organization of the industrialists, for their secret leadership in the struggle with the workers.[23]

In addition, the report recommended government financial aid to help enterprises struggling with strikes. In April 1914 the Ministry of Trade and Industry also suggested government measures to support lockouts, including the postponement of state orders and the like.[24] As will be seen shortly, many industrialist organizations were most eager to shoulder this responsibility, but steps in this direction also involved them in serious difficulties.

At the same time that the government attempted to work out measures to deal with strikes, it continued its Sisyphean efforts to enact permanent legislation to legalize worker organizations. Primary responsibility in this regard now belonged to the Ministry of Internal Affairs, whose official, A. D. Arbuzov, headed an interministerial conference to develop a law on unions in 1913.[25] The ministry had seven representatives in this conference; the Ministries of Justice and Trade and Industry had two each, and the Ministries of Finance, Transportation, and Education each had one. Once again, the government had contradictory goals. On one hand, it wanted "to strengthen the activity of professional societies in Russia, since, undoubtedly, with a certain reglementation it is possible to make of the professional societies strictly conservative organizations, similar to those which exist in many countries of the West."[26] At the same time, it found it necessary to add to the law "a whole number of new rules aimed at the regulation of the activity of the professional societies, at the weakening of the influence of Social Democratic teachings in them and at the elimination of their present-day dependence on revolutionary societies."

It was this latter consideration that occupied the attention of the conference, which amply displayed the usual official creativity in inventing rules. A new institution, the Main Factory Board, was to be created to coordinate all government measures with respect to unions and to oversee the activities of the local boards (which already existed). The minister of Internal Affairs would preside over the Main Board, which was to be composed of various officials, including the vice-director of the Department of Police, the St. Petersburg governor general, and various representatives from the Ministries of Internal Affairs, Justice, and Trade and Industry. Aside from this innovation, designed to increase the consistency of government policy, the conference's recommendations were overwhelmingly centered on new restrictions and controls. Its orientation can be inferred from its insistence that the phrase "clarification of the size of wages" be removed from the union's prerogatives, for, because of its imprecision, such a formulation might encourage the class struggle.[27] In addition, the conference explicitly included in the law the provision that all meetings of trade unions would be subject to the general rules about public meetings. Further, because "the most restless element among the workers is the youth," leaders of the future professional societies had to be at least twenty-five years of age. The legal project presented to the duma was twenty-four pages long and included 103 articles, together with appendices.[28] Forty-five articles, covering eleven very long pages, regulated the opening and closing of unions. As before, if the union's activity clearly threatened social peace and security or if it displayed immoral tendencies, it could be closed by the government. The only new check on potential arbitrariness was the authority granted to the Main Board, the potential effectiveness of which in this regard is questionable.

Beyond all of these defects, the project was marred by one overriding flaw: it was never enacted. We see it reappear in 1916 with a clarificatory report followed by seventy-three articles.[29] From there it fades from view. The same fate befell projects to legalize unions introduced in the duma by the Kadets and by the Social Democrats. The present law, noted the Kadet project, is "completely unsatisfactory. It is a law not about unions, but a law against unions."[30] On 14 February 1913 the Council of Ministers returned the compliment, finding both these duma projects completely unacceptable.[31]

Government policy toward trade unions and labor unrest in these years was both vacillating and ineffective. With great wariness the government did permit a certain amount of trade union activity, largely because of its own weakness, but it also conducted a policy of intermittent repression even against those unions that it formally authorized.[32] It struggled valiantly but vainly against the strike movement, which continued to gain strength until its crescendo in the massive unrest in the capital on the very eve of the war.

These signs of government impotence helped mobilize the factory owners, who were often driven to the point of despair both by the government's attempts to lay the blame on them and by its powerlessness. To these sources of discontent rooted in the government's labor policy was added a growing note of political criticism by industrialists outraged over the government's unwillingness to grant them broader political rights. Once again, political dissent was most intense among the Moscow industrialists, and their sharpest voice was the newspaper *Utro Rossii*, founded by Pavel Riabushinskii. On 4 April 1912 the newspaper proclaimed:

> It is high time for the merchant class to step into the political arena: it is already such an advanced economic force that it not only can but should possess commensurate political influence. The merchantry will be a force which, in its political demands, rests not only on certain ideals of justice, but—what is most important of all—on a certain economic strength. . . . Considering furthermore that the Russian merchantry has always been inspired by and has always shown liberal political tendencies and has not become bogged down in its own narrow "parish-pump" interests, then one can only welcome its wholly timely appearance on the political scene.[33]

A noteworthy political consequence of factory owner political dissent was the formation of the Progressive party after the 1912 duma elections. It sought to represent the emerging capitalist bourgeoisie in its struggle for a place in the sun. The Moscow industrialist Konovalov attempted to broaden the social base of the Progressives, first by means of a coalition of the right center (Octobrist, Progressives, and Kadets) and then, much more boldly, through a coalition of the duma opposition and the revolutionary parties. The first efforts never got off the ground, and the second failed after Progressive duma deputies voted to expel Social Democrat and Trudovik representatives for their obstructionism.[34] Ultimately the Progressive party was unable to forge political unity among the industrialists or significantly to broaden their influence among other sectors of Russian society.

Factory owner efforts at greater autonomy fared somewhat better in the class struggle. Much had changed since 1905: the industrialists as a class had become considerably stronger both economically and organizationally. In the 1912–1914 period government interference in factory affairs once again encouraged self-reliance in combating the strike struggle. Not since the 1905–1906 period had so much employer criticism of government policy been heard. Guzhon, for example, attacked Ministry of Internal Affairs predominance in labor policy, complaining that the Ministry of Trade and Industry had very little power.[35] There was also considerable friction between industrialists and factory inspectors, for the latter occasionally blamed the employers for worker discontent and took steps to force them to make concessions to the workers.[36] Discontent with government labor policy once again became linked with overall political opposition: even the conservative St. Petersburg Society rein-

troduced the old charge that labor protest stemmed largely from the country's unsatisfactory political situation.[37]

Disillusioned with government intervention, many factory owners also became aware of the limits to government repression. "There is no basis to count on help from outside," spoke L. I. Shpergaze in an August 1913 meeting of the St. Petersburg Society, "since the Minister of Internal Affairs does not find it possible to aggravate the situation by the application of repressive measures against the strikers." The Ministry of Trade and Industry, he said, actively abetted workers in their wish to control factory life by encouraging the establishment of sickness insurance funds.[38] The proposed remedy was for employer associations to develop a coordinated strategy and force their members to adhere to it. Various agreements were drawn up and sanctions announced for disobedience, a strategy that had considerable success, at least in the narrow sense of struggle against the workers' claims.[39] The St. Petersburg Society's convention, for example, interdicted trade union mediation in labor disputes and enjoined the strict application of fines during strikes. The Moscow Society of Factory Owners accepted the principle of trade union intervention in industrial conflict but rejected it in practice because of the immaturity of the unions. "And at the moment when the union achieves the necessary stability, the Society will agree to the proposal for mediation by the workers' union."[40]

In order to increase coordination, the Council of the Association of Trade and Industry promoted the creation of a united centralized industrialist organization. It supported its argument by referring to the broad scope of labor unrest and the presence of definite worker organization. Only through the creation of a central organization could they "direct the labor movement along a normal course on an exclusively peaceful basis."[41] The St. Petersburg Society rebuffed this initiative, however, arguing that a central organ was less effective than a number of local ones. It did agree, however, that there should be greater sharing of information among employer associations. The council quickly backed down from its proposals.

Employers also sought to strengthen their position through convincing the government to remove any restrictions on their freedom of action in the class struggle. Russian laws, claimed the St. Petersburg Society, did not grant factory owners the means to reestablish order easily, as did laws in Germany, Austria, and other countries.[42] The Russian government still saw the worker as a defenseless subject in need of protection, and consequently it limited the "general civil rights of the factory owners." Various measures were suggested to remedy the "powerlessness" of the factory owners: workers must be forced to give a monetary pledge to obey the terms of the labor contract; the rule requiring 14-day prior notification of

dismissal must be modified; fewer restrictions should be placed on fines; workers who were absent from work should be subject to firing regardless of whether their absence was willed or imposed by force; and partial strikes should terminate the wage contracts of all workers.

The factory owners' position in this period thus continued to be filled with contradictions. Many espoused political freedom, but they opposed freedom of association for the workers. Similarly, they claimed that they themselves should have complete freedom in the class struggle, but they rejected the workers' demands for elected representatives, even along the lines of the old starosta project.[43] Factory owners frequently embraced the principle of trade unionism but rejected it in practice even though they knew the difficulties of negotiating with "spontaneous" masses. Even those industrialists who sought to encourage trade unions were in an impossible situation. The director of the Lessner factory in St. Petersburg urged the workers to express their grievances through trade unions, as was done in the cultured countries of Europe and America. The worker delegation thanked the director for his advice but then answered "that for the Russian worker his proposed method of relationship is inapplicable because of the absence in Russia . . . of unions."[44]

In light of these contradictions, the results of the industrialists' strategy were predictable: they successfully countered the workers' demands in 1912–1914,[45] but they did not quell labor discontent. By their hypocrisy they also convinced the workers both that they could not trusted and that they were allies of the tsarist state. Through these actions they further undermined their already tenuous legitimacy within the context of the autocratic state. As a result, the claims of industrialists in February 1917 that they were part of the new Russia rang hollow to the workers, whose memories were not as short as the industrialists would have wished.

THE DILEMMAS OF GOVERNMENT INTERVENTION

From a comparative perspective, the remarkable feature of prerevolutionary Russian labor policy was the inability of the tsarist state to institutionalize any form of worker organization or even stable worker representation. I am unaware of any parallel inefficacy in any other country with such a significant degree of industrialization over so long a period. Although the magnitude of the failure is apparent, it is no easy matter to evaluate the relative weight of the many different forces conditioning this outcome. In previous chapters primary attention has been given to the impact of autocratic traditions, the ambivalence and divisions within the government, and the weakness of the industrialists, all of which are linked to the basic character of autocratic capitalist industrialization.

The interrelations among these underlying conditions, however, were

very different before, during, and after the 1905 revolution. Before 1905 hostile officials and fearful employers never dreamed of countenancing any significant degree of worker independence, and the possibility of legalizing trade unions was never seriously broached within the bureaucracy. The most significant experiment in worker mobilization, the Zubatov societies, that curious mix of disparate elements, quickly involved the government in a series of unresolvable dilemmas by activating the cleavages implicit in the whole contradictory pattern of development. The 1905 revolution created new possibilities—but also new dangers—for labor reform. The apparent failure of previous policies encouraged bold new initiatives on the part of a sector of government officials and industrialists, and the chances for liberal labor legislation looked brighter than ever before. Worker radicalism and the reestablishment of order, however, discredited these liberal voices much more effectively than the outbreak of the 1905 revolution had undermined their opponents. After the Stolypin coup, the requirements of order took precedence over the weak commitment to the partial autonomy of civil society. Class relations were once again largely shaped by the state, as the class struggle was not allowed to develop with any significant autonomy. The government and the industrialists, both chastened by their encounter with revolution, drew all the wrong conclusions, and neither showed any real desire to permit worker organization in anything but theory. The relationship between the state and the industrialists continued to be one of great tension, but their shared fear of worker independence made them desperate allies. The consequences of their choices became apparent in the 1912–1914 period, when a renewal of massive labor unrest showed the bankruptcy of their policies, the fragility of their alliance, and, at the same time, their lack of any new ideas.

Despite these important variations, the perspectives and interrelations of political and economic elites throughout this whole period were conditioned in a fundamental sense by the contradictory project of autocratic capitalist industrialization. This project did not predetermine the failure of the elites in any simplistic way: one can, for example, imagine a different policy toward trade unions in the 1906–1907 period, which might eventually have led to an entirely different outcome. However, an analysis focusing on the structural sources of elite strategy does serve to illuminate the underlying obstacles to reform and the relative likelihood of different policies. In this way, too, the study of elite strategies can be linked to the sociology of development, avoiding the twin dangers of structural determinism and historical voluntarism.

The failure to develop a coherent policy with respect to the labor question did not relieve the government of the necessity of responding to worker unrest. Its mode of action, devoid of stable principle, only deepened the breech between itself and the working class and exacerbated labor protest. In general terms its conduct suffered from three primary deficiencies. First, government officials, ranging from important ministers all the way down to local police and factory inspectors, incessantly made promises to protect the workers that they could not keep. Second, the absence of fixed norms and the lack of differentiation between politics and administration created great inconsistencies of conduct and deepened intragovernmental conflict. And third, the threat of labor protest did succeed in forcing sectors of the government to recognize the legitimacy of the workers' claims to greater independence, but the promise to free the workers, like the promise to protect them, was never consistently honored. All three of these flaws were of major importance in radicalizing the Russian labor movement.

Government officials tirelessly repeated that government tutelage was more beneficial for the workers than organization or political action. From Witte during the 1896–1897 strikes to Shuvalov in his 1903 report through the 1913 debates in the Council of Ministers, this theme was expressed time and again. The government has your interests at heart, workers were assured; refrain from protest and the government will protect you from exploitation. Under the conditions of rapid capitalist industrialization, however, this commitment proved impossible to fulfill. Thus, writing in 1908–1909, Bykov maintained that even though trade unions were much weaker than in Europe, making labor legislation all the more necessary, Russian labor law was much less developed than European legislation.[46] In Russia the scope of legislation was much narrower, whereas in Europe far more categories of workers were covered. Russian laws regulating worker safety were "almost absent," and those making provision for invalidism and old age were highly inadequate. The same, said Bykov, could be said for various other categories of labor legislation. Formally, he noted, the laws regulating the length of the workday were better in Russia than in England or Germany, but in fact the Russian workday was longer. As the worker Timofeev remarked, "If you ask a factory worker, 'How many hours do you work in a week?', he will probably answer in this way: 'We work as much as the foreman orders.' And I think he would be completely right."[47]

Thus even those laws that did manage to be enacted were very unevenly enforced, and there were no permanent worker organizations to ensure compliance. In addition, the factory inspectors, charged with overseeing the implementation of the laws, were simply not up to the task.[48] There were far too few inspectors effectively to enforce the meager legislation that did exist, and they were frequently opposed by both the factory owners and the local government officials. Sometimes the local factory boards or other officials did publish extensive administrative regulations, but the more detailed they were, the more unenforceable they became.

For example, in 1899 factory inspector V. I. Mikhailovskii was authorized by the Department of Trade and Manufacturing of the Ministry of
Finance to develop a set of rules to protect the safety and health of the
workers. He came up with no fewer than 445 articles covering various
branches of industry, types of machines, and living situations in factory
quarters.[49] Why, in the face of an obvious lack of staff for enforcement,
authorities continued to announce such regulations is difficult to explain.
Perhaps the bureaucratic penchant for control flourishes more in the face
of chaos. In any case, the discrepancy was bound to undermine the credi-
bility of the regulations and the prestige of the authorities. Who, for example, was going to enforce the 1897 Moscow rule that "in all factories
there must be good drinking water in vessels that are tightly closed and
have faucets;" or that in factories producing noxious gases the air inside
the factory must be renewed at least two or three times an hour; or the
thirty-one obligatory fire protection measures?[50]

An excellent example of the contradiction between the government's
tutelary claims and its virtual impotence in fact was the curious practice
of certification (literally, "witnessing"). The factory inspector was
obligated by law to certify piece rates in the factory—that is, officially
to confirm their level. The rates themselves were determined solely by
the factory owner. Understandably, this confused the workers, and they
often held the inspector responsible for the piece rates he had certified.[51]
For some reason the state wanted to be there, but it was there as a specta-
tor, a perfect metaphor for the coexistence of shadowy autocratic claims
and the reality of a capitalist wage relationship. This contradiction
provided an ideal opening for Social Democratic agitation. "Wages are
confirmed by an official of the government, by the factory inspector,"
proclaimed a leaflet from the Union of Struggle in July 1896. "This
means that the government thinks that it is legal for the workers to live
half starving."[52]

Government officials were by no means unaware of their inability to
protect the workers effectively. For example, the Smolensk governor
lucidly described the limitations of his power in reconciling an 1880
strike in comments that are relevant far beyond their immediate context:

> If, on the one hand, the disorders must be quickly stopped, then, on the other,
> it would seem that the violation of the workers' rights must be rectified with
> the same speed. But the representative of the administration, strong enough
> for the re-establishment of order, is completely powerless for the satisfaction
> of the just complaints of the workers, and he must convince the agitated popu-
> lace that the satisfaction of their petitions must be sought in court. This is
> almost impossible for the factory workers, because of the loss of time involved
> in going to the Justice of the Peace, for which they fear being fined for absence
> from work.[53]

It was just such considerations that convinced Trepov that police-sponsored worker organizations were essential for the protection of workers' rights, an explicit recognition that police tutelage alone was insufficient. Others, of course, drew the even more far-reaching conclusion that the solution to the labor issue demanded the legalization of independent worker organizations.

The government's recurrent assertion of autocratic protection as the ideal solution to the labor question had adverse consequences for its own authority. By failing to allow for the differentiation of a sphere of partially autonomous industrial relations, it simply took too much responsibility upon itself. The nature of the laws of the marketplace could not be blamed for low wages when the government explicitly promised to safeguard workers' welfare. In addition, in Western European countries legal labor organizations decentralized conflict and relieved the government of some of its responsibilities in social policy. In Russia because of the workers' weakness, the government became more accountable for the workers' welfare. By prohibiting worker independence the government assumed greater responsibility for protection—a principle inherent in the logic of the situation despite the Ministry of Finance's enunciation of the principles of freedom of contract and market determination of wages. These contrasting principles, however, could have no real moral weight when the autocracy stifled all the shoots of worker independence.

The revolutionaries made protracted efforts to disabuse workers of their faith in the tutelary authorities. They helped compose appeals to the highest authorities in the certainty that they would go unheeded. They tirelessly pointed out the discrepancies between the government's words and its deeds. Through these efforts, and aided by the government itself, the main source of the government's claim to legitimacy increasingly served to undermine it. "Gentlemen," exclaimed one worker with trembling voice after an explosion in a government plant, "today we bury six victims, killed not by the Turks, but by the tutelary authorities."[54] Such experiences had two frequently interrelated consequences: disillusionment with the government's tutelary claims, which was a rejection of government practice, and assertion of the need for worker self-reliance, which was a rejection of basic principles. Clearly many more workers drew the first conclusion than the second, for independent action required a degree of self-confidence and hope that the vast majority lacked. Disillusionment with government protection was nonetheless an initial step toward a commitment to independent action and helped weaken worker support for the tsarist regime.

The second dilemma, rooted in the lack of differentiation between politics and administration and the overreliance on administration, also damaged the government's authority. For centuries Russian political life had been characterized by a poorly developed legal system and a lack of differentiation between politics and administration. Indeed, there was an inherent tension between law and autocracy, given that law and the legal institutions necessary to protect it place limits upon the ruler's autonomy. In the Middle Ages in Europe royal absolutism was explicitly limited by law, which was held to be superior to the king. The king enforced and promulgated the law, but it was the community that declared what the law was.[55] Without an independent church or a natural law tradition, Russia was in a different situation, but the necessity of law was also affirmed by legal reformers and theorists such as Speransky and Korkunov. In Korkunov's discussion, law was grounded in the needs of the state more than in the rights of the community.[56] Without law the state could not rely on feelings of loyalty and moral duty from the subjects. In the absence of these, repression would become necessary, but it could be only exemplary and used in important cases, and so respect for the state would be undermined. Thus despotic governments, absolute governments not based on law, could never be firm in their foundations.

In addition, Korkunov maintained that law was necessary to regulate the interrelations among the different parts of the ruler's staff—otherwise they will become "independent sovereigns, each acting in its own special interest," thereby destroying the wholeness and unity of the government. It can be added that absolutism stands more in need of this kind of law than governments limited by custom or independent rights of the subject, for the more absolute the ruler, the less remains to regulate the relationships among subjects, between the people and the state, within the staff, and between the staff and the ruler. Korkunov thus declared it to be just and necessary that the Russian state be a state based on "objective right, custom, and law."

We have seen that the Russian state's labor policy was based not primarily on law—although the desirability of law was frequently asserted—but upon administration without fixed legal norms. In principle administration differs from politics in that it seeks solely to enact already enunciated goals. Whereas politics is inherently conflictual, ideally administration should be consensual. It involves not the selection of ends but the choice of means to enact these ends. In practice no complete separation between politics and administration can be made in any political system, because concrete institutions cannot correspond completely to particular functions. Observers since Weber have described the confusion between politics and administration in modern Western societies, decrying the decline of politics as an independent sphere.[57] As M. G. Smith has pointed out, this does not thereby eliminate politics but makes administration itself political.[58]

There were three new circumstances that rendered the traditional reliance on administration extremely harmful for government authority in rapidly modernizing Russia. First, the government's self-imposed tasks—to further the industrialization of the country and sponsor the minimum necessary changes in other areas of social life to support economic development—were far more complex than in earlier eras, partly because they implied a new degree of private initiative that depended on stable guarantees. Administrative decision-making served to encourage make-shift methods and personal whims and also to undermine the stable norms and expectations essential for the performance of these new tasks.

Second, reliance on administration fit poorly with the ministerial system of government developing throughout the nineteenth century. As the powerful ministries developed their own administrative apparatuses, the need for coordination between them increased proportionally, or they would become, in Korkunov's phrase, "independent sovereigns." This was precisely the situation in early twentieth-century Russia, as the rival satrapies fought each other over basic principles and matters of policy with very few efforts at consultation or coordination. In the eighteenth century the autocratic word of the tsar might have been able to rein in his personal favorites when rivalries became too intense, but the power of the different ministries was far too institutionalized for such simple methods to be effective. The result, predictably, was administrative chaos. Korkunov's insistence that consistent administration requires law applies in some measure to every kind of bureaucratic staff. It was especially necessary in the last decades of the tsarist regime, when the government had lost its ideological coherence. Thus conflicting principles were allowed to play themselves out in concrete practice, and these administrative conflicts further deepened political divisions within the bureaucracy. We have seen this process at work in some detail in previous chapters. Political and administrative incoherence fed upon each other, and the result was the further disorganization of the state apparatus. For this very reason coherent policy became less likely even as the corrosive effects of its absence became more evident. There was thus a kind of consistency to the political crisis of the tsarist regime: beginning with the tensions inherent in the project of modernization within a relatively stagnant political system, it ended with contradiction and inconsistency at the most minute administrative level as well. Undermining the public's confidence in its integrity, the government also lost the capacity to act with any vitality on its own.

Finally, reliance on administration was counterproductive because it violated the developing standards of public opinion, which increasingly demanded Western-style legal guarantees. Much of the press, many legal professionals, and educated Russians in general were outraged by the government's continuing reliance on administrative methods and its frequent violation of those laws that it did manage to enact. They could share Trotsky's disgust that "in Russia, 'provisional rules' of every kind are usually the most long-lasting forms of legislation."[59] Thus respect for law was one of the essential demands that drove a wedge between the government and a substantial portion of the privileged sectors in Russia, making the state more vulnerable to mass unrest.

In practice the reliance on administrative procedure corresponded to a devolution of discretionary powers to local officials. Two examples of their tactics will show the inconsistency and unpredictability of their actions, hardly traits capable of fostering labor peace—for, in the language of psychology, intermittent reinforcement is the most consistent method of prolonging a pattern of behavior.

The first tactic, arbitrary repression, is well exemplified by the government's handling of the May 1870 Nevskii cotton mill strike, the first major strike in postreform Russia. The case is instructive because it demonstrates the continuity between government policy at the dawn of the modern labor movement and after the defeat of the 1905 revolution. After leaving work because of a dispute over wage deductions, the Nevskii workers turned first to local police and then to Trepov, the municipal police chief, for adjudication of their grievances. After the workers refused to respond to the urgings of Trepov's deputy to resume work, Trepov promised to take "the most urgent measures."[60] He decided to prosecute them in the newly established court system, where he was certain that the workers would be rapidly and harshly punished. The sixty-two spinners were indeed found guilty of participating in a strike, but because of the improper conduct of the factory administration, the workers were given extremely light sentences. Obviously, such an outcome would not serve to discourage other workers, and Trepov sought and received permission from the Ministry of Internal Affairs to exile four of the leaders to their native provinces, thus bypassing the judicial system entirely. Later that year, illegal expediency was turned into administrative principle: provincial governors were authorized to exile strike instigators without court trials or even the prior permission of the ministry itself. In 1871 these administrative punishments were extended to all participants in strikes. An ironic twist to these events is that the Nevskii workers were in fact extremely moderate in their methods and demonstrated confidence in the impartiality of police officials. They apparently did not realize that the government was more concerned about the fact that they had acted together, "in a crowd," as the police liked to phrase it, than about the justice of their claims.

In other cases repression of independent action was combined with paternal solicitude for the workers' welfare. A fascinating example is provided by the actions of Moscow governor V. A. Dolgorukov in 1885.[61]

In a local factory there was a work stoppage accompanied by some disorder in response to an announced cutback in the number of working days. Dolgorukov reasoned that the main supporters of the strike were nonlocal workers; local workers would be more concerned with keeping the factory running. He dispatched troops into the village in order to take the outside workers to jail and then send them to their villages. The soldiers encountered no opposition, the disorders stopped, and no violence was used against the workers. During this time the workers and their families received soldiers' rations without charge. After the conflict Dolgorukov invited Ber, the director of the factory, to meet and informed him that the factory would remain closed until the just demands of the workers were satisfied. Not surprisingly Ber agreed to the demands, and many workers, including 71 of the 115 outside workers, were rehired on the old basis. According to the governor's report, all the workers held in the Moscow jail asked the jail supervisor and police superintendent to thank the governor for his concern for them and their families and his just treatment of them. After returning to their village and work, they celebrated a prayer of thanks in the church.

Neither of these types of government arbitrariness taught the workers positive lessons from the point of view of the authorities. Through actions such as Trepov's they learned that the government could not be trusted to honor even its own rules. Dolgorukov's tactics surely undermined the authority of the factory owner and subtly communicated to the workers that illegal action might still be effective. More generally, workers learned to look not to the law but to the goodwill of political authorities. Because the responses of government officials were inherently unpredictable, and also because the workers rarely had a viable alternative course of action, collective protest emerged as a fundamentally rational means of pursuing their goals—this despite the government's official pronouncements to the contrary.

Perhaps the most impressive examples of administrative arbitrariness in the labor question were the two major experiments in police socialism, the Zubatov and Gapon societies, in which the authorities fomented activities that were formally illegal and punishable by criminal law. With respect to the Gapon societies, there was a fundamental duplicity in the government's actions. Before the January 1905 strikes high officials were protecting and encouraging the societies; but then, without warning the workers that their peaceful march would be punished, they used unheard of violence against them. The great majority of the participants were firmly convinced that they had government approval for the march to the tsar to ask for his beneficence. In light of these unhappy experiences, it should occasion no surprise that broad sectors of Russian public opinion concluded that the problems of industrial life were fundamentally political.[62] The workers' reactions were even more intense: after 9 January a great many concluded that there was no longer either a tsar or a God, the two fundamental pillars of the traditional hierarchial system. Whereas the two previous dilemmas stemmed from the extension of autocratic principles and practices to a modern Russia where they were increasingly counterproductive, the final dilemma—the government's proclamation of new rights for the workers that it refused to honor— demonstrated how the growth of modern social relations forced the state to enunciate new principles that it could never fully accept. Thus it was unable to respect either its old principles or its new ones: the old because they were inapplicable to the demands of modern Russian society, and the new because modern social relations constituted a deep challenge to the integrity of traditional Russian politics.

The third dilemma thus illuminates the contradictions of autocratic capitalism from another angle. Many government officials were forced to recognize that some form of legal worker organization was essential to ensure social harmony, thus breaking with the autocratic prohibition of organized group activity. In addition, many accepted the logic that these rights of organization in turn required an expansion of civil and political rights. These convictions, in one or another variation, underlay the Zubatov societies, the starosta law, the Gapon societies, the legislative efforts culminating in the temporary rules on strikes and unions, and the issuance of the October Manifesto. The social and political groups and officials advocating these measures were strong enough to have them adopted but too weak to ensure their institutionalization. Just as the autocracy could not live up to its tutelary commitments, so it violated the liberal values that it half-heartedly avowed. The following remarks from the newspaper of the St. Petersburg Soviet in late 1905 are equally applicable to the whole period preceding the revolution:

Freedom of assembly is given, but meetings are surrounded by soldiers. Freedom of speech is given, but censorship remains untouched. Freedom of learning is granted, but the universities are occupied by soldiers. Inviolability of the person is granted, but the jails are overflowing with prisoners. Witte is given, but Trepov remains. A constitution is given, but autocracy remains. Everything is given, and nothing is given.[63]

Such hypocrisy and duplicity discredited both the government and the law in the eyes of the workers.[64] The violation of their recognized rights convinced them of the regime's injustice and also of the legitimacy of their own claims. The combination of these two themes is nicely expressed in the following poem written by worker Aleksei Piskarev, which he read at a huge mass meeting at the Technological Institute in late 1905. The sentiments expressed in it serve as a fitting conclusion to the previous analysis of government labor policy and also as an introduction to the following interpretation of the development of the Russian labor movement:

> They left us out of the Duma
> The guardians of the law.
> With the sanction of the throne
> They found us expendable.
> Just look, we are dirty and gray...
> May we not get used to it.
> Where it's necessary, we'll win by force
> We are full of faith in ourselves
> No one will indulge us,
> We'll take everything through struggle.
> Now we'll send a protest
> Or we'll announce a strike
> To the Shidlovskii Commission.
> They wanted to lead us,
> There to fool us:
> "You are the people," they said,
> "You're that sort."
> Although you're the head, you're mistaken, Senator
> We don't need an orator,
> But knowledge and rights.
> Without us you'll only ruminate there.
> We'll take everything by force.
> We'll send you to the devil
> And we'll all declare a strike.[65]

PART III

STRUCTURE AND BASIC TRAITS OF THE RUSSIAN LABOR MOVEMENT

INTRODUCTION

The Russian social and political formation, to which I have given the shorthand appellation *autocratic capitalism*, hindered any meaningful resolution of the labor question. This failure, together with other traits of autocracy and capitalism, decisively conditioned the emergence and development of the labor movement. It was within this structural context that the Russian labor movement acquired a distinctive physiognomy and pattern of organization and a high degree of solidarity and radicalism.

The key distinguishing feature of the Russian working class, then, was permanent and almost uninterrupted exclusion. And it was this exclusion, more than underlying sociological traits (rural-urban, skilled-unskilled, occupation), that defined the basic structure of the Russian labor movement. First, there was a large category of mass workers, without stable commitments or loyalties, who were denied organization and participation. Such workers existed in every industrializing country, but the lack of organization, weakness of civil society, and political despotism of Tsarist Russia ensured that massification would be more widespread and more profound.

In response to these conditions, as well as to the harsh economic and social deprivations of factory life, there emerged a second category of workers, a much smaller, self-defined elite of "conscious" workers. Under the influence of the intelligentsia, and partly in rejection of the way of life of the "gray" masses, conscious workers escaped from their mass situation through the elaboration of a new identity and new commitments. As role models, organizers, and transmitters of ideology, they made a critical contribution to the labor movement, particularly in periods of mass unrest.

Finally, nowhere else did revolutionary intellectuals play a more central part in the formation of a mass labor movement than in Russia. Exclusion also explains the difference here: without trade unions, a legal workers' press, or widespread educational or cultural opportunities, Russian workers could hardly generate their own leaders or ideals. Therefore, despite serious cleavages, they remained dependent on intelligentsia leadership. Each of these three groups was highly differentiated from the others culturally and socially, and mutual contempt often governed their interrelations. In periods of struggle, however, their very differentiation pushed them together in an uneasy though highly militant alliance.

A fourth group in the labor movement, reformist worker activists, had only marginal importance in Russia. After 1905 a potentially significant group of trade union organizers, many of them with roots in the milieu of the conscious workers, did make its appearance but was unable to overcome what Martov called "the infantile-romantic stage" of the Russian workers' movement.[1] Whereas in Germany moderate worker leaders provided much of the support for revisionist socialism and trade unionism throughout several decades, in Russia they were cast aside shortly after their tardy appearance, or, faced with the continuing reality of government repression, they embraced once again the ethos of the underground. Before this occurred, however, the Russian activists urged compliance with the existing repressive laws and viewed underground activity with skepticism, if not outright hostility. They frequently opposed strikes out of concern for union legality, preferring to devote themselves to organizational issues, mutual aid, and the resolution of industrial disputes.[2] During the period of effective repression of the labor movement, until 1912, reformist worker activists played a substantial role in the trade union movement, as evidenced by their leadership of the important St. Petersburg metalworkers' union. In the context of revived industrial protest after 1912 and continuing government repression, however, their position became increasingly untenable. By the eve of the war they had been largely replaced by Bolshevik activists hostile toward their moderate orientation. The underground and its associated structure— mass workers, conscious workers, and the socialist intelligentsia— proved itself more in line with the logic of Russian political life, which, despite itself, continued to generate an "infantile-romantic" social movement. Whatever their preferences might have been, committed worker leaders either joined in the upsurge of illegal labor militancy or lost their authority among the workers.

In contrast to the preceding analysis of tsarist labor policy, the organization of the following chapters is thematic, not chronological. The purpose here is not to write the history of the mass workers, conscious workers, and intelligensia but to sketch an ideal-typical portrait of their basic characteristics and interrelations. Generalization in this sense has the usual pitfalls, and some readers may have preferred more attention to nuance and historical change. However, whatever social and political changes may have occurred between 1895 and 1914, exclusion remained constant; and it was exclusion that determined the distinctive structure and traits of the Russian labor movement. The method of analysis, then, follows from the logic and purpose of the study as a whole: to analyze how the pattern of Russian development gave rise to a uniquely revolutionary labor movement. From this perspective fluctuations over time within the movement are ultimately less important than the fundamental differences that set it apart from other labor movements.

Given this distinctive structure of the Russian labor movement rooted in exclusion, its form of organization inevitably differed from Western European patterns. Local organizations could never come to control mass action based on territory and were themselves constantly under the influence of socialist leadership composed of conscious workers and the intelligentsia. The pattern of organization thus furthered the fusion of spontaneous mass action and class-based ideological action, a synthesis that was symptomatic of the combined pattern of Russian development and the dual pattern of the labor movement.

An extraordinary capacity for solidarity and radicalism was the outcome of this unusual structure and pattern of organization of the Russian labor movement. Many of the sources of fission characteristic of more institutionalized labor movements were largely avoided, and mass and class action supplemented each other. At the same time, the dearth of legal organizations and the lack of stable and moderate worker leadership exacted a high price: great unevenness. Periods of exceptional solidarity and militancy alternated with years of dramatic decline of the movement, the latter characterized by mutual recriminations and passivity imposed by force.

CHAPTER
7

Mass Workers

In terms of commitment to the labor movement, it is convenient to think in terms of two basic categories of workers: mass workers and conscious workers. This classification—or some variant of it—was commonly used by the worker elite and the revolutionary intelligentsia at the time to characterize the basic differences in political awareness and activism among workers. It is less likely that the mass workers also adopted this vocabulary. Almost all of what we know about the mass workers comes from the memoirs of the worker elite (many of them formerly "unconscious" and contemptuous of their own past lives) or the intelligentsia (who were separated from the mass workers by enormous social gulfs), so the mass workers were never able to give themselves their own name. The conscious workers often called them "gray" or "dark," terms that connoted indistinguishability, passivity, and ignorance.

The term *mass worker* is appropriate in two senses. First, it indicates that this was by far the largest category of worker. There is no possible way to estimate proportions, but all observers agree, and common sense suggests, that by any standard the mass workers were the immense majority. Standards, of course, could vary, and in individual cases categorization might be open to dispute. Usually, however, the distinction would not have been difficult to make, for the role of conscious worker became a relatively standardized and identifiable one. It was clear that the conscious worker stood out as a member of a separate minority both in his own mind and in the minds of others.

Second, mass workers were in what scholars call a mass situation: they formed a large category of people who were not integrated into any broad social groupings, including classes.[1] They had few organizational commitments or stable loyalties and were cut off from most basic social institutions. As opposed to conscious workers, they had not found a distinctive identity buttressed by social or organizational ties. They were indifferent to politics and generally sought relief from their frustrations through escape. As Kornhauser predicts, however, this did not mean that they were not "available" for mobilization into collective action. In fact, mass workers became an important part of the Russian labor movement without fully ceasing to be in a mass situation—just as, as a whole, the Russian labor movement was a complex amalgam of social movement and collective behavior. Even further, in strikes or crucial episodes of worker mobilization they often stood at the forefront of events because of their lack of commitment to long-term strategy or theory. In this sense neither mass workers nor conscious workers nor, indeed, the intelligentsia can be said to have led the labor movement. In addition, it should be emphasized that the category of mass worker is not static, some kind of ascribed state of being. Through their experiences in the workplace or through collective struggle mass workers might make the transition to consciousness.

Mass workers existed and exist in all industrial countries. In his discussion of workers in late Imperial Germany, Barrington Moore discusses the elite and masses among the workers. Much of his presentation is perfectly applicable to Russia.[2] Nonetheless, autocratic Russia was especially fertile in the creation of masses because of the prohibitions on organizational life. The state virtually decreed that the Russian population be nothing more than a mass. If many German or English workers had tenuous ties to parties, unions, or local government, the proportion of Russian workers without meaningful organizational affiliations was, of course, much higher. Passivity and indifference were all the more common in a social environment that virtually outlawed anything else.

Even religious enthusiasm was suspect. In his memoirs the worker Shapovalov tells an anecdote that reveals how passive workers were supposed to be even in religion, and how any active response to the surrounding world was regarded as dangerous. In complete despair and feeling "like a caged bird," he joined a religious temperance society to overcome his loneliness. He soon became an enthusiastic member, often preaching his views to other workers. Two of the best workers in the factory approached him:

They were both interested by my agitation. They came to my workbench and, becoming acquainted with what I said, they advised me: "Stop, Borovoi, don't preach, don't make a fool out of yourself. You start off on the right path, but it can end badly for you. You speak now about God, but look out, you'll become a socialist." "What do you mean, a socialist?" I asked, "That's right", continued Nikolaev quietly and in an even-tempered way. "In former times they were here. You, you see, began to read books and you will become engrossed in reading. . . . It's better to stop, or they will arrest and hang you."[3]

To Shapovalov's friends, any assertion of independence was the first step toward questioning the traditional hierarchies and so was inherently dangerous. The Zubatov experiment clearly demonstrated that any form of mobilization, even if based on religion or traditional ideas, went counter to the conservative emphasis on obedience.

In the following pages, using worker and some intelligentsia memoirs, I will sketch some basic sociological traits of the mass workers. I will also describe certain aspects of their relationship to the conscious workers and to the intelligentsia. My aim is not to describe their way of life completely but to explain how this "mass" could become part of a revolutionary class movement whose aims transcended their own.

DIVERSITY

The workers in his district, remarked factory inspector Gvozdev, were an extremely "motley mass." Their only shared characteristic was "their ignorance, their deep, almost impenetrable, darkness."[4] And although Gvozdev's remarks are certainly not free of class prejudices, they do suggest that the term *worker* masks an impressive richness of social experience. Such diversity of workers is typical of many industrializing countries because of the need to recruit a labor force rapidly. In Russia, however, social diversity had its distinctive aspects. Autocracy, with its emphasis on rank combined with its leveling tendencies and its prohibitions on association, sharpened the cultural importance of social differences. As in Germany or England, they became matters of extreme sensitivity and significantly shaped social relations. Their political import was greatly reduced, however, because they could rarely find organizational expression. In Western Europe craft unions could deepen occupational differences and divide workers in their struggles. Similarly, even modern German factories around the turn of the century often had a formally recognized hierarchy symbolized by separate costumes for each rank.[5] Religious differences could also give rise to different trade union and political party affiliations. In autocratic Russia, where society was so much less organized, rank could not become so institutionalized.

Perhaps the most important distinction was between workers of rural and urban origin. It was often argued that the peasant worker was not fully a worker—that his real ties were to the land, and he had no real commitment to factory work. Thus in the story "Dreamers" by N. Zlatovratskii, a populist writer, the peasant worker Dema still had not come to consider himself an industrial worker after ten years in the factory. He still dreamed of the countryside:

Before him in the hazy distance, as a longed-for haven, the countryside constantly came to him: instead of the sooty and gray walls of the workshop, in
the din and noise of the machines and instruments, he heard the trills of the
lark, the squeak of carts with hay and sheafs, the dialect of rural streets. He
saw his hut, his cow, horse, broad fields, the clean turquoise sky, the green
forest and . . . space, boundless space.[6]

It was widely felt that such workers would not struggle for general worker goals, that they were interested only in accumulating money for a future return to the countryside. Numerous government officials also held
this view, assuring themselves that the peasant character of the majority
of workers would save Russia from the calamity of a labor question as
Europe had experienced it.

Scholars have differed on the degree of permanent commitment to factory work; the intensity of the peasant worker's consciousness of himself
as an industrial worker; and the implications of continued links to the
village, including family ties and the possession of a plot of land.[7] L. M.
Ivanov has argued that by the turn of the century a large sector of the
industrial labor force had *de facto* severed any significant connection
with agriculture. In this respect he considers a worker's legal classification as a peasant as misleading, because a change in legal status was often
difficult and unnecessary. Similarly, he questions the significance of land-
ownership, as holdings were frequently worked by hired laborers or
leased out while the owner continued to work in industry. Even periodic
visits to the village were not a sign of enduring ties to agriculture or the
rural community—such visits were often only for vacation or rest. Yet
Ivanov also recognizes the great diversity in degree of commitment to
industry. For example, workers kept closer links to the village in less
mechanized industries and in those factories farther removed from important industrial centers.[8] Other scholars, such as Robert Johnson in his
study of Moscow workers, have argued that the peasant workers' ties to
the village were still quite strong and that most workers were firmly attached to both factory and village.[9]

Whatever the subtleties, there is no doubt that the distinction between
full proletarian and peasant worker was an important one for the workers
themselves. In Kanatchikov's factory, the peasant workers were called
"gray devils" and ridiculed whenever the opportunity presented itself.[10]
Kleinbort quotes numerous expressions and sayings used to deride rural
workers. They were scorned for their country ways, their humility before
the bosses, their immoderate drinking, and their visits to prostitutes.
They were also regarded as unreliable in times of strikes, or even as
strikebreakers, and hopelessly impermeable to socialist teachings.[11]

Occupation also provided a strong basis for stratification among workers. In Kanatchikov's factory, for example, the pattern-making workshop was considered an "aristocratic" one. The majority of pattern-makers were town dwellers, and they dressed well—on holidays some even wore bowler hats. "They bore themselves respectably, with an awareness of their own special worth."[12] Within Buzinov's factory there was a well-defined hierarchy: the workers of the machine shop, the fitters and turners, were at the top, whereas the workers in the "hot work-shops," including smelting, rolling, and metalsmith workers, were at the bottom because their work was more physical. It was said that the fitters were more thoughtful and educated, sharper and wittier in their speech, and held their heads higher.[13] In Petrov's factory the draughtsmen did not deign to associate even with the fitters or turners, considering them beneath their dignity. There were numerous fights among workers of different trades—among metalsmiths, turners, or boilermakers, for example. And Petrov had great difficulty convincing skilled workers to do agitational work among the carpenters and unskilled workers.[14] The unskilled workers, or "black workers," were always at the bottom of the hierarchy. Because of their very low salaries they were not strongly committed to the factory and changed jobs often. They were more likely to come from the countryside and to maintain their ties to it because of their economic insecurity.[15]

Age also seemed to be an important basis of differentiation. According to Kleinbort, the older workers who had worked twelve or fifteen years in the same place were much more conservative than the younger workers. They formed an isolated, closed group, having their own special privileges. They avoided politics and sometimes even informed about preparations for strikes to the factory administration.[16] There must have been some basis for this generalization, for we recall that conservative proponents of the starosta project in the government fought to raise the age qualification for election. Somov suggests the same general tendency in his observations on the workers in early 1905, although he emphasizes that even the older and more experienced workers became radicalized in the strike struggle. Ivanov makes similar comments about the older workers in the bakery in which he worked.[17]

These traits hardly exhausted the cleavages within the Russian working class. Religion, nationality, region, and ethnicity could each serve as the basis for social divisions within the workers. Isolated as they were from one another, and with such a fragile sense of personal dignity, it is not surprising that all such differences became bases of differentiation.[18] It is well to remember what cleavages were *not* present, however. Basically there were no craft workers with significant traditions, for the simple reason that guilds had never developed deep roots in Russia. Thus there was no category of workers with a sense of independence and dignity stemming from a preindustrial past. Further, there was no real workers' aristocracy in the sense that one developed in England.[19] For a basic precondition of the emergence of such a privileged group was strong and exclusive trade union organization.

Not only were these sources of diversity absent. In addition Russian workers were united by a powerful shared trait: they were all excluded from real participation in society. This was particularly true of the mass workers, even more than for their counterparts in England, France, or Germany, and it was this exclusion that made them such an appropriate base for a revolutionary movement centered on class.

LACK OF INTEGRATION

The meaning of integration will vary with the nature of a specific society. In medieval Europe, for example, serfs could be integrated into society through hierarchical relations and religion even though they were deprived of political rights. In nineteenth-century Europe, with the changes wrought by industralization and the decline of old-regime institutions and political structures, integration meant citizenship—the acquisition of civil, social, and political rights.[20]

By the late nineteenth century virtually all groups in Russian society were unintegrated to some degree. Old models of rule had declined and old interdependencies (including serfdom) had largely disappeared, but few new institutions or modes of participation had taken their place. This was true even for the nobility, many of whom chafed under the restrictions on their participation in public life and even joined oppositional circles. It was also true for the liberal professions, which were denied the prestige, prerogatives, and rights of their European counterparts. And it was true for the industrialists, who could only cast a wistful eye toward their German or French peers.

Of course, it was especially true for the lower classes, both for the peasants, whose old institutions had long been in decay, and for the workers, whose new status was yet to be recognized and granted appropriate rights. Among the workers it was truest for the mass workers, who did not have the political ideals and loyalties of the conscious worker. Becoming conscious paradoxically implied a kind of integration, for it involved a definite social role and a new personal identity.

When the young Kanatchikov left his village for the city, his father reminded him not to forget God, to honor his elders, to serve his boss honorably, and in particular to remember and care about his home.[21] The elder Kanatchikov thus hoped that the young man could live by the same rules as in the village and so find a recognized and honored, if subordinate, place in his new world. For the young Kanatchikov, as for so many others, the advice turned out to be unavailing.

Russian workers, even in the great cities, lived largely apart from major social institutions. They had some access to education in their youth, but this was cut short by the need to begin work. Sunday schools and night schools existed and at times flourished, but these were usually frequented by a small minority of workers, and in any case their activities were greatly curtailed when the government realized that many revolutionaries were teaching in the schools. In the period of reaction under Alexander III, in the late 1880s, the Church made attempts to win over the loyalty of the workers through sponsoring parish schools and temperance societies. In the capital it was a period of heightened religious sentiment, with rumors of miracles and talk of relics.[22] In no way could these efforts be compared to English Methodism, however, for they did not call forth the active participation and enthusiasm of the people, and many workers became disillusioned with the extreme conservatism of the teaching. I have seen no estimates of how widespread these institutions were, but as opposed to the night schools, they were hardly mentioned in the memoirs available to me.

It was also difficult for workers to lead a normal family life. They often lived together with other workers of the same sex in crowded quarters in the city, or else in factory barracks where there was no privacy and seldom any special quarters for families. Special provisions for child-rearing, such as nurseries or kindergartens, were almost nonexistent.[23] And many workers had left their spouses behind in the countryside.

Workers in all industrializing countries were cut off from major social institutions to some degree. Russia was simply an extreme case of a common phenomenon. Perhaps even more distinctive was the fact that in Russia workers had almost nothing of their own social institutions. Guenther Roth has described how German workers of the late nineteenth century were denied participation in German life as full citizens. Yet they did develop many of their own institutions and a rich subculture, with their own organizations, newspapers, cultural activities, and the like—a phenomenon Roth calls negative integration.[24] Even in comparatively backward China, traditional guild organizations and employer-dominated associations were far more important than in Russia, and although often conservative in orientation they did provide some framework for participation, and at crucial times, such as the 4 May movement of 1919, they could help lead industrial protest.[25]

For mass workers in Russia nothing of the sort could take place. There were mutual aid societies and cooperatives, but these played no great role, partly because they were largely controlled by the employers. Apart from these there was very little; no permanent legal worker press or legal worker parties, no established trade unions able to act freely. The only alternatives were the underground press and organizations, and of these the great majority of workers were understandably wary in normal times. It was to escape from this vacuum that Shapovalov joined the church's temperance society: "The separation among the workers was so great, the night was so dark, that the society, although run by the priests, seemed like a ray of light in the gloomy night." It was only by the complete absence of parties, unions, and self-help funds that he could explain to himself his attraction to what he later regarded as a trap that the priests created to help the tsar, landowners, and capitalists. "The proletarian instinct could not tolerate the isolation of workers and demanded association," as he would later express it in a new language.[26]

This institutional vacuum changed somewhat after 1905. As described in the previous section, during some periods (especially 1906–1907) trade unions were both legal and tolerated, and there was a flourishing worker press. Many cultural and educational societies arose, often initiated by the unions. The government never allowed these new institutions to develop naturally, however, and they all had a stunted, uneven history. Their progress was incapable of keeping pace with the workers' rising demands for a richer organizational and cultural life, and so, in a psychological sense, the situation was probably worse than it had been before. If, in addition, we consider the workers' bitterness over their illegal suppression, we can assume that they could hardly stimulate a sense of belonging to the larger society. Indeed, it has been persuasively argued that government repression of formally legal organizations was a major source of radicalism in the Russian labor movement in the prewar years.[27]

Work itself can also be a source of integration. Parsons and Smelser argue that a positive evaluation of the work role is an integrating mechanism in industrial societies and thus a noncontractual element of contract.[28] Kanatchikov had been admonished to serve his boss well, and presumably his father assumed that this would lead to mutual respect. The evidence from memoirs, however, is overwhelming that workers felt despised in their role, virtual outcasts from society, even though they themselves might have enjoyed their work and felt proud of their skill. This is one of the most prevalent of all of their complaints.[29] "We are not recognized as people, but we are considered as things which can be thrown out at any moment." "Outside Russia they say that even horses get to rest. Then our workers' existence is worse than a horse's." They complained that other social groups expected them to dress poorly and in general assumed the worst about and despised them. Workers resented the division of people into "black" and "white bone"—a survival of the serf era. The ruling classes, they said, could not imagine that a worker is also a human being.

The bosses and factory administration's treatment of the workers seemed to bear out their claims.[30] They swore at the workers and, assuming they were all thieves, searched them in a humiliating way upon leaving work. Taking it for granted that the workers were lazy, the bosses employed spies to watch them[31] and substituted piecework for daily wages.[32] The workers' feelings were not the result of overactive imaginations. Even the briefest inspection of archival records in which factory owners expressed their attitudes toward their workers shows that the workers were quite correct: their bosses distrusted them almost completely. The workers returned this sentiment with both hatred and fear.[33] "I avoided meetings with him," wrote Shapovalov about his boss, "but sometimes leaving the factory with a crowd of workers, I unexpectedly ran into him. At the sight of his fat belly and healthy red face I not only did not take off my hat, but in my eyes, against my will, there flared up a terrible fire of hatred when I saw him. I had the mindless idea of grabbing him by the throat, throwing him to the ground, and stamping on his fat belly with my feet."[34] We recall factory owner Belov's wall of isolation and fear, a sign of the missing bonds of civil society.

What about religion and loyalty to the tsar? Did these act as integrating forces? For some workers they clearly did. God, though not priests, and the tsar were still sacrosanct.[35] Religious faith of a fatalistic kind helped many workers resign themselves to their lot.[36] And it was often assumed that in his compassion the tsar cared for them, but in his isolation he was unaware of their travails or the injustices they suffered. "I do not blame my government at all. The government until now did not know," wrote one worker. "Everything was quiet and tranquil. I'll give an example from my own experience: my child does not cry and it doesn't occur to me to feed him."[37] As a result, some faith in the paternal benevolence of the government survived, as evidenced by the practice of sending personal petitions to the tsar or his ministers for help.[38] Indeed, the initial great popularity of the Zubatov and Gapon societies attests to the continuing strength of loyalty to the tsar.

The significance of traditional belief in God or loyalty to the tsar should not be overestimated, however. Such faith in both cases was attached to a distant object—so distant, in fact, that its lack of efficacy could be easily explained. Fatalism is, perhaps, a kind of negative integration. It does not appeal to everyone, however, particularly those with the most talent and initiative, and it is often replaced by more hopeful sentiments when change seems possible. It can also be destroyed if faith in the ultimate benevolence of the protector—either God or the tsar—is lost.

The experiences of workers with their little father, the tsar, led many of them to abandon this trust, and resignation often turned to anger.[39] For example, the Zubatov experiment showed the strength of royalism among many workers, but it also showed its limits: loyalty did not extend to the hierarchical social system that the tsar sought to order; and to be effective in reconciling the workers to the regime, it also became conditional because it implied an incipient contract. The Gapon movement taught a similar lesson: that monarchism and religious faith as sources of integration could be a double-edged weapon, quickly escaping the control of the authorities.

Resignation was one of the most healthy psychological reactions of mass workers to their situation. Often they developed much more self-destructive attitudes and habits. Many lost all their self-respect, internalizing society's attitude toward them as workers. As a young worker, Frolov sought associations with other kinds of people—railroad office workers, technicians, high school students. He was ashamed of being a worker and tried to hide the truth from his friends. He dressed well and washed his hands with strong detergent so they would not notice any factory grime. On workdays he was terrified of being seen by his friends in his worker's clothes. "I trembled, fearing that they, having noticed me in work clothes with other workers, whom everyone despised, would reject me. And then—goodbye to my wish to learn from them everything that they knew."[40] The baker Ivanov confessed that his fellow bakers were ashamed to tell prostitutes that they were bakers.[41]

Self-contempt, despair, a sense of meaninglessness: such feelings were very widespread among the mass workers.[42] Perhaps the most common reaction was escape through vodka. In Buzinov's factory vodka was everywhere. About one-third of the workers were drunkards in the full sense of the word, he claimed. Buzinov heard that formerly all workers had been drunkards, but by this time (the late 1890s) they were in the minority. The rest of the workers drank heavily but were not strictly speaking drunkards. For virtually all "vodka defined the content of life." There was much conversation about it, especially about ways of getting more money for it—advances, the reselling of goods, stealing.[43]

Self-contempt also implied contempt for others, and descriptions of the workers' relationships with their fellow workers often read like passages from Gorky. Swearing and fights were ubiquitous. Workers stole from the factory and robbed each other as well.

This cursed inheritance of Tsarist slavery [robbery] was implanted in the workers too. They took and stole from the factory everything that they could. They even stole tools from each other. The rule of life was: Keep your wits about you, keep your eyes peeled! . . . To steal, to deceive were considered good. The honest and just man who neither lied nor stole was looked upon as a fool or an oddity.[44]

There was thus some basis for the factory management's suspicions, if only in the sense of a self-fulfilling prophecy. In addition, it was not uncommon for workers to inform against one another to the authorities. Kleinbort recounts the case of a police official who had to announce that there would be no investigations of anonymous letters, thus trying to curb excessive denunciations.[45]

In this context of exclusion and self-contempt, mass workers felt helpless and without hope. "All of this so entered into the worker's flesh and blood that he somehow became accustomed to it and rarely even reflected on how to straighten out and improve his life."[46] "We are blind people, we're not smart enough to know how to act," lamented one worker to Professor Ozerov. "Show us the way, just as the Savior showed the way to salvation."[47] Offers of help from outside—from the police, as in the Zubatov experiment, or occasionally from the intelligentsia—could help dissipate this mood and give some hope. The general resignation also changed during periods of overall ferment and unrest. Often, however, these shifts in mood did not amount to a real change of consciousness—they were periodic and impermanent.

MASS WORKERS' CONSCIOUSNESS

Almost by definition mass workers lacked a well-developed political awareness. They were generally isolated from political discourse and institutions. Even in St. Petersburg they seldom had contact with revolutionaries except in times of ferment.[48] Conscious workers were a small minority, and in tranquil times, for reasons of safety, they formed a rather self-enclosed group the survival of which depended upon discretion.

Yet certain diffuse prepolitical sentiments seemed to have been widespread. We have already seen that there was general hostility toward the capitalists and capitalism deriving from traditional sentiments rooted in autocracy as well as the workers' dependent position in a capitalist system. They could readily accept an explanation of their misery in terms of exploitation because they largely viewed the capitalists as parasites. Speaking of the great display of wealth at a trade fair, the worker Petrov remarks: "Each worker and poor worker very well realized at the sight of these orgies that here is squandered the money created by his blood, and that things cannot continue in this way further. The parasitic class is too expensive!"[49] Other times similar sentiments were expressed in a more low-keyed manner. During an 1898 strike in Ivanovo-Voznesensk, the owner, Garelin, in negotiating with the workers, referred to his wife's charitable acts toward the workers. They thanked him but replied that if they didn't work, there wouldn't be money for these charitable institutions.[50]

Government officials occasionally recognized and reported on the workers' basic lack of respect for property rights. One September 1905 report even drew an explicit parallel between the peasants' claims to full ownership of the land and the workers' demands for an end to capitalist property in industry, though the author did not explore the possible interconnections between them.[51] Perhaps partly because the former peasants never accepted the legitimacy of the landlords, Russian workers, even more than other European workers, became convinced that labor was the source of wealth.[52] Finally, the radical implications of the traditional peasant myth of the good tsar deceived by his advisors but seeking to protect the interests of his loyal subjects has already been discussed. In Russia these sentiments had all the more potential danger because of the workers' lack of commitment to law, also a legacy of the autocracy. In this sense, too, there was considerable implicit radicalism in the mentality of politically unsophisticated mass workers.

Workers also developed a sense of injustice because of the treatment they received by bosses and the police. They did not come to view the whole social and political system as unjust, as did the conscious workers, but it led to the conviction that things were not as they should be. Mass workers saw how the police treated the upper classes differently, using the respectful form of "you" and handling them with decency. Many also seemed to be aware that workers were treated much better in other countries, and they often ascribed the difference to the workers' successful struggle for rights.[53]

Without any definite political views of their own, yet capable of anger over the injustices they felt, mass workers were receptive to new interpretations of their suffering. They flocked to the Gapon movement in St. Petersburg, and then in 1905 they gave great support to the Social Democrats. These commitments were temporary, however, made in the context of political ferment, and they seldom survived the defeat of the movements. Mass workers—and many conscious ones as well—became disillusioned with their leaders and even blamed them for involving workers in politics in the first place. At one meeting after Bloody Sunday, for example, the Social Democratic representatives were shouted at: "You pushed us into the abyss! It's necessary to hang you." Somov remarks that these cries were not supported by the crowd, but the mood was clearly dispiritedness, dismay, and disappointment.[54] If new ideals had not yet been firmly embraced, such experiences clearly weakened the hold of the old ones. "In the soul of the worker masses," wrote the memoirist Klaas, "the old faith perished, it perished irrevocably."[55]

Radical political ideas, with their connections to traditional political culture, were thus not foreign to mass workers, but neither were they absorbed. Indeed, real commitment to radical political ideas was difficult without greater organizational involvements—as it was, contact with organizations was only temporary and occurred in times of political unrest, when the organizations' resources were already overstrained and there was little opportunity for real political instruction. As one conscious worker confessed after 1905:

> Precisely now, in this time of stagnation, we understand the error which we committed. The fact is that little attention was paid to the very development of the worker. He would arrive at the labor exchange, he was propagandized, and he was right away considered a member. Well, even now some are not infrequently interested [in the movement], but unfortunately there are many who repent of their former sins. . . . To the conscious worker it is painful to look at this.[56]

Despite the transitory nature of their commitments, things were not as they had been before. As masses, the workers were still "available," but increasingly they were available only for certain kinds of movement and receptive only to certain kinds of appeal. Mass action was becoming more and more intertwined with class action. Even mass workers came to share the sentiments of Kanatchikov's timid co-worker Kvasnikov: "If everyone rose up and went against the Tsar and the bosses, then I would also go."[57] In the same way, Trotsky found that few workers in 1917 had a well-developed ideology, but he nonetheless recognized "elements of experience, criticism, initiative, self-sacrifice." Perhaps this did not quite amount to an "inner mechanics of the revolutionary movement as a conscious process," but it was evidence of the existence of something more than a completely disoriented mass.[58]

MODES OF ACTION

The traditional mode of action of the mass workers was the "bunt," the spontaneous act of violence. Unplanned and with little strategy or leadership, bunts were immediate responses to some provocation—a delay in the payment of wages, a lowering of wage rates, or some insult or coarse behavior by the factory administration or the police. If any longer-term emotion was behind the bunt, it was the desire for revenge for all the accumulated grievances that workers had no way of redressing.

Bunts were very common in Russian labor history and far from absent in Europe as well. Perrot writes that French strikes over labor discipline in the 1870s often bypassed economic rationality based upon calculation. They were frequently devoid of broader purpose, representing "the eruption of an anger usually controlled," and their purpose was revenge. They were savage and brutal, at times taking lives.[59] Such eruptions of violence in France, however, even before the rise of large-scale worker organizations, were a small minority. In Russia the balance seems to have been in the other direction. There are numerous accounts of bunts in the multivolume collection of documents on the nineteenth-century Russian labor movement and also in the memoir literature. Like happy families, bunts were much alike. There was generally much random violence, the workers arming themselves with rocks, metal pipes, tools, or anything at hand. The rioting workers broke windows, burned buildings, and beat up guards and factory administration. Robbery and stormings of the local store were common. Sometimes the violence could reach extremes, particularly when the vodka flowed freely. In one St. Petersburg bunt of 1890, for example, the workers almost drowned one engineer in a canal, and they got as far as constructing a gallows for the factory director.[60]

Bunts were, not surprisingly, the despair of the Social Democrats, those rationalists who believed in strategy geared toward history. And they were right that the bunt left few permanent traces. Bunts were usually ineffective. They did not accomplish much change in workers' political consciousness, and they alienated public opinion as well. They could be repeated endlessly without making any real change in the social or political life of the country.

Two qualifications are in order, however. First, the bunt could lead to certain changes in the workers' consciousness, even if seldom to real political reorientations. The first breach of the rigid authority structure of Tsarist Russia was often intoxicating and the workers could feel like heroes, if only for a time. When asked to identify some accused workers at their trial in 1900, an old woman responded: "Ah, batiushka! How could I recognize them? When this happened they were all giants, and now they sit there so small."[61] Similarly, in making plans to beat up a foreman, Kanatchikov and his fellows "felt ourselves to be heroes, having done a heroic deed in the interests of all the oppressed skilled workers."[62] After successful resistance to the boss after some fighting with a foreman, Ivanov remarked that "for the first time in our lives we felt that even we have human dignity."[63] Defiance could increase their solidarity, binding them together in danger (and perhaps in guilt, if we are to believe Freud). In this vein Ivanov wrote that "it seemed that some invisible threads united these twenty or thirty men into some single powerful body, and involuntarily for the first time in their lives they felt the power of labor before the strength of capital, and something new blew into their souls."[64] The very strong sense of loyalty to the collective among workers, which in normal times discouraged nonconformity and dissent, could become a powerful source of solidary protest.[65] Maybe their actions only took the form of retorts to the foreman's insults or demands for more polite treatment. Such changes were highly significant in the Russian context, however where subordination depended upon fear. A greater sense of personal dignity was truly subversive. For these reasons the bunt was politically dangerous, and the tsarist authorities knew it.

In addition, the bunt could easily turn into a strike. This mutation is easily explained. There were often conscious workers who acquired influence and prestige after the bunt had begun and so could infuse it with some organization and direction. Perhap the prototype of this kind of transformation was the famous Morozov strike of 1885, often regarded as the first real strike in Russian labor history. It began as a typical bunt, but under the leadership of a few experienced worker revolutionaries, it turned into a full-fledged strike with a list of formal demands. Thus in autocratic and capitalist Russia, just as mass consciousness became intertwined with class consciousness, so mass action in the form of bunts could not remain separate from class action in the form of strikes. Indeed, mass action often provided the impetus for extensive class mobilization.

RELATIONS TO CONSCIOUS WORKERS AND THE INTELLIGENTSIA

The worker Mironov narrates a curious incident in his memoirs.[66] In one factory the head foreman was regarded as a real scoundrel, especially because of his oppression of women workers, which included seduction using threats. The time came for his twenty-fifth anniversary in the factory, and the women workers were being forced to contribute toward a gift for him. A group of conscious workers from outside the factory decided to do what they could to prevent this. They prepared and distributed a leaflet describing his actions. Surprisingly, their agitation was effective: the women got their money back and the foreman was driven from the factory. The women workers were overjoyed and were ready to pray for their benefactors. A little later, however, when these same workers were arrested, the women gloated over their misfortune and said that they deserved it. This, said Mironov, "was one of many examples" of ambivalence and rapid change of disposition.

After the massacre of 9 January 1905, a survey was sent to St. Petersburg workers inquiring into their perspectives on a number of issues, including their attitude toward party workers and the intelligentsia. One worker's summation of the mass workers' attitudes is particularly suggestive: the workers felt "that they [the intelligentsia] help us, that they are educated people and they know what they are doing. But somehow they [the workers] look upon them [the intelligentsia] with hostility, not even themselves knowing for what reason."[67]

These attitudes suggest that the relationship between the mass workers and the politically committed workers and revolutionaries was clouded by considerable ambivalence. Zubatov, we recall, believed that the relationship between the intelligentsia and the workers was purely artificial, and he thought it would be a simple matter to wean the workers away from their influence. By contrast, the revolutionaries assumed a coincidence of interests and often naively anticipated that the workers would be grateful for their help. Let us look into the sources of the mass workers' ambivalence.

First, on the negative side, autocracy isolated groups from each other and accentuated cultural differences. The intelligentsia, as educated people from a different social class, were regarded with suspicion as outsiders. The ties between the worker masses and the intelligentsia could not be deep or permanent enough to overcome this basic suspicion. The workers often did not understand their motives and reacted with instinctive prejudice against the social differences. Conscious workers were also frequently regarded as outsiders. Buzinov describes the disquieting impact of a conscious worker on his fellow workers in the following way: his appearance was fierce, his gaze terrifying. It seemed "that he hated all the workers and therefore it was always empty near his workbench, as if it were a place infected by the plague."[68] Buzinov describes his own reaction as one of ambivalence toward him as an outsider, a person different from the other workers.

One of the most common sources of this hostility was that both the conscious workers and the intelligentsia were regarded as atheists. In a textile factory near Moscow the women workers began to circulate rumors about a worker activist in their factory. They said that he was an atheist, that he feared the Church because an unclean spirit was lodged in him. It was reported that he was related to the Antichrist, that he was "a troublemaker and confuses true men."[69] These rumors made their way to the factory administration, who understood what kind of Antichrist the man was and fired him. Such an identification of "consciousness" with atheism was far from mere prejudice—atheism was, with rare exceptions, one of the bases of the conscious workers' identity.

The mass workers' hostility toward conscious workers as outsiders was also linked to resentment.

The gray worker mass does not like and even hates those people from their midst who are beyond their understanding. They dislike them not because they consider them malicious or harmful people, but because they do not share their prejudices, customs, habits, and beliefs, because they live in contradiction to their ideas, in a word, because [the conscious workers] want to be more intelligent than they are.[70]

This was the other side of the conscious workers' view of mass workers as gray, as full of prejudice and ignorance. The conscious workers did regard themselves as superior and often made a point of their superiority. Such attitudes were bound to reinforce the existing cultural and ideological differences.

The mass workers' hostility was not based simply on social and cultural differences accentuated by isolation, however. The conscious workers and the intelligentsia were also dangerous people. They brought police and soldiers to the factories and exposed the workers to great risks. Mass workers often came to resent the activists for leading them in directions the consequences of which they came to regret. Carried away by enthusiasm and the taste of revenge in times of upsurge, the mass workers blamed their leaders for misleading them in times of defeat—even if their leaders had unsuccessfully tried to restrain them and had reluctantly given in to mass pressure. These shifts in mood, and the tendency to blame the conscious workers and intelligentsia for defeats, indicated an essential difference between them: the mass workers lacked a longtime perspective, created out of ideological conviction, that would have permitted them to absorb defeat as only part of a prolonged process of struggle. Just as they acted in response to immediate circumstances and the mood of the moment, so they wanted immediate results. They had no faith in anything else.

This pragmatic orientation worked both ways, for the conscious workers and intelligentsia often helped achieve immediate benefits. By the very fact that they brought greater attention to factory affairs and made them more of a public issue, workers felt less isolated and abandoned. Strikes brought punishment, but they also attracted government concern and sometimes condemnation of factory owners. Here is the reaction of a worker to the effect of revolutionary agitation in 1896: "Earlier we worked and worked, and saw no daylight. With your own eyes you saw how they swindle, and what could you do? Now it's not that way! Now when the inspectors or the police arrive, they begin to sniff around everywhere—the administration walks on tiptoe. It's miraculous!" "Lord, give good health to the people who print these leaflets," he concluded.[71]

Many mass workers also appreciated the moral qualities of the conscious workers and intelligentsia and respected them for their willingness to sacrifice themselves on behalf of others. One worker wrote of such feelings to Ozerov:

> There is still a spiritual ache for my comrades in my trade [who suffered]. . . . These comrades worked for the shortening of the workday and brought enormous benefits to us: thanks to them we work ten hours instead of twelve. These people are in great part morally developed, and I would be glad to forget about them. My soul aches, grief for their families unwillingly arises in our [sic] memory, unwillingly my body trembles when I recall the crying of their women and children.[72]

Another "gray" worker expressed similar feelings: be grateful to our intelligentsia allies, for "many of them suffer permanent exile for us, but we do not notice this and we did not appreciate our avengers."[73] According to Buzinov, despite the workers' hostility toward the conscious workers as outsiders, they still regarded the latter as the most intelligent and decisive people. "Unwillingly they believed each of their words."[74]

For the most part the mass workers had no alternative. They had no consistent rival interpretation of events. They had little leadership experience or self-confidence. Thoroughly repressed in their social and organizational activities, they lacked what only the more committed could supply: ideas, confidence, elements of strategy. Thus in January 1905 the newly mobilized workers were filled with questions and doubts. They wanted clear-cut and rapid answers, and they looked, often with disappointment, to the socialists to supply them. "The workers sought out the socialists, virtually courting them, even though previously they had insulted and scorned them."[75]

When the time was ripe for such contacts to be made, the intelligentsia sometimes modified their ideas and tactics in order to lessen the great cultural gaps between themselves and the mass workers. For example, in the Gapon movement the Social Democratic speakers adopted the religious tone of the mass meetings, leaving behind much of their intellectualism and socialist teachings. The worker masses could not even distinguish between them and the Gapon leaders—many of the socialists were called "Gapon Social Democrats."[76] Such rapprochements did not necessarily have to be merely tactical: the political activists were also susceptible to the fervor of the mass mood and could lose themselves in powerful feelings of solidarity. At such times, too, the masses could forget their previous skepticism and suspicion and accept the outsiders as comrades in struggle.

The links between the mass workers and the conscious workers and intelligentsia were thus tenuous but enduring. Abrupt shifts in mood were just as characteristic of this aspect of the mass workers' conscious-ness as of all others. They lacked a firm ideological or institutional framework for solid commitments. Was the link then artificial, as Zuba-tov believed? That is the same as asking whether autocracy was artificial, or capitalist industrialization. The question as posed makes no sense. If institutional contexts are real, then so are responses to them and their consequences. The institutional setting of late Tsarist Russia conditioned a mutual hostility between ordinary workers and worker and intel-ligentsia activists. It also ensured that mass workers would turn to the activists when conditions were right, for they had no alternative. As we will see, similar ambivalent interdependencies characterized the con-scious workers' relationship to the intelligentsia and the relationship of both of these categories to the mass workers. The parts of the labor movement were both highly differentiated and forced to act in concert.

Paradoxically, then, the very "mass" situation of Russian workers, their very exclusion, stimulated their involvement in a class movement, the aims of which both overlapped with and transcended their own. In a sense this was an analogue of Trotsky's combined development. Russian absolutism fused and blended forms of social action even while it divided actors from one another. Mass action could not remain separate from class action, even if ordinary workers often distrusted those who advo-cated and organized the latter. The mass workers' consciousness was similarly "combined": neither simply traditionalist nor socialist, their very traditionalism helped open them to new ideas that they seldom assimilated. No wonder the mass workers failed to fit the intelligent-sia's traditional categories, sometimes disappointing them, sometimes astounding them by their militancy. This incomprehension stemmed from the revolutionaries' adherence to Marxist categories, which did not sufficiently take account of the central fact of Russian development: the contradiction between capitalism and autocracy, which conditioned this complex fusion of mass and class action and consciousness.

CHAPTER
8

Conscious Workers

THE CONCEPT AND ITS DIFFICULTIES

Virtually all Russian workers, no matter how skilled, educated or well-paid, experienced the exclusion described in chapter 7. A minority of workers surely found satisfaction in family life, or perhaps in patriotic values inculcated during military service, or in their privileged position in the factory. For the great majority, however, the near institutional vacuum in which they lived had a powerful demoralizing effect.

Before their transformation, "conscious workers"—and this was a term in wide use at the time, together with "worker intelligentsia"[1]—also suffered from isolation and public contempt. Boredom and apathy were widespread, as were anger and bitterness. Perhaps these feelings were more intense among workers who would become conscious, for they tended to be from among those whom Walzer calls the "sociologically competent," and they made greater demands on life. Suicidal feelings, despair, and hatred seemed to be the other side of frustrated self-esteem.

Becoming conscious was one answer to the common plight of the workers. The conscious worker adopted an active relationship with the surrounding social world, one in which social values and institutions were not simply taken for granted but were interpreted more or less systematically and reevaluated according to new standards of justice. "No, comrades," proclaimed a worker at a May Day speech in 1895, "it is necessary to try to wipe away the stain of shame from ourselves; it is necessary to put new eyes into our enemies so that they will look upon us differently. It is time, gentlemen, to show our enemies that they are not our benefactors, but we theirs, that not we by their labor live, but they by ours, that all the luxury and wealth belong to worker hands."[2] "It is only necessary to understand where our poverty comes from," said another on the same day.[3] With such knowledge action could be taken, strategies developed, victories won. Each conscious worker, wrote Buzinov, "was already in some way a 'juridically thinking person', able to understand his surroundings. They all in greater or lesser degree understood the situation of the workers and their interrelations with the factory owners."[4]

Such a new conception of the social world involved a startling transformation of consciousness. For many it meant a rebirth, a new role in life, an escape from the hopelessness of their existence. " 'Everything as it is, so it must be and will be.' That's what I thought before I really began to live, when I was vegetating, indifferent to life around me."[5] For the worker Zalomov, "the possibility, even if in the distant future, of raising the economic and cultural level of the dark, laboring masses gave me a rich supply of life forces."[6] Their new conception of the world thus allowed workers to redefine social relations and their own place in the world, usually in terms of a broad worker community, the meaninglessness of paternal ties to the bosses or the government, and a life-giving sense of mission.

Becoming conscious was thus a subjective experience. It sometimes involved political commitments, but often it did not. Usually the conscious worker adopted outward signs of his convictions, and the role even became quite institutionalized. These objective dimensions do not define the role, however, although for sociological purposes they may be more significant than the subjective experience. The conscious worker was thus just as slippery a social type as the intelligentsia—for this category, too, membership was extremely problematic, and for the same reason: both concepts refer to a basic stance toward the world which is difficult to identify through external action. Fortunately, it is possible to recognize the essentially subjective reference of the concept without thereby denying the possibility of analyzing the conscious worker as a social type. For despite undoubtedly great subjective variations, there was enough of a standardized role to justify sociological generalization.

If, in the present usage, the term *conscious* is subjective (although not only subjective), this does not mean that it is evaluative. Social Democrats liked to think that only Social Democrats were conscious—that is, they truly understood the world around them. All other workers were dark and mired in ignorance, whatever their perceptions may have been of themselves. The present usage is not evaluative in this sense: I assume that there is no true understanding of the world by which "consciousness" can be objectively evaluated. A conscious worker could be an anarchist, a Tolstoyan, or a monarchist—although most would have identified themselves as socialists of one type or another. Indeed, the Zubatov worker leaders certainly qualify as conscious workers in this broad sense. Accepting Zubatov's ideas involved an active and thought-out response to the world, and it clearly called forth new energies and loyalties. Because of their espousal of monarchism, however, the Zubatov workers were certainly atypical, and like other minority currents, they did not fit completely into the generalized collective portrait to be shown here.

Consciousness was also not a permanent state. Conscious workers as well as mass workers could lose faith and shift loyalties. They could once again become mass workers, with no particular commitments and no trust in the future. The social world could once again become mysterious and unpredictable to them. This does not mean that they had somehow become less intelligent. Again, no evaluation is implied, as much as it was inherent in the usage of the period. Hindsight forces us to be a little more skeptical.

The phenomenon of the conscious worker was not restricted to Russia. In Spain the same terminology was used ("obrero consciente"), and there is much similarity between the two roles as well.[7] Probably the same correspondence exists in other languages and cultures, for the phenomenon of "consciousness" was inherent in the historicism (in Karl Popper's sense) of nineteenth-century labor movements. It was also inherent in the process that Karl Mannheim called "general democratization": acceptance of the legitimacy of the lower classes' views as identifiable and respectable alternatives.

Once again, however, Russia was distinctive. Conscious workers were part of all labor movements, yet Russia's labor movement and the political conditions in which it developed bore little similarity to the English, French, or German patterns. To be a labor militant in Russia was to take risks seldom incurred in Western Europe. It was also to isolate onself from one's fellow workers to a much greater degree. Thus the Russian conscious worker developed to an extreme traits found elsewhere in a less pronounced way. He had a great sense of separation, of distinctiveness, which was generally linked to an air of superiority toward other workers. He regarded himself as part of a knowing elite, one of the few who had been able to see behind appearances. This sense of separation was reinforced by the need for secrecy, which also had its psychological appeal. Membership in this elite involved a code of behavior and a symbolism, and the protection and cultivation of this new identity became so central to the worker's sense of himself that he was often willing to go to great lengths to preserve it. Underground work, jail, and exile became badges of honor, confirming the commitment of the conscious worker to his role.

Russia was different from Western Europe in another way as well. If, during the late nineteenth century, the lower classes in Europe were gradually acquiring their own voice in public life—Mannheim's general democratization—in Russia this process had only begun. Workers still had little access to education, and they had few opportunities to develop cultural expressions appropriate to their own experience. To take a key example: there was no mass worker press, and the underground newspapers that did manage to survive for a time were almost always controlled by the intelligentsia. Thus to a much greater degree than in Europe, conscious workers depended upon the intelligentsia to define their identity. Lacking the means to create their own subculture, including a range of political alternatives based on their own experience, they turned to the intelligentsia, specialists in ideology. In practice they even delegated to the intelligentsia the right to define who qualified as being conscious. Those workers who emphasized the economic struggle were labeled as dark, unenlightened, backward; those who accepted the intelligentsia's models were conscious, leading workers, the vanguard of the proletariat. For these reasons the Russian conscious worker tended to be much more ideological than his European counterpart. Also, his relationship to the intelligentsia, with its high degree of dependence, was both more profound and more ambivalent.

In the same way, tsarist repression and intelligentsia dominance virtually precluded the emergence of authoritative leaders from among the workers. Impressive figures there certainly were, but none who could achieve national prominence as spokesmen for their class. Garvi notes that in his many years as Social Democratic activist he met many outstanding workers in Russia capable of becoming real leaders, but they all "flashed like a meteor and left no traces."[8]

"CONSCIOUSNESS" AS A NEW IDENTITY

By the broad definition used earlier, the following typological description of the conscious worker is too narrow, for it does not take account of enough variations in consciousness. There were conscious workers who did not exhibit many of the traits to be mentioned later—the Zubatov worker leaders are a good example. Judging from memoirs, speeches, and other material, the general portrait given here seems to be broadly representative of the experiences and perspectives of workers who called themselves conscious. For although the defining trait of the conscious worker was a new subjective orientation to the world, this new orientation was quite standardized. Members of the new elite wanted to have at least some signs by which to recognize one another, for otherwise they could have no confirmation of their identity. As a result the role became institutionalized—not so much, perhaps, as occupational roles but certainly more than simply subjective orientations such as "lover of Greek philosophy." Therefore the following construction of the conscious worker as a type does not do too much violence to the definition.

BASIC TENETS

THE REPUDIATION OF HIERARCHY

In England many workers developed an alternative working-class ethic through rejection of the liberal idea of social harmony based upon the beneficial effects of the division of labor. To this they opposed the ideas of contradictory interests and labor as the source of all wealth. In Russia the ethic of conscious workers basically arose from rejection of hierarchical ties (which in England had been repudiated by the elites themselves). The idea of a harmonious self-regulating society never made much headway in Russia against the opposing assumption that only the tsar could harmonize social interests and keep the country from chaos. For a Russian worker the greater change in consciousness was a rejection of hierarchy, not of natural harmony. The paternalistic state, not the free market or liberal society, was the main impediment to Marxist ideas.

Hierarchy for the worker had three related dimensions: God (mediated through the Church), the tsar, and the boss. The transition to consciousness involved rejection of all three, although the major steps were the denial of religion and the legitimacy of the tsar. As we have seen, suspicion of the authority of social elites was a traditional theme in Russian political culture, and it was hardly a distinguishing trait of becoming conscious. At the same time, the conscious worker arrived at a new and more systematic understanding of why the bosses' authority was illegitimate, and so even here a transformation of traditional attitudes occurred.

The disclaiming of hierarchy also amounted to rejection of passivity. Indeed, this denial already implied a more active relationship to the surrounding world, for it was truly a choice, and traditional Russian institutions did not endorse active choice. The teachings of the Russian Orthodox Church, for example, were centered on other assumptions: the lower classes should reconcile themselves to suffering and submit to authority because God and their earthly superiors would take care of their needs.[9]

A small minority of workers probably accepted a view of religion more consistent with an active view of man. Mironov tells of some workers who interpreted religion as teaching opposition to authority. One of them had Mironov read from Isaiah, and he saw that Isaiah was condemning what priests did. The worker who showed him this passage explained to him, "You see, man cannot live without God. I believe in God and I understand him in my own way, that is, I have him in my soul, but only God the merciful, not God the policeman, as the priests made him out to be."[10] Other workers clearly felt a connection between themselves and the early Christians, who were also willing to forsake their own free wills and sacrifice themselves for the church.[11] Religious language even found its way into the 1879 program of the Northern Union, often regarded as the first major proletarian organization in Russia. Like the simple people who first responded to Christ's words, it proclaimed, "We are also called to the sermon, we also are summoned to be apostles of the new, but in essence only uncomprehended and forgotten teachings of Christ."[12] Whether these words expressed the true sentiments of the organization's leaders or whether they were merely designed to appeal to the worker masses cannot be determined.

By the end of the century, however, for most conscious workers religion probably meant submission to authority, reconciliation to oppression, and nonresistance to evil. Those who spoke in religious terminology, said Trotsky, "found that they were only a laughing-stock for the younger men." For the conscious worker, the religious standard with the cross was a symbol of slavery.[13] Nonetheless, the imprint of religious imagery upon the minds of defiantly anticlerical workers can be discerned in desires for secular salvation, in the appeal of a dualistic worldview stressing the struggle between good and evil, and in the concept of the fraternal worker community.

Loss of belief in God could occur in various ways. Education and acquaintance with science led many workers to doubt the naive versions of Christian doctrine that had been instilled in them. The influence of already conscious workers, more educated and sophisticated than their fellows, often was also a critical influence. And then there was the workers' version of the problem of theodicy: how to reconcile their own suffering with belief in an all-powerful and beneficent God.

With the disappearance of belief in God, much else disappeared as well. If God was a deception, then so was the tsar, who derived his authority from divine sanction. If the tsar was not the merciful protector of his people ordained by God, then neither did many Russian customs and institutions make sense. Such an interlocking of spheres is a basic trait of hierarchical societies, and it makes them particularly vulnerable in confrontations with the modern world. Thus Shapovalov writes that after his rejection of religion, he grew to hate Russian customs more and more:

Orthodoxy, tsarism, great Russian chauvinism, Russian poddyovkas [a light coat] and sheepskin coats, long beards and bobbed hair—all of this became hateful to me. Everything new and good, I thought, must be taken from the West, which had far outstripped us. Only one thing of hoary antiquity remained valuable and close. This was the sound of the veche's [medieval popular assembly] bell in Great Novgorod, with its veche and the democracy of the Zaporozhian Cossack host.[14]

If submission to authority was merely a deception and a trap, then it was necessary to struggle and use violence in order to change the world. Thus the rejection of religion was the linchpin in the overall denial of a hierarchical world view.

To reject the authority of the tsar could mean two things: to stop believing in tsarist paternalism and to oppose his regime. Both acts required moral courage. The belief in the tsar's protective role was a valuable moral crutch in a cruel and uncertain world. Like belief in God, it could provide faith in an eventual end to suffering and hope for a better future. To reject both God and the tsar was to expose oneself to despair. To oppose the regime politically was dangerous in another, more obvious sense. Workers were understandably hesitant to take either step.

Conscious workers rejected tsarist authority on two grounds: first, because if God did not exist, then neither did divinely ordained rule; and second, because they came to regard the tsar as protector of the capitalists and oppressor of the workers. It was the tsar who prohibited their self-development and outlawed free struggles to pursue their own interests. "In the struggle with the industrialists," spoke Zalomov at his trial, "workers collide against the industrialists' ally, the government. I saw that autocracy is the enemy of the Russian people. And that is why I wrote on my flags: 'Down with autocracy!' and 'Long live political freedom!'"[15]

There were fewer barriers in Russian political culture to the denunciation of the industrialists' authority and benevolence. Conscious workers, like many mass workers, regarded their bosses as parasites, often as foreigners preying upon the Russian people. They dismissed the possibility that the bosses might be concerned with the workers' welfare. Perhaps that might have been true in a previous time, said an 1895 brochure of the Moscow "Workers' Union." Then there was more contact between the workers and their employers, and all shared both good and bad times. Further, there was little distance between them, for the worker could always hope to save enough to buy his own tools and become independent. In this romanticized view, which perhaps owes more to the image of European guilds than to past Russian reality, the interests of the worker and his employer were the same. But capitalist industrialization, it was claimed, destroyed this formerly close bond. The main culprit was the machine, which threw workers out of work and allowed the employer to enrich himself as the worker became impoverished. Thus workers gradually come to understand that the capitalist system itself is at the root of their problems, and they become aware of the need to fight against it as a whole, not this or that boss or police official.[16]

It was this systemic analysis that distinguished the conscious worker from the mass worker. The mass worker might hope that a bunt would bring about changes, through either threats to the boss or government intervention in his behalf. In a given case workers' tactics might not be successful, but they did not believe their superiors were necessarily recalcitrant because of the latter's position in the class and political hierarchies. This is what the conscious worker (and the intelligentsia) taught. Only minor concessions could be won in the short run—within the system nothing could really change, although workers could gain hope and courage in their struggles by temporary victories. For the conscious workers, however, this was accompanied by a belief in the possibility of rational action to promote long-term social change. Mass workers held the opposite assumptions: that the bosses or government officials might be willing to act in their favor in the short term, but of long-term social transformation they had little conception.

THE TRANSFORMATION OF VALUES

In Russia, as elsewhere, conscious workers espoused a new set of values to pit against the dominant values labeling them inferior. Little was distinctive in the Russian version of this worker ethic, other than that it arose in an extraordinarily hostile environment and thus was more difficult to develop and to appropriate, and it appeared more subversive.

The first step was to neutralize the blame that other social groups imposed upon workers. The upper classes regarded workers as uneducated, culturally impoverished, lazy, and given to vices—in short, fully deserving of their low station in life. One worker response was to impute the same traits to the upper classes. What could be expected from workers if their so-called superiors provided such bad examples? The police, priests, and capitalists were themselves morally degenerate, engaging in drunkenness and prostitution and taking advantage of women workers.[17]

This implied only that the workers and the elites were on the same level. Conscious workers believed more than this: they held that workers were morally superior because industrialists and the authorities were responsible for most of the workers' bad traits. If workers were ignorant, this was because of the deficiencies of education and the lack of popular access to books. If they were lazy, it was because the bosses gave them no incentive to work and treated them poorly. If their productivity was lower than that of foreign workers, the fault lay not with them: "Take away from the French, English, and German workers their knowledge and their literacy, give them coarse, rude, and greedy industrialists, give them uneducated and heartless engineers, close the schools to them and put them into our Russian darkness—and then we will see what kind of things they produce."[18] Workers' housing and living conditions were bad not because they wanted to live like animals but because of merciless exploitation.[19]

Workers, they said, had many needs. This was the mark of civilized people, and the higher the level of needs, the more human were a person's aspirations. Workers needed not only the basic necessities but also access to culture and a sense of self-worth. With pride conscious workers noted that the workers' perceived needs were constantly growing, and they regarded this as a sign of the general development of the working class. It was not, therefore, that workers were indifferent to their own welfare. The problem was that the bosses cut short their efforts at self-improvement and made them live in an inhuman way.[20]

Some conscous workers even espoused a new general ethic based upon their own experience of oppression. They claimed that suffering had ennobled them and thus made them worthy to reconstruct the world in a more humane way. "For us workers," declared the program of the Northern Union,

> there lies a great task, the liberation of ourselves and our brothers. Upon us lies the obligation to renew the world, which is drowning in luxury and draining our strength, and we must do it. . . . We will renew the world, revitalize the family, establish property as it should be, and resurrect the great teachings of Christ about brotherhood and equality.[21]

These words echo Marx and Engels' remarks on the "bourgeois objections to Communism," which was reviled for its threats to property, the family, nationhood, and morality. For the leaders of the Northern Union, as for the authors of the *Communist Manifesto*, the task was not to destroy institutions and values but to reestablish them in a manner consistent with a new vision of community.

Such sentiments may provoke a knowing smile, but the conscious workers lived in a more innocent world in which beliefs could still seem untarnished, and some such version of a new moral vision was at the center of identity of the conscious worker. It gave him stubbornness, strength, and self-confidence. It allowed him to escape from the moral vacuum he had experienced before. And it gave him the courage to defy the government and suffer cruel punishments. Thus at a trial in March 1877, the accused worker did not deny his criminal responsibility from the government's point of view. He did not repent or believe he had done anything wrong. He proudly asserted that he had "only fulfilled the duty of an honorable worker, sincerely, with all his soul dedicated to the interests of his poor, tormented fellow workers! I have nothing more to say."[22]

A RATIONAL APPROACH TO SOCIAL CHANGE

In believing that they had come to understand the world, conscious workers also believed that they could change it. To do this, however, they had to have organization and unity, for the workers, unlike the capitalists, had no other source of power than their number.[23] Consequently, the workers' lack of unity and organization was a constant source of consternation to conscious workers. They were painfully aware of the obvious contradiction between their potential and actual power. Kanatchikov, reflecting on the enormous concentration of workers in the Nevskii Gate district of St. Petersburg, mused:

> Naturally, for every conscious worker, upon looking at these peacefully strolling workers, the question arose: what could this mass do if it were conscious? If by some miracle one were able to awaken this immense strength and direct it against the Tsarist autocracy, the police, the capitalists?! Why we would raze to the ground the old slave system![24]

This emphasis upon organization and unity was reinforced by the example of Western countries, which had immense influence on the perspectives of Russian conscious workers. Again and again worker activists spoke and wrote of the accomplishments of their Western brothers. They concluded that political struggle and broad class organizations were prerequisites to social change, the only way that workers could either gain benefits within the present system or bring about changes of the system as a whole. Again and again they lamented the lack of organization and unity among Russian workers. There was nothing to represent their common interests—common, because all workers were basically in the same position in the capitalist system.[25]

Organization was necessary for coordinating the wills of large masses of people, and also for developing effective tactics of struggle. Such leadership required knowledge, and conscious workers always emphasized their desire to know more. According to Plekhanov, this was a major source of contention between one sector of populists and a group of worker revolutionaries as early as 1876. The populists argued that every worker was a revolutionary by virtue of his social position, and there was little need of further knowledge. The workers responded that the worker "understands, but poorly. He sees, but not in the way that he should." Said one worker, "You will receive little worthwhile from a worker who knows nothing."[26] The high educational level of many conscious workers often surprised the intelligentsia, as when Martov was amazed by two St. Petersburg workers' ability to debate on Marx's critique of Hegel's *Philosophy of Right*.[27] It also astonished those government officials observant enough to be able to set the conscious workers apart from their fellows. In 1903 the director of the Department of Police spoke with some awe of the workers who read in three languages and had Marxist ideas. He was forced to admit that "in our factories some degree of culture exists"—quite a concession from a high government official.[28]

Discipline was just as necessary as education. Revolutionary workers must be serious and systematic, willing to subject themselves to the requirements of the overall cause. They must be expert in self-control, for otherwise underground work would not be possible. In this way Babushkin portrays an older conscious worker who was sizing him up for his suitability for revolutionary work: "I saw in front of me a man—self-reliant, energetic, courageous, wanting to test my sincerity, find out if I'm resolute and persevering, and if I'm really honest in claiming to serve the cause. Sensing that he was thinking on these lines, I took fright and couldn't utter a word."[29]

Thus both the movement and the individual were to be subjected to rational guidance and control. They were to be turned into instruments, renouncing their own impulses and wills. This new rational model required self-confidence and hope. Without these the worker could easily despair of the future and begin to doubt that all of his sacrifices were worthwhile. Indeed, in periods of repression and quiescence in the labor movement, many conscious workers did lose their faith and turned to terrorism, rejecting large-scale organization and strikes in favor of individual acts of heroism. The archetypical insight of the conscious workers remained constant, however; only through unity, organization, strategy, self-control, education, and discipline could the working class liberate itself.

Sources of the Conscious Worker's Identity

The conditions of factory life during industrialization created a multitude of sources of anger and discontent. Workers complained of the long hours, coarse treatment, arbitrary fines, and much else in the factory environment. In Russia there were no legitimate ways to combat these abuses effectively. For the great majority this powerlessness gave rise to anger, but also to resignation, for they had little sense that anything could be done to bring about change. For some workers, however, indignation was accompanied by a desire to do something, and it was these workers who were most likely to make the transition to consciousness.

Worker memoirs suggest that those who responded to their oppression in a more active way tended to be the most competent and self-confident. Of course, no surveys were taken, and the evidence cannot be more than impressionistic, but it is striking how many soon-to-be conscious workers were highly skilled, proud of their ability, relatively well-educated, and even economically well-off. For example, Kanatchikov remarks that

> the hard situation of the working class, about which he [a member of the intelligentsia] told us, we did not especially feel directly, for our wages were good, the workday was not long, and conversations about our living conditions bored us at home and in the factory. From an outsider, from a student, we wanted to hear something out of the ordinary, something novel which would open up new horizons before us.[30]

Similarly, Babushkin remarks in his memoirs that "I was not bad off economically." And summing up his impressions of St. Petersburg conscious workers around 1880, Plekhanov concluded "with surprise" that they lived no worse—and many lived much better—than students. Some workers were even well-off—they bought books, dressed well, and lived in nice apartments.[31]

Workers who would become conscious also seemed to be better educated and often passionately committed to books from a young age. This was true of Shelgunov, who worked in a bookbinding establishment from the ages of thirteen to eighteen and read Belinsky, Dobroliubov, Chernyshevsky, and Pisarev, as well as a great many old newspapers and journals.[32] While still an apprentice, K. Norinskii read the works of Uspenskii and Lafargue's *Religion of Capital* and also borrowed numerous books from an older worker.[33] Many other memoirs record the same love of books and thirst for knowledge, often acquired in early youth.

Workers who would become conscious also seemed to be skilled in their work and even to derive considerable satisfaction from it. Kanatchikov's memoirs include eloquent passages about the poetry of the great factory and his feelings of pride in being a master of his trade. "Precisely these feelings and experiences softened my drab, cheerless existence under the conditions of capitalist oppression and limitless exploitation."[34] With surprise, Social Democratic party worker Garvi noted "the affectionate opinion of each of the worker members of the [Odessa Social Democratic] Committee toward his occupation. . . . They were all...highly qualified workers in their specialty."[35] Perhaps the sense of power and control over their machines stemming from ability and training convinced them of the potential for changing society through a similar application of will, one that also involved skill, self-discipline, and knowledge.

It was precisely these people—more self-confident and independent, more convinced that they had rights and were free—who began to question hierarchical relations and chafed at any slight to their sense of dignity. When the foreman criticized Kanatchikov's work without justification, Kanatchikov felt hatred for him and the boss and for the "soulless machine" and his work as well.[36] Such workers were more likely to feel offended at the use of the familiar form of "you" and to bristle with anger at any slight to their sense of self-worth. They were indignant when not taken seriously—as when, for example, the intelligentsia argued that workers did not need education. Precisely this higher level of need was a source of pride for them. Fifteen Urals workers wrote in 1887 to the writer Uspenskii that

> it's time to stop seeing us as an uncomprehending herd of stupid people and to say that we are unable to understand the truth, that we don't need education or don't like to read good, useful books. It's time to stop telling us that we should only think about food and work. . . . We learned to think about our life, our comrades, about the life of diverse people, we learned to distinguish good from bad, the truth from falsehood.[37]

They were demanding nothing less than general democratization in a society in which even the revolutionary intelligentsia treated them with condescension.

Indignation—as opposed to anger or hatred—was a first key step in the transition to consciousness. It expressed a basic sense of injustice and an implicit rejection of accepted standards of judgment. The worker also had to acquire new ideas and find appropriate models of action. For this, contact with already conscious workers was of fundamental importance. These were often impressive people: aloof, self-contained, aware of their own distinctiveness, confident of their superiority. Upon the average worker they probably produced a rather negative impression because of incomprehension and resentment. To many young workers with more self-esteem looking for ways to affirm their dignity through a new sense of identity, however, they were a powerful magnet. Acceptance by them and induction into their secret mode of life would be a confirmation of their own worth.

Thus many young workers looked with awe upon these special colleagues. For example, upon arriving at the huge Obukhov plant in St. Petersburg in 1899, Sulimov felt ill at ease among the skilled, sophisticated workers: "I was an ignoramus, in the literal sense of the word. I didn't understand anything." He began to read—about the French Revolution, slave and peasant uprisings, and also literary classics by Zola, Dickens, Turgenev, and Tolstoy. "Now I became bolder in the company of comrades. I took part in discussions and arguments."[38] We recall, too, Babushkin's anxiety before the conscious worker in his factory. It was a test of worth. Would he measure up?

Acceptance of the young worker into the ranks of this self-defined elite could mean involvement in night school, worker study circles, and eventually participation in underground work as well. Study circles were sometimes led by the intelligentsia, sometimes by the workers themselves. Their "curricula" seemed to be fairly standard, including Russian literary classics, works on popular movements and revolutions in Russia and Europe, Marx (especially *Capital* and *The Communist Manifesto*), and popular scientific works. The theory of evolution was typically included in the course of study, exemplifying the rationalism and belief in progress that gave the workers hope in their struggles.

These circles were not for the purpose of education in a liberal sense. They were, rather, a form of sophisticated indoctrination, a revolutionary catechism, for the conclusions were already known. Workers were taught about the lawfulness of historical development, the essence of capitalist exploitation, and the necessity and possibility of social liberation. Mastery of these ideas became a kind of rite of passage to the status of worker revolutionary, and it created a common language and outlook among initiates. (Even non-Marxist conscious workers included Marx in their program of study, emphasizing his attack on capitalism rather than his insistence that its impact was ultimately progressive.) The classes also created strong social bonds among the workers, for they had participated in esoteric and illegal activities that separated them from the mass of workers. They had become members of a gnostic sect.

Similar sectlike organizations can be found throughout the history of European labor movements. In England, France, and Germany there were secret oaths, passwords, rites of initiation, esoteric ideas. In no other European country, however, were they so subject to persecution as in Russia, nor did they develop anywhere else such a closed character or play such a crucial role in a broad mass labor movement.

From the study circles the transition to underground work was not difficult. The necessary contacts had been made, and the young worker was often anxious to confirm his new identity through action. He had learned that the working class could change the world, and as a conscious worker he could no longer live as he had before.[39] The neophyte revolutionary would distribute leaflets and flyers, or perhaps serve as a courier for a revolutionary organization. His suitability for underground work would be scrutinized, and if he passed inspection he would gradually be given greater responsibilities in the organization. Many conscious workers did not make this transition to revolutionary activity, however, even though they may have shared many of the same ideas. Perhaps the risks were too high, or they had too many other commitments, such as family responsibilities. And some conscious workers, after having tasted underground work, became disillusioned and abandoned the organization. But they often retained their identities as conscious workers, and they could easily become active in times of ferment.

Beginning in the mid-1890s, the perspectives imbibed during this process of socialization were most often a version of popular Marxism. Populist and anarchist ideas were decidedly less influential, partly because Marxism was dominant within the intelligentsia, but also because it held greater appeal for conscious workers. Whereas populism emphasized the struggle of all the lower classes, including the peasantry, Marxism gave special importance to the workers and so appealed to their pride. Populism certainly had its advocates, particularly among workers with rural ties or among those who had become disillusioned with Marxist ideas and practices, but as represented by the Socialist Revolutionary party, it seldom offered an effective challenge to Social Democracy.[40] With respect to anarchism, most conscious workers had witnessed enough bunts to become convinced of the necessity of a mass labor movement. They valued, not denigrated, organization and control.[41]

Marxism was also influential because it was science, the latest advance in European social thought. The impact of European ideas and models upon the Russian conscious workers was enormous, just as it was for the intelligentsia. In their night classes and study circles workers read about the great advances of the German Social Democrats and the high living standards of the English workers. They learned about their political rights, their growing social acceptability, and their strong organizations, which could make the workers' voice a real force in public life. They saw that in Europe the worker was regarded as a human being and not a rightless slave, and they envied the achievements of their European counterparts. All of this knowledge gave them a sense of superiority with respect both to other workers and to those who claimed the right to regulate and control them. "You are a fool," said the worker Zhalkov to a police officer. "You never read Marx and you do not know what politics and economics are."[42]

Sometimes this abstract knowledge was buttressed by contact with foreign workers. In the repair depot of the railway where he worked, Shapovalov observed many German workers and noted their contempt for the Russians. The Germans were more skilled, dressed better, stole less, were more educated and cultured, and conducted themselves with greater dignity. "Encountering them, I asked myself: for what reason do they dislike us so, why do they despise us so? And this question stimulated reflection. It compelled me to think, to relate more critically to our Russian reality."[43]

In his memoirs the worker Svirskii records a worker friend's reactions to contact with an English worker temporarily employed in their factory. His reflections are worth citing at length:

> Mankind goes forward, it goes toward justice and happiness, but it's as if we Russians were lepers, we remain behind everyone. And in such moments my homeland, my great boundless homeland, appeared to me as a hero, whose eyes have been ripped out. Strong, wise, great-souled, he stands alone among the peoples of the world and does not move from his place. He is blind, he does not know where to go, to what to apply his giant's strength. . . . Slavery is the spiritual death of mankind. Thanks to many centuries of slavery we have died spiritually. The heavy oppression of rightlessness constantly tramples out of us all the best that nature has given to mankind. That is why other peoples call us barbarians, cannibals. . . . We constantly abandon goodness and truth. We become cruel to ourselves and to others, because they teach us to be haters of mankind. Not knowing in our darkness what we should do to save ourselves, in blind despair we commit unheard of atrocities which horrify the whole world. We have pogroms, we burn people and animals, we create martyrs the like of which have not yet been seen on the earth.[44]

Yet such strong feelings of inferiority also gave rise to counterreactions. Svirskii's friend ended on a note of hope: it will not always be this way. "Only the dead have a right to resurrection. . . . I deeply believe that the resurrection of my people is already close." Shapovalov, too, believed that in Russia suffering led to greater compassion and less complacency: "Only enormous suffering makes man more human, more sensitive to the suffering and pain of others."[45] Such feelings had their counterparts in the ideas of some populists, for whom Russian backwardness was a hidden advantage over the West, for it gave rise to a fuller kind of individuality (Mikhailovsky) or greater possibilities for radical change (Tkachev). Many Russian Marxists, even including such orthodox figures as Plekhanov, also espoused the idea that Russia had special blessings making it unnecessary to retrace Europe's steps. From here it was easy to argue that Russia had a special position in the world of nations, an idea dear to the hearts of monarchists like Zubatov as well. And we recall that for the Zubatov leader Slepov one of the appeals of Zubatov's ideas lay in the repudiation of foreign models and the emphasis on Russian nationalism. Russia could once more become an example to others and not simply an imitator.

Some conscious workers must have had just such ambivalent ideas about the Western model, even as they basically admired the achievements of the West and hoped that Russia would follow a similar pattern. The West's positive elements gave them hope in the future achievements of organized struggle. For some, however, a defensive sense of the special character of Russian institutions also provided a remedy against the despair that feelings of inferiority can engender. It gave them a different kind of hope, and it made social change seem less arduous and distant. And perhaps it made them willing to depart from Western organization and rationality in favor of "spontaneous" new paths of social change. After all, who were the Westerners to lay down ironclad laws of historical development? Belief in the advantages of backwardness may have helped convince some waverers among the conscious workers in 1917 that Marxism might be applied creatively in a crisis situation.

Becoming conscious did not have to be a gradual process of making contacts, participating in circle work, and socialization into a new world view. Some workers were "grabbed by the wave of the movement," as Buzinov put it.[46] Russian labor protest was characterized by its great unevenness. Years of tranquillity were followed by periods of immense ferment, such as 1905–1906 and 1912–1914. In these periods normal routines, expectations, and assumptions were swept away and new ideas appeared everywhere. Workers who had not previously been involved in strikes or political protest now joined their fellows, perhaps only half understanding what they were doing.

Participation in such events could have an impact similar to pride in work or the attainment of a higher cultural level. Ordinary workers became convinced that they had the capacity to act, that they did not have to be passive. Their self-esteem and sense of dignity rose and they were no longer so willing to take abuse from the foreman or the boss. At such times they were especially receptive to new ideas criticizing hierarchy, proposing a new set of values, and offering models of social change through struggle and organization. And it was also in these periods that many of the barriers between conscious and mass workers broke down. Conscious workers made speeches, drew up lists of demands, and gave advice. Their fellow workers listened to and followed them. In this process many became conscious workers themselves or even committed revolutionaries.

The Gapon movement, culminating in Bloody Sunday, and the 1905 revolution stimulated by the momentous events, probably produced more such conversions than any other period in Russian labor history. They had a sweeping effect on the consciousness of many St. Petersburg workers. "On this day [January 9] I was born a second time, but now not as an all-forgiving and all-forgetting child, but as an embittered man, prepared to struggle and be victorious."[47] "The events of January 9 completely changed my world view and left an indelible imprint on me for the rest of my life."[48] Workers had innumerable conversations about the events in their apartments. Even those who had been completely passive before were now willing to air their grievances. Buzinov himself ended up in the apartment of a conscious worker, who "was already able to answer any question." The workers' mood had been transformed, and the factory owner was forced to take account of this new mood and make concessions. The hierarchies of tsar and boss had both been challenged.

Workers' new mood, newfound power, and new contacts with conscious workers did not imply a mass conversion. For most workers the change was temporary, lasting only until the next major defeat or disappointment. For some, however, such intense events marked a major transition, the transition to a new identity as a conscious worker. They absorbed the right ideas, adopted the appropriate cultural style, and suffered the standard penalties.

STYLE OF LIFE AND CONFIRMATION OF THE CONSCIOUS WORKER

Conscious workers became an identifiable social type in Russian factory life. Aside from their social and political attitudes, they developed certain habits and customs that separated them from other workers. Much of this distinctive style was a conscious reaction to the "darkness" all around them—the ignorance, indiscipline, and violence of much of Russian factory life.

Conscious workers prided themselves on their self-discipline. They considered it a point of honor not to drink vodka. They were restrained in their personal mores, probably even in their sexual habits, though I have found almost no discussions of this theme in the memoir literature. They wanted to hold themselves up as models to other workers, as symbols of that self-respect and dignity which they felt all workers should feel. They could become prim and self-righteous, often insufferably so. Babushkin, for example, wrote the following of himself and his friend: "Kostya and I were of the opinion that no conscious Socialist should drink vodka, and we even condemned smoking. At that time we propagated morality in the strictest sense of the word. Briefly, we insisted that a Socialist should be an exemplary person in all respects and we ourselves tried to live up to this principle."[49] Such abstemiousness made conscious workers stand out in the factory environment, and by increasing their visibility, it augmented the risks involved in agitation. If there was trouble in the factory, everyone knew that the more serious workers—who read and who avoided vodka—were behind it.[50]

Similar characterizations emerge in other memoirs. Conscious workers were more reserved, often conversing only with trusted colleagues. They were serious about their reading, they followed politics, and they did not believe in God. They were concerned about their appearance and dressed well. Members of the intelligentsia, often affecting lower-class dress, sometimes criticized them for their bourgeois tendencies, failing to understand that both were rebelling against their social environment in the same way.

Many conscious workers were hesitant to marry, especially if they were involved in revolutionary activities. Garvi reports the sentiments of a worker revolutionary as follows: "But I, it is clear, will remain a bachelor for my whole life. . . . I think that a family is not a joke, it demands a man—a whole man. May God permit our Lev to combine a family and the revolution. But I feel that I will not be able to do it. And look, when some girl begins to attract me, I will step away and repress this feeling in myself."[51] Among women workers, recalled Mironov, words such as these were often heard: "They are good people, only they're socialists." And even the police paid special attention to workers who waited a long time to get married.[52]

Thus self-discipline often meant repression of feeling and everyday sentiments. The conscious worker, like the Puritan, lived in a world of temptation in which he was constantly being tested. He also lived in a dangerous world in which he could be harshly punished for his convictions at any time. Many conscious workers responded by acting discreetly and not getting involved in politics except in periods of massive unrest, when the danger was less. Older conscious workers were especially inclined to avoid doing anything to attract the attention of the authorities. But for those who chose to become politically active, there were various ways of reinforcing and validating their identities, thus affirming their positions as members of an elite.

Some of the most obvious reinforcements have already been mentioned: induction into special groups, mutual recognition of the like-minded, various kinds of service to the cause, danger and excitement surrounding their activity. Shapovalov explains his feelings: "The constant danger of arrest, which lay in wait for us, the secrecy which surrounded our meetings, the awareness that I was no longer an insignificant grain of sand, not the same worker who it was impossible to distinguish from the masses of others on the street, but a member of an organization dangerous and threatening to the government and the rich—all this was new and fascinating." He was also attracted by the feeling of brotherhood and sharing in the circle. He could rely on his comrades, and their dedication and mutual trust made him feel as if he were in a primitive Christian commune.[53]

Other memoirs also attest to the strong appeal of heroic ideals and the excitement of dangerous feats, particularly for the younger workers. "It was awe-inspiring and terrible [to read about earlier revolutionary feats], and at the same time we wanted to suffer for the overall cause, to sacrifice ourselves, as did the heroes told about in the books."[54] Working in a

Finnish factory, A. Shotman quickly became bored with the "phlegmatic Finns" and their monotonous trade union meetings. "I wanted real struggle, entailing great risk and danger, and my dear Peter pulled me back to it."[55]

Arrest itself was a source of pride and confirmation of revolutionary identity. After his arrest Kanatchikov was gratified to be in the "front rank of the attacking army," and Babushkin positively welcomed arrest for the opportunity to "show that I'm a man who would never betray the cause."[56] Undoubtedly the fear of arrest discouraged many conscious workers from political activity, and jail ended many revolutionary careers. Yet for some workers—who knows what proportion?—it was a trial to be endured in triumph and confirmation of their status as conscious workers.

Jail and exile had surprising effects on many workers. It is remarkable how lenient or inept the tsarist authorities were. This has often been noted with regard to the treatment of the privileged intelligentsia,[57] but it also seems to have been true of workers. The following poem scratched on a jail wall contained a good deal of truth: "Prison helps everyone: / It develops the mind / On the outside you don't read books / But here you fall apart without them."[58] "They put poorly developed workers in prison for correction," remarked Kanatchikov, "but prison became a university for them, it forged character and made of them firm revolutionaries. . . . There occurred a natural selection of revolutionaries—the weak in spirit left the revolution, and often life, but the strong and steadfast were tempered for future battles."[59]

Exile also brought revolutionaries together. Some workers had their first sustained contact with the intelligentsia in exile, and they did not always like what they saw.[60] The same factional disputes that created so much conflict in Russia were duplicated in frozen Siberian towns. For many workers, however, exile was a positive experience. Mikhailov recalled his time in exile "with great spiritual satisfaction" because he was able to carry on his revolutionary work in the presence of an "international commune."[61] The worker Kungarov felt similar emotions. "The month I spent in the Ekaterinburg prison was very good and useful for me. Here there were people of various parties and persuasions. Each day there were meetings with speakers. Here I learned to understand things that were inaccessible to me earlier." When he returned to his village, he immediately organized an underground study group and supplied it with literature. When he returned to his workshop, he was met in triumph.[62]

Jail and exile were by no means the lot of all conscious workers, but they were the extreme example of a general rule: every attempt to isolate and persecute politically aware workers had the paradoxical effect of tempering a certain proportion of them and making them more resolute in their convictions. Autocratic repression, like capitalism, was responsible for the formation of new and dangerous group identities. And although these identities significantly cut off the conscious workers from their fellows, they also prepared them for leadership roles when conditions were ripe.

MODES OF ACTION

Because becoming conscious was primarily a change in awareness, it did not correspond to any particular mode of action. Indeed, some workers, like some of the intelligentsia, went into a kind of internal exile, experiencing complete separation between their internal and external worlds. Spiritual development through literature was one possible response to the immense gap between ideal and reality in Russia. Such workers have left few traces, and it is impossible to know how many chose the path of internal development.[63]

Probably the majority of conscious workers saw as their ideal the Western worker leader: both politically committed and useful in the mass labor movement. The conscious worker was not to be isolated from the masses, but then neither was he to renounce his position of leadership as a member of an elite. In Russia this model was hard to duplicate, for in most periods tsarist repression drove a wedge between the conscious workers and the masses, and in periods of upsurge it was not clear who led whom.

Because this ideal model was not easily attainable, and because the Russian labor movement was so uneven and sporadic, conscious workers often shifted their modes of action. Sometimes conscious workers who had been committed to the gradual development of a mass labor movement and had abjured spontaneity and terror completely altered their views in the heat of battle or after defeat. Thus Garvi recounts the case of Vinogradov, a Moscow printer who in the September 1905 printers' strike had argued against the Mensheviks' decision to encourage street meetings and demonstrations in their districts. He argued that the workers were not ready to go into the streets, that there were too many gray workers. Two weeks later, however, he was ready to call people to the barricades, and in December, in the first days of the Moscow uprising, he was killed trying to disarm some officers.[64] Similarly, in times of political reaction or economic crisis, conscious workers were more likely to shift their positions. "What can be asked of the masses," asked one worker, "when they were shown the way [to opportunism] by our conscious workers? Look at Pavlov, Agafanov—they were eagles in our factory, they led the whole factory behind them. And they were the first to become scoundrels."[65] The point is that such abrupt shifts were not a psychological aberration. They were fully comprehensible in the context of the unevenness of the Russian labor movement and the difficulty of establishing firm ties to a mass base. The conscious worker was often isolated and had little except his faith to sustain him unless he was a member of an underground organization. These were not the conditions that fostered stable modes of action.

One constant temptation of conscious workers was to isolate themselves in small groups of the select and wait for the gradual maturation of the working class. Particularly if the worker was a Marxist this was a sensible strategy, for the Western model of social change often seemed so completely divorced from Russian reality. It was also consistent with the conscious workers' condescension toward the gray masses. And it was psychologically satisfying as well: the conscious worker could deepen his knowledge and awareness, confident that such enlightenment was in the best interests of the labor movement in this early stage of development. This pattern was characteristic of the Marxist circles of the early 1890s. In this period conscious workers were cautious and usually remained aloof from mass action. Their typical form of organization was the study circle made up of a carefully selected elite, and public action took the form of sophisticated speeches, the commemoration of May Day or anniversaries of respected figures, and the issuance of brochures. There was very little agitation in the factories; this would have required a lowering of tone.[66] The same type of conscious worker appears to have been prominent in the Gapon movement. These more cautious workers were alarmed at the overly rapid growth of worker militancy and strongly emphasized cultural development and education. They believed that the radicalism and spontaneity of the great mass strikes harmed the gradual evolution of the labor movement along Western lines.[67] Such workers, suggested Shapovalov—more knowledgeable, skeptical, cautious, and cold-blooded—may have provided the social base for Menshevism.[68]

Some conscious workers became politically cautious for less principled reasons. Perhaps they had become disillusioned after the many setbacks the labor movement had endured, particularly the defeat of the 1905 revolution. Sometimes disaffection with intelligentsia leadership led them to renounce open political activities. And many, having gotten older, had families, and established themselves in stable positions in their factories, came to feel that the risks of activism were simply too high. Such workers could, however, be mobilized in times of ferment: "If something big comes along we won't be left out."[69]

Aside from the advantages of moderation or quiescence, conscious workers could also succumb to the opposite temptation: adventurism and terrorism. The reason was often the same: despair that Russian workers could ever make gains through following the European example, or, more generally, loss of hope in the possibility of change in the rigid tsarist system. Repression was simply too fierce and workers too backward. The temptation of terrorism was especially strong after serious defeats, and it was fueled by intense feelings of hatred and revenge. These were Shapovalov's emotions upon leaving for a worker meeting in 1894:

> I took leave of life, which had given me nothing. I was certain that the nihilists, moved by the same hatred as I, would order me to take vengeance and perish for the humiliation, tears, and insults which the worker endures. I already saw the horror which seized the rich upon finding out that from a worker's hand the earthly god—the Tsar—had died. I saw myself in the hands of the crowd, who beat me up, led me to jail and then to the scaffold. But I die happy, because I have been avenged.[70]

Shapovalov was just beginning his career as an activist at this time, and so he still felt much of the despair of the mass worker who had not yet embraced a new revolutionary faith. The same emotions, however, could grip conscious workers who explicitly condemned terror. Garvi asked a leading worker activist why he had considered murdering the factory owner at the time of a violent strike. He reminded the worker that they all condemned terror for its deleterious effects on the labor movement. The worker responded that "even now I think that terror is harmful. But then I lost my head. The feeling of revenge was stronger than everything. I decided to avenge the comrades. When you personally experience abuse, then you don't always act according to theory."[71] It is sometimes more difficult to understand why *anyone* acted "according to theory" in Russia than to comprehend this, and other, departures from ideals.

Despite all the obstacles, some conscious workers were able to approximate the ideal: to lead the mass of workers in labor struggles on the basis of their experience and knowledge. This leadership was rarely more than an approximation, however. Strikes were seldom decided upon by leaders on the basis of strategy. They usually broke out unpredictably and with little attention to pragmatic considerations. Worker leaders were usually called upon to help after the outbreak of unrest, when the mass workers realized the need for ideas and experience. Conscious workers were often able to infuse the strikes with new elements: more organization, more ideology, more explicit demands, more rational calculation. These were the special contributions of the conscious workers to worker protest.[72] The intelligentsia were more isolated from the factory environment; in any case they often avoided involvement in the trifles of strike organization, for it was more prestigious to get involved in political events on a larger scale. There was thus a certain element of truth in government accusations that "half-literate" conscious workers terroristically led "all the backward, inert mass of completely law-abiding workers."[73]

Again, the degree of guidance and control should not be overestimated. The conscious workers often gave in to the mass mood and did things against their better judgment. As Moiseenko remarked of an important strike in 1879, "as far as possible, we held the workers back and carried on a policy of restraint. But when you see how the worker is exploding, you yourself are infected with his enthusiasm and willy-nilly go along with everyone."[74] And it is important to remember that the conscious worker had few institutional supports to buttress his authority, and until the outbreak of unrest had been looked upon with suspicion. He had a limited capacity to control events even if he had so wished.

Conscious workers were also instrumental in creating and staffing organizations when conditions favored their formation. It was during such periods that their dreams of a European-type labor movement seemed closest to realization. For such a change to take place, however, the whole structure of the labor movement—with the symbiotic relations among mass workers, conscious workers, and the intelligentsia—would have to be completely altered. Deprived of this legal role, conscious workers tended to withdraw, either into isolation or back into illegal work. In the underground ideology and intelligentsia tutelage once more substituted for the moderate organizational work denied conscious workers by the government.

RELATION TO MASS WORKERS

According to their beliefs, conscious workers should have looked upon the worker masses as their brothers and sisters, united to them by shared oppression in a capitalist system. The need for class unity was one of their central tenets, following directly from their systemic analysis of social life and their belief that they could effect change only through the mobilization of large numbers.

Ironically, however, the very decision to dedicate oneself to the workers as a class often led to rejection of the workers as people. Partly this was because the mass workers did not measure up to the conscious workers' new conception of the dignity of the working class. Perpetual drunkenness was hardly consistent with the challenge to redeem humanity. Like the early Christians, theirs was a conception of community that divided the community, for, not content with membership based on birth and shared characteristics, it demanded conversion and commitment. The conscious workers' hostility was also a product of the cultural differentiation that was part of becoming conscious. Status hierarchy thus resulted from class consciousness. New standards were applied to people, including to themselves, and by these standards the mass workers were uncouth, ignorant, and cowardly. Finally, their contempt was a response to their own isolation and the rejection by the other workers, which sometimes took the form of denunciations to the police. Thus one worker remarked to Kanatchikov: "And you want to achieve socialism with such people. . . . They'll hang you on the first lamp post."[75]

Such contempt for the mass workers stimulated some conscious workers to join the Socialist Revolutionaries in their terrorist methods. They simply despaired of any real change in the workers in the foreseeable future. "'You see,'" spoke Priiutov to Shapovalov, "'if we develop each worker individually, decades will pass, and nothing will come of this. Only individual workers will be able to comprehend the idea of revenge, of struggle, the idea which you have now arrived at after so many years. It's easy to recruit individuals into militant bands which, throwing bombs and killing the Tsar and ministers, compel the government to make concessions.'" "'Give me a bomb,' answered Shapovalov. "'I'm ready to throw it and die.'"[76]

Such a contemptuous view of the mass workers was not restricted to highly sophisticated conscious workers. Even a relatively untutored worker like Moiseenko became convinced that the masses' attitudes made only bunts possible. Giving examples of their conversations, he called them "superstitious" and an "ignorant mass."[77] Yet Moiseenko did not surrender to pessimism and continued to do agitational work for decades, despite jail and exile.

What sustained those conscious workers who maintained faith in the mass struggle? I doubt that any fully satisfactory answer can be given to this question. One source of hope, however, was that very spontaneity and unpredictability of the masses that they so condemned. After years of quiescence, the workers in a single plant, a region, or the whole country would rise up and demonstrate extraordinary courage and receptivity to radical ideas. Such unpredictable outbursts had an intoxicating effect upon conscious workers and clearly demonstrates that there was a reciprocal relationship between the two categories of workers, just as, for the same reason, there was interdependence between the workers as a whole and the intelligentsia.

The importance of mass spontaneity for reinforcing the conscious workers' faith was already evident in the early period of the organized labor movement in Russia. For example, members of a workers' circle of early 1880 were amazed, after an unexpected outbreak of mass defiance of the police, "that even the workers untouched by propaganda were fully capable of decisive and unanimous action. . . . It was only necessary for us not to let such moments slip by in order to guarantee ourselves the sympathy of the worker masses."[78]

A far more significant case was the mass unrest in St. Petersburg of late 1894, which led directly to the socialists' modification of their old strategy of painstaking propaganda and its replacement by active leadership of the strike movement, soon to register its first major successes in 1896–1897.[79] Most important of all, the 1905 revolution itself was ushered in by the militancy of relatively untutored masses fired largely by traditional expectations. The conscious workers and intelligentsia were astonished at the abrupt changes in consciousness of the previously "dark" workers, now, more than ever before, receptive to socialist ideas (although these changes would prove to be impermanent). Thus just as mass workers turned to conscious workers in times of need, so conscous workers were activated by the unexpected militancy of the mass workers. The two groups were interdependent precisely because of the extreme differentiation of roles that had arisen under tsarist absolutism, and so each needed the other to fuel its hopes for change.

These hopes were short-lived, but the experiences upon which they were based were enormously powerful. The conscious workers and the intelligentsia escaped from their isolation without having to give up their own identities. This merger of groups previously so separated must have had an indelible emotional impact, and not just for the promise it held forth for future victories. It has often been remarked that the Russian intelligentsia experienced deep feelings of guilt over its separation from the people. Similar feelings must have plagued the conscious workers. Periods such as 1896–1897 or 1905–1906 permitted these deeply stratified groups to merge into temporary unity—partly a mirage, certainly, because mutual isolation and cultural differentiation had created unbridgeable cleavages. It was partly real, too, for they were, after all, all workers in a capitalist system and downtrodden subjects of an oppressive state. The afterglow of this experience of unity was an important part of the revolutionary tradition that would sustain men's faith despite terrible setbacks.

RELATION TO THE INTELLIGENTSIA

Mass and conscious workers had many traits in common by virtue of their shared social position, but they were highly differentiated with respect to their cultural styles and political perspectives. The reverse was true of the relationship between the conscious workers and the intelligentsia. The social differences between them were often vast, but they shared a common outlook and sometimes participated in the same organizations. Just as the relationship between mass and conscious workers was filled with ambivalence, so was the relationship between the conscious workers and the intelligentsia, although the sources of strain differed.[80]

The most basic and unavoidable source of conflict between conscious workers and the intelligentsia was their class origin. Workers felt uncomfortable in the presence of their social betters, and attempts to bridge the gaps between them sometimes had comical results. Workers worried about mispronounced words, about where to place their napkins, and the like. It is understandable that in a society so riddled with hierarchy and in which formalities were so important the workers simply preferred their own company. Sometimes the workers interpreted these class cultural differences in a self-congratulatory way. Frolov remarks of the intelligentsia that "many of them spoke well, they knew much, but in their work there was not the soul, feeling, or warm comradely relationships which the workers' soul thirsted after."[81] Such sentiments, though arising partly from defensiveness, also stemmed from the workers' experience of being reborn into "consciousness."

Class differences went deeper than personal habits or cultural level, however, for they also shaped life experiences in the movement. Workers knew that the intelligentsia could always abandon the movement—a fact that was brought home to them every summer when a great number of student activists went away for vacation. For the intelligentsia, their commitment was a choice, not a fate, and although the workers admired (as well as puzzled over) their decision to a certain extent, they also knew it was revocable. This naturally led to suspicion and mistrust.

Conscious workers also resented the better treatment that the intelligentsia received from the public and at the hands of the authorities. Workers were called by the familiar form of "you" and treated coarsely; the intelligentsia were handled with much more respect. Similarly, jail was a different experience for the two classes: the intelligentsia frequently received help from home, whereas the worker was more likely to be on his own. Even the differences in image rankled: the intelligentsia were heroes who had chosen to sacrifice themselves for an ideal; the workers were upstart rabble who had no right to get involved in politics. Such sentiments based on class resentments flare up frequently in memoirs. For example, Petukhov describes how in 1905 some young revolutionary members of the intelligentsia came to their factory and told them to restrain themselves in the class struggle, for otherwise they would alienate the factory owners, who were necessary allies in the fight against tsarism. An old worker responded:

> Comrades, excuse me, an old man, perhaps it may not please you, but still I must say that we workers should not trust these mother's girls and boys and well-groomed idlers [beloruchki—literally, a person shirking physical labor]—who have come from the class of exploiters, since they and we don't have the same interests, and we must relate to them with great caution, since they can turn out to be false defenders of the workers' interests.[82]

Class differences did not disappear but took different forms in underground work. Worker activists constantly complained that they were not allowed to reach responsible positions in the party hierarchy.[83] Activists then and scholars now advance the reasonable explanation that underground work imposed a division of labor within the movement that was difficult to overcome.[84] Political surveillance made it natural for the workers to concentrate on tasks at the factory level which would arouse little suspicion, such as recruitment and handling of mutual aid funds, whereas the intelligentsia would specialize in providing political literature, maintaining contacts with other groups, and formulating political strategy. However much truth such arguments may have had, they could not neutralize worker resentment. And the workers' suspicion that much of the division of labor was a result of simple prejudice and condescension was undoubtedly true.

Conscious worker activists also blamed the party for failing to give due consideration to the workers' needs and goals. They were embittered by the party's tendency to downplay the importance of workers' economic aspirations.[85] It was not that the conscious workers wanted to ignore the political struggle, but they refused to sacrifice their material needs for purely political goals. This conflict, they suggested, was a good illustration of the implications of their different class positions. A worker colleague of Kanatchikov, Efimov, expressed these feelings well: "You despise the struggle for nickel and dime interests, but you yourselves live off your fathers and mothers. The worker has not only himself to support, but he must also create surplus value for your free and easy existence."[86]

Workers were also outraged by the factional disputes within the party. The intelligentsia preached the need for unity, but they fought bitterly over issues that few conscious workers even understood. These disputes were a major source of worker disappointment with the intelligentsia and led many conscious workers to abandon the party, for had not these selfless martyrs placed their own political ideas ahead of the interests of the workers whom they were claiming to defend?[87] When nothing came of their outrage, the workers could only complain of their intelligentsia associates, "they are incapable of being infused with the breadth and lawfulness of the proletarian forces. They became enclosed within themselves. They lost their tact, solidarity, sincerity."[88]

The variety and depth of these tensions suggest that Perlman was right—that there is an inherent conflict between workers and intelligentsia. In this case we are even referring to conflicts with the most politically aware workers, those who shared the same commitment to a mass political labor movement. Such dissension led to massive worker defections from the Social Democratic party, particularly in periods of the movement's downswing. Many conscious workers became involved with the anarchists or Socialist Revolutionaries, or they participated in the cooperative movement, mutual aid funds, cultural societies, or trade unions when possible. Or they abandoned political activities altogether. But they never realized the dream of workers like Fisher, one of St. Petersburg's leading conscious workers: to establish an independent worker voice within the party, which could sometimes restrain the intelligentsia, at other times push them forward.[89] The conscious workers either abandoned the party or continued to acquiesce, often bitterly, in the intelligentsia's domination. And when the movement ignited again, they had nowhere to turn than to the parties. In both 1905 and 1917 there was an enormous upsurge in influence and membership in the Social Democrats, even though shortly before they had been isolated and had little prestige. Why, then, did so many bitter conscious workers disclaim any desire to cut ties with the intelligentsia? And why did so many choose "exit" rather than "voice"?

The first and more obvious reason is that the intelligentsia virtually monopolized certain skills crucial for the success of the movement. They had wider contacts and more effective organizational and conspiratorial methods. They were better polemicists and orators, as even the workers themselves had to admit. Under tsarist conditions the workers could not easily have developed these talents, and so the growth of an independent worker tendency, such as existed in Western European labor movements, was stunted. Various attempts were made to establish independent worker organizations that could avoid intelligentsia dominance, but these were short-lived.[90]

There was another reason for the conscious workers' dependency, however. Many had accepted the basic claim of the intelligentsia: that history could be understood and controlled, and that abstract ideas and long-term strategies were consequently of fundamental importance in a social movement. Fisher, extremely bitter over the intelligentsia's role in the movement, nonetheless concluded that they were as necessary to the labor movement as "water to a fish": "Without deserters from the bourgeoisie to the proletariat, the working class would not have had the literature that it had then. The workers . . . would not be able to produce that mental material which the deserters gave. . . . A purely workers' movement cannot exist without turning into something similar to the

English labor movement."[91] Deprived of both ideas and the opportunity to act in pursuit of their own interests freely, the conscious workers over-estimated the necessity of ideology, just as the intelligentsia itself had turned to ideology in the absence of, and as a substitute for, concrete political action. Ideas became so important because the reality was so hopeless.

Ideology had another appeal for many conscious workers: it was, after all, the absorption of ideology that validated their own claim to superior-ity over their fellow workers. They, too, were part of a knowing elite, if only derivatively. They, too, professed to know how to act in accord with historical forces, and to be able to separate gray from conscious workers. Given these assumptions, how could they renounce ideology without reducing their own stature as well?

Thus in Russia, as in Western Europe, capitalist industrialization created many of the preconditions for a mass labor movement: a body of skilled, educated, and urbanized workers; the potential for communica-tion; and a shared class position that could serve as the basis for solidar-ity. The tsarist government, however, prevented the development of this movement along Western lines. Crucial resources were missing: the mass workers were more "massified" than in the West, more completely de-prived of organizational life; and the conscious workers were more iso-lated from the masses and less able to engage in independent activity vis-à-vis the intelligentsia. These deficiencies were responsible for great cultural and ideological divisions, but they also created interdependencies. Mass workers looked to the conscious workers and the intelligentsia for guidance, and conscious workers depended upon the ideas of the intel-ligentsia. In both cases ideology made up for the gaps and deficiencies in practical experience and became infused into the movement. Conscious workers played the crucial mediatory role, absorbing ideology from the intelligentsia and, in times of ferment, transmitting it to the masses, who, in the absence of anything else, were highly receptive to it, at least for a time. If it was the conscious workers who were the main "transmission belts" of ideology—and in an unfree society ideas always go from the top down—it was the intelligentsia who were its holy guardians. We now turn to their role in the labor movement.

CHAPTER
9

The Revolutionary Intelligentsia

"Between the two camps—the people and the intelligentsia—there is a line at which they can meet and agree. . . . But how tenuous this line is today between the secretly hostile camps!"

Alexander Blok[1]

The Russian revolutionary intelligentsia, unlike the workers, have never lacked public and scholarly attention. Whether celebrated or vilified, the intelligentsia—as borrowers or as conceivers of ideas, as ideologists or as political organizers—have been central to the debates on the Russian revolution. Indeed, parallel with this more general debate on the historical significance of the revolution, interpretations and polemics on the intelligentsia have raged on, seemingly insoluble for the past century.

In broad terms two general lines of interpretation confront each other. According to the first, the intelligentsia was, to its own and all other groups' misfortune, the demiurge of the 1917 revolution. "The Russian Revolution," wrote Szamuely, "was the product of the intelligentsia, and revolution was the intelligentsia's raison d'être."[2] The intelligentsia are portrayed as both isolated from the masses and capable of imposing upon the latter ill-understood and even alien goals. They were a "secular priesthoood" that shaped events on the basis of an ideological vision, and true to this vision and not to any mass base, they changed the course of history. For this reason, wrote Berlin, they constituted "the largest single Russian contribution to social change in the world."[3]

For those—including Marxists, but not they alone—who see the Russian revolution as a product of structured and coherent mass action, the significance of the intelligentsia is entirely different. Trotsky makes the argument with his usual lucidity: political leaders were not an independent element of the revolutionary process: they were like pistons driven by the energy of the masses.[4] The dynamic force of the 1917 revolution was not the party but the working class. Even further, in 1917 the party was not an instrument of an intelligentsia leadership, not an organizational weapon, but a democratic body expressing the will of its working-class base.[5]

Two issues have been at the heart of these debates. First, who led the revolution, a broad class movement or a minuscule elite? And second, how consonant or divergent were the perspectives and goals of the Russian working class and the intelligentsia, particularly the latter's Marxist branch?

The answers to these questions admit of less certainty than proponents of one or the other general interpretation are usually willing to recognize. The connections between the intelligentsia and the workers in the labor movement involved both shared goals and disaccord, both solidarity and conflict; and the question of who led whom also cannot be resolved simply. Appeals to the complexity of the issues and adherence to some kind of in-between position are also not satisfactory, however. For what is the origin of the complexity, and why do the polar positions sketched out previously fail to convince? Complexity, too, has its causes, and a theoretical compromise without any additional rationale or explication creates more problems than it resolves. In line with the overall logic of this study, the complexity and ambiguity of the relationship derive from autocratic capitalism. Autocracy isolated the intelligentsia from routine contact with a mass base and facilitated the emergence of a discrete intelligentsia subculture. In this respect the intelligentsia could not in any simple sense represent the masses. This very subculture, however, rooted as it partially was in the autocratic regime, also touched upon several traits of the workers' own culture that had parallel origins. The development of capitalism was also linked to a mosaic of discrepant social positions, elements of a shared modern culture, and differentiated—and so interdependent— roles in the movement.

Thus in their joint impact, autocracy and capitalism gave rise to a complex and shifting relationship between the intelligentsia and the workers. It was not simply a case of unprincipled manipulation by outsiders; nor did intelligentsia and worker aspirations coincide in a harmony of interests. Rather, the reality between these extreme views is far more interesting. Perhaps uniquely in Russia an ideological and sectarian revolutionary intelligentsia intersected in a profound way with relatively unorganized and highly militant worker masses. Such a convergence of sect and mass movement is rarer than it might appear. As they became transformed into a mass party, the German Social Democrats gradually lost their sectarianism. French sectarianism remained very much alive, but only in the context of a politically divided movement in which the worker masses largely went their own way. In the European context these were the two major possibilities: ideologists had either to modify themselves— to become a church more than a sect—or to sacrifice much of their mass base. It was only in a relatively closed political system such as Spain's that something approximating the Russian pattern emerged. This very pattern of development, however, which threw together such disparate elements, ensured that they could not be fused into a coherent movement. The aim of this chapter, then, is not to present new material on the Russian intelligentsia, nor is it to narrate the history of its different branches in their relationship to the workers. Rather, it seeks to use the general model of Russian development to trace a number of the main dimensions of the worker-intelligentsia relationship. In so doing it aims not only to elucidate this phenomenon but to suggest, just as was the case for government policy, how intergroup relations can be linked to a general model of development. The chapter will also show how the study of all of this together—structural contradictions, interelite relationships, government policy, and intergroup relations—is essential for the theoretical comprehension of revolutions.

THE EFFECTS OF AUTOCRACY

SOURCES OF DIFFERENTIATION AND CONFLICT

The autocratic system nurtured cleavages between the revolutionary intelligentsia and the workers first by fostering a distinctive intelligentsia culture, which, in their own minds, set the knowing elite apart from the masses. In addition, it shaped the social structure of the labor movement, imposing an internal division of labor and mutual isolation. As a result conflicts between the intelligentsia and workers within the movement multiplied, especially over the issues of hierarchy, sectarianism, and the selection of priorities. Third, by curtailing contact and making democratic procedures unrealistic, the autocratic system prevented changes that might have softened these divisions and established mutual accountability. The absence of overall democratization made it inevitable that, as many activists complained, the revolutionary underground would mirror the regime as a whole.

We need only detain ourselves briefly on the culture of the Russian revolutionary intelligentsia, the subject of countless historical and literary studies. In general terms it is well characterized by Ralf Dahrendorf's phrase, "the elite theory of manifest truth"—that is, the conviction that an enlightened elite uniquely possesses the key to what is universally valid.[6] Knowledge of the laws of history, of the inevitable destiny of mankind, as given by ideology—whether populist, Marxist, or Russophile—was deemed the fundamental requirement of leadership. Consequently, to an extraordinary degree intellectual virtuosity defined the elite of the Social Democratic movement. Young converts such as Lenin and Martov made pilgrimages to Europe to visit elders of Russian Marxism of the stature of Plekhanov and Axelrod, whose prestige was based not on their political skills but on their theoretical works. Those, like Axelrod himself and Vera Zasulich, whose theoretical contributions lacked originality and depth, suffered from a deep sense of inadequacy.[7] The ordinary Social Democratic intelligentsia were not expected to inhabit such heights, but they were still judged by their mastery of the canonical texts. Krzhizanovsky, a leading Marxist of the 1890s, declared in his memoirs that he was "firmly convinced that no good would ever come of anyone who had not gone through Marx's *Capital* two or three times."[8]

At least since Tocqueville, ideological politics have been traced to the absence of political freedom.[9] Lack of participation undercuts the tempering effects of debate and the sober discipline of reality. People turn inward, toward reflection and literature; ideas are evaluated for their profundity and revelatory character, not for their practicability. The abstract themes that become central to new personal identities cannot be tested against the stubborn facts of entrenched customs, interests, and institutions, the power of which is absurdly underestimated. Human nature and society can be reshaped at will in imaginations unobstructed by experience.

Stratification by knowledge gives a much firmer basis to elite leadership than that by interest; interests are both universal and plural, whereas knowledge is restricted and deemed unitary. The elitist character of knowledge in Russia was especially pronounced because of limits on the open expression and transmission of ideas. Knowledge was inevitably esoteric, whether based on high culture, modern European science, or proclaimed canonical texts, particularly as so much of the knowledge was imported from abroad, and so not rooted in Russian culture at all. Evaluating themselves by their gnosis, the intelligentsia were not ashamed to celebrate their own virtues,[10] as in these luxuriant cadences of Chernyshevsky, Lenin's great model

> the life of all prospers because of them, without them it would decay and turn sour. There are only a few of them, but they give breath and life to all people; without them people would suffocate. They are the quintessence of things, they are like the distinctive fragrance of a rare wine; from them comes strength and originality; they constitute the flower of the best people; they are the mover of movers, the salt of the salt of the earth.[11]

From this elevation of a knowing elite stemmed a lack of trust in the masses' ability to understand the world around them or act in favor of change. As Chernyshevsky declared, "the mass of the population knows nothing and cares about nothing except its material advantages, and rare are the cases in which it even suspects any relationship between its material interests and political change."[12] Axelrod, the most tractable of the leading Marxists because of his social origin, temperament, and ideology, was convinced that, as he expressed it in such un-Marxist terms, "even the most insipid liberalism of any intellectual still towers over the uncultured attitudes of the masses."[13] It was temporarily necessary, he added, for the workers to absorb bourgeois culture in their trajectory toward socialism.

Paradoxically, this low estimation of the masses was accompanied by great expectations of them. From those populists who yearned for a peasant revolution to Marxists who demanded a schooled class of worker-intellectuals, the intelligentsia imposed its own criteria on the dark masses. Without a reduction in their self-assigned role, many transformed themselves from makers of the revolution to preceptors of the future revolutionaries. The exalted hopes that the intelligentsia had for their charges demanded continued intelligentsia predominance in the movement. Thus for Lenin it was the impossibility of authentic class consciousness among the workers that required party tutelage. Notice, however, how impossibly high Lenin, no more than following Axelrod and Plekhanov, sets the standards of class consciousness:

> The consciousness of the working masses cannot be genuine class-consciousness, unless the workers learn, from concrete, and above all from topical, political facts and events to observe every other social class in all the manifestations of its intellectual, ethical, and political life; unless they learn to apply in practice the materialist analysis and the materialist estimate of all aspects of the life and activity of all classes, strata, and groups of the population.[14]

Lenin assigned to the party the responsibility for transforming this esoteric knowledge into shared convictions, but of course it was never able to perform this task. Despite Lenin's desiderata, in practice the appeal to consciousness and knowledge always implied guidance by the gnostic few.

One final point about the culture of the intelligentsia deserves attention: the tendency toward dogmatism and sectarianism. These traits, too, were grounded in the autocratic system, which did not permit open debate and the confrontation of ideas. Isaiah Berlin has contrasted Russian intellectual life with a more general European pattern.[15] Intellectual systems in nineteenth-century Europe, he claims, had to compete in a rich intellectual environment embracing a variety of ideas. Such pluralism, he holds, made European thought less absolute, less certain that final truths could be easily apprehended. Russia, which had not experienced the Renaissance, was an ideological vacuum by comparison, at least until the latter part of the century. Even then, however, ideas were not transmitted through public debate and open discussion in which they would have had to collide. Russian revolutionary intellectual life was esoteric and transmitted through selective contacts. Even when it became more diverse, the result was not the emergence of an authentic pluralism. Thus ideas, when they took root, became more absolute. With their sincerity, sense of purpose, and single-mindedness, the Russian intelligentsia took their ideas to their final consequences, relatively unaffected by the pragmatism often born of pluralism. In this way concrete knowledge and experience lost their capacity to guide thought, and ideas had a dynamic of their own.

In his various writings, particularly *From Under the Rubble*, Solzhenitsyn has poured scorn on the Western ideology of progress and its intelligentsia purveyors in Russia, so cut off from the roots of Russian culture and the people. Certainly the content of much of nineteenth-century Russian social thought—even, paradoxically, Slavophilism[16]—was of Western origin, but its tone and expression were still singularly Russian, the product of an autocracy that curtailed action and smothered debate. Nothing in Russia was more traditional, less Western, than the complex relationship between a despotic state and an ideological intelligentsia struggling for the hearts of the people.

The culture of the intelligentsia thus fostered hierarchy within the labor movement. The imperatives of conspiratorial work, stemming from autocratic repression, reinforced this same tendency by encouraging a rigid division of labor and minimizing contact among the differentiated parts. The intelligentsia tended to concentrate their efforts on what they regarded as the most important tasks: ideological discussions, decisions about overall strategy, the development of party organizations, the initiation of ties with other social groups, and action on the extralocal political arena. Worker activists tended to be restricted to the less important tasks and the least responsible positions.

These inequalities were only aggravated by the impossibility of routine open contact. Isolation inhibited the development of trust and left each side prey to its own images and fantasies about the other. Mutual reproaches based on these often unreal perceptions inevitably followed serious setbacks in the movement. For example, after the defeat of the 1905 revolution, many workers complained of the desertion of the intelligentsia; many intelligentsia activists, in turn, became convinced that "workers are ungrateful swine."[17] What Gorky said of Lenin—that "life in all its complexity" was unknown to him and that "he does not know the popular masses, he has not lived with them"[18]—was true, in different ways, for all social strata in Russia. Communication and understanding were universally distorted, and all groups operated by means of prejudices and caricatures, whether hostile or idealized. Because knowledge was distorted, so were expectations, and the resulting disillusionments led to dramatic shifts in judgment. Lenin's stalwart proletariat became, for him, by the late fall of 1917, a human swamp mired in bourgeois filth. The tacit dimension of routine understanding that social theorists have seen as both the foundation and prerequisite of stable interaction was utterly absent in the intelligentsia-worker relationship as it was shaped by the autocracy. Ideological knowledge substituted for routine knowledge, but ideological knowledge was the worst possible remedy for the conflicts and instability of the relationship. Whatever surface harmony may have existed at certain moments, and whatever the temporary capacity for solidarity, profound cleavages always lay very close to the surface in the Russian socialist movement.

The intelligentsia's emphasis on ideology led them to emphasize the political over the economic struggle[19]—a second source of cleavage between them and the workers, who always, even when (according to the intelligentsia) it was inexpedient, gave great weight to pressing material needs. The intelligentsia based their claims to leadership on the conviction that only they could guide workers in the political struggle, which, without their tutelage (it was claimed), could only degenerate into the crassest form of economic struggle. In debates among the intelligentsia about the relative weight to be given to political as opposed to economic goals, those who favored broad-scale political action won all the major victories. Ideology and politics were, after all, the métier of the most prestigious leaders, who had won their spurs by working out abstract political ideas and strategies and who, even if unaware, regarded the workers in terms of the historical mission that had been set for them, and not as concrete human beings with needs and goals.

Lack of contact exacerbated this worker-intelligentsia conflict over the movement's priorities. The emigrés, declaiming from abroad, interpreted all attention to the economic struggle as economism. The polarity between economic and political goals, so crucial in theory, lost its sharpness in practice, however; and the intelligentsia, isolated from the movement, simply failed to see the political implications of many of the events around them. "For us," wrote Garvi, "the underground processes of the accumulation of revolutionary energy, covered for the time being by the deceptive crust of silence and apathy, were unseen and unheard."[20] Much of the difference between workers and intelligentsia in the labor movement amounted to this: whereas the intelligentsia were at times willing to dampen the economic struggle for the sake of an overall political strategy, the workers refused to make this separation, even temporarily. To this refusal, which did not constitute a simple lack of political involvement, the intelligentsia gave the name "economism."

Ideology, with its emphasis upon doctrine and purity, especially when combined with mutual isolation, generated sectarianism among the intelligentsia. All standard histories of Russian socialism chronicle at length the various factional battles within and between populists and Marxists. Such personal and ideological differences plagued other socialist parties and labor movements as well, and no doubt they were particularly sharp among the intelligentsia. In France socialist parties preceded the growth of trade unionism, and the parties became dominated by intellectuals predisposed to ideological squabbling. In Germany the debate over revisionism was world-renowned, as, later, was the split between the party and the trade unions. Yet these conflicts had solid sociological roots in the position of the working class in German society, and they involved crucial points of ideology. What amazed Russian workers and foreign observers alike about Russian factionalism was, first, that the disputes seemed to be based on personal rivalries more than profound ideological differences.[21] In addition, these conflicts had no roots among the workers at all, for the great majority of workers did not even understand them— and yet the leaders remained intransigent and the splits irreconcilable.

The autocracy, just as it had done much to generate these breaches between the intelligentsia and the workers, was also the main guarantee that they could not be healed. Worker activists repeatedly attacked the intelligentsia for its hierarchical practices, its failure to become involved in economic struggles, and its sectarianism, but little came of worker outspokenness. The weakness of pressures for reform can be traced to the consequences of autocratic repression. First, the need for conspiracy disarmed much of the workers' critique of the party. In the face of tsarist repression, intelligentsia leaders claimed, with considerable justice, that centralization was a necessary part of underground work. Too much participation would threaten the necessary secrecy of the party's activities and expose the activists to arrest. Bitter experience convinced many workers that this rationalization was justified, although the issue never ceased to create great resentment. They grudgingly accepted the hierarchical practices of the intelligentsia, or else, in despair, they left the party organizations.

In turn, this lack of intraparty democracy had decisive consequences for the workers' ability to promote greater party unity or democratization.[22] With respect to the first issue, without consensual and institutionalized procedures for decision making, compromises were rare, for there was little autonomy of the organization as a whole from the factions that made it up. To encourage compromise the party would have to have enough resources to punish dissidence as well as mechanisms for arriving at authoritative decisions. In the persecuted Russian organizations, resources of all kinds were always meager, and so the first condition was absent. Similarly, because of its centralization, lack of democracy, and weak party ties to the mass base, there was no means of reaching a consensus by majority, for the nature and composition of the majority were always in dispute.[23] If a faction had a strong leader with a group of faithful activists, it could remain visible and make a claim to representativeness in a context in which such claims were not easy to challenge.

Party centralization had a further consequence: just as there was not enough democracy to develop consensus, so there was not enough mass pressure to force unification or greater democratization. Control from above was a self-reinforcing process: the more of it there was, the less it could be resisted. The intelligentsia, largely split off from the workers, could follow their innate tendencies without hindrance, particularly because, as a result of the weakness of liberalism in Russia, the workers had no realistic alternatives to the socialists.[24] Many Mensheviks after 1905 sought to reverse workers' dependence on the intelligentsia through encouraging the development of a mass labor movement—especially trade unions—and through the reconstruction of the party from the bottom up. In accord with this goal, they hoped to downplay the conspiratorial aspects of Social Democracy and take advantage of the possibilities for open legal activity among the masses and thus undermine all the old justifications for centralization and hierarchy in the movement. The tsarist state, however, by prohibiting such legal activity, unwittingly cooperated with the more ideological elements of Russian Marxism and prevented a more reciprocal interpenetration of the working class and the socialist parties. Autocracy and the radical intelligentsia opposition thus fed upon each other even while they jointly succeeded in weakening potential reformist alternatives.

SOURCES OF CONVERGENCE

The polarity of the ideological elite and the pragmatic masses is one of the clichés of the analysis of revolution. From here it is only a short step to the view that revolutionary intellectuals work upon or manipulate an otherwise indifferent and confused, even if militant, mass, and that revolutions inevitably culminate in the victory of a small elite separated from the people. Ironically, however, the very lack of freedom and participation that facilitates revolution also heightens ideological sensitivity among the masses, and so it is precisely in revolutionary situations that this pragmatic caste of mind among the lower classes is least likely to be encountered. Thus in *The Old Regime* Tocqueville clearly recognized that the influence of abstract intellectuals in French public life depended upon a general lack of political good sense and judgment among the people. Like the intellectuals, the masses had no idea what was sound policy or hopelessly impractical experimentation, and not understanding the solidity of customs and institutions, they were susceptible to programs of thoroughgoing metamorphosis. By contrast, declares Tocqueville, "any experience, however slight, of public affairs would have made them [the French masses] chary of accepting the opinions of mere theoreticians."[25]

Like the French masses, Russian workers suffered from a vacuum of political experience and a store of ideas built upon it. Tikhomirov, the ideologist of the Zubatov movement, recognized that the prestige of revolutionary ideas among the workers depended upon this void, and he urged the formation of a people's intelligentsia to develop an authentic popular world view. The independence and capacity for public action that he saw as vital to the development of this worker mentality were never allowed to develop, however. As a result, despite the many conflicts and divergences between workers and the intelligentsia, large numbers of workers continued to look to the intelligentsia for leadership and to accept at least some version of their ideological premises. As discussed previously, the meaning of this "acceptance" varied a great deal: among conscious workers it often constituted a willed choice based on a degree of knowledge; among mass workers it was more likely to be temporary and superficial agreement with the need for a complete transformation of their world. Whatever gradations may have existed, however, the conclusion stands that by depriving both workers and intelligentsia of the capacity for public participation, the autocracy unwittingly created "a line at which they can meet and agree."

This line was considerably widened by the cultural preconceptions that both groups, equally nurtured by autocratic institutions, shared with each other. In their different ways workers and the intelligentsia gave little priority to the values of bourgeois society: the rule of law (including the importance of rules and procedures); the sanctity of property; the elevation of political freedom over equality; the legitimacy of social elites; and an abhorrence of rapid social change. Whether in the form of literature or more systematic discussions, the intelligentsia gave to these presuppositions much greater clarity and explicitness, but their more developed accounts very often corresponded to the unspoken assumptions and latent ideas of the masses to whom they were frequently meant to appeal.

For example, at least since the emancipation of the serfs in 1861, Russian social thought distinguished between the people's freedom and their happiness and clearly taught that freedom without happiness—in the form of economic welfare and equality—was only a mirage. For this reason even in the first years after the new era the Russian intelligentsia was already largely socialist.[26] Herzen, the most eminent tribune of socialism before the predominance of Marxism from the 1890s, wrote in characteristic fashion: "Russia will never stage a revolution with the sole aim of ridding herself of Tsar Nicholas only to replace him by a multitude of other Tsars—Tsar-deputies, Tsar-tribunals, Tsar-policemen, Tsar-laws."[27] The average Russian peasant or worker would not, of course, have expressed the choice so clearly. Rather, schooled by the autocracy, he simply had no awareness of the significance of political freedom or the implications of the choice. Not having experienced liberty, he had not come to value it. The intellectual, having observed it from afar, had come to hold liberty in contempt for its partial nature and its conservative consequences. Neither perceived or accepted the possible connection between political freedom and the "people's happiness."

In addition, with social life dominated by the state, neither group had significant experience of society as composed of differentiated and interdependent elements related to one another in a complex interplay of conflict and cooperation. No more than government officials were they able to conceive of a partially self-regulating community operating with an independent logic. Community had to be mechanical, not organic; it was expressed in the desire for "metasocial bonds with others in unstructured collectivities."[28] The solidarity envisioned was of a primitive kind: for the intelligentsia, the unity of the "people" or the oppressed proletariat; for the workers, the community of brother workers bound together by shared oppression.[29] Neither could easily accept a vision of community compatible with conflict and diversity. Marxist doctrine taught the need to transcend civil society: thus both its relevance and irrelevance for a society only beginning to be "civil" in the classic sense.[30]

Just as the intelligentsia and workers could only begin to understand the complexities of a modern social order, so they had a fundamentally magical approach to the question of social change. Rational social movements depend on knowledge and experience to ascertain feasible strategies and goals. Autocracy, depriving people of knowledge, encouraged a very different image of change: it could abolish all evil; it could occur apart from a process of maturation; and leadership and the will could overcome objective obstacles. A tendency toward millenarianism, evident among the elite as well as the masses in Russia during periods of ferment, was the natural consequence of this constellation of assumptions. Revolutionary ideas of the total reconstruction of society through some mighty upheaval flourished in such soil.

Lack of knowledge thus accounted for certain shared assumptions about change. In addition, although mutual isolation conditioned the emergence of separate cultures and a general sense of apartness, it also had the reverse effect of allowing intelligentsia illusions about the people to bloom even in foul weather. A "proletarian mystique," parallel to the "go to the people" mystique of the early 1870s, flourished among the Marxist intelligentsia beginning in the 1890s.[31] On the basis of this idealization, leaders like Plekhanov or Lenin could assign to the proletariat a fantastic historical role. The frequent exaggerations of proletarian purity called forth Axelrod's reproach against "those who regard it as their duty in season and out of season to proclaim the proletariat as sinless and infallible, to lavish upon them all kinds of praise." Axelrod, at least on this occasion, sounded the other intelligentsia note: "On the contrary, I think it is our duty to point out to the workers with complete frankness that they, in the mass, are still very backward and that even their advanced elements are still only in the first stages of their political development."[32] Idealization clearly served to sustain the faith of revolutionaries despite disappointments and reverses, whereas a fuller knowledge might have led them to exclaim, as Plekhanov did in his first meeting with a real worker, that their "surprise knew no limits."[33] The intelligentsia's convictions, however, untempered by knowledge, assured that these distortions, a mixture of contempt and idealization, would endure whatever the actual state of mind of the workers.

Lack of contact and knowledge thus both separated the workers and the intelligentsia and also made it possible for them to perceive each other and interact on the basis of invalid assumptions. The polarization between the people and the intelligentsia fostered by the regime had a similarly dual effect, for the intelligentsia's understanding of themselves as an isolated and superior elite brought forth a number of well-known counterreactions: guilt, the obligation to pay back an unbearable debt,[34] helplessness,[35] and the desire to fuse with the masses.[36] The intelligentsia's deep reverence for the people, or the workers, was rooted in this traditional sense of their isolation and impotence, their fear of being "superfluous." Although in part they wanted to be the fathers who would elevate the worker children to their historical role, the intelligentsia also saw themselves as children before the masses. "We 'intelligentsia,'" wrote one self-proclaimed critical thinker in a letter intercepted by the police, "are as insignificant before life as children when they have only their own strength. We are only strong when the popular wave pushes on behind us."[37] Perhaps these feelings of impotence and low self-esteem diminished with the rise of the labor movement and the emergence of a new role for at least part of the intelligentsia. But was there not, as Lunacharsky also said of Martov, something of the Hamlet in many of these idealists? It was precisely such vacillation and inability to act that made Lenin despise the classical intelligentsia and ask for men of a new type. And perhaps also this basic sense of impotence provided a psychological undergirding for the Marxists' faith in the masses.

Taken together, the preceding dimensions of cultural convergence provided a not insignificant basis for rapprochement between the intelligentsia and the workers. Even had this overlap of beliefs not existed, however, out of necessity the two groups would still have found each other. Under the autocracy the workers could not produce sufficient leaders and substantial enough organization on their own. Consequently, as Martov recognized,

> Russian Social Democrats did what in free countries is accomplished by the mass organizations of the workers themselves—the trade unions, which direct the economic struggle. With the absence in Russia of any labor unions, the Social Democratic organizations, secret and protected from police raids, were the only means of tying together the uncoordinated masses, of uniting them by means of general slogans and leading them in struggle.[38]

Similarly, the intelligentsia, small in number and without independent sources of influence and power in a mature civil society, desperately needed the workers, their only potential mass social base, to help them realize their goals and confirm their beliefs. All the major events of the Russian labor movement, from the 1896 textile strikes to the 1905 revolution and including February 1917, were not only initiated by the workers themselves but caught the intelligentsia by surprise, forcing their leaders to scurry home from their European sanctuaries. In the intelligentsia's post factum efforts to explain and control events, they were capable of drawing conclusions full of historical irony. Of the outbreak of the 1905 revolution, the result of a movement headed by a priest with only belated participation of the Marxist parties, Trotsky wrote, "We had waited for it; we had never doubted it. For long years it had been for us the only logical conclusion of our 'doctrine' which was mocked by nonentities of every political hue."[39] However poor the fit may have been between the doctrine and the movement, for those convinced that "the whole of history is an enormous machine in the service of our ideals,"[40] the irony was not apparent. Such was the dependence of the Marxist intelligentsia on a revolutionary proletariat that would fulfill its appointed historical mission that many simply failed to perceive the essential ambiguity of the worker-intelligentsia relationship.

THE EFFECTS OF CAPITALIST INDUSTRIALIZATION

Capitalist industrialization under Russian political conditions brought forth its own peculiar mix of cleavage and shared interests between the workers and the intelligentsia. The breakdown of old social ties and the new possibilities for collective action and identity produced by capitalism stimulated the workers to seek participation in modern society. Some workers, of course, had fairly limited aspirations for participation, such as more education, higher wages, or better jobs. Others had broader participatory aims, including equality of rights with other subjects of the tsar or even a sweeping expansion of rights toward full citizenship. Finally, a minority of workers had explicitly revolutionary goals—participation was a means to explode the present system and found a new social order. Whatever the differences, however, all of these aspirations were quickened by the pace of capitalist development in Russia.

These new strivings, rooted in the desire to participate more fully in a modern society, led workers to turn to the products, bearers, and often would-be transformers of modernity: the intelligentsia. In the Sunday school movement, workers' circles, or courses for popular education in the Zubatov societies the intelligentsia taught the workers to understand the world around them through literature, history, economics, or sociology. They taught them new concepts, such as citizen or class, which encouraged the workers to think of their place in society in novel ways, and the intelligentsia showed them how to organize in order to change both their place and the society as a whole.

For their part, many of the intelligentsia came to realize that under modern conditions social change could no longer be the work of a small minority. A section of the populist intelligentsia had accepted this axiom even in the 1860s and 1870s and had sought to mobilize the peasantry to remove the still-remaining bonds of oppression. With the Marxist movement, the main target of efforts for mobilization came to be the proletariat, whom the Marxist converts regarded as fellow bearers of modern values. And so the hopes of much of the intelligentsia came to center upon this outcast class of modern society, whom the intelligentsia promised to lead to a better world. It was not, then, that the Marxist intelligentsia brought to life a previously nonexistent labor movement *ex nihilo*. Plekhanov, in his attacks on Lenin after the Second Party Congress, recognized that he himself (like Marx and Engels in the West) had developed his ideas in response to a class movement that already existed.[41] As Akimov, an "economist" party intellectual and Lenin's gadfly, expressed it, "the embryo of the future workers' party was the mass labor movement. And the Russian Social Democratic Movement . . . was born in the large industrial centres, the centres of sociopolitical life, and its first attempt at organization was the Northern Union of [Russian] workers."[42] Thus just as the complex of changes linked to capitalist industrialization led workers to turn to the intelligentsia, so they also kindled in the intelligentsia faith in the importance and historic mission of the workers.

If, in Martov's formulation, in Russia the Social Democrats were obligated to do what in Europe could be done by the workers' organizations themselves, then this convergence of modernizing goals between workers and intelligentsia necessitated a relationship of dependency. The intelligentsia could not simply instruct or lay the theoretical basis for action; they also had to take on the roles of agitators, propagandists, organizers, and leaders. Dependency, in turn, led to resentment, and just as workers came to question hierarchy and subordination in the factory and the state, so they challenged it in the socialist movement, even though the workers' own aspirations made dependency inevitable. Paradoxically, the workers' resentment was stronger the more they accepted the logic of class analysis, taught to them by the Marxist intelligentsia, according to which the privileged intelligentsia could be assigned to some category of the exploiting class. (We saw examples of conscious workers' class analysis of the intelligentsia in the previous chapter.)

By contrast, in some Western countries the workers' desire for organization or political freedom led to an inherently self-limited role for intellectuals, whose success eventually made them dispensable. In Russia the changes brought by capitalist industrialization perpetuated both the need for intelligentsia guidance and the frustrated desire on the part of the workers to supersede it.

The intelligentsia sought to resolve this dilemma and counter the workers' resentment by means of two related justifications. First, they imported into their ideologies, whether Marxist or populist, the traditional intelligentsia emphasis on the special role of the enlightened elite. Russian Marxism was thus a curious blend of the traditional revolutionary culture and the more modern, and Western, stress on mass politics and mobilization. Indeed, in his extraordinary emphasis on the conscious elite and the will, Lenin's ideas embodied the traditional ethos of the intelligentsia, forged by its opposition to the state and its isolation from the people. If, however, Lenin was the most extreme example of this traditionalism, almost all Social Democrats—even the most deterministic—attributed a more independent role to the party than did their Western counterparts.[43] Plekhanov, that model of orthodoxy, declared that the revolutionary party in Russia could shorten the stage of the bourgeois revolution and thus partly modify the historical process. Even Axelrod, the Marxist leader most sympathetic to the mass movement and least cut off from the masses in his own personal history, acknowledged the leading role of the intelligentsia in the movement. The Group for the Emancipation of Labor, he declared, should be preserved "as an independent cell, which would stand guard over the revolutionary traditions and theoretical stability of the movement."[44] Similarly, in a letter to the Iskraites in 1901 he wrote that he was "infused with the awareness of your historical right to the leadership of our movement"[45]—this without regard to the opinion of other sectors of the intelligentsia or the mass base of the party. From this perspective Maoism is not nearly as distinct from Russian Marxism as is often maintained. Maurice Meisner, for example, makes a convincing case that Mao was basically a populist.[46] In its emphasis on the moral virtues of an elite, however, Russian Marxism also had many populist elements; the great difference lay in the Russians' much more restricted ability to lead and educate, a difference that had enormous implications for the outcomes of the revolutions.

Second, and also in line with their traditions, the Russian intelligentsia gave a special interpretation to the idea of "consciousness." For example, if orthodox schools of Marxism taught the dependent and even epiphenomenal nature of consciousness, Russian Marxists viewed it both moralistically and voluntaristically.[47] Consequently, Social Democracy had both the duty and capacity to develop in the proletariat a revolutionary consciousness to replace its "spontaneous" and primitive instincts. And if, as Lenin taught, consciousness was more important than class origin for membership in the party, and if consciousness itself could be introduced from above regardless of the stage of historical development, then the proletariat's dependency on the intelligentsia was justified by the historical process itself. Now, however, as opposed to orthodox Marxism of the time, the historical process could be decisively shaped by the intervention of consciousness. To the extent that workers accepted this view of consciousness as *deus ex machina*, their commitment to an alternative vision of modern society required submission to the leadership of those who were its bearers. In thus combining Marxist goals with a traditional Russian emphasis on elite consciousness, the intelligentsia justified a dependent role for the class that in theory was actively to transform history.

For some workers the ambivalent relationship to the intelligentsia born of capitalist industrialization and modernization could be resolved through such explanations. If the trajectory of tsarist society had been different, the tension might also have been diminished through liberalization of the regime, difficult as this clearly was. First, workers might eventually have won enough autonomy to dispense with intelligentsia tutelage altogether. Second, the intelligentsia, as an educated elite and as professionals, might have reconciled themselves to an honored place within civil society and so turned away from the revolutionary underground and participation in the labor movement. Indeed, this dual process was partly initiated in the post-1905 period, when worker activists sought greater independence from the intelligentsia and the intelligentsia abandoned the revolutionary movement in vast numbers.[48]

There was a marked asymmetry, however, in the possibilities for change for the two groups in the political conditions of post-1905 Russia.

Whereas much of the intelligentsia could, and did, successfully abandon the revolutionary movement in order to pursue careers in a rapidly industrializing Russia, the workers remained rightless, and so dependent, as before, on outside leadership. With the upsurge of labor unrest in 1912–1914, they looked for guidance to the Bolshevik party, which, far more than the Mensheviks, had remained faithful to the traditions of the underground—this despite the fact that the Bolsheviks had always been hostile to a workers' movement independent of party control, a key goal of many worker leaders. The experience of 1912–1914 thus displayed in microcosm the paradoxical consequences for the workers of capitalist industrialization in Tsarist Russia: the very desire for independence delivered workers into a new state of dependence in order to achieve their own goals. Much of the intelligentsia could, conversely, be welcomed back to society, and their departure was interpreted by many workers as betrayal. To the resentments already built up toward the intelligentsia during the process of autocratic capitalist industrialization was added this new indictment. Little wonder, then, that the workers should give their allegiance in 1917 to the party that they came to view as the most purely proletarian, for they felt isolated even from the majority of their former allies. In the eyes of large numbers of workers, the intelligentsia, having abandoned their role as a guiding elite, came to be nothing more than "burzhui."

CONCLUDING REMARKS

In the past three chapters we have seen that the mass workers, conscious workers, and intelligentsia were all truer to type than elsewhere in Europe, and we have traced this relative purity largely to the effects of autocracy. We have also noted that this specialization forced them to be interdependent, thus creating an ambivalent relationship of symbiosis and conflict. The overall pattern was both reinforced and made more complex by the effects of capitalist industrialization, which stimulated the emergence of a modern mass movement requiring cooperation and organization but which also gave rise to new cleavages and tensions. In addition, interdependence introduced new elements into the actions and consciousness of each group, as the unpredictable militancy of workers forced the intelligentsia to adapt their self-enclosed party work to the exigencies of a leaderless mass movement; and contact with the revolutionary intelligentsia deepened the familiarity of workers with socialist ideas that were not entirely foreign to their own implicit political standards. These new elements facilitated the rise of a patterned movement, but one also made up of heterogeneous and poorly coordinated segments. These underlying conditions created in the movement a peculiar rhythm. By comparison with Europe, it was much more uneven, either more quiescent or more incandescently militant. It was the former when its highly differentiated parts were isolated from one another, each feeling powerless to act on its own and regarding the others with suspicion. When the movement came to life, however, stimulated by general political ferment or government repression, each sector made its special contribution to a powerful revolutionary wave, which nonetheless could never culminate in a profound synthesis of the different elements. Different categories of workers and the intelligentsia remained strangers to each other, divided by discrepant priorities of which the others had little awareness.

CHAPTER
10

Labor and Organization

Legal worker organizations were never permitted to develop freely in late Tsarist Russia, and so the dream of an organized socialist labor movement could never be brought to life. The prophecies of many populists in the early 1890s were realized: it was futile to try to organize a broad labor movement in the conditions of tsarist autocracy. The conclusions that they drew from this analysis were wrong, however. They supposed that such efforts were only a waste of strength, that they could accomplish nothing and would cost innumerable sacrifices in human lives. It was first of all necessary to overthrow the autocracy, and only then should organizational tasks be broached.[1] In fact, in the conditions of capitalist industrialization under the autocracy, a distinctive pattern of organization emerged that had considerable potential for guiding and encouraging revolutionary action. It was precisely because the Russian pattern of organization departed from the European model that the Russian labor movement had such a revolutionary character.

Organization in the Russian labor movement emerged from two separate but partly interdependent sources. First there were the various kinds of worker organization that emerged largely in the strike struggle—informal leadership, strike funds, strike committees, factory committees, and local trade unions. In normal times these organizations were fundamentally local, sometimes not even transcending a particular workshop and rarely going beyond a single factory. In times of militant struggle their geographical limitations were sometimes extended and efforts were occasionally made to connect them with more extralocal organizations, such as industrial unions or soviets. At such times worker organizations came into contact with the second source of organization critical for the labor movement: those organizations that had their origins in the intelligentsia. Whereas the purer type of worker organization involved the mutual interaction of mass workers and conscious workers, the intelligentsia-inspired organizations brought together conscious workers and the intelligentsia. Mostly these were party organizations, but in times of upsurge in the labor movement, nonparty though still socialistically inclined organizations were also formed. (The key example is, of course, the soviets.) During normal times these party organizations were largely cut off from the mass of workers, but in periods of militancy the two kinds of organization came to overlap, just as local worker struggles became interconnected with national politics. The nature of the relations between the two types of organization—a high degree of separation resulting in inefficacy in normal times, complementary interpenetration in periods of militancy—follows the same basic pattern as the worker-intelligentsia relationship. The products of autocratic capitalism, both embodied differentiation, symbiosis, and unevenness.

The extreme differentiation of these patterns of organization, as well as the interrelations established between them in times of unrest, were determined by the state's prohibition of open worker organizations, particularly trade unions. The organizations' forms and activities were thus defined politically. Only in a relatively liberal political context is organization defined primarily by technology, as Shorter and Tilly argue was the case for France. Their threefold typology of craft unionism, spark plug unionism (weak locals and highly centralized organizations at the regional and national levels) and science sector organization (which combines the solidarity of craft unionism and the organizational sophistication of large-scale proletarian organizations) is of little relevance to Russia, because state policy prohibited the different groups of workers from developing their resources. As there was relatively little organizational differentiation among different types of workers, so there was not as much variation in their modes of struggle, which Shorter and Tilly trace mainly to patterns of organization. In both these respects the state overwhelmed the working classes' potential for internal fragmentation.

In this chapter I will begin by reviewing the various views on worker organization. Then I describe the "spontaneous" worker organizations, followed by a portrait of the party-related organizations. I then show how the confluence of these two patterns in times of unrest created a distinctive pattern of worker organization and political action which brought together mass workers, conscious workers, and the intelligentsia. At the same time, collective behavior and social movement characteristics supplemented each other, as did economic struggle and ideology. All of these were fused: only in a freer political context could these elements have been differentiated.

THE DEBATE OVER ORGANIZATION

Intelligentsias and bureaucracies are alike in that they both have a pre-dilection for control from above. From their very emergence the Russian Marxists preached the need for worker organization in order to realize their model of historical change. It took Russian bureaucrats longer to come to understand the potential benefits of organization for the sake of control from above, and political dilemmas defeated efforts in this direc-tion. In opposition to the historic tendencies of both the bureaucracy and the intelligentsia, after the turn of the century voices from both camps began to call for more independent worker organizations. The idea that workers might have their own legitimate goals realizable only through organization gained a degree of currency.

All of the various ideas about organization were intimately connected with views about the implications of industrialization and the desired speed and direction of social change. In this context worker organiza-tions could not arise simply out of the needs of the workers as a "natu-ral" phenomenon under capitalism, for in fact the nature and desirability of organization were from the start a highly political issue. Nor could organizations develop relatively smoothly out of roots in precapitalist society, as they did in many countries, for there were few such roots. Thus in Russia the creation of organizations meant innovation and also political and ideological polarization. In the end the pattern of organiza-tion that emerged corresponded to the preferences of almost no one.

Perhaps the purest statement of a traditionalist bureaucratic view of the need for organization came from Plehve. In his intervention before the State Council, we recall, he expressed his sympathy for the economic complaints of the workers and declared that some form of worker orga-nization was necessary to make sure they were satisfied. Taking as his model the hierarchical organization of an army, he cited the great organi-zational successes of Napoleon. The tsarist government, however, never approached Plehve's vision of an organized worker army subservient both to the capitalists and to the political authorities, for it made little sense in a capitalist economic system. It required the victory of socialism and the party to bring these ideas to life with infinitely more sophisticated organizational resources than were at the disposal of the tsarist state.

Unlike Plehve, Zubatov was willing to go a considerable distance in granting the workers rights of association as long as their organizations pursued economic goals. Such a separation between economics and poli-tics was the ideal of many bureaucrats and industrialists around 1905, but, as opposed to Zubatov, many felt that this could be best accom-plished without state interference. They hoped that free trade unions might lead to a nonpolitical workers' movement. They perceived that organization was not necessarily a weapon in the hands of militant workers but could also serve as a mechanism of control by worker moderates who had a stake in the established system. Such a view was virtually heretical in Tsarist Russia; and, as we have seen, when the test came, few among the elite were willing to stake much on these assumptions.

It does not appear that many workers shared this view of a nonpolitical trade unionism pursuing purely economic interests. There was, however, considerable sympathy for an independent trade union movement, one separate from the parties but still sharing broad socialist goals. Such a movement could work within the contours of existing institutions at the same time that the preconditions for socialism were taking shape. This model would have had many advantages for the government and industrialists. Class struggle would take moderate forms in the short term, with a decline in bunts and their supersession by calculated strikes. Worker leaders would be able to formulate rational demands, the only ones for which they would risk organizational resources, and there would be fixed mechanisms for negotiation and conflict resolution. In this context would it really have mattered that at some distant point the trade unionists still might struggle for socialism? Had not Bernstein himself proclaimed that whatever the ideology, in German Social Democracy socialism as an end was nothing, and reform as a means was everything? The key point was that many Russian worker leaders wanted to promote organizations that had as their immediate goal the improvement of the workers' economic position using legal means of struggle.

Just as most government officials and industrialists lacked sufficient trust that such class organizations would become nonpolitical, a major part of the revolutionary intelligentsia was convinced that left to themselves, exactly this would happen. The only common feature in these differing evaluations of trade unionism was distrust of worker "spontaneity"—especially in an organized form. Their predictions about the workers' behavior were otherwise perfectly contradictory.

It was not until 1905 that the Social Democrats had to define their position with respect to the beginnings of an independent class movement with its own organizations, primarily trade unions and soviets. Prior to this the only important stable organizations had been connected with the party. Strike committees and other independent organizations had always been, with few exceptions, local and ephemeral. Thus the Social Democrats were faced with a new ideological task for which their Marxist assumptions prepared them poorly, for classical Marxism does not make problematic the relationship between party and class organizations.

Of course, the party had already split over precisely this issue of organization, but in 1903 it was purely a question of party organization and its relationship to the mass of workers. Now the question of the party's stance toward the workers' class organizations emerged. Social Democrats just as much as tsarist bureaucrats were forced to confront the question of industrialization, which was bringing forth the elements of independent class action. And this was just as inconsistent with many of their time-worn assumptions as it was with those of the government. How did an organized class, no longer entirely a spontaneous mass (though it never was this in an absolute way), fit with its revolutionary blueprints? This problem was not unique to Russia. In France and Germany, too, socialism as a political force preceded the emergence of a strong trade union movement. Russia was in some respects unique, however, for class and party were in fact more interdependent than elsewhere. In contrast to Europe, the party could not look to a large public and a broader political arena for the promotion of its goals, and the workers' class organizations could not accumulate as many independent resources for struggle. This interpendence, combined with a considerable divergence of goals, at least in the short run, ensured that the debate over the emergence of a mass labor movement and its political implications would be stormy.

The Mensheviks and the Bolsheviks eventually came to opposite conclusions about how class organizations and the party should fit together, although it is less clear how much the two parties differed in practice.[2] The Mensheviks remained closer to the Marxist heritage in arguing that the inherent tendency of the labor movement was toward socialism. The party did not have to instill socialism into a mass for whom it was foreign. Through their own struggles and organizations workers would come to accept socialism as a goal. Trade unions, cultural societies, and cooperatives would all supplement the party in its revolutionary role. The revolution did not have to be created from outside, merely unleashed and guided. In this view all worker organizations promoted socialism as an end, for they gave the workers greater capacity and experience, and there was no danger that they would divert the workers' basic political goals.[3] The Mensheviks, like the liberal bureaucrats, saw the outlines of civil society emerging in Russia, a society in which social groups would have the capacity to act on their own. Also like the liberals, they were convinced that such independent action would be consistent with their own values, for the workers would mature through experience. There is a final similarity: for both liberals and Mensheviks, this trust could be vindicated only in the future, after a period of transition. For the time being, the workers were still "unconscious"—not all of the old ideological legacy could be abandoned at once.

The Bolshevik position was in many ways parallel to that of Minister Plehve. It also favored organization along the lines of an army, assuming that people or classes would go astray if left on their own. Strict discipline was practically impossible for nonparty organizations, however, and so the question arose as to whether the Bolsheviks should support them. Given their suspicion of class organizations, the Bolsheviks' choice was not difficult to predict: in 1905, often through rather crude methods, they tried to subordinate nonparty organizations to party control. It was not until after the Stolypin years that they developed a more sophisticated method, their use of the party cell, although Lenin had already worked out this tactic theoretically in *What Is to Be Done?* In thus subordinating class organizations to political control, the Bolsheviks hoped to infuse all organizations with party ideology as well. This was their method of reconciling underground work with an open social movement.

Despite their differences, all of these views assumed that greater organization of the labor movement was necessary. Seldom did the virtues of organization itself come into question. One exception is the book by E. Lozinskii, *Goals and Perspectives of the Labor Movement*, which was part of the political debate after the defeat of the 1905 revolution.[4] Lozinskii's is a peculiar book; its basically anarchist sympathies have the virtue of revealing much about the assumptions shared by all the other viewpoints. Lozinskii attacked both trade union and party organizations. He argued that both Zubatov and the Social Democrats wanted to channel the instinctive fury of the workers, and that the revolutionary parties were no less the workers' enemy than the bourgeoisie. Trade unions divided the workers, separating out a narrow elite and subjecting the workers' rage to rational calculation. Like Rosa Luxemburg, Lozinskii asserts that capitalism itself creates enough revolutionary energy to topple the political regime, not through explicitly political action but through everescalating class warfare. Political revolutions require not broad and permanent organizations but only two basic prerequisites: the appropriate mass mood and a sufficient number of secret revolutionary circles able to make use of this mood. This mass mood is neither narrowly economic nor political: it is militant, and so, without being self-conscious, both economic and political at the same time. Lozinskii opposes sophisticated political instruction, for ideologies only divide a class inherently antagonistic to the whole economic and political system. Thus he charges that socialist political propaganda is responsible for the creation of reactionary workers, for it injects ideology, and therefore division, into class conflict. If left without broad-scale organization and divisive ideologies, the labor movement would be able to explode the entire framework of Russian society.

Lozinskii's ideal, then, is a model of mass action undertaken by a class, a celebration of fervor above calculation. In many ways it is a better guide to the actual pattern of labor militancy in Russia than the ideas of either Bolsheviks or Mensheviks, for all Social Democrats saw political organization and control of different kinds as the key to the future of the labor movement. By contrast, Lozinskii welcomes the consequences of a lack of organizational control, including radicalism and solidarity. At the same time, however, Lozinskii does not consider another possibility: that in Russia the special pattern of organization that emerged under tsarism minimized control and fueled worker militancy because it corresponded to none of the models of organization outlined earlier, or to Lozinskii's own view of organization. Lozinskii read too much of Germany or England into his interpretation of the Russian experience, failing to understand the distinctive role of organization in Russia. Organizations, either at the local factory or the party level, did not serve to restrain worker militancy and atomize struggles, and only the beginnings of a narrow trade unionist consciousness could be observed. Rather, organizations themselves were infused with the spirit of class warfare so prized by Lozinskii. Let us examine the emergence of this peculiar pattern, which embodied a form of relationship between class and party completely at odds with the preconceptions of the intelligentsia.

THE HISTORICAL DEVELOPMENT OF GRASS-ROOTS WORKER ORGANIZATION

Some degree of organization is inherent in any kind of worker protest, for as social action it involves expectations oriented toward the behavior of others and a differentiation of roles. Even crowd behavior has its rudimentary patterns that take shape through interaction. Worker protest, no matter how simple and uninstitutionalized, always goes beyond crowd behavior, because there is a preexisting social relationship of some kind before the emergence of the protest—networks of friendship, prestige hierarchies of individuals and occupations, and the like. Thus well before the beginnings of modern industrialization, industrial workers in Russia organized delegations of petitioners to the tsar (or other political figures) for the redress of their complaints. Surely these delegates played leading roles in other kinds of worker protest as well, trying to introduce some degree of discipline into protest when it emerged.

Capitalist industrialization created the prerequisites for a qualitative change in industrial protest and worker leadership, for all the reasons that Marx and many others have listed. First, worker protest came to concern specifically industrial issues: wages, authority relations within the factory, the enforcement of rules, and so on. In Russia industrialization began to have these effects at about the end of the 1860s, the decade of the great reforms. Until then worker protest had remained limited, and most unrest was linked to peasant demands unfulfilled by the terms of the Emancipation decree.[5] Such preindustrial demands continued to be heard throughout the period of Russian industrialization, particularly in areas such as the Urals, where workers were more closely tied to the land. Industrialization, however, caused a significant shift toward demands connected with the workplace. The implications of this change could be seen in the 1869–1872 period, when the first unmistakable signs of major industrial unrest emerged in the post-Emancipation period. The first real industrial strike had occurred in Orekhovo-Zuevo in 1863, but in 1869 and 1870 there was a dramatic increase in the number and seriousness of strikes, some of which occurred in technologically advanced factories. When using the term *strike*, however, we should keep in mind that there was still no advanced planning, and the level of organization went no further than the selection of delegates for meetings with the administration or police. As opposed to later years, such committees of delegates were not even intended to be permanent.

Until the late 1890s the organization of protest remained rudimentary in the great majority of cases. There were certainly no permanent worker organizations; conscious workers at this time were a very isolated minority as compared to later periods; and contacts with the populist or Marxist revolutionary intelligentsia were sporadic. Thus worker organization meant the emergence of some degree of coherence in the strike struggle through the choice of deputies to negotiate with the administration or factory inspectors. This choice of worker representatives was quite unsystematic—it could certainly not amount to anything like an election. Neither was it completely arbitrary, for the workers pushed forward their boldest or most sophisticated fellow workers to be spokesmen.[6] The chosen leaders accepted their charge with some hesitation, for it was common for the government to blame strikes upon a minority of instigators and arrest them. It took great courage to accept the role of informal spokesman for the strikers, and often the first demand of the workers was immunity from arrest for their representatives. Such immunity, when granted, was rarely respected.[7]

In exceptional cases worker protest displayed more sophisticated organization, even in the decades before the great St. Petersburg textile strikes of 1896–1897. Thus at the end of the 1870s the first planned and organized strikes broke out in St. Petersburg, and they involved the intelligentsia and also conscious workers who had participated in populist study groups. The strike leadership self-consciously selected itself, and it had goals that transcended the aims of the immediate conflict. The conscious workers had their own independent organization, the Northern Union of Russian Workers, which, we recall, had a very strained relationship with the populist intelligentsia because of its emphasis on worker goals inspired by the German labor movement. The Northern Union nonetheless cooperated with the populist intelligentsia of Land and Freedom to stimulate unrest, help shape workers' demands and tactics, and attempt to spread the strikes to other factories. For example, in the second Novaia textile factory strike in early 1879, strike leaders issued a proclamation requesting the support of all the workers of St. Petersburg, urging them to take up collections for the strikers, and in turn pledging their assistance to others in need of help. The appeal was extremely successful, and in addition similar proclamations and threats of strikes appeared in other factories.

The Northern Union could not claim to be the first militant worker organization—this honor must go to the Union of Workers of South Russia (active in 1875)—but it was the first to take an active part in strikes, and it distinguished itself from the populist intelligentsia most sharply. The Northern Union insisted that its membership include only workers, and it modeled its program on ideas from German labor parties. This meant an emphasis upon political struggle and civil liberties as a necessary adjunct to social transformation, a linking of class goals to political change that would become increasingly characteristic of the Russian labor movement in the following decades. The Northern Union's membership was composed largely of advanced workers—especially metalworkers, who, along with their skills, had acquired a strong sense of dignity and a willingness to act when it was violated.[8]

Government repression quickly put an end to the Northern Union, as it did to the unprecedented wave of strikes in St. Petersburg in the 1878–1879 period. However, the changes experienced by the St. Petersburg workers—metalworkers and textile workers alike—foreshadowed the direction of the Russian labor movement toward organization and political goals. Further, with the emergence of experienced worker militants, still very small in number, the groundwork was prepared for the spread of these ideas to other parts of the country. Thus in the great Morozov strike of 1885, two workers formerly in contact with the Northern Union were able to transform what started as a typical bunt in a provincial factory into an organized strike, with fixed demands and strategy. The Morozov workers' demands also showed evidence of the spread of a new class consciousness. They sought legislative regulation over the relation between labor and capital in general, especially with respect to the levying of fines and changes in wages and working conditions. Their demands thus transcended the immediate issues of their own struggle in order to promote the interests of all industrial workers.

Until the late 1890s, however, such organization and planning were quite exceptional. In fact, up through 1917 much worker protest took the form more of bunts than of true strikes, although the relative weight of these types of protest changed dramatically. The limitations of the bunt as an effective means of worker protest are obvious. They involved much random violence and so called forth police repression. Further, the absence of preparatory agreements and preestablished organizations led to an absence of unity and constancy in the demands of the workers. New demands could arise at any time during the unrest, and this meant that it was sometimes harder for the owners to meet the workers' demands and put an end to the incident. The bunt was also a purely local affair, sometimes involving only a single workshop, and so the workers could not count on any broader support.

Some of these limitations were gradually superseded as workers became more experienced in struggle. Intelligentsia influence certainly contributed to this change, but it could not simply be reduced to outside forces, for there were also great changes in factory life itself that facilitated new forms of plant organization. The difference was noticeable primarily in the metalworking factories. Surh has suggested that the metal factories, much more than the textile factories, approximated an artisan style of work.[9] Huge though some of them might have been, they were organized into workshops, and many of them were less mechanized than the textile factories. They demanded skill, and the high degree of interaction promoted shop solidarity and the emergence of known leaders. The metal factories were also the points of concentration of conscious workers who had made contact with the intelligentsia and had had some schooling in ideology. It was often these conscious workers who became recognized leaders in the workshop or factory. They could occupy no formal leadership positions and often were isolated from the rest of the workers, but in times of disturbance the other workers naturally turned to them. Occasionally one man would achieve exceptional prestige in the factory and command the loyalty of all of its workers, particularly during strikes. Sometimes the authority of such a figure would extend to a whole factory district. For example, Garvi describes the railroad worker Vinogradov as "the soul of his district" in Moscow in 1905. An extremely thoughtful and curious man who had participated in the early Social Democratic study circles for workers, Vinogradov had spent much time in jail and in exile. He participated in party work but was suspicious of the intelligentsia and often remarked that "we are not small children who need to walk on puppet strings."[10]

Such informal but often fairly permanent factory leadership was not always composed of conscious revolutionary workers. Somov informs us that the recognized leaders of the huge Putilov factory in 1905 were older, more highly paid workers who participated enthusiastically in the Gapon movement. At first they were more conservative and suspicious of Social Democracy, but they became radicalized by the January 1905 events and became quite militant, even lamenting the apathy of the worker masses.[11] Even as late as 1917 such shifts in orientation of a few key worker leaders, or sometimes even a single man, could change the political complexion of a whole factory. Such a leadership pattern was a natural counterpart to the workers' lack of organization and their inability to develop more permanent loyalties and commitments based on experience.

In large industrial centers patterned relationships also emerged among factories. As the strike struggle matured, some workshops or factories gained the reputation of being leading centers of labor militancy, and they were able to wield great influence on the factories in the surrounding area. Already in 1895 the governor of Vladimir reported to Minister of Interior Durnovo that "it is impossible to deny that there exist very consistent relations among factories, and the workers of one factory know very well what occurs in another. Therefore, any form of disorder not punished with the necessary strictness must be considered an extremely infectious phenomenon."[12] Such ties became much more developed in later years, however, and they were especially pronounced in St. Petersburg. Metalworking plants, with their concentrations of conscious workers, were especially likely to become such leading factories, and within them it was often the most prestigious workshops that led the way. It was enough to hear that the lathe workers, for example, were out on strike for the contagion to spread to the boilermakers or metalsmith shop workers, and the news that the Putilov workers had thrown down their tools was often enough to stimulate unrest throughout the district.

This tendency toward broader territorial organization becomes all the more interesting when we recall the tendency for the workers to form self-enclosed identities based on their workshops and factories. Fights between workshops were frequent, and it could be dangerous for a worker to enter another plant without taking proper precautions. Perhaps such rivalries decreased over time, but intense group identities surely endured. Bonnell has demonstrated the strength of both craft and factory patriotism among the workers. She has also pointed out that these particularistic identities were accompanied by broader loyalties, including a sense of class solidarity.[13] How did this new pattern of organization emerge despite these formidable localistic identities? One explanation is that territory tends always to become a basis for social organization when more elaborate connections are difficult to develop. Thus Evans-Pritchard emphasized the territorial bases of solidarity among the Nuer, a tribe with an extremely undifferentiated social and political structure. The "ideological" affinities of kinship became assimilated to the reality of territory. In Russia in the virtual absence of functionally based organization, intercommunication depended upon propinquity. Whereas in the modern United States an auto worker in Detroit is more interdependent with an autoworker in Los Angeles than with a textile worker in Detroit, the opposite was the case in Russia. Thus territoriality, rooted in the relative absence of other kinds of organization, could overcome the various social bases of differentiation. The result was that local worker organization began to extend itself and acquire new dimensions.

The pattern of change often took the following form. The outbreak of unrest in a large "leading" workshop or factory changed the conditions of struggle in the local area. Conscious workers would begin to agitate in other enterprises, or perhaps enter into communication with other conscious workers in the district. Conscious workers from various factories might have known one another from participation in study circles or even underground revolutionary work, and such ties could become a catalyst for unrest throughout the area. With large numbers of workers already on strike, the opportunity costs for collective action also changed: the risk of arrest was less and chances for concessions were perceived to be greater. As experience in the strike struggle accumulated, these channels of communication and influence tended to become more standardized, thus facilitating joint action in the future. As we will see, eventually region became a critical basis for worker militancy, and it was largely this subtle form of organization that underlay and supported it.

Together with the growing sophistication of factory leadership and ties among leaders went the gradual maturation of organizational forms. It is important to emphasize the word "forms," for individual organizations could not survive long enough to become well established in Tsarist Russia, and yet organizational experience accumulated rapidly. There were legal mutual aid societies that existed for a long time, but they were not very widespread and played only a minor role in the labor movement.[14] The major kinds of worker organization emerged in times of struggle and had a short life because of arrests and persecution. Even in these cases, however, there was a major qualitative change. If in the 1870s committees of delegates were not meant to be permanent, this was no longer the case for many worker organizations after the mid-1890s. And even if the individual strike fund, factory committee, or trade union disappeared rather quickly, it could also be revived with astonishing speed. Such organizations thus developed some traits of permanency, although certainly not of strong institutions.

The first such semipermanent worker organizations to emerge were the strike committees, which had their first major development in the empire among Jewish workers in the northwest region and in Russia itself at the time of the great St. Petersburg textile strikes in 1896–1897.[15] Together with the Union of Struggle, an underground intelligentsia organization, numerous worker coordinating committees and strike funds emerged during the strikes and their aftermath. Workers themselves, rather than the intelligentsia, played the dominant part in agitation, and they collected funds for support of the strike, for aid to imprisoned strikers and their families, and for the purchase of illegal literature.[16]

These strike committees showed notable potential for further development, but it could not be realized under the prevailing political conditions. For example, in the 1896 St. Petersburg strike—the most important and organized one—about one hundred worker delegates from factories throughout the city met in a park in order to work out a set of common demands, which turned out to include the shortening of the workday from thirteen to ten and a half hours, higher wages, and regular wage payments. After formulating this agreement, the workers gave it to the Union of Struggle, which published it a few days later.[17] This meeting showed a potential for the development of organization on a citywide basis without the constraints imposed by narrow craft unions. Further, the territorial base of the organizations and their emergence in struggle put an accent on numbers and solidarity and so also militated against exclusivity. Finally, the conscious workers who initiated these efforts were schooled in ideas of proletarian class consciousness, and exclusive organizations with a prestige hierarchy would have been anathema to them.

It was not until 1906–1907 that this potential for broad-scale organization would be realized on any significant scale. In the meantime, in the following years a plethora of short-lived, often militant class organizations emerged in the major industrial centers. Sometimes these aimed at citywide representation, and often they were extremely hostile toward the intelligentsia, insisting on the need for worker independence and militancy in the class struggle. They were also the stronghold of worker economism, for they insisted that improvements in the workers' well-being should not be subordinated to abstract political considerations. None of these organizations was able to survive government persecution for long, however, and so they could not effectively challenge intelligentsia hegemony.

The emergence of more stable leadership and more developed organizational forms reshaped grass-roots worker protest in significant ways. One observer noted these changes in a late 1897 strike: "The patience with which the strikers restrained themselves and the decisiveness with which the first strikers stopped work reveals that this is no longer such a dark mass, but one organized association determined to defend its interests."[18] Strikes, even if illegal (until 1905, and in fact repressed thereafter) became more institutionalized: demands, such as for the eight-hour day or more humane treatment, became more standard and methods of struggle more controlled. Such changes allowed some strikes, at least, to have much greater scope and to be more tenacious. These long-term changes should not obscure the fact that Russian strikes inevitably had much of the bunt about them. Factory-level leaders were seldom in a position to resist mass pressure, and frequently they had no such desire. Nor, as we shall see, did the central soviets or trade union organizations that emerged during times of upheaval have much greater independence. Indeed, they made their own contributions to the revolutionary synthesis of the Russian labor movement.

This brief sketch of grass-roots worker organization suggests that in Russia, as in Europe, there was a long-term tendency toward organization of the class struggle on the local level. In Europe, however, local-level organizations gradually became subordinated to more inclusive organizations. In addition, they lost the effervescence born of direct action and territoriality, for they became subordinated to bureaucratic control and calculation. In Russia grass-roots organization acquired some capacity to shape struggles but little ability to control them; it expanded beyond the individual workshop or factory without losing its territorial base; and it became linked to more inclusive organizations without being subjected to them. Nor were worker organizations permitted enough stability to provide a framework for internal differentiation within the working class and the labor movement. The history of trade unionism in 1906–1907 shows that such tendencies might have been immanent within the Russian unions, but they were never allowed to develop to any significant degree. Local organizations thus continued to make their contribution to the overall radical organizational pattern of the Russian labor movement, a fact that was painfully evident to the tsarist authorities during periods of massive unrest.

PARTY ORGANIZATIONS

The other major form of organization in the Russian labor movement was the party organization, which ranged from emigré groups of ideologists and propagandists to local party workers' circles tied to an intelligentsia organization. Party organization in prerevolutionary Russia was beset by a basic contradiction: in theory, the Social Democrats sought to form a broad mass labor party, but in fact, except in times of ferment (to be discussed in the following section) they were restricted to conspiracy. Consequently there was an unbridgeable gap between the programmatic emphasis on worker participation and the real situation of closed, sectlike, schismatic cells unresponsive to initiative from below. Party organizations were thus generally isolated from the grass-roots worker organizations discussed in the previous section, although Social Democratic ideas still often had enormous authority because of the influence of conscious workers. Such a bifurcation between party and local worker organizations was unparalleled in the other major industrial countries of Europe.

Party leaders sought to create a powerful organization that would counteract the tendencies toward fragmentation and indiscipline in the labor movement. The party in its organization too was to be the bearer of consciousness. As a result there was great sensitivity to organizational issues, as witnessed by the party split between the Bolsheviks and Mensheviks. Appropriate organization was all the more important in Russia because of the complexity of Social Democracy's tasks and all the more difficult to realize because of the political conditions of Tsarist Russia.

Part of Lenin's program of centralized control was embodied in actual institutions—even, ironically, by the Mensheviks: local party organizations were highly undemocratic. Membership in the local committees was by co-optation from above, not by democratic choice of the rank and file. The consequence was intelligentsia control over local organizations. For example, Garvi describes the organizatioin of Odessa party organizations around 1900 in the following way. The lowest level was a craft worker or factory worker group. In each of these there was a mediator (usually a worker) designated from above. These worker leaders formed an "Agitational Assembly," a kind of worker party committee. In Odessa in this period there were two such agitational assemblies, one each for factory and craft workers. These assemblies conducted the party's practical work, including the recruitment of new members and the establishment of ties in new enterprises. To each of these agitational assemblies the Odessa Committee sent its own intelligentsia mediator for ties and leadership.[19]

In Odessa and elsewhere socialist workers universally complained about their lack of incorporation into the local party organizations and their domination by the intelligentsia. Sometimes the party leaders were able to defend themselves. Garvi recounts an interesting example. In 1901 discontent among the worker agitators had reached a high pitch. They demanded more independence of action, and their anger was not diminished but rather increased after the arrest of a large number of local party leaders in August 1901. The workers' concrete goal was the election of all local party organs. The intelligentsia leadership appealed to the requirements of conspiracy—the impossibility of risking the fate of the Odessa organization, and even those of other cities, on elections. The workers rejected these pleas as simply an expression of lack of trust in them. The intelligentsia prevailed, however, when several workers came under suspicion of being informers. Because of this the workers' agitation assembly permitted the local committee to continue co-opting its members. Such reconciliations could not end resentments, however. The Odessa workers' opposition later formed "Workers' Will," an independent worker organization, which had an unsuccessful history before adhering to the committee again in 1903.[20]

The party's lack of democratic practices was not always so easy to justify. The following incident strikingly illuminates the extremes to which such tendencies could go. In early 1905 in Moscow, the entire central committee of the party was arrested except for one member. According to the party constitution, their remaining member had the right to co-opt a new membership according to his own initiative. Thus the composition of the main Moscow party organization, with its many rights and powers, depended entirely upon him. This individual was torn between the two factions, and both courted him. The Bolsheviks finally won his favor, and so there was a complete switch in the policy of the central committee, which until then had been dominated by the Mensheviks.[21] This was not a provincial organization or a district cell but one of the most important party bodies in all of Russia!

In a letter to Axelrod in February 1906, Martov described other dimensions of this lack of worker participation in party affairs and deplored its consequences. Trying to explain the relatively high level of support for the Socialist Revolutionaries in St. Petersburg in recent duma elections for the workers' curia, Martov pointed to worker discontent with the party's organizational practices. He claimed that Social Democratic local leaders acted despotically and in a partisan manner. The masses were unable to protest such conduct by demanding responsibility from the leaders, but they did express their discontent in any other ways that presented themselves. He claimed that this, more than sympathy for the Socialist Revolutionary program or even discontent with factionalism, explained the party's disappointing showing.[22]

From Lenin's organizational plans and the lack of intraparty democracy the inference has sometimes been made that party organizations were hierarchically organized. Democracy was sacrificed for the sake of the "organizational weapon." It seems truer to say, however, that only with respect to the relations between intelligentsia and workers was there a clear hierarchy of command, and even this was weakened during periods of mass unrest when the party organizations lost control of their membership and abandoned their previous hypercentralism. Otherwise observers tend to emphasize the confusion and lack of coordination among party organizations. Rabinowitch has proved this point conclusively for the Bolsheviks in 1917, and it seems no less true in previous periods.[23] There were often a multiplicity of competing local party organs with completely independent activities. They were frequently cut off from the nominal centers of party authority—neither knew what the other was doing or thinking, particularly as the most authoritative party leaders worked abroad. For example, the Mensheviks in 1905 were nothing more than a "federation of district organizations." Each local organization did what it pleased and was only weakly tied to the center. They published their own leaflets and developed their own study programs, which were often quite different from one another. In large districts even separate subdistricts carried on their work independently.[24] The worker Petrov, a member of the Bolshevik Petrograd Committee during the war, remarks that his committee received no instructions from the Central Committee and its Bureau on basic policy questions, with the minor exception of chance information and literature. The committee had no choice but to act on its own initiative.[25] Such situations were undoubtedly typical given the conditions of party work in Russia.

The reasons for this fragmentation are not difficult to discover in the dangerous conditions of underground work and the importance of individual personalities in the revolutionary movement. Its consequences for the influence of Social Democracy among the masses were not entirely negative: such decentralization could lead to greater flexibility and responsiveness to the mass mood in times of greater unrest. It allowed for the at least temporary reincorporation of disillusioned conscious workers into the party. These advantages never reconciled party ideologists to the strategic chaos that atomization entailed, however. The ideal of the hierarchical party was even more strongly embraced because of betrayal by a recalcitrant reality. Spontaneity and consciousness were also at war within the party itself.

WORKER AND PARTY ORGANIZATIONS IN TIMES OF FERMENT

Because of political repression, grass-roots factory organizations and the socialist parties were normally rather isolated, even though the socialists often had broad, if vague, ideological influence and prestige. Such bifurcation damaged both parts of the labor movement, for it left factory-level organizations localized and ideologically helpless and party organizations politically impotent. In times of ferment, however, both types of organizations became active in the struggle and were able to establish connections with each other. And just as in times of tranquillity the disadvantages of both were paramount, so in times of ferment each type of organization made its own contribution to revolutionary militancy.

In periods of great ferment, particularly 1905, relationships among various social groups had to be negotiated anew, as did the relationship of all to the state. Similarly, the different parts of the labor movement and their organizational expressions had to recast their modes of interaction. Old institutional patterns were threatened and new ones began to take form. These new tendencies encountered both enthusiastic support and wary concern among the main actors involved. Never did the revolutionary intermezzo last long enough to provide the context for a permanent reshaping of relationships, however. The Russian labor movement remained as before: highly volatile, with periodically great revolutionary potential. The most visible sign of the beginnings of a different pattern of relationship between grass-roots workers and party organizations in times of ferment was the emergence of new institutions connecting the two in unprecedented ways. Such institutional creativity could already be discerned in the 1896–1897 strikes, when the Union of Struggle and various worker committees cooperated in guiding the course of the strike.

Clearly the best examples of new institutional linkages emerged in the period of the 1905 revolution. Trade union organizations, which flourished in 1906–1907 and, to a lesser extent, in 1912–1914, together with the shorter-lived soviets, provide the best illustration. On the local level unions drew upon all previous kinds of organizational experience. Many local unions had their origins in strike committees, others in preexisting informal leadership patterns. In St. Petersburg in March 1905 workers had been encouraged to elect deputies to participate in the deliberations of the Shidlovskii Commission, designed to investigate the problems and needs of the St. Petersburg workers. The commission itself was still-born, but the worker deputies later often played leading parts in starting soviets and trade unions. Although these origins were diverse, they generally had one trait in common: they emerged during the strike struggle, around which most of their activities centered.

The weakness of local union activities can easily be imagined. According to Bulkin, the St. Petersburg metalworkers union in 1906–1907 had delegates in factories but not local organizations. Delegates were elected only by union members and were often unknown or possessed little authority in the eyes of the rest of the workers.[26] The Society of Workers of Graphic Arts, a Moscow printers' union the life span of which was September 1906 to June 1907, had the opposite arrangement: the worker deputies to the central organization were elected by both union members and nonmembers.[27] In neither case was there the basic prerequisite of a well-institutionalized union organization: a fixed leadership with a defined relationship to a specific mass base. In such circumstances either the mass base or organizational integrity had to be sacrificed. The St. Petersburg metalworkers elected the former option; the Moscow printers, the latter.

These difficulties were accentuated by the confused organizational context. Union activists shared leadership in the strike struggle with members of the soviets, party activists, and informal leaders with no official responsibilities. The interrelations of these different representatives were largely undefined, and one can easily comprehend the bitter disputes over authority, often exacerbated by factional political struggles. Competition among rival potential leaders also favored the rise of the most militant, who could bid more effectively for the workers' support. In this context union activists might well have been able to act as individuals in bringing organization to the strike struggle, but they could not coordinate their actions with the policy of the union itself, for they were not protected from the pressure of mass demands by an authoritative organization. The tsarist state never allowed Russian trade union leaders enough time to strengthen their organizations through the establishment of authoritative union leadership, and local unions continued to bear the mark of their origins in the pressures of intense conflict. Trade unionism in Russia was important, not mainly for its actual achievements but largely because it suggested the potential viability of Western-style organization—a development that was cut short by government policy.

In addition to the rapid proliferation of local bodies, periods of upheaval witnessed the formation of central organizations seeking to unite the workers of a whole industry in a large area, such as the succession of Moscow printers' organizations or the St. Petersburg metalworkers' central unions.[28] In various degrees these organizations were founded and run with the help of party intelligentsia—particularly the Mensheviks, who tended to be less ambivalent about unions than the Bolsheviks—but the real flesh and bones of their leadership came from conscious workers. The relationship between the unions and the parties was far from simple. Both the Mensheviks and the Bolsheviks, but especially the latter, subordinated unionization to the preparation for an insurrection during 1905, and in any case they were suspicious of formally nonparty organizations. Many had observed the tendency of Western European unionism to create worker aristocracies, and so they feared that unions might divide the working class. Thus much of the revolutionary intelligentsia opposed cooperation in the formation of unions. Others, however, either out of enthusiasm or the resigned sense that if Social Democracy did not cooperate the unions would only be more narrowly economistic, made important contributions to the union movement.[29]

For their part, the conscious workers in the union movement were no less ambivalent toward intelligentsia guidance. Many bitter memories of both intelligentsia dominance and neglect lived on, and the commitment to worker independence was strong. In the end, however, the unions generally accepted intelligentsia organizational aid while at the same time declaring themselves to be nonparty organizations with a commitment to socialism.

The second important example of new institutional links were the soviets, which began to appear in the second half of 1905. They were the perfect expression of that fusion of elements—workers and intelligentsia, grass-roots and party organization—that characterized the Russian labor movement in periods of great militancy. About forty to fifty soviets were formed throughout the country's industrial cities and regions, though many were hardly distinguishable from temporary strike committees. By far the most important of these bodies was the St. Petersburg Soviet, formed at the time of the October general strike. Soon it became the most authoritative revolutionary voice among the workers. In the October strike it formulated the main demands, calling for the convocation of a constituent assembly, the creation of a democratic republic, and the introduction of an eight-hour day in all factories and workshops, all of these as preliminary steps to the establishment of socialism. In addition, during the strike the St. Petersburg Soviet took on various governmental functions, including supervision over the press and giving orders to the post office and railroads.[30] All of these activities, together with its democratic practices, gave the St. Petersburg Soviet immense authority in the eyes of the workers. In Trotsky's view its prestige stemmed from its role as an explicitly class organ: "The Soviet's task was not to transform itself into a parody of parliament, not to organize equal representation of the interests of different social groups, but to give unity to the revolutionary struggle of the proletariat."[31]

The soviets had certain advantages over the trade unions in guiding worker mobilization in 1905, although they also suffered from serious deficiencies. They were more clearly a territorial organization, and they did not require strong local organizations to be effective. They were more like a workers' parliament than a union, although clearly local worker deputies participated in the strike struggle. The authority of the soviet, however, depended upon worker recognition of its general quasi-governmental authority over a given region. Their primary purpose was not guidance of the day-to-day struggle of a given category of workers but the strategic direction of the movement. The weak link between soviet members in the factories and the central city or district soviets was not so detrimental, for like any parliament the soviets did not depend upon organization as much as recognized authority. Their field of operation was inherently less confined to individual factories, especially in the case of the St. Petersburg Soviet, which played a national political role.

Menshevik intelligentsia leaders played a decisive role in the creation of the St. Petersburg Soviet. From the beginning of the strike they had made efforts to form a workers' committee to guide the strike and channel it in the direction of an uprising. Their efforts met with great success, and on 13 October the Petersburg General Workers' Committee met for the first time, with forty worker deputies. Over the next nine days they met seven more times, and on 17 October the body was renamed the St. Petersburg Soviet of Workers' Deputies. By mid-November it had 562 deputies from 147 factories, 34 shops, and 16 trade unions.[32]

The Soviet was composed predominantly of worker representatives from the city's most militant metal plants, certainly a high proportion of them conscious workers, but it was largely led by an executive committee controlled by the revolutionary intelligentsia. It was thus the example par excellence of the organizational linkage of factory-level organization (indigenous worker leadership through elections) and party organizations. These new connections helped make possible new forms of action on a wider and more militant scale than ever before.

Conscious workers played the key role as mediators in this new relationship, as they were in contact with both the worker masses and the intelligentsia.[33] This role was not without its complexities. On one hand, they owed their leadership at the factory level largely to their ability to guide the strike struggle, and so they had to be responsive to the workers' immediate demands, which in 1905 were often very militant. On the other hand, many of the intelligentsia tried to instill in the worker leaders the primacy of the political struggle and the need for self-discipline and strategy. Fortunately for them this pressure was less pronounced than it might have been in normal times, for in 1905 the workers infected the intelligentsia with their own enthusiasm, and the worker masses became highly receptive to political goals. Nonetheless considerable tension was inherent in the very nature of the role.

In addition to these new organizational forms that partly transcended the old boundaries, during 1905 factory-level worker organization flourished as never before. Organization was basically a response to the needs of the strike struggle, and a variety of strike committees, factory committees, and unions emerged at the factory level. Leaders in these organizations had little autonomy, for virtually everything that Robert Michels pointed to as bases of differentiation between leaders and led was absent in Russia. In fact, the worker leaders' only claim to authority was their ability to guide strikes, and so they would have been quite incapable of renouncing this role, no matter what their personal wishes. Thus throughout 1905 militant demands were channeled through worker leaders to the major organizations, certainly not controlled by them at the grass-roots level. Such crucial episodes as the eight-hour day campaign in November and the Moscow uprising in December had their roots in the mood of the worker masses, to which both worker and intelligentsia leaders had no choice but to respond.

Thus worker activism, often the angry action of "masses," pushed the intelligentsia forward, and often heightened its mood as well. The interrelation between mass action and party strategy took extremely complicated forms. The St. Petersburg Soviet was formed to guide a strike that was already taking shape through the initiative of worker organizations responsive to the mood of their mass bases. The Soviet in turn stimulated the development of the strike. Later it appealed for a general strike in early November to protest government action in Kronstadt and Poland, but this call helped stimulate the workers to undertake a strike campaign for the eight-hour day, which the Soviet initially opposed but was forced to lead. In this complex interaction party leaders were led to undertake actions that they would earlier have condemned.

Sometimes the pace of mass events created an appearance of more strength than the movement in fact possessed. In the midst of massive ferment there was no accurate way for the intelligentsia to measure the correlation of forces. Sometimes the intelligentsia supported worker militancy out of resignation, combined with a refusal to appear to have abandoned the workers in a time of need. Thus in late 1905 in Moscow, Ermanskii discovered that his Menshevik friends, who formerly disdained the very idea of a planned armed uprising as too conspiratorial, had been caught up in the rhythm of the movement and now supported it. He claimed that he himself knew that the Moscow uprising would fail, but he felt he had no choice but to support it. "For me it was clear that there was only one thing [to do]: the wine is uncorked—it is necessary to drink it."[34]

The intelligentsia were thus forced partially to abandon their tendency to insulate themselves in closed organizations and to develop ideal visions of change cut off from the concrete realities of Russian politics. No longer could they continue to be Turgenev's impotent Hamlets in search of an identity. In the grip of change they too became swept up in spontaneity and lost some of their drive (and more of their ability) to master and control. Such movements called into question the basic historical traits of the intelligentsia.

Worker organization and worker activism were thus a partly independent factor in the labor movement, but they were not autonomous. For intelligentsia influence, particularly through the socialist parties, also transformed the nature of grass-roots worker activity. Despite their separation from the masses, socialist party activists through the years had accumulated much experience in building bridges to the spontaneous mass movement: they had many experienced agitators, they knew how to propagate ideas and clarify goals, and they were expert in the organization of strikes. Such activities did not require deep trust rooted in prolonged contact on the part of the masses, but merely a more temporary coincidence of goals. The intelligentsia also exercised their influence through the conscious workers, many of whom were active in organizations or at least in touch with those who were. Consequently some degree of discipline and coordination was achieved, though it was always tenuous. Both the impact and limitations of this control were evident in the November strike called by the St. Petersburg Soviet. The workers' initial response to the Soviet's appeal was overwhelming, partly because it coincided with the workers' economic discontent. A few days later, on 5 November, the Soviet leaders decided to call off the strike, and again, perhaps even more remarkably, the great majority of workers heeded their appeal. Shortly afterward, however, on their own initiative and against the better judgment of the Soviet leaders (though not of the socialist parties), the workers began their strike campaign to win an eight-hour day. The campaign was an utter rout for the workers, who had badly overestimated their own strength. There was even considerable opposition to the campaign from among the workers themselves, and the employers were intransigent. Soon afterward the Soviet leaders were arrested, an event that helped precipitate the calamitous Moscow uprising in December.[35]

So it was true, as Garvi claimed, that in 1905–1907 the socialists "quickly became oriented to the circumstances of thunder and storm" and were able "to embrace the broadest masses and to direct their spontaneous movement into a relatively organized channel."[36] This period witnessed the culmination of organizational life among the Russian workers before the revolution. The soviets were not to make their appearance again until 1917. The trade union movement never reached the height that it had achieved in 1905–1907.

Between 1912 and 1914 the trade union movement did experience a significant revival. These were years of industrial progress, unlike the pre-1905 period, which was characterized by economic decline. Workers took advantage of the upswing in industrial life to press forward with their economic claims; and perhaps this, together with the bitter experience of previous years and the diminished role of the party intelligentsia in the labor movement, explains the more pragmatic cast to worker struggles in this period. This more pronounced pragmatism was not accompanied by political moderation, however. In fact, Bolsheviks were far outstripping Mensheviks in support among the organized workers despite the Mensheviks' more explicit espousal of an open labor movement. The Mensheviks' more legalistic approach clashed too dramatically with continuing political repression to be convincing to many workers, and the Bolsheviks benefited from the participation of a number of effective worker activists in their ranks.[37] This modest revival of trade unionism, which demonstrated an unquenchable thirst for organization among the workers, also never gave rise to as much centralization as in the earlier period: the state was now more effective in preventing such a development. In recompense trade unionism, without serious organizational rivals and restricted in its scope, was perhaps able to develop more roots in the local factories than before. This tendency, if real, was soon to be cut short by renewed repression following the outbreak of war.

CONCLUDING REMARKS

Periods of mass ferment thus brought local worker organization and party organization together in new ways, in large part through stimulating the creation of novel organizational forms. In these periods local militancy and a degree of centralized direction strengthened each other. In addition, the mutual influence they exercised upon each other created the possibility of a transformation of both. In 1905 many of the self-enclosed party organizations were considerably opened up. Not all: some local party bodies attempted to continue to operate in secret using conspirational methods. For example, the leaders of the Narva district organization in St. Petersburg wanted to stick to circle work and were hesitant to participate in mass events, particularly out of fear that party members would be exposed. They played little role in strikes and tended to occupy themselves purely with party matters, not reaching out to the mass movement.[38] However, the new opportunities offered by worker militancy led to changed policies on the part of many party organizations.[39] Petukhov remarks that in Moscow "the revolutionary explosion was so strong that it was impossible to draw a border between members of the party and the ranks of non-party workers."[40] Somov complements his portrait of the Narva district organization with a completely opposing description of that of the Moscow Gate region of St. Petersburg. This organization consisted largely of workers recently recruited into the party who had not gone through a long period of preparatory work in circles. They had become mobilized in the process of the strike struggle itself. In turn, they sought to bring any active, influential worker into the party, regardless of ideological preparation—a policy that was formally illegal because new members were supposed to be chosen by the main intelligentsia figure in the district. This rule became a dead letter, however, as the organization acted quite independently and guided itself by the needs of the mass struggle. Following this policy the local party cell had enormous influence in the local plants, leading strikes and winning many concessions.[41]

These changes were forced upon many party organizations by "life itself," in the Russian expression. They signified the beginnings of an authentic mass labor party, an incipient transformation of old party practices. This new pattern raised the organizational question anew for the intelligentsia, and after 1905, as we shall see, there were numerous proposals to reorganize the party, particularly among the Mensheviks. As so often before, however, "life itself"—or, more prosaically, the autonomous development of social forces—was cut short by government policy.

Grass-roots labor organizations also underwent changes in times of mass unrest. The challenges in this case were different: to create authoritative leadership, to break out of the pattern of local action, and to link discontent with overall political strategy. Here, too, new beginnings were made, largely through the mediation of the new institutions discussed earlier. The isolation of individual shops and factories began to be broken down not only through joint participation in strikes but also through more comprehensive organizations. Conscious workers from different plants and districts could meet one another more freely, share ideas, and devise more general tactics. They could learn about the mood of workers in various sectors of industry and parts of the city. Potentially they could begin to make a reality their commitment to a "common worker family." Their challenge, in a sense, was the reverse of that facing the party organizations, which suffered at times from too much organization.

These new organizational patterns among the workers, however, were also not permitted to develop very far, in either length of time or degree of complexity. They were largely restricted to periods of militancy, and so the kind of discipline that they might have injected into the labor movement could only begin to show itself. Few in the government or among the industrialists were willing or able to see the tendencies toward moderation for the sake of self-interest. The old pattern of worker organization, with all its weaknesses and its potential for militant leadership in times of upsurge, was never really overcome, despite promising beginnings.

Either of the changes mentioned earlier would have had momentous implications for the structure of the Russian labor movement. The relations among mass workers, conscious workers, and intelligentsia would have been transformed, and gradually each group would have lost its distinctive features. The truly ideological intelligentsia would have declined in importance as the party became more responsive to a mass base and more committed to pragmatic aims. Worker organizations most probably would have developed in the direction of those of Western Europe, toward centralized bureaucracies with a cautious attitude toward change and a great gap between leaders and led. Because neither of these parallel sets of changes went very far, however, the pattern of Russian labor organization remained revolutionary in a special sense, one that did not correspond to the ideals of either the Mensheviks or the Bolsheviks.

What, then, was the essence of this revolutionary pattern of organization? Essentially it synthesized many of the advantages of localism and a degree of centralism without incorporating their drawbacks. On the local level organization was characterized by territoriality, slight separation between leaders and led, and little institutional autonomy from the mass base. All of these traits made organization a channel for expressing mass discontent, not a means for containing it. Central organizations also supplemented, rather than restrained, the autonomy of local organizations. They could not discipline and control them through formal channels of authority, but they could help the local organizations break out of their isolation and give them a sense of their great power through numbers. The central groups could also give a more inclusive meaning to the workers' local struggles by locating them as part of the overall battle for socialism. Such ideological labeling of what could have been regarded as no more than localized class conflict expanded the time frame of worker action and imbued many workers with a sense of historical mission.

In Russia this pattern of organization was not so much willed as it was the unintended consequence of tsarist policy. It bears a striking resemblance to the consciously chosen organizational structure of the Spanish anarchists, however, another archetypal example of a mass revolutionary movement. The Spanish anarchist leaders after World War I confronted the same dilemmas as the Russian Social Democrats: they wanted to transform their party into a mass organization, but they also wanted to maintain its revolutionary purity. Previous experience had also made them suspicious of trade unionism because of its narrowness and tendency toward reformism. They themselves were committed not simply to the mass strike (as were the French anarchosyndicalists) but to the revolutionary uprising, for which mass revolutionary militancy was a prerequisite. Their programmatic solution to this dilemma was entirely different from Lenin's theory but approximated the actual organization of the Russian labor movement. Lenin sought to keep party and class separate but to organize the party so that it could mobilize and control the class. The Spanish anarchists chose to organize the party as a mass movement that would embody revolutionary elan. In important congresses in 1918 and 1919 they decided to organize unions on a territorial (not craft) basis and to eliminate union dues and paid union officials. They also refused to promote organizational centralization, preferring loose organizational links and much local autonomy. Yet there was enough central direction to permit the organization of numerous general strikes and uprisings, which generated great revolutionary enthusiasm. This central strategic guidance depended on the prestige of the National Workers' Central (CNT) leadership and not its organizational leverage. The CNT made use of, rather than stifled, local revolutionary initiative.[42]

Such a pattern of revolutionary organization is not effective for the indoctrination of masses or the initial creation of a revolutionary mood. It cannot so much initiate as further stimulate and channel militancy; it cannot so much control as orient. It depends on the prior existence of a volatile mass mood, which in postwar Spain was created by economic hardship and the international political climate. Given these prerequisites, however, it is most effective in sustaining the revolutionary temper and giving it organized expression, for links between local militancy and central control are established without sacrificing the advantages of either level of organization to the other.

Leninist theory and the organization of Spanish anarchism contrast with a pattern of revolutionary organization that was impossible in Russia: the model of the revolutionary army as developed in Maoism and in South Vietnam by the National Liberation Front. In this case revolutionary leaders exercise more complete control over the mass base and have the power to instill revolutionary values and discipline. With the ability to transform values and institutions and so completely reshape the participants' worlds, this latter kind of organization is highly effective in creating revolutionary situations. It can only develop in a context of civil war, however, in which the revolutionaries control territory, create elements of a new state, and have the power to make use of particularistic loyalties to family or place by integrating them into their movement.[43] In other situations organization is more porous and the ties between leadership and the mass base less definite. Revolutionary action depends upon a more subtle interaction between party and masses and a looser organizational structure. Spanish anarchism and the Russian labor movement both exemplify this complex organizational synthesis of grass-roots organization and centralized political leadership.

Neither the Mensheviks nor the Bolsheviks were satisfied with this pattern of organization. Lenin, committed to making use of spontaneity rather than to transforming it, wanted to strengthen party control through the conversion of the Bolsheviks into a "party of the new type."[44] The union he envisioned of party control and mass activism depended on the continued immaturity of the workers as a class.[45] The Mensheviks tended to welcome the new tendencies among the working class toward organization and consciousness, as embodied after 1905 in the rise of trade union activists and other authentic worker leaders. They argued that it was time for intelligentsia hegemony over the workers to end, and for the party to be transformed into a mass workers' party in more than name. In their proposals for a workers' congress or workers' self-government, Axelrod and Martov sought to overturn the bifurcation of factory-level worker organization and the party that characterized the past. They argued that the revolution was developing within the proletariat itself, that it was only a matter of the self-development of the labor movement's own inherent energies. As Martov wrote in *Iskra* on 27 January 1908, the task was "not so much to 'organize' a people's revolution as to 'unleash' one. The revolution existed already potentially in the thoughts and feelings of the broad masses of the people. It required only to be given an outlet into an open movement, to realize it."[46]

The Menshevik leaders' position left many questions unanswered. Could Russia avoid the split between party and trade unions evident in Germany? Could the trade unions go beyond the relatively narrow interests of their own members? Was organization compatible with the masses' revolutionary enthusiasm? Lenin, ever distrustful, was dubious on these points. Historically the question is moot, but for many of the most committed workers, the tsarist government suggested another answer. Confronted by repression of even moderate tendencies, they concluded that the Mensheviks' emphasis on open struggle and the modification (though not abandonment) of conspiracy was either foolishness or cowardice. The Mensheviks lost support even among those to whom they wanted to pass the mantle. The old model of organization was never superseded in practice, even if no one embraced it theoretically. It was not superseded, that is, until after the October Revolution, when Lenin's party transformed the uneasy relations between grass-roots and party organization that had existed before.

CHAPTER
11

Solidarity

The nature and sources of solidarity
have been classic themes of sociology, arising, as did sociology itself, in a
period in which older forms of solidarity and community had lost much
of their authority. The cohesion of modern society had become problematic, both in social life and, in a reflected way, in social theory. Social
thinkers as diverse as Marx and Durkheim sought to understand the
changes that had come about and to lay bare the sources of conflict and
cohesion in modern society.

The major unit of analysis was society as a whole. The classic formulation was Durkheim's: whereas solidarity in simpler societies had been
based upon mechanical likeness and common values, in modern society it
was based upon interdependence and the division of labor, buttressed by
new kinds of shared norms legitimating individualism. Other thinkers
offered related schema. In this case as well, many Russian thinkers
followed the European trend. For example, Russian populist Lavrov
distinguished among the unconscious solidarity of custom, emotional
solidarity based on uncritical impulses, and "conscious historical solidarity" based on common efforts to pursue rationally chosen goals.[1] For
Lavrov, as for Durkheim, solidarity in modern societies was of a higher
kind, more powerful in its capacity to bind, more closely connected to
freedom and choice.

The nineteenth century witnessed the emergence of social movements
on a new scale, partly because of the decline of old forms of solidarity.
With respect to them, too, the question of solidarity was posed but with
an added dimension: under what conditions will people act together in
the pursuit of common goals in conflict with other groups? For Marx it
was largely a matter of mechanical solidarity: shared positions in the
relations of production would lead to the emergence of a solidary community willing to struggle for social revolution. Lenin was more in the
tradition of Lavrov, for whom solidarity emerged in the community of

"critically thinking individuals," which, for Lenin, was the party. Consciousness and will replaced Marx's natural community.

Solidarity in nineteenth-century Western European working classes underwent an important transition, one unanticipated by Marx and deeply disturbing to Lenin to the extent that he appreciated it.[2] In the early period of industrialization solidarity among workers was of a mechanical kind, rooted in the local workshop and based on common craft identities supported by guilds or similar organizations. The sense of community within a craft or shop was often very strong, but these loyalties were narrow, local, and exclusive. They provided little basis for the development of a broader class identity. Worker struggles could evince intense commitment, and workers could endure great deprivation for the sake of solidarity, but such struggles were small in scope and unconnected with broader class issues.

This model fits craft workers and skilled artisans better than textile workers, for the greater mechanization of textile factories, with the relative homogeneity of the labor force, already prefigured a new pattern. The rise of mechanization and the decline of artisan skills created the basis for a broader solidarity and more extensive organization. "Here, no borders, no hierarchies."[3] Shared ideas and feelings could diffuse throughout the factory, or even the district, because there were fewer barriers or privileges. Thus whereas in France metalworkers were characterized by a narrow particularism and strikes remained within an establishment and often only in a particular workshop, textile workers had a broader identity, and their struggles were less bounded geographically and by profession.[4] With the deepening of industrialization, the new pattern came increasingly to predominate. It was accompanied by organizational changes: no longer the guild, with its localism and particularism, but the trade union, extending ever wider geographically and functionally, was the basic institution. The intensity of solidarity declined, but its scope increased. Solidary action was less rooted in the norms of a cohesive community and more and more in the rational response to calls for joint action by broad representative bodies. Class solidarity was now more real than it had been before—there was nothing in the nineteenth century to equal the general strikes in Britain in 1926 or in France in 1936—but it was based less on an inclusive identity. It was also more subject to calculation and rationality, mediated as it was by bureaucratized organizations.[5]

Solidarity in the Russian labor movement never became transformed in this way. In the early period of industrialization solidarity was rooted to a much lesser degree in craft and guild traditions. Later it was less mediated by broad representative organizations. Ironically, the cause of the departure from the European model was the same in both cases: the lesser autonomy of social groups, with the slighter possibilities for their organized self-expression.[6] Solidarity of neither the guild nor the trade union type could flourish in Russia. The social and political conditions of Tsarist Russia facilitated the emergence of a very different, and in many ways more explosive, pattern of solidarity, one rooted in the special structure of the Russian labor movement and its distinctive mode of organization. Solidarity in the Russian labor movement had a strong local basis in the factories during episodes of collective action, which recapitulated something of the intense solidarity of crafts struggle in Europe, though for very different reasons. It also had the capacity to extend outward to other factories, districts, cities, and even nationwide without sacrificing this intensity. This synthesis was not without its costs, however, just as the transition between crafts-type and trade union-type solidarity had its trade-offs. In Russia the cost was the great unevenness and unpredictability of worker solidarity.

THE LOCAL BASES OF SOLIDARITY

In Russia solidarity at the plant level could not be based upon a homogeneous and cohesive community. There were too many social differences among the workers, particularly the gap between workers of rural and urban origin and those rooted in different levels of skill. There were also too few means of communication to bridge these gaps. And the relative absence of organizations impeded the growth of a communal consciousness, for shared symbols and traditions could not be born and nurtured through the resources of organized action.

Because of these impediments arising from the autocratic regime, in Russia worker solidarity did not so much precede and promote collective action as emerge from it. The act was primary, but emerging out of a relative void, it in turn engendered new conditions that led to its own transformation. Collective action had a developmental dynamism that made its end point very different from its beginning in ways that few would have predicted.

The beginning of collective action was usually unplanned, its impetus often an event that unleashed anger and the desire for vengeance. Even what later came to be great strikes often began as such bunts. If they were initially successful, they created an atmosphere propitious for the further development of collective action. The workshop or factory might be taken over and thus opened up to mass meetings and demonstrations. In such circumstances an extraordinary atmosphere of danger, challenge, and exhilaration could emerge. Contagion, persuasion, and force in different modes and combinations could operate in this new environment in which the old rules had already been broken.

First let us address contagion. The initial break in routine and the challenge to the authority structure could embolden previously passive workers, for if others were already involved, the risk to new participants was now perceived to be less. And nonparticipation might be a mark of shame, showing lack of courage. Matters of principle—Was the strike justified? Should the uncommitted worker line up behind avowed socialists?—receded in importance. The atmosphere of ferment had its own logic. Plekhanov successfully depicted this mood in his description of an encounter between a worker and a member of the intelligentsia during the 1878 Novaia strike in St. Petersburg. At the height of the strike, Ivan, an energetic and bold worker with a passion for showing off, arrived at the apartment of the intelligentsia leader Gobbst. He announced to one of the revolutionaries: "'Petr Petrovich, it's necessary to make a public appearance!' 'What kind of public appearance?' 'Well, to go out on the street, to look at the people, to show ourselves. The people are getting bored!'" The two went out on the street, and spectators witnessed the following scene:

> Hundreds of strikers covered the embankment, forming a solid wall along it. In front of this wall, slowly and triumphantly, Petr Petrovich marched, and behind him, at some distance, Ivan went forward, having slightly turned his humbly bowed head to the side, as if to have at least one ear closer to the authorities, and no orders were uttered. Everywhere where this amazing pair passed, the workers took off their hats, politely bowing and making various approving remarks about them. "There they are, our eagles, they're stirring!", affectionately exclaimed one old worker several steps away from me [Plekhanov]. Those around him were silent, but it was evident that the appearance of the "eagles" gave them great satisfaction.

Plekhanov remarks that Ivan's act showed a true understanding of the mood of the masses, for "the 'people' really were 'bored' without the revolutionaries. They felt more cheerful and more bold in their presence."[7]

New possibilities for persuasion also emerged. The workshop and perhaps the factories and the streets became worker territory. New ideas could circulate and ferment within the festive atmosphere of challenged authority. Conscious workers now had the opportunity to make speeches to stir the enthusiasm and raise the militancy of the masses. Mass meetings had their own logic, encouraging ardor and unanimity. Resolutions were formulated and decisions made by universal acclaim.[8] Persuasion shaded imperceptibly into coercion, the coercion of mass enthusiasm.

The militant workers temporarily in control had the power to use force to ensure solidarity. This was frequently the government's explanation for the solidarity of large strikes: a small group of instigators intimidated the unwilling mass of workers into obeying their commands.[9] And this was frequently the case, though rarely the full story. On 8 December 1905 a group of outside workers wrote to factory owner G. Rops that his workers were guilty of reactionary views and that decisive measures with respect to them were necessary. They threatened that if his workers did not adhere to the general strike by 9 December at 12:00, there would be a boycott and further repressive action against them.[10] One of the most effective weapons was public shaming. Worker S. Balashov, describing Ivanovo-Voznesensk in 1905, gives us an idea of the strength of this punishment: "In a word, this was the military proletarian camp, with its leadership and its discipline, for the infringement of which people were subject to strict punishment: putting them forward on the tribune before the whole mass and the clarification of the misdeeds committed. Such a punishment was considered very severe, and everyone feared, like fire, public denunciation before the mass."[11]

Underlying this collective solidarity were a number of deeper conditions that transcended the enthusiasm of the moment. First there was the hostility shared by mass and conscious workers alike toward private property and the authority of the industrialists. Even though the bases of these sentiments were somewhat different, they buttressed common action. For example, the anticapitalist sentiment arising out of autocratic traditions was one of the causes of the 1896 textile strike. Recall that according to Witte's report of July 1896, the strike had been preceded by rumors that on the day of the coronation the tsar would proclaim the shortening of the workday, thus giving Social Democratic agitators an entree.[12] Similarly, the Gapon orators, with the strong religious tone of their views, initially looked upon the Social Democrats with suspicion but soon saw that their views were similar and began to depend on the Marxists for their ideas.[13] Of course, both Marxist and traditional religious ideas of community alone could provide an underpinning for solidarity. The strength of shared religious sentiment is evident in the Northern Union (an explicitly revolutionary organization) as well as in the Gapon movement, and references to it occasionally crop up in descriptions of strikes. For example, in Vladimir in 1898 striking workers asked the local priest to say a prayer for them and also to take their oath to stand together until they reached their goals. The priest performed the first but refused the second, so instead of taking an oath, the workers kissed the cross.[14]

Collective action, even supported by larger ideological images of solidarity, might have become fragmented had it not been for the peculiar institutional features of the Russian labor movement. There were no particularistic organizations to channel action along narrow paths. Commitments to political parties were seldom divisive, for there were few worker adherents of the right or center parties, and the workers understood the differences among the Socialist Revolutionaries, the Mensheviks, and the Bolsheviks—if they understood them at all—in a nonsectarian way.[15] Further, as opposed to countries such as Germany or Brazil, the government had done almost nothing to create cleavages among the workers by introducing exclusive corporate privileges for different categories.[16] Consequently collective action, highly infectious at the grass roots, was less likely to become diluted by more narrow loyalties.

As the strike developed new elements were introduced that could also increase local solidarity. Although conscious workers, the intelligentsia, and organizations may have had little impact on the emergence of the strike, their participation in it could significantly shape its development.[17] In large factories conscious workers, with their ties to comrades in other workshops, could help break down the isolation of these often self-contained units. Further, the authority enjoyed by both conscious workers and the intelligentsia, stemming from their greater political experience and self-confidence, permitted them to promote the ideas of unity and solidarity, one of the major themes of Social Democratic agitation. The workers, declared the Workers' Committee of the Kiev Union of Struggle in late 1897, "have one powerful resource—union. While each worker seeks some kind of concession in isolation, then they will not begin to listen to him. . . . The more developed, intelligent, and conscious the workers, the better they understand that they must unite and stand together all for one and one for all."[18] In addition, they frequently emphasized goals common to all workers and not just certain categories—the eight-hour day and political liberties, for example.

This generalization of demands through the agency of the conscious workers and the intelligentsia could be observed already in the early years of the labor movement in the Morozov strike, which began without specific grievances and ended with formal demands for the government to regulate the labor contract in general. The Morozov strike also shows that these shared demands often emerged during the struggle itself. In the same way, in St. Petersburg in 1905 conscious workers "made heroic efforts to develop in the masses the sense of solidarity."[19] Similarly, conscious workers and the intelligentsia often supplemented these general goals with calls to struggle especially for the improvement of the wages of the "black workers," thus appealing to an overall sense of solidarity even when focusing on the needs of one particular category. In all these ways the conscious workers and intelligentsia reinforced the tendencies toward solidarity inherent in the dynamics of the mass movement itself.

A brief account of two renowned examples, the Obukhov defense and the Gapon movement, can serve to illustrate the interaction of these forces and tendencies at the local level in the Russian labor movement.

The Obukhov factory around the turn of the century was an important state-owned armaments factory under the administration of the Navy Department.[20] Located in the outskirts of St. Petersburg, it had a labor force of about 6,000. As was typical of large metal plants, it was divided into many workshops, which constituted self-contained worlds largely isolated from one another. Working conditions and wages were comparatively good, though they varied greatly by skill and workshop. There was an important sector of privileged workers who had been with the factory a number of years and benefited from state-supplied housing and other advantages. Agitation among them, and among a great many of the factory's workers, encountered severe obstacles.

Nonetheless, by 1901 workers' circles existed and underground literature was available in almost all the workshops. There had been a celebration of May Day that year, an event that provided the immediate context for the "defense." At a meeting of various members of workers' circles on 7 May it was decided to stop the factory after lunchtime in protest over reprisals against workers who had participated in the May Day events. Shortly after the lunch whistle the agitators assembled at the factory gate and tried to delay the workers' return by various pretexts and diversions, but they did not immediately communicate their ultimate purposes. They managed to gather a crowd of two or three hundred workers, who began to demand the arrival of the military authorities in the plant. A delegation was sent, and meanwhile members of their organization carried on agitation among the crowd, encouraging the fearful and calling on people to be staunch. Five or six of the activists began to compose a list of demands. For Shotman, a worker leader in the events, the belatedness of this action showed "to what extent we were unprepared for the strike which was gushing over us."[21]

The delegation returned with Colonel Ivanov, to whom the demands were read. The workers demanded the attention of the head authority in the factory, General Vlas'ev; Ivanov returned with him shortly afterward. Meanwhile, the activists attempted to stop work in the gun-carriage workshop. When Vlas'ev appeared in full parade uniform, however, many workers abandoned the struggle out of respect and fear. Only thirty or forty workers remained, and they too soon had to disperse after unsuccessful discussion with the general.

Shotman returned to his own workshop, the target of mocking and hostile glances. He, along with a few other workers, refused to return to his bench and renew work. Despite the outward antagonism, he detected considerable sympathy among the workers, but it seemed that the efforts to orchestrate a strike had failed. He prepared to go home and await the next day's dismissal or his arrest.

Then shouts were heard, and Shotman went to the window and saw that the strike had begun. Workers in the gun-carriage workshop had been able to stop work in their own workshop and had gone to other shops in order to broaden the struggle. Shotman and his supporters began to shout and threatened those workers who did not stop work willingly. What was now a large crowd went toward the gun-carriage workshop. The leader was a man named Iunikov: "Tall and well-built, with shining light blue eyes and wind-tossed blond curls, in rolled-up sleeves and with an enormous stick in his hand, he was inexpressibly beautiful at that moment, and unintentionally attracted the crowd behind him."[22] Work in all the workshops was halted, and a crowd of about 6,000 workers poured through the gates. They were met by about twenty police, who were completely helpless, and the chief of police was beaten. The workers went home triumphantly after stopping work at a large neighboring factory.

The leaders of the strike had little idea of what to do next. Throughout all these events there had been no participation of the intelligentsia or ties to any central organizations. Ideas would have been of little avail, however, for events continued to develop with their own momentum. Later that day Shotman joined a large crowd on the way to Shlissel'burg Road. There they met columns of police on foot and horseback. Crowds of strikers as well as women from a nearby factory walked up and down the street. Subjected to insults from the workers and after one of their number had been struck, the police lost patience. They charged the workers near the railway barriers, then the strolling public. The public panicked and many fled, but a number of workers defended themselves against the police by throwing cobblestones. The police opened fire with revolvers, and the workers continued to defend themselves. "Together with me," remarked Shotman, "fought my old friend A. Shul'ts, who kept right up with me in throwing stones—this man who only a year ago cursed me as a fool and an idiot for reading and distributing illegal literature."[23] The battle continued; the workers seemed to have the upper hand until the police were reinforced by about forty sailors, before whom the workers had to retreat.

In all, the "defense" lasted about three hours, from six until nine o'clock in the evening. Only three workers were wounded. Skirmishes occurred later that night, and soldiers and police entered many worker quarters, breaking and stealing household possessions. There were numerous arrests, which continued throughout the next day and night.

Despite their defense, reputed to be the first case of armed worker resistance to the authorities in the era of modern industry, the bunt-strike accomplished nothing. Many workers were stunned by the violence and the arrests, and the mood was one of depression. Older workers turned particularly hostile toward the instigators. Shotman continued to work in his workshop for a few weeks, but threats from other workers and fear of arrest led him to leave the factory.

The Obukhov defense became a legendary episode in the labor movement, part of the heroic tradition of resistance to the government. And yet in its genesis and progress there was little "consciousness." Conscious workers did create the atmosphere that eventually gave birth to the violence, but their activities were only tenuously connected to the actual events, which had a momentum of their own. Further, there was little plan or purpose, and even the list of demands belatedly drawn up played no role in the defense. Solidarity was a function of the logic of mass action, and there were no organizations, such as trade unions, to channel it in other directions. The social structure of the factory, with its hierarchy and inequalities, was also of little significance for the course of events, nor were the individual psychologies of the workers crucial. Conservative shops and workers were for the moment on strike as much as the militants. Workers like Iunikov, with his shining blue eyes and enormous stick, and the police, armed and afraid, set the tone.

The Gapon movement, which culminated in Bloody Sunday, was in many ways quite different, demonstrating the potential for the extension of solidarity in the Russian labor movement. Conscious workers had played an important part in the leadership of the Assembly for several months, and in the period immediately preceding 9 January the Marxist intelligentsia had begun to play an increasing role. Gapon and his lieutenants had also developed a basic platform for the workers' struggles, though it was secret until the eve of the great events. These important differences permit us to see how grass-roots solidarity became heightened through the influence of new ideas from conscious workers and the intelligentsia, a result, once more, of the dual character of the Russian labor movement.

Gapon's Assembly was an experiment in worker organization similar in some respects to the Zubatov societies, in that the organization had close ties to the police and was originally meant to be a way of coopting workers by increasing their loyalty to the regime. There were also important differences: police control was not as complete; the Assembly concentrated more on cultural matters and was less of a proto-trade union; and in the early stages the role of former revolutionaries was less central. Like the Zubatov experiment, however, Gapon's Assembly soon went beyond the original intentions of either the police or Gapon himself and provided a dramatic demonstration of the potential for solidarity and militancy inherent in the labor movement.

Gapon's Assembly has often been interpreted as a traditional religious movement led by an unscrupulous police agent. In fact, as Surh has persuasively argued, the reality was quite different: its membership embraced many skilled and educated workers; its leadership included a group of conscious workers with considerable experience in the Social Democratic movement; and Gapon himself was sincerely committed to the workers' welfare, becoming, in the last months of his organization, more and more politically radical.[24]

The great transformation of the Gapon Assembly from what was to most participants only a self-help and self-improvement society occurred after the outbreak of conflict in the Putilov factory. Meetings were held in workshops and taverns throughout many of the working-class areas of the city, and the mood of the participants reached extraordinary emotional levels. Not just in numbers but also in this exaltation of mood, the January strike was virtually unprecedented in the history of the Russian labor movement. Accounts of these events are unanimous in their evocation of a quasi-religious ecstasy involving a profound sense of solidarity and a willingness for self-sacrifice for the sake of the movement. Of the meeting which he attended, Buzinov wrote that each word "ignited the soul and fused everyone into one compact, solid mass. . . . The reading [of the petition] brought the listeners to a frenzy." At the high point of the petition, after the words "we have only two paths: either to freedom and happiness, or to the grave," "unprecedented ecstasy seized everyone. Some shouted 'two paths', others 'we will die here', others something else, but all this merged together, everyone burned, as in a fever."[25] The mood was religious—at times messianic—in tone. Hands were raised to vote with fingers shaped in the sign of the cross to show that the demands were holy; images of martyrdom, of the willingess to die for the just cause, intensified the atmosphere. "'Do you all swear to die?' asked an orator. 'We swear'. 'Let all who swear raise their hands.' Hundreds of hands simultaneously were raised into the air."[26]

Such solidarity emerged from a powerful synthesis. First there was the atmosphere created by the strike itself, with all of the effects discussed earlier. Groups of the most energetic workers made the rounds of workshops and factories, persuading and forcing other workers to participate. The strike embraced conscious and dark, prepared and unprepared, workers. Gurevich cites the following account by a participant:

> On January 5 I arrived in the workshop at seven in the morning. We humbly sang a prayer. . . . I lit a candle, I gripped the oil-can in the vice and began to saw. In two to three minutes a certain lathe-operator N. came up and said: "Get dressed, comrades! Let's go to find the truth with the Putilov workers." I heard him and assumed that he was joking and, not paying attention, I began to work. Suddenly I heard a whistle, then another, and I thought: something's not normal. I looked around—the workers were getting dressed, and I among

them. We went to the next workshops and suggested that they stop work. Without any opposition they also got dressed and left.[27]

Striking was not a decision of individuals but a collective act. Such solidarity alone might have led to nothing more impressive than the Obukhov defense. What distinguished the January 1905 strikes and meetings was the participation of recognized leaders with a makeshift platform within the context of a preexisting organization. The solidarity born of contagion could be augmented and interpreted in terms of more definite ideas embodied in the petition; and it could be channeled according to a plan of action: the march to the tsar for the presentation of the petition. This leadership and these ideas had been developing within the Assembly for months, unknown to the great majority of its participants.

Father Gapon had been acquainted with conscious workers who had participated in the Social Democratic movement almost from his earliest encounters with St. Petersburg workers.[28] Such workers were attracted to Gapon and his movement because of the possibilities for reaching out to the worker masses inaccessible to the radical political parties. The politically naive Gapon was greatly swayed by these sophisticated and educated workers, and their influence grew to the point where Gapon became fearful of their predominance in the movement. An important early sign of the changes wrought in Gapon was the first version of the petition that he showed to the four Assembly leaders in a secret meeting in March 1904. The five men decided to keep the program secret but at the same time "to conduct future work only under the aegis of this program, not revealing it all at once, but gradually, on every convenient occasion, instilling it into the consciousness of the assembled workers."[29] The program itself was reportedly very close to the petition presented in January 1905, including basically liberal demands that were, of course, truly revolutionary in the Russian context: for example, civil liberties, ministerial responsibility, and freedom to unionize and strike. In addition, it included more specifically socioeconomic goals: land redistribution, establishment of the eight-hour day, and a progressive income tax. The conscious workers in the Gapon Assembly acted very much like their socialist party counterparts, emphasizing political education and self-improvement. There was a difference, however: they were more subtle in their methods, and they understood the need for gradual persuasion. Throughout 1904, but particularly after August, when censorship was relaxed, these workers held numerous conversations with the rank-and-file members of the Assembly, their tone gradually becoming more radical as the year wore on. Thus the solidarity of the Putilov strike and the march to the tsar were partly the result of a process of gradual maturation. It was not simply, as many Social Democrats liked to think, the result of the explosion of mass rage and spontaneity.

After the outbreak of the strike the Assembly made another contribution to solidarity: it provided an organizational context for the spread of ideas. Such a context had been largely lacking in the Obukhov defense, in which the conscious workers had to act under pressure of the mass movement in the factory and streets. In the January events in St. Petersburg there were definite places to meet and recognized leaders. The energy of the strike could be channeled along strategic paths. There was a huge influx of previously passive, dark workers into the meetings, where they came under the influence of the Assembly's leaders and its long-time members, who patiently explained to them their goals and purposes. It should be clear, however, that such leadership was a long way from the bureaucratic control of a modern trade union. The worker orators and leaders were subject to the exalted mass mood that they had helped to create. In such a context plans could be developed, but rational calculation based on means-ends criteria was hardly predominant.

Until the Putilov strike the revolutionary intelligentsia had condemned the Assembly as Zubatovist and had purposely kept their distance. This attitude cost them dearly, for they had no inkling of the increasing ferment among the workers; and unlike the group of conscious workers within the Assembly, they were incapable of understanding its potential for class struggle. The situation changed somewhat in the last days before Bloody Sunday. Social Democrats finally awakened to what was happening before their eyes, and they sought permission to speak in the meetings. Rather than use the language of Marxism, these Social Democratic agitators seem to have gradually adopted the tone of the Assembly, making use of shared cultural conceptions, such as the need for redemptive social change. At the final moments, then, the intelligentsia played a role in the creation of solidarity, but their main impact would come after the great massacre of Bloody Sunday, when the whole political environment was transformed.

The combination of these various elements, of the street and the meeting, of traditional religious ideas and the desire for radical transformation, of mass and conscious workers, of collective action and organization, created a movement of imposing solidarity. There were no partisan struggles to decompose this unity, no organizations to channel the energy along divergent paths. The massive January strike and the march to the tsar were truly the work of the St. Petersburg proletariat as a whole, comprehensible only in terms of the structural and organizational traits of the labor movement. In the following section we will see how these basic traits allowed such solidarity to be expressed on an even grander scale, embracing whole regions or, as in 1905, the whole country.

THE EXTENSION OF SOLIDARITY

The Gapon movement, culminating in the January 1905 strikes, illustrates the powerful forces generating solidarity at the local level. It also gave hints of how solidarity could be extended, as it was in the 1903 strikes throughout the south, in the all-national 1905 upheaval, and in the 1912–14 period. In these periods, and particularly in 1905, other conditions came into play that transformed the nature of the strike movement.

There was first a change in the overall political atmosphere of the country. This could occur through the emergence of a crisis external to the labor movement or through the deepening of the strike movement itself. The best example of the first is the war with Japan, and particularly the Japanese seizure of Port Arthur in late 1904, which so angered and humiliated the Russian public and added to the conviction of many that the regime was corrupt and incompetent. This anger was certainly felt among the capital's workers, many of whom worked in war-related industries and had served in the armed forces themselves, and it was part of the background of worker militancy in December and January. Also of major significance in transforming the atmosphere was the outbreak of the strike. After all, there was great strike solidarity in 1903 and 1912–1914 even without an external political crisis. In both cases, once the strike movement had passed beyond a certain threshold it created a political crisis that further encouraged worker solidarity.

The first stage in the emergence of the new political atmosphere was a period of widespread contagion. Great events like the Morozov strike, the Obukhov defense, the Odessa strike in 1903, Bloody Sunday, or the Lena massacre in 1912 echoed throughout the country and stimulated sympathy strikes or strikes of protest. Such contagion had various roots, including the challenge to the regime's authority structure, which itself helped to undermine that authority and encouraged further defiance, and the anger over repression, especially when it took very violent forms. The contagion also stemmed from the excitement of new prospects for action in a society that offered few avenues for public expression. Protest now seemed more possible, more morally justified, and more promising.

If protest was able to deepen, this contagion eventually took the form of a normative rule implicitly recognized by many categories of workers. To prove that they were in tune with the most advanced currents, many workers believed they should participate in the movement. Activism was a form of self-justification. Thus Korolev reports in his memoirs that after their April 1905 strike, the workers felt that they were not "an empty space in the ranks of the proletariat."[30] Similarly, Surh records the anxious queries of some St. Petersburg typesetters in January 1905:

"'There's a general strike in Petersburg, we're being shut down, but where are our typographical organs? Why do they know nothing and do not participate in the movement? Why have we, who for a number of years have had several of our own institutions, our own journal, turned up in the rear of the movement?'"[31] In 1905 such sentiments spread across the empire and among all categories of workers, even including such nonproletarian groups as personal servants.

One implication of the moral pressure for solidarity was an explicit ideological commitment to action for the sake of solidarity. Workers often struck on the basis of abstract principle. According to Varzar, such solidarity was especially common among metalworkers,[32] but it was hardly confined to them. A good example of the force of such a norm of solidarity can be found in the report of the factory director Ivan Gippius of the Nevskii Shipbuilding and Mechanical Factory on a strike in his factory in St. Petersburg in February 1905.[33] On Saturday, 5 February, there was an unexpected work stoppage in one of the workshops, which particularly disturbed Gippius because the previous Thursday the workers' elected representatives had explicitly agreed that work in the factory should be continued. Gippius, and then the workers' own representatives, spoke to the striking workers, trying to convince them that a strike could only do harm. In response there were scattered replies from the workers that "we are obligated to support our comrades of the Putilov factory who are seeking political rights, and we don't have the right to abandon our comrades." Gippius concluded that the workers were not acting according to their own will and purposes but had come under the control of outside forces with political goals. In a sense he was right, although he distorts the nature of the influences involved.

Another aspect of the changed political context was the softening of the isolation among groups imposed by autocracy. Mass and conscious workers could now associate with one another more freely, and the intelligentsia could partially overcome their isolation in the underground. Similarly, workers could come in contact with students or liberal intellectuals, and the beginnings of a real public began to emerge. This was true in some of the 1902 and 1903 strikes in the south, where meetings took place in the open and were attended by a diverse public. There was considerable public sympathy for the workers' cause. Again 1905, the year of revolution, provides the most striking examples, especially the opening of the halls of institutions of higher education to public meetings and discussions without government control. Such changes strengthened the conviction that a decisive turning point had been reached and that, far from going backward, the government would have to promote even more change. The new political atmosphere thus gave birth to a crucial precondition for further solidarity: the belief that change was possible, or even that it was inevitable. The new society, with its greater freedom and more open contacts among groups, seemed already to exist in embryo. With such widespread public action, the government's capacity for repression was weakened and the fear of reprisals declined dramatically. This change could be observed both for the actions of individuals and for organizations. Opportunities for action on a new scale opened before them. Old organizations played a new role and new organizations emerged to fill new needs for which the old organizations were ill-suited.[34] Such organizations increased the potential for solidarity partly because they facilitated links between different cities and regions. The best example was the St. Petersburg Soviet of 1905, which played a crucial role in the success of the October and November 1905 general strikes. Party organs and trade union central organizations also fostered solidarity, as the Moscow printers' strike in September and the railway strike in October clearly demonstrate. Printers in Moscow or textile workers in Ivanovo-Voznesensk could be more stubborn in their struggles with the knowledge that their actions might be supported by their fellow workers in other cities.

It was the conscious workers and the intelligentsia who created these organizations, and by means of them many of their ideas were filtered to the worker masses. For example, the St. Petersburg Soviet advocated over-all political change and also such general proletarian goals as the legalization of the eight-hour day. As mass strikes developed these ideas became more and more current and themselves provided a basis for further solidarity. Worker demands were not specific to any particular group and thus not divisive. A report of a group of Urals factory owners on the 1905 strikes describes this dynamic for their own region very well:

> Together with the growth of the movement in scope, the demands of the workers also grew. At first purely economic, often very minor, they broadened and turned into political ones. . . . In this way, the uncoordinated demands announced during the year by workers in individual plants evidently took on the character of overall demands by the end of the year.[35]

As a result of these interrelated processes, local action in factories could become part of citywide unrest, and protest in one city became linked to protest in others. In times of massive unrest events echoed across the country, with unpredictable consequences for social change. In 1905, for example, there seemed to be a complex dialogue between St. Petersburg and Moscow that culminated in the December armed uprising in the Presnia district of Moscow. The printers' strike in Moscow, the railway strike, the October general strike supported and publicized by the St. Petersburg Soviet, the November strike called by the Soviet to protest events in Poland and Kronstadt, the arrest of the St. Petersburg Soviet, and the defiant response to this arrest in Moscow were all part of one drama of completely interconnected elements. Such impressive displays of solidarity, of the capacity for joint action for shared goals, was built upon and did not substitute for the local bases of solidarity. This precisely was its strength.

CONCLUDING REMARKS

Western Europe has also witnessed general strikes, though none that predated the 1905 general strikes in Russia, nor any that were as all-embracing.[36] In France, home of the theory of the mass revolutionary strike, the first successful general strike did not occur until 12 February 1934, and this was explicitly a one-day strike in defense of the republic. Called by the General Labor Confederation, its aims and method "were limited, defensive, and orderly, not revolutionary."[37] Prior to this there had been solidarity strikes, many large-scale strikes led by labor federations, and impressive strike waves, but nothing that could really be termed a general strike. Clearly the 1934 general strike was of a very different nature from the October and November 1905 Russian strikes, for it was always under the control of the central labor organizations and always directed toward a specific political purpose. The 1936 strike wave, reaching its peak in June, was somewhat closer to the Russian pattern. It was led not by centralized trade union organizations but by local political militants, and it emerged in a context of general political ferment (the left's electoral victories). It was a strike wave, however, not a general strike, and the solidarity displayed, no matter how great in its context, was of a different flavor and had entirely different political implications. And even granted certain similarities, it was quite exceptional in French labor history to that time in its lack of direction by organizations, in this sense going back to labor struggle in the middle decades of the nineteenth century and prefiguring the 1968 explosion.[38]

Of the 1926 general strike in Britain Perlman said that "it has revealed the greatest display in history of labor solidarity."[39] Led with some vacillation by the newly organized General Council of the Trade Union Congress, the strike completely paralyzed the British economy. Local union leaders displayed great resourcefulness and initiative, and the worker participants became so enthusiastic that despite great sacrifices, they were angry when the national leadership ended the strike in defeat. For the fervor of the worker participants was not matched by that of their leaders, who were anxious for a compromise with the government. The leadership was able to convince the workers to surrender, but only at the cost of great disillusionment with their policies and mass defection in the membership.[40]

Solidarity in the Russian labor movement clearly had different sources and different traits from either France or England. It was rooted more in the dynamics of collective action than in the calculation of organizations. Further, it reinforced and took strength from radicalism, unlike many situations in which radicalism divides and isolates. For example, Schorske notes that in 1905 "the very intensity of labor conflict in Germany, which encouraged radicalism in the radicals, produced a more-than-normal caution in the trade-union leaders."[41] In Russia solidarity was not so much the result of a decision based upon political principle as a process that had its own logic. Workers and revolutionary intelligentsia both felt engulfed in a wave that swept them along whatever their own inclinations. This is not to say that solidarity was purely spontaneous. On the contrary, we have seen that it was heightened by the activists' political teachings and goals and it was consistent with the movement's organizational structure. It was precisely the combination of these various elements that made solidary action seem so overpowering.

If these traits made solidary action powerful and intense, however, they also implied that it could not be controlled and directed so easily. Nor could it be so constant in its expression. On the contrary, solidarity was highly uneven, as was the labor movement itself. The 1905 events were followed in the succeeding years by an absence of joint action and even by mutual recriminations and denunciations to the police. As Buzinov expressed it, the working class was like a bottle of water with various seeds in it: when you shake the bottle, all the seeds of different weights are mixed together, giving an impression of homogeneity. But when all is quiet again, the seeds return to their places, separate as before.[42]

After 1905 this unevenness greatly disturbed many of the intelligentsia, particularly the Mensheviks. For example, the Menshevik writer Cherevanin (whose views Trotsky subjected to a vitriolic critique) criticized a writer from Kiev who praised the Russian workers for their solidarity in strikes, in the sense that all categories of workers struck at once. Cherevanin objected that it could not be a case of "unconditional solidarity" when the movement started and stopped spontaneously. The Western European workers, he charged, had much greater solidarity in their constant organized struggle, in the unity combined with discipline with which their movement was imbued. Not just in times of extreme action, he claimed, but in their everyday struggles the workers feel themselves to be part of a single fighting army.[43]

Instead of invidiously comparing the Russian labor movement in terms of solidarity, as did Cherevanin, it makes some sense to distinguish it as embodying a wholly different type. Its distinctiveness from the European pattern has been emphasized throughout this discussion. In a theoretical sense it was neither mechanical nor organic, traditional nor modern, for Russian society did not go through the historical transition to which these terms refer. Its political implications also clearly differed from those of European movements: solidarity in Russia was part of a general revolutionary pattern, whereas English or even French solidarity was firmly within the context of reform.

CHAPTER 12

Radicalism

The gradual extension of civil, political, and social rights to the lower classes in most Western European countries led to a significant decline in worker radicalism. This tendency could be best observed in England, where the extension of rights was accompanied by economic improvements and by the emergence of an egalitarian, individualist ideology that helped depoliticize class conflict. Workers could still be militant, as exemplified by the "New Unionism," but it was militancy in the class struggle, not in the struggle for a radical new social and political order.

The transition was more complex in France and Germany. In France the industrialists often stubbornly refused to recognize unions or the formal equality of the two contending sides, and class conflict often became exceptionally bitter. Revolutionary traditions also lived on in a way that they did not in England, and socialist sectarianism flourished. Among the workers there was much revolutionary rhetoric, the language of the mass revolutionary strike. As Perrot warns us repeatedly, however, appearances were deceptive. In fact reformism was also triumphant in the French working class, a tendency observable even in the 1871–1890 period, before the rise of mass unionism and union bureaucracies. The first change was in the workers' consciousness itself. Workers as individuals and the labor movement as a collective enterprise had a recognized place in society, with rights and access to knowledge and power. Gradually a "worker consciousness of the conjuncture" was emerging,[1] an emphasis on rational calculation based upon an awareness of the political and economic circumstances. At first short term, based upon immediate signs of surrounding conditions, this awareness also extended over longer time frames, including evaluations of employer profits over time spans of several years. The counterpart of this new rationality was the delegation of power to specialists, particularly in the union bureaucracy. More and more choice eluded the mass base. "The large factory is a disguise that takes away from the worker even his most elementary weapon: the feeling of need that he has about himself, cement of the first proletarian consciousness."[2] "The street becomes empty and rooms fill up."[3] Speech remains radical, but it belies practice. "Violence is proclaimed when it is not accomplished; one speaks of the Revolution when one does not make it. Discourse fulfills, like the dream, a repressive and compensatory function."[4] The working class, as a whole, is closed to radical messages, particularly from outside revolutionary intellectuals, who are considered to be distant "gentlemen."[5]

In Germany, too, the working class was far from achieving full political and cultural integration, but even under the antisocialist laws the same process observed by Perrot was well under way. The party, even under these repressive conditions, was shifting to parliamentarian tactics, which took precedence over the semi-underground activities on the grassroots level. The party's leadership prudently avoided actions that could lead to violence and even discouraged strikes. True, there was radical dissent within the party and formal commitment to a revolutionary doctrine, but radicalism was a minority current, and the doctrine merely buttressed and made acceptable reformist practice by theoretically linking it to the eventual triumph of socialism. Within the trade unions, too, moderation and prudence were triumphant, even more than in France.

In Russia there was perhaps less revolutionary talk—this, after all, was prohibited, though none too effectively. Radicalism, however, was built into the very structure and institutional context of the labor movement. On the absence of talk, Trotsky wrote of the St. Petersburg Soviet that its every step "was determined in advance. Its 'tactics' were obvious. The methods of struggle did not have to be discussed, there was hardly time to formulate them."[6] The relation between word and act was clearly different from that in France or Germany. The differences, once more, can be traced to the distinctive culture, structure, and organizational pattern of the Russian labor movement as these were rooted in the autocratic capitalist system.

THE EFFECTS OF AUTOCRACY

Autocracy made its contribution to the radicalization of the labor movement largely by fostering certain attitudinal and institutional preconditions. These preconditions, when combined with elements of the modern class struggle, proved to be explosive.

The Zubatov experiment already showed how monarchist ideas in the context of industrial class relations could lead to extreme worker militancy. This was not yet political radicalism, but it did prepare the ground for it because it helped make the class struggle intractable. Seldom did workers embrace monarchist ideas very consistently or explicitly, but many traces and implications of them could be found in labor struggles. Simply the general belief among many workers that the government had the responsibility to protect them was a source of both hope and then disillusionment. Such ideas were clearly present in the Gapon movement—it was from the tsar that the workers could receive a just solution to their sufferings.

Such sentiments were probably strongest among workers of peasant background, and in their minds claims for the tsar's attention to their needs as industrial workers was often fused with claims over the land question. Plekhanov gives a good illustration of this fusion in the passages in his memoirs describing the Novaia textile strike in St. Petersburg. After the outbreak of discontent, the workers expected the revolutionaries to compose a petition for the redress of their needs to the tsar. After it was composed and approved by the local workers' circle it was presented for discussion to a general workers' meeting in the factory yard. The petition began with references to the small size of peasant allotments and the heavy dues placed upon them. As a result, "need drives us to work for wages in the city, and here factory owners and police oppress us at every step."[7] The workers, it said, saw no other source of protection than the successor to the throne, whose help they awaited. If he gave no attention to their request, however, then it would be clear that they only could rely upon themselves, a conclusion that the workers found very reasonable. The successor did not help them, and the workers soon became disillusioned. Plekhanov remarks that they lost their political prejudices brought from the countryside. Perhaps it would be truer to say that workers' anger over the tsar's refusal to protect them in the countryside now became combined with anger over his protection of the capitalists in the city. The workers' new conviction was embodied in a story of unknown origin that "the successor to the Throne was intimately connected with the wife of the manager and, besides that, had his share in the factory capital. Hardly anyone of the strikers seriously believed this tale, but everyone willingly repeated it."

Another example of the fusion of agrarian and industrial discontent can be seen in the following. The Urals worker, noted a Urals industrialist group in 1907, is generally conservative politically, still seeing the necessity of tsarist power. Teachings about the seizure of land and factories receive an enthusiastic response, however.[8] The linkage of peasant and worker discontent was also occasionally noted by government officials. For example, in his September 1905 report government administrator Chikolev recognized the rural population's right to enough land to satisfy its necessities and, in a parallel way, the worker's claim to a whole series of rights "not compatible with the contemporary sense of justice" based on the prerogatives of private property. Like the peasant, the worker would seek "freedom and equality also in economic relations."[9]

Rumors of the kind described by Plekhanov embodying implicitly monarchist ideals frequently circulated during strikes. Often they consisted of concrete promises said to have been made by the tsar or his ministers to improve the workers' situation. I have already noted Witte's reference to the rumors that at his coronation the tsar would announce a shortening of the workday. Recall also that similar rumors were rampant in the Moscow region during the Zubatov experiment—that, for example, some of the Zubatovite worker leaders were tsarist agents in disguise sent to redress their grievances.

The traditionalist cast of much worker protest can also be seen from the following example: In his 1901 report the factory inspector for Moscow province remarked that the only source of worker discontent was wages. In their great majority these complaints arose before the Christmas and Easter holidays, and they were rooted in the workers' belief that the government had established a minimum wage of seventy to seventy-five kopeks per day. "It is difficult to say," remarked the inspector, "from where this rumor appeared, but it is held to stubbornly."[10] As Plekhanov's example suggests, the Social Democrats were not beyond making use of these traditionalist sentiments to spur worker unrest. For example, Garvi reports on the Odessa Committee's use of an old law limiting the workday from Catherine the Great's time for agitational purposes.[11] The problem for the government was that even though government officials might sympathize with these sentiments, they were in basic conflict with capitalist relations in industry and could cause nothing but trouble.

A further contribution of autocracy to the long-term radicalization of the labor movement was the ignorance that its repressive policies spawned. The French worker described by Perrot developed a "consciousness of the conjuncture" partly through a growing understanding of the economic context of the firm. Trade unions played a key educative role in this process. Workers gradually developed a better understanding of which demands made sense because they understood the position of their opponents. Similarly, they came to have a better sense of what the law was and the scope of their rights. Action and its consequences could thus be assessed in rational terms. In Russia workers were generally ignorant of the law, and, it bears emphasis, they could not predict how the law would be enforced because this was often a matter of whim. For example, in the Sormov factories in February 1908 the workers presented a long list of demands, including the eight-hour day, worker control over hiring and firing, and freedom of organization and assembly. At the end of the list they referred to these as legal aspirations to create acceptable living conditions—when, of course, they went far beyond the law.[12]

Demands were made not only in ignorance of the law but also in ignorance of their practicality. Without trade unions there was no possibility for workers to learn about the firm's economic situation. In the period of the 1905 strikes, Gvozdev castigated the workers in one factory under his supervision for their lack of realism. "'Gentlemen! You mustn't present such demands! Look, they make no sense at all.'" He received the following reply, in a hostile tone: "'And who is guilty for not giving us any knowledge?! Did anyone teach us anything?! Well now, let those who are guilty in this matter pay for what they didn't teach us!'"[13]

Because of their isolation from the factory owners, because of the wall of which Belov and others spoke, the workers also were ignorant of the functions of management and the technical complexity of at least some tasks. Such ignorance buttressed their underlying suspicion that the factory owners were nothing more than parasites. Thus the Urals report mentioned earlier declares that the workers and employees of the Urals factories were convinced that they could administer the factory far better than the existing management, whose high pay was nothing more than waste.[14]

Left in ignorance, the workers had other sources for their beliefs: the popular culture of the factory and socialist teachings from conscious workers and the intelligentsia, which were much more systematic and powerful when they could be heard. No matter how different in other ways, these two sources were alike in that they embodied values hostile toward capitalism.

Autocracy also created fertile ground for militancy by prohibiting organizations that in other industrial countries stabilized relations with factory owners and the state and also transformed the labor movement in a moderate direction. Further, instead of worker leaders with a stake in the system, strike leadership in Russia tended to be composed either of hot-headed young workers or committed conscious workers. As a result of a lack of institutionalized means of struggle, the workers were forced to resort to bitter mass strikes, even if this was against their inclinations.[15] In this context workers even feared that external calm could be mistaken by the government and factory owners for indifference or satisfaction, a fear that played into the hands of militants.[16] Just as the factory owners came to rely on the coercive power of the state, so workers had to rely on the coercive power of the strike.

THE UNINSTITUTIONALIZED CLASS STRUGGLE

These underlying effects of autocracy were interwoven with the dynamics of uninstitutionalized conflict that, just as it gave rise to solidarity, also stimulated radicalism. With little susceptibility to calculation beforehand or to control during the course of the struggle, Russian strikes were more frequently shaped by the dynamics of conflict itself.

Much of what was suggested earlier about the genesis of solidarity also holds for the emergence of radicalism. Collective action in Russia had a built-in dynamism because of the lack of set purposes and organizations and the infectious nature of action in a repressive social context. Direct action and face-to-face contact created a new mood that gave rise to new kinds of action. The break in authority encouraged further challenges to it. In periods of great ferment the workers' mood was heightened by the action of other groups, including students, intellectuals, white-collar workers, occasionally even the industrialists themselves. The new atmosphere of exhilaration and hope emboldened workers to the point that anything seemed possible. Rational calculation, difficult in any case in the context of autocracy, was even more unable to keep up with the pace of events. Trotsky, who better than anyone communicates a sense of the dynamism and unpredictability of class conflict in Russia, scorned those who would be the schoolmasters of the revolution. He wrote of 1905:

> The spirit of mutiny swept the land. A tremendous mysterious process was taking place in countless hearts: bonds of fear were being broken, the individual personality, having hardly had time to become conscious of itself, became dissolved in the mass, and the mass itself became dissolved in the revolutionary élan. Having freed itself from inherited fears and imaginary obstacles, the mass did not want to, and could not, see the real obstacles in its path. Therein lay its weakness, and also its strength. It rushed forward like the ocean tide whipped by a storm. Every day brought new strata of the population to their feet and gave birth to new possibilities.[17]

One of the most explosive consequences of collective action was the workers' heightened sense of dignity. Moscow baker Korolev described the effects of the April 1905 strike as follows: "Now the bakers looked on themselves differently: each had a vivid memory of the April strike and the panic it caused among Moscow residents. Therefore the workers bore themselves with pride, with dignity even at the factory gates. . . . Yes, the bakers even turned out to be people, even more—important people. They only had to leave work and immediately all Moscow, from the aristocrat to the simple day-laborer, became alarmed."[18] By giving the workers a sense of worth, collective action taught them that they had the right to act. Buzinov remarks that after 9 January, "it was as if the workers considered it their duty to speak their mind on every occasion."[19] A perceived right of citizenship emerged during collective action, to which the government was unable to respond in a constructive way.

Until the 1912–1914 period, when political strikes with specific purposes became more common, the typical Russian strike began with poorly formulated demands. The immediate cause of the strike, an insult by a foreman or the arbitrary firing of workers, may have been clear, but the workers' aspirations were usually unfocused and underlaid with a desire for revenge for past abuses. The lack of organizations was clearly the decisive factor in this regard. Demands came to be worked out in the heat of conflict, and as the workers' actions became bolder, so did their aspirations.[20] The constantly changing character of worker demands and their increasing radicalism made the resolution of conflict much more difficult. It is understandable that even the best-intentioned employer could become exasperated with the workers' inconsistency.[21] The workers accused the government of bad faith and deception, and the same charge was made against the workers. Such instability on both sides was part of the price paid for lack of institutionalization.

The illegality of strikes and the risks that they entailed shaped the kind of leadership that emerged. Perrot shows that in France worker leadership changed with changes in the mode of struggle. The bold orator gradually gave way to the careful and specialized negotiator.[22] In Russia strike leadership came to fall upon two distinct types: the worker rebel and the conscious worker. The first, young and fiery, led by virtue of his bold example. The second relied upon his ideas and links to the party and intelligentsia in a context in which there was otherwise a vacuum of ideas. Interaction frequently occurred between these two types of leaders: angry young radicals came to adopt the language, if not the inner sense, of socialism,[23] and, as discussed earlier, conscious workers often came under the influence of "spontaneity," at times even espousing terror. Such a pattern of leadership obviously contributed to the radicalization of goals and mood during the course of collective action.

Strikes and demonstrations on any significant scale involved workers in conflict with the government. Police repression could suppress protest, at least temporarily, but it could also make protest even more militant. Anger or the allure of heroism might stimulate more resistance. In times of special ferment many workers probably believed that all was lost anyway, and the prospect of further clashes with the police inspired no additional fear. Alternatively, many were convinced that eventually victory was inevitable, and they were willing to be martyrs in the cause. They interpreted police violence as a sign of the regime's weakness and took more strength in the knowledge of its imminent fall.[24] Thus in December 1905 in Moscow and July 1914 in St. Petersburg, many workers seemed to take no account of the threat of police repression. Nor did concessions from the government at crucial moments seem to be of use in stemming the tide of protest. Buzinov remarked that the October Manifesto only showed the workers that their demands were beginning to be taken into account, and virtually everyone understood the manifesto itself as a call for renewed pressure.[25] Part of the problem was the workers' lack of trust in the government—they did not necessarily believe that concessions would be enacted after unrest had died down. Thus various workers from a St. Petersburg printing house announced to Witte at the end of their letter that "we also consider it necessary to inform you that, at the present time, on the basis of your actions in internal politics, we decisively do not trust you."[26] Such convictions, often born of long experience of government inconsistency and treachery, also underlay much worker militancy.

Because of government interference and the emergence of radical leadership, strikes quickly became politicized. Perrot remarks of France that "very rarely political in the end, the strike of this epoch is frequently so in its beginning."[27] In France class conflict—not revolutionary political change—was the issue, and this was implicit in the logic of conflict even if the actors were not always aware of it. The reverse was true in Russia: until shortly before the war strikes seldom began as political protests but often ended up with radical political demands. The source of this politicization was not just government interference but the workers' realization that they had to have political rights to protect themselves in a capitalist society. When it became clear that government tutelary claims were largely ineffective, there was no realistic choice but to struggle for political rights—that is, for radical change.

Thus the class struggle itself brought workers up against the political foundations of the tsarist state. Workers learned both a negative and a positive lesson from the class struggle: that the government generally played a repressive role and that organization was necessary to protect their interests. Implicit in both lessons was the need for overall political change. Thus the logic of capitalism encouraged the fight against autocracy, just as the logic of autocracy gave rise to opposition to capitalism. As a result, little distinction was made between these two spheres, a comprehensible outcome given the relative lack of differentiation of politics and economics. Workers made economic demands on the government and political demands on the factory owners, for which each disclaimed responsibility. Reinforcing this tendency toward fusion, the factory owners blamed the government for stimulating class conflict by making promises to the workers and using police coercion; government officials blamed the industrialists for provoking political unrest through their economic exploitation. The resulting complex fusion between economic and political conflict meant that worker unrest threatened both class and political domination.[28]

THE CONTRIBUTION OF CONSCIOUS WORKERS AND THE INTELLIGENTSIA

Radicalism was not rooted only in preconditions created by autocracy or in the logic of uninstitutionalized struggle. It also stemmed from events in the larger political context, such as military defeat or general changes of political mood and atmosphere.[29] In addition, it depended on ideas and leadership coming from the intelligentsia and the conscious workers.

It has been noted in previous chapters that workers were forced to turn to conscious workers and the intelligentsia for leadership because of the lack of institutionalization of the labor movement. Further, both worker and intelligentsia leaders were able to maintain themselves as bearers of revolutionary doctrine and practice. There were opposing moderate tendencies, but the political conditions of tsarism ultimately strengthened the positions of the most radical leaders. As early as 1906, Martov perceived the dangers: "In the moment of political tranquillity and with a complete absence of 'freedom' the Bolsheviks must win, for the 'spontaneity' of revolution is for them; for them is the slight consciousness of the 'conscious' workers and the cursed, lifeless psychology of the circles and conspiracy developing in the underground."[30] Worker leaders who might have supported the Mensheviks were unwilling to return to the underground, to engage in heroic activities at great risk. There was great apathy; attendance at meetings was poor; spirits were low. The Bolsheviks, he said, were better able to withstand such trials.[31] Thus there was a dual process: the Bolsheviks would gain the support of those workers who chose to remain active, and the more moderate worker leaders would tend to abandon the movement. Both of these processes led to a self-selection of militant leaders.

What role did these worker leaders play in stimulating worker radicalism? The answer is by no means simple. Recall that some of the great instances of worker militancy began without the awareness or initial participation of socialist leaders, although their indirect influence often was still significant, as in the case of the Gapon movement. Further, the intensity of the mass mood frequently overcame any efforts to lead the movement in terms of long-term strategy or ideology. It is also true that leaders, both workers and intelligentsia, often tried to restrain the movement. Even the Bolshevik leadership in St. Petersburg in July 1914 feared the consequences of further militancy.

Conversely, conscious workers and the revolutionary intelligentsia often did assume the mantle of leadership, far from always against their will. Like the worker masses, they often got caught up in the mood of the moment, overestimated their strength, and cast aside considerations of consequences. In this they approximated Luxemburg's ideal of the role of leadership in the mass strike: it was to give direction to the struggle, to regulate tactics and guide action, but not to "command over its origin" or to reckon costs.[32] This is a fairly accurate description of the role of the St. Petersburg Soviet at the end of 1905. Further, even when party leaders attempted to restrain the masses, this was not for the motives common among the Germans—the desire to work within the system—but simply in order not to divert attention from the major task, which they saw to be armed insurrection. Both Mensheviks and Bolsheviks were reluctant to support the strikes in late 1905 for this reason. Thus despite certain ambiguities, there can be little doubt of the overall impact of worker and intelligentsia leadership. Indeed, here too there was a process of selection at work: leaders who tried to "command over its origins" or reckon costs were discredited.[33] "It is not only the party that leads the masses," wrote Trotsky, "the masses, in turn, sweep the party forward."[34]

The movement's leaders did more than shape the course of collective action, however. They also helped to change the workers' perspectives on themselves and their role in society. We have seen that many traditional worker views of justice were antithetical to capitalism and the regime's sponsorship of it. The demands that stemmed from these beliefs were radical only in the weak sense that they were inconsistent with basic aspects of the social structure and impossible to fulfill within the status quo.[35] The conscious workers and the intelligentsia were instrumental in many workers' transition to the second type of revolutionary commitment: the willingness knowingly to use illegitimate means to change the political system for the purpose of changing society. In order to accomplish this goal they had not only to lead the workers in strikes but to impart to the workers new meanings for their action, changing accepted frameworks of reference. In doing this they often made use of traditional worker values and expectations, asking the workers to think about their implications, to compare them with what they saw, and to change them. They thus sought to convince the workers that their traditional assumptions were inadequate for judging the real situation, and they offered a rival interpretation. This interpretation, especially its Marxist variant, offered a basis for sustained radicalism and not merely spontaneous militancy. In short, the conscious workers and the intelligentsia played an indispensable part in the formation of an authentic social movement.

The Union of Struggle's leaflet at the time of the 1896 St. Petersburg textile strikes provides a typical illustration of this struggle over interpretations.[36] On 15 June Witte had appealed to the striking workers, portraying the strike as a result of instigation by ill-intentioned people. Workers should turn for protection to the government, for whom "the affairs of the factory owners and workers are equally dear." The Union of Struggle responded as follows.

The strikes have so frightened the government that it seizes any means to stop them. First it tried repression, and now it adopts more moderate means, such as talking with us, which it refused to do earlier. It tells us to live according to the truth of God, and claims that it has our interests at heart as much as the factory owners'. Let's look, comrades. The capitalists go on strike to raise the prices of goods and have congresses for the discussion of their affairs. But for the workers to discuss their needs together is illegal. The government promised to compensate the capitalists for their losses during the strike. Soldiers and police were called out against the workers. The capitalists were called to the minister, the workers—to jail. "And all this because the minister is concerned about the improvement of our living conditions and work, insofar as this is possible and profitable for us ourselves. So, we ourselves do not understand our own interests, it's all the action of plotters and instigators. We ourselves cannot understand how hard it is to work fifteen hours at a time without rest, we ourselves cannot understand how difficult it is to live always half-starving. What's with us! Instigators taught us this." We are told that the minister and factory inspectors are our protectors and defend all our "legal" demands. "Bravely said: 'legal' demands. As if we didn't know the laws! As if we didn't know that our demands about our essential needs, the shortening of the workday and the increase of wages, are considered illegal. And what there is in the law, is it really observed?" Recently the government sent out a secret circular to justices of the peace ordering them to investigate the affairs of the factory owners and the workers, not according to the law but according to the customs that prevail in the factory—or, more simply put, as the factory owner wants. "Look, brothers, enough listening to the Minister! Let's laugh about his appeal and continue our difficult and glorious task. As before, we ourselves will tirelessly and firmly struggle for our own interests, and in addition we will teach our young and inexperienced comrades. All our working life has taught us that we have no friends besides ourselves, that only by harsh struggle can we get anything from the capitalists and the government. No threats or sacrifices frighten us. We will struggle until we reach our great goal—the liberation of the working class."[37]

Such a new framework of interpretation lies between traditional expectations and a full-fledged ideological consciousness, but it is closer to the second because it involves a rejection of accepted views and prepares the way for additional socialist teachings. The spread of such a new account of everyday experience was perhaps the most important ideological contribution of the movement's leaders, reaching a broader sector of workers than socialist doctrine itself. For example, the rejection of hierarchy made sense to many workers to whom the idea of the "bourgeois revolution" or the dialectic made little sense. Such workers might even be more radical than their more fully conscious comrades because they were less restrained by visions of how social change was supposed to occur. It may be conjectured that "intermediate" workers were more likely to adhere to the Bolsheviks, whereas more sophisticated socialist workers tended toward the Mensheviks.[38]

The distinction among these different sources of radicalism made little difference for the dynamism of the movement itself. Workers acting out of hostility to capitalists based upon autocratic promises of protection could be just as threatening to the regime as committed socialist workers. Further, the transition from one type of radicalism to another was not terribly difficult. Faith in government tutelage could turn into hatred of the government, for unlike societies with more differentiation between state and society, the promise of protection had been made. Similarly, a new intepretation of experience could be supplemented by ideological glosses on the new interpretation. All of these changes were facilitated by the outbreak of worker unrest, which allowed for greater communication. The Russian institutional context made worker radicalism highly synthetic and dynamic, and thus explosive. Once again, as in the case of solidarity, different kinds of action and types of consciousness were fused, not differentiated as in freer societies.

THE CIRCULARITY OF RADICALISM

Worker protest in Russia, once it passed a certain threshold, thus had a tendency to become more and more radical. These factors made compromise difficult and heightened worker radicalism over the short term: changes in the overall political atmosphere; shifts in the workers' mood, including a new sense of their political importance, their increased daring, mounting anger over harsh government responses; the increased communication among different groups, which facilitated the spread of radical ideas; the increased impact of organizations, which could seldom play a restraining role; the inability to calculate resources, and thus the tendency to overestimate their own strength. Many of these traits were also present to some degree in European labor movements at times of crisis, but they were counterbalanced by stronger organizations and also by governments the mediatory role of which was regarded as relatively legitimate. Thus the general strikes in 1926 England and 1936 France were both ended through negotiations between governments and centralized labor organizations. In Russia the late 1905 strikes were put down by force after they culminated in the Moscow uprising, and for obvious reasons no higher-level negotiations between the government and the labor movement ever took place. Once protest was initiated there was little inside the movement in Russia to brake the course of militancy. The Russian labor movement had an inherent internal dynamic toward radicalism—a radicalism that did not depend upon a specifically radical consciousness.

A change in this short-term tendency toward radicalism would have required an alteration of the basic structure of the labor movement, a change that in turn depended on a new direction in government policy. Circularity was also built into the long-range course of the labor movement, however. Short-term radicalism reinforced long-term radicalism by making reform seem almost impossible. As was shown in part II, many government officials and factory owners simply abandoned any hopes that the labor movement could be dealt with by means other than repression. Looking at the apparent calm achieved by violence, they also managed to convince themselves that reform was unnecessary. Even those who continued to hope for reform argued that it could take place only after a transition period in order to ensure the emergence of a peaceful labor movement. They failed to appreciate that during this transition the old pattern of the underground organization linked to a volatile mass movement would reassert itself and prevail over the moderate tendencies they hoped to encourage.

As a result, worker radicalism and government repression reinforced each other. After 1905 workers became more isolated from the rest of society, and worker protest, when it reemerged after 1910, garnered no political support from other classes.[39] Fear of the workers united the government and industrialists in an uneasy alliance that belied all hopes of a "bourgeois revolution." Cherevanin's interpretation of the significance of worker radicalism in late 1905 is surely correct: "The proletariat actively works to push the capitalists into the embrace of the government, but it also does not forget the latter, and in the same way actively begins to push the government into the embrace of the capitalists."[40] For the Bolsheviks, who denied the reality of bourgeois revolutionism, this result was inevitable, hardly the product of errors in calculation by the labor movement. For the Mensheviks it stemmed from a lack of schooled political consciousness among the workers: once more spontaneity had won the upper hand. In a sense it is difficult not to agree with the Bolsheviks, but for a different reason. Given the contradictions of autocratic capitalism and the nature of the labor movement that it shaped, a successful moderate strategy had few chances either to emerge or to attain its goals. Responsibility for strategic errors must be laid at the door not of the workers but of the tsarist state, which augmented long-term risks for fear of confronting short-term ones.

In such a context where could the proponents of a two-stage revolutionary strategy find support for their views? An answer—nowhere—is given in the speech of a worker in 1906 responding to Axelrod's call for a workers' congress:

"Here Comrade Iurii [Garvi] tells us that the workers' congress is the best means of assuring the independence of the proletariat in the bourgeois revolution; otherwise, we workers will play the role of cannon fodder in it. So I ask: what is this insurance for? Is it possible that we will spill blood twice—once for the victory of the bourgeois revolution, and the other time for the victory of our proletarian revolution? No, comrades, it is not found in the party program [that this must be so]; but if we workers alone will spill our blood, then only once, for freedom and for socialism.[41]

THE PROBLEM OF CONTINUITY

With its lack of stable organizations, with its dependence on collective moods, and with the lack of permanent contact among its different elements, the Russian labor movement was subject to dramatic reverses. Its history was highly discontinuous, more a series of powerful outbursts than a gradual evolution. In times of ferment participation reached massive proportions and militancy became the norm. Leadership and organization developed with amazing speed, so quickly and in such circumstances that they could not become really institutionalized. With defeat and reverses, however, everything seemed to change, to revert to the past of impotence and passivity. The best example is the period following the defeat of the 1905 revolution, of which Trotsky writes:

The sharp ebbs and flows of the mass struggle had left the Russian proletariat after a few years almost unrecognizable. Factories which two or three years ago would strike unanimously over some single arbitrary police action, to-day have completely lost their revolutionary colour, and accept the most monstrous crimes of the authorities without resistance. Great defeats discourage people for a long time. The consciously revolutionary elements lose their power over the masses. Prejudices and superstitions not yet burnt out come back to life. Grey immigrants from the village during these times dilute the workers' ranks. Sceptics ironically shake their heads. So it was in the years 1907–11.[42]

Kleinbort describes conditions in a similar way:

This was the destruction of the past, the ruin of tradition, a break with the family foundations. There is anger, often expressed indiscriminately, a lack of trust, disconnectedness. The awareness of the semi-intelligentsia, of the worker, of the peasant, is still there, but the cold of hopelessness penetrates the soul, freezes the mood. Ferment continues within, and it is as if small islets in the broad watery expanse remain as they were. But precisely that link between them, that living pulse which beat in each of them, is not present. The old power of darkness, which the defense of one's own dignity dissolves, returns. The same moral solitude looms over everyone.[43]

It is common for social movements to experience changes in fortune. Sometimes, of course, whole movements disappear, leaving little residue on which to build future struggles. The Russian labor movement survived, but not on the same basis as other European labor movements with their mass organizations, labor press, and relatively stable constituencies. What, then, were its sources of continuity, the elements of stability that allowed it to survive as a recognizable movement?

On the most elementary level, a degree of continuity was ensured simply by the long-term participation of many individuals. It is true that the Russian working class itself was characterized by great instability in its composition, with massive influxes of new peasant workers and great geographical mobility. There was also great discontinuity in participation in the labor movement: in periods of defeat even many conscious workers became inactive, and after 1905 much of the revolutionary intelligentsia abandoned the movement as well.

Despite such changes, however, a core of experienced activists remained, together with many workers who had had prior experience in the movement. It is impossible to estimate percentages, but there are indications that the proportion was high enough to make a considerable impact upon the movement when it revived. For example, many worker organizations in 1917 were founded by activists who had had prior personal experience in the movement. The Third Conference of trade unions, meeting in June 1917, was called by members of the Organizational Committee selected in 1906 at the Second Conference. The committee had ceased to exist in 1909, but its individual members, returning after February 1917 from exile and emigration, completed the duties entrusted to them eleven years earlier.[44] A fifth of the delegates present at this meeting also participated in the Second All-Russian Conference.[45] Here is another example: worker G. K. Korolev noted that various delegates to a worker conference held in April 1917 in the Ivanovo-Voznesensk industrial area emphasized the leaders' prior participation in the movement, often going back to 1905. He adds that in their 10 June trade union conference it was determined that of the seventy-two formal participants giving information about themselves, sixty-seven had taken part in the labor movement before 1917, twenty-two had been in jail, and twelve in exile. These representatives, it was claimed, were virtually all workers.[46] Among the intelligentsia leaders the proportion of veterans was probably higher. In both cases it was certainly significant enough to ensure substantial continuity in leadership.

Aside from continuity of personnel, there was also continuity of organizational forms. The history of the organizations themselves was clearly ruptured by repression, but the experience accumulated in prior years allowed for their reemergence when conditions permitted. This was obviously true for trade unions, an internationally recognized type of organization with evident functions in the labor movement. Impressively, it was also true of the soviets, a more original organizational form. Thus of the February days of 1917, worker-Bolshevik Shliapnikov writes that "at the victory of the uprising, even at its first success, we proposed the calling of a soviet of workers' deputies. The workers knew very well how to create it from their experiences in 1905. It was difficult to think up another, more authoritative center. . . . Ideas about the creation of a soviet of workers' deputies in Petersburg arose during the war frequently (1915–16), almost with each large strike movement."[47] In addition to such specifically class organizations, the political parties contributed to organizational continuity. The organizational traits that would emerge in 1917 had already been shaped by the movement's prior history.

Patterns of leadership had also been institutionalized. The conscious worker, the revolutionary intelligentsia, the militant factory, the spark-plug district—all had long since been established in the movement by the time of the 1917 revolution. They had definite roles that endured through time. Ironically this permanence was ensured by government repression, which did not allow for substantial evolution. If an open labor movement had been permitted, patterns of leadership would have had to adapt to change. The conscious workers and the intelligentsia would not have been able to maintain their complex role as both leaders and outsiders, which allowed them to guide the movement without being absorbed in it. Thus just as the English trade union leader or the German Social Democratic Reichstag deputy developed a definite role in his respective labor movement, so did the parallel figures in Russia. Whereas in England or Germany permanence was ensured by integration, in Russia it was sealed by repression.

In a complex way socialism—especially its most systematic variant, Marxism—was also a source of continuity. Among many of the intelligentsia, of course, the continuity was clear-cut: they adhered to social-

ism as a faith that could explain short-term reverses within the context of
eventual victory. Marxism in particular could accommodate the unevenness of the Russian labor movement better than less historicist ideologies.
Among conscious workers, I have suggested, Marxism was often the crys-
tallization of a set of powerful sentiments and definitions of the situation,
a kind of popular *Weltanschauung*: the rejection of hierarchy in state and
society, the bitterness of class feeling, faith in the growing importance
and perhaps redemptive role of the working class, and the like. Experience in struggle and in the movement made these sentiments quite permanent for many conscious workers, and they were easy to awaken in new
generations of workers embittered by the combined repression of state
and capital. Finally, even for mass workers Marxism provided continuity, for they embraced its ideas and accepted the leaders espousing them
during times of struggle. It played a role perhaps similar to Buddhism
among the Vietnamese: relatively insignificant during normal times, during times of ferment it expressed and gave shape to opposition.[48] Hence
despite changes in the composition of the workers, shifts in mood, and
disillusionment with the intelligentsia, socialist ideas remained without
serious challenge in the Russian labor movement, accepted in different
ways by both main categories of workers.

The Russian labor movement also gained greater coherence through
the development of a heroic tradition. This tradition, like the movement
itself, had a number of complex and interrelated strands. First there were
the legends of peasant rebellions and worker bunts that provided an
authentic mythology of struggle for many unsophisticated workers. With
his customary condescension, Babushkin noted with dismay that the
workers thought often of bunts but seldom of strikes. "I never heard
anything said about past strikes, but someone was sure to remember a
revolt of some kind, and would talk about past repressions by the authorities, although all this got us nowhere."[49] These discussions could refer
to the great peasant rebellions of Razin or Pugachev, or they could
be memories of bunts from the workers' own past experiences. Such
memories were often reawakened by current struggles, as when the older
workers in the 1896 St. Petersburg strikes began to recall the actions of
former revolutionaries, telling stories of agitation and rebellion years ago
in the factory. There was of course much exaggeration and enthusiasm,
and the legends that emerged strongly influenced the overall mood.[50]

In breaking the silence of passivity, such revived memories seem to
have had a kind of magical power. They had the aura of great events and
danger, frightening the timid and emboldening the brave. Their magical
properties helped them to survive vividly in the memory, and they surface
in many worker memoirs. For example, the worker Mikhailov, writing
many years later, still recalled the rumors circulating in his St. Petersburg

factory in the early 1890s about the great strike that had occurred there in 1878. He particularly recalled the trick of a local official which led to many beatings, arrests, and exiles.[51] Evocation of such events had almost a fetishistic power. Shapovalov recalls the panic in his workshop in 1885 when the word "revolution" was spoken. "When I turned around because of these incomprehensible words, I noticed that the copper worker Sokolov suddenly turned pale. He grabbed Semenov by the hand and whispered to him in terror: 'What's the matter with you, have you lost your mind! . . . Be quiet! . . . ' The word 'revolution,' which was then incomprehensible to me, evidently at that time, when the noise from the bombs of People's Will had still not abated, was known to many. I automatically recalled how even my father, despite all his passivity, knew this word."[52]

Such memories surely gave some sense of continuity to struggles and reinforced the belief that resistance was possible. As Babushkin suggested, however, by themselves they were not altogether appropriate for a modern labor movement, for they were unfocused and essentially passive. In the same way Kanatchikov, writing in 1901, complained that the workers had no real idea of how to struggle because of the lack of tradition. "Our misfortune was that in Russia there had been no revolution, and consequently we had no revolutionary tradition and organized class struggle."[53]

Such amorphous traditions never disappeared, but their importance was eclipsed by the development of a more specifically proletarian heroic tradition. This tradition was made up of many elements: for example, the celebration of May Day and the anniversaries of key events in Russian labor history, such as the Obukhov defense, Bloody Sunday, or the Lena massacre[54]; the use of certain songs or slogans, such as the funeral song "You Fell Victim" or the invocation of the words of famous martyrs[55]; or the renown of certain factories or districts, such as the Putilov plant,[56] the Vyborg district in St. Petersburg, or the Presnia district in Moscow. Such symbols and celebrations, denoting landmarks in the history of the labor movement, touched deep emotions.[57] In the vast majority of cases they are hidden from view, but they occasionally emerge in memoirs. For example, Sapronov recounts that on 1 May 1913 workers of the Liuberetskii plant stopped work and together, singing revolutionary songs, went to the "brotherly grave" of victims of the 1905 revolution.[58] Attached to momentous events rather than to organizations or institutions, they were a powerful source of solidarity and continuity, forging links over time between temporally disconnected moments.

Other elements of the heroic tradition linked the movement to previous revolutionary generations in Russia and to European labor movements. These aspects of tradition were especially strongly preserved and felt by the intelligentsia, although many conscious workers shared in them as well. Marxist revolutionaries saw populist martyrs as their ancestors despite their ideological disagreements.[59] Martov illustrates this continuity in a striking way: after graduation from his gymnasium he spent a great deal of time in the library reading old newspaper accounts of the trials of populists in the 1870s. He learned the names of all the accused and the sentences they received, and they impressed him to such an extent that he still knew them by heart when writing his memoirs decades later.[60] The revolutionaries also saw themselves as part of an international revolutionary movement, and they appropriated many of the key events of the class struggle in Europe the French Revolution, 1848, and the Commune, for example. This broadening of the scope of the revolutionary tradition reinforced their beliefs in the permanence and viability of their struggle, of the historical necessity of their victory.

A heroic tradition rooted in the early years of repression was undoubtedly strong in all labor movements. The traditions of most labor movements also included many other elements, however, some of them (such as guild traditions) rooted in the preindustrial past, others connected with modern institutions such as parties or parliaments. In Russia little endured beyond the heroic tradition of martyrdom and struggle. The great trials, massacres, and periods of revolutionary ferment provided the most lasting sense of the continuity of tradition. "The ghastly consequences that attend the spoken word in Russia," wrote Herzen, "inevitably increase its effectiveness,"[61] a remark that applies equally well to other aspects of the revolutionary tradition. In its own way such a pattern was very effective. It imbued participants in the labor movement with a sense of heroism and solidarity, and it gave them the courage to continue their struggles. For example, in jail Kanatchikov reflected that "it was enough to read on a wall somewhere during a walk the name of a comrade and I no longer felt myself to be 'alone, abandoned'. . . . I felt myself to be a leading fighter for the cause of the working class, which every year sends us more and more new fighters for help. I became ashamed of my momentary faint-heartedness."[62] The tradition thus reinforced hope and faith, and it helped channel action and crystallize sentiments. It emerged from the state's harsh repression of the labor movement and took shape as a fitting response to it. It was part of the dialectic of oppression and uncompromising opposition that gave birth to both solidarity and radicalism in the Russian labor movement and made labor unrest so dangerous. It helped make of the uneven alternations of outbursts and quiescence an institutionalized pattern of its own.

For in a certain sense discontinuity was itself a form of continuity, and it corresponded to rhythms often seen to be characteristic of Russian life. Wright Miller refers to the traditional Russian pattern of "dumb plodding interspersed with furious bouts of activity."[63] If this was indeed a general cultural pattern, then, despite ebbs and flows, disparate events might still be understood as part of one underlying process. With respect to the labor movement, the events of 1917 were not so much a break with previous history but one more period of great ferment, with its own traits but still part of a long-term historical process.

PART IV

PERSPECTIVES ON THE URBAN REVOLUTION IN 1917

INTRODUCTION

The 1917 revolution was not inevitable, nor was the victory of the Bolsheviks foreordained before October or ensured thereafter. Scholars who point to the decisive impact of World War I on the collapse of the old regime and on the political radicalization of workers in 1917 are right to be skeptical of the theory of "the deep natural inevitability of the October Revolution."[1] Yet to deny the revolution's historical inevitability is not to embrace the contrary view that it was simply the product of the war and war conditions, and so historically "accidental."[2]

The argument to be developed in the following chapters rejects both of these polar alternatives. From this perspective the urban revolution grew out of a contradictory pattern of development that weakened the elites' capacity to respond to the crises confronting them and facilitated militant worker protest. With the overthrow of the tsarist state, labor protest took on much of its classical pattern and the workers, government officials, industrialists, and intelligentsia largely recapitulated their old pattern of relationships. The 1917 revolution thus confirms Marx's dictum that "just when they [men and women] seem engaged in revolutionizing themselves and things, in creating something that has never yet existed, precisely in such periods of revolutionary crisis they anxiously conjure up the spirits of the past."[3]

The following account does not aim to be a full description of the events of 1917. Rather, it demonstrates how an analytical perspective sheds light on certain crucial aspects of the 1917 revolution, especially urban class relations and the relationship of the workers to the socialist parties and the Provisional Government. It argues the following points: that the radicalism of the labor movement in 1917 can be understood in terms of the two sources of radicalism and the pattern of organization rooted in the autocratic capitalist regime; that despite important changes the class struggle between workers and industrialists took on much of its accustomed shape; that the workers' growing hostility toward the Provisional Government can also be understood largely in terms of their political experience under the tsarist regime; that the eventual triumph of Bolshevik ideas fed upon many of these prerevolutionary class and political patterns, and also upon traditional worker-intelligentsia ambivalence; and that despite temporary solidarity among various categories of workers and, by October, overwhelming support for the Bolsheviks, the same old antinomies produced by autocratic capitalist industrialization lay close to the surface.

To affirm the revolution's origins in the old regime is not to deny the significance of the discontinuities in the labor movement brought on by the war. A significant part of the male industrial labor force, roughly one-fifth to one-fourth, was drafted, and the percentage of females and minors working in industry accordingly increased.[4] There was a huge influx of callow peasant workers into wartime industry, many of them without a sense of proletarian identity or identification with the labor movement. The organized labor movement and the socialist parties suffered crushing blows from police repression that limited their activities and threatened to cut their ties with the worker masses.

Yet in another sense wartime repression served only to reinforce the classical pattern of unorganized mass protest and a socialist underground and so ensure that protest, when it broke out, would take radical forms. As opposed to other European countries, particularly Germany with its famous *Burgfrieden*, the Russian government made no significant concessions to the workers. In the beginning of the war governors were given almost dictatorial powers in dealing even with formally legal worker meetings. As early as the end of July 1914, Minister of Internal Affairs Maklakov explained that the law allowed authorities to exceed their legal rights if such measures were justified by extraordinary circumstances. Considering that such conditions were present throughout Russia, Maklakov assured local authorities that their zeal in protecting society "will always meet with the approval and support of the Ministry."[5] When strong measures such as the firing, exile, imprisonment, and drafting of striking workers failed to end worker unrest, various government bodies proposed the militarization of labor, with the subjugation of workers to military justice and regulation. Such proposals were rejected by the Council of Ministers for a variety of reasons, including fear of the widespread protest that they might have engendered and industrialist opposition to further state intervention in the factories.[6]

The war witnessed a repetition of many of the old debates over the proper way to handle the labor question. The interministerial splits were reactivated, and the government and industrialists reproached each other for their respective failures. Projects to permit the development of worker organizations—which were, after all, formally legal even if repressed in fact—were introduced but not passed in the Ministry of Internal Affairs.[7] The only liberal initiative to make any progress during the war was the formation of workers' groups attached to the industrialist-led war industries committees.[8] At first moderate in orientation, the workers' groups became radicalized in the general labor ferment of late 1916, showing once again how little scope for moderation there was in the Russian labor movement.

Political exclusion thus guaranteed the continuity of Russian labor protest. Beyond this, as will be shown in the following chapters, the cultural expectations and definitions of the situation fostered by the old regime continued to exercise their power. None of the major actors could reconcile themselves to a liberal system in which outcomes were the product of a balance of forces regulated by law. None of the major classes and parties understood or trusted one another, and their mutual fears and hatreds virtually ruled out compromise. The Provisional Government saw itself as the above-class mediator of social and political life, but the contending sides, hoping for an unconditional ally, both saw betrayal in its policies. Because of this matrix of interpretations, chances for the emergence of a liberal democratic society were slim. The possibility of a right-wing military dictatorship representing the threatened elites probably ranked somewhat higher, but the victory of the alliance of a militant class movement and a radical intelligentsia is far from astonishing.

The bearers of these interpretations and expectations were of course real people, and although the war removed a large number of activists, many experienced leaders remained to give shape to events. For example, despite changes in the composition of the labor force, a significant proletarian core survived in industry, particularly in Petrograd, the historic center of the labor movement, where only about 17 percent of industrial workers were drafted.[9] Further, Petrograd workers in highly modern defense-related factories, such as many of those in the Vyborg district, with its particulary strong tradition of militancy, were especially likely to be exempt from conscription.[10] Even in those areas, such as the south, where these skilled experienced workers became a small minority, their absolute number could remain stable because of the wartime expansion of industry, and so they could constitute enough of a critical mass to exercise considerable influence.[11] It was this maintenance of a basic kernel of experienced workers that has allowed Soviet scholars to argue that a potent nucleus of Russian worker activists survived throughout the war and gave direction to the reviving labor movement.

The point can be generalized. Millions of workers, industrialists, socialist party activists, and government bureaucrats survived from the prewar years into the revolution, and they brought with them established practices and memories from the past that shaped their activities and goals in the new Russia. Thus after February workers demanded the dismissal of administrative personnel whose actions they had resented under the old regime. Industrialists distrusted worker organizations because of their perceived role in previous revolutionary events. Committed socialists feared mass spontaneity and harbored suspicions toward revolutionaries of other factions.

The labor movement's revolutionary tradition was also able to survive on the basis of these continuities. A notable feature of the strikes of late 1916 and early 1917 was the celebration and reaffirmation of labor traditions, including 1 May and the anniversaries of Bloody Sunday and the Lena massacre. Present struggles were thus fused with past ones and identified as forming part of a larger historical sequence, one that would obviously extend into the revolution as well.

The February revolution provides the best evidence for the basic continuity of the Russian labor movement after nearly three years of war. For those who emphasize the contingent nature of the revolution, February was brought about by wartime deprivation and the collapse of the army. The revolution was spontaneous, the unexpected consequence of food riots initiated by hungry women. There was no guiding hand directing the February events, and the decisive factor was the rebellion of the garrison. This general interpretation has something to recommend it. The February revolution was clearly unexpected, just as much for the socialist parties as for every other social group. Similarly, party leaders did not direct the course of events and often tried to restrain worker militancy. Finally, the emphasis on the impact of the war and the incompetence of the tsarist state are certainly not misplaced.

Ultimately, however, the spontaneity and discontinuity theses distort the nature of the February revolution.[12] The hungry women who inadvertently initiated the revolution were textile workers who had previously participated in wartime strikes. Their factories were located in the Vyborg district next to two metal factories with militant traditions. More generally, the long-term interpenetration of the mass labor movement and the actions of small activist minorities had meant that few, if any, cases of worker protest were spontaneous in any simple sense. As Trotsky remarked, "the insurrectionaries [of February] were not human locusts. They had their political experience, their traditions, their slogans, their nameless leaders."[13] Their prior experience allowed them to contribute a degree of leadership to the February revolution as well. It was certainly true that this leadership was not firm enough to define the shape of events, much less to provide the basis for a new form of government. The labor movement had always been strongest at local levels, and February was no exception. As Hasegawa's account shows, however, leaders were clearly capable of channeling and stimulating mass unrest, avoiding, at least to some extent, unnecessary excesses and giving it a political focus.[14]

It is also an exaggeration to say that because of war weariness and government incompetence, the Petrograd garrison simply fell apart. First, as Wildman has argued, the mass defections of the troops had "deep and unalterable" historical causes in the social and political cleavages of Russian society.[15] Second, the garrison only rebelled when confronted with an extreme choice forced upon it by the mass movement: to disobey higher authorities or to shoot upon masses of militant demonstrators willing to risk death. The violence of Sunday, 26 February, was not sufficient to deter thousands of militant workers from further protest and so could not save the soldiers from this excruciating choice. In this sense the February revolution resembled, on a smaller scale, the Iranian revolution. Further, it was far from bloodless: more than 400 people were killed and over 1,200 wounded in Petrograd.[16]

Various aspects of the February revolution are thus explicable only within the context of the labor movement as it had developed historically. Even the spontaneous, unexpected outbreak of unrest resembled the beginnings of the 1905 revolution. The weakness of leadership and organization throughout the February days also repeated the traditional pattern, as did the rapid spread of solidarity and radicalism. The February revolution thus exemplifies the basic unbrokenness of the Russian labor movement despite the war. It also foreshadowed the future, as the cleavages revealed in February and present for decades before were never repaired. February initiated the revolution, but the revolution had already been shaped by larger historical forces.

If Russian workers acted in terms of perspectives and expectations created under the old regime, it is wrong to impose on them ahistorical schema of action and consciousness. They were neither simply "politically ignorant people" motivated by "envy and hatred" nor rational actors engaged in a "realistic mulling over of means and ends,"[17] but a social group interpreting events and acting in terms of their cultural understandings and prior experiences, which defined for them what was "rational" and what was not.

Nor, as will be seen, were the workers simply manipulated by the Bolsheviks. Various groups in 1917 offered the workers new definitions of Russian society and their own place in it. The industrialists proclaimed themselves staunch opponents of the old regime and bulwarks of a new European-style Russia. They hoped that this new definition would replace the older perceptions and so enhance the class harmony that could emerge from the growth of a responsible labor movement. They offered a new definition of the workers as well: free citizens in a liberal political regime who accepted the basic institutions of a capitalist society. The new Provisional Government also promised to renegotiate the relationship between state and society and to allow social groups more autonomy to struggle and cooperate with one another on their own terms. The revolution thus saw an apparent widening of possibilities, the chance for a recasting of relationships. New roles and definitions were at least proposed in what seemed to be an intoxicatingly new society.

Despite these new possibilities, however, by October the old definitions had triumphed over the new. Political and class relations came to be defined much as they had been in the late tsarist period. In particular, after several months the workers increasingly regarded the industrialists as counterrevolutionaries cooperating with a hostile state; they saw the

Provisional Government as a closer and closer approximation to the tsarist regime; and they played out their traditional ambivalence toward the revolutionary intelligentsia and parties in a massive shift from moderate socialism to the Bolsheviks. The workers eventually opted to support the Bolsheviks in overwhelming numbers because of the party's consistently class interpretation of events, which corresponded with their own.

The Bolshevik seizure of power in October thus stemmed from one aspect of the traditional worker-intelligentsia relationship, part of that "line at which they [could] meet and agree." Post-October Russian political life would bring into focus the other dimension of their relationship: the tenuousness of the line "between the secretly hostile camps."

CHAPTER
13

Radicalism in the Class Struggle

In overthrowing the tsarist state, the February revolution removed the very foundation of social relations— and thus the foundation of the class struggle—in Russia. Now, after February, it seemed that Russian society might truly be transformed, that civil society might become relatively self-regulating. The pattern of spasmodic outbursts followed by artificial tranquillity might be replaced by a more continuous and moderate adjustment of interests according to relative power.

Despite some early signs that such a transition might occur, the class struggle in 1917 proved to be largely consistent with its past. The previous organizational patterns, attitudes toward industrialists and private property, relationships with the socialist parties, and perspectives on the state and its role in class conflict survived the change in regime and even came to be reinforced by the crisis atmosphere of the revolution. Class conflict was thus still rooted in the historical dilemmas of autocratic capitalist industrialization, the effects of which endured longer than the autocracy itself. The class struggle also continued to be a major source of the political radicalization of Russian workers. Factory politics were intimately bound up with national politics, as the workers increasingly identified the industrialists with the Provisional Government.

Worker radicalism has probably been an important element in all modern revolutionary situations in countries with a significant level of industrialization. This was certainly the case in post-World War I Germany, Republican Spain, and Allende's Chile, three celebrated periods of worker militancy. Segments of the labor movement actively struggled to take over factories and establish proletarian power in the workplace and the state. In none of these cases, however, and perhaps nowhere else than Russia did previous patterns give birth to an almost uniformly radical labor movement (which is not to say working class) during the revolution.[1] On the contrary, in these other cases radicalism engendered significant opposition within the labor movements themselves.[2] These divisions corresponded to crucial sociological cleavages the expression of which had historically been permitted by mixed government policies toward labor. Only in Tsarist Russia had the state been so impotent in integrating industrial workers, and only there did the labor movement have the peculiar physiognomy described in earlier chapters.

Radicalism was not merely a conscious choice based on ideology for Russian workers in 1917. Barrington Moore is probably right that such principled decisions have been relatively rare among the masses even in the great revolutions. Perhaps in Germany radicalism depended to a high degree upon an aggregation of such individual decisions, and for this reason it was always a minority current. In Russia, however, radicalism did not stem only from such explicit choices, even though these were far from absent. Instead it was implicit in the preexisting attitudes, assumptions, institutions, social structure, and traditions of workers and the labor movement. Thus it was not, as many have averred, reducible to the anger of confused masses, any more than it was solely the product of schooled proletarian revolutionaries. As P. N. Durnovo wrote in a secret memorandum to the tsar in February 1914, "here the masses of the people unquestionably believe in the principles of unconscious Socialism."[3] Conscious ideological radicalism, one part of the labor movement before 1917 (though lacking the scale that it would assume during the revolution), only served to reinforce this "structural" radicalism rooted in the previous regime of autocratic capitalism.

The legacies from the past that would shape the class struggle in 1917 have already been discussed at length. From autocracy stemmed the weakness of organizations; the meager development of civil society (with its consequences: lack of trust, weak attachment to private property, the tenuous authority of elites); and the low commitment to pluralism and democracy. The growth of modern capitalist industry had added its very different complex of ingredients: conscious workers, socialist ideology, new forms of organization, demands for workers' control, and new types of collective action. The interdependence of these sources of radicalism was expressed in the complementarity of mass and class action, of spontaneity and consciousness, of mass and conscious workers. Radicalism was a synthesis of all of these opposing pairs, and it was sealed by a revolutionary tradition that kept alive the example of direct action and the authority of socialist ideals. Moderation had virtually no historical grounding either in meaningful paternalism by the tsarist state or in the integrative mechanisms of modern liberal capitalism. Quite the contrary: both autocracy and capitalism had given rise to their own forms of radicalism, both of which are essential for understanding the radicalization of the labor movement in 1917.

The radicalism in the Russian labor movement in 1917 was an emergent property of the movement, not a trait of all or perhaps even the
majority of Russian workers. Many workers remained passive, uncertain
of the future and afraid of action. Similarly, militancy in 1917 came in
waves: periods of temporary calm or disillusionment alternated with outbursts of combativeness. As in the Kornilov affair, workers often perceived their actions to be defensive, necessary for the preservation of the
revolution. On all these counts it would be wrong to picture a highly
ideological and united working class anxious at all times and at all costs
to vanquish its enemy. Such a revolutionary movement did not exist in
Russia, or in any other revolutionary situation. The Russian labor movement was revolutionary in a more nuanced way, the product of a peculiar
historical development combined with events of great turbulence and
conflict.

THE RADICALIZATION OF THE CLASS STRUGGLE
IN 1917: A DESCRIPTION

THE INITIAL SITUATION

In no period do we, therefore, find a more confused mixture of high-flown
phrases and actual uncertainty and clumsiness, of more enthusiastic striving
for innovation and more deeply-rooted domination of the old routine, of more
apparent harmony of the whole of society and more profound estrangement of
its elements.

—Karl Marx, *The Eighteenth Brumaire*[4]

Many factory owners and officials of the new government perceived
the precarious position of private enterprise after the February revolution. An article in the *Trade Industrial Gazette* from early March contained a warning about the danger of economic and political class struggle in the new regime, concluding that "the clear golden days of freedom
can easily become darkened by gray storm clouds."[5] And of course for
many years liberal industrialists had feared the prospect of confronting
the workers, as Konovalov had said, face to face, and they had perceived
that the isolation of workers from the industrialists was a great danger
for "the normal political development of the country."[6]
    In order to counter this threat of sharpened class conflict, political
leaders and economic elites developed a number of strategies. First they
tried to portray themselves as authentic revolutionary leaders legitimated
by militant past struggles against tsarism. "Comrade Citizens," began an
appeal by the Trade Industrial Committee of Ekaterinburg, in the Urals.

"Understand that among the most outstanding organizations of democracy is the merchant industrial class, which in the course of long years took the most active participation in the preparatory work of the liberation movement."[7] In a similar statement Zubatov's old nemesis Guzhon referred explicitly to the industrialists' defense of the workers' group of the war industries committees during the war. "We were not revolutionary when we began," he asserted, "but the government made us so."[8] In accord with these claims, factory owner organizations collected donations to support freed political prisoners: "The rebirth of Russia was prepared by those for whom we now gather funds."[9]

Beyond this the Provisional Government and industrialists hoped that with the tsarist state gone, the class struggle could develop in an organized fashion. "The revolution swept away the oppression of the police regime which hung over the labor movement, and the liberated working class can by its own class solidarity and unity defend its economic interests."[10] Such interests, it was assumed, included the preservation of industry, upon whose prosperity the workers' livelihoods depended. Organizations, rationally calculating and defending these interests, would give rise to a purely economic class struggle and a healthy economy. Thus in word and often in deed, the government and many factory owners supported the creation of worker organizations and also supplementary bodies, such as conciliatory chambers and arbitration courts, which would ensure that they had a proper voice in factory affairs.

A third strategy was to appeal to worker patriotism. The war required a healthy economy, and this in turn necessitated high productivity and strict labor discipline. Heightened class struggle would harm the cause of the nation and thus threaten the survival of the revolution itself by undercutting the economy.

Finally, factory owners made significant concessions in the early days of the revolution, especially in the capital, where they led the way in accepting the eight-hour day and recognizing the soviets and factory committees. By the end of March even the more wary industrialists of the Donets Basin had recognized the eight-hour day, at least in principle, though they made an exception for factories where it would lead to a decrease in production.[11] Obviously these were not purely voluntary agreements,[12] but they did include an element of willing sacrifice based on the hope that initial concessions might create an atmosphere of harmony. In addition, at least some categories of workers received significant wage increases after the revolution, especially organized workers who could better press their demands.[13]

Moderate socialists supported all of these attempts of the political and economic elites to control the class struggle. They defined the revolution as bourgeois, thus emphasizing the industrialists' revolutionary role until the complete democratization of the country had been achieved. They also advocated organization in the name of a controlled class struggle. Similarly, the great majority of moderate socialists supported the continuation of the war, and they urged workers to support their brother soldiers at the front through hard work. They welcomed and ratified factory owner concessions as a sign of the latter's willingness to compromise and hoped that they would have a moderating effect upon the workers' demands.

It is true that there were many signs in the labor movement in the early weeks of the revolution to encourage optimism among partisans of a bourgeois revolution. A new patriotism born of the revolutionary struggle was evident, leading Shliapnikov to remark on how easily the "broad worker masses gave themselves up to the lure of 'all-national brotherhood' or the unity of 'revolutionary democracy.'"[14] Workers passed resolutions promising to make sacrifices for the sake of the war effort, often with the proviso that the war be regarded as purely defensive.[15] This mood partly explains the workers' willingess to recognize the legitimacy of the Provisional Government, even if this recognition was itself provisional and partly at the behest of the Soviet. Similarly, the great prestige of the Soviet, dominated as it was by the moderate socialists, was also a sign of forbearance, although the workers by no means slavishly obeyed its commands. The tempo of the strike movement declined significantly, even if not as dramatically as earlier scholarship maintained.[16] Further, despite the enactment of the eight-hour day, overtime work was often accepted out of the conviction that the war required sacrifice. The workers' sense of responsibility resulted in a probable rise in productivity in this early period, although the evidence in this regard is incomplete.[17]

When the workers were accused of indiscipline and irresponsibility, their reactions often showed great concern for the condition of industry and their own honor as a class. For example, in a meeting of representatives of several Petrograd factories, the workers reacted indignantly to the bourgeois press' "vile slander" and the factory owners' 7 March declaration, which attempted to "pass responsibility for the collapse and disorganization of industry to the workers." They called for a series of meetings to clarify "the true cause of the industrial collapse" and to expose those who impeded economic recovery.[18] Such phenomena indicated, declared the *Trade Industrial Gazette*, that the people were with the government. "It is easy to construct on such a basis," it concluded. "In such an atmosphere it is easy to work."[19]

These signs of moderation were superficial, however, a product of the evanescent atmosphere of revolutionary solidarity and of the absence of political experience among workers. Lenin saw more deeply: "Instinctively, emotionally, and by attraction, the bulk of Russia's population, namely, the proletarians and semi-proletarians, i.e., the workers and poor peasants, are in sympathy with a revolution against the capitalists."[20] Indications of the irreconcilable industrial conflicts to come were far from absent even in the earliest period of the revolution.

The implicit radicalism of the workers was evident first in the range of issues at stake in the revolution. The major definitions of what could be contested derived from the recent past, when the tsarist state had itself taught the workers the weakness of an independent civil order. In 1917 the survival of the basic institutions of capitalist Russia was posed automatically. The demand for workers' control or the nationalization of industry came readily to the minds of people who had never accepted the legitimacy of capitalist industry. In the German revolution, an episode useful for highlighting the distinctiveness of Russia, issues were not as consistently posed in such an uncompromising way, and there was widespread worker acceptance of private property and entrepreneurial authority. Such definitions of what is at stake in social change, of what it makes sense to contest, are historically based.

The historical linkage between economic and political demands within the labor movement provides a particularly important example of a radical posing of issues in the Russian revolution. The dominant role of the autocratic state in economic life had led to an interpenetration of economic and political goals in social protest under the old regime. For this reason from the first days of the revolution it was difficult for rank-and-file workers to accept the moderate socialists' claims that February had ushered in a bourgeois, not a socialist, revolution. Workers demanded an eight-hour day, higher wages, and the removal of personnel repugnant to them. They assumed that the capitalists would oppose their demands, as they had done historically, and so saw them as their enemies and thus enemies of the revolution as well. A gathering of 4,000 workers in the Petrograd Cartridge factory adopted the following resolution in a meeting to commemorate the fifth anniversary of the Lena massacre (4 April):

> The autocratic government is overthrown, but on the path to a bright future for the laboring masses stands a threatening enemy—the capitalist bourgeoisie. We trust that, similar to how the autocracy, guilty of this barbaric shooting, was overthrown, the laboring class will eliminate the hated dominance of capital and on its ruins it will bring forth the desired kingdom of worldwide brotherhood and equality.[21]

Although the ideological thrust of this resolution was unusual, there was very broad sentiment that the political revolution also entitled the workers to economic gains. Korolev reports that by the end of February the workers in his factory had elected a factory committee and authorized it to enact the eight-hour day, a twenty percent salary bonus for the past year, and a one hundred percent wage increase, and had also instructed it to fire "toadies," spies, and the like.[22] It is clear from such demands that civil society had no separate rules and principles of legitimacy. In the minds of the workers capitalism was historically and morally linked to the tsarist state, and the downfall of the autocracy prepared the way for victory over the capitalists, whose privileges had been secured only by government repression. For Russian workers who, unlike many of their counterparts in more democratic countries, had never learned to value parliamentary procedures, February was a great deal more (and also less) than a bourgeois revolution.

As in previous years, the initial hostility toward the capitalists had both an "unconscious" dimension based on the mass workers' experiences under the autocracy and a more self-consciously radical aspect identified with the socialist tradition. Manifestations of the first type of radicalism were often branded as anarchy, but it must be emphasized that such "spontaneity" partly derived from the workers' political culture—an alternative to "bourgeois" assumptions—and so could not merely be defined by the absence of "consciousness." Their consciousness, no matter how nonideological, had already been partly shaped by the autocratic regime. As a consequence of the workers' fundamental assumptions and also the breakdown of authority, instances of the spirit of anarchy, if seldom its doctrine, abound in the early weeks of the revolution. Workers often obeyed the directives of their organizations either hesitantly or not at all. For example, it was only with great difficulty that the Petrograd Soviet managed to convince workers to return to their factories after the February strikes.[23] Similarly, there was a disconcerting amount of violence in local factory affairs, particularly over the removal of factory administrators unacceptable to the workers.[24] Many wage increases were gained through intimidation and fear.[25] Such incidents could even take place in factories where the management made extraordinary concessions to the workers, such as the Skorokhod factory in Petrograd, where the owners had donated a great deal of money to support the cause of the workers.[26] Cases of worker spontaneity were also part of a general atmosphere of hostility toward what, even in early April, was occasionally referred to as "our counterrevolutionary bourgeoisie."[27] Workers sometimes suspected that factory owner complaints about the lack of fuel and raw materials were simply attempts to conceal a policy of lockouts, a good example of the basic lack of trust inherited from the former regime.[28]

Early worker radicalism did not only assume this "spontaneous" form, however. Sometimes it was directly sponsored by worker organizations.

For example, in many defense-related state factories in Petrograd the factory committees administered the factories until mid-April. Their actions were not strictly an indicator of revolutionary militancy, for much of the motivation was to ensure continued military production after the fall of the tsarist state. There was certainly an element of revolutionary ambition as well, however, for the worker leaders in these factories, many of them Bolsheviks, were committed to democratizing their factories. Moderate worker leaders eventually succeeded in curtailing the rights of the factory committees in this sector, but their efforts did not resolve the basic dilemma of reconciling actual worker power and nominal managerial authority.[29] The same dilemma was visible in the Urals, where worker organizations also took on managerial functions, often because the managers were incompetent or absent. Worker organizations were surprised at the criticism they received, for they saw themselves as safeguarding production in conditions of managerial irresponsibility.[30]

The first month or so of the revolution thus revealed that the workers' definitions of the class struggle still lacked clarity and consistency. Workers were not entirely certain whether the factory owners were their allies in a bourgeois revolution or their enemies in a socialist one. They did not know whether their initial hostility toward their class enemy should be channeled into cooperation for the sake of protecting the revolution or deepened in order to ensure its further development. By late summer, however, the revolutionary process would eliminate the ambiguities and crystallize an almost exclusively radical definition of class relations among politically active workers. The vast majority came to believe that, as one Bolshevik worker expressed it in early October, "there's no middle course—either be completely for the bourgeoisie, or against it, with us, right up to bringing out the proletariat into the street for the decisive battle."[31] Worker radicalism, implicit in the revolution from the beginning but initially diluted by the appeals of moderate socialist leaders and the general revolutionary effervescence, quickly became the organizing principle of the class struggle in 1917.

THE CRYSTALLIZATION OF RADICALISM

Worker attitudes and actions in the class struggle were transformed in the course of 1917 primarily under the influence of three interrelated processes: the continuation of the war, the deepening economic crisis, and the perceived hardening of the industrialists' stance toward the workers. Workers blamed the capitalists and, with them, the Provisional Government, for all three of these conditions, rapidly coming to view them all as agents of willed sabotage of the revolution.[32] However, the causes of worker radicalism go much deeper than these facilitating conditions, which, in a different historical context, might have led to very different reactions. Military defeat, for example, could have permanently undermined the leftists who might conceivably have been seen as traitors to the country and the revolution. In 1917 Russia such sentiments did emerge among the workers against the Bolsheviks after the July days, but they quickly all but vanished. Similarly, economic crisis and a tougher industrialist stance could potentially have divided or demoralized the working class. In Russia, however, the social topography of class relations and of the labor movement had developed in such a way as to select in favor of radical interpretations and actions. Thus after the following capsule description of the process of radicalization, this outcome will be discussed in terms of the long-term consequences of autocratic capitalism.

Despite the pleas of the government and industrialists, who sought to convince the workers that victory over Imperial Germany was necessary for the consummation of the revolution, the workers saw an end to the war as one of the basic goals of the revolution from the beginning. As mentioned earlier, many workers supported a short-lived purely defensive war, but this compromise could not mask overwhelming emotional hostility toward its continuation. The war did not end, however, and because of incidents like the Miliukov note in late April there was a widespread sense that the government was pursuing aggressive aims.[33] Such suspicions were reinforced by the June-July offensive, which, despite initial successes, by early July had ended poorly for the Russians. It may have been true that workers mostly blamed the government for the continuation of the war, but, as had been true under the old regime, workers tended to identify the government with the capitalists.[34] Thus the industrialists were certainly held partly responsible for the continuing carnage, particularly as the war dragged on toward October.[35] Apart from this, no matter how blame was assigned, the war had the indirect effect of intensifying the economic crisis and so exacerbating class conflict.

The late spring and early summer of 1917 also marked a turning point in the economic condition of the country. The economy had long since shown signs of great strain during the war, and food shortages had been partly responsible for precipitating the February revolution. By early summer, however, the economic crisis had reached a new level. In June the Ministry of Trade and Industry prepared a bleak report on the economic situation of the country. "The disruption of Russia's national economy has reached its peak at the present moment," it began. "The country is facing economic and financial bankruptcy. These menacing symptoms appear with special vividness in the main branches of industry, which have completely lost their equilibrium."[36] The crisis of industrial production stemmed partly from shortages of fuel: in the south the production and transport of coal and anthracite was significantly lower in the second third of the year than the first.[37] And it was exacerbated by what the ministry's report termed "the dreadful situation in transport," which caused acute shortages of food and other basic necessities in the cities.[38] The inevitable consequence was a runaway inflation that far surpassed increases in wages.[39] The industrialists also suffered from the shortages. According to ministry figures, factory shutdowns started to increase dramatically in May.[40] Undoubtedly many of these closings were politically motivated, but of a sample of 568 factories closing between March and July, Soviet historian Volobuev attributed 375 (66 percent) to a lack of fuel.[41] This desperate and constantly worsening economic situation provided the context for the sharpening of class antagonisms in the spring and early summer of 1917. By raising the stakes of the struggle and by forcing both sides into actions that reinforced the suspicions of the other, the economic crisis further channeled class relations into their historical patterns.

It was approximately at this time (early summer) that a hardened strategy on the part of some factory owners began to embitter the workers even more, leading to the dissipation of the earlier ambivalent mood. As will be discussed in more detail, the actual response of the industrialists to the intensification of the class struggle was complex and diverse, by no means purely aggressive. Much of their apparent militancy arose from a sense of desperation, the result of a desire to survive in a seemingly hopeless situation. Whatever the nuances, however, with a noticeable increase in lockouts and urgent calls for repression, the workers came to have an almost monolithic view of the factory owners as ardent counterrevolutionaries. By October there were few workers who granted them any property rights or legitimacy, and the only question concerned the best strategy for opposing and neutralizing them.

These three factors, then, helped crystallize many previously implicit preconceptions into conscious anticapitalist attitudes in the course of 1917. The capitalists were accused of economic sabotage, of willfully creating shortages and stopping plants for political purposes.[42] Lack of factory maintenance and failure to replace raw materials were interpreted as Italian strikes by management. Plant closures were merely disguised lockouts. The factory owners, who, said the workers, denounced the economic ruin of the country even though they themselves created it,[43] were thus identified with economic chaos. Such chaos helped the industrialists, charged the workers, because it would weaken the workers' resolve to struggle and turn the rest of the population, especially the soldiers, against them. All of this showed that the factory owners, with their international economic ties and often foreign backgrounds, cared little for the fate of Russia—a lack of concern evident in their commitment to the war. Thus chaos was identified with the class enemy and the working class stood for order—the transposed but otherwise identical view that the factory owners had of the workers.[44] Both sides thought that the other sought to bring Russia to ruin for the sake of its own interests. Workers felt that these weapons were employed not just for the sake of the class struggle but also as part of an overall counterrevolutionary policy.[45] In the late spring such suspicions were mainly evident in the widespread hostility toward the evacuation of Petrograd and the transference of industry to safer locations. Although the government and many factory owners proclaimed the necessity for this policy in order to protect industry from the Germans, the workers saw it as a plot to destroy revolutionary Petrograd. The goal, they felt, was simply to clear the revolutionary workers from the city. It would be more appropriate, proclaimed one resolution signed by 700 Putilov workers, to evacuate the idle bourgeoisie whiling away time in restaurants on the Nevskii Prospect.[46]

Workers also saw the specter of counterrevolution behind the factory owner's attempts to curtail meetings of worker organizations during working hours and their efforts to stop paying wages to worker representatives. The industrialists claimed that they should not have to subsidize their class opponent. The workers interpreted this refusal as a sign of their bosses' unrelenting hostility toward the gains legitimately won in the revolution. These suspicions were especially widespread from late spring, when, as noted earlier, a substantial number of factory owners embarked on a more aggressive policy. Workers seemed to be convinced that, as one trade union newspaper put it, this "coterie of overfed exploiters" was ready to attack the proletariat at the first favorable moment and "to wipe off the face of the earth all of its victories won by blood."[47]

The workers' recriminations reached their apex in the Kornilov affair, which many powerful factory owners did indeed support. On this basis the workers drew the extreme conclusion that the industrialist class was uniformly counterrevolutionary, that there was not even a pro-February bourgeoisie. Here are some excerpts from an unsigned article entitled "Traitors" from the printers' newspaper *Pechatnik*, whose union remained one of the few remaining outposts of Menshevism in the labor movement and thus relatively moderate.[48] It opens with the declaration that "the punitive expedition"[49] of the organized bourgeoisie was not successful, thus identifying the industrialists with the worst excesses of the old regime. For the previous six months, continued the article, the factory owners had been undermining the revolution by destroying the economy and attacking the soviets, seeing in the latter a truly strong organized force (and not just anarchy). Now the Kornilov plot revealed them openly for the counterrevolutionaries that they had always been, ready to plunge the country into fratricidal war to maintain their privileges and so make the front vulnerable to the Germans. They were thus traitors to the people. By contrast, "we workers do not claim to be patriotic as this is understood in a philistine way, but we must be true patriots of our revolution. . . . The recent events [the Kornilov affair] and our relation to them speak in favor of our political maturity; they reveal our ability to submit ourselves to the interests of the general whole. Let it be so and not otherwise." The bourgeoisie, the enemies of the working class, were thus the enemies of the people as well.[50]

In this way were class and nationalism linked in the eyes of Russian workers in 1917. Perhaps in no other modern revolution was this linkage so clear. In China, Vietnam, and Iran nationalism was probably a stronger force than in Russia, but in none of these cases was nationalism given such a narrow class interpretation, either by the leadership or by the mass movement. The connection between class and nationalism was just as powerful a synthesis in Russia as the orthodox Marxist linkage of class and socialism. Both combinations had roots in the tsarist order, in which the autocracy had nourished the idea that the factory owners were both outsiders and exploiters. Now in 1917 all three components were joined in a polarized vision: workers came to feel that the salvation of the nation required a socialist state representing their own interests. Freedom—for them—could be made consistent with the need for order, one of the strongest strivings of Russian workers. Order required the control of sabotage, speculation, and counterrevolution, and thus of the bourgeoisie. The factory owners were nothing more than "internal Germans," and so without any rights in revolutionary Russia.[51] Such control would allow the workers to enjoy material advantages (deprivation was the product of disorder) and the freedom to organize and participate. Freedom, then, was also given a class interpretation, one very far removed from the rules of formal democracy. If February brought freedom, October was to bring both freedom and order.

The radicalization of attitudes corresponded, in a complicated way, to the radicalization of action in the class struggle. By radical action, I mean efforts to curtail or eliminate the property rights of the industrialists. From a comparative standpoint, the Russian labor movement in 1917 was in some ways not as radical as its counterparts in other revolutions. The movement for socialization among workers in early 1919 Germany was stronger than in pre-October Russia. In the last years of Allende's regime in Chile more factories were seized by the workers than ever occurred in Russia.[52] The distinctiveness of Russia lies in the weakness of moderation within the labor movement and, correlatively, the lack of serious internal splits. This is not to say that Russian workers were uniformly radical or that radicalism was a fixed quality. As opposed to

Germany or Chile, however, little support for the status quo or deep-seated hostility toward the radical left could be found during the 1917 revolution.

As had historically been the case, worker radicalism in the 1917 revolution had two basic dimensions: the "spontaneous" attack on property rights and the more programmatic attempt to alter capitalist relations through workers' control or nationalization of industry. Throughout 1917 the relative weight of these two modes of action, the first more typical of the "backward" workers, the second favored by their more conscious fellows, changed in favor of more planned and considered radicalism. From the early period of the revolution, however, there existed a degree of conscious radicalism, and spontaneous direct action remained after October to haunt Lenin.

In the first month or so of the revolution, the implicit anticapitalism of the workers emerged as radical direct action without explicit radical attitudes. This form of radicalism was encouraged by the relative absence of state power and the weakness of worker organizations—and it is the mode of action most frequently mentioned by Western scholars. It was also quite appropriate for the main aspirations of the workers in this early period: wage increases, the eight-hour day, and the removal of unacceptable administrative personnel. The first goal would eventually require greater organization and tactical coordination, but in the first weeks of the revolution direct action was quite effective in inducing concessions from worried employers, and strikes in the proper sense were quite rare. The eight-hour day and the purging of the administration could often be carried out by the workers on their own, even without the consent of the employer, and "spontaneity" in the early period proved especially effective in achieving these purposes, as the frequent complaints of employers attest.

Newspapers and archival records give vivid descriptions of direct action in 1917: attacks against the factory or its personnel, the use of violence to resolve disputes, the failure to obey directives from organizations and even assaults upon their leaders. Such acts appear to have been most widespread among the least proletarian elements of the labor force, particularly women, peasants, and unskilled workers.[53] In part they attest to anarchy, to the lack of effective state power. They were also rooted, however, in the lack of legitimacy of capitalism and the weakness of civil society, which historically had given the labor movement such a strong mass character.

There were some signs of organized radicalism even in the early period of the revolution, but these were either inspired by minority party activists or largely defensive in character. As an example of the former phenomenon, in early March some Bolshevik activists called for a continuation of the strike that had overthrown the tsarist state and urged a policy of class warfare against the bourgeoisie.[54] Such radicalism was an isolated current even within the Bolshevik party, however.

Instances of defensive radicalism were more significant, especially, as noted earlier, in the state sector of the capital's industry and in the Urals. Encouraged by moderate leaders, after a short time the workers renounced the goal of worker management, but they arrogated to themselves extensive rights of interference in labor relations and managerial policy. Clearly the workers saw their new powers as matters of right justified by their past suffering at the hands of management.[55] The appropriation of these new rights was accomplished with little debate and in an atmosphere of complete assurance of righteousness. Similar conclusions seem justified even in the relatively isolated cases of early workers' control in backward factories. For example, in the Treugol'nik factory, with its largely peasant and unskilled labor force, beginning in early April the council of elders began to take on many management functions in an effortless and natural way. It began to investigate delays in production, to control access to the factory, and to elect worker representatives to sit on the board of directors.[56] In the Kolomenskii machine-building factory the executive committee of the council of elders complained to the factory inspector when the new manager tried to strip it of some of its formally illegal powers. It was wrong, appealed the council, for the new manager to conduct an open struggle with their organizations, which, they ingenuously claimed, were of a purely economic nature.[57]

The temporary triumph of the moderate socialists in the labor movement dampened much of the early worker radicalism. As noted earlier, the socialist parties, the labor press, and the renascent worker organizations all urged tactical moderation in the class struggle, and their appeals were not without effect. An organized, extraplant strike movement with some ability to calculate and control did emerge. Conciliatory chambers were formed and achieved some very limited success in resolving disputes. The boundaries to this moderation were always visible in several respects, however. First, the workers did not fail to proclaim that their restraint was only tactical and would be abandoned when convenient for them. For example, an article couched in military language, with references to "diplomatic relations" with the enemy and the like, concludes as follows: the more organized, serious, and disciplined the worker army, "the sooner will the future open class struggle lead the proletariat to a 'victorious end.'"[58] In addition, no matter how reasonable and moderate the workers' demands may have been in their own eyes, often they simply could not be fulfilled, a consequence of the economic crisis.[59] Finally, many workers, particularly the unskilled, never accepted the logic of conciliation and often threatened to undermine accords made by worker organizations.[60] One understands why many factory owners became skeptical about the promises of worker organizations.

By late summer principled radicalism based upon a commitment to organized action had become more prominent in the labor movement. Calls for workers' control, factory requisitions, and the nationalization of industry under the auspices of a socialist government multiplied. The immediate causes of this change are not difficult to locate: the transformation of worker attitudes; the failure of controlled class struggle to resolve basic problems, particularly in the context of the worsening economic crisis; and the growing influence of Bolshevism, with its commitment to an all-socialist government. Now more than ever, the class struggle became intertwined with radical politics.

The change was evident, for example, in the nature of the strike movement in the final period before October. Strikes no longer implicitly assumed the continued existence of capitalist relations, and their demands became more politically radical. In some regions of the country strikes of a size unprecedented in the history of Russian labor broke out.[61] The railway workers' general strike of 23–27 September numbered approximately 600,000 workers; 300,000 workers participated in the central industrial region textile strike beginning in late October; and in September and October literally the whole south of Russia was in great turmoil. These strikes were notable not only for their massive size but also for the uncompromising attitudes of the workers participating in them. For example, the president of the strike committee of the Ekaterinskii railway line assured Kerensky that he "must understand that we will carry on the struggle to the end. Let him know that even victory over us is the death of the Russian railways. Let him know that madmen inspire him, that a refusal of the union's demands even without our opposition is the ruin of the railroads. Our struggle has as its goal the salvation of the country."[62]

Such threats were far from empty, for the weapons at the disposal of the strikers by this stage of the revolution were most impressive. This was the case even for such relatively weak groups as the textile workers. For example, on 18 October the Ivanovo-Voznesensk textile workers' union announced the following methods of struggle for its upcoming strike: (1) A telegram was to be sent to Moscow and Petrograd textile workers with a request to support their action. (2) Worker organizations would not allow products to leave the factories. (3) Control over the shipping of products on the railways would be established by means of Red Guards after an agreement with the railway workers. (4) Delegations were to be sent to the Ministry of Labor, the Central Executive Committee of the Soviet, and the all-Russian Council of Trade Unions to inform them of the situation and win their support. It was no wonder that the strike went very well. "In these days the authentic bosses of the enterprises were the workers themselves. . . . The factory owners, yesterday bosses, one after another abandon their old haunts and flee to Moscow."[63]

As against this general picture of militancy the strike movement in both Petrograd and Moscow declined after the Kornilov affair in late August. For Petrograd, Mandel's explanation for this apparent anomaly, supported by a number of examples, is that the worker leadership was able to prevent the masses from conducting such pointless struggles. Rather, it was able to persuade them to wait and channel their efforts into the preparations for a seizure of power.[64] Of course, it was only a small minority of workers who actively enlisted in the workers' militia or Red Guards, but their rapid growth in September and October in various industrial centers of the country lends weight to Mandel's explanation.[65]

In another sense, too, the workers' opposition to the factory owners went beyond the bounds of the strike movement. As a response to lockouts, the owners' unwillingness to meet the workers' demands, and the impotence of the Provisional Government, in the final months before October workers' control took increasingly developed forms, including intervention in sales and financing. The reason for many of these actions was simply to continue production and save jobs, but the line between defensive and offensive motives cannot be drawn in a clear-cut way. The workers' very efforts at self-defense led them to actions that were understandably perceived by their opponents as highly aggressive.

Workers' organizations participating in workers' control faced a terrible dilemma in this final period. Given the catastrophic economic situation in many firms, layoffs and partial shutdowns were unavoidable. Management and the government often asked for the cooperation of worker leaders in order to gain acceptance for these measures. Anguished debates were held about the advisability of worker organizations' taking on administrative functions, for they would clearly assume some of the responsibility for the crisis.[66] One way of resolving the dilemma is evident in the rationale of the leadership of the Petrograd metalworkers' union: the union should help raise productivity and undertake substantial worker control in order to help develop industry and therefore hasten the triumph of socialism: "The working class will burst apart the shell of capitalism and from the kingdom of darkness it will pass into the kingdom of light and freedom."[67]

The basic outlines of the old Menshevik conception are still evident in the metalworkers' strategy, but for many worker leaders the dissonance could be only resolved by workers' control within the context of state control over the whole economy. This would require an all-socialist government acting in the interests of the working class, which workers perceived to be the real interests of the whole country. This was also the position on workers' control advocated by Lenin: workers' control was to operate through worker representation in government institutions regulating the economy and through worker participation in local activities. He saw worker initiative and socialist direction of the state as complementary rather than contradictory processes.[68] Both worker organizations and the Bolshevik party rejected a syndicalist model of worker self-management and local autonomy.

Although worker sentiment about workers' control and the desirability of a socialist government shifted dramatically toward the Bolsheviks in the final months, workers' control and workers' self-management still remained rather limited phenomena. Without adequate financial support and with only limited administrative experience, workers preferred to wait until a socialist government was actually established. At that time the bourgeoisie would be truly superfluous. This, indeed, was the conclusion reached by a metalworkers' conference held in early November 1917. The bourgeoisie, it resolved, had shown itself unwilling and unable to save the country from economic disaster.

> In such conditions the heroic efforts of the working class are necessary in order to organize the whole economy of the country. To the bourgeoisie's counterrevolutionary economic policy, the workers' organizations, in particular the trade unions, must oppose their own class policy, which at the present moment more than ever responds to the needs of the enormous majority of the population.[69]

That such a decision could only be resolved after the Bolshevik seizure powerfully supports the conclusion that the movement for workers' control was only part of the an overall socialist vision of state and society, and not at all an independent movement with syndicalist aims.

The radicalism of the last two months before the October revolution embodied a new unity between the conscious worker leadership and the worker masses. Worker leaders openly espousing the idea of a prolonged bourgeois revolution almost disappeared from view, either through revision of their ideas or by replacement through reelection. Few worker organizations opposed the formation of an all-socialist government that would take direct control over the economy. At the same time, under pressure of the revolution the political ideas of the worker masses had congealed as never before, and there was overwhelming support for socialism as they understood it, as well as for that party which most clearly espoused it. "Consciousness" and "spontaneity" were temporarily joined, both within the labor movement and as a unity of outlook between the workers and the Bolshevik party.

This commitment to organized radicalism did not encompass all workers, however. In fact, there was much commentary at the time about the passivity and indifference of many workers.[70] Such apathy, it may be suggested, stemmed from the extreme choice facing the workers: not whether to strike but whether to take power. The triumph of radicalism as the only realistic alternative thus led to the marginalization of many workers from the movement. In addition, the desperate economic and political situation strengthened the appeal of anarchist direct action methods, particularly among unskilled workers. As Mandel points out, however, very few workers were converted to a principled commitment to anarchist views.[71] Workers, schooled under the old regime, tended toward a statist perspective emphasizing order and control from above, now to be based on a new class and new ideas. The challenges to this overall viewpoint were not theoretical and hardly threatened to undermine the solidarity of the labor movement in any consistent way.

LONG-TERM SOURCES OF RADICALISM

Behind the class conflict of 1917 lay several decades of capitalist industrialization and many centuries of autocratic rule. The workers' experiences in capitalist factories and with the despotic tsarist state that underwrote modern industry provided the most important context for their understanding of class relations in revolutionary Russia. In addition, the organizational patterns of the labor movement and the workers' political loyalties, whether schematic or deeply considered, were a legacy of the past that impinged on the present. Taken together, these shaped the workers' responses to the immediate crises facing them in their relationship to the factory owners in 1917 and explain the radicalism described earlier.

THE AUTOCRATIC LEGACY: CLASS POLARIZATION

Because of the weak development of civil society under the autocracy, workers had little sense that managerial authority could be rooted in factory relations. Authority was politically defined, relatively unconnected to the role of elites in civil society. The civil order was not seen as determinant, and consequently there was lack of agreed-upon rights on the part of both parties. Property rights and authority had depended upon the state much more than had been the case in Western Europe. After the fall of the autocracy the factory owners were left to confront a working class oblivious to their claims to legitimacy.

In the new situation workers did not accept private property and the rights claimed for it. The Socialist Revolutionary worker Voronkov, a delegate to the late May Petrograd factory committee conference, expressed the rival view with unusual clarity: all the noise of the bourgeois press about anarchy and the seizure of factories is based on the principle of "'the inviolability and sanctity' of property. For the bourgeoisie this principle is above the interests not only of any single class in the state, but above the interests of the state as a whole. Of course, workers cannot bow down before such a principle."[72] Consequently, factory owners had no right to dispose of their property as they wished, firing workers or closing plants to the detriment of the workers.[73] Following this same logic, the Petergof Soviet ordered the owner of the Zakorko factory not to fire workers because of a shortage of fuel or orders. Further, they told him to take back three workers already fired and sent into military service. Firing, they said, could not be justified purely by the search for profits.[74]

There was also skepticism among workers about the value of the industrialists' contribution to the factories' performance. In the view of the council of elders of the Dinamo factory, their enterprise could be administered perfectly well "without high-cost mediators between the government and the workers in the person of the stock society": on its own the factory committee could guarantee satisfactory production with the cooperation of government representatives.[75] Private entrepreneurship was not regarded as a scarce resource entitling the factory owners to authority or profits.[76] Recall that factory owners had historically been regarded as parasites living off the largesse of the government. Further, just as in the past, factory owners had often reinforced this view by appealing to the government for intervention in labor relations; so out of a sense of their own weakness, they continued to do this in 1917.[77]

In addition to their weak legitimacy, the industrialists bore the onus of being identified with the old regime and the war. Undoubtedly many factory owners had opposed the February strikes that had toppled the government,[78] and workers remembered the cooperation that many had offered to the government during the war. Workers, said one worker representative,

know how the propertied classes look on our organizations, they know how they looked [on them] earlier in the days of the reign of the Romanovs, and how they look now, when already much has changed for the better for us. . . . The factory owners wait for something better for themselves, they hope . . . that they will again take everything into their hands and return to the former times.[79]

These suspicions were exacerbated by the widespread belief that the factory owners favored the war for reasons of self-interest. This belief had existed during the war and was even shared by the relatively moderate workers' group of the war industries committee,[80] but by October 1917 it had become almost axiomatic.

All of these assumptions gave rise to a basic mood of mistrust and a sense on both sides that an unbridgeable gulf separated them. Such sentiments as those expressed by the factory committee of the Raditskii plant surely must have been widespread. The committee declared that the many problems of their enterprise could be resolved, except that "even before the revolutionary period, and up until the present, there existed a sharp gap between the factory administration and the workers, and therefore it is not possible to undertake these tasks and stop the entrepreneur's encroachments on the interests of the working class."[81] From very early, many workers suspected the factory owners both of mismanagement and sabotage within the plant and of counterrevolutionary activities in the broader political arena. Such was the substratum of preconceptions and expectations that would provide the basis for radical action and the rapid emergence of new, more explicit interpretations, a transformation in which the Bolsheviks, as Lenin had hoped, would play a major part.

Social polarization had already been given a moral interpretation well before the revolution. Under the autocracy, many Russian workers had begun to see themselves as a unique group, entitled to special privileges because of their outcast status and their worldly suffering. On one level such sentiments were exposed among mass workers in the Zubatov and Gapon experiments, where, particularly in the latter case, the mood became truly millenarian. For conscious workers the teachings of Marx and his Russian followers also created a strong sense of separateness and a belief in a special destiny. The autocracy, by isolating groups from one another and oppressing virtually all of them, created especially fertile ground for the emergence of such convictions. After the February revolution they were strongly reinforced by the workers' sense that because they had led the revolution, they had a special status, with accordingly greater rights and privileges. This belief was expressed frequently in the labor press and in public statements of worker leaders. In the Special Committee of the Ministry of Labor to discuss labor legislation, the worker representative Lurin-Lur'e opposed the project on unemployment insurance because "both in general and for economic reasons we cannot be behind Germany, where the government makes the contributions. And indeed, in Germany there was no revolution."[82] Surprisingly, it was also affirmed by Minister of Finance Shingarev in a meeting with merchants and industrialists. In a flight of rhetoric he assured the worried listeners that "however strong the insults that you hear seem to you, remember the state of the worker masses earlier, remember that the wages of labor were insignificant. Workers were literally pariahs. Remember, that by their hands Russian freedom was won, do not fear them."[83]

This new sense of self-esteem was visible in the workers' attempts to eliminate from the factory all those who were not "pure" proletarians, including many individuals from other classes who had worked in factories to avoid the draft.[84] It also surfaced in the workers' hostility toward the dumas, which represented other classes of the population and for this reason had tenuous legitimacy. Workers opposed themselves, worthy beneficiaries of the state, to the "philistines," the middle classes who had no real place in revolutionary Russia.[85] High-handed attitudes also often shaped the workers' relationship to the peasantry. According to the reports of the Main Land Committee, workers in factory districts and areas adjacent to them controlled peasant elections and public life. They acted more energetically and also terrorized the villagers by their threats, claiming that earlier they were the last, but now it was their turn to be first. Their attitude was summed up in the following way: "What we want we'll do, and he who goes against us is an adherent of the old regime."[86]

Such beliefs could find expression in a number of different ways. One consequence was an uncompromising insistence by workers on their own point of view and rights. Worker Pavel Budaev, writing in *Pravda*, asked his readers if the conciliatory chambers could help improve the workers' situation. To his own question he answered: "Yes, they can, if only the industrialists fully meet the demands of the workers."[87] The proceedings of conciliatory chambers often revealed this same perspective.[88] The workers in one factory sent a note to the chamber investigating the case of a certain Shtalmeister, asserting that the matter had already been resolved by a general meeting of all the workers. They claimed that this was a completely legal way of resolving the question of his removal, and that the decision of the general meeting could not be changed.[89] The note was composed in a completely matter-of-fact, nonpolemical tone, indicating that for the workers the decision was simply a matter of unquestioned right.

In another case worker Gal'berg, in a hearing before soviet, factory committee, and Ministry of Labor representatives, declared that he was willing to see a dispute over the firing of two administrators go to a conciliatory chamber, but if the chamber refused to satisfy the workers' demands fully, the government should confiscate the factory and operate it itself.[90] Such intransigence indicates a basic lack of acceptance of the legitimacy of the opposing viewpoint, a sentiment that was probably just as common among the industrialists.

Among conscious workers this sense of special worth reinforced the conviction that workers should be moral exemplars to the community as a whole. In, but not of, bourgeois society, they should embody the virtues of the new socialist society to come. In some cases courts of honor were established in factories as a way of upholding these new standards.[91] The implications of this new morality could be seen in incidents such as the following. Reacting to a report from a worker, the executive committee of the Petrogradskii Soviet became concerned about a worker who had raised the rent on a boarder by twenty rubles. They sent a representative to his factory committee to convince it to put pressure on him, to tell him that such conduct was impermissible on the part of a worker.[92]

Undoubtedly measures of this kind implied a large degree of self-righteousness and even puritanism, qualities that were also evident in the strict artistic canons favored by many conscious workers. For example, the Nobel works theater group proclaimed: "We exist not to amuse [rav-lechenie] but to foster spiritual growth, to enrich consciousness. . . . All that does not serve the development of Humanity is vain and empty."[93] Such moral earnestness must have continued to arouse considerable resentment among the backward masses, as it had done in the previous history of the labor movement. For mass workers the revolution itself had already given all workers new privileges. For conscious workers it had provided workers with the opportunity to build a new society, a task that required discipline and seriousness. Despite their divergences, both perspectives entailed radicalism in the class struggle.

Worker radicalization was not, then, simply a "rational" response to the crisis of 1917. It was not, properly speaking, either rational or irrational but was rooted in more general assumptions developed under the tsarist regime. These assumptions served to filter the workers' perceptions and make compromise nearly impossible. Partly because of the workers' own experience, the revolution had a "we or they," "all or nothing" quality; the Bolsheviks would play upon, not invent, these preconceptions.

THE ROLE OF ORGANIZATION

The autocratic regime had never permitted the development of moderate worker organizations that might have tempered the class struggle. The industrialists, many of whom had supported the government's repressive policy, reaped the harvest of this long-term failure in 1917. The pattern of organization that emerged after February contributed to the radicalization of the labor movement in two ways. First, because of their youth and weakness, organizations had little capacity to control the class struggle. Second, because of the growing class polarization and the influence of the Bolsheviks, the organizations themselves became radicalized, thus making a mockery of the moderate socialists' hope that organization was the key to well-paced and controlled change. These two characteristics parallel the distinction between implicit and conscious radicalism and, like it, ultimately derive from the dual nature of the Russian labor movement described in part III.

The Problem of Organization in 1917

"The world has not yet seen an organized revolution," wrote Shliapnikov, a Bolshevik worker leader who had been in the thick of events in the February revolution in Petrograd.[94] And yet all revolutionary leaders, both moderates who want to restrain the explosion of participation and radicals who want to encourage and direct it, celebrate organization as the keystone to a revolution's success. They do so because revolutionaries must always counteract potential opposition and also create support for the new institutions and great challenges on the horizon. In the modern world of the nation-state these tasks require mass participation, and it is only through organization that mass participation can be channeled. Without organization revolutionaries may be weakened both internally and externally by the mass movement that ostensibly supports them.

Shliapnikov's remark thus suggests a formidable dilemma: revolutions both demand and complicate effective organization. Perhaps only when revolution is accompanied by foreign or civil war, as in China and Vietnam, can this predicament be resolved. Thinkers like Luxemburg and Pannekoek, secure in their faith in the eventual triumph of revolutionary mobilization, tend to downplay the difficulties of combining mass participation and organizational control. Yet the revolutionary experiences of many other countries, including post-World War I Germany, Spain, Brazil, and Chile, suggest the intractability of the problem. Mobilization is both dangerous and essential for revolutionary leaders.

The need for organization was felt particularly strongly in Russia among very broad sectors of the public. Many groups were well aware of the effect that the tsarist regime's restrictions on organization had had for their own interests as well as their interrelations with other groups. The rapid creation of new organizations seemed to be a panacea for the social and political chaos bequeathed by the old regime. In this sense the revolution was made in the name not only of freedom but of order: a less corrupt government, better management of the economy, the elimination of economic speculation and sabotage, and the softening of political polarization. It was felt that organization would lead to the emergence of a viable society no longer deformed by an arbitrary state. It would also, however, protect social groups against their opponents and so was necessary for self-defense. Organization, it was felt, served the interests of both society as a whole and those of individual groups.

Throughout 1917 both of these themes were frequently sounded, though in different tonalities. Organization would lead to the renovation of society and simultaneously allow for social groups to defend their own interests. The emphasis of government officials was clearly on the link between organization and order. In early March, Minister of Trade and Industry Konovalov echoed the ideas that he had espoused during the war: resolution of the labor question in Russia was urgent and could be accomplished only by the "free independence and organization" of the workers. The widespread development of trade unions would be one of the main ways of realizing the economic rebirth of Russia, for it would put industrial relations on a healthy foundation.[95] Minister of Labor Skobolev, a Menshevik, speaking at the first Congress of Soviets in early June, appealed for organization in even more forceful terms: Revolutionary democracy, he said, "must be organized from head to toe, and any rank and file member of the working class and other sectors of democracy still not a member of his class, economic, and political organizations commits a crime against the revolution." Otherwise the government would never be able to regulate the interests and demands of the separate classes of the population or establish effective control over the economy. In addition, organization would lead to a greater correspondence between the workers' demands and the economic possibilities of industry. If wage claims were pursued in an unorganized fashion, economic chaos could lead other groups to turn against the workers, who, Skobolev reminded them, were only a small minority in society.[96]

Many factory owner organizations accepted the view of government officials like Konovalov and Skobolev that organization was the precondition of healthy class relations in the new Russia. "The completely changed interrelations between employers and workers require energetic and rapid work for the introduction into enterprises of a new order and the most rapid reestablishment of the normal course of work for defense needs," said a circular of the St. Petersburg Society, which had been so adamant in its opposition to trade unions in the past. To bring about this new order, the St. Petersburg Society mandated that employers willingly assist in the creation of worker and employer organizations in order to clarify and satisfy their mutual needs.[97] The first important step in this direction was the 10 March agreement between the St. Petersburg Society and the Petrograd Soviet, which, among other measures, formally recognized the legitimacy of the factory committees and affirmed the need to create conciliatory chambers at the plant level.[98] Although many smaller and provincial industrialist associations resented the society's unilateral action, the action embodied the widespread recognition that, as the "bourgeois" newspaper *Russkiia Vedemosti* expressed it, "freedom of associations and assembly is as indispensable to Russia as light and air." Only through them could the revolution consolidate itself and provide security for "the conservative elements of the Russian public."[99]

Sometimes the industrialists went further than pronouncements. In mid-March the management of the important Skorokhod factory in Petrograd donated 10,000 rubles to the union of tanners to underwrite its work and 100,000 rubles to a fund to assist newly freed political prisoners.[100] (Naturally support for worker organization had its limits. For example, the factory owners almost universally insisted that workers not be allowed to interfere in managerial functions.) Despite great disappointments, many industrialists kept this commitment throughout the long period of growing class polarization, after worker organizations had frequently failed to meet their expectations. Thus in early September in a circular to its members, the Presidium of the All-Russian Union of Societies of Factory Owners reiterated that because in the future "correct" industrial relations would require strong organizations, factory owners should encourage the formation of trade unions. This, it was emphasized, was one of the measures essential for the salvation of Russian industry.[101]

For quite different reasons socialist party and worker leaders added their own voices to the chorus of appeals for organization. Mensheviks recalled the disastrous consequences of hypermobilization in 1905, when workers struggled for democracy and economic gains at the same time. Workers in 1917 should not repeat these mistakes and for the time being should concentrate on the creation of a free and democratic Russia. For unlike 1905, now capitalists and workers could confront each other directly, without the mediation of the tsarist state. To fight this powerful and dangerous opponent, workers must be internally united. Restraint, discretion, and calculation would be necessary to avoid the fiasco of another failed general strike similar to the one of November 1905.[102]

Many worker leaders were also convinced that the time was not yet ripe for a socialist revolution. According to an article published in the newspaper of the glassworkers' union, entitled "It's Necessary to Organize," factories could not be seized right away. Capitalism had to develop further and workers required organization. In the meantime workers could make great economic gains through the struggles of their class organizations.[103] The metalworkers' union newspaper took the argument one step further. Worker organizations were necessary to raise worker productivity and to intervene in factory affairs so that industry might develop more rapidly, for without advanced industry socialism could not triumph. To this end the union leadership sent union organizers to the Donets Basin in the hope that they might improve the workers' economic performance.[104] Similar appeals came from the Bolsheviks, who seem to have overcome their 1905 reservations about supporting the formation of nonparty organizations. In March, *Pravda* even adopted the scolding tone more characteristic of the Mensheviks: "In the factories and plants of Petrograd a completely abnormal phenomenon is noticeable. There are no strikes, but the process of production is disorganized, work goes poorly. Sometimes it is not even known why they don't work." Such disorganization was dangerous, *Pravda* warned. It created an anarchistic mood and led to fruitless actions harmful for unity. Workers should create trade unions and clubs and strengthen local party organizations.[105] For the Bolsheviks, organization was essential for the strengthening of the working class and the party for an eventual attack on the new regime. Unlike the Mensheviks, they had no interest in fortifying either the state or civil society, even temporarily.

If the Russian labor movement had been well organized, such pleadings would have been gratuitous. Shliapnikov is probably right that no revolution has really been organized. Because of tsarist oppression, however, Russia was distinctive in the complete absence of well-established organizations to guide the mass movement.

A brief contrast with the post-World War I German revolution will serve to highlight some of the implications of this difference. The German Social Democratic party and the major trade unions were already relatively old, well-established organizations, with many of the traits that Samuel Huntington ascribes to strong institutions. They were also deeply conservative in many respects, with significant commitments to the economic and political status quo. Changes during the war had only accentuated these long-term tendencies. The party and union leadership had made great compromises with the ruling groups with respect to the war and industrial policy. These concessions cost the majority socialists considerable support within the ranks of the workers and also embittered the more radical elements within the party, some of whom founded the USPD in the spring of 1917 in reaction. After the November 1918 revolution the radicals enthusiastically embraced workers' councils as an alternative to the more conservative trade union and moderate party leadership. In many regions the council movement gained significant grass-roots support among the workers, but they were never able to displace the older organizations. Rather, through a policy of skillful compromise the moderates managed to channel the workers' councils away from the radical demands supported by some of their members.

Established working-class institutions thus contributed to moderation in the German labor movement. The rise of militancy led to a split with the majority position, not to the triumph of radicalism.[106] This split corresponded to deep-seated divisions within the labor movement itself, and was not simply an expression of partisan quarrels among the leadership. The moderates did not organize or control the revolution in any simple sense, yet the strength of their institutions allowed them to counter the radical challenge effectively.

In Russia many Mensheviks certainly wished to enact the role later played out by the German majority socialists, and there were many activists in worker organizations who wanted to retard the revolution's pace. Yet there were no established organizations to promote this policy, and there was no real mass base to support it. Organization mainly served to aid the overall process of radicalization in 1917.

Types of Organization in 1917

Fired by the atmosphere of freedom, workers embraced their new organizations with impressive enthusiasm. Responding to the numerous appeals addressed to them, and also acting on their own initiative, workers began to form organizations of various types from the first days of the revolution. Behind these efforts lay the experience and models of many years of activity, and both intelligentsia and worker militants played an important role in the creation of organizations.

Factory committees were often the first organizations to be formed, many in the two capitals even antedating the calls for their formation from the city soviets. Emerging as they did from local initiative, their origins were diverse. Sometimes they grew out of already existing councils of elders, sometimes from strike committees; and sometimes they were newly elected together with worker delegates to the soviets.[107] Because they required little organization beyond the local level and because of their obvious utility in local factory affairs, factory committees generally emerged before trade unions, which had a more complicated rationale and required more organizational effort and sophistication. The widespread appeal of factory committees was based upon their ability to represent the needs of all categories of workers in an individual workshop or plant without the need to coordinate their activities with more inclusive class groupings. The committees were thus rooted in local factory affairs and drew much of their vitality from this localism. Localism was a disadvantage on the national scale, however, and in the course of the revolution factory committees attempted and were able to transcend it to some degree, although the centralizing impulse was never as strong as it was for the trade unions.

In large factories there might be several factory committees and a great many commissions mandated to deal with a wide range of issues— including, for example, wage struggles, internal discipline, and supplies of fuel and raw materials. The well-deserved revolutionary reputation of many factory committees—they led the way among organizations in going over to the Bolsheviks—should not obscure the fact that much of their day-to-day activity was nonpolitical and routine. The protocols of factory committees in four Petrograd factories in 1917 show that they often concerned themselves with issues such as the formation of factory canteens, refuse disposal, permission for work leaves, wood supply, and the like. Occasionally an interesting issue such as the legal status of civil marriages was discussed. In addition, of course, extremely serious political matters were broached, including the creation of Red Guards in the factory, the approval of political resolutions, and the desirable degree of worker control over management.[108]

The soviets, including local soviets, also played a key role in factory affairs. In fact, the differentiation of functions was often unclear and depended upon the initiative of local activists. In some cases, such as the Petergof district soviet in Petrograd, where the giant Putilov works were located, the soviet was so dominated by a single factory that it really amounted to a factory committee.[109] In general, however, as opposed to the factory committees, the soviets were charged with representing the interests of all the workers in a given district.[110]

The scope of soviet activities differed greatly according to local political and economic conditions. For example, in outlying areas of the Urals they had great significance in local affairs from the beginning of the revolution because of the relative absence of competing organizations and the weakness of elites.[111] In Petrograd, with its proliferation of other working-class organizations and institutions representing the public at large (for example, local dumas), the soviets' activities were more restricted. Many attempts were made to distinguish between the responsibilities of city and district soviets, and between soviets and factory committees and trade unions. This was not an easy task, for like trade unions and factory committees, the soviets regarded the defense of the professional needs of workers (and soldiers) as one of their key goals. They created commissions to deal with industrial conflict and often took part in local conflicts. They actively intervened in the early struggles over the eight-hour day (the Petrograd Soviet at first trying to restrain the workers) and in the general issue of workers' control.[112] At the same time, they were committed to such broader issues as the "democratization" of rival local organizations (which meant ensuring that they were composed mainly of the "laboring class"), educational and cultural activity among the masses, and leadership of the mass political action of the working class.[113] They also played a key part in forming and coordinating the activities of other worker organizations, and in so doing were an important link between the political parties and local organizations.

Finally, trade unions became increasingly central in the class struggle throughout 1917. At the time of the February revolution union membership was negligible, but it rose dramatically after the overthrow of the tsarist state.[114] Unions were generally quickest to form among artisan trades, but they eventually became established in virtually all branches of industry. In some areas they were slower to take root because of the lack of union traditions and the active role played by the soviets, but by October their geographical spread was impressive. By virtue of their rapid proliferation and through the central union organizations formed to coordinate them, they brought considerable planning and organization to the class struggle. Some unions, such as the metalworkers and leatherworkers, were able to conduct prolonged campaigns for carefully chosen goals.

The union movement embraced a number of diverse organizational forms. There were industry unions, craft unions, and enterprise unions, the last hardly distinguishable from factory committees except that they usually existed only in nonurban areas. In the cities the prior existence of factory committees usually precluded the emergence of enterprise unions.[115] Trade unions faced particularly difficult tasks throughout 1917, for their presumed goal was to coordinate the economic struggle. More than the factory committees and soviets, the accent of trade unions was on control, not mobilization, and economic tasks, not political struggles. In Germany, where trade unions had a larger membership than either socialist parties or the council movement, they were a considerable brake upon radical action.[116] The events of 1917 did not offer the most promising conditions for keeping union activities either moderate or purely economic.

Organization and Control

All social movement organizations aim to exercise some control over their members, for only through such control can they acquire power for their goals, which are often distinct from those of their constituencies. Wherein lies the strength of the Petrograd Soviet? asked the Menshevik newspaper *Rabochaia Gazeta* rhetorically. Only in the fact that the revolutionary masses follow it. If the Provisional Government were to become convinced that it had no control, then its power would come to nothing and the revolution would be dead.[117] And yet neither the ferment of 1917 nor the prior history of the labor movement augured well for the emergence of a class struggle controlled by organizations. It is true that organizations, no longer worried about the threat of the tsarist state, had virtually complete freedom to develop during 1917. But the labor movement was at heart still a synthesis between a militant, unorganized mass—many of them recent wartime entrants into industry—and a small worker elite committed to organization in the name of one or another ideological vision of change. If the opportunities for organization were greater, so were its challenges, for the mass workers were freer to express their disaffection than under the old regime. With this new freedom they put unrelenting pressure upon worker leaders who, staffing poorly institutionalized organizations, were often pushed in directions they opposed. Either this, or they were replaced. As a consequence, throughout 1917 organization had only limited, though perhaps growing, ability to direct grass-roots worker struggles.

Worker organizations certainly tried to control what they regarded as worker spontaneity. They struggled against drunkenness, gambling, and other moral pecadillos that had long been the bane of the worker elite and that now threatened to turn the revolution into chaos. In the name of centralized control, they opposed unplanned and merely localized action unconnected to larger purposes. All demands were to be processed through authorized worker organizations, which would analyze their viability and compatibility with the overall goals of the movement. Similarly, leaders were concerned with maintaining worker discipline and worker productivity, partly in order to deflect the attacks of other social groups against the workers. Partly, too, skilled conscious workers had already begun to develop an ethic of productivity, celebrating the machine and the expertise connected with it.[118] For reasons such as these, the word "organization" acquired almost mystical power in 1917—it signified maturity, knowledge, consciousness. It was the symbol of the historic new role of workers in Russian society, and it was seen as basic to securing the revolution. A remark by a soldier to a local soviet reveals much about the spirit of the time. Replying to worker criticism of his appeal for workers to disarm, he remarked: "Get to know our resolution a bit better. We are organized."[119] It was a kind of all-purpose virtue that communicated seriousness and commitment.

Organization often required bitter words and harsh actions. Factory committees and soviets sometimes decreed fines and even firing for drunkenness, absenteeism, and failure to attend meetings.[120] They authorized piece rates, hated by the workers for decades, in order to raise productivity.[121] They felt a responsibility to educate the masses and to draw them into the movement, by compulsion if necessary: "Only when we compel [the workers] to enter into our ranks will we be able to educate and develop the best fighters among them."[122] They adopted military language to describe the required discipline and obedience of the worker masses:

The labor army prepares its martial banners. By the will of the delegate meeting the general of this worker army is the central strike committee. It has the responsibility, if necessary, of leading the worker battalions into battle for the defense of the demands announced to the factory owners on October 13. In fulfillment of this will the central strike committee sends you its "Order no. 1."[123]

Sometimes this army was urged to bide its time until conditions were more promising, and sometimes it was urged to attack immediately. But always the expressed goals were coordinated action, planning, and discipline.

Often worker organizations did manage successfully to introduce elements of planning and strategy into the class struggle in 1917. As late as September, the writer for the "bourgeois" *Trade Industrial Gazette* recognized the enormous number of labor conflicts resolved by the unions, which, he said, had tried to avoid strikes and deflect unrealizable demands.[124] The labor press reported numerous instances in which soviet or union officials had restrained the workers' actions, and there were also significant cases of organized negotiations (for example, in favor of industrywide wage scales) and well-directed strikes (the Moscow leatherworkers' strike).[125] On the whole, however, worker organizations could not make of the young Russian labor movement anything like a labor army. Perhaps they were more successful in Petrograd or Moscow,[126] but even in the two capitals they were too weak as institutions and faced too many obstacles to keep the rank and file satisfied with tactics of control and discipline. As had been true over the past decades, grass-roots worker militancy put constant pressure on the weak organizations and so helped to turn them in a more radical direction. As a result worker organization, even when effective, was often far from moderate.

Much of the organizations' vulnerability stemmed from their youth, for although many had fairly long traditions, almost none had any continuous histories. As a result the worker rank and file, lacking organizational experience, often failed to understand the responsibilities, possibilities, and limitations inherent in their participation.[127] These deficiencies were particularly evident among workers from the countryside, many of whom were unfamiliar with the rudiments of organization and not permanently committed to industrial work. Rank-and-file apathy and irresponsibility seemed to be a serious problem among all categories of workers, however. Although they certainly supported the principle of organization, they often refused to support or even accept actual organizations in concrete ways. Thus, for example, there were numerous complaints that workers showed little interest in participating in local soviet, factory committee, or union activities.[128] The printer Aleksandr

Kastov, a union member writing in the union's newspaper *Pechatnik*, complained that workers were concerned only about pay, to the virtual exclusion of other union matters. Many workers left the meetings after this issue was discussed, and many more simply stayed home. Rumors charging that the union board was in the pay of management and betrayed the workers' interests were rampant.[129]

If such indifference was present among one of the most educated and experienced categories of workers in the capital, it seemed to be all the more characteristic of the situation in the provinces. Thus, of the condition of unions in the Urals in late September, a local newspaper reported that attendance at meetings was very low, that dues were seldom paid, and that only the union boards did any work. The masses, in short, were largely indifferent to their activities.[130] With respect to Moscow, Koenker has assembled a large amount of evidence suggesting that worker apathy toward their organizations was particularly marked after July and seemed especially pronounced in the soviets and the unions.[131]

The same complaints about workers' lack of participation and the shortage of people to work in the factory committees and trade unions were voiced numerous times by delegates during the second conference of Petrograd factory committees held in early August.[132] This last evidence is particularly telling, for if any organizations should have avoided these problems, it was the factory committees; and if any place could have inspired mass enthusiasm, surely Petrograd would have been it.[133] Even in the capital, however, how could workers have learned that organization required participation? Perhaps through cultural and educational activities worker leaders might have taught this lesson, but in 1917 these dimensions of organizational work were poorly developed. Leaders and organizations spent too much time on other, more pressing matters, such as conflict resolution, avoiding what seemed to be a long-term and secondary goal.

Because of the lack of prior experience, workers also often misconceived the prerogatives and powers of their organizations and so made unreasonable demands upon them. They rejected the factory committees' mediatory role, regarding them as responsible for realizing all the workers' demands without delay or compromise. This was the complaint of the Putilov factory committee in an appeal to the workers to understand that the factory committee was not an executive body capable of achieving all the workers' goals on its own. It grumbled that the workers blamed the committee for not defending workers' interests when there were obstacles or delays in the fulfillment of their demands.[134] Such suspicion and lack of trust of their own leaders appear to have been widespread during 1917. Caution and circumspection were interpreted as inexcusable foot-dragging, or, as in the earlier example, collusion with management. It was difficult for worker leaders to allay these suspicions, and their calls for restraint or discipline were often contemptuously shouted down.[135] Even when leaders were able to negotiate successful agreements, rank-and-file workers sometimes refused to recognize them as binding commitments, perhaps partly because of limited experience with contracts negotiated through representatives, a lack that was bound up with the general weakness of civil society in Russia.[136]

As a result, worker leaders frequently had little autonomy of action, knowing full well that the workers did not trust them enough to let them use their own judgment. They were often replaced, usually after they took a decision out of touch with the immediate demands of the moment. The overall consequences for the leaders' authority are evident in the caution shown by worker representatives to a conciliatory commission examining conflict in the Mal'tsevskie factories. They asserted that their mandates were limited, that they were not authorized to make any compromises, and that if their demands as stated were not met, they had to return to the general meeting of workers in their district to receive further instructions.[137] Such procedures were perhaps admirably democratic, but they also attested to the low autonomy of worker leadership. Left-wing socialists like Luxemburg and Pannekoek celebrated such arrangements, arguing that they ensured the predominance of direct action and thus radicalism. Pannekoek writes: "Leaders cannot make revolutions: labor leaders abhor a proletarian revolution. For the revolutionary fights the workers need new forms of organization in which they keep the powers of action in their own hands." Examples of such new organizational forms were strike committees and the Russian soviets. "Such committees are not bodies to make decisions according to their own opinion, and over the workers; they are simply messengers. . . . They cannot play the roles of leaders, because they can be momentarily replaced by others."[138] It is easy to understand why, as the Menshevik Grinevich charged, many worker leaders made no attempt to educate the workers or reject irresponsible demands but, in order to remain in their positions, simply "swam with the current of spontaneity and lack of consciousness."[139] In this, said Grinevich, was the crisis of the Russian trade union movement.

Worker leaders, worried about their lack of authority and the mass pressures to which they were subject, sometimes tried to institutionalize more orderly procedures for dissent. For example, in the Franko-Russkie factories, the factory committee determined that dissatisfied workers should make a formal complaint to the factory committee's bureau if they could gather the signatures of at least one-fourth of the workers, after which the complaint would be discussed at a factorywide meeting. If the meeting gave a vote of no confidence in the leadership, the committee would be dismissed and obliged to hold new elections. The committee also tried to restrict dissent within its own ranks by prohibiting minorities from criticizing its policies in the factory as a whole—a tactic reminiscent of Lenin's "democratic centralism".[140] Clearly leaders recognized the problems, but effective solutions were not easy to find. Delegates to the Third Trade Union Conference suggested measures such as compulsory union membership and further organizational centralization, but these steps had to await the further development of the revolution after October.[141]

Such grass-roots distrust of leadership is easily comprehensible within the context of the labor movement's prior history, which precluded the emergence of long-standing patterns of leadership based on trust. The workers simply had had very little experience in delegating authority to others, and they had no reason to believe that the leaders deserved their trust. Often experienced conscious workers had been chosen as strike representatives because of a lack of alternatives in situations in which some leadership was an obvious necessity. As noted earlier, however, they often suffered the rebukes of the rank and file if the outcome was not favorable, and their resentment even if it was. Some hostility toward leadership in 1917 was undoubtedly rooted in such traditional suspicions of the mass workers for their conscious counterparts. In addition, it cannot be assumed that the worker leaders always earned the trust of their constituents, for many of them, too, had had little practice with ongoing organizational work and some were dishonest.[142]

Other difficulties inherent in young organizations also afflicted the workers' new representative bodies. One might mention, for example, the lack of strict differentiation of functions among trade unions, factory committees, and soviets, leading to overlap, rivalry, and poor use of scarce resources.[143] In addition, local organizations of a single type were often poorly articulated with one another and with central organizations claiming a broader jurisdiction.[144] Similarly, particularly in backward areas workers often trusted individual leaders more than organizations, and such personalism hindered routine work.[145]

In addition to these endogenous weaknesses, however, worker organizations faced constraints from their external environment. These obstacles to effective performance also weakened the organizations' authority in workers' eyes and undermined their ability to control events. Perhaps the most important of these impediments was simply economic need— for Hannah Arendt the impasse that hinders the creation of new institutions in all revolutions. As the economic crisis worsened, and as workers experienced actual hunger, they became impatient with organizations that could not fulfill their pressing needs. The situation was equally bad, or perhaps even worse, in factories that had significant workers' control. In the Brenner plant in Petrograd, which had witnessed an experiment in workers' self-management, the worker leaders had completely lost the workers' trust by September because of the lack of payment. The workers wanted to replace them, and the factory committee wanted government requisition of the plant, which was in fact announced by the Ministry of Trade and Industry in early September.[146]

Factory owner hostility also impeded organizational control. Many industrialist organizations had initially placed great hope on the moderating effects of organization, but their experiences sobered them considerably. Many concluded that, as one of their representatives put it, "essentially there are no workers' organizations." The speaker elaborated as follows: "The workers change the composition of their committees monthly, and if the latter announce moderate demands, then they are blamed for their counterrevolutionary tendency. In this respect it is characteristic that the larger the organization, the more prudent are the decisions it takes, but such organizations quickly lose their authority."[147] The tone of such factory owner complaints was often truly apocalyptic. One important industrialist newspaper complained in mid-October that in Russia there was no organized struggle of classes as a whole, but merely the decentralized economic and physical violence of an unorganized crowd. It was necessary to save industry and the country, it declared, and for this new forms of class cooperation were an urgent necessity.[148]

Despite such complaints, however, the actions of factory owners frequently contributed to the very organizational weakness that they condemned. There was factory owner "spontaneity" just as much as worker "spontaneity," for neither side had yet learned the rules of controlled conflict within a context of some degree of trust. Thus factory owners were often unwilling to recognize the legitimacy of the soviets and accept their participation in labor disputes.[149] In addition, factory owners sometimes dragged out wage negotiations interminably, showing less flexibility than worker organizations. The *Trade Industrial Gazette*, certainly not partial to workers, reported on one such case, the negotiations between the textile section of the Petrograd Society of Factory Owners and the trade union of workers in fiber production of the northern industrial region. By mid-September negotiations had been in progress since late June about collective wage scales, and the dispute had been given over to an interdepartmental conference of representatives from various ministries in order to arrive at a binding decision. The union leadership agreed with the decision, though they were not entirely satisfied, but the factory owners refused to accept it until price increases could be guaranteed for their products. The worker representatives lost patience and demanded an immediate answer; otherwise they would have freedom of action. The factory owners finally agreed.[150] There were also cases in which individual factory owners did not recognize worker organizations authorized by industrialist organizations or did not accept their own organizations' agreements with workers.[151] Thus high-handed tactics and uncompromising attitudes could be found among the factory owners as well as among workers. In such circumstances why should rank-and-file workers have listened to the appeals of their representatives when the formal agreements appeared to be useless in practice?

Factory owners undercut the independence of worker organizations in other ways as well, trying to prohibit them from holding meetings during working hours or refusing to pay worker representatives for their activities. It should be recalled that the fledgling organizations did not have funds to pay many of their leaders, who thus depended upon their regular salaries. Even though the industrialists' opposition to subsidizing union activities is understandable, workers interpreted it as an attack. To this were often added the factory owners' open expressions of hostility, sometimes in the form of angry statements in public forums. The workers reacted to these criticisms with burning indignation. Thus the board of the Moscow Printers' Union responded furiously to the change voiced by one factory owner that worker organizations engaged in unauthorized activities—the insinuation was that workers lacked organization and were basically spontaneous.

> The struggle, comrades, is conducted not only for the raising of our wages, but also for the recognition of our organizational existence. We will never forget the words uttered about the unauthorized organizations of the working class by one of the major representatives of the industrialists at the Moscow Conference! . . . Forward! To organization! Long live the unity of the working class. This must be our answer.[152]

Factory owner attacks upon worker organizations may not have unambiguously damaged the organizations. As the foregoing appeal indicates, they may even have encouraged the workers to rally behind their representatives more. If through such attacks the organizations were in some ways strengthened, however, it was not as legitimate brokers engaging in controlled struggle within an accepted framework of capitalist relations. Rather, the industrialists' actions reinforced the aura of semilegality that the organizations inherited from the past. In essential ways local worker organizations continued to resemble the strike committees of tsarist times, with their instability and unpredictability, much more than they did the powerful English or German worker organizations, the very institutionalization of which made them predictable and reliable. Not only Russian workers but also Russian worker organizations continued to be capable of acting "spontaneously"—that is, immoderately and without sufficient deliberation. Many would have agreed with the resolution of the First Urals Regional Conference of Trade Unions that the unions must "remain foreign to any idea of interclass truce, any recognition of the possibility of joint work with the bourgeoisie."[153]

This radical orientation became more pronounced as the revolutionary crisis ripened and as moderate socialists were replaced as leaders by Bolsheviks, who made no attempt to identify control and moderation. The Mensheviks' appeals for organization became, from their own point of view, increasingly hollow and pointless. Trotsky exposed the nerve with his usual acuity. In criticizing anarchy, strikes, and radicalism, he said, the moderate socialists were actually criticizing the worker organizations that in fact were leading them. Trotsky noted that the Socialist Revolutionary Rudnev at the State Conference attacked the anarchic elements who called a general protest strike in Moscow. "But who organized the strike?" asked Trotsky. "The Moscow trade unions." Worker organizations, he noted, were all headed by Bolsheviks. In what sense was this anarchy? Only in that Bolshevism was itself identified with anarchy.[154]

The Bolshevization of worker organizations suggests the incompleteness of the preceding analysis of the radicalization of the class struggle, for this process must also be interpreted within the larger political context. First, increasing worker hostility toward the Provisional Government was an important factor in class polarization because of the workers' identification of the industrialists with the state. Second, the influences of the socialist parties—by October, largely the Bolsheviks—were inseparable from the transformation of the workers' political role and the radicalization of the class struggle. These two issues, the workers' relationship to the Provisional Government and the role of the socialist parties, both crucial for understanding the development of industrial relations, will be considered in the following two chapters.

Excursus: The Role of the Factory Owners

In explaining the radicalization of the class struggle in 1917, the emphasis throughout has been on the historical shaping of class relations, particularly with respect to the workers' own conceptions and the movement's long-term traits. The validity of this approach receives further support if the activities of factory owners are taken into account. They were not at all a powerful, monolithic, and reactionary class inhospitable, in principle, to the workers' aspirations. At times their policies were certainly harsh, but the severity stemmed largely from desperation. The radicalization of the class struggle was thus not simply a response to a reactionary bourgeoisie. Indeed, the role of the factory owners in 1917 does not admit of easy generalization. There is a simple account available: Soviet scholars tend to portray them as implacable foes of the revolution and the working class, a judgment that is occasionally accepted by Western scholars as well.[155] It is more accurate to view them, however, as a highly fragmented class that shared little except an acute sense of their own weakness and a desperate uncertainty about how to act in the new Russia. These attitudes conditioned all of the factory owners' contradictory responses to the perceived chaos around them.

From the very beginning some factory owners saw the workers as lawless, socialistic,[156] and insatiable in their demands. This judgment was only strengthened as the revolution developed and as the economic crisis helped make agreement over wages nearly impossible. In their meetings, statements to the government, and public declarations the factory owners repeatedly referred to workers' wage demands as irrational and completely out of line with economic conditions. Further concessions, they declared, would lead to the bankruptcy of their firms. For example, in early May a group of important metallurgical and metalworking industrialists reported to the Provisional Government that a group of eighteen key enterprises of the Donets Basin held 195 million rubles worth of basic capital, which in the previous year gave them a gross profit of 75 million rubles and dividends of 18 million rubles. The workers, they charged, demanded wage increases totaling 240 million rubles. The factory owners agreed to raise wages by 64 million, but the workers, they said, recognized nothing apart from their own demands.[157] Many would have agreed with the principle expressed by a Urals industrialist group that the level of wages must not be determined by workers' demands, for their claims were limitless, but by the market prices of goods.[158] Often they interpreted workers' excessive demands as socialistic or socialist-inspired,[159] and they supported these claims by references to worker anarchy: workers allegedly did not respect private property or the law and freely used violence against the factory administration. They intervened in factory affairs in ways that directly contravened both the law and the agreements signed by their own organizations, even claiming these prerogatives as their right.[160] The industrialists concluded that, in the words of several factory owners at a conference in Petrograd in early April, "the workers consciously and systematically try to bring the entrepreneurs to a state of complete ruin," often in the hope that the factories would be taken over by the state.[161] "In the present moment the dictatorship of the working class has been realized in its most primitive form," declared a group of factory owners from the south of Russia in late May.[162]

Many factory owners ascribed the workers' anarchy and lawlessness to lack of organization. This judgment afforded them a measure of hope, for they could expect that the labor movement would gradually become better organized. Others blamed a small minority of agitators, principally

Bolsheviks.[163] This, too, provided some consolation, for agitators could eventually be rooted out. Toward October, however, it had become clear that radicalism was rooted in worker organizations themselves and was hardly the product of isolated Bolshevik agitators. In the words of one industrialist leader, the industrialists, and also broad sectors of other social groups, had come to feel "that not only the main, but almost the only goal of all the above-designated organizations of the so-called revolutionary democracy is . . . struggle with the industrialists."[164] As a result, they came to conclude that authorized and well-established organizations were even more dangerous for them than weak ones.[165] The liberal solution to labor conflict—the development of civil society—had proved unworkable.

Besieged by what they regarded as impossible worker demands, the factory owners also became convinced of their own impotence. They saw themselves as poorly organized, even more so than the workers, whose strength they sometimes exaggerated.[166] They had trouble recruiting people to their organizations and finding enough representatives to present their views before the government.[167] This was a severe handicap in a period in which there were no paid lobbyists or media campaigns, two contemporary ways of translating money into power. The industrialists also had no moral or intellectual tradition in Russia to support their claim to a strong political voice. They felt isolated from the rest of society, which evinced little commitment to private enterprise and often saw the factory owners as culpable for their own plight. The lead article of the first issue of the All-Russian Union of Societies of Factories and Plants' official publication eloquently expressed factory owners' sense of isolation and despair. Industry always depends on the support of the country in which it operates, the article began. Russian industry, however, was now without a fatherland. "The fatherland renounced Russian industry, it placed it almost 'outside the law.'" Industry is attacked from all sides. "Neither the government, nor the people, nor the intelligentsia, nor the workers reflect on the fate of Russian industry." "From one side, there is prolonged disorganization from below, from the other, mortal blows from above, and from all sides blindness, enmity, hatred."[168]

Previously the industrialists had been well aware of their weakness, but they had been able to rely on the support of an oppressive state. This was now no longer the case, and, as the foregoing passage indicates, factory owners felt betrayed by the Provisional Government. They accused the government of passivity in the face of worker lawlessness and of one-sidedness in the settlement of disputes and in the preparation of legislation.[169] The government, claimed industrialist Bublikov, "hears only the voice of the left, and not voices from the right. The government does not have ears to hear the will of the whole country."[170]

Attacked from all sides, some industrialists comforted themselves with the thought that ultimately they would survive, for industry was indispensable to the welfare of the country. This failure of imagination seems less obtuse when it is recalled that there were no historical precedents for the expropriation of the capitalists. Still, it is strange to see them retreat into illusions, such as the assertion that, as S. Kondratenko put it in the newspaper cited earlier, not one reasonable Social Democrat advocated the socialization of factories or the expropriation of capital. After all, reasonable men agreed that capitalism could not be eliminated. There were no more class contradictions, for both sides depended upon the survival of industry and so must be against anarchy. This article appeared on 28 September 1917.[171] The factory owners simply could not imagine that they, the bearers of human progress and culture, of science and technology, of human genius and organization, were dispensable.[172] Worker-run industry would be tantamount to an opera production with a chorister in place of Chaliapin in the title role.[173] The growing economic crisis, the closure of plants, and, in a famous phrase, "the bony hand of hunger" would make workers come to their senses and finally rally behind private industry.[174]

This passive response at least had some elements of optimism. Sometimes the factory owners simply gave up, abandoning their enterprises or pleading with the government to take them over. Even the irrepressible Guzhon seemed to have lost much of his former stamina. He reported to the Ministry of Trade and Industry that the board of directors of his factory had proposed to ask the state to administer it because of the gravity of the problems. He complained that the governmental body, the Factory Conference, had refused to act upon this offer—because, he said, it was composed of people hostile toward private property![175] In many industrialist organizations there were debates about the desirability of some form of direct governmental control or administration.[176] Many industrialists simply wanted to relinquish their property: in Kherson province, according to the local factory inspector's report, they did not take such a step purely out of fear of worker terror against them.[177]

Other factory owners continued to hope that concessions would undermine worker militancy and lessen support for the Bolsheviks.[178] Optimists held on to the belief that worker organizations would gradually establish control over the labor movement, and so they urged industrialist support for them.[179] In addition to these passive or moderate responses, many factory owners declared war on the labor movement and its organizations. They adopted such a posture on the basis of a similar sense of desperation, but they were not yet ready to give up. In declaring their intentions to fight back, they called upon their traditional arsenal of weapons. First they appealed for government intervention, including the use of force and repression, to eliminate anarchy and lawlessness.[180]

"Give us good politics, and we will give you good economics in the Donets Basin," pleaded the Council of the Congress of Mining Industrialists of the south on 2 August.[181] The government was often unable or unwilling to defend them,[182] however, and the more perspicacious of the industrialists realized that state aid would ultimately be counterproductive, for it would undermine the authority of the Provisional Government.[183] Many industrialist organizations also asked the government to intervene more profoundly in the industrial life of the country in order to buttress their tenuous authority. Indeed, important industrialist leaders called for a remarkable degree of state control over factory affairs. In mid-May, Von Ditmar declared that the government must accept a very active role in economic life, regulating salaries and wages, prices, and factory owner profits.[184] Other important industrialist organizations made similar requests.[185]

Still other industrialist groups trusted little in the different coalitions of the Provisional Government and emphasized the need to rely on their own strength. Steps were taken to form united national industrialist organizations, such as the Committee for the Defense of Industry, the Main Committee of United Industry, and the All-Russian Societies of Factories and Plants. None of these succeeded in uniting Russian industry into a coherent political force, as the old divisions continued to make themselves felt, but the impulse for stronger organization was clearly present. Internally, the different organizations tried to tighten their rules and instill greater discipline in their members.[186] They struggled to adopt common policies toward worker unrest, hoping thereby to present a united front before their opponents. For example, the Third Conference of Industrialists of the south of Russia adopted a ten-point resolution on policy toward workers' demands that later became the basis for similar resolutions by various other industrialist associations.[187]

On the basis of these battle plans, many industrialist organizations conducted a bitter struggle with the worker organizations. Conflict was especially strong over whether worker committees could meet during work hours and whether factory owners had the obligation to pay their leaders for time spent engaged in committee responsibilities. Here the divergence of views was total: factory owners saw worker organizations as unauthorized usurpers, whereas workers saw them as vital forces for the health of their factories. Factory owners also rejected any worker interference in hiring and firing and sought to limit worker organizations' initiatives in the area of workers' control.

Many of their other options exhausted, some industrialists found lockouts and factory closures to be an increasingly useful tactic in the class struggle. Beginning in May the lockout as a planned tactic was used more extensively, and there was widespread talk of an all-Russia lockout.[188]

Offensive closures and lockouts seemed to be particularly prevalent in areas in which industry was weaker.[189] In Petrograd, by contrast, the industrialists were better able to withstand worker pressures and postpone such extreme measures.[190] For although closures and lockouts could occasionally be effective in curbing worker demands,[191] they also had major drawbacks, which the factory owners well recognized. They knew that they risked the alienation of public opinion, and they also understood that as opposed to former times, factory closures might stimulate worker self-management or government requisition. Lockouts and closures would also deepen class conflict and so appealed only to those who felt in a position to combat further worker militancy. Thus they were often acts of desperation undertaken only after there was little prospect of government aid,[192] and they were sometimes explicitly rejected as general methods of class struggle.[193]

By late summer it had become clear to a great many leading industrialists that neither by their own strength nor by appeals to the government could they reestablish order in the factories. Some began to perceive the need for a more explicit political role for their class. Similar convictions had emerged earlier in the war as a response to the crisis of the tsarist state, particularly among certain key Moscow industrialists. Disunity precluded any significant progress along these lines, however, and the industrialists had remained politically marginal, with no political organizations or mass base to support them. Now, in the new situation, there were renewed calls for a more active and explicit political stance. The industrialist class should stop hiding within the folds of the various political parties' flags, wrote one author in the journal of the Society of Factory Owners. It should act in terms of a full awareness of its historic role in developing the productive forces of the country, and so should become conscious of itself as a political class.[194]

Despite such grandiose hopes of national leadership, the political role of the industrialists was largely confined to intrigues.[195] The most notable of these was widespread industrialist support for the counterrevolutionary plot of General Kornilov. Key leaders of large Petrograd firms, including Putilov, Vyshnegradskii, Kutler, and Meshcherskii, founded the Society for the Economic Regeneration of Russia with the express aim of supporting Kornilov's plans against the Kerensky government.[196] Far from all major industrialist groups adhered to his counterrevolutionary goals; Riabushinskii and his All-Russian Association of Trade and Industry, for example, kept their distance. Ironically, this was the closest the factory owners ever came to becoming a "political class" in 1917.

In sum, the factory owners' weakness made many of them aggressive, particularly toward the end of the year. Chernov, the Socialist Revolutionary leader, was perhaps right to speak of the "two Maximalisms"—

"industrial-feudal Maximalism" and "the Maximalism of expropriation, the absolutism of the proletarians."[197] It is well to remember, however, that the industrialists' maximalism emerged only after they concluded that February had given birth to much more than a bourgeois revolution, that radicalism was implicit in it from the beginning. Many industrialists had welcomed the February revolution, misinterpreting its nature, but they were soon to feel what the workers had experienced after 1905. Although the development of trade unions after 1905 indicated that a reformist solution to the labor question was feasible in Russia, the industrialists, allied with the government, used repression to regain the upper hand. Now, when the new political situation encouraged industrialist moderation and led them to hope for an organized civil society, the workers took advantage of their relative strength to settle old scores and achieve long-held aspirations. The result was a stiffened resolve on the part of many factory owners and, in response, a further radicalization of the workers' perspectives. Both after 1905 and after February 1917 the stronger party was unwilling to make compromises based on the conviction that it had some interests in common with its opponent and that both sides could regulate conflict in a context of social and political pluralism.

CHAPTER
14

The Workers and the State in 1917

The dramatic destruction of the tsarist state gave birth to the momentous challenge of creating an entirely new political system. Every revolution requires the reconstitution of political authority and the foundation of novel political insitutions—for Hannah Arendt these political tasks were more essential to revolutionary change than equality or the satisfaction of need. Probably in no other revolution did the old regime leave behind such a vacuum of political leadership and such a high degree of social polarization as in Russia. These peculiarities of the Russian revolution in its early stage were direct consequences of the history of autocratic rule, which left little room for independent political leadership and, in the context of rapid capitalist industrialization, fostered class polarization. Even in autocratic Iran, the shah's regime had been unable to stamp out rival organizations that had broad constituencies, and these had the capacity to focus opposition and provide leadership in the postrevolutionary period. In addition, in Russia the very suddenness of the revolution's victory added to the intractability of the problem, for there had been very limited opportunies for an opposition movement to gain authority through its leadership of a prolonged struggle.[1] No firm links were established before the revolution with a mass opposition movement.

The period from February to October 1917 culminated in extreme political polarization. By October the vast majority of workers supported some form of soviet government representing the lower classes, and in this they were supported by a large part of the politically active peasantry. Privileged Russia desperately prayed for some kind of alternative, whether democratic or dictatorial, civilian or military. These processes of radicalization and polarization provided the social and political context for the Bolshevik seizure of power in October. The Bolshevik insurrection turned out to be the first step in a long process of re-creating state power to fill the near political vacuum left after February.

The political radicalization of the Russian working class meant rejection of liberal democracy in favor of a class government. It was intertwined with the radicalization of the class struggle in the sense that the two processes of radicalization had common roots and influenced each other. Russian workers rejected the Provisional Government for many of the same reasons that they rejected capitalism, and they increasingly regarded the Provisional Government as the defender of capitalist interests and the capitalists as the bulwark of a counterrevolutionary alliance against them.

The political radicalization of the labor movement was a complicated process that, at least for Petrograd and Moscow, has been well described by historians.[2] It had an uneven rhythm, broken by the temporary outburst of anti-Bolshevik sentiment after the July days and accelerated by the failure of the Kornilov putsch. Its geographical pattern was also complex. Petrograd was naturally the center of ideological radicalism because of its revolutionary traditions, immense concentration of political activists, large contingent of metalworkers, and the influence of a rebellious garrison. In this respect Moscow fell far behind the capital, but it still sheltered a respectable core of militants and possessed a large industrial labor force with a tradition of struggle.

It would be wrong, however, to contrast the radical capitals and the conservative provinces. Petrograd and Moscow also contained an array of groups and institutions espousing political moderation that effectively impeded the extension of soviet power—government organs, soviets dominated by moderate socialists, city dumas, and the like. In many provincial centers, however, both the bourgeoisie and government administrative organs were virtually absent, and soviet power filled this vacuum without regard to parties or ideologies. To the delight of Lenin, many local Bolshevik activists at the April Petrograd Conference and the Sixth Party Congress in late July reported that in their areas the soviets were all-powerful. "Here in Petrograd," declared the Penza delegate Kuraev, "the question stands: to take or not to take power, but in the provinces it's already taken."[3] "All power in Orekhovo-Zuevo is in the hands of the workers," declared Efimov. "The Petrograd Soviet lags behind and fails to defend the interests of the workers and soldiers."[4] In smaller towns in the Volga region and in central Siberia, it was reported, the soviets also had complete governmental authority. Eduard Dune, working in a factory outside Moscow, noted that "somewhere in Peter there was a Provisional Government, in Moscow there was the city duma and other organizations of the new government, but this government was not real: it was only possible to get something through the soviet. Formally this was dual power, but we did not feel this."[5] The party resolutions at the April conference recognized this anomaly. It was declared that soviet power was more problematic in Moscow and Petrograd because of the strength of the bourgeoisie and the moderate socialists, and so renewed efforts to change the big-city soviets were recommended.[6]

And yet it was not true that soviet power in many parts of the provinces reflected a radical political consensus. Bolsheviks like Preobrazhensky who criticized the party's Central Committee after the July Days for its failure to take account of the isolation of radical Petrograd from the provinces surely had a point.[7] For soviet power had not yet become programmatic in the provinces, and the political complexion of the soviets was still frequently indefinite. "When life puts forth a question, the provinces answer: 'Let's listen to what the center says.'" There's no party loyalty [partiinost]. "Today they accept one resolution, tomorrow another. It's a jumble."[8] Provincial activists, not to speak of the worker masses, were often poorly schooled in party doctrines and unable to appreciate the overall political context. Such considerations led party leaders to insist that the Central Committee should not act merely according to the wishes of the provinces but should lead events from its more considered standpoint.[9]

It was not until late summer that a rapprochement between the capital and the provinces was consummated. The underlying economic, military, and political conditions mentioned in the previous chapter were decisive in this transformation, and so were the repressions following the July Days and the failure of the Kornilov putsch. The latter event in particular garnered immense sympathy for the Bolshevik party. The general had been decisively outmatched by the united action of worker, soldier, and sailor organizations. Of their resistance Rabinowitch has written that "it would be difficult to find, in recent history, a more powerful, effective display of largely spontaneous and unified mass political action."[10] Soviets, trade unions, factory committees, party organizations, and a newly founded Committee for Struggle Against the Counterrevolution all acted to mobilize the masses against the army units advancing on Petrograd. Trenches were dug, barricades erected, and new units of Red Guards formed. Preparations for the defense of the capital proved to be unnecessary, however, as Kornilov's forces simply dissolved under the influence of agitators sent to win over the army. Within a couple of days many of the general's units were ready to arrest their commanding officers. After the failed putsch ecstatic reports to the Bolshevik party secretariat from all over the country chronicled the workers' dramatic change of mood. By early fall little worker enthusiasm could be found anywhere for any program other than the demand for soviet power.

The massive scope and depth of the workers' political radicalization in 1917 is not open to doubt, but the correct interpretation of this process is still contested. One view, well represented by Leonard Schapiro's *The*

Russian Revolutions of 1917, focuses on anarchic workers, the mistakes of the Provisional Government, and the agitation of the Bolshevik party. The alternative, whose pedigree needs no elaboration, celebrates the Bolshevik party's leadership of a class-conscious labor movement against the government of the bourgeoisie. The perspective to be developed here, stemming from the model of autocratic capitalist development, connects the political radicalization of Russian workers to their strong sense of class isolation rooted in the old regime. From this vantage point Russian workers formed neither an anarchic mass nor a self-conscious class in the Marxist sense, but a combined movement quite united in its radicalism yet socially fragmented. The Provisional Government was not simply guilty of tactical errors, nor was it the uncompromising representative of the bourgeoisie; rather, it was in the impossible position of mediator between irreconcilable sides. And the Bolshevik party both benefited from and stimulated the development of worker political radicalism, although in a deeper sense its relationship to the workers was rife with tensions.

THE WORKERS' POLITICAL STANCE

The general cast of mind that underlay the political radicalization of workers in 1917, a synthesis of traditional and socialist ideas, has been described at length in earlier chapters. The tsarist regime had taught workers a general lesson about the state, that its duty was to protect them. The government's staggering departure from its own promises had weakened its legitimacy more than it had destroyed the principle. The regime, with its ambivalence toward the capitalists based upon its statist worldview, had also taught the workers something more specific: that they had been unjustly treated under the capitalist system and accordingly deserved special treatment. Socialists gladly adapted their agitation to these traditional assumptions for their own purposes, and thereby propagated a new set of interpretations: the tsarist state would *always* violate its promises because it protected the industrialists' interests; capitalism as an economic system was based on exploitation; and the workers could save themselves only through their own efforts. Thus, helped by the socialists and also on the basis of their own experiences under the old regime, a great many workers developed a sense of isolation, of injustice, and of mission. The revolution reinforced these sentiments and gave a powerful impetus to the class polarization that already existed.

These assumptions and beliefs did not augur well for the acceptance of social pluralism or political liberalism in 1917. In the eyes of the workers a just government did not mediate between conflicting interests but took the role of the weaker side. Following this logic, the worker representatives to the Special Commission of the Ministry of Trade and Industry's Department of Labor disputed the government's claim that it must conciliate the interests of both sides: the task of the Department of Labor, they claimed, should be defense of the interests of labor. In any case, they continued, workers did not really care about such details, only about the confirmation and strengthening of the rights they had won. (We already saw that their conception of rights went far beyond political rights to embrace a number of crucial socioeconomic aspirations, such as the eight-hour day and workers' control.) The worker representatives then proposed to postpone the sessions until all members of the commission had received and studied the Soviet's project on organization. If it were to be decided otherwise, the workers, obeying the directives of the Soviet, were obligated to leave the meeting.[11] In a later session of the Department of Labor, worker representatives S. Monoszon was even more explicit: the question of which side is weaker is clear to all in a "capitalist state." In order to redress the balance, the government must definitely be on the side of the workers.[12]

Just as workers assumed that a legitimate government would act to protect their interests, so they felt that a government should be judged only according to the end result of its policy. They were not concerned with what the workers considered to be the "details" of procedure. "When our opponents," wrote Miliukov, obviously referring to the Bolsheviks, "who by then had become everyone's enemies, began to use word-shibboleths which charmed the masses, simple words like peace, land, rights of labor, class struggle, we had nothing to oppose to them. Our words were taken from us: constitution, rights, law, equality."[13] Miliukov portrays the process as one of seduction and despoilment, and he implies that there was a real contest. In fact, liberal ideas, focusing on process and formal equality, never found any support among the workers in 1917.

In this regard workers simply had had almost no familiarity with the logic or procedures of liberal democracy. They had no reason to believe that an emphasis upon rules might protect both sides or to accept that formal law in a democracy would have to involve compromises. Nor, for that matter, was there anything in their experience to suggest that a government would be bound by the laws it made. Law as both an expression of social pluralism and a means to regulate it was completely unfamiliar to them. So was the concept of a semiautonomous civil society the logic of which the government, by means of law, was bound to respect. The state, if it was the right kind of state, could and should violate the existing pattern of social relations in the interests of a higher form of justice: to redress past abuses, to protect the weak, and to create a more egalitarian society. Social relations had no independent integrity.

The Provisional Government, by insisting on formal procedures and democratic representation, violated all of these assumptions about the proper role of the government in class relations. Thus it was not just the government's actual policies—its impotence and its gradual move to the right—that the workers found objectionable but its very vision of how ideally it should act. Disappointed in their expectations, workers gradually came to accept that the state solely represented the interests of its enemy, as many had believed in the prerevolutionary period. The seeds of this belief were already present in the assumptions inherited from the past. It is for this reason that shortly after the February revolution workers gave notice that "the people and the army came out on the street not to replace one government by another, but to carry out our slogans in reality. And these slogans are the following: freedom, equality, land and liberty, and an end to the war—to us, the propertyless class, the bloody carnage is not necessary."[14]

Given these political premises, a third conclusion ineluctably followed: the workers did not want an absence of government but a strong state that would represent only their interests and do so in a way that would achieve immediate results.[15] An authentic revolutionary government had the responsibility to struggle against chaos as the workers interpreted it; that is, against bourgeois sabotage, the continuation of the war, and economic anarchy. For this struggle a dictatorship of the proletariat was indispensable in order to defeat the counterrevolution and institute a new revolutionary order.[16] In this regard Moscow worker-memoirist Dune remarked that for workers, the whole issue was much simpler than it was for sociologists [sic]. They wanted only one thing: the creation of a revolutionary government that they could trust, in the form of a dictatorship of the proletariat. Such a government, they felt, was more than desirable—it was a necessity.[17]

The strength of this desire for a proletarian state among Russian workers does not contradict the observation that many workers acted in an anarchic manner. Clearly indiscipline and the spirit of anarchy were rampant in 1917, but acceptance of the principles of anarchism was another matter. Toward October hunger, unemployment, and frustration over what appeared to be a political stalemate increased the appeal of direct action and led to disillusionment with organized politics, particularly among the less proletarian elements among the workers.[18] In the political struggle, as in the class struggle, the labor movement continued to be "combined" in 1917. Nonetheless, anarchism as the principled rejection of centralized state power found little articulate support among Russian workers, and it was obviously outdistanced by overwhelming backing for the Bolsheviks, whose expressed goals in 1917 were far from anarchic.

In sum, the workers' political perspectives and aspirations in 1917 followed an almost exclusively class logic, the result of their prior experiences under the tsarist regime. Class conflict thus turned out to be the most powerful motor of political events in urban Russia in 1917, determining the political loyalties of both workers and industrialists. Class conflict has also been vital in the political life of other revolutionary situations with a significant proletarian element, but not in such a determinant way as in Russia. Because of greater internal class differentiation and the deeper roots of rival political parties and institutions in countries such as Germany, Spain, or Chile, the workers' political goals and allegiances during the revolution were also differentiated. Class alone could not explain the political action of the labor movement, for civil and political society were both more highly developed. In Russia class polarization shaped political polarization—in a sense, the reverse of the prerevolutionary situation, when it was the tsarist state that largely determined the nature of the class struggle. Although the relationship may have been inverted during 1917, however, the close connection between class and political conflict followed the traditional logic of state-society interaction in Russia.

All three of the previous political assumptions were fortified by what the workers interpreted as their victory in February, and it is not surprising that numerous signs of political radicalism, implicit or explicit, were already visible in the early weeks of the revolution. Some workers, particularly Bolshevik activists, favored the immediate creation of a revolutionary government representing the popular classes, and they rejected the Provisional Government from the start.[19] More frequently, however, the workers' class point of view took the form of marked distrust of the Provisional Government and the Duma without explicit rejection of them. The eminent Soviet historian Burdzhalov described the complex mood in Petrograd as follows: subjectively, few workers and soldiers advanced the goal of a revolutionary government in the early days of the revolution. Objectively, however, in their suspicions about the new bourgeois leaders they were struggling for this goal.[20]

From this point of view, dual power, according to Trotsky the "riddle" of the February revolution, was not merely an ambivalent accord between the Provisional Government and the Petrograd Soviet. More deeply, it was the reflection of two basic conditions of post-February Russia bequeathed by the old regime, the vacuum of power and class polarization. No political organization—neither the Duma nor the Petrograd Soviet—had enough power or authority to govern on its own. Partly this condition was a result of the lack of political parties with an organized mass base; partly it was because of the class divisions that militated against consensus. As a result the institutional representatives of the rival forces of liberalism and some form of socialism had to cooperate, yet their cooperation had to involve bitter opposition. The weakness of both sides entailed the first; class polarization and the pressure of the masses, the second.[21]

The underlying contradictions in the formal system of dual power expressed themselves even in the early weeks of the revolution in occasional criticisms of the agreement and in underlying suspicion.[22] Workers expressed their loyalty to the new government not unconditionally but only insofar as it enacted the will of the Soviet and, by implication, their own will. How conditional this support could be is indicated by the following resolution from the Guzhon factory:

> Taking into account that—thanks to the pressure of the Soviet of w[orkers] and s[oldiers] d[eputies] on the Provisional Government, Russia was saved from the renewed oppression of Tsarism, which the Provisional Government wanted to thrust on Russia by installing Mikhail as monarch instead of Nicholas, and thanks to the pressure of the Petrograd Soviet. . . . Nicholas the Bloody was arrested together with all his gang, and by this Russia was saved from preparation for a counterrevolution—we express our full solidarity with the Petrograd Soviet.[23]

If in the early weeks of the revolution only a small minority of workers expressed open support for a class government, by late summer the same events that had precipitated the radicalization of the class struggle had had the identical effect on the workers' political perspectives. Economic crisis, the continuation of the war, the acceleration of class conflict, and the Kornilov putsch transformed the vast majority of politically active workers into enemies of the Provisional Government in its various incarnations. It represented the class enemy, and this identification led many workers to another conclusion with deep historical roots. They came to see no essential distinction between the new government and the old tsarist regime, except that the Provisional Government was now more clearly a "bourgeois dictatorship."

One of the most extreme statements of this position came from the worker delegation in the Ministry of Labor's Committee of Labor in the Ukraine. "In the political area," it said, "we see a complete restoration of the system of Tsarist autocracy, a system leaning today on the support of foreign occupation. In the economic region, the basis of all government policy is in fact the decisions of the May congress of representatives of industry, trade, finance, and agriculture." The results of this policy, it continued, had been disastrous for the country, and the masses were in despair. The government responded with the use of repression against peaceful and unarmed strikes, and it encouraged lockouts. The police cruelly repressed trade unions, arresting and exiling their leaders, while it tolerated and even aided factory owner organizations. Even the Ministry of Labor failed to defend the workers, and at times it took initiatives deeply harmful to their interests. The workers' participation in legislative work also reflected this policy, for the Provisional Government, like the tsarist regime before it, would better be able to identify and arrest worker leaders. The only hope for the workers, therefore, was organization and solidarity, for the government would give them nothing.[24] Such an extreme indictment is unusual, but it is not difficult to locate more measured expressions of the same sentiment. The reintroduction of the death penalty in the army was particularly effective in stimulating many workers to identify the two governments.[25] The assignment of Cossacks to the Donets Basin and the many threats to use force against strikes clearly had the same effect, even though the government was in no position to follow through in these matters.[26] As the declaration summarized earlier indicates, the workers' past experience was just as crucial for shaping perceptions as were current realities.[27]

Within this context the ideal of a Constituent Assembly as the prelude to a democratic republic made little sense to workers. Workers rejected liberal democracy partly because they rejected social pluralism. Just as the industrialists were not necessary in the factories, so the privileged classes were not necessary in the state. Sometimes this parallel was explicitly drawn, as when the Bolsheviks urged that the transfer of state power to the soviets was identical to what already existed inside many factories. Together they constituted the dictatorship of the proletariat. As Dune described the sentiment at the time, "If we were able to organize a new revolutionary government in one factory, we must create roughly the same order for Russia as a whole. Let the bourgeoisie trade and construct factories, but power must be in the hands of the workers, not of the factory owners, merchants, and their servants."[28] As in Lenin's vision, politics was reduced to administration and administration was to serve the ends of the favored class. Factory and state could thus operate according to the same logic.

The revolution was now wholly identified with the workers and peasants—it was "our" revolution—and the privileged classes, opposing it tooth and nail, had no right to expect anything from it. Local soviets and Bolshevik party organizations continued to talk of the Constituent Assembly, urging workers to organize themselves for the upcoming elections. They did not accept its basic principles, however, embracing it only to the extent that it would legitimate a class-based government. The contradiction between their espousal of elections to the assembly and the demand for soviet power was evident in debates and resolutions at the time. For example, at the Fourth Congress of factory committees, several speakers defended the Constituent Assembly against the attacks of those who wanted an all-soviet government. Responding to the expressed fear that landowners and priests might be elected, the worker Iusis remarked that it was the job of the workers to ensure that such people were not elected. Skrypnik assured his listeners that a freely elected Assembly would truly express the will of the proletariat and all the urban and rural poor. It is not clear, however, if any of these supporters of the Assembly would have embraced it if the election results were not to their liking.[29] An indication to the contrary is the resolution adopted by the Obukhov factory, which celebrated the need for class unity and harmony within the Constituent Assembly: "Only the class struggle exists, the struggle of labor against capital, and there is no room for dissension in the Constituent Assembly."[30] The true measure of the workers' commitment to the Constituent Assembly was obvious in January, when it was dispersed by the Bolsheviks with virtually no worker opposition, despite Menshevik efforts to drum up support for it.

The demand for soviet power, extremely widespread among workers by October, was the most clear-cut political expression of the underlying logic of class. For radical theorists it was precisely this class nature of the soviets that elevated them over parliamentary democracy as a basis for the future form of government. Further, the soviets were built upon the direct involvement of the masses in political life and thus, for men like Lenin or Pannekoek, they were far more democratic than bureaucracies removed from the will of the masses and parliamentary institutions based upon an abstract notion of representation. The soviets thus embodied the workers' impatience with mere procedure—their aim was to realize the goals of the working class—and they perfectly expressed the widespread sense that only the workers and their allies should have political rights. For it was clear to all that a government of soviets was a class government with little or no room for the workers' opponents. In these respects the soviets were not as different from the Bolshevik party as is sometimes claimed. Both favored the dictatorship of the proletariat; both embraced the idea of a unitary proletarian will; and both devalued political debate and democratic procedures as ends in themselves, standing instead for class interest and ideology. For both, too, politics was hardly distinguishable from administration; for Dune, as for Lenin, the state and the factory could be run in the same way. The work of the revolution was not to secure subjective rights but to institutionalize mass participation in administration and expropriate the class enemy. From their instrumentalist and class point of view, the workers, by October, had overwhelmingly come to support the Bolshevik party and a soviet government, in many cases failing to make a distinction between the two.

The workers' overwhelming transfer of loyalty to the Bolshevik party is the final key example of the triumph of a class point of view in the political radicalization of the Russian workers, for it was the Bolsheviks

who decisively cut themselves off from any semblance of class collabora-
tion. The process of Bolshevization is thus thematically part of the present discussion, but it will receive the more extended treatment that it
deserves in the following chapter. Before turning to this theme, the dilemmas of the Provisional Government will be considered in light of the
workers' inherited political preconceptions and their rapid radicalization. It will be seen that the Provisional Government failed not out of
stupidity or because of its class bias but because no experiment in liberal
democracy had much chance against a mobilized mass of workers hostile
toward its basic principles.

THE DILEMMAS OF THE PROVISIONAL GOVERNMENT

THE OVERALL FAILURE OF THE PROVISIONAL GOVERNMENT

From the early days of the revolution, members of the emerging government and the parties that represented them, especially the Kadets,
were well aware of their tenuous legitimacy in the eyes of the masses.
They could proclaim to the ends of the empire that they had been the
courageous leaders of the revolution, even that the revolution had been a
heroic exploit of the Duma.[31] They could try to convince themselves that
what the Russian people desired most of all after the fall of the Romanovs was the reestablishment of strong central authority, a goal to which
they were willing to devote themselves without hesitation.[32] As the negotiations over the form of the new government in early March demonstrated, however, they were also profoundly aware of the many divisions
between themselves and the "revolutionary people." They felt the people's hatred of the old regime and their deep distrust of the privileged
classes who had collaborated with it. They were surely aware that
demands for political reform would be accompanied by pressure for immediate changes in class and economic relations as well, as they had been
in earlier episodes of revolutionary ferment. They knew that the workers
and soldiers regarded the revolution as their work and claimed new
rights in accord with their achievements. It was clear to all with any
political perspicacity that taming the revolution and governing the
impatient workers and peasants would be an arduous and dangerous
assignment.

One potential remedy, the investment of the new regime with some of
the authority of the old, failed miserably. This was the tactic of Paul
Miliukov, leader of the Kadets and the guiding force behind the formation and program of the Provisional Government in the early stage of the
revolution. From his own political experience and his knowledge as a

historian, he was profoundly aware of the dangers of mass movements during revolutions, and his preference was for a parliamentary and constitutional monarchy under Grand Duke Mikhail to replace Nicholas.[33] He sensed that a liberal regime was insufficient to satisfy the aspirations of a mobilized mass movement, and so he sought to undergird parliamentary democracy with old and, he supposed, still partly venerated symbols of authority. Miliukov clung to this idea after it had been rejected by many of his colleagues, but even he was forced to abandon it when his colleague Guchkov "went directly to the railroad workshops, made an announcement to the workers about Mikhail—and just barely managed to escape getting beaten or killed."[34] After Mikhail's refusal to assume the position of constitutional monarch, it was clear that the new government had failed in its efforts to connect itself to the old regime. Left to itself, it was forced to deal with the new forces of the revolution on its own. Ironically, many workers soon came to identify the new government with its predecessors, with consequences contrary to Miliukov's hopes.

What, then, was the program of the new government, and how did it hope to establish its right to rule in the eyes of the masses? The Kadets were the central party of the government (they had six ministers, whereas the Progressives and Octobrists had two each, and the Centrists and Socialists had one). At the time the Kadets were accused of being a bourgeois party, the party of the capitalists. The claim has some truth, but is also a bit misleading. The party, and by extension the government, certainly favored capitalism and some form of liberal republic. Consequently, they hoped for the emergence of a pluralistic civil society that could provide the basis for private property and capitalist development. In their view this vision required the tutelage of the liberal intelligentsia and the continued predominance of privilege, for, as Miliukov retorted to an angry jibe, "propertied society is the only organized society, which can enable other strata of Russian society to organize themselves too."[35]

However, despite the two (if one includes Guchkov, three) industrialist ministers in the cabinet and the heavy representation of industry among the new administrative personnel,[36] the new government did not represent the industrialist class in any simple sense. The political parties represented in the cabinet were mainly composed of the liberal intelligentsia, and for many years there had been hostility and suspicion between them and the factory owners.[37] The Kadets in particular saw themselves in the classical mold of the intelligentsia: above class egoism, able to represent the interests of the nation as a whole because of their superior ideological vision.[38] In accord with this view, and also with Russian political traditions, they placed more emphasis on state intervention in the economy than many industrialists would have wished. Thus the Provisional Government represented the factory owners in much the same qualified sense as the socialist parties represented the workers.

Armed with this perspective, the new government approached class relations gingerly. It did not want to risk the exacerbation of class polarization, and it had a principled commitment to the participation of all affected groups in the formation of policy. In this context fundamental reform was placed in the background, to be accomplished, perhaps, after careful study and the organization and participation of the contending sides.[39] The principle might have been admirable in the abstract, but its application could not satisfy the urgent demands of Russian workers: this would have required a partisan policy. In the absence of significant government initiatives, many workers eventually came to conclude that "it's now about time to perceive behind these 'all-national' principles the simple betrayal of the motherland"—which meant the betrayal of their concept of the revolution.[40] From late spring onward growing worker radicalism and hostility toward the Provisional Government in fact helped push the Kadets to the right, to the outright defense of the industrialists and, later, to the sponsorship of counterrevolution. By the end of the year the Kadets had indeed come close to being a bourgeois party.

The various transformations of the Provisional Government and their efforts to solve the twin problems of power and legitimacy have been expertly recounted many times and need be reviewed only briefly here. The pure model of dual power, with no significant socialist participation in the government, could survive only as long as there were no major conflicts between the government and the Petrograd Soviet. The requisite concord lasted only until April, when it was revealed that Minister of Foreign Affairs Miliukov had sent a secret note to the allies undermining the expressed "defensist" aims of the government. On 20 and 21 April massive protest demonstrations broke out in Petrograd. There were some outcries against the Provisional Government as a whole, but most of the demands of the demonstrating workers and soldiers centered on the replacement of Miliukov and War Minister Guchkov as pledges of the government's commitment to peace. These protests precipitated a crisis in the socialists' strategy of dual power and heated debates over the desirability of formal participation in a coalition cabinet. Advocates of a coalition government, with Kerensky the most visible spokesman, argued that the socialists were now strong enough to shoulder the burdens of government without falling under the dominance of the bourgeoisie. At first their arguments failed to convince the necessary number of Menshevik and Socialist Revolutionary representatives, many of whom feared that a coalition government would, in the words of Tseretelli, "weaken revolutionary enthusiasm."[41] Only a plea from a representative of the

Petrograd garrison convinced enough socialists that such a step was the only way to avoid political crisis.

From this dramatic change the neutral observer would have concluded that the government had made a clear shift to the left, that it was no longer "bourgeois," and he would have felt confirmed in his judgment by its 5 May declaration of principles, which affirmed the policy of "a peace without annexations or indemnities" and its energetic support for "measures for the protection of labor in every possible way."[42] But he would have been wrong in two senses. First, the socialists in the government still accepted the basic concept of a bourgeois revolution and so continued to argue that workers should accept their place in a capitalist society in order to develop the economy. One of the bluntest statements of this position can be found in the speech of Kolokol'nikov (an important Ministry of Labor official) before the Third Petrograd factory committee conference. Arguing that the revolution was democratic, not socialist, he announced that "capitalist oppression will exist and even intensify, since class contradictions will become sharper and sharper." Workers should not place too much hope in the Ministry of Labor but should instead seek to develop their own independent power.[43]

Second, there were indeed divergences between the liberals and the socialists in the coalition government, but these did not lead the government to move to the left so much as to lose its coherence almost entirely. In the face of economic crisis, the socialists called for increased government regulation of industry, heavy taxation of profits, and broad social reforms in industry and agriculture. Responding to the same conditions, and also to their perceptions of growing worker anarchy, the Kadets turned to the right and strengthened their ties with industrialist groups. The conflict, in some ways reminiscent of the old tsarist splits between the Ministry of Internal Affairs and the Ministry of Finance, proved intractable. On 16 May the Petrograd Soviet demanded state control over the economy. Two days later Konovalov resigned, to be replaced by Stepanov, who openly called for a rapproachement with the bourgeoisie. The cabinet rejected Stepanov's plan.[44] The coalition government thus failed to satisfy the goals of the workers, the moderate socialists, and the liberals. In many senses it ceased to be a government at all, collapsing into warring factions seeking outside support.

There followed a second coalition government (23 July), and then a third (25 September), with Kerensky assuming ever more visible roles against a background of growing class polarization and political stalemate. What Sukhanov said of the second coalition, the product of prolonged negotiations after an acute political crisis, that it was "hanging in the air," with no roots in society and no internal unity, was just as true of the third.[45] Government without a coalition was impossible for the time being, and yet no coalition proved to be workable. Within this context of political decay, in which some members of the government clearly favored counterrevolution, the workers increasingly came to support a class government of soviets.

THE PROVISIONAL GOVERNMENT'S LABOR POLICY

The relationship between the Provisional Government and the labor movement was not so profoundly shaped by government labor policy as had state-labour relations been in the last decades of tsarist rule. Laws regulating strikes, the labor contract, or worker organization would have required some time to transform class relations even in a calmer atmosphere. Thus the government's inability to push through a significant labor program was rather incidental to its overall failure. Much more important was the ultimate lack of viability of the various incarnations of the Provisional Government in the context of Russian class conflict and politics. Yet it is worthwhile to cast a glance at government labor policy in order to understand the nature of the constraints operating against the government. Such an examination shows the untenability of the argument that the government's failure was mainly a result of tactical errors. In fact, the Provisional Government was trying to square a circle: to enact policy relying on democratic participation. As is well known, however, democracy requires some degree of consensus between opponents, a consensus that, for reasons examined earlier, did not exist in Russia. Toward October the various factions in the government abandoned their commitments to democracy and class conciliation, thus recognizing the failure of the whole program of dual power.

In his early statements on labor policy, Minister of Trade and Industry Konovalov recognized that the resolution of the labor question was an urgent task. He promised a broad program of reform to be conducted by a new Ministry of Labor. The ministry was to have an associated collegial organization with representatives of worker, factory owner, and social organizations. He summarized the government's ideals in the early period thus: reform should be accompanied by organization, participation, and law. Both sides would be consulted through their organizations, and this democratic process would ensure that legislative changes were in accord with social forces. The program of reform that he envisioned was a broad one: many old laws would be canceled, and new legislation would be enacted on organizations, the length of the workday, the protection of labor, insurance, conciliatory chambers, and labor exchanges.

Such a program, Konovalov announced, depended upon the correct functioning of the economy.[46]

In a later statement Konovalov clarified his views. The person to head the new ministry would be chosen by the socialist parties, and he must enjoy the complete trust of the "laboring masses." The nomination of such a person would serve to strengthen the "national cabinet" charged with governing the country until the Constituent Assembly was convened.[47] Konovalov was thus apparently willing to violate the Kadets' policy of nonpartisanship and make the ministry a spokesman for the workers. As far as direct economic reforms are concerned, such as the eight-hour day and wage increases, he was more chary, preferring to allow the two rival sides to resolve such issues.

Until the creation of the Ministry of Labor and the formation of the coalition government—both in early May—the Department of Labor of the Ministry of Trade and Industry busied itself with preparing legislation, but none was actually enacted. The major reform of the early period, the agreement on the eight-hour day between the Petrograd Soviet and the Petrograd Society of Factory Owners, was never legislated by the government. In general the ministry's commitment to consultation and democracy prohibited the rapid issuance of new laws, and it insisted that law should be the basis of policy.[48] The press occasionally gave glimpses of the legislative process and its difficulties under the new regime. For example, the *Trade Industrial Gazette* reported on a 25 April conference of the Department of Labor on the department's project to legalize strikes. Representatives were included from the sick funds, Petrograd worker organizations, the Petrograd Soviet, and industrialist organizations. The Minister's offical, M. V. Bernatskii, declared that the goal of the conference was to clarify the classes' points of view and to find a middle course that would satisfy both sides. Such a compromise would help channel the workers' economic struggle and keep those efforts within legal limits. The factory owners advocated compulsory conciliation. The workers objected that the coming political system would not yet be socialist but bourgeois, so they would need all possible weapons to defend themselves. Bernatskii remarked that he sensed an atmosphere of mistrust on the part of the worker organizations toward the Provisional Government, and particularly the Department of Labor.[49] The contradiction between democratic procedures and class polarization was already evident at this relatively early date.

In appearance, government labor policy became more activist with the political changes of early May and the creation of the Ministry of Labor. The ministry embodied to the fullest all the contradictions of moderate socialist policy, however, and little was accomplished in the way of reform. In fairness, the new ministry was given little time to enact its program, and most of its efforts during this short time were directed toward the mediation of conflicts.[50] But the ministry also shared some of the blame. Its socialist leaders clearly saw the workers as their main constituency, but their conception of the revolution and the tasks of revolutionary democracy made no concessions to the popular mood. Quite the contrary: officials lectured and scolded the workers that their refusal to embrace a policy obviously contrary to their perceived interest was a sign of betrayal of the revolution.

Both in content and in style the Ministry of Labor's policy was completely at odds with the workers' goals. Numerous pronouncements by Minister Skobolev and his high officials at worker conferences and in the labor press were disarmingly blunt and unyielding. Skobolev's assistant Kolokol'nikov, a right-wing Menshevik, was particularly outspoken. In his speech at the First All-Russian Congress of factory inspectors in mid-June, he emphasized the government's commitment to rapid reform of the previous backward labor legislation. Immediately afterward, however, he declared that the central point of the government's domestic policy was the struggle with the economic crisis, and if the legislative protection of labor interfered with the struggle against economic ruin, a temporary retreat from reform must be permitted.[51] Kolokol'nikov spoke even more directly at the First Congress of Soviets: some measures would have to be postponed, including the eight-hour day, although it would be recognized in principle. The legislation he advocated, such as changes in insurance laws and worker participation in government policymaking, was certainly worthwhile, but it did not touch the workers' major immediate demands. Nonetheless he urged them actively to support the work of the ministry.[52] Three months later Skobolev defined the tasks of the revolution in the same (to the workers) limited way: the formation of a new political system, the salvation of the country from economic ruin, and the creation of firm state power for the transitional period. Revolutionary democracy could have mechanically taken power long ago, as early as 28 February, he said, but it understood that power had to be shared by all the elements that would benefit from a bourgeois revolution. It could not, and still cannot, break its coalition with the commercial-industrial bourgeoisie.[53]

The fulfillment of these tasks—in the ultimate interests of the working class—depended upon strong and independent state power. Ministry of Labor officials thus rejected any suggestion that the workers themselves should be responsible for policy. In fact, despite their view of themselves as advocates for the working class, they showed a marked distrust for workers, even for worker organizations. Kolokol'nikov declared that giving regulatory control to factory committees and trade unions was dangerous, for "these organs will approach these issues from a local and small-group point of view, and not from a statewide viewpoint."[54] Skobolev voiced the same concerns to worker and industrial representatives in a session of the Ministry of Labor's committee to discuss labor legislation. The formation of the committee, he announced in words reminiscent of Kokovtsov, did not deprive the government of its right to make policy independently, particularly if the two sides did not agree. Ideally, any project would have the approval of both, "but if we do not obtain this, we will have to introduce them to the Provisional Government by our own responsibility or delay a whole number of legislative projects until another time." The government, responded a worker representative, "did not at all have to say that if the committee agrees with you, then fine, but if it does not, then you will all the same act in your own way."[55]

The workers were thus called upon to participate in the formation of labor policy, and they were urged to support the ministry against their class enemies. In so doing, however, they were to accept a very limited program of reform basically formulated by the government independently of their input. They were to trust that a policy of government control over the economy best served their interests in the intermediary stage of the revolution. The state should be responsible for organizing production and distribution, and "only state power can say where the limits of the economic improvement of individual classes of the population are."[56] Much was being asked of the workers, and it is not difficult to understand their suspicion that little had really changed since the fall of the old regime. Previously state solicitude and paternalism had been proclaimed, but the workers were denied immediate benefits in the interests of capitalist development and order. With the advent of democracy, a tutelary ministry warned them that their aspirations had to be subordinate to more overriding goals. The main difference was the degree of participation, but the ministry wished to deny workers the direct benefits even of this. For, as always, social groups were too immature to define and regulate their own affairs: the classical assumption of both the tsarist state and the intelligentsia.

The ministry thus had a limited agenda of legal reforms, but even these limited goals went unrealized. Again, part of the problem was a lack of time and resources. In addition, however, the minister himself admitted that the ministry's method of work was responsible for considerable delay. Legislation went slowly, said Skobolev, because it had to be done democratically. All relevant legislative proposals were examined in special committees representing both labor and capital.[57] When we recall that it was precisely during the first months of the Ministry of Labor's existence that the class struggle was acquiring ominous new traits, it requires little imagination to understand the sterility of these committees. According to one industrialist representative in the deliberations, thanks to the "harsh criticism" of the industrialists, the majority of projects "were returned to the Department of Labor for reworking, from where they did not return."[58] Although industrialist opposition indeed played a significant role in delaying legislation such as the project on strikes, worker intransigence was just as strong and probably just as decisive.

Interministerial conflict also did its part to inhibit government initiatives on the labor question. There were now three ministries concerned with the functioning of the economy and the state of industrial relations: Finance, Trade and Industry, and Labor. Although I am unaware of any thorough study of the matter, it is doubtful that the powers and responsibilities of the ministries were any better defined than were those of the old tsarist ministries. In addition, there were serious disagreements on crucial issues, such as the necessary degree of government regulation of the economy, with the Ministry of Labor clearly taking the most activist position.[59] Cleavages were also evident in their differing perspectives on labor policy. The Ministry of Trade and Industry tended to represent the factory owners' point of view, criticizing, for example, the Ministry of Labor's project on strikes for being too one-sided in favor of the workers. It requested that the proposals be reexamined in a special conference with the participation of representatives of factory owners and Trade and Industry.[60] With the ripening of the revolution, Trade and Industry became even bolder in its proposals to tame the labor movement: a report by a high official in the ministry suggested the possibility of forced labor at wages determined by the government.[61] The idleness and indiscipline of the workers had been a favorite theme of the ministry for months, without Skobolev's appeals to socialist morality or comradely discipline. Already on 16 May Minister Konovalov inveighed against "the slogans which are being thrust into the midst of the workers, exciting the dark instincts of the mob, [which] are followed by destruction, anarchy, and the annihilation of public and national life."[62] Even the Mensheviks were forced to conclude that the Ministry of Trade and Industry was an agent of the industrialists and that it directly opposed the program of revolutionary democracy.[63] Further, their main newspaper declared that the Kadets supported the Ministry of Trade and Industry's policy, which was directed against both the national economy and the workers. It concluded that the alliance with the bourgeoisie must be with leftist elements only, for only they understood the needs of the revolution.[64]

Clearly the Ministry of Labor was far from radical in its goals, accepting the basic logic of the Ministry of Trade and Industry. It differed greatly on specifics, however, as the previous examples indicate, and it was forced to take account of the will of the Soviet and the mood of the masses. Its intermediate position between the "bourgeois" Ministry of Trade and Industry and the aspirations of the worker masses, symptomatic of the situation of the moderate socialists as a whole, paralyzed the government yet failed to win for it mass support. The result was a stalemate, part of the general polarization and decay that affected the government as a whole and forced it to reconstitute itself two more times after the first coalition. Legislative reform could hardly be expected in the political chaos of the months before October.

What, then, did the Provisional Government accomplish in the area of labor reform? The Ministry of Labor summed up its achievements in its August report.[65] Not surprisingly, the results were not impressive. On 11 July, local commissars of labor were established in order to mediate industrial conflict, enforce compliance with labor laws, and carry out the policy of the ministry on the local level. This was regarded as a preliminary step toward the creation of a new Inspectorate of Labor, which was to include working-class as well as factory owner representatives. In the meantime, the labor commissars were to cooperate (in an unspecified way) with the factory inspectors and trade unions. The underlying purpose of this new office was to create closer ties between government officials and the labor movement, for the factory inspectors were clearly regarded as an anachronism left behind by the old regime. To this end the decree gave commissars the right to coopt workers into the enforcement of labor laws. Further, in his comments on the decree Kolokol'nikov remarked that the commissars would need to lean upon local worker organizations to nominate and then confirm the candidates, although they were at all times to be guided by the ministry's directives.[66] It is thus clear that on the local level the ministry was willing to give a considerable (and perhaps unfair) degree of influence to worker representatives, as long as this delegation of authority would not harm its autonomy in the policy realm. It is understandable that the government issued the measure in the form of a decree, thus bypassing the endless debates of the legislative commissions.

The Ministry of Labor also managed to enact a few other measures. On 15 July regional insurance and factory boards were authorized to establish average yearly earnings for work paid by the day. Two days later a new health insurance law was passed that extended the 1912 law to a great many more workers and gave the sick funds more independence. On 5 August the government approved a law on conciliatory chambers in factories not controlled by the government, which, in accord with the wishes of the workers, made arbitration nonbinding. Night work by women and minors under age seventeen in nondefense factories was banned on 8 August. Finally, after strong opposition from the industrialists and the Ministry of Trade and Industry, the Provisional Government accepted Minister of Labor Gvozdev's project to limit the factory owners' freedom to fine workers.[67]

Although many of these measures touched upon questions central to the welfare of the workers, the most important projects to reconstitute labor relations on a new basis never went beyond the stage of proposals and discussions. No new laws were passed on strikes, worker organizations, or the nature of the labor contract. Legislative proposals were drawn up, debated, and resubmitted, but time and differences of opinion prevented their passage as laws. For what it was worth, the Ministry of Labor's projects often tended to favor the workers—for example, by espousing a virtually unlimited right to strike—although it is doubtful that the worker representatives recognized this slant. And any credit to the ministry was probably canceled by its unwillingness to let the workers (or the industrialists) participate in the actual drawing up of the projects.

As discussed in part II, tsarist authorities had also been unable to legislate in the area of labor relations. The cost for them, in terms of consistency of administration and the ability to channel class conflict, was also paid by the Provisional Government, although with this difference: it is highly unlikely that law could have controlled class conflict in the circumstances of 1917. Governmental paralysis was more a result than a cause of social polarization. Nonetheless it is worth noting some interesting similarities with tsarist labor administration.

Tsarist officials were caught between the incompatible goals of honoring the government's claim to protect workers' interests and its rival commitments to social order and industrial growth. The Ministry of Labor, and to some extent the Provisional Government as a whole, had to try to maintain its worker constituency even while supporting capitalist relations and defining economic recovery as the revolution's main immediate task. Like the tsarist administration, it could not be guided by law in its decisions, so local officials enjoyed (or were burdened with) considerable autonomy. As before, at times government officials even evinced an indifference to law, in part because the extant laws were still those of the tsarist state.[68] Antinomianism also was rooted in the traditional political culture of the intelligentsia (many of whom were now in the government), with its emphasis on basic social forces and historical trends (evident in the very ideas of the bourgeois revolution and dual power) and its elevation of morality and ends above law and procedures.[69] Just as Ministry of Internal Affairs officials had often proclaimed the moral rights of the worker in attacking factory owner exploitation, so Ministry of Labor officials were capable of basing decisions on their own moral standards regardless of the law. For this reason the following exchange in the conciliatory commission of the Otto Kirchner factory has a familiar ring. The session was discussing the rights of workers dismissed because of the economic crisis. A factory owner representative quite correctly objected that the matter rested within the realm of managerial authority. After all, new legislation on the labor contract had not yet been passed. The official from the Ministry of Labor replied that the issue was not legal but moral. He then lectured the factory owners in much the same tone as tsarist officials had been accustomed to adopt: the wealth of the enterprise was not created by the factory owner as such but was the product of the labor of a whole range of "co-workers." Many of the workers who had been fired had worked there for a long time, contributing to the factory's wealth but receiving only a bare subsistence. Besides this, they had damaged their health, and so, upon firing, they had "complete rights" [polnoe pravo].[70]

Given the divisions within the government, the lack of firm governmental authority, the emptiness of law, and the heightened atmosphere of crisis, government labor policy was inevitably inconsistent, subject to the judgment of individual officials and shaped by local circumstances more than by principle. Partly on this basis, both workers and factory owners came to see the government as serving the interests of their opponents, and both sides could support their claims with telling evidence. Government officials were often unable or unwilling to protect property rights or even the personal safety of factory administrative personnel—so much was clear from the first days of the revolution. Factory owners often concluded that the government, particularly the Ministry of Labor, had little sympathy for private property and was cooperating in the ruin of Russian industry.[71]

The Provisional Government's labor policy also helped to estrange the workers from the government. Even had it been less ambivalent, the government would have faced great obstacles in winning over the workers, who at heart rejected a nonpartisan policy. The government, however, including both the Ministry of Trade and Industry and the Ministry of Labor, gave the workers incontrovertible cause for suspicion. On 22 August and 28 August, Skobolev issued two circulars (as of old, recourse to circulars!) severely limiting the prerogatives of the factory committees, in particular with respect to hiring and firing and the convocation of meetings during working hours. To the outrage of the workers, these edicts were then used by the industrialists as a weapon in their attack against the workers' organizations. The fact that the circulars were issued in the period of the Kornilov putsch was of course not lost on the workers, and for them it became an indictment against the whole policy of socialist participation in the government. Thus, contrary to his wishes, Skobolev exacerbated rather than softened class conflict, though it was of course class conflict that had made his ministry's middle course so treacherous.

In addition, government officials and organs issued various harsh condemnations and threats to use violence against the workers.[72] The government seldom had the power to carry out these threats, and when it did, its actions were often counterproductive. For example, it sent Cossack troops into the Don region in October, provoking a huge general strike and encouraging the formation of new cadres of Red Guards. By this time it was clear that dual power remained nothing more than a formality, that in fact the Provisional Government no longer existed as a coherent entity. Once again, in trying to control class polarization by threats, the government, in its impotence, only sharpened it.

In sum, despite the hopes of moderates, labor policy proved incapable of reconstructing class relations in Russia. Its failure is only an interesting sidelight to the major social movements and political events of 1917, for at no time was it able to play an independent role. Class polarization was too pronounced and governmental authority too fragile to permit any other outcome. Besides, as had been true after 1905, only the weaker class supported the rule of law, and opponents of formal legality could be found even within the government. The only effect of government labor policy was further to convince both sides that the government did not represent their interests and thus encourage them to support other political solutions. Even in this case the specific impact of labor policy was far less central than other key events in the class and political struggle. What the failure of labor policy mainly serves to illustrate is the shaping of political life in 1917 by class conflict and the survival of old assumptions and patterns of relationship. Deeply rooted in prerevolutionary Russian society and politics, class polarization virtually ruled out moderation, which would have required a truce in the class war under the rule of law.

"Instinctively, emotionally, and by attraction," Lenin had declared, the Russian lower classes, the workers and poor peasants, supported a revolution against capitalism. In the previous two chapters we have seen how the conceptions and organizations of Russian workers rooted in the past shaped their stance in the class and political struggles of 1917 in the direction Lenin suggested. And then he continued: "So far, however, there is no clear consciousness of this, and, as a result, no determination. To develop this is our chief task."[73] To accomplish this task meant to bring together spontaneity and consciousness, to give direction to the workers' revolutionary energy and to whip the party into action. It also meant to reinforce the revolutionary patterns of the past based on an alliance of mass action and a revolutionary underground. In promoting this program, in refusing to accept social pluralism or support parliamentary politics, Lenin's party both accelerated the process of class polarization already described and, after temporary reverses, won the overwhelming support of Russian workers. To the role of the socialist parties in the radicalization of Russian workers in 1917 we now turn.

CHAPTER 15

Workers and Social Democracy in 1917

The combination of autocracy and capitalism led in the late tsarist period to a deep inner connection between socialism and the labor movement. It conditioned the emergence of a committed core of conscious socialist workers who acquired great influence at times of unrest, in large part because the mass of unintegrated and unorganized workers had nowhere else to turn. Similarly, ideology and the party intelligentsia substituted for an absent mass labor movement that might have facilitated the social, political, and ideological differentiation of the working class. There was also an "elective affinity" between traditional political assumptions and the ideals of socialism, for both were alternatives to the liberal emphasis on the autonomy of civil society, the independence of the industrial elite and private property, and a neutral, noninterventionist role of the state. All of these connections had been fortified by government repression, which inadvertently furthered the emergence of a revolutionary labor movement and a heroic revolutionary tradition.

This uneasy coordination of highly disparate elements provided the historical basis of the initial overwhelming sympathy of workers for socialism after February. It was reinforced by the workers' complete separation from privileged Russia, which virtually excluded adherence to liberal, not to mention right-wing, political tendencies. It was not at all clear, however, what the implications of these connections would be for the future, for the interdependence of the labor movement and socialism was based upon conditions, particularly the autocratic state, that were now partly superseded. Further, both the workers and the parties would be confronted with new tasks the solution of which would challenge the old patterns: participation in the new political system, the formation of new organizations, the mobilization of large numbers of untutored participants, and the consolidation of ties between party and class organizations and their mass bases. The requirements of the underground had pushed these issues into the background for many years, but the revolution brought them to the fore with unprecedented urgency.

Difficult choices had to be made in dealing with these issues, for there was no easy compatibility among them. A few such tensions follow. First, choices had to be made between building up party organization and recruiting a mass membership. These were not wholly consistent, for both made great demands on the limited resources of the parties, and the recruitment of masses of inexperienced members augmented the difficulties of organization building. Second, the need to garner mass support was in some tension with the goal of protecting the parties' basic values, for the parties had never had sufficient opportunity to inculcate their values in the masses. Third, the parties had to determine their own desirable degree of participation in the fledgling political system and how to make this participation compatible with a revolutionary stance. Finally, the goal of an immediate seizure of power was not necessarily compatible with the eventual socialist transformation of society. Marxism had taught that the opportunities for socialism would coincide with the ripeness of social forces, but the special conditions of Russian development had separated these two. The seizure of power was potentially closer at hand than socialism, but this made the question of their interrelationship all the sharper. All of the previous issues had both short-term and long-term dimensions, and this duality added further complexities. For example, policies that would win the short-term sympathies of the masses were not necessarily compatible with the parties' long-term goals, whereas strategies centered on long-term socialist goals might well conflict with the immediate aspirations of the masses. Similarly, as the experience of German Social Democracy had suggested, immediate participation in power might lessen the eventual chances for a fully socialist government by transforming both the party and the mass base.

It was amid these uncertainties and dilemmas that the socialist parties had to develop their strategies and policies in 1917. They had to make their calculations in a period of feverish change and uncertainty and without the benefit of the kind of detailed knowledge that an extensive party organization might have given. In this context decisions were made on the basis of ideology and previous experience but an interpreted previous experience that was consonant with ideological presuppositions. The workers' response to these party positions was at first rather inchoate because of their own lack of experience and knowledge, but they also soon began to evaluate party policies in terms of their previous interpretive frameworks. Thus despite the overwhelming novelty of the revolutionary situation, there was an impressive transference of assumptions and perspectives—more homogeneous, perhaps, than in other revolutions because of the relative poverty and uniformity of past experience, narrowed as it had been by autocratic repression. Previous experience thus weighed heavily upon the present, but in very different ways for the two Marxist parties: the Mensheviks were increasingly identified with basic ills of the old regime; the Bolsheviks more and more stood forth as the champions of both the past's worthy ideals and the future's bright promises. Because it was they who offered the two major ideological alternatives in 1917, the contest between the Mensheviks and the Bolsheviks provides the focus for this chapter. The Socialist Revolutionaries, despite their great popularity—especially, it may be assumed, among workers with a peasant background—were not able to offer a distinctive and coherent alternative.[1]

THE INITIAL RELATIONSHIP

Workers' perspectives on the merits of the various socialist parties were initially much less defined than their attitudes toward the factory owners or even toward the new government. General sympathy regarding socialism was combined with almost complete lack of knowledge of or interest in doctrinal differences. This lack of partisan definition was most pronounced in the early weeks of the revolution, particularly in the provinces, but it was never completely replaced. Even in Petrograd, on the eve of the 18 June demonstrations, nominally Socialist Revolutionary and Menshevik workers passed Bolshevik resolutions in their factories.[2] In July according to the report of Volodarskii to the Petrograd Committee, one Bolshevik worker in the Narva district asserted that it was necessary to hang Lenin.[3] This lack of ideological sophistication surely lasted much longer in the provinces, where political life did not have the sharpness that it did in Petrograd and Moscow. In the early days, of course, partisan commitments were especially vague. This was true even of a great many worker activists and even more true of rank-and-file workers. Provincial Bolshevik activists frequently reported in March and April that in local soviets nonparty people predominated.[4] In the Urals there were cases of workers inscribing themselves by mistake in peasant unions, and resolutions often failed to distinguish between Socialist Revolutionary and Social Democratic positions.[5] Later one Bolshevik activist in Central Asia pleaded for the publication of a brochure entitled "On Bolsheviks and Mensheviks" in order to explain the differences between the two factions in simple language.[6] As late as October, Bolshevik leaders reported that workers made complaints such as the following: "We are the best activists of the district, and can we explain the difference between us and the Socialist Revolutionaries? No."[7]

Naturally, there were significant exceptions to this generalization.

A committed core of worker activists had had previous experience in different types of labor organizations, and so they brought well-defined political loyalties from the first days of the revolution. This was most obviously true of many party members, but often nonparty trade union activists also had clear-cut partisan political loyalties.[8] Even some soviets identified themselves with a particular party faction from their formation, as in the cases of the Bolshevik-dominated Vyborg district soviet and the Menshevik-Socialist Revolutionary Porokhovskii Soviet.[9] Such nuclei of party activists soon came to be highly effective in promoting partisan consciousness and loyalties. They could do this partly because many workers continued to feel a dependence upon outside leaders, whom they saw as more capable of defining appropriate strategies. Thus even the workers in a remote textile factory in the Urals, the Zhiriakov factory, ascribed the ineffectiveness of their struggles to the absence of "ideological workers."[10] Sometimes, workers complained, there was even a lack of literate people in their midst, and so outside help was essential.[11]

In addition, two new aspects of Russian social and political life in the months of revolutionary ferment fostered greater ideological awareness among the mass of workers. First, the very flux and coexistence of competing definitions of the situation (characteristic of all revolutions) demanded choice where none was possible before. Strong pressure was felt for systematization and coherence, and thus for ideological awareness, because ideologies help make sense of puzzling situations. Ideological commitment was thus a felt need of the workers themselves, a response to the uncertainty around them, and not simply an artificial contribution of intellectuals. Second, ideological clarity stemmed from the flowering of party competition and the relatively free political debates of the time. Under these conditions workers and peasants could acquire new sophistication in the linking up of interpreted experience and abstract ideas.

In thus turning to ideologies, workers (and others) were also in a sense turning to the past, for although ideological debates were partly about images of a future society, their emotional resonance was more profoundly rooted in their interpretations of social relationships based upon past experience.

As opposed to the pressures toward party identification, there was also among workers a strong commitment to explicit nonpartisanship, a stance that was never completely extinguished even in the face of the ripening of party loyalties.[12] At heart it was connected with the workers' sense of weakness and isolation in Russian society, which seemed to make any internal differences less weighty than external ones.[13] Even in Petrograd local soviets expressed their fervent hope for an end to the schisms. In this spirit, for example, a 1 August general meeting of the

Narvskii district soviet in the capital declared that the conflicts and dis-unity within revolutionary democracy were impermissible and danger-ous. All political groups and the numerous political tendencies had emerged from above, never really understood by people at the grass roots. The resolution called upon workers to adhere to nonpartisan organizations, particularly those that held dear their "young freedom" threatened by reaction. "We propose to the leaders that they find a com-mon language so that we can struggle with the enemies of the revolution in a united way."[14]

The deepening political consciousness of the workers challenged this fundamental belief in unity and led to a number of difficult accommoda-tions. If at first nonpartisanship was based upon a general lack of politi-cal knowledge, it later had to be upheld by explicit decisions and concrete arrangements that recognized factional competition. In a debate in the Gorodskoi district soviet, for example, each socialist party was to choose one orator who could speak for up to twenty minutes.[15] Similarly, facto-ries often made equal contributions to the three main parties, sometimes bending over backwards to accommodate minorities.[16] United socialist blocs with candidates equally chosen from each socialist party were often favored at the local level. Soviet members were asked to emphasize the soviet's lack of partisanship among socialist parties and were urged to make clear when they appeared as soviet and when as party members.

Yet such arrangements and appeals could not prevent the emergence of partisan conflict within factories and worker organizations, and this often reached extreme heights of acrimony, particularly toward Octo-ber. In a 5 October meeting of the Kolomenskii Soviet, after some very bitter exchanges, a Bolshevik speaker exclaimed: "It's necessary to build, say the Socialist Revolutionaries. Look what the Socialist Revolution-aries built . . . gallows. They sent out punitive expeditions."[17] There were occasions when disagreements in the local soviets became so intense that party delegations left the meeting, foreshadowing the famous departure of the Socialist Revolutionaries and Mensheviks from the Second Con-gress of Soviets.[18] The executive committee of the Porokhovskii Soviet issued a remarkable threat in late May. It accused the Bolsheviks of making work in local organizations impossible and demanded that they support the program of the Petrograd Soviet. If the Bolsheviks refused, the Mensheviks cautioned, they themselves would resign and turn over all responsibilities to the Bolsheviks.[19]

This unresolved tension between unity and partisanship was rooted in two basic conditions of the 1917 labor movement, both legacies of the past: its solidarity and its dependence on parties for direction. Both the Mensheviks and the Bolsheviks tried to resolve this tension by presenting themselves as the party of proletarian unity, the Bolsheviks, by October, with considerably more success than their opponents. Neither, however, could entirely eliminate the deeply held belief that there was something illegitimate about factional struggles. For this reason, despite approval for their policy, many workers continued to reject the idea of a Bolshevik dictatorship.

Both of these former traits—the workers' lack of political sophistication and their belief in class unity above party loyalties—were linked to a third basic aspect of the initial situation: the scarcity and poor preparation of party intelligentsia. Many potential party activists removed themselves from local affairs through involvement in the work of the soviets or trade unions, and of those that remained many were of poor quality, often unable themselves to distinguish among the different party programs.[20] This shortage of schooled cadres continued to be felt throughout the year, and, for the Bolsheviks at least, it was probably more acute toward October, when the demand for leadership swelled dramatically. By this time, however, party newspapers and brochures could at least partially fill the void, even though complaints about the lack of literature continued to flood in. This deficiency turned out to be not entirely detrimental to party work, for it virtually removed the potential tension between workers and intelligentsia in local party organizations. It did help perpetuate the early nonpartisan mood of the workers, a great bane from the point of view of most party leaders.

Instead of parties as such, then, workers in the early weeks tended to follow whichever leaders were available, and particularly those who had great personal prestige in local affairs. The leaders' party affiliation was at first a secondary matter, even in the relatively sophisticated factories of the capital.[21] Thus the predominance of any one faction in a factory or soviet did not indicate support for its program so much as the greater initiative and visibility of its cadres. Loyalty was not rooted in firm organizational ties but in the shifting sands of individual attachments, chance, and mood. This state of affairs may not have been propitious for party pluralism, for it encouraged uniformity within party organizations and extreme, rather than partial, changes of orientation.[22] It is unlikely that any other labor movement entered a revolution with such a peculiar combination of weak partisanship and a strongly fixed class orientation. Nor anywhere else did a class orientation eventually come to determine partisan loyalties in such an impressive way.

If local initiative and personalities largely determined factional attachments in the weeks after February, how can the initial dominance of the Mensheviks and Socialist Revolutionaries be reconciled with the prewar Bolshevik predominance in the labor movement? This question troubled Bolshevik activists at the time, who tended to ascribe their poor showing to the voluntary departure of many old Bolsheviks from the organization, to massive arrests, or to the party's preoccupation with revolutionary tasks more than with elections in the early period.[23] Contemporary Soviet scholars have rightly continued to insist on the importance of these factors, but it is also often recognized that the views of the Menshevik-Socialist Revolutionary majority better corresponded to the workers' early mood. The revolution had just been victorious, and there was widespread, if superficial, sentiment for class cooperation and moderation.[24] Disillusionment with moderate socialism would not progress as rapidly as disaffection with the industrialists or the Provisional Government, but despite the emphasis on worker unity, it would follow the same general trajectory.

This, then, was the situation confronting the socialist parties: a set of difficult political decisions arising in a time of great uncertainty and flux, and a worker mass malleable in terms of its partisan loyalties but very insistent in its expectations from the revolution. The Mensheviks and Bolsheviks, true to their traditions, adopted opposite interpretations of the revolution and very different political strategies, differences that provided the foundation for the workers' evaluation of their relative merits. As with their judgment on the industrialists and the government, however, they also interpreted the parties within the context of frameworks derived from the past. In this assimilation of present and past experiences the Mensheviks clearly lost, as the workers increasingly identified them not just with antiworker policies in the present but also with many of the ills of the old regime.

THE MENSHEVIKS' REVOLUTIONARY PROGRAM

It is an irony of some significance that the Mensheviks were less revolutionary toward the revolution but more revolutionary toward the labor movement than the Bolsheviks. They did not favor such a radical break with prerevolutionary Russian society as their rivals, but they did advocate a more dramatic transformation of the labor movement's organization, goals, and place in society. The latter change was seen as a prerequisite for the former, a view that was directly contrary to that of the workers, who, implicitly or explicitly, gave pride of place to the revolutionary transformation of society. The Mensheviks thus sounded the traditional intelligentsia note of the priority of politics over economics, despite the fact that historically they had been more sympathetic to the workers' economic struggles than the Bolsheviks.

The cardinal assumptions of mainstream Menshevism were, first, the precarious nature of the revolution, even in its bourgeois dimensions. They feared the possibility that as in 1905, the bourgeoisie would desert the revolution and thus, in 1917, prepare the way for the restoration of a repressive state. They also wanted to maintain a broad alliance with such forces as the peasant movement, the zemtsvos, and the cooperatives. The difficulties of this orientation became excruciatingly clear during the late summer, particularly after the Kornilov fiasco, which many liberals had clearly supported. What sense did it make to continue the alliance with the bourgeoisie when it itself had deserted the "bourgeois revolution"? The answer of moderates like Tseretelli was none too convincing: "All the census elements that could help Kornilov to victory have realized that he can bring nothing but ruin."[25] This new awareness, he believed, would now make of the liberals responsible coalition partners, willing to follow the logic of the bourgeois revolution. Many other Mensheviks rejected this line of reasoning, however, declaring that the bourgeoisie had deserted the bourgeois revolution. Coalition with the liberals, they urged, was preventing reform and in fact promoting the popularity of the idea of proletarian dictatorship. As an alternative they advocated the formation of a socialist government to run the bourgeois revolution![26] This painfully twisted idea was the only solution for the dilemma that many Mensheviks had discerned: continuation of the proletarian revolution would isolate the workers and drown them in blood, yet the alliance with the liberals for a program of moderate reform had led to paralysis.

The second basic tenet of the Mensheviks in 1917 was the impossibility of an immediate transition to socialism. In numerous speeches key Menshevik leaders such as Tseretelli and Skobolev hammered on the same set of themes: industry was not yet sufficiently developed in Russia to provide the necessary material base for socialism; the war and the economic crisis made increased productivity and the reconstruction of industry top priorities; and the workers were not yet sufficiently united or organized to administer industry. For these reasons, too, the revolution had to remain bourgeois, although it could transcend the limitations of other bourgeois revolutions because of the relatively larger role of the proletariat in the Russian revolution. It is true that this crucial difference signified that the establishment of formal political freedoms was not enough, that they had to be accompanied by broad social reforms in accord with the workers' demands. For example, the all-Russian conference of Mensheviks, held in early May, supported many immediate demands in the struggle for the elimination of "hired slavery," including freedom of unions, the eight-hour day, changes in the role of factory inspectors, and the strengthening of worker organizations.[27] These measures hardly fitted the industrialists' conception of the bourgeois revolution, however, and, as with their political views, this strategy led the Mensheviks into irresolvable contradictions.

Despite these difficulties, many Mensheviks continued to believe that their views were rooted in the reality of the situation and that their Bolshevik opponents were a "sectarian circle of believers in miracles."[28] The masses who listened to the Bolsheviks' appeals, they said, were ignorant and dark, totally unaware that Russia did not have the necessary prerequisites either for a socialist revolution or even for worker control over production. They asserted that only a thin layer of the proletariat, the leading worker intelligentsia, could perceive the emptiness of the Bolsheviks' tantalizing appeals and relate to their "chatter" ironically. Unfortunately this flower of the proletariat was attacked as nothing more than elitist English trade unionists.[29] So once again party leaders could take solace in their special gnosis, regarding all deviation from their own perspective as rooted in ignorance or deceit. Given his superior knowledge, "the conscious worker, the socialist worker, must always try to lead the masses in the struggle for proletarian ideals, but never to adapt himself to the moods of the mass wherever these moods go."[30]

For mainstream Mensheviks an authentic socialist awareness among the masses could be implanted only through organization, which they saw as vital to their revolutionary strategy in 1917. Only organization could counteract the signs of anarchy in the worker masses and devitalize Lenin's irresponsible appeals, which brought discord into the labor movement and threatened it with schism. The Bolsheviks, those "dark personalities and groups,"[31] were thus objectively working for the counterrevolution through their policy of class isolation and their partisan appeals.[32]

In his memoirs left-wing Menshevik Ermanskii charged the Bolsheviks in 1917 with Don Quixotism, the Mensheviks with Hamletism.[33] But in many ways the Mensheviks' quest was far less tempered by reality than the Bolsheviks'. They demanded from workers nothing less than that they act in terms of the norms of a liberal bourgeois society that did not yet, and never was to, exist. In so doing the workers were temporarily to abandon the demands rooted in both their traditional assumptions and their modern socialist ideas as these had been legitimated by the revolution. Like Don Quixote, the Mensheviks entered the battle with old and worn-out weapons. Like him, too, they were soon to be identified as relics of an older time, whose ideas were either irrelevant or harmful in the present.

The Mensheviks' fundamental problem was that their image of the revolution was diametrically opposed to that of the workers, whose vision was not concentrated on the long term and who had no interest in becoming only full-fledged contenders in a liberal society. In this, of course, the Mensheviks shared the plight of the Provisional Government —for, as the Soviet's policy of conditional support for the government indicated, their parting of the ways was not to come until later. The

Mensheviks had the advantage that they were not branded as bourgeois from the beginning, but the dark side of this favorable circumstance was the tension between their final goals and their immediate strategy. At first this tension was not generally seen as a contradiction, but it nonetheless took its toll on worker support for the Mensheviks. As one Ministry of Trade and Industry report expressed it in late April, "the workers of these districts [Vasiliostrovskaia, Vyborg, and Petrograd], although as a whole belonging to the Menshevik tendency, are under the strong influence of the most active part of the Bolsheviks."[34] Later in the revolution the tension was increasingly resolved in favor of the Bolsheviks: the Mensheviks, many workers concluded, favored the rich and their government. Once again, political differences, this time among the socialists, became condensed into the idiom of class.

This substantive divergence between the workers and the Mensheviks was exacerbated by the latter's participation in the Provisional Government. On the local level the party's cooperation often took the form of attempts to mediate industrial conflicts, and, as with the government in general, their efforts frequently met with the hostility of both sides. There must have been many incidents like the one described by Grunt in the Moscow area, where a whole factory was converted to the Bolsheviks because of Menshevik efforts to resolve a labor dispute. In such cases workers came to share Grunt's conclusion that "the Mensheviks, on orders from above, noticeably defended the interests of the factory management to the detriment of the workers."[35]

In high politics, too, the Mensheviks often suffered for their inability to separate themselves from government policy. A notable example was the Menshevik duma fraction's refusal to vote on the question of reintroducing the death penalty, a measure violently opposed by the workers. According to a report at the Bolsheviks' Sixth Congress, this even evoked a protest from the small number of Menshevik workers.[36] The effect of the Skobolev circulars has been described in the previous chapter. Example after example could be adduced, all leading to the conclusion that the Mensheviks had abandoned the workers. As Bolshevik worker Naumov declared in a workshop on the eve of October, it was felt that

carried away by their fleeting successes, the Socialist Revolutionaries and Mensheviks turned away from those who took them to the summit of power: they forgot about the workers and peasants. . . . These gentlemen concentrated all their attentions on negotiations with the Kishkins and Buryshkins, with the Kornilovs and the Alekseevs. They had to, as they say, unite "all the live forces of the country," but in the strength of the workers, in the strength of the soldiers, these gentlemen never believed, nor do they believe in it now. So, we will show them where the real strength is.[37]

And in this Naumov was clearly right, for it was true, as the Mensheviks tirelessly repeated, that they did not believe in the isolated strength of the workers. Their own participation in the coalition government did not succeed in bridging the gap between the workers and privileged society, however, but only widened that between themselves and their mass base, an outcome already predicted by some Mensheviks before the party's entrance into the government.[38]

The participation of many Menshevik activists, both intelligentsia and workers, in governmental affairs also helped weaken the party in organizational terms, for it drew energies away from political work with the masses. And yet such political work was essential if the Mensheviks were to win the masses over to their viewpoint, which ran so counter to the workers' own assumptions. Even more than the Bolsheviks, the Mensheviks needed a strong party organization able to win and transform a mass base. According to the Menshevik leaders themselves, however, little was done in this regard. In a declaration to all members of the party, the Organizational Committee warned of the weakness of Petrograd's party organization, partly because of its members' work in nonparty bodies. If energetic measures were not taken to reverse this pattern, it warned, the masses would be lost to the Leninists, anarchists, the dark socialism of the Socialist Revolutionaries, and even to the Black Hundreds.[39] The same complaint was voiced a month later by Iamaiker, a member of the Narvskii district committee, who charged that virtually no attention had been given to the organization of the party, which appeared as some kind of "formless, indistinct mass." It was imperative to adapt to the conditions of life in a free country and create a true organization made up of interdependent bodies connected by formal rules and procedures. The alternative, he said, was continuation of the organizational disunity that threatened the complete destruction of the party.[40]

Iamaiker was surely right that lack of unity threatened the organizational effectiveness of the Menshevik party, but the sources of internal conflict went far deeper than the lack of established rules and procedures. The basic cause was growing dissatisfaction among the Mensheviks over their overall revolutionary strategy, particularly their participation in the Provisional Government. After the Kornilov putsch a new party majority against the policy of coalition with the Kadets emerged—despite which the new coalition government included Menshevik ministers. As before, the apologists for coalition, including Tseretelli, Dan, and Skobolev, pointed to the weakness of democracy and the isolation of the workers. Their arguments, however, could not be an effective counterweight to many Mensheviks' conviction of their own growing weakness because of their failure to adopt a class strategy. The conflict between the two sides was completely unresolvable and threatened to split the party, which for the previous six months, and even twenty years, had been preaching the importance of unity. If a split should occur, wrote P. Golikov, "the worker masses entering into our ranks will not understand us and will leave us."[41] Facing this prospect, the Mensheviks were hardly in a position to transform the workers' perspectives and counter the Bolsheviks' appeal.

In this general process of political decay, the Mensheviks also suffered from identification with the intelligentsia,[42] toward whom the workers had been highly ambivalent for decades. During 1917 much of this ambivalence seemed to disappear as workers, and the lower classes in general, increasingly associated the intelligentsia with the bourgeoisie: "intelligent and burzuj soon became almost indistinguishable synonyms."[43] The Mensheviks appeared to be the main target of their hostility among the socialists for a number of reasons. First, more obviously than the Bolsheviks, Menshevik intellectuals occupied public leadership roles, which made them highly visible and also exposed divergences between them and the workers. In addition, both their ideology and the tone of their discourse emphasized the gap between the conscious few and the spontaneous many, and so reinforced the traditional hostilities discussed earlier. *Rabochaia Gazeta* constantly lectured workers on their immaturity and unfitness for the immediate construction of socialism. Its issues were laden with didactic articles, often very abstract, by intelligentsia party leaders. Relatively few worker contributions appeared in its pages, in contrast to *Pravda*, which took pains to publish worker opinions and even belles-lettres.

Through all of this the Menshevik press and leaders communicated the time-honored assumption that knowledge was superior to class membership and experience. To workers who believed they had made the revolution, such a supposition was antiquated and offensive. They resented the charges that they understood nothing about the issues of workers' control or socialism, that their cultural level was too low, or that their immaturity derived from their rural backgrounds.[44] Even in the February days worker activists expressed contempt for the "chatterboxes" who talked while they fought in the streets. They also recalled that many intellectuals had abandoned the labor movement during the years of repression.[45] Later, with the glaring discrepancies in goals, workers could understandably draw conclusions such as the following: "The intelligentsia can in no way represent the interests of the workers, they will be able to twist us around their little finger and [then] surrender our interests."[46]

Apart from roles, ideas, and tone, it is probably true that workers comprised a lower proportion of the Mensheviks than of the Bolsheviks. No definite conclusions are possible, in part because of the survival of many local united Social Democratic organizations and in part because of insufficient data. There were, however, occasional references to the greater weight of the intelligentsia within the Mensheviks, a conclusion that makes sense given the party's program and, later in the year, its declining worker base.[47] Many workers continued to see the Mensheviks as a fraternal party, struggling, even if perversely, for their class goals, but it was less and less perceived as their own party, the reflection of their will and the product of their efforts.

In confronting the erosion of their mass base, Mensheviks responded in different ways. Some, as noted earlier, sought to change the party's line, abandoning the idea of coalition and advocating the creation of an all-socialist government. Others hoped that soon a new Menshevik alliance would emerge among the workers, a coalition between the conscious workers and the worker masses, sure to become disillusioned by the Bolsheviks' erroneous course. The former, they believed, had never been entranced by the Bolsheviks' empty promises and stood ready to assume leadership of the movement.[48] The worker masses, they hoped, would eventually come to consciousness through Bolshevik irresponsibility. Disappointment would lead at first to apathy and despair but then might be transformed into support for a more responsible socialist program.[49] In this respect the Mensheviks never lost faith in the force of their own ideas or the power of consciousness.

Which workers *did* continue to support the Mensheviks? The Mensheviks hoped to build their influence among the masses partly on the basis of a core of conscious workers who could perceive the workers' long-term interests and who understood the challenges of socialism. Such a stratum was to be both independent and influential—two traits difficult to bring together in any revolutionary situation, and particularly one with a paucity of established organizations. These conscious workers were also to provide the backbone for the network of new organizations that were to discipline and instruct the workers in the class struggle. Thus the traditional role of the conscious worker was to be combined with the less established role of the organizational leader in a broad labor movement. Unfortunately for the Mensheviks, this synthesis was difficult to realize: conscious workers who tried to remain independent in the Mensheviks' sense soon ceased to be leaders; and the leaders who came to represent the workers' aspirations did not embody the Mensheviks' model of consciousness.

There was, it is true, a stratum of workers who fit the Menshevik prescriptions to a certain extent. They agreed that the revolution was in its bourgeois-democratic stage, that the workers must not isolate themselves from the peasantry, and that the threat of counterrevolution from the right was menacing in the extreme. They feared the risks of precipitate action, for if the workers overstepped the proper limits, then "over our corpses the captains of industry will take control of the ship of state and will be at the helm of government."[50] They prided themselves on their higher cultural level, calling themselves the conscious minority, and cast aspersions on the masses' lack of understanding and realism, which led them to shift from one party to another on the basis of temporary moods and appealing slogans.[51] For all of these reasons, this category of workers was drawn to Menshevik ideas, which also emphasized the manifold weaknesses of the labor movement.

Along with their critique of the mass workers, this conscious stratum also sought to distinguish themselves from the intelligentsia, scoring the latter for the same vices they had exhibited for the past two decades.[52] Golikov, identified by *Rabochaia Gazeta* as a member of the workers' intelligentsia, attacked the intelligentsia both for their abandonment of the workers in the repressive years 1907–1912 and for their overbearing dominance of the labor movement after the outbreak of the revolution. As a consequence, he declared, the independent worker leaders who had begun to emerge between 1905 and 1917 were once again relegated to a secondary position, as Social Democracy was "taken into captivity by a new stream of radically minded intelligentsia." The intelligentsia reintroduced their customs, traditions, and psychology into party life, and the workers' intelligentsia, "this authentic and real framework of the workers' party," were pushed to the side. With pain in the heart, they watch how the "new masters lord over their domain [votchina], how they mercilessly and extravagantly deal with the accumulation of wealth." This exploitation, he claimed, could not continue, for the absurdity of their unrealistic dreams, based on imported ideas foreign to the masses, would become evident. Workers must replace ideology with an orientation toward concrete tasks and objective circumstances. Those workers who never broke their ties with the masses even during the period of reaction must take the initiative and create a united front that "will take the fate of their own party into their own hands."

This emphasis on the need for unity, an echo of the worker-intelligentsia conflicts at the turn of the century, was affirmed by an appeal from the newly formed group "Free Labor," which also blamed the intelligentsia for their squabbling and divisions. Each party leader, it charged, formed his own little party around him: "the Martovites, Leninists, Plekhanovites, Potresovites, Trotskyists, and so on and so forth."[53] The termination of such factional struggles was the goal of their new organization, which would represent the workers' own interests on the basis of a broad Social Democratic platform. Golikov, too, had proposed a break with the existing factions and announced the creation of a new journal, *Workers' Thought*, as the first step in the creation of an authentically workers' party.[54] Undoubtedly there were other similar proposals for new groups, organizations, or newspapers, but they had no more impact than either Free Labor or *Workers' Thought*, which have left hardly a trace and had no impact on the course of the revolution.[55]

Workers with these ideas were probably drawn more to the Mensheviks than to the Bolsheviks, for the Bolsheviks seemed to them to be more given to romantic dreams and prone to play upon the workers' irresponsibility.[56] They saw the Bolsheviks as anarchistic and charged them with spontaneity, warning that their actions served to strengthen the counterrevolution. Further, in the early months of the revolution the moderate socialist coalition seemed to represent the great majority of the Russian masses, and so support for the Bolsheviks could be seen as a source of disunity and enmity within the labor movement.[57] Ironically, then, the stigma of the intelligentsia seemed to lie most heavily upon the Bolsheviks in the eyes of conscious workers, while the mass workers increasingly identified the Mensheviks and the intelligentsia.

As the revolution developed, however, new circumstances emerged to weaken the alliance between the workers' intelligentsia and the Mensheviks. First, there was growing disillusionment with the model of the bourgeois revolution, as, for exactly the same reasons, there was disillusionment among Menshevik party leaders. The bourgeoisie were increasingly seen as incapable of performing their positive task of developing the country's industry and as committed to counterrevolutionary politics. Thus even skeptical conscious workers were led to favor proposals such as an all-socialist government and worker control over industry, positions that lessened the gap between them and the Bolsheviks.[58]

Second, it was more and more difficult for the Mensheviks to appear to be the party of proletarian unity as their support among workers rapidly dwindled and as internal factional struggle sharpened. The party's halfhearted policy of cooperation with repression of the Bolsheviks after the July days also did not help their image in this regard, as even Menshevik worker activists condemned the Provisional Government's policy of searches and arrests.[59] Consequently, many conscious workers must have accepted the logic of the Menshevik Internationalist Larin in his speech at the Bolsheviks' Sixth Congress: "The organization of the Bolsheviks represents the undoubted majority of the Russian proletariat, and its mistakes are the latter's mistakes. If this majority errs, then we must err together with it."[60]

Third, the very strength of the increasingly Bolshevik mass mood surely weakened the convictions of many conscious workers, creating in them the same fear of isolation that their counterparts had felt so strongly in the past. Was their higher level of consciousness an adequate justification for opposition to what they saw all about them? "Make things easier for us," wrote a provincial Menshevik organization, "give us permission to become less intelligent."[61] In any case, with the glaring impotence of the government, a socialist or Bolshevik government seemed indispensable for the protection of the workers from counterrevolution. Thus many conscious workers, who might have wished things otherwise, accepted the Bolshevik tide with great reservations: "The Bolsheviks acted and spilled blood, but, comrades, there was nothing else left for the Bolsheviks to do except to take power. Otherwise the Soviet would have been disbanded. I doubt that suitable people will be in power, but I think that we must create a government that will rest upon the popular masses."[62]

Not all conscious workers were so resigned. Various unions with Menshevik influence berated the Bolsheviks for their seizure of power and urged the formation of an all-socialist government and the convocation of a Constituent Assembly. Neither after October nor earlier in the revolution, however, could the Mensheviks' hopes in the leadership of this stratum materialize. It was precisely their separation from the mass of workers that had given them their previous identity, and joint action had been possible only when they abandoned their own ideas and put themselves at the head of mass militancy. Nor had they been able to establish independence from the party intelligentsia, except when repression made separation inevitable. In 1917 the situation was different only in that the chances for an independent role were even weaker. With elimination of the tsarist state, the mass movement and the political parties both acquired new opportunities for action. At first it seemed that conscious workers might have an independent niche as well in the network of organizations that they did so much to create. But, as described earlier, these organizations quickly came under the dual pressures of the mass mood and party politics, particularly as these were shaped by the intensifying class struggle. In these circumstances conscious workers standing for the traditional values of their stratum had to choose between surrender or isolation. A united workers' party tied to the workers' own interest and free of intelligentsia tutelage was simply not attainable.

The failure of the Mensheviks in 1917 cannot be ascribed to the universal impotence of moderates in revolutionary situations. The German experience after World War I shows both that moderates may prevail in a revolutionary situation and that labor movements themselves may be a crucial source of moderation. Rather, the Mensheviks' weakness stemmed from the basic traits of the labor movement as these had been shaped by the basic pattern of Russian industrialization. Nor should the Mensheviks be summarily criticized for their "mistakes," for these same mistakes were part of a profound insight into the long-term difficulties of the revolution in backward Russia. To have abandoned this insight would have been to betray their own interpretation of Marxism and their vision of socialism, and so to negate their own identity. These were the sources of the tragic dilemma facing the Menshevik party: to be impotent or to be right.

THE BOLSHEVIKS' REVOLUTIONARY CONSERVATISM

> But human thought is conservative, and the thought of revolutionists is at
> times especially so.
>
> —Trotsky[63]

The experiences of workers in the last decades of tsarist rule had given
rise to a political vision of class and a class vision of politics. The capitalists were the superfluous stepchild of the tsarist state, and the tsarist state
blatantly protected the privileges of the capitalists. The "worker collective" could easily do without either oppressor, and it had a moral right to
replace them with a government more responsive to its sufferings. Thus
implicitly or explicitly, workers came to apply a rigid class point of view
to social and political questions. As the implications of this view became
clearer during 1917, the great mass of workers came to embrace Bolshevism, by far the purest expression of a consistent class perspective. The
Bolshevik party had also made the cleanest break with liberal society
and, by extension, with the tsarist past. In the eyes of the workers they
came to represent the working class, the revolution, and the future. At
the same time, the Bolsheviks embodied the revolutionary past, with its
traditions of uncompromising militancy and emphasis on class division.
In this sense more conservative than the Mensheviks, who sought the
integration, and thus transformation, of the labor movement, the Bolsheviks both depended on and further exacerbated the cleavages inherited
from the past.

The consonance of views between class and party was thus much deeper than is usually recognized,[64] but at the same time this congruence of
perspectives was not accompanied by deep organizational and ideological interpenetration. The party had little capacity to resocialize the workers and shape their community according to its ideals; the workers were
unable to develop an independent vision and shape the party according
to their own goals. In this regard neither the classic Menshevik nor Bolshevik interpretations do justice to the complexity of the relationship.
For it is not enough to emphasize, as does the former, that the ties between the proletariat and the Bolshevik party were shallow, although this
is true. Nor can one stop at the assertion that the workers overwhelmingly came to accept the Bolshevik interpretation of the revolution. The old
regime had made possible a correspondence of assumptions and perspectives but not the emergence of an integrated movement based on
shared experience. The discrepancy between these two dimensions of
the worker-Bolshevik relationship gives a highly distinctive note to the
Russian revolution, distinguishing it from the Chinese and Vietnamese
pattern, where the party was able to create the mass movement, and also

from the European pattern, where labor movements had been able to reorient parties.

At the prodding of Lenin after his arrival in April, the Bolshevik party adopted a policy "distinguished by the fact that we demand, above all, a precise class characterization of events."[65] Class conflict, the party stressed, was the master key for the comprehension of social relations, politics, and even factional struggles among the socialist parties. For example, there were no national tasks to unite the capitalists and the workers, for the capitalists merely impeded the development of Russian industry and undermined Russian democracy with their counterrevolutionary aims and plots. For Lenin, the bourgeois revolution had ended almost as soon as it had begun, and the country was entering the first stage of the proletarian revolution. The capitalists no longer had any useful role to perform. Accordingly, Lenin declared, in remarks at the First Congress of Soviets that became famous, "fifty or a hundred of the biggest millionaires" might just as well be arrested as a means to combat anarchy and ruin.[66] It followed that the Bolsheviks solicited support only from the working class and its allies in the poorer strata of the population, making no efforts to widen their appeals to win a broader social base. "We call on you to vote for the party of the revolutionary proletariat, which defends the interests of the working class . . . the party which goes against the factory owner-lockoutters and their representatives. . . . Vote for the party of workers and the poorest peasants, for the Russian Revolutionary Social Democratic Workers' Party!"[67]

If there were no national tasks, there also could be no national government. Indeed, in general governments always represent classes, never the people as a whole.[68] The Provisional Government, like the tsarist state before it,[69] clearly defended the interests of the capitalists. Liberal democracy, like freedom of the press, was merely freedom for the rich to deceive the exploited masses.[70] Those who proclaimed the bourgeois-democratic character of the revolution had forgotten an elementary "truth of Marxism": "It is precisely within a 'democracy' that the gulf between the capitalists and the proletarians is widest."[71] The soviets, as a higher form of government, a class government representing the mass of the population, could not possibly coexist with an ordinary bourgeois government such as the Provisional Government. Because the two types of government were completely incompatible, soviet support for the Provisional Government was nonsensical. Lenin was the most vocal and consistent advocate of these views, but, as early issues of *Pravda* suggest and as the victory of Lenin's position in April proves,[72] they represented the most profound tendencies within the Bolshevik party as well.[73]

This same class analysis was also applied to the factional struggles within Russian socialism. The Mensheviks and Socialist Revolutionaries, despite their claims, were betrayers of the proletarian revolution and represented the petit bourgeoisie. Bolshevik activists in the trade union movement felt justified in demanding a partisan choice from the workers, for they identified the workers' class interests with the positions of the Bolshevik party.[74] For the same reason, a complete break within Social Democracy was inevitable, for the deepening of the revolution would sharpen class conflict within united Social Democratic organizations. In this respect the cooperation of Mensheviks and Bolsheviks in local party work only served to dampen class conflict and blur the correct view of the revolution as the first stage of a proletarian revolution.[75] By October many Bolsheviks had come to agree with Lenin that support for the Mensheviks was virtually criminal, for by their continued participation in the coalition government they had shown themselves to be the workers' class enemies.

Two separate sets of dichotomies thus came to coincide. The workers' experiences in Tsarist Russia had given them a strong sense of class polarization. For the workers, wrote Lenin approvingly, "the whole world is divided into two camps: 'us', the working people, and 'them', the exploiters."[76] Lenin's own political vision—and that, no doubt, of many other Bolsheviks—was also centered on a manichean partition between good and evil, truth and error, friend and enemy. During 1917 the Bolsheviks succeeded in persuading large numbers of workers that the two sets of opposition were the same, that the dichotomy between the workers and their enemies was the same as that between the Bolsheviks and their enemies. The party, they claimed (with considerable truth), was the only undeviating champion of the workers' class interest. The workers' dualistic vision became ideologically interpreted in terms of the party's dualistic vision, and, in mass meetings and demonstrations, party leaders and workers could share in the mood of millenarian expectation.[77]

The Mensheviks, we recall, had rejected a purely class interpretation of the revolution because they were convinced that the workers were too immature and isolated to create a socialist society whose prerequisites had not yet been created. The Bolsheviks, playing upon the long-term cleavages in Russian society, exulted in the workers' isolation and gambled their fate upon it. Opponents of the Bolsheviks tried to take comfort in the party's choice: "Soon they will stand outside the framework of Russian reality. . . . Look how with each day more allies leave them, how their tactical methods alienate those whom they considered their army. . . . Under such conditions the Bolshevik crisis can be resolved without a catastrophe—or with a catastrophe on the level of an average street scandal."[78] This article was published on 19 October, shortly before the Bolsheviks proved that isolation in polarized Russia had its own advantages. As Trotsky sarcastically remarked, "The misfortune of the proletariat and the garrison was that they were 'isolated' from those classes from whom they intended to take power!"[79]

Staking everything on the workers, the Bolshevik party opened itself to a flood of new proletarian members barely acquainted withe the rudiments of Marxist ideology.[80] As a result, even in the Petersburg Committee it was reported that there were very few intelligentsia activists and that workers themselves did all the organizational and a significant part of the agitational work.[81] The unprecedented increase in party membership completely outstripped the leaders' capacity for organizational control. "In the organization there are many insufficiencies," said Tomskii at the July conference, "in the underground we had a stronger organization."[82] Many provincial activists, not to speak of rank-and-file members, sorely lacked ideological sophistication. What they did know can be inferred from the following cases.

V. F. Babkin, a local party member from the village of Chernava, sent a plea to the party secretariat for help in deciphering the foreign words in the books he was trying to master, for otherwise he could not "understand the whole book correctly and also I cannot struggle against the bourgeoisie in the right way."[83] Similarly, Sapronov reports that many new party members, when queried about their knowledge of the program, simply answered, "Our program is struggle with the bourgeoisie."[84] In earlier years new recruits would have been taken under the wing of conscious workers or undergone preparation in study circles or routine party work. In the ferment of 1917 gradual apprenticeship was obviously precluded, and in this sense the importance of the party intelligentsia declined. Although this was not a major impediment to the party's revolutionary leadership in 1917, particularly because of the correspondence between the party's tactics and the workers' own convictions, it indicated a grave weakness in the party's ties to the masses.

As the party became overwhelmingly proletarian in composition, it did everything possible to identify itself as the sole representative of the working class. On the programmatic level it supported workers' control and a soviet government, and, because it did not emphasize the problematic relationship between short-term and long-term goals, its actions were in accord with the values it proclaimed. In addition, *Pravda* published a number of worker poems, as well as poems and songs from the revolutionary tradition. It gave prominence to the anniversaries of key events in the labor movement's past, including Bloody Sunday and the Lena massacre. Above all it refused to criticize worker spontaneity, the favorite *bête noire* of the Mensheviks. The usually cautious Zinoviev explained its rationale: Those who cry out against anarchy have a bureaucrat's view of the revolution as an orderly process of achieving political rights. The spontaneous acts of the workers, peasants, and urban poor, which are called anarchic, in fact serve to develop the revolution further. "Do you want to struggle against anarchy, gentlemen? Then don't hinder the workers, soldiers, and peasants, led and controlled by their soviets."[85] Similarly, what Lenin would later call (and had earlier called) anarchy he now greeted as revolutionary enthusiasm. He was delighted that the workers, soldiers, and peasants were "carried away by enthusiasm" and enjoined his Central Committee colleagues to "arouse their enthusiasm further."[86] "Revolutionary measures" against the capitalists were necessary to stir up this enthusiasm and embolden the workers further, and also to help prepare for socialism, which required the enthusiastic participation of the masses. "Failing this, your promised [workers'] control will remain a dead, capitalist, bureaucratic palliative."[87] This enthusiasm was not merely egoistic, declared Shliapnikov at the Democratic Conference. The working class was full of idealism, and it would show what it could give the world when a truly revolutionary government came to power.[88]

This praise of the workers went along with denigration not just of the bourgeoisie and the Provisional Government but also of the intelligentsia, whom the Bolsheviks sought to identify with the Mensheviks. The intelligentsia, the traditional repository of consciousness, was now seen as too doctrinaire and cautious, too cut off from the militant masses who had purer revolutionary instincts. It may seem odd to find such statements in the speeches of Lenin and in resolutions of the Bolshevik Central Committee, themselves thoroughly steeped in the traditions and culture of the intelligentsia. In an important sense, however, they were only following the traditional practice of assigning a moral, not sociological, meaning to the concept. And this particular meaning—the intelligentsia as impotent Hamlets unable to connect themselves to the masses—was also hallowed within the revolutionary movement. There was no innovation in Lenin's recipe to purify the party by purging it "of a dozen or so spineless intellectuals." By thus uniting the ranks of the revolutionaries, the party would be able to "go forward with the revolutionary workers."[89] Similarly, after the October revolution the Bolshevik Central Committee referred to its socialist opponents as "groups of intellectuals who are not backed by the masses."[90] It was these isolated groups, the Bolsheviks said, who were threatening the unity of the working class, which had overwhelmingly given its support to the Bolsheviks. They were also charged with keeping themselves aloof from the day-to-day struggle of the working class at the time of its greatest need.[91]

The Bolsheviks' appeals to the workers in 1917 were judged by their opponents at the time as the crassest opportunism, a view shared by numerous historians afterward. However, the party's stance in 1917 in fact followed from Lenin's theoretical analysis of the prospects for social-ism in the era of imperialism.[92] The capitalist system was now interna-tional, Lenin argued, and therefore Russia's relative backwardness de-clined in significance: socialism is "gazing at us from all the windows of modern capitalism."[93] The revolution would encompass all of Europe, and the more advanced countries would come to the aid of their poorer neighbors. In addition, capitalism and the bourgeoisie in the era of im-perialism were no longer progressive and were only capable of leading their peoples into unparalleled slaughter. It was pointless to expect an imperialist bourgeoisie to make a bourgeois revolution, and so the Men-sheviks' reliance on the old two-stage model was deemed misguided in the new era. To the objection that the workers' political and cultural levels were very low—a view Lenin shared[94]—Lenin answered that the experience of revolution and socialist practice would develop socialist consciousness. In any case, in the divided Russia of 1917, with its weak and ineffectual bourgeoisie, the workers had no realistic alternative to the seizure of power.[95] And once the workers controlled the government, why could not the prerequisites for socialism be created by the proletariat and socialism itself gradually be introduced?

In early fall, after the defeat of the Kornilov putsch and the avalanche of worker support for the Bolsheviks, Lenin became convinced that the times were auspicious for a seizure of power. The country's social, polit-ical, and economic conditions and the mood of the vast majority of the workers favored it, Lenin argued. Not all Bolshevik leaders agreed with the diagnosis, however, and some urged, as they had since the early weeks of the revolution, that the party and the workers were too isolated and weak to govern overwhelmingly petit bourgeois Russia. The appar-ent apathy of the masses, their low level of consciousness, and the weak-ness of the party organization also greatly troubled moderate Bolsheviks like Kamenev and Zinoviev even on the eve of the October revolution.[96] The party, activists often remarked, had enormous influence but little organization. To compound the problems, the "general staff" lacked dis-cipline almost as much as the rank and file; and even when, after bitter debates, the party's Central Committee did take a position, it was often disobeyed—if it was known at all—by lower-level party organizations.[97] Instances of indiscipline were not confined to petty details but also ex-tended to central political issues such as whether and how to act in the July demonstration or whether to take power in Petrograd in October. Service and Rabinowitch are probably right that local initiative brought many advantages to the party and was in tune with the spirit of the revolution, but it also generated much dismay among the party leaders.

The victory won by the party in October, after doubts and opposition within the party had been overcome, was not, it is clear, the product of a uniformly militant working class led by a disciplined party. The misgivings of the moderates about the workers and the party hit the mark, but they were politically secondary in October. The workers, if not a united proletarian army, were at least not divided; they were overwhelmingly sympathetic to the Bolsheviks' program, and there was truly a revolutionary core of worker activists. The party, despite its weaknesses and inability to reeducate the worker masses, certainly became, in Trotsky's words, a "quite adequate instrument of revolution"[98]; and, to its advantage, it faced a divided and decomposed opposition.

The opportunity could not be ignored. A political party "would have no right to exist...if it refused to take power when opportunity offers."[99] The impressive, if temporary, convergence of the Bolshevik party and the working class could by no means eliminate tensions inherent in their relationship, however. Party leaders still assumed that they had a historic mission that transcended the immediate goals of the workers. "One cannot be guided by the mood of the masses for it is changeable and not to be calculated," declared Lenin in mid-October.[100] Whatever these shifting winds, "we have the advantage of being a party which knows very well where it is going."[101] Other Bolsheviks also praised the party for the clarity and unity of its outlook,[102] and dissenters were in constant danger of being branded as heretics.[103] The strength of the norm (as opposed to the reality) of uniformity is evident from the numerous cases of proffered resignations by those who disagreed with party policy on critical issues.

In addition, Bolshevik leaders continued to display their traditional condescension for both the party rank and file and the worker masses, attitudes that, as had historically been the case, uneasily coexisted with romanticized views of their radicalism.[104] All of this indicates that the massive transformation of the party during 1917 did not entirely suit party leaders, who knew both that mass mobilization into the organization was essential to their cause and that it brought alarming dangers to the party's integrity. The gap between the reality and ideal of the party strengthened, rather than weakened, the ideal.

Under Nicholas II the precarious unity of the different parts of the labor movement had been based upon interdependence rooted in a high degree of differentiation of roles, this differentiation itself shaped by the severity of tsarist repression. The year 1917 witnessed the emergence of a new link between socialism, now most clearly represented by the Bolsheviks, and the workers, based now, more than ever before, on an explicit correspondence of viewpoints. The mass labor movement became more "conscious" as workers with implicitly radical assumptions, influenced by their politically more sophisticated fellow workers and stimulated by the intensity of class conflict, came to understand the implications of their historically shaped assumptions. At the same time, the Bolshevik party, partly by choice and partly through force of circumstance, shed much of its intelligentsia character and championed the aspirations of the workers more clearly than ever before. In this process of convergence, class and political perspectives from the past became the framework for interpreting contemporary events, much to the advantage of the Bolsheviks, who encouraged this identification, and to the detriment of the Mensheviks, who proclaimed that Russia was now in a new stage of development.

The Bolsheviks, then, in a sense peculiar to Russia were less ambitious than the Mensheviks, for they paid scant attention to the creation of close links between their social base and the party leadership, and they completely rejected the institutionalization of intraclass and intraparty pluralism. These challenges, in a deep sense revolutionary, were perhaps the most difficult of all, for as opposed to the development of a strategy based on class conflict, they required a renunciation of aspects of the past exactly when this appears most difficult—in a time of acute crisis. In the context of Russian history this most difficult of revolutionary feats was to lay down the initial bases of civil society. It is an irony of Russian Marxism, at least of its Bolshevik variant, that although it illuminated brightly the class conflict that eventually destroyed so many remnants of the old regime, it left its adherents completely unprepared for this greater task of political construction. In light of this unmet challenge it is understandable why the development of the state under communism often seems counterrevolutionary.

Conclusion

REVOLUTIONARY OUTCOMES

Fractured Solidarity

The revolutionary process in 1917 reinforced the unusual sense of class solidarity that had emerged from the isolation and exclusion of workers in prerevolutionary Russian society. Confronting their enemies, workers appealed to one another as members of a worker collective, a worker family, or a worker army. "Each of us felt himself to be not a 'free' atom, but only an electron," wrote Dune. "Workers jumping out from the overall orbit were rare phenomena. Each of us forfeited a certain portion of his freedom in favor of this collective."[1] Self-discipline within the worker collective was also demanded by the perceived need to struggle against the class enemy. As a result, discipline and self-sacrifice were frequently regarded as among the highest political virtues: "The recent events [the defense against Kornilov] and our relation to them speak in favor of our political maturity; they reveal our ability to submit ourselves to the interests of the general whole. Let it be so and not otherwise."[2] The logic of solidarity had the consequence of establishing the ideal of a general will capable of embodying the goals of all workers. This will of the proletariat was extended to mean the will of the people and the will of the revolution. It was unitary and so should command the loyalty of all workers. This logic was not exclusively Bolshevik; when they were in the majority, the Mensheviks also appealed for unity and discipline, to the submission of the minority to the majority. Those who disagreed were guilty before the revolution.[3]

Early in the revolution this general will was not identified with any particular party, and in fact it was poorly defined. Nevertheless the assumption was made that there should be a unitary worker interest deeper than partisan politics. In the course of 1917 this unitary interest came to be identified with the Bolshevik party, as worker support for the Mensheviks effectively vanished and the Socialist Revolutionaries proved unable to define and develop alternative worker loyalties. The decline of the Mensheviks also showed the weakness of firm institutional pluralism within the labor movement, a pluralism that, as in Germany, would have made the idea of a unitary will unrealistic. In Russia there was no set of established worker institutions arising out of social differentiation that could ensure internal pluralism (or, in the worst of cases, create the basis for civil war within the working class). The idea of solidarity did not have to confront the reality of diversity and so could support the appeal to unanimity. If such a unitary will was deemed to exist, it followed that politics within the working class was unnecessary, for divergent views were rooted in ignorance or bad faith, not in the nature of organized social life. Participation would remain, but participation in Lenin's sense: based not on politics but on administration.

The sentiment in favor of a unitary will was thus very strong, and it was to some degree realized in practice. Overwhelming worker support for the Bolshevik party and the impressive number of resolutions passed in worker meetings, including large assemblies, by huge majorities, even unanimously, provide telling evidence for this assertion. The very emphasis on mass participation, with its face-to-face interaction and the pressure of majorities upon minorities, facilitated this outcome, as did the accelerating tempo of class conflict. In this sense a shared workers' will developed as a synthesis between past experience and the turbulent events of 1917. Neither the past nor the present favored the emergence of an alternative vision based on the rootedness and legitimacy of diversity and participation based upon it.

The political process was thus deemed irrelevant, for if there was consensus among the workers, there was little need for debate and formal procedures to resolve conflicts. Further, this general will, to the extent that it existed, was not the outcome of a political process but preceded and transcended debate. It preceded politics in the sense that it was in part based upon pressing economic necessity, which accounts for the striking unanimity of demands after the February revolution. It transcended politics insofar as the general will was partly based upon ideological gnosis the source of which was the parties. In this regard, if shared goals are based upon a generally accepted claim to knowledge, there is no need for political pluralism or representation, for there can be no meaningful disagreement. Again, political pluralism depends upon the assumption that rival values and goals have a claim to a hearing. Need and knowledge as sources for action profoundly undercut this assumption, however. Consequently the political process did not impress itself as a means for ascertaining political values, for these had their sources in class conflict and party ideology.

Yet despite the strength of solidarity among Russian workers in 1917, the labor movement hardly constituted a revolutionary brotherhood of unity and community. On the most basic level workers were fragmented according to disparate class positions. Before the revolution their internal differentiation had relatively modest consequences, for the tsarist state prohibited its organizational expression. After February, however, workers could often achieve their goals through very localized action, and industrial protest no longer had such a strongly expansive tendency.[4] The plethora of newly formed local organizations reinforced this pattern of more sectional action. The organization of the labor movement appeared to be heading toward the atomization of trade union struggle typical of many European countries. Class organization appeared as if it might pose a threat to class solidarity. Such a tendency during the revolution has frequently been noted.[5] Soviets, factory committees, and trade unions were susceptible to fissure along regional or functional lines. The relative lack of a tradition of association, a result of the policies of the tsarist state, was another factor encouraging sectionalism. Thus both the old and new regimes made their contributions to atomization.

Many worker and intelligentsia leaders recognized the danger of sectionalism and took active steps to counteract it. The trade union press scolded workers for their craft egoism and urged the adoption of an egalitarian collective wage agreement. They fought organizational fission along what they regarded as narrow professional lines by struggling for industrial unions and centralization. They called for coordinated strategy during strikes and condemned the undisciplined action of separate workshops or factories seeking their own ends.[6] They appealed to the workers' sense of class consciousness, solidarity, and egalitarianism—and also to their own self-interest. For by standing together for egalitarian values and united organizations, "we eliminate friction and enmity among ourselves, the most dangerous instrument for our defeat and the most favorable for the entrepreneurs."[7]

Such appeals appear to have had a measure of success. Worker organizations formally adopted demands for a more egalitarian pay scale, with the greatest increases going to the least well paid. Even a general meeting of the relatively "aristocratic" Petrograd printers' union criticized comrades who refused to accept the egalitarian wage agreement. A leveling policy was necessary, the meeting resolved, because of the war and the economic crisis, which made the situation of the most poorly paid workers extremely precarious. They asserted that it was the strategy of the factory owners to increase the wages of skilled workers in order to reduce solidarity and demoralize the union. Further, criticism of the agreement would lower the strength and prestige of the union in the eyes of the enemy.[8] Even the *Trade Industrial Gazette* recognized that one of the main objectives of the wage struggles was the establishment of a higher minimum wage for the lowest-paid workers and a reduction of inequality among all workers.[9]

Such successes did not eliminate the egoism of sectional demands. Worker leaders often complained that the principle of solidarity built into their agreements encountered frequent opposition. With respect to collective contracts, workers criticized the rates determined for their own category and sought to change the standards of categorization. Solidarity was clearly strongest when workers were united against a common enemy, and it sometimes reached impressive dimensions. Nonetheless, internal class fragmentation was strong enough to arouse the suspicions of a great many worker and intelligentsia leaders.

We have also seen that the gaps between conscious workers and the masses, and between workers and the intelligentsia, by no means closed in 1917. Historic ambivalences reasserted themselves in the charged political atmosphere of the revolution. The revolutionary anger of the masses both exhilarated and dismayed the "conscious" elements of the revolution. The masses, in turn, both needed and resented guidance from worker and intelligentsia leaders. These intergroup tensions were rooted in a set of time-honored oppositions within the labor movement: party and class, consciousness and spontaneity, discipline and revolutionary enthusiasm, control from above and grass-roots democracy. These dichotomies did not vanish but were temporarily submerged in an ephemeral unity. Workers came to regard the Bolsheviks as their own party; many conscious workers minimized the reservations they may have had in the interests of proletarian solidarity; and the Bolsheviks, severing all ties with the other socialist parties, temporarily shed many of their historic intelligentsia traits. The worker army temporarily acclaimed its general staff without realizing that all officers seek discipline and control in the name of their own goals.

THE DUAL ROLE OF ORGANIZATION

Organization arises from, expresses, and pursues collective purposes, and so in any social movement the pattern of organization partly reflects the nature of social solidarity. The fractured solidarity of the Russian labor movement gave rise to two distinct and partly inconsistent dimensions of organization: organization as an expression of solidarity that already existed, and organization as an attempt to create a higher level of principled unity transcending internal fragmentation. The first was connected to egalitarian attempts at representation and participation in the general will and efforts to unite in order to overcome the external enemy. The second emerged as a reaction against cleavages within the labor movement and sought to soften or overcome them through education or control. Both favored centralization and bureaucratization, which was thus inherent in the labor movement itself and not simply imposed by political parties. In addition, the attempt to diminish fragmentation and so enforce solidarity justified leadership by a special elite.

Working-class solidarity in 1917 expressed itself in the formation of representative organizations meant to embody the will of the masses. Many scholars who have examined the soviets, factory committees, and trade unions have been impressed by their direct democracy and their responsiveness to the will of their members. According to Oskar Anweiler, author of a well-known study on the soviets, "self-government by elected factory committees and peasant cooperatives represented an economic democracy within a political framework of decentralized autonomous communes."[10] Hannah Arendt was inspired by Anweiler's interpretation to regard the soviets as a form of representative self-government inherently opposed to parties and ideologies.[11]

There was much in the practice of grass-roots organizations— especially factory committees and soviets—that was consistent with the commitment to class solidarity, internal democracy, and participation. All workers had the right to vote in factory committee elections, and the elected representatives could be recalled at any time by general meetings. Organizations were formally responsible to these general assemblies, and at least sometimes this responsibility was not a mere formality.[12] Before October reelections were held in many Petrograd factory committees, and in many more cases individual committee members were replaced. The proportion of workers taking part in elections is difficult to determine because of lack of data, but Smith suggests that in most Petrograd factories a majority of workers did vote.[13] The implications of these procedures can be deduced from Grinevich's complaint, cited earlier, that the worker leaders became engulfed by "spontaneity." Even Marc Ferro, skeptical of the representative nature of worker organizations, admits that new worker leaders had to be more radical than the mass base, for otherwise they would not be elected.[14] Grinevich's remarks suggest that whatever flaws in democratic procedure there might have been—and it should be remembered that many worker organizations also had commissions to check the validity of elections and the credentials of candidates—rank-and-file workers did have real choices.

In addition, in line with the general atmosphere of the revolution, there was the sense among many worker leaders that they had an obligation to express the will of the majority. Liubimov, upon being elected president of the executive committee at the Baltic plant in Petrograd, addressed these words to his colleagues:

> Comrades, I thank you for electing me as president of the committee, for the high honor you have given me. Having so trusted me, I ask you to remember that I am called upon to fulfill the will of the majority and, depending only on the majority, I will boldly carry out the great task you have placed upon me. But comrades, I give you notice that I will not stay at my post for a single moment as soon as a decline in trust becomes noticeable.[15]

Such sentiments led leaders to keep in touch with the moods of their constituents in order to be certain that they continued to enjoy their trust.[16] Worker leaders may not have perfectly represented the membership's views or have been absolutely accountable to them, but such a conception of democracy is largely utopian. More to the point, worker organizations do seem to have fulfilled Schumpeter's more limited conception of democracy as competition for leadership.

Clearly, however, organizations were not merely the expression of grass-roots solidarity or the result of mass democratic participation. Organization was also an instrument: first, to defeat the workers' enemies; and second, to realize the purposes of leaders claiming to represent the workers' authentic interests. It was thus partly a product of the historic cleavages of the labor movement. It followed that for instrumental reasons, centralization and bureaucratization developed in opposition to the more egalitarian and democratic dimension of organizations. Worker leaders were acutely aware of the limitations of purely local organizations for coordinating tactics on a broad scale. Thus the leaders who convened the First Petrograd Conference of Factory Committees on 30 May referred to the working class' great tasks in the revolution and asserted that

> working individually, without a general direction, not united, they [the factory committees] do not constitute a force capable of intervening in the economic life of revolutionary Russia and leading it from the morass into which Russia has fallen. The might and power of the organization of the workers themselves must be set to work.[17]

So even the leaders of factory committees, by nature those most localized of worker organizations, espoused greater centralization of action, and they quickly took steps toward what Ferro calls the "horizontal extension" of the factory committee movement.[18] First, there was the convocation of the citywide Petrograd Conference, which set up an embryonic national executive, the Central Committee of Factory Committees of Petrograd, which immediately sent instructors to other regions to help set up similar bodies elsewhere. Regional conferences were then held in major industrial centers such as Moscow and Kharkov. In mid-August a Petrograd factory committee conference elaborated plans for a more complex organizational structure for the CCFCP. Two more citywide conferences were held in Petrograd in September and October, and on 17 October the first All-Russian conference of factory committees was convened, the culmination of the efforts toward centralization of the previous months.

Centralization came even more naturally to the trade unions and the soviets. In fact, for both types of organization the formation of central bodies preceded the establishment of local organizations. In Moscow, for example, intelligentsia and party activists, primarily Bolsheviks, organized a Central Bureau of Trade Unions, which became an important center of working-class power before unions were well organized on the local level.[19] In the Urals, too, a regional council of trade unions was established without a base in strong local organizations.[20] The same phenomenon was characteristic of Petrograd, where the predominance of the intelligentsia in the central organizations, with their factional squabbles, was particularly notable.[21] As a result, by the time of the first general trade union conference after the revolution (in June) there were already said to be fifty-one central bureaus in existence.[22] A temporary All-Russian Central Council of Trade Unions, which then elected an executive committee, was also established at this conference.

Tendencies toward centralization were also easily observable in the soviets, and they have been abundantly documented in the literature.[23] Centralization took two primary forms. First, a network of central organizations, culminating in the All-Russian Central Executive Committee, gradually took shape. Second, within these organizations the executive committees and even bureaus of the executive committees came to dominate over the organizations as a whole. Thus there was a strong central hierarchy both among and within the soviets. In an important sense the soviets had, like the trade unions, been centralized from the beginning, for the Petrograd Soviet, controlled by the moderate socialist intelligentsia, exercised overwhelming authority from the moment of its foundation. The leadership of the All-Russian Central Executive Committee, for example, was largely drawn from the Petrograd Soviet. And as in the case of the trade unions, this early centralization was at the behest of the intelligentsia leaders, who were crucial in the foundation and organizational development of the soviets and always supported greater coordination and control.

With centralization inevitably came bureaucratization. There was a proliferation of offices within workers' organizations as their responsibilities expanded. Food supply, cultural-educational, credentials, and conflict commissions, to name only a few, all had their authorized representatives. Many of these offices were occupied by full-time paid officials, who, according to Ferro, quickly became a self-selecting and closed elite with a style of life different from their former comrades. This self-anointed new elite were known to refuse to hold new elections and make decisions without quorums,[24] clearly contradicting the egalitarian and participatory norms also rooted in the nature of the labor movement.

Thus the beginnings of oligarchy were clearly visible in 1917, but it would be too much to say, with Ferro, that oligarchy already triumphed. Rather, both radical democracy and elite domination were rooted in the prior history of the "combined" labor movement, which had always embraced contradictory elements. Weak institutionalization had implied that leadership would be poorly insulated from mass pressures, but the historical separation between mass workers, conscious workers, and intelligentsia activists ensured that leaders would seek to control their constituencies whenever possible. The historical vitality of localism had favored democracy, but the traditional disjunction between local and central organizations also created a commitment to centralization and control from above. The atmosphere of 1917 also reinforced both conflicting tendencies. There was a general commitment to democratization, one of the central promises of the revolution, which was accompanied by an explosion of participation; but the chaos of the revolutionary year also taught the need for strong central authority to regulate the economy and establish political harmony. During the revolution the two poles even nurtured each other, as ordinary workers resisted privilege and control from above and as worker and intelligentsia leaders struggled against spontaneity. The tension between the two polar dimensions of organization would not diminish until the consolidation of Bolshevik power resolved it in favor of an oligarchical model based on unambiguous principles.

THE BOLSHEVIKS AND THE DICHOTOMIES OF THE OLD REGIME

The Bolsheviks came to power on the basis of the workers' strong sense of solidarity and the radical class conceptions of politics connected with it. They did not as yet constitute a disciplined party or have at their disposal a powerful administrative apparatus. But, in the workers' own sense of isolation, class polarization, and moral righteousness, reinforced by the civil war, as well as in the traditions of the party and many soon to be absorbed remnants of the tsarist bureaucracy, the Bolsheviks had a formidable basis on which to construct a powerful new state.

Bolshevik policy in the early years of the regime was a product both of certain basic ideological goals (attacks on old and new elites, the nationalization of large industry, the curtailment of capitalism, and the like) and of the circumstances in which the Bolsheviks found themselves, particularly international isolation and civil war. Historical circumstances thus combined with Bolshevik assumptions to facilitate a certain set of responses to the dilemmas born of autocratic capitalism that had afflicted the old regime. First, the previously unresolvable contradiction between the logic of the state and the logic of capitalism was largely eliminated (to reappear, in a milder form, under the NEP) in favor of a consistent statist model of political and economic rule. The capitalists that remained were either servants or enemies of the state; no intermediate category of self-interest and private accumulation for its own sake remained, at least not officially. No longer would state policy be strongly conditioned by the interests of a capitalist class, thus undercutting the state's own premises. Nor would any liberal movement rooted in the claim to autonomy for social groups be able to help coalesce worker discontent against the state, as it did in 1905. With the attack on capitalist Russia the whole political configuration was altered, with corresponding effects on the nature of the labor movement.

A key dimension of the transformations in the labor movement and the potential for worker protest was the changed role of the intelligentsia. To simplify, but not distort, the intelligentsia either became absorbed into the state apparatus or lost their ties to the masses. The complex position they occupied in the last decades of Imperial Russia was no longer available to them; their relative immunity was removed; and the working class now had an entirely different relationship to the regime. Potential dissident intelligentsia were thus deprived of any conceivable mass base and the workers of any significant dissenting leaders or ideas. The fractured social structure of tsarist Russia had made possible a "thin line" of agreement between the workers and a revolutionary intelligentsia; under the new regime, with its greater consistency, no such potential existed.

Great changes were in store for the working class, too. Much of it disappeared in the ruralization, deindustrialization, and sheer slaughter of the Civil War period. Many of the most talented worker leaders became part of one of the many burgeoning bureaucratic machines, whether party, state, soviet, or trade union. That distinctive stratum of potential activists—the conscious workers—disappeared as a visible element in factory life, whether through absorption into state service, purges, or death. Nor was it possible for the regime to tolerate the passivity and lack of organizational ties that characterized the mass workers. They were called, if necessary by coercion, to aid in the construction of a new world; and to serve this end they came under the control of expanding bureaucracies. These changes did not eliminate discontent, but they did close off effective channels for its expression. The more consistently statist model of industrial organization was in some ways a throwback to old Russia, the Russia that antedated the emergence of a capitalist elite partly independent of the state. In its emphasis on resocialization and mobilization, however, it was indubitably novel.

In this process of violent conflict and change, which culminated in the Stalinist period, the Bolsheviks solved problems that the autocratic capitalist system proved unable to handle. They cut the Gordian knot, but at great cost: the near destruction of civil society. The contradiction between an emerging civil society and a traditional autocratic regime was resolved through the further incapacitation of civil society and the upgrading of the tools of state control. Ironically, many of the contradictions of the old regime facilitated these transformations, as the positive evaluation of "consciousness" and "organization" was held to entail centralization and state control against their deeply rooted opposing tendencies.

This response to the dilemmas of Russian development may have temporarily resolved one set of dichotomies, but it exacerbated another: the discrepancy between archaic and modern Russia. In Marxist theory the revolutionary movement was supposed to embody modernity; the capitalist class had already made its contributions to history and so was superfluous. In Russia, however, this was not the case. There was much in the revolutionary movement that was decidedly archaic—a necessary consequence of Russia's dualism. And the capitalist class, as well as its associated "bourgeois" specialists, far from being obsolete, had vital and extremely scarce skills to contribute to Russia's modernization. Consequently, the virtual elimination of civil society only shifted the terms of the dilemma, importing the debates into the party and widening the gap between the modernizing party and an even more backward Russia. Within the party there was a cleavage between those who wanted to make use of the potential contributions of the old capitalist Russia and those who advocated a deepening of the model of uncompromising state control. The contradictions of autocratic capitalism were therefore not so much resolved as displaced, and it was this brokenness, this duality, of the party itself that created part of the climate of the purges.

The Bolsheviks' solution to the dilemmas of autocratic capitalism prepared the way for further polarization and conflict in another way as well. By reducing the role of the capitalist class and the middle sectors, the party-state became the only force for Russia's modernization. Meanwhile, as Lewin has shown,[25] after the revolution the peasants withdrew more and more into their traditional world, reducing their ties with the cities and strengthening their communal traditions. The statist solution had thus spawned its opposite, and there was no mediation. In this sense, too, the Bolsheviks' rash solutions to the central issues of Russian development did not allow them to sidestep conflict. Under the tsarist regime conflict between old and new and between the state and capitalism had led to inconsistency, impotence, and the bankruptcy of the regime. In Soviet Russia it led to purges and bloodshed on a scale that the tsarist authorities could not even have begun to comprehend.

THE RUSSIAN REVOLUTION IN PERSPECTIVE

The solidarity that allowed the Bolsheviks to take power in October was the product of a dual society that had lost its coherence. The fragmentation within the labor movement and the cleavages between the workers and privileged society that provided the impetus for so much of Bolshevik policy—its emphasis on centralized control, on demarcating friends and enemies, on exclusion and purges—also had their sources in the failed attempt to combine autocracy and capitalist industrialization. Both the revolution and its outcome were the consequence of duality, brokenness, and contradiction. Under the old regime, contradictions had immobilized the government, sapped the unity and legitimacy of elites, and shaped the rise of a revolutionary movement that was also dual in nature.

If the contradiction between old and new was at the heart of the old regime's failure and also fashioned the perspectives and priorities of the new rulers, monocausal interpretations of Russia's crisis and its denouement are inadequate. For Richard Pipes, for example, modern Russian history is marked by an essentially unbroken patrimonialism that consolidated itself into a police state as early as the 1880s. Expansionist and totalitarian tendencies are built into the historical texture of Russian politics, and communism flowed naturally from tsarism. The processes at the center of the present account—the development of capitalism and the challenges of an emerging civil society, especially from the 1890s to the outbreak of World War I—hardly figure in Pipes's major work, *Russia under the Old Regime*.[26] Pipes treats Western influences such as private property as "loopholes" in the power of the police state, whereas in my view the beliefs, practices, and institutions of derivative capitalist modernization combined with the traditional political model to give rise to a new and insoluble set of social and political challenges. Similarly, although the Bolsheviks certainly made use of techniques and even personnel from the past, they defined the problems and solutions of Russian political life in an entirely new way. They "knew what they wanted and how to fight for their aims," boasted Trotsky,[27] and these aims were not simply the re-creation of a traditional police state but the construction of a new society cleansed of the impurities of the past. Just as there was an essential discontinuity introduced by the development of advanced capitalist industry, so the new regime created a further break with the past through the construction of a consistent statist model of modernization based on a rigid doctrine of harmony. Neither the statism nor the emphasis on artificial harmony can be understood apart from the tensions and conflicts to which they were both a reaction and a solution. The thesis of historical continuity, of an unbroken chain between Peter the Great and Stalin, underplays the impact of the distinctly modern crises underlying the effort to cauterize and then totally reconstruct a fragmented society.

An emphasis on the dualism of Russian development in the decades before the revolution has implications for the sociology of revolution as well as for the interpretation of Russian history. The idea of contradiction, in my view, ought to be restored to its pride of place in theories of revolution. If properly grasped for a given pattern of change, it delivers the key to understanding the crisis of the old regime and the nature of the opposition movements that emerge to contest it. The proper theoretical questions should not be of the order of states or social movements, elites or masses, economics or culture, internal versus external circumstances, chance versus inevitability. Rather they should be as follows: How can a theoretical analysis of basic social and political contradictions illuminate the relationships among the main actors? Within this structural context, how do the purposes and actions of elites and masses shape and constrain each other? How does the cultural definition of interest give rise to insoluble conflicts that culminate in revolutions? How do internal and external pressures cause and transform the central contradictions? And how do individual events reflect and modify long-term beliefs and institutions?

It may be objected that such a synthetic analysis cannot provide conceptual clarity; the complexity of reality is not sufficiently reduced by theoretical simplification. It is indeed true that theory necessitates simplification, but simplification does not dictate a one-sided choice of poorly defined alternatives. Rather, it should mean an explication of the essential through which a whole range of empirical phenomena become intelligible. This was the strategy of both Tocqueville and Marx, who used an analytic model of structural contradiction to classify and explain ephemeral historical events and processes.

The present model of autocratic capitalism has combined insights from Tocqueville on despotic states and Marxism, especially Trotsky's variant, in order to understand the dilemmas of late tsarist society and politics as expressed in government policy, the nature of worker organization, relations between the intelligentsia and the workers, intraclass differentiation, and a wide range of other issues. In so doing it has treated Russia as part of the general category of countries undergoing capitalist industrialization, but it has also insisted on the comparative uniqueness of the autocratic state's sponsorship of capitalism. Rapid capitalist industrialization has occurred in many backward countries, but only in Russia and, to a lesser degree, Iran, did a largely unreconstructed autocratic regime sponsor rapid industrialization based on private initiative. This was the contradiction that generated a revolutionary labor movement and so gave rise to the closest approximation in history to a proletarian revolution.

Notes

1. Introduction: The Proletarian Revolution in Russia

1. The temptation is particularly strong for Marxist historians but is not restricted to them. Thus for Gerschenkron, the 1917 revolution was a peasant, not socialist or bourgeois, revolution. See Alexander Gerschenkron, "Reflections on Economic Aspects of Revolutions," in *Internal War*, ed. Harry Eckstein (New York: Free Press, 1964), p. 200. Also see Bertram Wolfe, speaking of Lenin: "But the leading organizations of the proletariat, the powerful trade unions, would oppose his seizure of power, while the land-hungry peasants, above all the peasants-in-uniform, the peasants-under-arms, would assure victory to his side." *Three Who Made a Revolution* (New York: Delta Books, 1964), p. 116.

2. Leon Trotsky, *History of the Russian Revolution* (London: Sphere Books, 1967), 1: 144.

3. Alec Nove, *An Economic History of the U.S.S.R.* (Harmondsworth, England: Penguin, 1976), pp. 11–17.

4. Victoria Bonnell, *Roots of Rebellion* (Berkeley, Los Angeles, London: University of California Press, 1984), pp. 362–363.

5. Trotsky, *History*, 3: 270.

6. Steven Smith, *Red Petrograd* (Cambridge: Cambridge University Press, 1983), p. 259.

7. *The Bolsheviks and the October Revolution. Central Committee Minutes, August 1917—February 1918* (London: Pluto Press, 1974), pp. 58, 63.

8. Thus with respect to Russia, Tilly remarks that Russia is a "type case" of one of the two main paths to the "revolutionary outcome": "The absorption or weakening of a government's repressive capacity by war, coupled with a decline in the government's ability to meet its domestic commitments, encourage its enemies to rebel." Charles Tilly, "Reflections on the History of European State-making," in *The Formation of National States* in *Western Europe*, ed. Charles Tilly (Princeton: Princeton University Press, 1975), p. 74.

9. For Skocpol on urban workers, see "Explaining Revolutions: In Quest of a Social-Structural Approach," in *The Uses of Controversy in Sociology*, eds. Lewis Coser and Otto Larsen (New York: Free Press, 1976), p. 13.

10. See her comments in "Rentier State and Shi'a Islam in the Iranian Revolution," *Theory and Society* 11 (1982): 266.

11. Victoria Bonnell argues that trade union practices in 1906–1907 indicated a considerable potential for reformism, much as in other European countries. See *Roots of Rebellion*.

12. For these reasons I find Skocpol's dichotomies misleading. One can easily agree with her criticism of the naive view that social revolutions have been "caused" by revolutionary movements. That revolutionary movements have often been central to the crisis of the old regime and, in highly complex ways, to the formation of the new society, however, is undeniable and will be demonstrated for the Russian case throughout this book.

13. See, in particular, Robert Devlin, *Petrograd Workers and Workers' Factory Committees in 1917* (Ph.D. diss., Department of History, State University of New York at Binghamton, 1976); David Mandel, *The Petrograd Workers and the Fall of the Old Regime* (London: Macmillan, 1983); and idem, *The Petrograd Workers and the Soviet Seizure of Power* (London: Macmillan, 1984).

2. Autocratic Capitalism as a Model of Industrialization

1. Max Weber, *Istoricheskii Ocherk Osvoboditel'nogo Dvizheniia v Rossii i Polozhenie Burzhuaznoi Demokratii* (Kiev: Chokolov Press, 1906), p. 144.

2. In general the Iranian state relied much less on a national capitalist class than did the tsarist regime. The changed international context had much to do with this crucial difference. First, the shah had before him the experiences of many successful statist industrialization programs, whereas the tsarist state had none. In addition, the role of foreign capital was immeasurably greater in Iran. The shah's oil revenues gave him an independence from the indigenous capitalist class that Russian proponents of the "above-class" state would have envied. It was perhaps for these reasons that the Iranian state could go much further in its populist attacks against the industrial bourgeoisie than tsarist officials. For example, with the severe oil-induced inflation of 1976, the shah's government arrested a number of "industrial feudalists" and subsequently waged a campaign against small businessmen and traders. (For a brief description of these events, see Ervand Abrahamian, *Iran between Two Revolutions*, [Princeton: Princeton University Press, 1982], pp. 497–498.) In Russia, where the regime was wedded to the capitalist class, nothing on such a scale ever occurred.

3. Louis Dumont, *Homo Hierarchicus* (Chicago: University of Chicago Press, 1980), p. 3.

4. Quoted in Andrzej Walicki, *A History of Russian Thought from the Enlightenment to Marxism* (Stanford: Stanford University Press, 1979), p. 431.

5. Albert Hirschman, "Obstacles to Development: A Classification and a Quasi-Vanishing Act," in *A Bias for Hope* (New Haven, Conn.: Yale University Press, 1971), pp. 312–328; Alexander Gerschenkron, *Economic Backwardness in Historical Perspective* (Cambridge: Harvard University Press, 1962).

6. Talcott Parsons and Neil Smelser, *Economy and Society* (New York: Free Press, 1956), p. 82; see also, Dumont, *Homo Hierarchicus*.

7. However, according to Tocqueville, the French nobility's loss of its political functions was one of its main sources of weakness in prerevolutionary France. Many of Tocqueville's analyses in *The Old Regime and the French Revolution* apply *a fortiori* to Russia.

8. See Tibor Szamuely, *The Russian Tradition* (New York: McGraw-Hill, 1974), p. 114: "Once they had wriggled out of their obligations their property rights became illegal, and they themselves superfluous."

9. Quoted in Szamuely, *The Russian Tradition*, p. 131. Also see Marc Raeff, *Plans for Political Reform in Imperial Russia, 1730–1905* (Englewood Cliffs, N.J.: Prentice-Hall, 1966), pp. 18, 23–24.

10. In his famous book Tugan-Baranovsky rejects the notion that modern capitalism in Russia was artificial, arguing that the state had traditionally played a predominant role in Russian economic life. State-subsidized capitalism was thus fully consonant with the Russian past. M. I. Tugan-Baranovsky, *The Russian Factory in the Nineteenth Century* (Homewood, Ill.: The American Economic Association, 1970).

11. Nove, *An Economic History of the U.S.S.R.*, p. 18.

12. This was a basic theme of the Zubatov movement, to be analyzed in the next chapter.

13. According to Speransky's memorandum, "under autocratic rule there can be no Code of Laws, for where no rights exist there can be no constant balance between them. What these governments call codes and laws are nothing but the arbitrary decisions of the sovereign authority." Quoted in Szamuely, *The Russian Tradition*, p. 130. Also see Walicki, *History of Russian Thought*, pp. 26–34 and various selections in Raeff, *Plans for Political Reform in Imperial Russia*.

14. See Richard Wortman, *The Development of a Russian Legal Consciousness* (Chicago: University of Chicago, 1976), pp. 285–288.

15. Leon Trotsky, *1905* (New York: Random House, 1971), p. 350.

16. Wortman, *Development of a Russian Legal Consciousness*, p. 288.

17. For a discussion of contract in these terms, see Parsons and Smelser, *Economy and Society*, pp. 104–113.

18. See Niklas Luhmann, *Trust and Power* (Chichester, U. K.: John Wiley, 1979), pp. 18–22.

19. Michael Walzer, *The Revolution of the Saints* (New York: Atheneum, 1968), pp. 210–215.

20. Ibid., pp. 212–213.

21. Ibid., p. 210.

22. Reinhard Bendix, *Work and Authority in Industry* (Berkeley, Los Angeles, London: University of California Press, 1974), pp. 99–116.

23. Thus according to Moore, the greater traditionalism of the coal miners encouraged them to protest against factory rationalization, and the ironworkers' and steelworkers' lack of an implicit contract helps explain their greater passivity. See *Injustice: The Social Bases of Obedience and Revolt* (White Plains, N.Y.: M. E. Sharpe, 1978), pp. 233–274.

24. See Wildman's remarks on the peasantry: "The existing hierarchy of au-

thority and the social classes that shored it up were, in peasant eyes, fundamentally alien and illegitimate. The Tsar—Batiushka—was revered precisely because it was felt that he sanctioned the peasants' way of life." Allan Wildman, *The End of the Russian Imperial Army* (Princeton: Princeton University Press, 1980), p. 37.

25. Joseph Schumpeter, *Capitalism, Socialism, and Democracy*, 3d ed. (New York: Harper & Row, 1962), pp. 134–139.

26. See Roberta Manning, *The Crisis of the Old Order in Russia* (Princeton: Princeton University Press, 1982), p. 369. In the postrevolutionary regime, "the political role of all such 'bourgeois' elements remained strictly curtailed, however, because their inclusion would undermine the gentry's hegemony in local affairs and open up the possibility of competition for government funds that might restrict or even terminate the program of state subsidies to gentry agriculture upon which the provincial gentry had come to depend."

27. Max Weber, *Economy and Society*, eds. Guenther Roth and Claus Wittich (New York: Bedminster Press, 1968), 3: 1094.

28. Montesquieu, *The Spirit of Laws* (Berkeley, Los Angeles, London: University of California Press, 1977), p. 143.

29. Ibid., p. 154.

30. Ibid., p. 143.

31. Weber, *Economy and Society*, 3: 1106–1107.

32. Macpherson makes a similar argument about "possessive individualism" and the need for compensatory social control. See C. B. Macpherson, *The Political Theory of Possessive Individualism* (London: Oxford University Press, 1962).

33. Alexis de Tocqueville, *The Old Regime and the French Revolution* (Garden City, N.Y.: Doubleday/Anchor, 1955), p. 107.

34. See Iulii Martov's brilliant analysis in *Sovremennaia Rossiia* (Geneva: Tipografiia "Soiuza Russkikh Sotsial'demokratov," 1898), pp. 2–5.

35. N. M. Korkunov, *Russkoe Gosudarstvennoe Pravo* (St. Petersburg: M. M. Stasiulevich, 1899), 1: 209.

36. Martov, *Sovremennaia Rossiia*, p. 2.

37. Weber, *Economy and Society*, 3: 1106.

38. P. S. Squire, *The Third Department* (Cambridge: Cambridge University Press, 1968), p. 78.

39. Quoted in Andrzej Walicki, *The Controversy over Capitalism* (Oxford: Oxford University Press, 1969), p. 83.

40. The massacre of 9 January 1905 is traditionally regarded as the great event definitively destroying the myth of the tsar as the benevolent autocrat deceived by a treacherous elite. It is highly significant that a case of working-class rather than peasant mobilization provided the occasion for this great change in consciousness. For decades peasants had witnessed the government's unwillingness to grant them land and freedom, and yet to an unknown degree the mythic image of the tsar lived on. The peasants' relative isolation, lack of resources for struggle, and inability to generate another ideological model to give them hope for the future may be adduced as plausible reasons for the difference. For an illuminating study of peasant monarchism, see Daniel Field, *Rebels in the Name of the Tsar* (Boston: Houghton Mifflin, 1976).

41. For a vivid description see V. N. Kokovtsov, *Out of My Past*, ed. H. H.

Fisher (Stanford: Stanford University Press, 1935), pp. 32–33. (Kokovtsov will be discussed in later chapters in his capacity as Minister of Finance.)

42. TsGAOR, DPVI, 1902 g., d. 7a, l. 2.

43. Sipiagin's statement can be found in TsGAOR, DPVI, 1902 g., d. 7a, l. 19; the second is cited in Jeremiah Schneidermann, *Sergei Zubatov and Revolutionary Marxism* (Ithaca, N.Y.: Cornell University Press, 1976), p. 29.

44. See P. A. Zaionchkovskii, *Rossiiskoe Samoderzhavie v Kontse XIX Stoletiia* (Moscow: Mysl', 1970), pp. 197–204.

45. TsGIA, f. 1276, g. 1906, op. 2, d. 116, l. 27.

46. Theodore Von Laue, *Sergei Witte and the Industrialization of Russia* (New York: Atheneum, 1969), p. 217.

47. *Rabochee Dvizhenie v Rossii v XIX Veke*, vol. 4, p. 1 (1895–1897), ed. L. M. Ivanov (Moscow: Izdatel'stvo Sotsial'no-Ekonomicheskoi Literatury, 1961), p. 824. Hereafter referred to as *RD*.

48. Cited in A. F. Vovchik, *Politika Tsarizma po Rabochemu Voprosu v Predrevoliutsionnom Periode* (L'vov: Izdatel'stvo L'vovskogo Universiteta, 1964), p. 90.

49. See Geoffrey Hosking, *The Russian Constitutional Experiment* (Cambridge: Cambridge University Press, 1973), p. 7.

50. Weber, *Istoricheskii*, p. 149.

51. Thus even the liberal Moscow industrialists who, in 1905, had so sharply condemned the autocratic government were forced to turn to it in order to reestablish order in their factories and society as a whole. By 1907 little was left of the vaunted liberalism of the "young" Moscow industrialists.

52. V. Sharyi, "Pravo soiuzov," in *Narodnoe Khoziaistvo*, year six, book one (January–February 1905), pp. 84–100.

53. See Clark Kerr, John Dunlop, Frederick Harbison, and Charles Myers, *Industrialism and Industrial Man* (New York: Oxford University Press), 1960.

54. See Carlos Waisman, *Modernization and the Working Class* (Austin: University of Texas Press, 1982), pp. 15–16.

55. See Leonard Krieger, *The German Idea of Freedom* (Boston: Beacon, 1957), pp. 12–22.

56. See Geoffrey Barraclough, *The Origins of Modern Germany* (New York: Capricorn, 1963), p. 429; Alexander Gerschenkron, *Bread and Democracy in Germany* (New York: Fertig, 1966).

57. The report of an unidentified industrialist conference of early 1905 from the Soviet archives is instructive. The report casts an envious eye on the German government's acceptance of industrialists as a fundamental basis for German power and the unity of the German nation. TsGIA, f. 150, g. 1905, op. 1, d. 484, l. 107.

58. Barrington Moore, *Social Origins of Dictatorship and Democracy* (Boston: Beacon, 1966), p. 437.

59. Ibid., p. 229.

60. See William Lockwood, "Asian Triangle: China, India, Japan." *Foreign Affairs* 52, no. 4 (1974): 818–839; also see David Landes, "Japan and Europe: Contrasts in Industrialization," in *The State and Economic Enterprise in Japan*,

ed. William Lockwood (Princeton: Princeton University Press, 1965), pp. 113, 150.

61. Landes, "Japan and Europe," p. 153.

62. The contrast between industrializing Japan and colonial Vietnam parallels the distinction between Japan and Russia. In Vietnam the French state refused to permit the organization of workers and so there was an immense gap between employers and workers. French colonialism thus prohibited what might otherwise have developed into some form of Confucian paternalism. For interesting contrasts between Japan and Vietnam, see Alexander Woodside, *Community and Revolution in Vietnam* (Boston: Houghton Mifflin, 1976), pp. 207–209.

63. See Alain Touraine's suggestions in *Les Sociétés Dépendantes: Essais sur l'Amérique Latine* (Paris: Gembloux, 1976), pp. 14–15 and passim. Also see Francisco Weffort, "State and Mass in Brazil," in *Masses in Latin America*, ed. Irving L. Horowitz (New York: Oxford University Press, 1970) pp. 385–407; and Robert Adams, *The Second Sowing* (San Francisco: Chandler, 1967), pp. 116 ff.

64. Touraine, *Les Sociétés Dépendantes*, p. 15. Also see idem, *Vie et Mort du Chili Populaire* (Paris: Editions du Seuil, 1973), p. 75; and Tim McDaniel, "Class and Dependency in Latin America," *Berkeley Journal of Sociology* XXI (1976–1977): 51–88.

3. THEORETICAL PERSPECTIVES ON THE RUSSIAN LABOR MOVEMENT

1. Vernon Lidtke, *The Outlawed Party. Social Democracy in Germany, 1878–1890* (Princeton: Princeton University Press, 1966).

2. Samuel Huntington, *Political Order in Changing Societies* (New Haven, Conn.: Yale University Press, 1968), pp. 284–285.

3. Selig Perlman, *A Theory of the Labor Movement* (New York: Augustus Kelley, 1949), p. ix.

4. Martin Malia, *Alexander Herzen and the Birth of Russian Socialism* (Cambridge: Harvard University Press, 1961), p. 115.

5. Adam Ulam, *The Unfinished Revolution* (New York: Vintage, 1960), pp. 58–90.

6. Moore, *Injustice*, p. 351.

7. Rosa Luxemburg, "The Mass Strike," in *Rosa Luxemburg Speaks*, edited by Mary-Alice Waters (New York: Pathfinder Press, 1970).

8. See Edward Shorter and Charles Tilly, *Strikes in France* (Cambridge: Cambridge University Press, 1974), pp. 29–33; also see Michelle Perrot, *Les Ouvriers en Grève, France 1871–1890* (Paris: Mouton, 1974), 1: 180, 196.

9. V. E. Varzar, *Statisticheskiia Svedeniia o Stachkakh Rabochikh na Fabrikakh i Zavodakh za Desiatiletie 1895–1904 Goda* (St. Petersburg: Tipografiia V. Kirshbaum, 1905), pp. 41–42.

10. K. A. Pazhitnov, *Polozhenie Rabochego Klassa v Rossii* (Leningrad: Put' k Znaniiu, 1924), 3: 146.

11. Reginald Zelnik, "Essay Review: Russian Workers and the Revolutionary Movement," *Journal of Social History* 6, no. 2 (1972–1973): 214–237.

12. See Henry Landsberger and Timothy McDaniel, "Hypermobilization in Chile, 1970–1973," *World Politics* XXVIII (July 1976): 504–542.

13. Tocqueville, *Old Regime*, p. 137.

14. For example, see Leopold Haimson, "The Parties and the State: The Evolution of Political Attitudes," in *The Structure of Russian History*, Michael Cherniavsky (New York: Random House, 1970), pp. 309–341.

15. Alexis de Tocqueville, *The European Revolution* (Garden City, N.Y.: Doubleday/Anchor, 1959), pp. 44–45.

16. TsGIA, f. 1276, g. 1906, op. 2, d. 116, l. 27–28.

17. Two suggestive contrasts: in the leading capitalist countries class conflict did not so clearly lead into the struggle against the state; by contrast, in Iran the struggle against the shah's political regime was also directed against foreign-linked capitalism, but not so much against capitalism or capitalists as such—these, too, had often been the victims of the shah's arbitrary power. Again, what was crucial in Russia was the closer interdependence of autocracy and capitalism.

18. Moore, *Injustice*, pp. 227–275.

19. S. Gvozdev, *Zapiski Fabrichnogo Inspektora. Iz Nabliudenii i Praktiki v Period 1894–1908 gg*, 2d ed. (Moscow-Leningrad: Gosudarstvennoe Izdatel'-stvo, 1925), p. 189. See also the discussion of Zubatovism in the following chapter.

20. Vladimir Akimov-Makhnovets, "Pervoe Maia v Rossii," part 1. *Byloe*, no. 10 (October 1906): 185.

21. I use these terms roughly in the way that Herbert Fingarette reinterprets Freud: in the transition from unconscious to conscious ideas, "I do not discover unfelt feelings; I reinterpret the feelings I felt (and this may lead me to have new feelings and responses now)." Unconscious events are not secret but simply those whose meaning we could not fully see or interpret. See Herbert Fingarette, *The Self in Transformation* (New York: Harper & Row, 1965), p. 35.

22. Lidtke, *The Outlawed Party*, pp. 213–241.

23. Perrot, *Les Ouvriers en Grève*, 1: 199; 2: 607, 725–726.

24. For example, see William Kornhauser, *The Politics of Mass Society* (New York: Free Press, 1959), pp. 76–90.

25. Perlman, *Theory of the Labor Movement*, p. 49.

26. See, for example, Trotsky's *History*, 1: 432; 2: 252–254.

27. George Rudé, *The Crowd in History* (New York: John Wiley & Sons, 1964), p. 5.

II. AUTOCRATIC CAPITALISM AND TSARIST LABOR POLICY

1. This is the argument of Victoria Bonnell's *Roots of Rebellion*. The author shows that the beginnings of a reformist trade union movement clearly emerged in Russia in 1906–1907, but the government refused to allow it to develop. Clearly, then, the government did have options; it was not simply trapped within an inevitable cycle of repression and revolutionary threat.

4. GOVERNMENT LABOR POLICY BEFORE 1905

1. See Bendix, *Work and Authority*, p. 47.

2. See Reginald Zelnik, *Labor and Society in Tsarist Russia* (Stanford: Stanford University Press, 1971), pp. 119–159, 285–300.

3. I. Kh. Ozerov, *Politika po Rabochemu Voprosu v Rossii za Poslednie Gody* (Moscow: Izdatel'stvo Tovarishchestva I. D. Sytina 1906), p. 28: "In Petersburg they looked upon the factory as a highly dangerous place, subject to strict supervision. In ministerial circulars it was ordered to report by telegram to the Ministry of Finance about all instances of dissatisfaction in the factories, and then to make detailed reports; all these matters were considered completely secret; the telegrams which the local factory inspectorate and the Ministry of Finance exchanged were encoded."

4. TsGAOR, DPVI, g. 1902, d. 7a, l. 19.

5. Statement of Ministry of Internal Affairs representative Shcheglovitov in debates on the law regulating the workday. See *Kommissiia dlia Sostavleniia Proekta Zakona o Normirovanii Rabochego Vremeni v Fabrich-zavodskoi Promyshlennosti. Tainye Dokumenty Otnosiashchiesia k Zakonu 1-go Iiunia 1897 Goda* (Geneva, 1898), pp. 19–20.

6. For example, *RD*, vol. 3, pt. 2, pp. 614–617 (edited by A. M. Pankratova; Moscow: Gosudarstvennoe Izdatel'stvo, 1952): Report of Vladimir governor M. N. Terenin to the Ministry of Internal Affairs.

7. Sipiagin report (see note 4), l. 17.

8. TsGIA, f. 1282, op. 1, d. 696, ll. 3–4. For similar comments see the 30 September 1896 circular by St. Petersburg governor Kleigel's to various police authorities: TsGIA, f. 1282, god 1906, op. 1, d. 700, ll. 13–14.

9. This was one aspect of the Ministry of Finance's 23 June 1898 response to Panteleev's report. TsGAOR, f. 543, op. 1, d. 509, l. 24. Sometimes, however, Ministry of Finance officials recognized the justice of the allegations. For example, in his report to the tsar on the causes of the 1896 textile strikes, no less a figure than Witte pointed to the deplorable working conditions in the textile factories and the employers' infringements on workers' legal rights. For these reasons, he claimed, the workers had no real cause to value their jobs. TsGIA, f. 40, op. 1, d. 48, l. 113.

10. *Kommissia dlia . . .* , p. 13. For Sviatopolk-Mirskii (soon to be named minister of Internal Affairs) the most basic cause of worker unrest was the tireless labor of revolutionary elements who had formed a cadre of revolutionary workers, "far from cultured and extremely worthless in a mental sense." These revolutionary workers, in turn, operated on the mass of workers, who had no real understanding of the ideas they preached. TsGIA, f. 1282, op. 1, d. 699, l. 14 (June 1901). Such views were in complete harmony with the bureaucracy's traditional disdain for individual judgment, particularly in the case of the lower classes. Alexander III's government had a special department to censor theatrical works in popular theaters, for, "because of the level of their mental development, opinions, and ideas, simple people are often capable of completely misinterpreting things that present no temptations for educated people." Quoted in Zaionchkovskii, *Rossiiskoe Samoderzhavie*, p. 303.

11. TsGAOR, f. 543, op. 1, d. 509, ll. 26–30. Also see Witte: "The basic, main cause of the observed unrest among the workers is, in my opinion, outside propaganda," TsGAOR, DPVI, 1897, d. 43, l. 10.

12. For examples see RD, vol. 2, pt. 2, p. 635 edited by A. M. Pankratova, (Moscow: Gosudarstvennoe Izdatel'stvo) Politicheskoi Literatury, 1950); TsGIA, f. 150, op. 1., d. 646, ll. 44–45; TsGIA, f. 1284, god 1898, op. 223, d. 59, l. 4–5.

13. TsGAOR, f. 543, op. 1, d. 509, l. 30 (early 1897).

14. TsGIA, f. 23, No. 25, op. 30, god 1895–1897, l. 112. These sentiments also found expression in the Odessa Governor General Shuvalov's 1903 report, in which he repeated Benckendorff's promise that the "tranquillity and rights of citizens will not be violated by any private power and the illegal predominance of strong individuals" (TsGIA, f. 1,281, op. 1, d. 711, l. 3).

15. See Daniel Orlovsky, The Limits of Reform: The Ministry of Internal Affairs in Imperial Russia, 1802–1881 (Cambridge: Harvard University Press, 1981), pp. 10–11.

16. Shuvalov's report is a good example of this hostility toward organization. "The path of government intervention in the protection of labor must be recognized as more correct than the way of the organization of trade unions"—for proof one need only look at the sharpness of the labor question in Western Europe. Further, the English workers themselves had begun to recognize their inability to achieve their goals by their own efforts and had begun to turn to the government (Shuvalov report, l. 7). This hostility toward organization, here given a quasi-populist justification, was already enshrined in Russian law, which had various provisions against almost all forms of collective action, including even the collective presentation of petitions. A listing of these laws can be found in TsGAOR, DPVI, g. 1901, d. 56, l. 39.

17. Squire, The Third Department, p. 59. Also see Sidney Monas, The Third Section (Cambridge: Harvard University Press, 1961) p. 19.

18. See Perrot, Les Ouvriers en Grève, vol. 1, pp. 192–193.

19. Shuvalov report, l. 2.

20. TsGAOR, 1902 g. d. 7a, ll. 7–82. Proposals in the same spirit were already being made in the 1860s and 1870s. For examples, see Vovchik, Politika Tsarizma, pp. 108–109; Gaston Rimlinger, "Autocracy and the Factory Order in Early Russian Industrialization," Journal of Economic History 20 (1960): 76; and Zelnik, Labor and Society, pp. 374 ff.

21. TsGIA, f. 1282, op. 1, d. 696, l. 4.

22. TsGIA, f. 1282, god 1906, op. 1, d. 700, ll. 10–11.

23. For a good example see RD, vol. 4, pt. 2, pp. 110–111. In addition, TsGIA, f. 23, god 1902, op. 24, d. 1175 has numerous worker petitions to higher authorities for a redress of their grievances. It is also remarkable that these petitions sometimes reached important ministers, who sometimes acted upon them. For examples see the 4 March 1904 note from the minister of Internal Affairs to Kokovtsov enclosing a petition over a wage dispute, or the note from the same minister to Witte about a firing at the Putilov plant. (This delo has over 600 items, including hundreds of these petitions from the 1902–1909 period.)

24. See the Shuvalov report, l. 8–9 and Sviatopolk-Mirskii, l. 14–15.

25. There were isolated cases of successful conciliation chambers. See Pazhitnov, *Polozhenie Rabochego Klassa*, pp. 131–132.

26. This was part of the Ministry of Finance's response to Panteleev's report cited earlier. See especially ll. 30–33. Also see Witte's 15 April 1898 letter to Goremykin (TsGAOR, DPVI, 1897, d. 43, l. 10).

27. This was already an old dilemma in Russian industry. See Bendix, *Work and Authority*, p. 169.

28. See chapter 8 ("Conscious Workers").

29. The foregoing statement was made after the failure of the experiment but expresses well one of his main themes: the insufficiency of legal remedies. The quotation comes from A. P. Korelin, "Krakh ideologii 'politseiskogo sotsializma' v Tsarskoi Rossii," *Istoricheskie Zapiski* 92 (1973): 112–113.

30. Cited in Schneiderman, *Sergei Zubatov*, p. 116.

31. A. P. Korelin, "Russkii 'politseiskii sotsializm' (zubatovshchina)," *Voprosy Istorii* (October 1968): p. 50. In the beginning of 1902 there were almost 1,800 members in Moscow.

32. Bonnell, *Roots of Rebellion*, p. 83–84.

33. TsGAOR, f. 63, op. 1, d. 1090, god 1901, t. 1, l. 197.

34. Bonnell, *Roots of Rebellion*, p. 81.

35. Woodside, *Community and Revolution in Vietnam*, pp. 207–208.

36. Schneiderman, *Sergei Zubatov*, pp. 49–51, discusses all that is known of Zubatov's early life. Also see the recollections of M. R. Gots, "S. V. Zubatov," *Byloe* year 1, #9 (September 1906) 63–69, esp. p. 65.

37. From a speech made to factory owners on 26 July 1902. TsGIA, f. 150, op. 1, d. 481, l. 88.

38. Ibid., l. 88.

39. Ibid., l. 91.

40. Ibid., l. 88.

41. He was well-read in European social thought, with a particular enthusiasm for Eduard Bernstein. See Korelin, "Russkii 'politseiskii sotsializm'," p. 45.

42. TsGAOR, DP00, 1898, d. 2, ch. 1., l. v (2), str. 152–153. (21 August 1900 report).

43. P. A. Valuev, Minister of Internal Affairs under Alexander II and one of Russia's most important statesmen in the last half of the nineteenth century, had strikingly similar ideas, but his basically conservative policy ruled out their application. Like Zubatov, he was aware that Russian autocrats needed to allow new forms of participation in order to shore up their authority. He recognized the dangers inherent in the reform movement of the 1860s but believed that the government alone was incapable of combatting it: "There are times," he wrote, "when the suppression of ideas that are undermining social order cannot be accomplished by the use of government power alone precisely because of the limited number of unconditionally subordinate weapons at the government's disposal. What is needed is the cooperation of that part of society that is imbued with or may be imbued with opposing ideas. Pitting one side against the other, the government may rule over both and retain for itself appropriate space for its

own power." Quoted in Orlovsky, *The Limits of Reform*, p. 72.

44. Quoted from an article by Zubatov cited in Korelin, "Krakh ideologii," pp. 112–113.

45. Philippe Schmitter, "Still the Century of Corporatism?" In Frederick Pike and Thomas Stritch, eds., *The New Corporatism* (Notre Dame, London: University of Notre Dame Press), p. 103.

46. Lasalle's ideas have interesting parallels with those of Zubatov: both believed in a kind of cult of the state and distrusted bourgeois liberalism. Lasalle, however, advocated universal suffrage. See Lidtke, *The Outlawed Party*, pp. 18–25. There are also parallels with German theorists of state socialism, who rejected the democratization of the German Reich and wanted to solve the social question in purely economic terms. Ibid., pp. 62 ff and p. 156. See also Lidtke's discussion of Stoecker's Social Christians, pp. 161–163.

47. Korelin, "Russkii 'politseiskii sotsializm,'" p. 45.

48. Quoted in Schneiderman, *Sergei Zubatov*, p. 62. For more information on Trepov's background, see ibid., pp. 61–62.

49. TsGIA, f. 1282, god 1902, op. 3, d. 704, ll. 86, 88.

50. TsGAOR, f. 63, d. 1090, 1901, t. 2, ll. 152–155.

51. TsGIA, f. 1282, god 1902, op. 3, d. 704, l. 85.

52. TsGAOR, DPI, god 1898, d. 25, l. 40, l. 23. (Trepov's 8 April 1898 report to the Moscow governor general, based largely on Zubatov's ideas.)

53. These views were expressed in a report in early 1902. It can be found in TsGAOR, DPVI, 1902, d. 7b, ll. 76–94.

54. Ozerov, *Politika*, p. 228.

55. Ibid., p. 229.

56. Ibid., p. 217.

57. See Ozerov's report, cited in note 52.

58. This was not as strange a conversion as might appear. Many populists had believed that the autocracy could protect the lower orders against the oppression of elites. In addition, many had a nonpolitical conception of democracy, emphasizing the welfare of the people over formal institutions.

59. The most important document is "Zapiska o zadachakh russkikh rabochikh soiuzov i nachalakh ikh organizatsii" (TsGIA, f. 150, god 1901, op. 1, d. 678, ll. 1–9). Also see "Professional'naia organizatsiia rabochikh" (f. 150, g. 1901, op. 1, d. 678, ll. 10–25); and "Znachenie 19-go fevralia 1902 goda dlia Moskovskikh rabochikh" (TsGAOR, DP00, 1901, d. 801, l. 8–11). The following account is a synthesis of the views expressed in these sources.

60. "Zapiska. . . ," l. 3–4.

61. "Znachenie. . . ," l. 10.

62. Zubatov was much impressed with Tikhomirov's ideas. In the long statement of a "Group of Conscious Workers," attributed to Zubatov, the themes are very similar to those outlined earlier. TsGAOR, DP00, 1901, d. 801, l. 1–7.

63. Korelin, "Krakh ideologii," p. 116, for quotations from Zubatov.

64. TsGAOR, god 1901, d. 1090, l. 34.

65. These themes can be found in the "Letter of Sixty-five Workers to Afanas'ev, the First FOUNDER of the Society." TsGAOR, f. 63, op. 11, d. 1090, god 1901, t. 1, l. 66.

66. Ibid. l. 66.

67. TsGAOR, f. 63, d. 1090, 1901 g., t. 2, l. 228.

68. A leaflet of the Odessa Zubatovites has a particularly good discussion of the role that purely economic trade unions should play in the labor movement. They could satisfy various needs: economic interest, self-respect, the reinforcement of solidarity, independence. The example of our foreign "comrades" already proved all of this. For the leaflet, see N. A. Bukhbinder, "O zubatovshchine," *Krasnaia Letopis'* #4 (1922): 306–308.

69. "Letter of Sixty-five Workers," l. 66. One of the clearest examples of this hostility toward the intelligentsia, judging by the standards of the European trade union movement, comes from the Zubatov movement in Odessa. In a proclamation of 3 April attacking socialists, movement members declared that the workers' real need was for organization and made the following appeal: "Stop your outcry about the revolutionary struggle, allegedly necessary for freedom of economic struggle, abandon the terrible words concentration, expropriation, and proletarianization and look at life with your own eyes, not fearing to violate the preaching of Marx's gospel" (TsGAOR, f. 102, 00, god 1901, d. 801, ch. 4, l. 19). Also see Ainzaft, *Zubatovshchina i Gaponovshchina* (Moscow: VTsSPS, 1922), p. 28, for another example.

70. Schneiderman, *Sergei Zubatov*, p. 196.

71. TsGAOR, f. 63, op. 11, d. 1090, god 1901, t. 1., l. 383. The speech, dated 1 February 1902, can be found in ibid., l. 384–386.

72. "Letter of Sixty-five Workers," l. 66.

73. In his "Essay. . . ," l. 38.

74. Ibid., l. 384.

75. Later Slepov occasionally changed his tone. In a newspaper article located in the archives from 21 February 1903 he asserted that the time was close when the factory owners would unite with workers and fraternally work for the welfare of Russia (TsGIA, f. 150, op. 1, d. 644, l. 5). Three months later, however, he once again excoriated the capitalists for their merciless exploitation of the workers, claiming also that the factory owners and revolutionaries were equally opposed to worker organizations with purely economic goals (TsGAOR, f. 63, op. 11, d. 1090, t. 6, 1901, l. 188–193). It is not difficult to guess the nature of Slepov's real convictions.

76. TsGAOR, f. 63, op. 11, d. 1090, god 1901, t. 1, l. 384.

77. TsGAOR, f. 63, op. 11, d. 1090, god 1901, t. 1, l. 322. Also see Schneiderman, *Sergei Zubatov*, pp. 141–142.

78. Iu. Martov, *Razvitie Krupnoi Promyshlennosti i Rabochee Dvizhenie v Rossii* (Petrograd-Moscow: Kniga, 1923), pp. 213–216.

79. TsGAOR, f. 63, god 1901, d. 1090, l. 34.

80. Martov, *Razvitie*, p. 229; TsGAOR, f. 63, d. 1090, 1901, t. 2, l. 108–109 (27 March 1902 report of Moscow governor to Moscow governor general); TsGIA, f. 1282, god 1902, op. 3, d. 704, l. 62–63 (factory inspector report to the Department of Industry).

81. Bonnell, *Roots of Rebellion*, pp. 83–84.

82. V. V. Sher, *Istoriia Professional'nogo Dvizheniia Pechatnogo Dela v Moskve* (Moscow: Nauka, 1911), pp. 133–134.

83. These rumors were referred to, without specification of place or category of worker, in a report by Zubatov to L. A. Rataev on 3 April 1902 (TsGAOR, f. 63, d. 1090, 1901, t. 2, l. 136).

84. See Field, *Rebels in the Name of the Tsar*. P. A. Valuev wrote in 1897, in words equally applicable to the Zubatov experiment, that "the masses are easily reached by malign rumors or promises of a grant to them of some new favors or material benefits. Under the influence of these rumors and promises, they are capable of refusing to submit to the proximate governmental authorities, and they seek out enemies where these authorities do not perceive any." Quoted in Field, p. 22.

85. These rumors are described in TsGIA, f. 1282, god 1902, op. 3, d. 704, l. 53–54, l. 62–63 (factory inspector Astaf'ev's report).

86. Reference to the first can be found in Witte's report to the tsar on the strikes (TsGIA, f. 40, op. 1, d. 48, l. 113); the second report was delivered in a Ministry of Finance conference on 9 April 1901 (TsGAOR, DPVI, 1901, d. 56, l. 11). In the latter it was remarked that "it is difficult to say where this rumor [about a government-decreed minimum wage] comes from, but it is stubbornly adhered to."

87. The most extensive report was that of Astaf'ev. It can be found in TsGIA, f. 1282, god 1902, op. 3, d. 704, l. 26–64 (17 March 1902). The report included a brief history of the Zubatov societies and then proceeded to the subject of industrial unrest. Astaf'ev, pointing to the unusual number of strikes and disagreements, explicitly blamed the Zubatov Council. He also described a growing atmosphere of fear among the factory owners in the region.

88. Quoted in Schneiderman, *Sergei Zubatov*, p. 149. Schneiderman has an exhaustive account of the strike and its importance; see pp. 141–172.

89. Bonnell, *Roots of Rebellion*, p. 84.

90. Astaf'ev report, l. 54, 55.

91. Ibid., l. 53.

92. Ibid., l. 53.

93. TsGAOR, f. 1282, god 1902, op. 3, d. 704, l. 4.

94. V. V. Sviatlovskii, *Professional'noe Dvizhenie v Rossii* (St. Petersburg: Izdanie M. V. Pirozhkova, 1907), pp. 65–66.

95. TsGAOR, f. 63, op. 11, d. 1090, god 1901, t. 1, l. 370.

96. TsGAOR, f. 63, d. 1090, 1901, t. 2, l. 18.

97. TsGAOR, f. 63, op. 11, d. 1090, god 1901, t. 1., l. 288–296 (1 December 1901).

98. For a description of the celebration, which was proposed and organized by the workers themselves, see Schneiderman, *Sergei Zubatov*, pp. 128–135.

99. These events have been well covered in other works and need only be summarized here. In English see Schneiderman, *Sergei Zubatov*, chaps. 5 and 6.

100. Quoted in ibid., p. 153.

101. In fact, these conflicts between the Ministries of Finance and Internal Affairs dated from the prereform period, well before active government sponsorship of industrialization under the Ministry of Finance. See Tugan-Baranovsky, *The Russian Factory*, p. 129.

102. These reports can be found in TsGAOR, god 1898, d. 25, l. 1–14, 34–

38. Trepov's responses are on l. 15–28 and 44–47.

103. Reply to Panteleev's report (TsGAOR, f. 543, op. 1, d. 509, l. 14).

104. Witte briefly reviewed the history of the disputes until May 1900 in a report to Sipiagin located in TsGIA, f. 20, op. 13a, d. 56, l. 121–123.

105. The organization of the government into self-contained units made the conflicts even more intractable. According to Kokovtsov, "at that time [around 1904] there was no co-ordination among the ministers. Each ministry was a closed, self-contained entity, managing all by itself the business within its competence. . . . There was never any preliminary discussion except when friendly relations existed between separate ministries" (*Out of My Past*, p. 32).

106. Trepov's views can best be seen in two reports to the Moscow governor general from mid-April 1902: TsGIA, f. 1282, god 1902, op. 3, d. 704, l. 84–88 and l. 89–93. Zubatov's reactions are expressed in various documents, particularly two April 1902 reports to his superior Rataev and his address to a meeting of Moscow factory owners (TsGAOR, f. 63, d. 1090, 1901, t. 2, l. 112–7 and 136–138; TsGIA, f. 150, op. 1, d. 481, l. 88–91).

107. Just as the factory owners and Ministry of Finance claimed that police interference was inconsistent with the logic of capitalism.

108. TsGAOR, f. 63, d. 1090, 1901, t. 2, l. 136.

109. TsGAOR, DPVI, 1902 g., d. 7b, l. 119–120.

110. Schneiderman, *Sergei Zubatov*, p. 165.

111. Quoted in Korelin, "Russkii politseiskii," p. 57. Another indication is his evaluation of the reading program for the Zubatov societies sent to him in September 1902. He praised, in principle, instruction in the glorious history of the tsarist state and the "popular spirit" but believed it was dangerous. "It would be safer to define the goals of the readings more simply and modestly" (TsGAOR, DPVI, 1902 g., d. 7b, l. 160–161).

112. All of these changes are expertly discussed by Schneiderman, *Sergei Zubatov*, especially pp. 181–190.

113. Sviatlovskii, *Professional'noe Dvizhenie*, pp. 386–388.

114. TsGAOR, f. 63, op. 11, d. 1090, t. 6, 1901, l. 79–80.

115. Struve's preface to *Russkii Zakon i Rabochii. Materialy po Rabochemu Voprosu*, vol. 1 (Stuttgart, 1902), p. iv.

116. Quoted in Israel Getzler, *Martov: A Political Biography of a Russian Social Democrat* (Cambridge: Cambridge University Press, 1967), p. 35.

117. I disagree with Schneiderman's assessment that Zubatov's program was "well tailored to fit the needs of a Russian working class then in an early stage of development." Schneiderman misses the major conflict between Zubatov's own ideals and those of the workers who joined the societies (see pp. 365–366).

118. Cited in Getzler, *Martov*, p. 35.

119. Martov, *Razvitie*, p. 233.

120. Ozerov, *Politika*, p. 234.

121. TsGIA, f. 150, god 1905, op. 1, d. 484, l. 66–68. The document has no date on it, but it clearly comes from early 1905.

122. Bonnell, *Roots of Rebellion*, pp. 85–86. Also see Sher, *Istoriia*, p. 136; Martov, *Razvitie*, p. 233.

123. Quoted in Bonnell, *Roots of Rebellion*, p. 86.

124. Occasionally the need for worker representatives had been espoused by government officials or factory owners. Recall that the Shtakel'berg Commission advocated urban industrial courts with worker representatives and rudimentary workers' associations. Also see *RD*, vol. 4, pt. 1, pp. 138–42 for the letter of a Yaroslav textile factory director to the Ministry of Internal Affairs advocating the legalization of worker representatives and at the same time "the establishment of more real control over the workers," indicating his deeply conservative intentions. References to already existing elections of worker deputies can be found in the debates on the project; see, for example, TsGIA, f. 1153, g. 1903, op. 1, d. 153, l. 73–74 and f. 150, op. 1, d. 481, l. 17.

125. See Albert Hirschman, *The Strategy of Economic Development* (New Haven, Conn.: Yale University Press, 1961), passim.

126. A good source for these arguments is the project itself (or any of its preliminary versions). For example, TsGIA, f. 150, op. 1, d. 481, l. 21–43. They can also be found in virtually all discussions of the project.

127. TsGAOR, DPVI, 1901, d. 56, l. 27 (record of Ministry of Finance conference of 9 April 1901).

128. Thus the legal project explicitly refers to the Ministry of Internal Affairs' "undesirable" formation of trade union organizations in Moscow (TsGIA, f. 150, op. 1, d. 481, l. 29–30).

129. See Struve's introduction, note 115, p. iii. Struve dates the original project from about the time of the 1897 law. It is interesting that this early project included ideas that would later give rise to the starosta project. It referred to worker organization "which has the goal not of self-help, but assistance to the members of the factory inspectorate in the clarification of various kinds of disagreements between employers and workers." *Osvobozhdenie* #6 (2 September 1902); the project is reprinted in *Osvobozhdenie* #4–6. Witte himself argued that the law allowed for stopping work under some conditions and that the police should not be permitted to punish all workers who participated in strikes. The report with these views is in TsGIA, f. 1282, op. 1, d. 696, l. 28–35. No date is given, but from the context it is clearly sometime in 1898.

130. TsGAOR, f. 543, op. 1, d. 509, l. 9.

131. See the perceptive remarks by Martov on Witte, in *Razvitie*, pp. 165–166.

132. Trepov's defense of the Zubatov council has already been mentioned. Sviatopolk-Mirskii's advocacy of worker representatives can be found in his June 1901 report, TsGIA, f. 1282, op. 1, d. 699, l. 15.

133. TsGIA, f. 1153, g. 1903, op. 1, d. 153, l. 97–98 (Plehve's defense of the starosta project).

134. *Uchrezhdenie Starost v Promyshlennykh Zavedeniiakh* (St. Petersburg: "St. Petersburg Zeitung," 1903).

135. The journal of this conference can be found in TsGAOR, DPVI, 1901, d. 56, l. 26–30.

136. This first version of the starosta project can be found in TsGAOR, DPVI, 1901, d. 56, l. 2–3; also TsGIA, f. 1276, g. 1905, op. 1, d. 50, l. 77–78.

137. TsGIA, f. 1276, g. 1905, op. 1, d. 50, l. 70.

138. Industrialists participated in the following formal deliberations: a 28

April 1903 Ministry of Finance conference on the proposal (TsGIA, f. 150, op. 1, d. 481, l. 16–20); a 2 May meeting with N. M. Chikhachov, a member of the State Council (TsGIA, f. 1153, g. 1903, op. 1, d. 153, l. 63–86); and several sessions of the State Council (2, 7, and 9 May: TsGIA, f. 150, op. 1, d. 481, l. 44–87; TsGIA, f. 1153, g. 1903, op. 1, d. 153, l. 87–128). Glezmer's report can be found in the last source, l. 18–24. I am not certain whether factory owners who were not members of the State Council were invited to participate in these sessions.

139. Of course it is difficult to generalize from the industrialist leadership to the people they were supposed to represent, for the industrialists also did not have a well-organized and reliable system of representation. Thus one Moscow factory owner wrote to Witte denying that the majority of Moscow factory owners were in favor of the project. In fact, he and his colleagues had never heard of it before reading news reports of debates on it within the government. And, he continued, if the news reports were accurate, it would lead to no good, according to the Russian saying, "Laws are holy, but people are satanic" (TsGIA, f. 150, op. 1, d. 481, l. 98–99). Whatever the real sentiments of their constituencies, in the public debates the St. Petersburg industrialists generally opposed the project, whereas their Moscow colleagues tended to favor it.

140. Plehve made this latter suggestion: TsGIA, f. 1153, g. 1903, op. 1, d. 153, l. 100. It is also suggested by Alfred Rieber, *Merchants and Entrepreneurs in Imperial Russia* (Chapel Hill: University of North Carolina Press, 1982), p. 254.

141. See references in note 138.

142. TsGIA, f. 1153, g. 1903, op. 1, d. 153, l. 64.

143. Ibid., l. 70.

144. TsGIA, f. 150, op. 1, d. 481, l. 20. It may be true that they tended to come from the more independent and nationalistic group of Moscow entrepreneurs, as the cases of Morozov and Iakunchikov, the two main defenders of the project, suggest.

145. TsGIA, f. 1153, g. 1903, op. 1, d. 153, l. 97–98.

146. The major source for his views is the protocols of the 2 May 1903 meeting of industrialists with State Council members. Witte made a speech and participated in the debates. See TsGIA, f. 1153, g. 1903, op. 1, d. 153, l. 63–86.

147. TsGIA, f. 1153, g. 1903, op. 1, d. 153, l. 71. Iakunchikov expressed his confidence that the factory owner could influence the workers' choice of a representative.

148. This difference between Plehve and Witte was noted by Prince Viazemskii in the State Council debates. His own reaction was interesting: if labor protest is threatening, this project will not satisfy the workers; if it is not, the project will only stir the workers up. See ibid., l. 101.

149. Witte's speech in ibid., l. 79.

150. TsGIA, f. 150, op. 1, d. 481, l. 70–87.

151. See Struve introduction, p. ix.

152. Bonnell, *Roots of Rebellion*, p. 96.

153. Ibid., p. 96.

154. Ozerov, *Politika*, p. 281.

155. Bonnell, *Roots of Rebellion*, p. 96.

156. TsGIA, f. 150, god 1901, op. 1, d. 49, l. 41.

157. For example, Ogranovich rejected the need for mediation. Factory owners already knew the needs of the workers, and all rights and obligations, he said, were well known and defined by the law (TsGIA, f. 1153, g. 1903, op. 1, d. 153, l. 64). This, of course, is a version of the old model of conservative tutelage.

158. See Shorter and Tilly, *Strikes in France*, p. 34.

159. Perrot, *Les Ouvriers en Grève*, 1: 305.

160. See Ozerov, *Politika*, p. 241. In a similar way, Yaney argues that the state under Alexander III supported gentry privilege only because it believed that the gentry best served its own interests. George Yaney, *The Urge to Mobilize* (Urbana: University of Illinois Press, 1982), pp. 75–79. For both gentry and industrialists this support had to be substantial, for on their own they had little authority.

5. LABOR POLICY IN 1905–1907

1. TsGIA, op. 1, d. 36, l. 28.

2. Korkunov, *Russkoe Gosudarstvennoe Pravo*, 1: 204–214.

3. This distinction is made by Korkunov.

4. Witte expressed this view in an 1898 report criticizing police punishment of strikers under all conditions. TsGIA, f. 1282, op. 1, d. 696, l. 29. Also see the June 1898 Ministry of Finance report responding to Panteleev (TsGIA, f. 543, op. 1, d. 509, l. 16).

5. Ozerov, *Politika*, pp. 21–22.

6. TsGIA, f. 1153, g. 1903, op. 1, d. 153, l. 84.

7. TsGIA, f. 1282, god 1902, op. 3, d. 704, l. 7 (11 March petition to Kovalevskii).

8. Schneiderman, *Sergei Zubatov*, p. 166. This example also points up the great ambiguity of these liberal ideas—recall that Plehve's interpretation of the starosta law was far from liberal.

9. Gerald Surh, "Petersburg's First Mass Labor Organization: The Assembly of Russian Workers and Father Gapon, part two," *Russian Review* 40, no. 4 (October 1981): 435.

10. This document can be found in S. B. Okun et al., eds., *Putilovets v Trekh Revoliutsiiakh: Sbornik Materialov po Istorii Putilovskogo Zavoda* (Leningrad: Gosudarstvennoe Izdatel'stvo "Istoriia Zavodov," 1933), pp. 62–65.

11. The appeal can be found in TsGIA, f. 40, op. 1, d. 59, l. 106–108.

12. The 16 January report can be found in TsGIA, f. 40, op. 1, d. 59, l. 99–101 (which refers to the 14 January report); the major 19 January 1905 report can be found in TsGIA, f. 22, g. 1902, op. 2, d. 2218, l. 1–8.

13. Throughout these reports there is a striking mixture of paternalistic and liberal ideas. Kokovtsov never doubted that the state had the right to determine social relations, but he had become convinced that state interests dictated the granting of new rights, to be strictly defined by the state. A number of examples of this paternalistic perspective will appear in the following discussion.

14. TsGIA, f. 22, g. 1902, op. 2, d. 2218, l. 3.

15. See *Rabochii Vopros v Kommissii V. N. Kokovtsova v 1905 g.*, B. A.

Romanov, ed. (Moscow: Voprosy Truda, 1926), pp. 18–34, for the "special journal" of the Council of Ministers' meetings. (This collection is hereafter referred to as *KK*).

16. TsGIA, f. 1276, g. 1906, op. 2, d. 116, ll. 26–50. The commission is discussed in V. Ia. Laverychev, *Tsarizm i Rabochii Vopros v Rossii, 1861–1917* (Moscow: Mysl', 1972), pp. 201–206. This document is the only one I encountered in the archives and the only one cited by Laverychev.

17. *KK*, p. 200.

18. *KK*, p. 32.

19. TsGIA, f. 150, god 1905, op. 1, d. 492, l. 8.

20. Karl Mannheim, *Ideology and Utopia* (New York: Harvest Books, 1936), pp. 118–119.

21. TsGIA, f. 150, god 1905, op. 1, d. 492, l. 15.

22. Kokovtsov, *Out of My Past*, p. 45.

23. Stenographic report of December 1906 Ministry of Trade and Industry conference (TsGIA, f. 23, op. 27, god 1906, d. 321, l. 9). Litvinov-Falinskii, director of the Ministry's Department of Industry, elaborated the ministry's rationale further. The workers, he said, should exercise their influence through their organizations, the press, and the duma representatives. We in the government, he said, are a "neutral side, and we, the government, are obligated to stand for general state interests. We must protect the interests, not only of the workers and employees, but also of the population" (TsGIA, f. 150, g. 1905, op. 1, d. 492, l. 17). Why, then, invite the industrialists?

24. TsGIA, f. 150, op. 1, d. 496, god 1906, l. 142.

25. Romanov introduction to *KK*, pp. ix–x.

26. *KK*, p. 198. Also see Kokovtsov's interview with the newspaper *Novoe Vremia* (TsGIA, f. 150, god 1905, op. 1, d. 492, l. 15; 4 April 1905).

27. TsGIA, f. 150, god 1906, op. 1, d. 496, l. 132 (7 October 1906 speech).

28. *KK*, p. 111. For a similar argument, see the report of the Kostroma Committee of Commerce and Manufacturing in TsGIA, god 1905, op. 1, d. 484, l. 64–65 (8 April 1905). See also Laverychev, *Tsarizm*, pp. 194–196.

29. TsGIA, f. 150, god 1905, op. 1, d. 488, l. 79–90 (8 April 1905).

30. *KK*, pp. 235–237. Kokovtsov's response and the factory owners' reactions to it can be found on pp. 238–244.

31. TsGIA, f. 150, op. 1, d. 496, god 1906, l. 115 (14 December speech).

32. The council was the executive body of the newly formed (in 1906) Association of the Representatives of Trade and Industry, which claimed to represent industrialists throughout the empire but the leadership of which was opposed by various other entrepreneurial groups, including the recently renamed St. Petersburg Society. Despite its tenuous overall authority, it played a key role in the Filosofov Commission, attempting to develop a unified industrialist perspective and preparing reports and recommendations. As noted in the text, it was less hostile toward the legislation than the St. Petersburg Society and attempted to support the ministry's efforts.

33. TsGIA, f. 150, op. 1, d. 496, god 1906, l. 137.

34. TsGIA, f. 150, op. 1, d. 496, god 1906, l. 138.

35. See, for example, the comments of Von Ditmar, TsGIA, f. 23, op. 27, god

1906, d. 321, l. 13 and A. A. Vezhbitskii, ibid., l. 153.

36. TsGIA, f. 150, op. 1, d. 496, god 1906, l. 139.

37. TsGIA, f. 150, g. 1905, op. 1, d. 483, l. 26–49 (24 March 1905).

38. *KK*, pp. 257–267 (21 June).

39. TsGIA, f. 23, op. 17, d. 648, l. 1–5.

40. The decree permitting strikes was published on 2 December 1905. Criminal punishment was retained for incitement to strike, intentional damage to property, compelling other workers to stop work, and participation in societies that seek to organize strikes in vital enterprises or those that might damage society (TsGIA, f. 23, op. 17, d. 648, l. 21).

41. The text can be found in *KK*, pp. 133–140. An excellent analysis of the law and its modification is in Sviatlovskii, *Professional'noe Dvizhenie*, pp. 345–361. The relevant archival materials will be cited later.

42. Sviatlovskii is wrong in assigning the responsibility to the State Council in its later deliberations.

43. TsGIA, f. 1405, d. 543, op. 913, l. 286. The Ministry of Justice project was on societies and unions in general; the Ministry of Finance project was on professional societies and unions. The distinction was artificial and led to the strange division of the temporary rules into two overlapping parts.

44. The State Council debates are in TsGIA, f. 1405, d. 543, op. 913, l. 334–366. They are summarized in Sviatlovskii, *Professional'noe Dvizhenie*.

45. TsGIA, f. 1405, d. 543, op. 913, l. 362–366.

46. TsGIA, f. 23, god 1906–1907, op. 17, d. 650, l. 18.

47. Ibid., l. 18.

48. Von Ditmar included an astute criticism of the December 1906 rules in his report. The goals envisioned for the organizations were too narrow, he said, and there was no justification for the prohibition of their transformation into trade unions. He was particularly wary of the vagueness of the causes for closing societies, fearing that this could lead to administrative arbitrariness. Finally, he objected to the proliferation of regulations, arguing that the law should regulate only the most essential matters (TsGIA, f. 150, op. 1, d. 494, l. 324–326).

49. TsGIA, f. 1282, op. 1, d. 717, l. 70–79.

50. TsGIA, f. 1276, god 1906, op. 2, d. 131, l. 5.

51. Sviatlovskii, *Professional'noe Dvizhenie*, pp. 364–365.

52. See Bonnell, *Roots of Rebellion*, pp. 278–279.

53. Sviatlovskii, *Professional'noe Dvizhenie*, p. 333–334; Bonnell, *Roots of Rebellion*, pp. 280–281.

54. Bonnell, *Roots of Rebellion*, p. 201.

55. Ibid., p. 205. The following information also comes from this definitive study of prerevolutionary trade unionism.

56. Ibid., chap. 6.

57. Ibid., p. 237.

58. Ibid., p. 256.

59. It is noteworthy that the desirability of boards of conciliation was less controversial in Russia than in Germany and France, where it was sometimes held that they undermined the class struggle. See ibid., p. 291 (quotation from Grinevich).

60. Quoted in ibid., p. 303.

61. Paraphrased from TsGIA, f. 150, g. 1907, op. 1, d. 495, l. 453.

62. These generalizations are based on the works of Rieber, *Merchants and Entrepreneurs*, and Thomas Owen, *Capitalism and Politics in Russia* (Cambridge: Cambridge University Press, 1981).

63. Rieber, *Merchants and Entrepreneurs*, p. 233.

64. Ibid., p. 255.

65. Owen, *Capitalism and Politics*, p. 173.

66. The Moscow industrialists' view was also unmistakably in their own self-interest, and this obvious connection led government officials to see their position as a means of delaying economic concessions. Thus in its 1905 survey the Ministry of Trade and Industry claimed that the argument that overall political change must precede economic improvements was only an attempt to win time (TsGIA, f. 23, god 1905, op. 16, d. 3, l. 55).

67. This account, including the quotations, comes from Owen, *Capitalism and Politics*, pp. 175–177. The memorandum dates from 27 January.

68. TsGIA, f. 150, god 1905, op. 1, d. 484, l. 9–12.

69. The sources for these views are a 30 January report by Tripolitov and a 31 January report of St. Petersburg factory owners to the Ministry of Finance (TsGIA, f. 150, op. 1, d. 646, l. 76–78; f. 150, op. 1, d. 646, l. 84–86). Also see Rieber, *Merchants and Entrepreneurs*, pp. 345–346.

70. TsGIA, f. 48, op. 1, d. 233, l. 8–20 (February report to Ministry of Internal Affairs).

71. TsGIA, f. 150, god 1905, op. 1, d. 484, l. 69–80 (9 March 1905). Another interesting report, which made many of the same points, was prepared by I. I. Iasiukovich (TsGIA, f. 150, op. 1, d. 652, l. 28–34; 12 April 1905).

72. The bitterness of the disputes can be judged from the following incident. In early July the Moscow Stock Exchange Committee sponsored a nationwide meeting of industrialist representatives to create a clear economic and political program. After the radicals raised the question of a legislative duma, Naidenov, the conservative head of the committee, reported on their action to the police and demanded that the police close the meeting. See Owen, *Capitalism and Politics*, p. 185.

73. A summary of its activities can be found in TsGIA, f. 150, op. 1, d. 646, l. 158–60.

74. TsGIA, f. 150, g. 1905, op. 1, d. 487, passim, esp. l. 119, 123, 176.

75. TsGIA, f. 65, op. 1, d. 156, l. 286–288 (3 November 1905, meeting of St. Petersburg Society).

76. TsGIA, f. 150, god 1905–1906, op. 1, d. 653, l. 158.

77. TsGIA, f. 150, god 1905–1906, op. 1, d. 653, l. 156.

78. In midsummer Guchkov was an important member of the liberal minority.

79. Quoted in Owen, *Capitalism and Politics*, p. 202.

80. TsGIA, f. 150, op. 1, d. 654, passim.

81. Owen, *Capitalism and Politics*, p. 199.

82. TsGIA, f. 65, op. 1, d. 156, l. 115 (pamphlet from late 1905).

83. TsGIA, f. 150, god 1905, op. 1, d. 484, l. 105.

84. Rieber, *Merchants and Entrepreneurs*, pp. 354–358.

85. TsGIA, f. 150, op. 1, d. 646, l. 118–119 (11 February memorandum of Glezmer).

86. TsGIA, f. 32, op. 2, d. 72, l. 50–51; ibid., l. 53–55.

87. The following comes from Von Ditmar's lengthy report on the labor question delivered to the 31st Congress of Mine-Industrialists of the south of Russia (TsGIA, f. 150, op. 1, d. 494, l. 290–386).

88. Examples can be found in TsGIA: f. 150, g. 1906, op. 1, d. 424, l. 562; f. 65, op. 1, d. 156, l. 10; f. 150, op. 1, d. 495, g. 1907, l. 452; f. 150, op. 1, d. 494, god 1906, l. 276; f. 48, op. 1, d. 233, l. 30.

89. TsGIA, f. 150, op. 2, d. 69, l. 7.

6. LABOR POLICY AT A DEAD END

1. At this time Stolypin dissolved the Second Duma and announced a new electoral law ensuring the dominance of the provincial gentry in future elections.

2. See Gladstone's speech in Thomas Barnes and Gerald Feldman, eds., *Nationalism, Industrialization, and Democracy, 1815–1914* (Boston: Little, Brown & Co., 1972), p. 207.

3. TsGIA, f. 1282, god 1908, op. 1, d. 722, l. 1–29. This report is also discussed in Bonnell, *Roots of Rebellion*, pp. 276–278.

4. Needless to say, this is a bizarre picture of the 1905 revolution, in which the popular masses were deeply involved, to the point of putting considerable pressure on the Socialist party leadership. See chapter 12.

5. TsGIA, f. 1282, god 1908, op. 1, d. 722, l. 6.

6. For this information see Bonnell, *Roots of Rebellion*, p. 319–320.

7. Ibid., p. 323.

8. The insurance laws were finally passed in June 1912. The proposals had been discussed in the 1907–1908 Ostrogradskii Conference, and the Ministry of Trade and Industry passed them over to the duma committee on labor legislation in June 1908. They were not debated in the duma as a whole until April 1911. As finally enacted, they were limited in their coverage to heavy factory and mining industry and large railway and water transport in European Russia and the Caucasus regions, thus touching only a minority of the empire's workers. Tailored to meet the objections of some groups of factory owners, expressed through duma representatives, they represented a marked retreat from the government projects of 1905–1907.

9. Elise Kimerling, "The Disintegration of the Tsarist Order: The Worker Question, 1905–1912" (unpublished honors thesis, Brandeis University, 1977), pp. 91–95.

10. Paul Miliukov, *Political Memoirs 1905–1917*, ed. Arthur Mendel (Ann Arbor: University of Michigan Press, 1967), p. 215.

11. The political impasse of the 3 June system is well described in Hosking, *Russian Constitutional Experiment* and Manning, *Crisis of the Old Order*.

12. Kimerling, "Disintegration of the Tsarist Order," pp. 54–59.

13. TsGIA, f. 23, g. 1907, op. 27, d. 381.

14. TsGIA, f. 150, op. 1, d. 495, god 1907, l. 459–461.

15. TsGIA, f. 32, god 1909, op. 1, d. 1863, l. 4–47. For the fragmentary minutes of another conference to work out a law on societies and unions see TsGIA, f. 23, op. 14, d. 446, l. 1–2 (11, 18, and 22 May 1910).

16. TsGIA, f. 32, god 1908–1917, op. 1, d. 1905, l. 3 (29 April 1908 session of Ostrogradskii Commission).

17. Laverychev, *Tsarizm*, pp. 256–269, has much material on this theme. I have also examined various documents from the archives, of which the most important are the following. TsGIA: f. 23, op. 17. d. 648, l. 23–25 (8 August 1913 meeting of the Council of Ministers); f. 23, op. 17, d. 648, l. 15–22 (24 October 1913 meeting of the Council of Ministers, the richest source); and f. 23, god 1913, op. 20, d. 293, l. 145–174 (24 April, 1, 8, 22, 29 May 1914 Ministry of Trade and Industry conference on the strike movement).

18. 8 August 1913 Council of Ministers meeting, l. 23.

19. 24 October 1913 meeting of Council of Ministers, l. 16–17.

20. 24 October meeting, l. 17–18.

21. Ibid., l. 20–21.

22. Laverychev, *Tsarizm*, p. 257.

23. Quoted in ibid., p. 262.

24. Ibid.

25. The journal of this conference can be found in TsGIA, f. 1276, op. 1, d. 79, l. 201–215; the Ministry of Internal Affairs sent a long report on it to Minister of Finance Kokovtsov on 29 October: see f. 1276, op. 1, d. 79, l. 183–229.

26. Ibid., l. 210.

27. Ibid., l. 211. Only the Ministry of Trade and Industry objected to this change.

28. The text can be found in ibid., ll. 188–229.

29. TsGIA, f. 1405, d. 543, op. 913, l. 694–705.

30. TsGIA, f. 1276, op. 1, d. 79, l. 179–80.

31. Ibid., l. 182.

32. For examples see Bonnell, *Roots of Rebellion*, pp. 346–348.

33. Quoted in Hosking, *Russian Constitutional Experiment*, p. 191.

34. Rieber, *Merchants and Entrepreneurs*, p. 331.

35. I. A. Menitskii, *Russkoe Rabochee Dvizhenie i RSDRP Nakanune Voiny (1912–1914)* (Moscow: Krasnaia Nov', 1923), pp. 36–30.

36. G. A. Arutiunov, *Rabochee Dvizhenie v Rossii v Periode Novogo Revoliutsionnogo Pod"ema 1910–1914 gg.* (Moscow: Nauka, 1975), p. 165.

37. The 27 May 1914 report of the St. Petersburg Society refers to the frequency of political strikes not caused by circumstances internal to the factory (TsGIA, f. 150, op. 1, d. 651, l. 37).

38. TsGIA, f. 150, op. 1, god 1907, d. 660, l. 173; also f. 150, op. 1, d. 651, l. 38–41.

39. For example, on 21 June 1913 the machine-building division of the St. Petersburg Society worked out a set of measures claimed to be most effective against strikes. When workers are taken back after strikes, they must sign a statement that they will submit to the authority of the factory administration; no concessions should be made, but factories should be closed and then only selected workers should be rehired; no wage payments for time lost during strikes; when

signs of unrest are noticed, an announcement warning of dismissals should be posted; no hirings should be done when there are strikes anywhere in the factory owner's own branch of industry (TsGIA, f. 150, op. 1, d. 660, god 1907, l. 162). Also see M. Balabanov, "Rabochii klass nakanune revoliutsii," in *Professional-'noe Dvizhenie v Petrograde v 1917 g: Ocherki i Materialy*, ed. A. Anskii (Leningrad: Izdatel'stvo Leningradskogo Oblastnogo Soveta Profsoiuzov, 1928), p. 8; Bonnell, *Roots of Rebellion*, pp. 381–382; and TsGIA, f. 150, op. 1, d. 651, passim.

40. Quoted in Bonnell, *Roots of Rebellion*, p. 387.

41. TsGIA, f. 150, op. 1, god 1907, d. 660, l. 169–170.

42. TsGIA, f. 150, op. 1, d. 651, l. 38–41 (June 1914 document of St. Petersburg Society on means to struggle with the strike movement).

43. For examples see Bonnell, *Roots of Rebellion*, p. 384.

44. V. Kaiurov, "Rabochee dvizhenie v Petere (1914 god)," *Proletarskaia Revoliutsiia*, no. 9 (September 1925): 186.

45. See Bonnell, *Roots of Rebellion*, p. 383.

46. A. K. Bykov, *Fabrichnoe Zakonodatel'stvo i Razvitie ego v Rossii* (St. Petersburg: "Pravda," 1909), pp. 269–272.

47. P. Timofeev, *Chem Zhivet Zavodskii Rabochii* (St. Petersburg: N. N. Klobukov, 1909), p. 34.

48. See Frederick Giffin, "The Formative Years of the Russian Factory Inspectorate, 1882–1885," *Slavic Review* 25, no. 4 (1966): 641–651; Theodore Von Laue, "Factory Inspection under the 'Witte System': 1892–1903," *The American Slavic and East European Review* XIX (October 1960): 347–362.

49. TsGIA, f. 20, god 1899, op. 13, d. 192, l. 54–86.

50. Examples from TsGIA, f. 20, op. 13a, d. 56, l. 16.

51. Gvozdev, *Zapiski Fabrichnogo Inspektora*, p. 77.

52. *RD*, vol. 4, pt. 1, p. 271.

53. Quoted in M. Balabanov, *Ocherki po Istorii Rabochego Klassa v Rossii. Kapitalisticheskaia Rossiia.* (Kiev: Izdatel'stvo Sorabkop, 1924), p. 202.

54. G. V. Plekhanov, *Russkii Rabochii v Revoliutsionnom Dvizhenii. Sochineniia*, vol. 3, ed. D. Riazanov (Moscow-Petrograd: Gosudarstvennoe Izdatel'stvo, 1923), p. 157.

55. Fritz Kern, *Kingship and Law in the Middle Ages* (New York: Harper 1970), p. 140.

56. See Korkunov, *Russkoe Gosudavstrennoe Pravo*, 1: 204–213.

57. See Sheldon Wolin, *Politics and Vision* (Boston: Little, Brown & Co., 1960).

58. M. G. Smith, "On Segmentary Lineage Systems," *Journal of Royal Anthropological Institute* 86 (1956): 39–80.

59. Trotsky, *1905*, p. 148.

60. Zelnik, *Labor and Society*, p. 352. This account is based on ibid., pp. 340–369.

61. *RD*, vol. 2, pt. 2, pp. 574–582.

62. Two excellent statements to this effect based on the Zubatov and Gapon experiments are TsGIA, f. 1276, g. 1905, op. 1, d. 50, l. 97–100—a 23 January 1905 statement of 186 engineers and technicians to the Committee of

Ministers—and f. 150, god 1905, op. 1, d. 484, l. 66–68—an undated report of a group of industrialists from the central industrial region.

63. Quoted in A. El'nitskii, *Istoriia Rabochego Dvizheniia v Rossii*, part 2 (Moscow ?: Izdatel'stvo Proletarii, 1924), p. 41.

64. Ozerov, *Politika*, p. 292, writes: "Has a feeling for legality developed in the population? No and no again: it was trampled under at each step."

65. P. F. Kudelli and G. L. Shidlovskii, eds., *1905. Vospominaniia Chlenov SPB Soveta Rabochikh Deputatov* (Leningrad: Rabochee Izdatel'stvo Priboi, 1926), p. 21.

III. Structure and Basic Traits of the Russian Labor Movement

1. Quoted in Bonnell, *Roots of Rebellion*, p. 398.
2. See the description of the "liquidators" in ibid., pp. 343–344.

7. Mass Workers

1. Kornhauser, *Politics of Mass Society*, p. 14.
2. Moore, *Injustice*, pp. 191–196.
3. See A. I. Shapovalov, *Po Doroge K Marksizmu. Vospominaniia Rabochego Revoliutsionera* (Moscow: Gosudarstvennoe Izdatel'stvo, 1922), p. 30.
4. Gvozdev, *Zapiski Fabrichnogo Inspektora*, p. 33.
5. Moore, *Injustice*, p. 197.
6. I. N. Kubikov, *Rabochii Klass v Russkoi Literature* (Ivanovo-Voznesensk: Osnova, 1926), pp. 131–132.
7. For general overviews of the debate, see Theodore Von Laue, "Russian Peasants in the Factory 1892–1904," *Journal of Economic History* XXI, no. 1 (March 1961): 61–81; and Reginald Zelnik, "Essay Review."
8. L. M. Ivanov, "Vozniknovenie rabochego klassa," in *Istoriia Rabochego Klassa Rossii, 1861–1900*, L. M. Ivanov, ed. (Moscow: Nauka, 1972), pp. 38–47.
9. Robert Johnson, *Peasant and Proletarian* (New Brunswick, N.J.: Rutgers University Press, 1979).
10. S. Kanatchikov, *Iz Istorii Moego Bytiia*, vol. 1 (Moscow: Izdatel'stvo "Staryi Bol'shevik," 1932), pp. 41–42.
11. L. M. Kleinbort, *Kak Skladyvalas' Rabochaia Intelligentsiia* (Moscow: Izdatel'stvo VTsSPS, 1925), pp. 54 ff.; Kubikov, *Rabochii Klass*, p. 132; S. N. Prokopovich, *K Rabochemu Voprosu v Rossii* (St. Petersburg: Izdanie E. D. Kuskovoi, 1905), p. 70.
12. Kanatchikov, *Iz Istorii*, 1: 37.
13. Aleksei Buzinov, *Za Nevskoi Zastavoi* (Moscow-Leningrad: Gosudarstvennoe Izdatel'stvo, 1930), p. 21.
14. A. K. Petrov, *Rabochii Bol'shevik v Podpol'e* (Moscow: Novaia Moskva, 1925), pp. 58–60.

15. Timofeev, *Chem Zhivet*, pp. 12–13.

16. Kleinbort, *Kak Skladyvalas'*, pp. 51–52.

17. S. I. Somov, "Iz istorii sotsialdemokraticheskogo dvizheniia v Peterburge v 1905 godu (Lichnye vospominaniia). Part 1, *Byloe*, no. 4 (16) (1907): 49–52; Boris Ivanov, *Zapiski Proshlogo, Povest' iz Vospominanii Detstva: Iunoshestva Rabochego-Sotsialista* (Moscow: Gosudarstvennoe Izdatel'stvo, 1919), pp. 67–68.

18. Alexander Woodside makes similar remarks about Vietnamese rubber plantation workers under the French: "Starved for effective points of reference in their lives [they] might develop such intense group feelings that lethal quarrels would break out between 'villages.'" See *Community and Revolution in Vietnam*, p. 213.

19. Although the term is sometimes used in memoirs. Shapovalov, for example, identifies the metalworkers, assistants to the metalworkers, and machine-building workers as the aristocracy in his plant. They were distinguishable by their dress and customs and imitated the European workers in the workshop. "Their pocket watches were a luxury seldom accessible to workers. In order not to be late for work, they arrived at the factory gates twenty to thirty minutes before the whistle." Some of the older "aristocrats" looked back to the era of serfdom with nostalgia, for in modern times people had no fear of God or respect for elders. See *Po Doroge*, p. 19.

20. This is the central theme of Reinhard Bendix's *Nation-Building and Citizenship*, 2d ed. (Berkeley, Los Angeles, London: University of California Press, 1977).

21. Kanatchikov, *Iz Istorii*, 1: 15.

22. Shapovalov, *Po Doroge*, pp. 27–28.

23. Johnson, *Peasant and Proletarian*, pp. 52–56.

24. See Guenther Roth, *The Social Democrats in Imperial Germany* (Totowa, N.J.: Bedminster Press, 1963).

25. Jean Chesneaux, *The Chinese Labor Movement, 1919–1927* (Stanford: Stanford University Press, 1968), pp. 119–121, 153.

26. Shapovalov, *Po Doroge*, p. 29.

27. Bonnell, *Roots of Rebellion*, pp. 434–438.

28. Parsons and Smelser, *Economy and Society*, p. 110.

29. Kleinbort, *Kak Skladyvalas'*, pp. 45–49; V. F. Shishkin, *Tak Skladyvalas' Revoliutsionnaia Moral'* (Moscow: Mysl', 1967), pp. 57–58; Timofeev, *Chem Zhivet*, p. 46; Boris Ivanov, *Zapiski Proshlogo*, p. 49.

30. See *RD*, vol. 4, pt. 2, pp. 193–194, for a good example.

31. Shiskin, *Tak Skladyvalas'*, p. 57.

32. Timofeev, *Chem Zhivet*, p. 46.

33. For example, see A. Frolov, *Probuzhdenie. Vospominaniia Riadovogo Rabochego*, vol. 1 (Gosudarstvennoe Izdatel'stvo Ukrainy, 1923), p. 19; S. Balashov, "Rabochee dvizhenie v Ivanovo-Voznesenske 1898–1905 gg," *Proletarskaia Revoliutsiia* no. 9 (44) (September 1925): 147.

34. Shapovalov, *Po Doroge*, p. 69.

35. Kanatchikov, *Iz Istorii*, 1: 148, 154.

36. Balashov, "Rabochee dvizhenie" p. 147; Shapovalov, *Po Doroge*, p. 28.

37. TsGAOR, DPVI, 1902, d. 7b, l. 89.

38. Examples can be found in TsGIA, f. 23, god 1902, op. 24, d. 1175.

39. For several accounts of such a change after the massacre of Bloody Sunday, see B. Pozern, ed., *Putilovtsy v 1905 godu: Sbornik Vospominanii Rabochikh* (Leningrad: OGIZ Priboi, 1931).

40. Frolov, *Probuzhdenie*, p. 27.

41. Ivanov, *Zapiski Proshlogo*, p. 49.

42. For examples see, ibid., pp. 48–49; Balashov, "Rabochee dvizhenie," p. 147; Shapovalov, *Po Doroge*, pp. 27–28.

43. Buzinov, *Za Nevskoi Zastavoi*, pp. 22–25.

44. Shapovalov, *Po Doroge*, p. 22.

45. Kleinbort, *Kak Skladyvalas'*, pp. 57–58.

46. Ivanov, *Zapiski Proshlogo*, p. 49.

47. TsGAOR, DPVI, 1902, d. 7b., l. 89.

48. Somov, "Iz istorii," p. 49.

49. Petrov, *Rabochii Bol'shevik*, p. 66.

50. *RD*, vol. 4, pt. 2, p. 125.

51. September 1905 report of Chikolev: TsGIA, f. 1205, op. XVI, d. 1, l. 301.

52. See Werner Sombart, *Socialism and the Socialist Movement* (New York: Dutton, 1909), p. 25.

53. K. M. Taktarev, *Ocherk Peterburgskogo Rabochego Dvizheniia 90-x Godov*, 2d ed. (St. Petersburg: Tipografiia B. Ia. Mil'shtein, 1906), pp. 38 ff. The leaflet "Advice by a 'gray worker'" is reprinted.

54. Somov, "Iz istorii," p. 42.

55. G. K. Klaas, *Moi Pervye Shagi na Revoliutsionnom Puti* (Leningrad: Rabochee Izdatel'stvo Priboi, 1926), p. 17.

56. Quoted in Kleinbort, *Kak Skladyvalas'*, p. 203.

57. S. Kanatchikov, *Iz Istorii Moego Bytiia*, vol. 2 (Moscow: Moskovskoe Tovarischestvo Pisatelei, 1934), p. 32.

58. See Trotksy, *History*, 1: 153.

59. Michelle Perrot, *Les Ouvriers en Grève*, 1: 297.

60. *RD*, vol. 4, pt. 2, p. 41.

61. A. Martynov-Piker, "Vospominaniia revoliutsionera," *Proletarskaia Revoliutsiia*, no. 11 (46) (November 1925): 273.

62. Kanatchikov, *Iz Istorii*, 1: 142.

63. Ivanov, *Zapiski Proshlogo*, p. 48.

64. Ibid., p. 48.

65. The explosive implications of collective norms among Russian workers is suggested in Eduard Dune, "Zapiski Krasnogvardeitsa" (unpublished ms., Nicolaevsky archive, Hoover Archive, Stanford University), p. 9.

66. K. Mironov, *Iz Vospominanii Rabochego* (Moscow: Izdatel'stvo Molodaia Rossiia, 1906), p. 21.

67. Liubov' Gurevich, *Deviatoe Ianvaria* (Kharkov: Izdatel'stvo Proletarii, 1926), p. 16.

68. Buzinov, *Za Nevskoi Zastavoi*, pp. 29–31.

69. I. Petukhov, "Moi kratkie otryvochnye vospominaniia o lichnykh perezhivaniiakh i o prokhozhdenii surovoi shkoly zhizni," in *Put' k Oktiabriu: Sbornik*

Statei, Vospominanii i Dokumentov, ed. S. Chernomordik, Vypusk 3 (Moscow, 1923–1926), p. 53.

70. Mironov, *Iz Vospominanii,* p. 21.
71. Takhtarev, *Ocherk Peterburgskogo,* p. 30.
72. TsGAOR, DPVI, 1902, d. 7b, l. 89.
73. Taktarev, *Ocherk Peterburgskogo,* p. 39.
74. Buzinov, *Za Nevskoi Zastavoi,* p. 31.
75. Ibid., pp. 48–49.
76. Somov, "Iz istorii," p. 34.

8. CONSCIOUS WORKERS

1. Some authors, such as Gvozdev, distinguish between the two, but any such conceptual distinctions are not important for present purposes.
2. *RD,* vol. 4, pt. 1, pp. 158–159.
3. Ibid., p. 170.
4. Buzinov, *Za Nevskoi Zastavoi,* pp. 102–103.
5. Ivan Babushkin, *Recollections (1893–1900)* (Moscow: Foreign Languages Publishing House, 1957), p. 22.
6. *Rabochee Dvizhenie v Rossii v 1901–1904 gg. Sbornik Dokumentov* (Leningrad: Nauka, 1975), p. 90. For similar sentiments (which are common in worker memoirs) see Ivanov, *Zapiski Proshlogo,* p. 78.
7. See Gerald Brenan, *The Spanish Labyrinth* (Cambridge: Cambridge University Press, 1964), p. 174.
8. P. A. Garvi, *Vospominaniia Sotsialdemokrata* (New York, 1946), p. 88.
9. Shapovalov, *Po Doroge,* pp. 29–31, 40; Petr Moiseenko, *Vospominaniia Starogo Revoliutsionera* (Moscow: Mysl', 1966), p. 95.
10. Mironov, *Iz Vospominanii Rabochego,* p. 8.
11. Leon Trotsky, *My Life* (New York: Pathfinder, 1970), p. 107; and Dune, "Zapiski Krasnogvardeitsa," p. 9.
12. *RD,* vol. 2, pt. 2, pp. 239–242.
13. Trotsky, *My Life,* p. 107; also see Shapovalov, *Po Doroge,* p. 38.
14. Shapovalov, *Po Doroge,* p. 46.
15. *RD, 1901–1904,* p. 93.
16. *RD,* vol. 4, pt. 1, pp. 72–90.
17. Babushkin, *Recollections,* pp. 179–181.
18. A. I. Svirskii, *Zapiski Rabochego* (Moscow-Leningrad: "Zemlia i Fabrika," 1925), p. 71.
19. See, inter alia, *RD,* vol. 2, pt. 2, pp. 44–47; Babushkin, *Recollections,* pp. 196–224; *RD, 1901–1904,* pp. 90–93.
20. *RD, 1901–1904,* pp. 90–93; Svirskii, *Zapiski Rabochego,* pp. 33–39; Plekhanov, *Russkii Rabochii,* p. 132.
21. *RD,* vol. 2, pt. 2, pp. 239–242.
22. Ibid., p. 43.
23. *RD, 1901–1904,* p. 92.
24. Kanatchikov, *Iz Istorii,* 1: 156.

25. *Rabochaia Mysl'*, cited in Taktarev, *Ocherk Peterburgskogo*, pp. 91–92.

26. Plekhanov, *Russkii Rabochii*, p. 130.

27. Iu. Martov, *Zapiski Sotsial-Demokrata* (Cambridge: Oriental Research Partners, 1975, reprint of 1922 Berlin edition), p. 282.

28. TsGIA, f. 1153, g. 1903, op. 1, d. 153, l. 82.

29. Babushkin, *Recollections*, p. 35.

30. Kanatchikov, *Iz Istorii*, 1: 148.

31. Babushkin, *Recollections*, p. 22; Plekhanov, *Russkii Rabochii*, p. 132.

32. M. Rozanov, *Vasilii Andreevich Shelgunov*, 2d ed. (Leningrad: Lenizdat, 1976), pp. 21–25.

33. *Ot Gruppy Blagoeva k "Soiuzu Bor'by"* (Rostov na Donu: Gosudarstvennoe Izdatel'stvo Donskoe Otdelenie, 1921), p. 9.

34. Kanatchikov, *Iz Istorii*, 1: 35–37, 86. See Reginald Zelnik, "Russian Bebels: An Introduction to the Memoirs of Semen Kanatchikov and Matvei Fisher, Part One," *The Russian Review* 35, no. 3 (July 1976): 249–290. See also Kirill Orlov, *Zhizn' Rabochego-Revoliutsionera, ot 1905 k 1917 g.* (Leningrad: Rabochee Izdatel'stvo Priboi, 1925), p. 4; Petrov, *Rabochii Bol'shevik*, p. 40; Shapovalov, *Po Doroge*, p. 23. For a secondary account see Shishkin, *Tak Skladyvalas'*, pp. 44–49.

35. Garvi, *Vospominaniia Sotsialdemokrata*, p. 96.

36. Kanatchikov, *Iz Istorii*, 1: 37.

37. Cited in Kubikov, *Rabochii Klass*, pp. 135–136.

38. Sulimov, "Vospominaniia obukhovtsa (1900–1903)," *Proletarskaia Revoliutsiia*, no. 12 (1923): 145–146.

39. Iakov Mikhailov, *Iz Zhizni Rabochego. Vospominaniia Chlena Peterburgskogo Soveta Rabochikh Deputatov 1905 Goda* (Leningrad: Priboi, 1925), p. 13.

40. For example, see Bonnell, *Roots of Rebellion*, pp. 167, 251–254, 398–400.

41. For interesting material on Marxism's meaning to conscious workers, see Shapovalov, *Po Doroge*, pp. 65–66; Kanatchikov, *Iz Istorii*, 1: 178; A. V. Fisher, *V Rossii i v Anglii* (Moscow: Gosudarstvennoe Izdatel'stvo, 1922), pp. 15–16; and Rozanov, *Vasilii Andreevich Shelgunov*, pp. 42–43.

42. T. Sapronov, *Iz Istorii Rabochego Dvizheniia* (Moscow-Leningrad, 1925. Reprinted by Oriental Research Partners, Newtonville, Mass., 1976. With a new introduction by Victoria Bonnell), p. 35.

43. Shapovalov, *Po Doroge*, p. 18.

44. Svirskii, *Zapiski Rabochego*, pp. 46–47.

45. Shapovalov, *Po Doroge*, p. 28.

46. Buzinov, *Za Nevskoi Zastavoi*, p. 28.

47. Ibid., p. 41.

48. S. Adashev in Kudelli and Shidlovskii, eds., *1905*.

49. Babushkin, *Recollections*, p. 51.

50. For an example, see Martov, *Zapiski Sotsial-Demokrata*, pp. 286–287.

51. Garvi, *Vospominaniia Sotsialdemokrata*, p. 96. See also Shapovalov, *Po Doroge*, p. 76; Frolov, *Probuzhdenie*, pp. 61–62; Mironov, *Iz Vospominaniia*, p. 23.

52. Mironov, *Iz Vospominaniia*, p. 23.
53. Shapovalov, *Po Doroge*, pp. 53–54.
54. Kanatchikov, *Iz Istorii*, 1: 145.
55. A. Shotman, "Zapiski starogo bol'shevika, Part one," *Proletarskaia Revoliutsiia*, no. 9 (1922): 148.
56. Kanatchikov, *Iz Istorii*, 2: 85; Babushkin, *Recollections*, p. 61.
57. As, for example, with respect to Lenin in Adam Ulam, *The Bolsheviks* (New York: Collier Books, 1968), p. 124.
58. Sulimov, "Vospominaniia obukhovtsa," p. 168.
59. Kanatchikov, *Iz Istorii*, 1: 7–8.
60. Fisher, *V Rossii*, pp. 42–43.
61. Mikhailov, *Iz Zhizni*, p. 76.
62. P. Kungarov, "Zapiski rabochego," *Proletarskaia Revoliutsiia*, no. 4 (1922): 250.
63. Peshekhenov cites a letter of one such individual at length. See A. B. Peshekhonov, *K Voprosu ob Intelligentsii* (St. Petersburg: Russkoe Bogastvo, 1906), pp. 60–61.
64. Garvi, *Vospominaniia Sotsialdemolerata*, pp. 545–546.
65. Quoted in Kubikov, *Rabochii Klass*, p. 250.
66. See S. Valk, "Materialy k istorii pervogo maia v Rossii," *Krasnaia Letopis'*, no. 4 (1922): 250–288; V. Karelina, "Na zare rabochego dvizheniia v S-Peterburge," ibid., pp. 12–20.
67. Ainzaft, *Zubatovshchina i Gaponovshchina* (1924 ed.), p. 43.
68. Shapovalov, *Po Doroge*, p. 11.
69. Quoted in Garvi, *Vospominaniia Sotsialdemokrata*, p. 496.
70. Shapovalov, *Po Doroge*, p. 50.
71. Garvi, *Vospominaniia Sotsialdemokata*, p. 87.
72. Evidence for the leadership of conscious workers in the crucial episodes of labor protest will be provided in chapters ten, eleven and twelve. The most clear-cut examples are the early January 1905 strikes connected with the Gapon movement and the late 1905 ferment, when conscious workers played a leading role in the St. Petersburg Soviet.
73. TsGIA, f. 1282, op. 1., d. 699, l. 14 (June 1901 memorandum of Sviatopolk-Mirskii, soon to be minister of Interior). A similar analysis was made by Chikolev in September 1905 (TsGIA, f. 1205, op. XVI, d. 1, l. 288). Both reports emphasize the crucial importance of these "highly developed, strongly committed people" (in Chikolev's phrase). Lenin also emphasized the centrality of "a few educated workers whom the masses will follow." Such advanced workers, he claimed, determined the character of the labor movement. Quoted in Neil Harding, *Lenin's Political Thought*, vol. 1 (London: Macmillan, 1983), p. 173.
74. Moiseenko, *Vospominaniia Starogo*, p. 38.
75. Kanatchikov, *Iz Istorii*, 1: 155.
76. Shapovalov, *Po Doroge*, p. 51.
77. Moiseenko, *Vospominaniia Starogo*, p. 70.
78. Plekhanov, *Russkii Rabochii*, p. 159.
79. See Takhtarev, *Ocherk Peterburgskogo*, pp. 14–16.
80. In Russian the literature on this subject is vast. Nearby all revolutionary

intelligentsia and worker memoirs touch upon it, often at length. In English there are some outstanding works, including Allan Wildman, *The Making of a Workers' Revolution: Russian Social Democracy, 1891–1903* (Chicago: University of Chicago Press, 1967); and Reginald Zelnik, "Russian Bebels" (in two parts), *The Russian Review* 35, no. 3, (1976): 249–290 and 35, no. 4 (1976): 417–448. (The second part is particularly valuable for this theme.) I have relied on these works, as well as numerous memoirs—especially those of Fisher, Kanatchikov, and Garvi. Kleinbort's book is also a very valuable source.

81. Frolov, *Probuzhdenie*, p. 71.

82. Petukhov, "Moi Kratkie," p. 61.

83. One of the most eloquent examples is the pamphlet by Golub, a disillusioned Social Democratic worker. Stepan Golub, *Cherez Plotinu Intelligenshchiny. Pis'mo Rabochego k Intelligentam i Rabochim Nashei Partii* (Publication by the author, no place given, 1908).

84. See Wildman, *The Making of a Workers' Revolution*, pp. 90–93; N. Baturin, *Ocherk Istorii Sotsial-Demokratii v Rossii* (Moscow: Moskovskii Rabochii, 1922), pp. 104–105; Garvi, *Vospominaniia Sotsialdemokrata*, passim.

85. This and other issues mentioned here will be discussed from the intelligentsia's point of view in the next chapter.

86. Kanatchikov, *Iz Istorii*, 2: 37.

87. See the pamphlet *Rabochie o Partiinom Raskole* published by the Central Committee of the Russian Social Democratic Party (Geneva: "Party" Publisher, 1905). See particularly the second part, "Letter to all conscious worker comrades" from "A worker—one of many."

88. Golub, *Cherez Plotinu*, p. 81.

89. Fisher, *V Rossii*, p. 49.

90. For example, see Wildman, *The Making of a Workers' Revolution*, pp. 112–115; Garvi, *Vospominaniia sotsialdemokrata*, pp. 107–108.

91. Fisher, *V Rossii*, pp. 42–43.

9. THE REVOLUTIONARY INTELLIGENTSIA

1. From "The People and the Intelligentsia," an address given in 1908. Reprinted in Marc Raeff, ed., *Russian Intellectual History. An Anthology* (New Jersey: Humanities Press, 1978), p. 360.

2. Szamuely, *Russian Tradition*, p. 143.

3. Isaiah Berlin, *Russian Thinkers* (New York: Pelican, 1979), p. 116.

4. Trotsky, *History*, 1: 17.

5. Among recent scholars, David Mandel has gone furthest in developing this view. In particular, see *Fall of the Old Regime*, p. 240, on the role of the Bolshevik Central Committee.

6. Ralf Dahrendorf, *Society and Democracy in Germany* (New York: Norton, 1979), pp. 151–152.

7. On Axelrod see Abraham Ascher, *Pavel Axelrod and the Development of Menshevism* (Cambridge: Harvard University Press, 1972), pp. 103–105.

8. Quoted in Harding, *Lenin's Political Thought*, 1: 72.

9. See Tocqueville, *The Old Regime*, pp. 138–148. For the application of many of these ideas to Russia, see Martin Malia, *Alexander Herzen.*

10. As will be seen shortly, this self-aggrandizement gave rise to its opposite, self-abasement, as well.

11. Quoted in Nikolai Valentinov, *The Early Years of Lenin* (Ann Arbor: University of Michigan Press, 1969), p. 129.

12. Quoted in Szamuely, *Russian Tradition*, p. 156.

13. Quoted in Ascher, *Pavel Axelrod*, p. 138.

14. V. I. Lenin, *What Is to Be Done?* (New York: International Publishers, 1969), p. 69.

15. Berlin, *Russian Thinkers*, pp. 122–124.

16. See Alain Besançon, *The Intellectual Origins of Leninism* (Oxford: Basil Blackwell, 1981), pp. 65–78.

17. Statement of a contemporary observer cited in Bonnell, *Roots of Rebellion*, p. 333.

18. Quoted in Harrison Salisbury, *Black Night, White Snow: Russia's Revolutions 1905–1917* (Garden City, N.Y.: Doubleday, 1978), p. 540.

19. In fact, the question of the proper relationship between political and economic goals caused considerable dissension among the intelligentsia, some of them supporting the economic struggle as the best way to develop political consciousness. In general, however, the orthodox view on the priority of the political held sway, in large part because of the preeminent role of ideology for the intelligentsia.

20. Garvi, *Vospominaniia Sotsialdemokrata*, p. 520.

21. According to Harding, even the most famous and consequential of these splits—that between the Mensheviks and Bolsheviks—arose largely over personal rivalries, not different perspectives on organization. See Harding, *Lenin's Political Thought*, 1: 189–196.

22. See Iu. Martov, *Proletarskaia Bor'ba v Rossii* (St. Petersburg: N. Glagolev, n.d.), p. 132: "Stability of policy and firmness of organization are all the stronger the deeper are the foundations of the party laid in the very class struggle of the masses."

23. *Rabochie o Partiinom Raskole*, pt. 1, p. 7.

24. See Paul Miliukov, *Russia and Its Crisis* (New York: Collier, 1962), pp. 245, 248, for remarks on the predominance of socialism in Russia: "Russian socialism met with no opposition from the individualistic spirit, and found no organized democracy." Ermanskii also refers to the weak political influence of "bourgeois democracy": "And this made us in a certain sense the monopolistic possessors of the political 'souls' of the proletariat." O. A. Ermanskii, *Iz Perezhitogo (1887–1921 g.g.)* (Moscow: Gosudarstvennoe Izdatel'stvo, 1927), p. 99.

25. Tocqueville, *The Old Regime*, p. 141.

26. R. V. Ivanov-Razumnik, *Istoriia Russkoi Obshchestvennoi Mysli*, vol. 2, 3d ed. (St. Petersburg: M. M. Stasiulevich, 1911), pp. 3–4.

27. Alexander Herzen, "The Russian People and Socialism" in *From the Other Shore* and *The Russian People and Socialism* (Oxford: Oxford University Press, 1979), p. 200.

28. Dahrendorf, *Society and Democracy*, p. 293. Dahrendorf's remarks are relevant far beyond the immediate German context to which they refer.

29. This theme has already been explored in the discussion of the Zubatov workers and will resurface in different contexts, including the 1917 revolution itself.

30. See Plekhanov's comments on Lenin (August 1917): "Those things which bourgeois liberalism must bring to a country and everywhere in Europe has already brought, never occurred to Lenin." Valentinov, *Early Years of Lenin*, p. 245.

31. See Ulam, *The Bolsheviks*, p. 148. Also see Nicholas Berdiaev, *The Russian Idea* (London: The Centenary Press, 1947), p. 30, for characteristic remarks on this theme.

32. Both quotations from Ascher, *Pavel Axelrod*, p. 246.

33. Plekhanov, *Russkii Rabochii*, p. 127.

34. Nikolai Mikhailovsky, one of the most important populist thinkers, wrote as follows: "We have come to realize that our awareness of the universal truth and of universal ideals could only have been reached at the cost of the age-old suffering of the people. . . . We have come to the conclusion that we are the people's debtors. . . . We may argue about the size of the debt or the best method of repayment, but this debt weighs down on our conscience, and return it we must." Quoted in Szamuely, *Russian Tradition*, p. 152. For Kropotkin's sense of guilt, see Samuel Baron, *Plekhanov* (Stanford: Stanford University Press, 1963), p. 10.

35. The intelligentsia's sense of its own helplessness before the people is also a theme of nineteenth-century Russian literature. For example, Turgenev has his young sculptor Shubin complain in *On the Eve* that "we haven't got anyone among us, no real people, wherever you look. It's all minnows and mice and little Hamlets feeding on themselves in ignorance and dark obscurity." Ivan Turgenev, *On the Eve* (Harmondsworth, England: Penguin, 1950), p. 197.

36. Any well-known account of the intelligentsia, such as those by Haimson, Ivanov-Razumnik, Walicki, Szamuely, or Wolfe, touches upon these central themes of the culture of the intelligentsia.

37. TsGAOR, f. 102, g. 1898, d. 2., ch. 3, l. D., s. 2.

38. Martov, *Proletarskaia Bor'ba*, p. 93.

39. Trotsky, *1905*, p. 78.

40. Ibid., p. 351.

41. See Baron, *Plekhanov*, pp. 250–251.

42. Quoted in Jonathan Frankel, ed., *Vladimir Akimov on the Dilemmas of Russian Marxism. 1895–1903* (Cambridge: Cambridge University Press, 1969), pp. 86–87.

43. Leopold Haimson, *The Russian Marxists and the Origins of Bolshevism* (Boston: Beacon, 1966), p. 213.

44. The Group for the Emancipation of Labor was the main emigré Marxist group in the first two decades of Russian Marxism. The quotation comes from Ascher, *Pavel Axelrod*, p. 120.

45. P. B. Axelrod, *Pis'ma P.B. Aksel'roda i Iu. O. Martova* (The Hague: Europe Printing, 1967), p. 37.

46. See Maurice Meisner, "Utopian Socialist Themes in Maoism," in *Peasant Rebellion and Communist Revolution in Asia*, ed. John Wilson Lewis, 207–252 (Stanford: Stanford Univerity Press, 1974).

47. The moralistic and voluntaristic aspects of Russian Marxism have been treated in numerous works on the subject, including Szamuely, Baron, and Dan. Dan, passim, has an especially interesting analysis of how the emphasis on consciousness solved the theoretical problems of introducing Western Marxism into backward Russia. See, for example, Theodore Dan, *The Origins of Bolshevism* (New York: Schocken, 1970), p. 330, for representative comments.

48. For a description of these changes for both workers and intelligentsia, see Kleinbort, *Kak Skladyvalas'*, pp. 225–226. For the intelligentsia, Haimson has some especially interesting reflections on their integration into postrevolutionary society. See Haimson, *The Russian Marxists*, pp. 217–218.

10. Labor and Organization

1. See Takhtarev's paraphrase of the views of the People's Will (*Ocherk Peterburgskogo*, p. 7).

2. See Solomon Schwarz, *The Russian Revolution of 1905* (Chicago: University of Chicago Press, 1967), pp. 170–171 and passim.

3. The fate of these ideas will be discussed later.

4. Evgenii Lozinskii, *Itogi i Perspektivy Rabochego Dvizheniia* (St. Petersburg: Tipografia V. Bezobrazova, 1909).

5. See L. M. Ivanov, B. S. Itenberg, and Iu. N. Shebaldin, "Nachalo puti," in *Istoriia Rabochego Klassa Rossii, 1861–1900 gg.*, ed. L. M. Ivanov (Moscow: Nauka, 1972), p. 69.

6. In her comments on French strike leaders in the 1871–1890 period, Perrot makes some very relevant suggestions about the characteristics of strike leaders in struggles not yet regulated by organizations. Single workers are more likely to be strike leaders, for example, and the young, the latter particularly in those branches of industry (such as textiles) without a strong skill hierarchy. By contrast, in factories with skilled workers age means knowledge and prestige, and older workers often played a leading role in conflicts. Whether such generalizations hold for Russia, in a context in which gaps in knowledge are even greater than those in France, is not certain. See Perrot, *Les Ouvriers en Grève*, 2: 460–463.

7. For a good description of such a process of leadership selection in a strike in Saratov in 1901, see Kanatchikov, *Iz Istorii*, 2: 76–79.

8. The Northern Union's program can be found in *RD*, vol. 2, pt. 2, pp. 239–242.

9. See Gerald Surh, "Petersburg Workers in 1905: Strikes, Workplace Democracy, and the Revolution" (Ph.D. diss., University of California, Berkeley, 1979), pp. 77 ff.

10. Garvi, *Vospominaniia Sotsialdemokrata*, p. 523.

11. Somov, "Iz istorii," pt. 1, p. 46.

12. *RD*, vol. 3, pt. 2, p. 615.

13. Bonnell, *Roots of Rebellion*, p. 151.

14. See Sviatlovskii, *Professional'noe Dvizhenie*, pp. 21–51.

15. For a brief description see S. Ainzaft, *Rabochee Dvizhenie do 1905* (Moscow: Izdatel'stvo MGSPS, 1924), pp. 71–74.

16. Among many descriptions see Takhtarev, *Ocherk Peterburgskogo*, pp. 34–56.

17. The text can be found in ibid., p. 36.

18. *RD*, vol. 4, pt. 2, p. 130.

19. Garvi, *Vospominaniia Sotsialdemokrata*, pp. 24–25.

20. Ibid., pp. 107–112.

21. Somov, "Iz istorii," pt. 2, p. 163.

22. Axelrod *Pis'ma*, pp. 155–158.

23. Alexander Rabinowitch, *The Bolsheviks Come to Power* (New York: Norton, 1976).

24. Somov, "Iz istorii," pt. 2, p. 163.

25. Petrov, *Rabochii Bol'shevik*, p. 26.

26. F. Bulkin, *Soiuz Metallistov 1906–1918 gg.* (Moscow: Izdanie TsKVSRM, 1926), p. 100.

27. Sher, *Istoriia*, pp. 376–377.

28. See Bonnell, *Roots of Rebellion*, pp. 266–272.

29. The article by S. Gusev corrects the tendency of Schwarz to present the Bolsheviks' position in too simple a way. Gusev shows that even among the Bolsheviks there was considerable debate and uncertainty about the proper relations of party and unions. See S. Gusev, "Odessa v 1905 g." *Proletarskaia Revoliutsiia* 2, no. 49 (February 1926), pp. 168–169.

30. Oskar Anweiler, *The Soviets* (New York: Pantheon, 1974), p. 58.

31. Trotsky, *1905*, p. 259.

32. All these data are from Surh, *Petersburg Workers*, pp. 423–424.

33. For examples of conscious workers as trade union leaders, see Bonnell, *Roots of Rebellion*, p. 164. Also see p. 113 for comments on the weight of conscious workers among the Shidlovskii electors.

34. Ermanskii, *Iz Perezhitogo*, pp. 85–86. Also see Trotsky, *1905*, p. 185.

35. For an excellent account of the November strike see Surh, *Petersburg Workers*, pp. 464–485.

36. Garvi, *Vospominaniia Sotsialdemokrata*, p. 558.

37. See Bonnell, *Roots of Rebellion*, chap. 10.

38. Somov, "Iz istorii," p. 2, pp. 156–158. For another example, see Buzinov, *Za Nevskoi Zastavoi*, pp. 63–64.

39. Lenin, incidentally, was completely in favor of opening up the party to masses of new recruits in 1905, as he was in 1917. He advocated more democracy in party affairs and criticized those Bolsheviks who continued to adhere to his own hierarchical organizational ideas as excessively formalist. See Wolfe, *Three Who Made a Revolution*, pp. 306–308.

40. Petukhov, "Moi Kratkie," p. 58.

41. See Somov, "Iz istorii," pt. 2, pp. 158–160.

42. For an excellent account see J. Romero Maura, "The Spanish Case," in *Anarchism Today*, eds. David Apter and James Joll (Garden City, N.Y.: Doubleday, 1972), pp. 71–97, esp. pp. 87–91.

43. See Woodside on Vietnam: "Communist organizers, as early as the 1920's, engaged in a pertinacious search for existing personal ties, primordial social attachments, and existing corporate bodies in Vietnam which they could exploit and expand in the interests of their world revolution." Woodside, *Community and Revolution*, p. 179.

44. See Schwarz, *Russian Revolution of 1905*, p. 245.

45. Haimson, *The Russian Marxists*, pp. 214 ff.

46. Cited in Getzler, *Martov*, p. 101.

11. SOLIDARITY

1. See Walicki, *History of Russian Thought*, pp. 241–242.

2. These ideas are derived largely from the works of Perrot and Shorter and Tilly, but they seem applicable to other Western European countries.

3. Perrot, *Les Ouvriers en Grève*, 1: 341.

4. Ibid., 1: 341; 1: 384–389; 2: 508–513.

5. The 1936 strikes in France, which were most intense among newly unionized workers, are partial exceptions to this. See Shorter and Tilly, *Strikes in France*, pp. 127–137.

6. Partly, too, it was a matter of the different pattern of Russian industrialization, with its quicker tempo and the predominance of large enterprises at a relatively early stage.

7. Plekhanov, *Russkii Rabochii*, pp. 161–162.

8. For some astute remarks on the unanimity of mass meetings, see Robert Michels, *Political Parties* (New York: Dover, 1959), p. 25.

9. For a good example of such an interpretation, see district attorney Kichin's report on the 1896 textile strike in *RD*, vol. 4, pt. 1, pp. 253–264. Kichin also recognized the importance of persuasion.

10. TsGIA, f. 150, god 1905–1906, op. 1, d. 653, l. 138.

11. Balashov, "Rabochee dvizhenie,", p. 170.

12. TsGIA, f. 40, op. 1, d. 48, l. 113.

13. Somov, "Iz istorii," pt. 1, p. 37.

14. *RD*, vol. 4, pt. 2, p. 112.

15. The evidence for these statements is overwhelming in memoirs and secondary accounts alike. For the weakness of the right wing, particularly the "Black Hundreds," see *Istoriia Putilovskogo Zavoda, 1789–1917*, ed. V. A. Bystrianskii (Moscow: OGIZ Gospolitizdat, 1941), p. 266; and Gerald Surh, *Petersburg Workers*, p. 494, although many writers refer to its existence in their factories. Sviatlovskii (*Professional'noe Dvizhenie*, p. 375) attests to the weakness of liberalism among workers. There are numerous references to the relative lack of partisanship among workers. For a good example see Liza Vol'shtein, "Zapiski fabrichnoi rabotnitsy," *Proletarskaia Revoliutsiia* no. 9 (1922): p. 166.

16. For Brazil see James Malloy, "Social Security Policy and the Working Class in Twentieth-Century Brazil," *Journal of Interamerican Studies and World Affairs* 19, no. 1 (February 1977): 45–46. In Vargas's program workers were organized by regional professional categories, and social welfare protection was

granted on this divisive basis. Moore writes of the government-protected benefits of some categories of German workers in *Injustice*.

17. As well as on extralocal levels, the subject of the following section.

18. *RD*, vol. 4, pt. 1, p. 762. This example could easily be multiplied.

19. Kudelli and Shidlovskii, *1905*, p. 20.

20. This account is based on the two articles by worker memoirist A. Shotman, "Zapiski starogo bol'shevika, Part 1," *Proletarskaia Revoliutsia*, no. 9 (1922): 138–153; Part 2, ibid., no. 11 (1922): 91–116.

21. Shotman, "Zapiski Starogo bol'shevika, part 2," p. 95.

22. Ibid., p. 96.

23. Ibid., p. 99.

24. See Surh, *Petersburg Workers*, and his two part article, "Petersburg's First Mass Labor Organization: The Assembly of Russian Workers and Father Gapon", Part 1, *Russian Review* 40, no. 3 (July 1981): 241–262; Part 2, ibid., 40, no. 4 (October 1981): 412–441.

25. Buzinov, *Za Nevskoi Zastavoi*, p. 35. For another description of the millenarian mood, see Klaas, *Moi Pervye Shagi*, p. 15. Klaas refers to the "influence of some kind of hypnosis," "some old faith, outmoded, but nonetheless strong enough to unite these tens of thousands of people."

26. Ainzaft, *Zubatovshchina*, 1924 ed., p. 143. See also Gurevich, *Deviatoe Ianvaria*, pp. 23–24; Somov, "Iz Istorii," pt. 1; and V. Nevskii, "Ianvarskie dni v Peterburge v 1905 g," *Krasnaia Letopis'*, no. 1 (1922): 31–33.

27. Gurevich, *Deviatoe Ianvaria*, p. 18.

28. Most of the information that follows comes from the second part of Surh's article.

29. Shilov, quoted in Surh, "Petersburg's First Mass Labor Organization," pt. 2, p. 415.

30. P. Korolev, *V Podvale* (Moscow-Leningrad: Gosudarstvennoe Izdatel-'stvo, 1926), p. 102.

31. Surh, *Petersburg Workers in 1905*, p. 274.

32. Varzar, *Statisticheskiia Svedeniia*, p. 59. This marked a great change from the 1896 textile strikes, to which the metalworkers did not adhere, often out of contempt for the more rural and backward textile workers.

33. TsGIA, f. 1205, op. xvi, d. 1, l. 88–89.

34. See the previous chapter for more discussion of this point.

35. TsGIA, f. 48, op. 1, d. 233, l. 23. For similar comments on the Moscow printers' strike of September 1905, see Laura Engelstein, *Moscow in the 1905 Revolution: A Study in Class Conflict and Political Organization* (Ph.D. diss., Stanford University, 1976), p. 135. Also see Garvi, *Vospominaniia Sotsialdemokrata*, pp. 539–544.

36. "No strike in history in any land has ever been as 'general' as this one." Wolfe, *Three Who Made a Revolution*, p. 321.

37. Val Lorwin, *The French Labor Movement* (Cambridge: Harvard University Press, 1954), p. 69.

38. See Shorter and Tilly, *Strikes in France*, pp. 104–146; Frederick Ridley, *Revolutionary Syndicalism in France* (Cambridge: Cambridge University Press, 1970), pp. 117–118.

39. Perlman, *Theory of the Labor Movement*, p. 152.
40. For an account see G. D. H. Cole and Raymond Postgate, *The British Common People, 1746–1946* (London: Methuen, 1961), pp. 576–587.
41. Schorske, *German Social Demorcracy 1905–1917: The Development of the Great Schism* (New York: John Wiley, 1955), p. 40.
42. Buzinov, *Za Nevskoi Zastavoi*, p. 101.
43. N. Cherevanin, *Proletariat v Revoliutsii*, vol. 2, of V. Gorn, V. Mech, and N. Cherevanin, *Bor'ba Obshchestvennykh Sil v Russkoi Revoliutsii* (Moscow: Izdatel'stvo Dvizhenie, 1907), pp. 16–17.

12. RADICALISM

1. Perrot, *Les Ouvriers en Grève*, 1: 148.
2. Ibid., 1: 148.
3. Ibid., 1: 308.
4. Ibid., 2: 724.
5. Ibid., 2: 602.
6. Trotsky, *1905*, p. 106.
7. Plekhanov, *Russkii Rabochii*, pp. 169–170. The petition and the strike are described on pages 163–171.
8. TsGIA, f. 48, op. 1, d. 233, l. 25.
9. TsGIA, f. 1205, op. xvi, d. 1, l. 301–302.
10. TsGAOR, DPVI, 1901, d. 56, l. 11.
11. Garvi, *Vospominaniia Sotsialdemokrata*, p. 84.
12. TsGIA, f. 23, op. 20, d. 1, l. 24–25.
13. Gvozdev, *Zapiski Fabrichnogo Inspektora*, p. 55. Also TsGIA, f. 150, op. 1, d. 652, l. 30, for a complaint from a factory owner about the workers' ignorance: "The workers are in no state to know the real situation of the industrial branch in which they participate, and even of the situation of the establishment in which they work. In such conditions there arose in Russia the kind of labor movement whose witnesses and passive participants we are forced to be."
14. TsGIA, f. 48, op. 1, d. 233, l. 25.
15. As it was for the representatives of the Baku workers in their statements on the strike movement in 1906. TsGIA, f. 23, op. 27, d. 377, l. 87–88. The workers, they said, are powerless; "they are forced to be silent, and in silence to prepare a new strike."
16. As reported by a St. Petersburg factory inspector in early 1905. TsGIA, f. 23, op. 20, d. 1, l. 132.
17. Trotsky, *1905*, pp. 197–198.
18. Korolev, *V Podvale*, p. 103.
19. Buzinov, *Za Nevskoi Zastavoi*, pp. 58–59.
20. Varzar notes the hidden and shifting character of demands in Russian strikes, also tracing it to the lack of organization. See Varzar, *Statisticheskiia Svedeniia*, pp. 47–48.
21. An excellent account by a factory owner of his puzzlement over what the

workers really wanted and his dismay over their inconstancy can be found in TsGIA, f. 1205, op. xvi, d. 1, l. 88–89.

22. Perrot, *Les Ouvriers en Grève*, 2: 459.

23. The resolution of a group of young Bolshevik radicals opposing the Bolshevik Petrograd Committee's decision to end the July 1914 strikes illustrates the intertwining of primitive socialist ideas and popular anger. Note the use of such terms as "laboring population" and "the people," which indicate a rather incomplete assimilation of Marxism. "The government led by the capitalists has announced in earnest a merciless war with the laboring population; everywhere, in both political and economic strikes, the bloodthirsty police heroes have appeared. They inflict unpunished violence and make mass arrests, sometimes shooting, and close professional and also cultural-educational organizations. But even this doesn't help them. Each day in Russia there grow up, like mushrooms, jails. Each day the newspapers are full of news of the exile of our comrades to the most remote places! Everywhere we see that strikes take on colossal proportions. The peasants do not pay their quit-rents, they chop down the forests of the state and landowners, they burn down estates. Soldiers don't take their oaths, they are rude to the authorities, they read harmful newspapers. The government wavered, fearful because around it there grows, not daily but hourly, the laboring army, which is also preparing for the decisive battle with its age-old enemy. But in vain are your efforts to maintain the people in chains. You only show once again that you are powerless, and by increasing your violence against the people you only lay a deeper trap for yourself. In vain you—bloodthirsty breed—took arms against the laboring masses. The government struggles with bayonets, the capitalists with money, and the clergy with sermons. But the people take no account of this. They no longer believe the tales, and in answer the whole laboring class announces to you, perpetrators of police violence, that your song is sung. We are on the eve of great events. One day now your luxurious palaces will be turned into people's clubs and unions . . . Factories will give work only for those who labor. The jails will be filled by you . . . Forests, meadows, fields, all will pass from you into the hands of those whom you humiliated. Comrades! Pay attention and prepare for anything. Wait and endure—away with these words! Our slogans—long live the merciless struggle with the Tsarist government and with the capitalists! Down with capital! Comrades, prepare yourselves! Long live socialism." This document is an excellent example of the theme to be discussed later: how Marxist ideas helped crystallize world views and interpretations of social life for many workers even when they did not fully understand them doctrinally. The document is from "Iul'skie volneniia 1914 g. v Peterburge," *Proletarskaia Revoliutsiia* (August-September 1924): 318.

24. See note 23.

25. Buzinov, *Za Nevskoi Zastavoi*, pp. 80–81. For corroborating evidence, see Engelstein, *Moscow in the 1905 Revolution*, p. 239 and Surh, *Petersburg Workers*, p. 249.

26. TsGIA, f. 1276, op. 1, god 1905, d. 164, l. 61.

27. Perrot, *Les Ouvriers en Grève*. 2: 722.

28. The Mensheviks and Bolsheviks tended to react differently to this fusion of

economic and political struggles. The Mensheviks sought to control the economic struggle in order to maintain an all-class alliance against autocracy. Lenin and the Bolsheviks had much less faith in the revolutionary potential of the bourgeoisie, and so were less concerned that the potential alliance might be broken.

29. This was particularly the case up to and during 1905. In the next upsurge, from 1912 to 1914, worker protest was isolated from larger social ferment, either from the peasants or privileged groups.

30. Martov letter to Axelrod, 17 February 1906, in Axelrod, *Pis'ma*, p. 150.

31. Ibid., p. 149.

32. Luxemburg, *Rosa Luxemburg Speaks*, p. 189.

33. Thus railway officials in mid-1906 complained that "positive elements" refused to become worker representatives. The worker representatives argued that they were threatened by the masses unless they supported the workers' demands. As a result, said the officials, only unscrupulous workers and party militants would become leaders. TsGIA, f. 273, g. 1905, op. 13, d. 361, l. 97, 103–104, 107–108.

34. Trotsky, *1905*, p. 264.

35. For this distinction see Moore, *Injustice*, p. 167.

36. *RD*, vol. 4, pt. 1, pp. 264–266. Numerous similar examples could easily be cited.

37. This is a paraphrase with some direct quotations.

38. This is in line with Martov's complaints cited earlier on the low level of the conscious workers' level of awareness.

39. See Leopold Haimson, "The Problem of Social Stability in Urban Russia, 1905–1917," part 1, *Slavic Review*, 23, no. 4 (December 1964): 619–642; ibid., part 2, 24, no. 1 (March 1965): 1–22; also see G. Lelevich, "Lenskii rasstrel," *Proletarskaia Revoliutsiia*, no. 5 (1922): 21–22.

40. Cherevanin, *Proletariat v Revoliutsii*, p. 68.

41. Cited in Ascher, *Pavel Axelrod*, p. 255.

42. Trotsky, *History*, 1: 50.

43. Kleinbort, *Kak Skladyvalas'*, p. 199.

44. Iu. Milonov, Introduction to stenographical account of *Tret'ia Vserossiiskaia Konferentsiia Professional'nykh Souizov* [Hereafter referred to as *Tret'ia*] (Moscow: Izdatel'stvo VTsSPS, 1927), p. vii.

45. *Rabochaia Gazeta*, 30 June 1917, p. 2. (Hereafter RG). This Menshevik newspaper thought this proportion small, but it seems rather impressive to me, given the intervening years and the effects of the war.

46. G. K. Korolev, *Ivanovo-Kineshemskie Tekstil'shchiki v 1917 Godu* (Moscow: VTsSPS, 1927), pp. 22–28. For more examples see T. Shatilova, "Petrogradskoe obshchestvo zavodchikov i fabrikantov v bor'be s rabochim dvizheniem v 1917 godu"; and K. Bruk, "Organiztsiia soiuza metallistov v 1917 g.," both essays in Anskii, *Professional'noe Dvizhenie v Petrograde*.

47. Aleksandr Shliapnikov, *Semnadtsatyi God* (Moscow-Petrograd: Gosudarstvennoe Izdatel'stvo, 1923), 1: 119.

48. See Frances FitzGerald, *Fire in the Lake* (New York: Vintage, 1973), pp. 176–178.

49. Babushkin, *Recollections*, pp. 108–109.

50. Taktarev, *Ocherk Peterburgskogo*, pp. 15–16.

51. Mikhailov, *Iz Zhizni Rabochego*, p. 10.

52. Shapovalov, *Po Doroge*, p. 20.

53. Kanatchikov, *Iz Istorii*, 2: 5.

54. The importance of such events for the labor movement was clearly recognized by the government. In March 1905 a factory inspector filed a report considering the advisability of including 1 May as an official holiday in the Sormov factory. Because of the very tense mood among the workers, he thought it was dangerous to establish it as a holiday—after all, in Western Europe it was celebrated in memory of workers who perished in the Commune. He also feared that if 1 May were to be included, workers would soon demand the recognition of 9 January. Further, a victory for the Sormov workers would lead to similar demands in other factories, and then the day would almost always be accompanied by worker disorders and demonstrations. If other factories were not given it as a holiday, however, the Sormov workers would probably compel them to stop work anyway. Because of all these considerations, it was "impossible" to establish 1 May as a holiday. Conversely, given the workers' present mood, he feared that refusal to recognize the day would also cause unrest and lead to a general strike, for which the factory inspector would be blamed. Given these quandaries, he concluded that the matter should be resolved by the governor. (TsGIA, f. 23, op. 20, d. 1, l. 26–27.) Fearing responsibility for any consequences the governor referred it to the factory board (ibid., l. 43). The problem was solved as follows: 1 May would be a nonworking day, but it would not be formally recognized in the rules, a compromise to which the workers agreed.

55. Such as the end of the speech of the weaver Alekseev: "The muscular hand of millions of working people will rise and the yoke of despotism, protected by soldiers' bayonets, will scatter into dust." For the speech see *RD*, vol. 2, pt. 2, p. 47; for examples of its use in later agitation, see *RD*, vol. 4, pt. 1, pp. 203–204 and vol. 4, pt. 1, p. 333.

56. In February 1916 the Bolshevik Petrograd Committee proclaimed, "The government considers the Putilov plant the most dangerous for it, knowing that it always was the instigator of revolutionary acts of the Petersburg proletariat. And it is not wrong: so it always was, so will it be now." Quoted in E. N. Burdzhalov, *Vtoraia Russkaia Revoliutsiia* (Moscow: Nauka, 1967), p. 33.

57. For a moving example see the letter from a worker (Karelina) written eight years after Bloody Sunday. It can be found in *Krasnaia Letopis'*, vol. 1 (1922): 124–125. "Today is January 9. A momentous day for me personally, and this day for me will remain such for all my life, since hardly again in my life will it be necessary for me to live through what I experienced on January 9, 1905. Each year on this day I am possessed by a special feeling of some kind of burning anguish and sadness."

58. Sapronov, *Iz Istorii Rabochego Dvizheniia*, p. 15.

59. Akimov-Makhnovets, "Pervoe Maia v Rossii," p. 180.

60. Martov, *Zapiski*, p. 61. For another striking example, see pp. 115–116.

61. Herzen, *The Russian People and Socialism*, p. 194.

62. Kanatchikov, *Iz Istorii*, p. 190.

63. Wright Miller, *Russians as People* (London: Phoenix House, 1960), p. 35.

IV. PERSPECTIVES ON THE URBAN REVOLUTION IN 1917

1. Trotsky, *History*, 1: 425.

2. See George Katkov, *Russia 1917. The February Revolution* (New York: Harper & Row, 1967), p. 34. In an article summarizing the major points of view on the causes of the collapse of the Russian autocracy, Arthur Mendel discusses both the sources of breakdown attributed to the tsarist system itself and those connected with World War I. See "On Interpreting the Fate of Imperial Russia," in Theofanis Stavrou, ed., *Russia Under the Last Tsar* (Minneapolis: University of Minnesota Press, 1969), pp. 26, 34–36.

3. Karl Marx, *The Eighteenth Brumaire of Louis Bonaparte* (New York: International Publishers, 1963), p. 15.

4. See P. V. Volobuev, *Proletariat i Burzhuaziia Rossii v 1917 g.* (Moscow: Mysl', 1964), p. 20; and V. Ia. Laverychev, "Vliianie voiny na chislennost', sostav i polozhenie rabochego klassa," in Laverychev, ed., *Rabochii Klass Rossii, 1907–Fevral' 1917 g.* (Moscow: Nauka, 1982), pp. 290–293.

5. Laverychev, "Vliianie Voiny," p. 274.

6. For explanations of the rejection of proposals to militarize labor, see Lewis Siegelbaum, "The Workers' Groups and the War-Industries Committees: Who Used Whom?" in *Russian Review*, 39, no. 2 (April 1980): 153–154.

7. TsGIA, f. 1405, d. 543, op. 913, l. 694–705.

8. The war industries committee was created mainly at the initiative of Moscow industrialists as a foil to the St. Petersburg magnates for the purpose of organizing industry for the war effort. In addition to their economic activities to supplement the work of the often incompetent government, their explicit purpose was to foster a new climate of class cooperation in order to prevent anarchy in Russian industry. Despite considerable official skepticism, and for reasons that are not entirely clear, the Council of Ministers permitted the election of worker representatives to the committee.

9. I. P. Leiberov and O. I. Shkaratan, "K voprosu o sostave petrogradskikh promyshlennykh rabochikh v 1917 godu," *Voprosy Istorii* (January 1961), p. 52.

10. Ibid., p. 54.

11. Iu. I. Kir'ianov, *Rabochie Iuga Rossii. 1914—Fevral' 1917* (Moscow: Nauka, 1971), pp. 35–37.

12. The best account of the February revolution can be found in Tsuyoshi Hasegawa, *The February Revolution. Petrograd 1917* (Seattle: University of Washington Press, 1986). My conclusions are largely derived from Hasegawa's exhaustive analysis.

13. Trotsky, *History*, 3: 272.

14. For example, almost immediately after the striking women had marched to the neighboring metal factories (New Lessner and Erikson), socialist worker activists began to provide some leadership to the movement. Again the pattern was traditional: organizations did not initiate mass actions so much as guide them after they had broken out. With considerable ambivalence worker leaders in the metal factories decided to support the women and urged the workers in their factories to join the strike. "The spontaneous strike movement with economic demands now began to be transformed into a highly political demonstration led

by experienced, conscious elements of the working class" (Hasegawa, *February Revolution*, p. 218). The party intelligentsia, both Menshevik and Bolshevik, were initially completely cut off from events. In Ermanskii's phrase, they were nothing more than "specks of dust" in these stormy days (Ermanskii, *Iz Perezhitogo*, p. 148). They would only begin to guide the movement later.

15. See Allan Wildman, *The End of the Russian Imperial Army*, pp. 154–155.

16. Hasegawa, *February Revolution*, p. 567.

17. For the first view see Schapiro, *The Russian Revolutions of 1917* (New York: Basic Books, 1984), p. 81. Schapiro's account is typical of many works that emphasize the anarchic, unconscious, irrational actions of the workers, treating them as if they had arisen out of nowhere, with no prior conceptions or assumptions. For the second view see Mandel, *Fall of the Old Regime*, p. 3. Mandel does recognize the importance of culture, but the burden of his argument is to defend the means-end rationality of the workers during 1917.

13. RADICALISM IN THE CLASS STRUGGLE

1. Of course, this is not to say that all Russian industrial areas were equally radical. For example, Petrograd clearly outstripped Moscow. But if the rhythm of events was different, the outcomes were broadly similar. For the radicalization of Moscow workers, see Diane Koenker, *Moscow Workers and the 1917 Revolution* (Princeton: Princeton University Press, 1981). The same conclusion can probably be drawn for less important provincial centers as well, with the necessary qualifications. See Ronald Suny, *The Baku Commune 1917–1918* (Princeton: Princeton University Press, 1972); and idem, "Toward a Social History of the October Revolution," *American Historical Review* 88, no. 1 (1983): 47.

2. For the Chilean case, certainly the least known of the three, see Henry Landsberger and Timothy McDaniel, "Hypermobilization." In the case of Spain, after the Civil War began there was initially almost universal support for strong state power and the temporary sacrifice of the revolution in order to fight the war. The reemergence of radicalism in the spring of 1937, particularly in Barcelona, exacerbated the split within the labor movement, a process that culminated in the government's repression of the anarchists. These divisions were not simply partisan splits within the leadership but involved the worker rank and file. See Pierre Broué and Emile Temime, *The Revolution and the Civil War in Spain* (London: Faber and Faber, 1972), pp. 280–281.

3. Quoted in Dan, *Origins of Bolshevism*, p. 399.

4. Marx, *Eighteenth Brumaire*, p. 22.

5. *Torgovlia-Promyshlennaia Gazeta* [hereafter *TPG*], 7 March 1917, p. 2.

6. The Central War Industries Committee's response on 31 January 1917 to the arrest of the workers' group. This document can be found in Shliapnikov, *Semnadtsatyi God*, 1: 280–283.

7. *Rabochii Klass Urala v Gody Voiny i Revoliutsii v Dokumentakh i Materialakh* (Izdanie Uralprofsoveta Sverdlovsk, 1927), 2: 69. [Hereafter referred to as RKU]

8. *Rech'*, 9 March, pp. 5–6.

9. Examples can be found in TsGIA f. 150, op. 1, d. 685, l. 13; f. 48, op. 1, d. 38, l. 31; and A. Sivtsov, "Profdvizhenie sredi rabochikhkozhevnikov 1917–1918 g. g." in Anskii, *Professional'noe dvizhenie v. Petrograde*, p. 137.

10. Statement by Minister of Labor in *Vestnik Ministerstva Truda*, nos. 1–2 (August 1917): 1–2.

11. *TPG*, 8 April 1917. However, the mining industrialists of the Urals continued to oppose it because of its effects on production. Their 20 March memorandum can be found in TsGIA, f. 48, god 1917, op. 1, d. 39, l. 57–58.

12. Sometimes they were made in the interests of continuing production for the sake of national defense. See the Omsk Exchange Committee's memo in V. L. Meller and A. M. Pankratova, eds., *Rabochee Dvizhenie v 1917 Godu* (Moscow: Gosudarstvennoe Izdatel'stvo, 1926), p. 50. This organization regarded its concessions as a selfless sacrifice dictated by "state necessity."

13. For evidence on Petrograd, see Smith, *Red Petrograd*, p. 68. Koenker is more tentative for Moscow. She is surely right to point out the difficulty in coming to any general conclusions. Koenker, *Moscow Workers*, pp. 118–119.

14. Shliapnikov, *Semnadtsatyi God*, 1: 224.

15. For example, *Rech'*, 5 April 1917, p. 6; also *RKU*, 2: 56.

16. See L. S. Gaponenko, *Rabochii Klass Rossii v 1917 Godu* (Moscow: Nauka, 1970), p. 386; Koenker, *Moscow Workers*, pp. 295–296. Part of this decline was surely a result of the effectiveness of direct action.

17. G. L. Sobolev, *Revoliutsionnoe Soznanie Rabochikh i Soldat Petrograda v 1917 Godu* (Leningrad: Nauka, 1973), p. 80; Mark David Mandel, "The Development of Revolutionary Consciousness among the Industrial Workers of Petrograd between February and November 1917" (Ph.D. diss., Columbia University, 1977), pp. 184–185.

18. L. S. Gaponenko et al., eds., *Revoliutsionnoe Dvizhenie v Rossii Posle Sverzheniia Samoderzhaviia* (Moscow: Akademia Nauk, 1958), pp. 527–528.

19. *TPG*, 8 March 1917, p. 2.

20. V. I. Lenin, *Collected Works*, 4th ed. (Moscow: Progress Publishers, 1964), 24: 361.

21. *Delo Naroda*, 5 April 1917, p. 4.

22. G. K. Korolev, *Ivanovo-Kineshemskie Tekstil'shchiki*, p. 19. For other resolutions expressing the workers' demands for economic improvements, which were very common, see RG, 11 March 1917, p. 3, and *Pravda*, 27 April, pp. 3–4. As these examples show, some of these appeals were quite militant.

23. See the complaints of the Petrograd Society to the soviet on 17 March 1917. This agreement, it said, has quieted workers "only to the most insignificant degree." TsGIA, f. 150, op. 1, d. 511, l. 5.

24. Sobolev, *Revoliutsionnoe Soznanie*, pp. 70–72, and B. M. Friedlin, *Ocherki Istorii Rabochego Dvizheniia v Rossii v 1917 g.* (Moscow: Nauka, 1967), p. 248, claim that such removals were generally accomplished in an organized and disciplined manner. It is difficult to know how representative their examples are.

25. See the retrospective complaint in the socialist *Delo Naroda*, 11 August 1917, p. 1. Also see TsGIA f. 150, op. 1, d. 511, l. 5.

26. See Sivtsov, "Profdvizhenie sredi rabochikh kozhevnikov," pp. 137–138.

27. *Delo Naroda*, 7 April 1917, p. 4.

28. For examples, see Meller and Pankratova, *Rabochee Dvizhenie v 1917 Godu*, p. 42 and *Raionnye Sovety Petrograda v 1917 Godu*, 3 vols., ed. S. Valk et al. (Moscow-Leningrad: Nauka, 1964–1966) [hereafter referred to as *RS*] 1: 130–131.

29. See the excellent discussion in Smith, *Red Petrograd*, pp. 60–64.

30. *RKU*, 2: 57–58.

31. Statement of the worker Pakhomov at a general meeting of the Kolomenskii district soviet, October 5. *RS*, 1: 354.

32. Excellent accounts of the transformation of the labor movement in 1917 are now available for both Petrograd and Moscow. It is now no longer possible seriously to sustain Schapiro's view that the revolution was "in large measure that of the Lumpenproletariat" (Schapiro, *The Russian Revolutions of 1917*, p. 214). For Petrograd I have drawn primarily on the cited works of Smith, Devlin, and Mandel. Koenker gives a persuasive account of the radicalization of Moscow workers. Readers who want more than the present summary of these changes should consult these works.

33. On 18 April, Minister of Foreign Affairs Miliukov sent a note to the Allies assuring them that Russia would respect all of its obligations toward them. He did not mention Russia's new commitment to "peace without annexations or indemnifications." The note infuriated the moderate socialist leaders as well as large numbers of workers. On 20 and 21 April there were demonstrations in the capital demanding that the Soviet should take charge of the government's foreign affairs and that Miliukov and Guchkov be replaced. The crisis eventually led to the formation of the coalition government with the socialists.

34. Evidence for this assertion will be presented in the next chapter.

35. For an example of a strong worker statement blaming the bourgeoisie for for the war, see *RS*, 1: 150. The capitalists, it was alleged, directly profited from the war.

36. R. P. Browder and A. F. Kerensky, *The Russian Provisional Government, 1917: Documents* (Stanford: Hoover, 1965), 2: 672.

37. A. L. Sidorov et al., eds. *Ekonomicheskoe Polozhenie Rossii Nakanune Velikoi Oktiabr'skoi Sotsialisticheskoi Revoliutsii; Dokumenty i Materialy, Mart-Oktiabr' 1917 g.* [hereafter *Ekon. Pol.*], 2: 87.

38. For information on this see Koenker, *Moscow Workers*, p. 138.

39. Devlin, *Petrograd Workers*, p. 130; Koenker, *Moscow Workers*, pp. 118–119; Smith, *Red Petrogrod*, p. 116.

40. *Ekon. Pol.*, 2: 146.

41. Cited in William Rosenberg, *Liberals in the Russian Revolution* (Princeton: Princeton University Press, 1974), p. 139.

42. In addition, they were blamed for the war, the ultimate source of many of these evils. Sometimes workers also recognized their partial responsibility for the economic crisis, but this was clearly a secondary theme. See, for example, *Fabrichnozavodskie Komitety Petrograda v 1917 Godu. Protokoly* (Moscow: Nauka, 1979), pp. 81–82, [hereafter *Protokoly*], for a factory committee discussion on 1 August that admits the importance of the eight-hour day and the decline in intensity of work as key causes of the factory's declining productivity.

43. "From you, capitalists who cry crocodile tears, we demand that you stop

weeping about the catastrophe, when you yourselves created it." A resolution of Putilov workers from early August, in Okun, *Putilovets*, pp. 364–365.

44. Arguments along these lines are ubiquitous in documents and in the contemporary press.

45. The following resolution from 21 August expressed the perceived link between economic sabotage and political counterrevolution particularly clearly: the factory owners had the goal "not only of stopping the development of the revolution, but also of eliminating all the rights and property of the people and the working class won through it. To attain this goal they create masses of unemployed by closing factories and enterprises or by cutting back on work to an enormous degree. By means of repression they know that they can make obedient slaves from the hungry and disorganized masses of workers thrown out into the streets." D. A. Chugaev et al., eds., *Revoliutsionnoe Dvizhenie v Rossii v Avguste 1917 g. Razgrom Kornilovskogo Miatezha* (Moscow: Akademiia Nauk SSSR, 1959), p. 226.

46. 19 May resolution in Okun, *Putilovets*, p. 340.

47. *Golos Truda*, 6 May 1917, p. 2.

48. *Pechatnik*, 8 September 1917, pp. 2–3.

49. A reference to the tsarist state's repression of the remnants of the revolution after 1905.

50. The idea that the interests of the workers were the interests of the nation as a whole is found frequently in documents and resolutions. A good example is the appeal of the organizational bureau for the late May factory committee conference in Petrograd. See Meller and Pankratova, *Rabochee Dvizhenie v 1917 godu*, pp. 75–77.

51. For an excellent example, see Mandel, *Soviet Seizure of Power*, p. 268.

52. It is also worth noting two further considerations. The German workers had a prior model of socialization (Russia), and so in some ways their actions were less daring. Chilean workers had the benefit of an ambiguously sympathetic government, and the danger of repression appeared to be much less.

53. Smith, *Red Petrogrod*, pp. 190–196.

54. For an account of a meeting of a group of worker radicals in Moscow, see T. Sapronov, *Iz Istorii Rabochego Dvizheniia*, pp. 124–126.

55. For example, on the matter of interference in hiring and firing, the Organizational Bureau of Artillery Plants declared; "This is that right for which workers always struggled so hard and for which still not so long ago many of them paid cruelly." P. N. Amosov et al., eds., *Oktiabr'skaia Revoliutsiia i Fabzavkomy* (Moscow, 1927), 1: 31 (13 March meeting of Organizational Bureau).

56. See the description in V. Belokurova, "Ot rabochego kontrolia k rabochemu upravleniiu (Zavod 'Treugol'nik')," in Anskii, *Professional'noe Dvizhenie v Petrograde*, pp. 279–280.

57. TsGIA, f. 23, op. 29, d. 84, l. 6–7 (no date but appears to be late spring).

58. *Golos Truda*, 18 June 1917, p. 1.

59. A striking example of how the economic crisis made conflict irresolvable in the context of mutual suspicion is provided by the report of the board of directors of the I. I. Gen'' factory to the Ministry of Trade and Industry. Since late spring the workers had been making wage demands that even worker representa-

tives recognized were beyond the economic possibilities of the factory. A commission composed primarily of workers concluded that worker demands must be lowered by 30 percent in order to avoid bankruptcy. The board of directors agreed to make a variety of other concessions if the workers would agree, including a complete renunciation of the profits until 1 November (should there be any). The workers were not convinced, however, and continued to blame factory management, threatening them with violence. The board appealed to the government to protect it, for otherwise the factory would be obliged to close. TsGIA, f. 32, op. 1, d. 1892, l. 8–9 (24 August report).

60. See the account in Smith of the negotiations over the Petrograd metalworkers' collective contract, which the unskilled workers came close to jeopardizing. *Red Petrograd*, pp. 121 ff.

61. See Volobuev, *Proletariat*, pp. 239–243.

62. A. L. Sidorov et al., eds., *Revoliutsionnoe Dvizhenie v Rossii v Sentiabre 1917 g. Obshchenatsional'nyi Krizis* (Moscow: Akademiia Nauk SSSR, 1961), pp. 336–337.

63. See the fascinating account in Korolev, *Ivanovo—Kineshemskie Tekstil'shchiki*, pp. 41–44.

64. See Mandel, *Development of Revolutionary Consciousness*, pp. 495–501.

65. See John Keep, *The Russian Revolution—A Study in Mass Mobilization* (New York: Norton, 1976), pp. 84–95.

66. Vivid documents on the Putilov debates can be found in Okun, *Putilovets*, pp. 386–391 and 395–399. Worker leaders wanted to exercise control without taking responsibility for difficult measures. Their uncertainty and confusion are evident in these documents. Some workers wanted only partial control, whereas others favored the creation of a tripartite organization with government, industrialist, and worker participation.

67. *Metallist*, 18 October 1917, p. 12.

68. See the discussion in Smith, pp. 153–156. Smith convincingly refutes the traditional treatment of the movement for workers' control. According to this view, a syndicalist or anarchist labor movement demanded workers' management of industry. They were temporarily lured into support for the Bolsheviks, who squashed their ideals after the October revolution. Smith shows that worker sentiment was overwhelmingly in favor of strong central control of the economy. My own reading of the sources is in complete agreement with his judgment. See pp. 139–167.

69. This document can be found in Meller and Pankratova, *Rabochee Dvizheniev v 1917 Godu*, pp. 303–306.

70. See Alexander Rabinowitch, *The Bolsheviks Come to Power*, p. 218. Also see *RG*, a report on the Petergof united Social Democratic party meeting. Representatives spoke of the disappointment, apathy, and drunkenness of the workers. *RG*, 30 September, pp. 3–4.

71. Mandel, *Soviet Seizure of Power*, p. 282.

72. See 30 May speech in Amosov, *Oktiabr'skaia Revoliutsiia*, 1: 101. Voronkov received the most votes of any candidate in elections to the presidium of the conference.

73. Such views, we recall, also were often held by workers during the tsar's

reign, and they were occasionally expressed by government officials as well.

74. *RS*, 2: 106, 17 March general meeting of Petergof Soviet.

75. TsGIA, f. 1600, op. 1, d. 29, l. 20.

76. Another case suggesting the same conclusion can be found in TsGIA, f. 150, op. 1, d. 560, l. 45. The worker representatives to a conciliatory chamber hearing simply denied that the manager of the factory had much to do with plant productivity. Ferro suggests that these ideas were somehow related to the agrarian background of many workers. Just as the land should belong to those who worked it, so should the factory be run by the direct producers. Ferro offers little evidence, but it is certainly worth considering whether the peasant view of the nobility was connected with the worker view of factory administrators. See Marc Ferro, *La Révolution de 1917. Octobre. Naissance d'une Société* (Paris: Aubier-Montaigne), p. 289.

77. A good example can be found in TsGIA, f. 150, op. 1, d. 560., l. 33.

78. For example, see the remarks of Korolev *Ivanovo-Kineshemskie Tekstil-'shchiki*, p. 15.

79. *Tret'ia*, p. 207.

80. The workers' groups' view of the capitalist and the war can be found in TsGIA, f. 23, op. 27, d. 377, l. 84. For another example of a class interpretation of the war by workers (in spring 1916) see Burdzhalov, *Vtoraia Russkaia*, p. 34.

81. TsGIA, f. 1600, op. 1, d. 33.

82. TsGIA, f. 32, op. 1, d. 1928, l. 68. Later, the same representative declared: "We did not make the revolution and we did not struggle with counterrevolution in order to turn back from social reforms." Ibid., l. 82.

83. *TPG*, 21 May 1917, an 18 May speech in Rostov-on-Don.

84. See Volobuev, *Proletariat*, p. 58.

85. See Mandel, *Soviet Seizure of Power*, pp. 297, 325, for characteristic examples of references to the workers' "philistine" opponents.

86. See "Agrarnoe dvizhenie v 1917 godu po dokumentam glavnogo zemel-'nogo komiteta," *Krasnii Arkhiv* 14 (1926): 42–43.

87. *Pravda*, 27 April, p. 4.

88. See the comments of N. Dmitriev in "Primiritel'nye kamery v 1917 godu," in Anskii, *Professional'noe Dvizhenie v Petrograde*, pp. 79–80.

89. TsGIA, f. 150, op. 1, d. 560, l. 22.

90. TsGIA, f. 1600, op. 1, d. 28, l. 124.

91. Smith, *Red Petrograd*, p. 94.

92. *RS*, 3: 91.

93. Quoted in Smith, *Red Petrograd*, p. 97. Smith remarks that "there was a widespread belief within the labour movement that education and amusement were mutually exclusive."

94. Shliapnikov, *Semnadtsatyi God*, 1: 69.

95. *Rech'*, 8 March 1917, #57, p. 5.

96. *Pervyi Vserossiiskii S"ezd Sovetov Rabochikh i Soldatskikh Deputatov*, vol. 2, ed. V. N. Rakhmetov and N. P. Miamalin (Moscow-Leningrad: Gosudarstvennoe Sotsial'no-Ekonomicheskoe Izdatel'stvo, 1931), pp. 90–95.

97. TsGIA, f. 150, op. 2, d. 17, l. 1.

98. For this agreement see L. S. Gaponenko et al., eds., *Revoliutsionnoe*

Dvizhenie Posle Sverzheniia, pp. 242–243. It is discussed at length in Devlin, *Petrograd Workers,* pp. 44–50.

99. Browder and Kerensky, *Russian Provisional Government,* 2: 717.

100. Sivtsov, "Profdvizhenie sredi rabochikh Kozhevnikov," p. 137.

101. TsGIA, f. 126, op. 1, d. 4, l. 165–167.

102. For examples of these views, which are very widespread in the Menshevik press, see *RG,* 9 March 1917, p. 1 ("1905–1917") and 20 May 1917, p. 1.

103. *Proletarskii Prizyv,* 19 July 1917.

104. *Metallist,* 18 October 1917, p. 12.

105. *Pravda,* 25 March 1917, pp. 3–4.

106. For accounts of the conservatism of the unions and majority socialists and the development of a radical reaction to them, see Richard A. Comfort, *Revolutionary Hamburg* (Stanford: Stanford University Press, 1966), pp. 84–108; and David Morgan, *The Socialist Left and the German Revolution* (Ithaca, N.Y.: Cornell University Press, 1975), pp. 31–80.

107. See the introduction to *Protokoly,* p. 7.

108. *Protokoly,* passim.

109. *RS,* 2: 91.

110. The majority of soviets had more comprehensive responsibilities and constituted something more along the lines of a workers' parliament.

111. *RKU,* 2: 24, 36.

112. See A. M. Andreev, *Sovety Rabochikh i Soldatskikh Deputatov Nakanune Oktiabria* (Moscow: Nauka, 1967) pp. 97–111, for a description of many of these activities.

113. For good examples of local soviets' definitions of their tasks, see *RS,* 1: 183, 2: 113.

114. Estimates from the Third Trade Union Conference in June are as follows: 967 unions and 51 central bureaus, with 1,475,429 members. Rosenberg, using data from the Central Statistical Board, gives much lower figures: 650,000 members by July and 1,650,000 by the end of the year. William Rosenberg, "Workers and Workers' Control in the Russian Revolution," *History Workshop 5* (1978): 93. According to K. F. Shchatsillo, "Rabochee dvizhenie v gody pervoi mirovoi voiny," in Laverychev, *Rabochii Klass Rossii,* p. 365, more than 2,000 unions were formed in the first two months of the revolution.

115. Introduction to *Tret'ia,* p. vii.

116. See Morgan, *Socialist Left,* pp. 270, 272.

117. *RG,* 11 March 1917, p. 2.

118. Smith, *Red Petrograd,* pp. 132–133.

119. *RS,* 2: 226.

120. For examples see TsGIA, f. 150, op. 2, d. 61, l. 4; f. 1600, op. 1, d. 33, l. 18; and *RS,* 2: 286–287.

121. *TPG,* 8 September 1917, p. 2; *Metallist,* 18 October 1917, pp. 8–9; *Protokoly,* pp. 172–174.

122. The union representative Zholnerovich in *Tret'ia,* p. 218.

123. Meller and Pankratova, *Rabochee Dvizhenie v 1917 Godu,* p. 179. Also see *Pechatnik,* 11 June 1917, p. 3, and *Golos Truda,* 18 June 1917, p. 1.

124. *TPG,* 8 September 1917, p. 2.

125. See Koenker, *Moscow Workers*, pp. 320–325.

126. In many provincial centers the comments of Danilov, chairman of the Kostroma soviet executive committee, were probably apposite (November 1917): "In the provinces we are dealing with a backward mass of people unaccustomed to organization. The factory committees enjoy extremely little authority and trade unions are weak; and the same may be said of the party organizations." See *The Debate on Soviet Power, Minutes of the All-Russian Central Executive Committee of Soviets*, trans. and ed. John Keep (Oxford: Oxford University Press, 1979), p. 109. Nonetheless, organizations in the provinces sometimes faced less organized opposition and so played a large role in public affairs.

127. Not only new organizations have such problems. Michels held that the apathy of the masses was a general phenomenon encouraging bureaucratization. More established organizations, however, develop ways of minimizing the impact of grass-roots indifference—paid staffs emerge, dues become automatically deducted, and the like. Older institutions even thrive upon certain forms of mass apathy. The point at issue here is not so much a comparative one: it is simply that without professional staffs and a secure source of funds, and in great need of mass support because of the difficult tasks facing them, worker organizations in 1917 suffered from a disappointing level of mass commitment.

128. In addition to the examples given later, see *RS*, 2: 153, 220; *RS*, 3: 59, 61, 73.

129. "Moi zapiski" in *Pechatnik*, 6 August 1917, pp. 6–9. For similar remarks see the carpenter's statement cited in Smith, p. 196.

130. A newspaper report from *Ural'skii Rabochii* given in *RKU*, 2: 247–249. Also see this source, pp. 206–249, passim, for many other examples.

131. Koenker, *Moscow Workers*, pp. 171–183. Koenker's examples are mainly from soviets and unions.

132. Amosov, *Oktiabr'skaia Revoliutsiia*, 1: 163–254, especially pp. 187–192.

133. By contrast, Smith emphasizes the high percentage of workers who voted in factory committee elections, see *Red Petrograd*, (pp. 205–206). Perhaps his figures support a different judgment from the one given earlier, but it should also be noted that voting requires a relatively small degree of commitment, particularly if elections are held during working hours.

134. Okun, *Putilovets*, pp. 367–368.

135. An excellent example comes from the protocols of the secretary of the Putilov factory committee C. Ia. Bogdat'ev from 14 July. Bogdat'ev was unsuccessful in defending the factory committee from the complaints of workers over its alleged slowness in achieving wage increases. See Okun, *Putilovets*, pp. 352–357.

136. For such a complaint see *Pechatnik*, 8 September 1917, p. 8. Also, for examples of workers' failures to recognize collective wage agreements, see Smith, *Red Petrograd*, pp. 127–129. Smith sees impressive worker adherence to the wage agreements given the severity of the economic crisis.

137. TsGIA, f. 1600, op. 1, d. 33, l. 54 (5 August).

138. Serge Bricianer, *Pannekoek and the Workers' Councils* (St. Louis: Telos Press, 1978), pp. 273–274.

139. *Golos Truda*, 10 September 1917, p. 1.

140. TsGIA, f. 150, op. 1, d. 513, l. 8–10.

141. *Tret'ia*, pp. 197–198. Some delegates also expressed opposition to compulsory membership—see, for example, the statement of Volkov on p. 214. In the Urals some unions adopted a policy of compulsory membership even before October. Nonmembers were threatened with expulsion from the factory. See *RKU* 2: 42.

142. For several examples of irresponsible worker leadership, see Koenker, *Moscow Workers*, pp. 177–178. Also instructive is the 4 August incident at the Petergof district soviet, which ended in delegates' challenging each other to a duel (*RS*, 2: 235). The protocols of the local soviets include numerous complaints of poor attendance by elected worker representatives.

143. For examples see *RS*, 2: 218, and Smith, *Red Petrograd*, p. 66. For general remarks on this theme see *RG*, 16 May 1917, p. 2. The interrelations among the different kinds of organizations were a matter of great discussion and debate. The question was not resolved until after October. See Smith, *Red Petrograd*, pp. 185–189.

144. See *RG*, 7 June 1917, p. 2, which complained of the lack of interconnectedness of the unions. The situation was probably worse for factory committees.

145. For an example from a provincial factory near Moscow, see Ia. Grunt, "Kolomenskaia organizatsiia R.S.D.R.P (b) i oktiabr' 1917 g.," in *Put' k Oktiabriu. Sbornik Vospominanii, Statei i Dokumentov*, ed. S. Chernomordik and S. Polidorov (Moscow, 1923), p. 332.

146. See *RS*, 2: 259, 263. Also see Smith, *Red Petrograd*, p. 178. For other examples of worker organizations undermined by economic need, see Smith, ibid. p. 124, and Okun, *Putilovets*, p. 367.

147. *Ekon. Pol.*, 1: 563–564. A speaker in the session of the Special Conference of 23 September.

148. *Izvestiia Vserossiskogo Soiuza Obshchestv Zavodchikov i Fabrikantov* (19 October 1917), p. 1. [Hereafter *IZF*]

149. Several examples are given in Meller and Pankratova, *Rabochee Dvizhenie v 1917 Godu*, pp. 99–102.

150. *TPG*, 6 September, p. 3, and 12 September. For another example, see *Protokoly*, p. 300.

151. For examples, see *RG*, 11 August 1917, p. 4; *Pechatnik*, 8 September 1917, p. 8; *RS*, 2: 218; Smith, *Red Petrograd*, p. 127; TsGIA, f. 150, op. 2, d. 39, l. 68.

152. *Pechatnik*, 8 September 1917, p. 2.

153. *RKU*, 2: 240.

154. *Proletarii*, 18 August 1917, pp. 3–4. "With blood and iron. . . ."

155. For an authoritative Soviet view, see Volobuev, *Proletariat*, pp. 184–190. For hostile Western judgments see Ferro, *Octobre*, pp. 253–260 and Leo Lande, "The Mensheviks in 1917," in Leopold Haimson, ed., *The Mensheviks* (Chicago: University of Chicago Press, 1974), p. 41.

156. Even though socialist demands among the workers were very infrequent in the early period. Ferro, *The Russian Revolution of February 1917* (Englewood

Cliffs, N.J.: Prentice-Hall, 1972), p. 121.

157. TsGIA, f. 48, op. 1, d. 38, l. 78–80. For some examples (among many) of factory owner complaints about workers' extreme demands in May and June, see *TPG*, 21 May 1917, TsGIA, f. 1600, op. 1, d. 31, l. 14; f. 48, op. 1, d. 38, l. 88–89; f. 48, god 1917, op. 1, d. 39, l 104–105.

158. TsGIA, f. 48, op. 1, d. 38, l. 88.

159. For examples see Mandel, *Development of Revolutionary Consciousness*, p. 208; and TsGIA, f. 48, g. 1917, op. 1, d. 39, l. 104.

160. TsGIA, f. 150, op. 1, d. 683, l. 81.

161. Ibid., f. 150, op. 2, d. 25. There were, it is true, some opposing voices. These could sometimes be found in newspapers expressing the general viewpoint of the industrialists, such as *TPG* and *IZF*, but the specific articles appear to be written by members of the so-called bourgeois intelligentsia rather than by factory owners. For examples see *IZF*, 28 September 1917, pp. 1–2, and *TPG*, 14 June 1917, pp. 1–2.

162. *TPG*, 1 June 1917, p. 3.

163. For an example see TsGIA, f. 32, op. 1, d. 63, l. 177–178 (1 June statement of industrialist Fedorov at a conference of representatives of various industrialist organizations).

164. *RKU*, 2: 86.

165. TsGIA, f. 32, op. 1, d. 1943, l. 1.

166. See the statement of S. I. Khoronzhitskii, a factory owner representative to a board of conciliation: "Workers have old organizations, which now grow stronger from day to day; these organizations already have professional secretariats doing preparatory work, while we are in the sessions with empty hands, completely unprepared." The industrialists must organize quickly in order "to be equal with the workers, who at the present moment are stronger than us both politically and morally, and in all senses better organized." TsGIA, f. 150, op. 1, d. 562, l. 30.

167. TsGIA, f. 48, op. 1, d. 38, l. 85–86.

168. *IZF*, 14 September, p. 1.

169. The minister of Labor was attacked particularly harshly. For other examples of antigovernment sentiment, see TsGIA f. 48, op. 1, d. 38, l. 123; f. 1600, op. 1, d. 31, l. 132; f. 32, op. 1, d. 63, l. 109, l. 152; f. 32, op. 1, d. 27, l. 129–130; f. 23, op. 27, d. 377, l. 119–122; *TPG*, 27 September, p. 3. The second to last document, by Guzhon, is particularly bitter. After describing worker violence in his factory, he concludes: "And if this violence were to go further than the current removals in wheelbarrows, assaults, and other insults, then the role of the Moscow administration would be limited only to the registration of the fact that such great excesses were for the first time committed at the Moscow Metallurgical Plant."

170. TsGIA, f. 32, op. 1, d. 1943, l. 42.

171. *IZF*, 28 September, pp. 1–2.

172. *IZF*, 14 September, p. 1.

173. TsGIA, f. 32, op. 1, d. 63, l. 88.

174. For examples of the view that the economic crisis would resolve the labor question, see *TPG*, 1 June, p. 1; TsGIA, f. 32, op. 1, d. 63, l. 177–178; *Ekon.*

Pol., 1: 196–201. The last example is Riabushinskii's "bony hand of hunger speech" made to the Second All-Russian Trade-Industrial Congress on 3 August. After a gloomy account of the country's economic situation and the inefficacy of government policy, Riabushinskii declared that the industrialists were at that time powerless to influence the course of events. Their only alternative was to await with resignation the coming economic collapse, during which the "bony hand of hunger" would bring people to their senses. Only at that time could the industrialists act forthrightly to "save the Russian land" from the "deceivers of the people." The workers were quick to interpret the speech as an active threat rather than an expression of political helplessness.

175. TsGIA, f. 23, op. 27, d. 377, l. 121. No date is given, but it appears to be from July or August.

176. For example, *RKU*, 2: 275 (June 1917); TsGIA, f. 32, op. 1, d. 27, l. 121–122 (29 May).

177. TsGIA, f. 23, op. 29, d. 84, l. 44. No date is given, but it appears to be from July or August.

178. *RKU*, 2: 275–276; TsGIA, f. 32, op. 1, d. 27, l. 117–118.

179. TsGIA, f. 126, op. 1, d. 4, l. 165–167 (4 September); TsGIA, f. 32, op. 1, d. 240, l. 31.

180. "By mid-August both merchants and entrepreneurs were clamoring for a show of military force." Rieber, *Merchants and Entrepreneurs*, p. 411.

181. Council of the Congress of Mining Industrialists of the south on 2 August, *Ekon. Pol.* 1: 192–195.

182. The factory owners must have been truly disconcerted after incidents such as the following. In the Schliesselburg gunpowder factory, the local administration called in about 150 Cossacks to help protect the factory (in particular, its liquor supply). Unfortunately, the Cossacks quickly established good relations with both the local garrison of soldiers and the workers. They even started to go to factory meetings and to take an active part in them. "The administration is in despair. The factory director has been removed." *RG*, 18 August, p. 4. Some factory owners clearly recognized that the government simply did not have the power to defend them. See the remarks of Tret'iakov in TsGIA, f. 32, op. 1, d. 63, l. 119.

183. See the remarks of A. E. Gutt in *RKU*, 2: 275–276.

184. TsGIA, f. 32, op. 1, d. 27, l. 117–118.

185. TsGIA, f. 48, op. 1, d. 38, l. 88–89 (Urals); *TPG*, 1 June 1917, p. 3 (the south); f. 32, op. 1, d. 63, l. 184–186. The first of these proposals was particularly interesting. Price regulation should be brought about by means of industrial syndicates the activities of which would be controlled by government organs. It should be noted that there was no consensus among industrialists on this issue. Just as there had been major conflicts among different groups of industrialists during the war over the appropriate degree of government intervention in private industry, so such disputes continued throughout 1917. For example, the Petrograd Society of Factory Owners espoused considerable cooperation with the government, whereas the Committee for the Defense of Industry (composed of thirteen different financial and trade organizations) rejected any limitations on

private enterprise. These different approaches led to the Petrograd Society's refusal to join the new organization. TsGIA, f. 150, op. 1, d. 513, l. 14–150.

186. T. Shatilova, "Petrogradskoe Obshchestvo," describes how the society worked to ensure greater discipline among its members (pp. 102–103).

187. *Ekon. Pol.*, 1: 212–213, 585. The All-Russian Union of Societies of Factory and Plant Owners and the Main Committee of United Industry also attempted to work out a set of common principles. TsGIA, f. 126, op. 1, d. 4, l. 165–167; f. 48, op. 1, d. 38, l. 140.

188. V. I. Selitskii, *Massy v Bor'be za Rabochii Kontrol'* (Moscow: Mysl', 1971), p. 135; Volobuev, *Proletariat*, pp. 305–307. Of course, it is not easy to distinguish closings for economic reasons from closings as a strategy to restore discipline.

189. Many precarious factories must simply have been unable to meet the workers' demands. For example, the management of the Bogoslovskoe factory announced to the workers that it would not raise wages even if such increases were mandated by conciliatory chambers. They claimed that there was no money for further increases, and so informed the workers that the factory would be closed if further increases were awarded. TsGIA, f. 48, god 1917, op. 1, d. 39, l. 161–162.

190. Smith, *Red Petrograd*, p. 169.

191. A Ministry of Labor commission traced improvements in worker productivity in the Dinamo factory of Petrograd to threats to close the plant. The workers began to look on things differently, the report claimed, and there had been a significant increase in productivity. TsGIA, f. 1600, op. 11, d. 29, l. 24 (July).

192. Sometimes the threat of plant closures was intended to make the government restore order. For example, the Urals industrialist organization warned that if the local administration did not defend the legal demands of the owners, the latter would be forced to close factories as the only means of combating worker militancy. TsGIA, f. 48, op. 1, d. 38, l. 138.

193. TsGIA, f. 48, op. 1, d. 38, l. 177–178.

194. *IZF*, 14 September 1917, p. 1.

195. This was true even for the Petrograd Society. See Shatilova, "Petrogradskoe Obshchestvo," p. 106.

196. Rieber, *Merchants and Entrepreneurs*, p. 411.

197. Victor Chernov, *The Great Russian Revolution* (New York: Russell and Russell, 1966), p. 228.

14. THE WORKERS AND THE STATE IN 1917

1. In this the situations in France, China, Vietnam, and Iran (among others) were very different. In *The European Revolution* Tocqueville points out that the nobility was able to gain much popular support before the revolution because of their outspoken criticism of the government, despite the fact that their goals were totally at variance with those of the masses (p. 44). Something similar happened in the Russian revolution with the mounting criticism of the government by the

liberal opposition, but their public role was much less preponderant than that of their French counterparts.

2. See the works of Devlin, Koenker, Keep, Mandel, Rabinowitch, and Smith. Readers are referred to these works for accounts of the major events.

3. *Sed'maia (Aprel'skaia) Vserossiiskaia Konferentsiia RSDRP (Bol'shevikov). Protokoly* (Moscow: Gosudarstvennoe Izdatel'stvo, 1958), p. 132. [Hereafter referred to as *April Conference*]

4. *April Conference*, p. 134. The Moscow city delegate at the April conference denied that Moscow and Petrograd had a "corrupting" influence. The soviets still had many complicated tasks to accomplish, such as the unification of the soldiers and workers. Life had to be reconstructed on new principles, and the revolution had to be broadened and deepened. In the meantime, the bourgeoisie could share some of this burden (pp. 136–137).

5. Dune, "Zapiski Krasnogvardeitsa," pp. 32–33.

6. *April Conference*, pp. 259–260; also see Lenin, *Collected Works*, 24: 295–296.

7. *Shestoi S"ezd RSDRP (Bol'shevikov). Protokoly* (August 1917) (Moscow: Gosudarstvennoe Izdatel'stvo, 1958), pp. 21–22. [Hereafter referred to as *Shestoi*.]

8. *April Conference*, p. 139.

9. So said Stalin, representing the Central Committee, in his defense of its policies after the July days. *Shestoi*, p. 27.

10. Rabinowitch, *The Bolsheviks Come to Power*, p. 139.

11. TsGIA, f. 1600, op. 1, d. 3, l. 66–67 (24 March).

12. TsGIA, f. 32, op. 1, d. 1843, l. 23 (27 March).

13. Miliukov, *Russia and Its Crisis*, p. 66.

14. In Meller and Pankratova, *Rabochee Dvizhenie v 1917 Godu*, p. 31. A Pavlovskii officer described the mood of the soldiers in a similar way: "In their eyes, what has occurred is not a political but a social revolution, which in their opinion they have won and we have lost." Wildman, *End of the Russian Imperial Army*, p. 245.

15. The anarchy of the Russian workers used to be a virtual postulate of Western work on the revolution. More recent work has shown that whatever the incidence of indiscipline and disorder, there was also a desire for a strong workers government to control spontaneity. Also there was little principled adherence to anarchism.

16. For examples, see *Metallist*, 18 October 1917, pp. 5–7; and *Proletarskii Prizyv*, 20 September, p. 4.

17. Dune, "Zapiski Krasnogvardeitsa," pp. 35, 42; also see Amosov, *Oktiabr-'skaia Revoliutsiia*, 1: 123.

18. See Mandel, *Soviet Seizure of Power*, p. 282.

19. Other isolated groups of socialist intelligentsia had similar ideas. See Hasegawa, *February Revolution*, pp. 332–334.

20. Burdzhalov, *Vtoraia Russkaia Revoliutsiia*, p. 306.

21. Hasegawa, *February Revolution*, has an illuminating discussion of this deeper meaning of dual power. My analysis owes a great deal to his argument. See, for example, his remarks on p. 583.

22. Sometimes the criticism came from local soviets. For examples see *RS*, 3: 10, and 2: 28.

23. Friedlin, *Ocherki*, p. 56.

24. TsGIA, f. 1600, op. 1, d. 3, l. 3–4. No date, but from the context it seems to be late September or early October.

25. For powerful statements in this regard see *RS*, 2: 203–204 and 3: 203–204.

26. The resolution of the workers of the Dar'inskoe Donets corporation is interesting for the light it sheds on the workers' new mentality: "We, accustomed to carry our labor to the altar of the fatherland not under the bayonet or the whip, not under arbitrary violence, but as free citizens" protest against the dispatch of Cossacks "with all the fibers of our soul." Meller and Pankratova, *Rabochee Dvizhenie v 1917 Godu*, p. 231.

27. For other resolutions and statements see *RS*, 1: 341; Amosov, *Oktiabr-'skaia Revoliutsiia*, vol. 2, speech of Evdokimov at Third Petrograd factory conference, 10 September; Meller and Pankratova, *Rabochee Dvizhenie v 1917 Godu*, pp. 97–98. Also see the statement by the anarchist Voline cited in Ferro, *Octobre*, pp. 58–59. This was also a favorite theme of Lenin's. He frequently used phrases such as "The 'Stolypins' Kerensky and Co." See 26: 122. Other examples are in 24: 57–59, 122, 162.

28. Dune, "Zapiski Krasnogvardeitsa," pp. 33–34.

29. See the debates in Amosov, *Oktiabr'skaia Revoliutsiia*, 2: 127–128. For another example see *Perepiska Sekretariata TsK RSDRP (b) s Mestnymi Partiiny-mi Organizatsiiami (Mart—Oktiabr' 1917)* (Moscow: Gosudarstvennoe Izdatel-'stvo, 1957), p. 213 [hereafter *Perepiska*]. Workers and soldiers from Cheliabinsk accepted the upcoming elections but nonetheless avowed that the participation of Kadets and privileged groups in it was unacceptable. The new government, they declared, should be drawn solely from the revolutionary proletariat and laboring peasants, and it should take "merciless" measures against the capitalists. Also see V. Kaiurov, "Oktiabr'skie Ocherki." *Proletarskaia Revoliutsiia*, No. 7 (July 1925): 149.

30. Mandel, *Soviet Seizure of Power*, p. 352.

31. That is how the Council of the Association of Representatives of Trade and Industry addressed the Duma on 2 March. It referred to the great feat of the Duma, "which led the army and the people to victory over the old regime and to the freedom of Russia." TsGIA, f. 32, op. 1, d. 27, l. 40.

32. For this reason, said a report on the situation in the provinces after February, there was great sentiment against dual power. People were willing to support any strong authority no matter what its source. "Agrarnoe dvizhenie," p. 36.

33. See his revealing remarks on revolutions in his memoirs: "I was still [during World War I] a historian—and I studied the history of social movements. I could not help knowing that a certain dynamism existed in these movements which was independent of personal will. Even if I had not known this, my own experience of 1905 would have taught it to me. At that time I had sensed the vanity of my own personal efforts to direct the impulsive current of revolution into a channel for conscious utilization. And now what was in the making threatened to take on much greater dimensions than before. It was precisely in

these months that I reread Taine—with a different attitude than when I had compared him to Michelet during my student years. Our Russian experience was sufficient to snatch the halo from 'revolution' as such and to destroy its mystique, in my eyes at least. I knew that my place was not there." Miliukov, *Political Memoirs*, p. 320.

34. Ibid., p. 410. Also see Hasegawa, *February Revolution*, pp. 532–533.

35. N. N. Sukhanov, *The Russian Revolution 1917*, vol. 1 (New York: Harper, 1962), p. 145.

36. Rosenberg, *Liberals*, p. 137.

37. According to an April 1916 police report, the industrialists' suspicions were the following: (1) they feared an alliance between the liberal intelligentsia and the workers and revolutionaries; and (2) they opposed the Kadets' emphasis on state intervention in the economy. These suspicions were evident in their hostility toward the workers' groups of the war industries committees. For the police report see B. Grave, *K Istorii Klassovoi Bor'by v Gody Imperialisticheskoi Voiny* (Moscow-Leningrad: Gosudarstvennoe Izdatel'stvo, 1926), pp. 99–100.

38. Miliukov writes: "It [the Kadets] was not a party of the 'capitalists' nor was it a party of the 'landowners', as hostile propaganda tried to portray it. It was a 'supra-class' party which did not exclude even those supraclass elements which were found in socialism." *Political Memoirs*, pp. 414–415.

39. See, for example, Rosenberg's comments on Minister of Finance Konovalov's economic policy. Rosenberg, *Liberals*, p. 81.

40. An unsigned comment in *Rabochii Put'*, 6 September 1917, p. 3.

41. Quoted in Ferro, *February 1917*, p. 222. Ferro gives a good account of the debates in pp. 219–226.

42. Browder and Kerensky, *Russian Provisional Government*, 3: 1267–1268.

43. Amosov, *Oktiabr'skaia Revoliutsiia*, 2: 18–21.

44. See Rosenberg, *Liberals*, pp. 138–142.

45. Quoted in Lionel Kochan, *Russia in Revolution 1890–1918* (London: Granada, 1970), p. 256.

46. *Rech'*, 8 March, p. 5. The connection between reform and labor productivity was also a favorite theme of the Mensheviks—for example, see Tseretelli's remarks in *Vserossiiskoe Soveshchanie Sovetov Rabochikh i Soldatskikh Deputatov* (Moscow-Leningrad: Gosudarstvennoe Izdatel'stvo, 1927), p. 43.

47. *Rech'*, 30 March 1917, p. 2.

48. For this reason Ministry of Trade and Industry official Varzar refused to consider the Soviet's request for the requisition of a firm owned by the John Graves Stock Co.—it was against the law. *Delo Naroda*, 3 May 1917, p. 3.

49. *TPG*, 27 April, p. 2.

50. According to Minister Skobolev, virtually all the efforts of his ministry from its first days of activity were directed toward resolving labor conflict. See his 7 June speech in *Pervyi S"ezd*, 1: 230. An activist stance at this early stage might have convinced the workers that the ministry was ready to defend their interests.

51. *Vestnik*, p. 65.

52. *Pervyi S"ezd*, 22 June session, 2: 252.

53. 16 September speech at the Democratic Conference as reported in *RG*, 17 September 1917, p. 2.

54. Quoted in Koenker, *Moscow Workers*, p. 120.

55. TsGIA, f. 32, op. 1, d. 1928, l. 66–68. Skobolev may well have been convinced that the two sides were irreconcilable, perhaps mostly because of worker intransigence. A prominent industrialist, I. K. Kul'man, reported that Skobolev had told him privately that the workers had no ideology, only class egoism of a zoological nature. TsGIA, f. 32, op. 1, d. 63.

56. Skobolev speech at *Pervyi S"ezd*, 1: 92. For other examples of the minister's statist point of view see the 27 June appeal reprinted in *Vestnik*, pp. 1–2, and the summary of his speech in the protocols of the 30 May conference of factory committees in Amosov, *Oktiabr'skaia Revoliutsiia*, 1: 83. With admirable consistency Skobolev made the same basic points on all of these occasions.

57. *Pervyi S"ezd*, 1: 235. Earlier in the same congress Tseretelli had justified the delays in the same way. Ibid., p. 62.

58. Volobuev, *Proletariat*, p. 333.

59. See the report on an interministerial conference in *TPG*, 17 May, p. 4.

60. TsGIA, f. 23, op. 27, d. 360, l. 125–126 (June). Some of the grounds for the industrialists' opposition are of interest: factory owners were not allowed to use lockouts or blacklists; they could not fire workers during strikes; vital branches of industry were not protected from strikes; and only individuals, not organizations, were punishable for excesses.

61. TsGIA, f. 23, op. 27, d. 346, l. 1–2. (This was an 11 October report, "The labor question in the Ministry of Trade and Industry").

62. Browder and Kerensky, *Russian Provisional Government*, 2: 669.

63. *RG*, 2 July 1917, p. 1.

64. *RG*, 4 July, p. 1.

65. See *Vestnik*, especially the final section, "Activity of the Ministry of Labor."

66. See the description in *Vestnik*, pp. 3–10. Among the commissars listed in the *Vestnik* we find the name of S. I. Kanatchikov, the worker memoirist (p. 45).

67. See the description in *RG*, 13 October 1917, p. 3.

68. The attitude to tsarist labor laws was also ambivalent. On one hand, the Ministries of Trade and Industry and of Labor both committed themselves to the development of a whole new set of basic principles. Meanwhile, in the absence of new legislation they often had to rely on the old. Thus at the Third Petrograd Factory Committee Conference Kolokol'nikov, with his customary lack of tact, said that the Ministry of Labor must observe the old laws that had not been canceled, even if they were bad. Amosov, *Oktiabr'skaia Revoliutsiia*, 2: 18–21.

69. Kolokol'nikov also remarked, in good Marxist or classical liberal fashion, that the government was powerless to change the position of the working class, for any improvement must stem from a basic change in the relations of social forces in the society. Workers should not place much hope in the Ministry of Labor but should develop their own source of independent power. Ibid.

70. TsGIA, f. 23, op. 27, d. 355, l. 9. (7 August). Similarly, the following example of disregard for the law is interesting for its pedestrian character, indicating that abuses were a matter of course. The Ministry of Labor's Department of Labor and Capital wrote the Perm labor commissar that worker organizations were prohibited from exercising "control functions" unless the factory

owner agreed or the government gave its authorization. Because the government had no legal right to make such an authorization, the Urals Industrialist Association decided to lodge an official protest. TsGIA, f. 48, op. 1, d. 38, l. 153. See Hannah Arendt, *On Revolution* (New York: Penguin, 1977), p. 90: "Measured against the immense sufferings of the immense majority of the people, the impartiality of justice and law, the application of the same rules to those who sleep in palaces and those who sleep under the bridges of Paris, was like a mockery."

71. Factory owner complaints abound in the documents. An almost hysterical example is Guzhon's 9 June letter to the Ministry of Trade and Industry: TsGIA, f. 23, op. 27, d. 377, l. 119–122.

72. A number of examples can be found in *Ekon. Pol.*, 1: 544–571.

73. Lenin, *Collected Works*, 24: 361.

15. Workers and Social Democracy in 1917

1. The Socialist Revolutionaries, heirs of the Populists, had a great deal of support but little capacity to lead. Unlike the two Marxist parties, they had no coherent ideology, and worker support for them in 1917—especially in the early period—often signified support for the revolution in general. Workers who nominally supported the Socialist Revolutionaries very frequently favored the Bolshevik interpretation of the revolution without being aware of the contradiction with the party's official moderate position. (For evidence see Mandel, *Soviet Seizure of Power*, pp. 252, 291; also see Trotsky, *History*, 1: 173.) Trotsky's judgment on the nature of SR support remains unsurpassed: "A party for whom everybody votes except that minority who know what they are voting for, is no more a party, than the tongue in which babies of all countries babble is a national language. The Social Revolutionary Party came forward as a solemn designation for everything in the February revolution that was immature, unformulated and confused." (Trotsky, *History*, 1: 217) Toward October the party became increasingly divided and even less able to lead the workers or the revolution.

2. Alexander Rabinowitch, *Prelude to Revolution. The Petrograd Bolsheviks and the July 1917 Uprising* (Bloomington: Indiana University Press, 1968), p. 104.

3. In *Vtoraia i Tret'ia Petrogradskie Obshchegorodskie Konferentsii Bol'shevikov v Iiule i Oktiabre 1917 g.*, ed. P. F. Kudelli (Moscow-Leningrad: Gosudarstvennoe Izdatel'stvo, 1927), pp. 61–64 [hereafter referred to as *July POK* and *October POK*]. Volodarskii cites this as one example of the general lack of knowledge of party differences among the mass base.

4. For example, see *Perepiska*, p. 108, 114, 121.

5. *RKU*, 2:30.

6. *Perepiska*, pp. 164–165.

7. *October POK*, 8 October. Statement by Kharitonov.

8. For example, in Petrograd many trade union activists had Menshevik leanings, whereas in Moscow the Bolsheviks had a strong base from the beginning. Bonnell, The Politics of Labor in Pre-Revolutionary Russia: Moscow Workers' Organizations 1905–1914 (Ph.D. diss., Harvard University, 1975), p. 352.

9. *RS*, 1: 123, 3: 179–180.

10. *RKU*, 2: 94–95.

11. TsGIA, f. 32, op. 1, d. 1941, l. 20–2. This statement was made in a government commission on the rights of workers' committees. Factory owners claimed the right to control the admission of people from outside the factory.

12. For a similar judgment see Leonard Schapiro, *The Communist Party of the Soviet Union*, 2d ed. (New York: Vintage, 1971), p. 25. Also see Lande, "The Mensheviks in 1917," pp. 12–13. The masses' wish for socialist unity "was not to die easily even after October." Also see Koenker, *Moscow Workers*, p. 190.

13. See Moiseenko's remark: "I hoped that all parties could be combined into one for the good of the people and not fan party squabbles which could lead us to ruin" (*Vospominaniia Starogo*, p. 226).

14. *RS*, 2: 46.

15. *RS*, 1: 212–217.

16. Thus the Tube factory decided to give the following donations at a 28 June general meeting: All-Russian Congress of Peasant Deputies—20,000 rubles; All-Russian Congress of Workers and Soldiers Deputies—20,000 rubles; Petrograd Soviet of Workers and Soldiers Deputies—15,000 rubles; Socialist Revolutionary party press—5,000 rubles; Bolshevik press—5,000 rubles; Menshevik press—5,000 rubles; Internationalist press—3,000 rubles; Maximalists—2,500 rubles; anarchists—2,500 rubles; Bureau of Trade Unions—5,000 rubles; the organization of Red Guards—5,000 rubles; Vasiliostrovskii district soviet—2,000 rubles. *RG*, 13 July, p. 4.

17. *RS*, 1: 350–355. The quotation is from p. 354.

18. For examples see *RS*, 1: 201–203, 9, 15.

19. *RS*, 3: 192.

20. Grunt recounts the story of a young Socialist Revolutionary leader who, either out of "simplicity of soul" or stupidity, wrote an article advocating the Bolshevik land program. This gave Grunt the chance to accuse the Socialist Revolutionaries of stealing the Bolshevik program and to undermine their influence. Grunt, "Kolomenskaia," p. 333.

21. See Smith, *Red Petrograd*, p. 160; Trotsky, *History*, 1: 391. For Petrograd trade unions see Bruk, "Organizatsiia soiuza metallistov," pp. 118–119. Also see Koenker, *Moscow Workers*, p. 193, for Moscow.

22. Thus Kubikov, a Menshevik, complained that the workers' personalism meant that individual party organizations became either all Menshevik or all Bolshevik. See *RG*, 17 August 1917, pp. 1–2.

23. For examples see *Shestoi*, p. 81; *April Conference*, p. 126; Sapronov, *Iz Istorii*, p. 123; Shliapnikov, *Semnadtsatyi God*, 1: 203–204.

24. Shliapnikov also pointed to the importance of the all-national mood. See *Semnadtsatyi God*, 1: 203–204. For a recent Soviet analysis see Shchatsillo, "*Rabochii klass v fevral'skoi Revoliutsii*," p. 350. Smith and Mandel agree that the general revolutionary mood influenced workers' attitudes.

25. Quoted in Lande, "The Mensheviks in 1917," p. 27.

26. Ibid., p. 26.

27. *RG*, 12 May 1917, p. 3. This resolution also justified the need for a broad program of labor reform by appealing to the workers' historical weakness as an

organized movement—all the more reason, it was argued, for a broad government program.

28. *RG*, 5 April 1917, pp. 1–2.

29. See, for example, Ivan Kubikov's article in *RG*, 31 May, p. 3. For a similar view of the workers' backwardness and low cultural level, see N. Rostov's article in *RG*, 29 June 1917, pp. 1–2.

30. V. Grinevich in *Pechatnik*, 28 November 1917, pp. 2–4.

31. From an 11 July worker resolution in *RG*, 23 July 1917, pp. 3–4.

32. *Rabochaia Gazeta* sometimes published accounts of violence among workers, including threats of drowning or incinerating opponents, always portraying the "anarchistic" elements as betrayers of worker unity. The unity they celebrated, however, was based on a partisan vision that had increasingly less relevance to the workers themselves. For a good example see *RG*, 20 May 1917, p. 1.

33. Ermanskii, *Iz Perezhitogo*, p. 74.

34. TsGIA, f. 23, op. 24, d. 84, l. 146.

35. Grunt, "Kolomenskaia," p. 335.

36. *Shestoi*, p. 56.

37. I. K. Naumov, *Zapiski Vyborzhtsa* (Leningrad: Lenoblizdat, 1933), p. 24.

38. For example, in B. I. Gorev's article in *RG*, 25 April, pp. 1–2. The moderate socialists, he warned, "would lose that influence, that moral authority, which they have among the masses."

39. *RG*, 11 July, p. 3.

40. *RG*, 8 August, p. 2.

41. *RG*, 27 July, p. 2.

42. Mandel makes this point. See *Development of Revolutionary Consciousness*, pp. 423 ff., for evidence.

43. Charles Rougle, "The Intelligentsia Debate in Russia 1917–1918," in *Art, Society, Revolution. Russia 1917–1921* Nils Nilsson, ed., (Stockholm: Almquist & Wiksell International, 1979), p. 68. For examples see pp. 68–69. For peasant hostility toward the intelligentsia, even to teachers whom they had previously elected to represent them and whom they respected, see "Agrarnoe dvizhenie," p. 42.

44. For an excellent example of such allegations, see Rostov's article in *RG*, 29 June, pp. 1–2.

45. Hasegawa, *February Revolution*, p. 338.

46. The anarchist worker Renev, quoted in Devlin, *Petrograd Workers*, p. 313. For other examples see Mandel, *Soviet Seizure of Power*, pp. 317, 341.

47. For example see *April Conference*, p. 153. Also Koenker shows that in the June Moscow duma elections, the Bolsheviks had significantly more worker candidates than the Mensheviks or the Socialist Revolutionaries. Mandel strongly agrees that the Bolsheviks were much more a workers' party than their rivals.

48. For an excellent expression of this view, see Grinevich in *Pechatnik*, 28 November, pp. 2–4.

49. See Lande, "The Mensheviks in 1917," pp. 36–37. The parallel with the views of some industrialists is clear: in both cases, a refusal to believe that social-

ism was conceivable in Russia at the time, and thus a faith that things would turn in their favor.

50. Speech of the worker Tkachenko in 30 May factory committee conference. His speech is an excellent example of the reasoning of this stratum of moderate workers. Amosov, *Oktiabr'skaia Revoliutsiia*, 1: 102–104.

51. For examples see *Proletarskii Prizyv*, 3 August 1917, p. 11; *RS*, 1: 354; *RG*, 25 July 1917, p. 2; *Pechatnik*, 28 November 1917, p. 6.

52. The clearest examples of this viewpoint I have located are in *RG*, 20 August 1917, p. 2, article by P. Golikov; and *Proletarskii Prizyv*, 3 August, p. 4.

53. *Proletarskii Prizyv*, 3 August 1917, p. 4.

54. *Rabochaia Mysl'*, it will be recalled, was the name of the newspaper so heavily attacked by Lenin and others for its economism around the turn of the century. Two issues of the new *Rabochaia Mysl'* appeared, one dated 25 August 1917, the other 23 September 1917. The goal of the new journal, proclaimed the editorial announcement, was the consolidation of the forces of the "workers' intelligentsia," in order to free the labor movement and its vanguard, the Social Democratic party, from the "counterrevolutionary influence of anarcho-syndicalism, which is fed by the economic backwardness of the country and the political immaturity of the masses." It sought to combat all utopian tendencies in the labor movement, which should be founded on the principles of scientific socialism and the experience of the Western and Russian labor movements. See no. 1 (25 August 1917), p. 1.

55. The pages of *Rabochaia Mysl'* are a rich source for the views and sentiments of the Menshevik workers' intelligentsia. The articles chronicle the despair of this narrow stratum, superior in consciousness (the journal claimed) to its Western counterparts, yet isolated between the dark masses, motivated purely by passion, and the utopian Leninists, who only wanted to use the workers for their own unrealizable goals. "There is something terribly painful in his influence on the masses not of the leading proletariat, tied in one degree or another to workers, but of people completely foreign to them" (25 August 1917, p. 6). But the worker elite should not give way to "spiritual exhaustion." Though weak in numbers, it is armed with knowledge and experience, and so can counter the work of the Leninists to some degree. "And if our work is powerless to create a change in the mood of the worker masses, then we will be vindicated before the court of history, for then we can say: for our part we did all we could in the name of the salvation of the revolution" (ibid., p. 7).

56. For a similar judgment see Lande, "The Mensheviks in 1917," p. 37.

57. For such a charge see the factory resolution in *RG*, 23 July, pp. 3–4.

58. Examples can be found in *Pechatnik*, 8 September 1917, pp. 2–3; *Metallist*, 18 October, p. 12; *RS*, 3: 195–196 (17 August).

59. See, for example, *RG*, 26 July 1917, p. 4.

60. *Shestoi*, p. 72 (28 July speech).

61. Sapir gives this paraphrased version of the letter. Boris Sapir, "Notes and Reflections on the History of Menshevism," in Haimson, *The Mensheviks*, p. 372.

62. Speech of the worker Iuknevich, *RS*, 1: 277.

63. Trotsky, *History*, 1: 298.

64. Even Charles Bettelheim underestimates it in his judgment that the workers' and Bolsheviks' views corresponded only to an agreement on "immediate tasks." Charles Bettelheim, *Class Struggles in the USSR. First Period: 1917–1923* (New York: Monthly Review Press, 1976), p. 95. According to Getzler, the Bolsheviks made "an all-out effort to pander to the primitive needs, class-instincts and hatreds of the masses and to win them over to their side." (*Martov*, p. 165) This latter kind of judgment, common in Western interpretations, is a completely inadequate account of the nature of the workers' political beliefs and culture. Further, it is difficult to take seriously the concept of "class instinct."

65. *April Conference*, p. 65.

66. Lenin, *Collected Works*, 25: 21. At the April Conference there had been long debates on the question of the nature of the Russian revolution. Kamenev disagreed with Lenin's contention that the bourgeois revolution had already ended.

67. An appeal of the Kolomenskii district committee about elections to the city duma (no date given). Grunt, "Kolomenskaia," p. 337.

68. Lenin, *Collected Works*, 25: 29–30. This is one of Lenin's recurrent themes.

69. Lenin sometimes charged that the Provisional Government was preparing the ground for the restoration of the monarchy. For example, *Collected Works*, 24; 32.

70. For pungent remarks on the evils of freedom of the press and suggested measures to combat it, see Lenin, *Collected Works*, 25: 378–383.

71. Ibid., 24: 547 (31 May).

72. See Robert Service, *The Bolshevik Party in Revolution* (London: Macmillan, 1979), pp. 53–54.

73. See, for example, *Pravda*, 7 March 1917, pp. 2–3. The Provisional Government was different from the tsarist government only in that it was more flexible and willing to make concessions. "It does not stand for the revolution, but · against it." Also see 9 March, p. 3, lead article, "Taktiki revoliutsii," 11 March, p. 1, "Vtoroe napadenie." The arrival of Stalin and Kamenev led to the paper's less militant stance toward the government. Also, see Trotsky's argument that Lenin's positions accorded with "the living tradition of the party—its irreconcilable attitude to the ruling classes and its hostility to all half-way measures." Trotsky, *History*, 1: 304.

74. *Tret'ia*. See the opening speech by Miliutin, who demanded a choice between the Bolsheviks and their opponents on this basis.

75. See "Protokoly Moskovskogo Oblastnogo Komiteta RSDRP (b) za mai i iiun' 1917 g," *Proletarskaia Revoliutsiia*, 4 (April 1927): 257. [Hereafter MOK]

76. Lenin, *Collected Works*, 25: 120.

77. In this regard see ibid., 24: 236.

78. *IZF*, 19 October 1917, p. 1.

79. Trotsky, *History*, 3: 170.

80. T. H. Rigby, *Communist Party Membership in the USSR, 1917–1967* (Princeton: Princeton University Press, 1968), pp. 63–68; Service, *The Bolshevik Party*, pp. 43–44. Even at the Sixth Party Congress 70 out of 171 people answering the survey were workers (23 were without definite professions); the next most

numerous category was white-collar workers, with 22 representatives. See *Shestoi*, pp. 294–300.

81. *Shestoi*, p. 45.

82. *July POK*, p. 12; also see *October POK*, p. 111, for similar complaints that "the organization is truly experiencing a tragedy."

83. *Perepiska, p. 273.*

84. Sapronov, *Iz Istorii*, p. 126.

85. *Pravda*, 4 May, pp. 2–4, "Ob 'anarkhii.'"

86. *Minutes*, p. 48.

87. Lenin, *Collected Works*, 24: 358.

88. *Rabochii Put'*, 19 September, p. 10.

89. *Minutes*, p. 119 (19 October).

90. Ibid., p. 147 (5–6 November).

91. Thus *Novaia Zhizn'*, a newspaper of the Menshevik Internationalists, was accused of being schismatic. The Petrograd Bolshevik organization, it was claimed, had more than 40,000 organized workers, whereas only 4,000 or so followed the Internationalists, who were thus guilty of dividing the workers. In addition, they were defective in their refusal to dirty their hands in the class struggle. See *Proletarii*, 16 August 1917, pp. 5–6, article by V. Volodarskii.

92. See the powerful argument in Harding, *Lenin's Political Thought*, 2: 142–167, from which this account is taken.

93. Lenin, *Collected Works*, 25: 362. Also see *ibid.*, 26: 106.

94. The proletariat "has never been socialist, nor has it the slightest idea about socialism, it is only just awakening to political life." Ibid., 24: 236.

95. For Lenin's argument, see Trotsky, *History*, 1: 301–302; also see Lenin, "Can the Bolsheviks Retain State Power?" *Collected Works*, 26: 90–130 (1 October).

96. See *Minutes*, pp. 90–91.

97. Service, *The Bolshevik Party*, pp. 56–62.

98. Trotsky, *History*, 3: 134.

99. Bubnov, objecting to Nogin's arguments at a meeting of the Moscow regional party committee. See *MOK*, p. 264. Lenin says virtually the same thing: a political party "would have no right to exist . . . if it refused to take power when opportunity offers" (*Collected Works*, 26: 90).

100. *Minutes*, p. 97.

101. Ibid., p. 62. (Lenin letter from mid-September).

102. See, for example, Stalin's recorded remarks in *Minutes*, p. 185 (19 January 1918). "Comrade Stalin feels that it has been our Party's whole strength up to now that we have taken a very clear and definite position on all issues."

103. The most dramatic example was Lenin's excoriation of Kamenev and Zinoviev as strikebreakers. See *Minutes*, pp. 116–120.

104. See Service, *The Bolshevik Party*, pp. 45–46.

CONCLUSION

1. Dune, "Zapiski Krasnogvardeitsa," p. 9.

2. *Pechatnik*, 8 September 1917, pp. 2–3.

3. For example, see the 11 June resolution of the Menshevik-controlled Porokhovskii soviet, *RS*, 3: 193–194.

4. Smith, *Red Petrograd*, p. 70: "The month of March saw a plethora of small-scale, short, sometimes sectional struggles for higher wages." These were often very effective. Later wage struggles did not involve the dynamic extension of local solidarity as much as organized struggles on a broad scale.

5. For a sample of such remarks, see *Pechatnik*, 11 June 1917, p. 3; K. Bruk, "Organizatsiia soiuza metallistov," pp. 121–122; T. Shatilova, "Petrogradskii soiuz stroitel'nykh rabochikh v 1917–18 g.g.," in Anskii, *Professional'noe Dvizhenie v Petrograde*, pp. 178–180; Koenker, *Moscow Workers*, pp. 184–185; Rosenberg, "Workers and Workers' Control," pp. 93–96.

6. For example, the executive committee of the Baltic plant factory committee responded to a plea for solidarity from the Putilov workers in the following way: they should strike only when all peaceful means had been exhausted and when called upon by the metalworkers' union. Any isolated action, it urged, was tantamount to defeat. *Protokoly*, p. 270.

7. *Pechatnik*, 6 August 1917, pp. 3–4.

8. In Meller and Pankratova, *Rabochee Dvizhenie v 1917 Godu*, pp. 186–187.

9. *TPG*, 8 September 1917, p. 2. Also see Smith, *Red Petrograd*, pp. 72–73.

10. Anweiler, *The Soviets*, p. 255.

11. See Arendt, *On Revolution*, esp. pp. 246–248.

12. This seemed to be the case in the Petergof district soviet. See *RS*, 2: 91–92; also, in the Petrograd district soviet, ibid., p. 7.

13. Smith, *Red Petrograd*, p. 205. Keep, *Russian Revolution*, pp. 81–82, questions the democratic nature of factory committee elections but offers no evidence to support his claim.

14. Ferro, *Octobre*, p. 318.

15. *Protokoly*, p. 305 (27 July).

16. For a good example, see *Protokoly*, pp. 311–312. The factory committee leaders sponsored meetings in the factory so that workers could express their views on the leaders' performance. Later the factory committee itself suggested the need for reelections, in part to buttress its own authority (p. 351).

17. Quoted in Devlin, *Petrograd Workers*, p. 127.

18. Ferro, *Octobre*, p. 302.

19. Koenker, *Moscow Workers*, pp. 148–149.

20. *RKU*, 2: 240.

21. Devlin, *Petrograd Workers*, pp. 173–174.

22. *Tret'ia*, Introduction, p. vii.

23. In particular see Keep, *Russian Revolution*, pp. 128–140 and Ferro, *Octobre*, pp. 291–362.

24. Ferro, *Octobre*, pp. 312–317.

25. Moshe Lewin, *The Making of the Soviet System* (New York: Pantheon, 1985), pp. 49–56, 298.

26. For his very sketchy remarks see Richard Pipes, *Russia under the Old Regime* (New York: Scribners, 1974), pp. 313–318.

27. Trotsky, *History*, 3: 322.

Bibliography

ARCHIVES

Hoover Institution on War, Revolution, and Peace. Stanford, Calif. Nicolaevsky archive.

    Dune, Eduard. "Zapiski Krasnogvardeitsa." MS.

Tsentral'nyi Gosudarstvennyi Arkhiv Oktiabr'skoi Revoliutsii (TsGAOR). Central State Archive of the October Revolution. Moscow.

    f. 63   Secret Police (Okhrana)

    f. 102 Department of Police (Includes DPOO, DPI, and DPVI)

    f. 543 Investigatory Commission of the Supreme Revolutionary Tribunal of VTsIR.

Tsentral'nyi Gosudarstvennyi Istoricheskii Arkhiv (TsGIA). Central State Historical Archive. Leningrad.

    f. 20   Ministry of Finance

    f. 22   Ministry of Finance

    f. 23   Ministry of Trade and Industry

    f. 32   Association of Trade and Industry

    f. 40   Ministry of Finance

    f. 48   Association of Urals Mining-Industrialists

    f. 65   Lys'venskii Stock Society

    f. 126 All-Russian Union of Factory Owners

    f. 150 St. Petersburg Society of Factory Owners

    f. 273 Ministry of Communications

    f. 1153 State Council

    f. 1205 State Council

    f. 1276 Council of Ministers

    f. 1281 Ministry of Internal Affairs

    f. 1282 Ministry of Internal Affairs

    f. 1284 Ministry of Internal Affairs

f. 1405 Ministry of Justice

f. 1600 Ministry of Labor

Note: The archival references given in the text were copied directly from the documents. For this reason, the annotations, the order in which they are given, and the use of full words versus abbreviations vary. It was thought better to adhere to these as they appear in the documents rather than to systematize them. For example, *god* (year) usually precedes *delo* (file), but not always; *god* often appears as g.

DOCUMENTS

1905. Vospominaniia Chlenov SPB Soveta Rabochikh Deputatov. Edited by P. F. Kudelli and G. L. Shidlovskii. Leningrad: Priboi, 1926.

"Agrarnoe Dvizhenie v 1917 Godu po Dokumentam Glavnogo Zemel-'nogo Komiteta." *Krasniii Arkhiv* 14 (1926): 182–226.

The Bolsheviks and the October Revolution. Central Committee Minutes, August 1917–February 1918. London: Pluto Press, 1974.

The Debate on Soviet Power. Minutes of the All-Russian Central Executive Committee of Soviets. Edited by John Keep. Oxford: Oxford University Press, 1979.

Ekonomicheskoe Polozhenie Rossii Nakanune Velikoi Oktiabr'skoi Sotsialisticheskoi Revoliutsii. Dokumenty i Materialy, Mart-Oktiabr' 1917 g. Edited by A. L. Sidorov et al. 3 vols. Moscow-Leningrad: Akademiia Nauk SSSR, 1957–1967.

Fabrichno-Zavodskie Komitety Petrograda v 1917 Godu. Protokoly. Moscow: Nauka, 1979.

"Iiul'skie Volneniia 1914 g. v Peterburge. Arkhivnye Materialy." Edited by S. N. Valk and S. E. Livshits. *Proletarskaia Revoliutsia*, no. 7 (July 1924): 181–214; and nos. 8–9 (August–September 1924): 306–322.

Kommissiia dlia Sostavleniia Proeketa Zakona o Normirovanii Rabochego Vremeni v Fabrich-zavodskoi Promyshlennosti. Tainye Dokumenty Otnosiashchiesia k Zakonu l-go Iiunia 1897 Goda. Geneva: Union of Russian Social Democrats Abroad, 1898.

Leningradskii Rabochii v Bor'be za Vlast' Sovetov 1917 g. Edited by P. F. Kudelli. Leningrad: Gosudarstvennoe Izdatel'stvo, 1924.

Oktiabr'skaia Revoliutsiia i Fabzavkomy. Edited by P. N. Amosov. 2 vols. Moscow: VTsSPS, 1927.

Ot Gruppy Blagoeva k "Soiuzu Bor'by." Rostov-on-Don: Gosudarstvennoe Izdatel'stvo Donskoe Otdelenie, 1921.

Perepiska Sekretariata TsK RSDRP (b) s Mestnymi Partiinymi Organizatsiiami (Mart-Oktiabr' 1917). Moscow: Gosudarstvennoe Izdatel'stvo, 1957.

Pervyii Vserossiiskii S''ezd Sovetov R. i S. D. Vol. 1. Edited by V. N. Rakhmetov. Moscow-Leningrad: Gosudarstvennoe Izdatel'stvo, 1930.

Pervyii Vserossiiskii S''ezd Sovetov R. i S. D. Vol. 2. Edited by V. N. Rakhmetov and N. P. Miamalin. Moscow-Leningrad: Gosudarstvennoe Sotsial'no-Ekonomicheskoe Izdatel'stvo, 1931.

Petrogradskaia Obshchegorodskaia Konferentsiia RSDRP. Protokoly. Moscow: Gosudarstvennoe Izdatel'stvo, 1958.

"Protokoly Moskovskogo Oblastnogo Komiteta RSDRP (b) za Mai i Iiun' 1917 g." *Proletarskaia Revoliutsiia* 4 (April 1927): 235–281.

Putilovets v Trekh Revoliutsiiakh: Sbornik Materialov po Istorii Putilovskogo Zavoda. Edited by S. B. Okun et al. Leningrad: Gosudarstvennoe Izdatel'stvo "Istoriia Zavoda," 1933.

Put' k Oktiabriu: Sbornik Statei, Vospominanii i Dokumentov. Edited by S. Chernomordik. Moscow: Kooperativnoe Izdatel'stvo Moskovskii Rabochii, 1923–1926.

Putilovtsy v 1905 Godu: Sbornik Vospominanii Rabochikh. Edited by B. Pozern. Leningrad: Priboi, 1931.

Rabochee Dvizhenie v Rossii v XIX Veke. Vol. 2, pt. 2 (1875–1884). Edited by A. M. Pankratova. Moscow: Gosudarstvennoe Izdatel'stvo Politicheskoi Literatury, 1950.

Rabochee Dvizhenie v Rossii v XIX Veke. Vol. 3, pt. 2 (1890–1894). Edited by A. M. Pankratova. Moscow: Gosudarstvennoe Izdatel'stvo, 1952.

Rabochee Dvizhenie v Rossii v XIX Veke. Vol. 4, pt. 1 (1895–1897). Edited by L. M. Ivanov. Moscow: Izdatel'stvo Sotsial'no Ekonomicheskoi Literatury, 1961.

Rabochee Dvizhenie v Rossii v XIX Veke. Vol. 4, pt. 2 (1898–1900). Edited by L. M. Ivanov. Moscow: Izdatel'stvo Sotsial'no Ekonomicheskoi Literatury, 1963.

Rabochee Dvizhenie v Rossii v 1901–1904 gg. Sbornik Dokumentov. Edited by L. M. Ivanov. Leningrad: Nauka, 1975.

Rabochee Dvizhenie v Gody Voiny. Edited by M. G. Fleer. Moscow: Voprosy Truda, 1925.

Rabochee Dvizhenie v 1917 Godu. Edited by V. L. Meller and A. M. Pankratova. Moscow: Gosudarstvennoe Izdatel'stvo, 1926.

Rabochii Klass Urala v Gody Voiny i Revoliutsii v Dokumentakh i Materialakh. Vol. 2 (February–October 1917). Vol. 3 (October Revolution). Sverdlovsk: Izdanie Uralprofsoveta, 1927.

Rabochii Vopros v Kommissii V. N. Kokovtsova v 1905 g. With an introduction by B. A. Romanov. Moscow: Voprosy Truda, 1926.

Raionnye Sovety Petrograda v 1917 Godu. Edited by S. Valk et al. 3 vols. Moscow-Leningrad: Nauka, 1964–1966.

The Russian Provisional Government, 1917: Documents. Edited by R. P.

Browder and A. F. Kerensky. 3 vols. Stanford: Hoover, 1965.

Russkii Zakon i Rabochii. Materialy po Rabochemu Voprosu. Vol. 1. Preface by P. Struve. Stuttgart, 1902.

Sed'maia (Aprel'skaia) Vserossiiskaia Konferentsiia RSDRP (Bol'shevikov). Moscow: Gosudarstvennoe Izdatel'stvo, 1958.

Shestoi S''ezd RSDRP (Bol'shevikov). Protokoly. Moscow: Gosudarstvennoe Izdatel'stvo, 1958.

Tret'ia Vserossiiskaia Konferentsiia Professional'nykh Soiuzov. Moscow: Izdatel'stvo VTsSPS, 1927.

Uchrezhdenie Starost v Promyshlennykh Zavedeniiakh. St. Petersburg: St. Petersburger Zeitung, 1903.

Velikaia Oktiabr'skaia Sotsialisticheskaia Revoliutsiia. Dokumenty i Materialy: Revolutsionnoe Dvizhenie v Rossii Posle Sverzheniia Samoderzhaviia. Edited by L. S. Gaponenko. Moscow: Akademiia Nauk SSSR, 1957.

Revoliutsionnoe Dvizhenie v Rossii v Aprele 1917 g. Aprel'skii Krizis. Edited by L. S. Gaponenko. Moscow: Akademia Nauk SSSR, 1958.

Revoliutsionnoe Dvizhenie v Rossii V Mae-Iiune 1917 g. Iiun'skaia Demonstratsiia. Edited by D. A. Chugaev. Moscow: Akademiia Nauk SSSR, 1959.

Revoliutsionnoe Dvizhenie v Rossii v Avguste 1917 g. Razgrom Kornilovskogo Miatezha. Edited by D. A. Chugaev. Moscow: Akademiia Nauk SSSR, 1959.

Revoliutsionnoe Dvizhenie v Rossii v Sentiabre 1917 g. Obshchenatsional'nii Krizis. Edited by A. L. Sidorov. Moscow: Akademiia Nauk SSSR, 1961.

Vserossiiskoe Soveshchanie Sovetov. Edited by M. N. Pokrovskii. Moscow-Leningrad: Gosudarstvennoe Izdatel'stvo, 1928.

Vtoraia i Tret'ia Petrogradskie Obshchegorodskie Konferentsii Bol'shevikov v Iiule i Oktiabre 1917 g. Edited by P. F. Kudelli. Moscow-Leningrad: Gosudarstvennoe Izdatel'stvo, 1927.

Vtoroi Vserossiiskii S''ezd Sovetov. Edited by M. N. Pokrovskii. Moscow-Leningrad: Gosudarstvennoe Izdatel'stvo, 1928.

BOOKS AND ARTICLES

Abrahamian, Ervand. *Iran Between Two Revolutions.* Princeton: Princeton University Press, 1982.

Adams, Robert. *The Second Sowing.* San Francisco: Chandler, 1967.

Ainzaft, S. *Rabochee Dvizhenie do 1905.* Moscow: Izdatel'stvo MGSPS, 1924.

————. *Pervyi Etap Professional'nogo Dvizheniia v Rossii (1905–1907)*. 2 vols. Gomel: Gomelskii Rabochii, 1924, 1925.

————. *Zubatovshchina i Gaponovshchina*. Moscow: VTsSPS, 1922, 1924.

Akimov-Makhnovets, Vladimir. "Pervoe Maia v Rossii." Part 1. *Byloe*, no. 10 (October 1906): 163–192.

Andreev, A. M. *Sovety Rabochikh i Soldatskikh Deputatov Nakanune Oktiabria*. Moscow: Nauka, 1967.

Anskii, A., ed. *Professional'noe Dvizhenie v Petrograde v 1917 g.: Ocherki i Materialy*. Leningrad: Izdatel'stvo Leningradskogo Oblastnogo Soveta Profsoiuzov, 1928.

Anweiler, Oskar. *The Soviets*. New York: Pantheon, 1974.

Arendt, Hannah. *On Revolution*. New York: Penguin, 1977.

Arutiunov, G. A. *Rabochee Dvizhenie v Rossii v Periode Novogo Revoliutsionnogo Pod"ema 1910–1914 gg*. Moscow: Nauka, 1975.

Ascher, Abraham. *Pavel Axelrod and the Development of Menshevism*. Cambridge: Harvard University Press, 1972.

Axelrod, P. B. *Pis'ma P. B. Aksel'roda i Iu. O. Martova*. The Hague: Europe Printing, 1967.

Babushkin. Ivan. *Recollections (1893–1900)*. Moscow: Foreign Languages Publishing House, 1957.

Balabanov, M. *Ocherki po Istorii Rabochego Klassa v Rossii. Kapitalisticheskaia Rossiia*. Kiev: Izdatel'stvo Sorabkop, 1924.

————. *Ot 1905 k 1917 Godu. Massovoe Rabochee Dvizhenie*. Moscow: Gosudarstvennoe Izdatel'stvo, 1927.

————. "Rabochii Klass Nakanune Revoliutsii." In Anskii, *Professional'noe Dvizhenie v Petrograde v 1917 g.*: 5–28.

Balashov, S. "Rabochee Dvizhenie v Ivanovo-Voznesenske 1898–1905 gg." *Proletarskaia Revoliutsiia* 9, no. 44 (September 1925): 144–175.

Baron, Samuel. *Plekhanov*. Stanford: Stanford University Press, 1963.

Barnes, Thomas, and Gerald Feldman, eds. *Nationalism, Industrialization, and Democracy, 1815–1914*. Boston: Little, Brown & Co., 1972.

Barraclough, Geoffrey. *The Origins of Modern Germany*. New York: Capricorn, 1963.

Baturin, N. *Ocherk Istorii Sotsial-Demokratii v Rossii*. Moscow: Moskovskii Rabochii, 1922.

Belokurova, B. "Ot Rabochego Kontrolia k Rabochemu Upravleniiu. (Zavod 'Treugol'nik')." In Anskii, *Professional'noe Dvizhenie v Petrograde v 1917 g.*, 279–283.

Bendix, Reinhard. *Work and Authority in Industry*. Berkeley, Los Angeles, London: University of California Press, 1974.

————. *Nation-Building and Citizenship*. Berkeley, Los Angeles, London: University of California Press, 1977.

Berdiaev, Nicholas. *The Russian Idea*. London: The Centenary Press, 1947.

Berlin, Isaiah. *Russian Thinkers*. New York: Pelican, 1979.

Besançon, Alain. *The Intellectual Origins of Leninism*. Oxford: Basil Blackwell, 1981.

Bettelheim, Charles. *Class Struggles in the USSR*. New York: Monthly Review Press, 1976.

Bonnell, Victoria. *The Politics of Labor in Pre-Revolutionary Russia: Moscow Workers' Organizations 1905–1914*. Ph.D. diss., Harvard University, 1975.

———. *Roots of Rebellion*. Berkeley, Los Angeles, London: University of California Press, 1984.

Brenan, Gerald. *The Spanish Labyrinth*. Cambridge: Cambridge University Press, 1964.

Bricianer, Serge, ed. *Pannekoek and the Workers' Councils*. St. Louis: Telos Press, 1978.

Broué, Pierre, and Emile Temime. *The Revolution and the Civil War in Spain*. London: Faber and Faber, 1972.

Bruk, K. "Organizatsiia Soiuza Metallistov v 1917 g." In Anskii, *Professional'noe Dvizhenie v Petrograde v 1917 g.*, 116–130.

Bukhbinder, N. A. "O Zubatovshchine (Po Neizdannym Arkhivnym Materialam)". *Krasnaia Letopis'* 4 (1922): 289–335.

Bulkin, F. A. *Soiuz Metallistov 1906–1918 gg.* Moscow: Central Council of the Union of Metalworkers, 1926.

Burdzhalov, E. N. *Vtoraia Russkaia Revoliutsiia*. Moscow: Nauka, 1967.

Buzinov, Aleksei. *Za Nevskoi Zastavoi*. Moscow-Leningrad: Gosudarstvennoe Izdatel'stvo, 1930.

Bykov, A. K. *Fabrichnoe Zakonodatel'stvo i Razvitie ego v Rossii*. St. Petersburg: Pravda, 1909.

Bystrianskii, V. A., ed. *Istoriia Putilovskogo Zavoda, 1789–1917*. Moscow: OGIZ Gospolitizdat, 1941.

Cherevanin, N. *Organizatsionnyi Vopros*. Geneva: Social Democrat Party Press, 1904.

———. *Proletariat v Revoliutsii*. Vol. 2, *Bor'ba Obshchestvennykh Sil v Russkoi Revoliutsii*, edited by V. Gorn, V. Mech, and N. Cherevanin. Moscow: Izdatel'stvo Dvizhenie, 1907.

Chernov, Victor. *The Great Russian Revolution*. New York: Russell and Russell, 1966.

Chesneaux, Jean. *The Chinese Labor Movement, 1919–1927*. Stanford: Stanford University Press, 1968.

Cole, G. D. H., and Raymond Postgate. *The British Common People,*

1746–1946. London: Methuen, 1961.

Comfort, Richard. *Revolutionary Hamburg*. Stanford: Stanford Uᴿ˙ versity Press, 1966.

Dahrendorf, Ralf. *Society and Democracy in Germany*. New York: Norton, 1979.

Dan, Theodore. *The Origins of Bolshevism*. New York: Schocken, 1970.

Devlin, Robert. *Petrograd Workers and Workers' Factory Committees in 1917*. Ph.D. diss., State University of New York at Binghamton, 1976.

Dmitriev, N. "Primiritel'nye Kamery v 1917 Godu." In Anskii, *Professional'noe Dvizhenie v Petrograde v 1917 g.*, 78–100.

Dumont, Louis. *Homo Hierarchicus*. Chicago: University of Chicago Press, 1980.

El'nitskii, A. *Istoriia Rabochego Dvizheniia v Rossii*. Part 2. N.p.: Izdatel'stvo Proletarii, 1924.

Engelstein, Laura. *Moscow in the 1905 Revolution: A Study in Class Conflict and Political Organization*. Ph.D. diss., Stanford University, 1976.

Ermanskii, O. A. *Iz Perezhitogo*. Moscow-Leningrad: Gosudarstvennoe Izdatel'stvo, 1927.

Ferro, Marc. *The Russian Revolution of February 1917*. Englewood Cliffs, N. J.: Prentice-Hall, 1972.

———. *La Révolution de 1917. Octobre. Naissance d'une Société*. Paris: Aubier-Montaigne, 1976.

Field, Daniel. *Rebels in the Name of the Tsar*. Boston: Houghton Mifflin, 1976.

Fingarette, Herbert. *The Self in Transformation*. New York: Harper & Row, 1965.

Fisher, A. V. *V Rossii i v Anglii*. Moscow: Gosudarstvennoe Izdatel'stvo, 1922.

FitzGerald, Frances. *Fire in the Lake*. New York: Vintage, 1973.

Frankel, Jonathan, ed. *Vladimir Akimov on the Dilemmas of Russian Marxism. 1895–1903*. Cambridge: Cambridge University Press.

Friedlin, B. M. *Ocherki Istorii Rabochego Dvizheniia v Rossii v 1917 g.* Moscow: Nauka, 1967.

Frolov, A. *Probuzhdenie*. Gosudarstvennoe Izdatel'stvo Ukrainy, 1923.

Gaponenko, L. S. *Rabochii Klass Rossii v 1917 Godu*. Moscow: Nauka, 1970.

Garvi, P. A. *Vospominaniia Sotsialdemokrata*. New York, 1946.

Gerschenkron, Alexander. "Reflections on Economic Aspects of Revolutions." In *Internal War*, edited by Harry Eckstein, 180–204. New York: Free Press, 1964.

———. *Economic Backwardness in Historical Perspective*. New York: Praeger, 1965.

————. *Bread and Democracy in Germany.* New York: Fertig, 1966.

Getzler, Israel. *Martov: A Political Biography of a Russian Social Democrat.* Cambridge: Cambridge University Press, 1967.

Giffin, Frederick. "The Formative Years of the Russian Factory Inspectorate, 1882–1885." *Slavic Review* XXV, no. 4, pp. 641–651.

Golub, Stepan. *Cherez Plotinu Intelligenshchiny. Pis'mo Rabochego k Intelligentam i Rabochim Nashei Partii.* N. p.: Publication of the author. 1908.

Gots, M. R. "S. V. Zubatov." *Byloe*, year 1, no. 9 (September 1906): 63–69.

Grave, B. *K Istorii Klassovoi Bor'by v Gody Imperialisticheskoi Voiny.* Moscow-Leningrad: Gosudarstvennoe Izdatel'stvo, 1926.

Grunt, Ia. "Kolomenskaia Organizatsiia R. S. D. R. P. (b) i Oktiabr' 1917 g." In Chernomordik, *Put' k Oktiabriu.*

Gurevich, Liubov'. *Deviatoe Ianvaria.* Kharkov: Izdatel'stvo Proletarii, 1926.

Gusev, S. "Odessa v 1905 g." *Proletarskaia Revoliutsiia* No. 2, 49 (February 1926): 162–177.

Gvozdev, S. *Zapiski Fabrichnogo Inspektora. Iz Nabliudenii i Praktiki v Period 1894–1908 gg.* Moscow-Leningrad: Gosudarstvennoe Izdatel'stvo, 1925.

Haimson, Leopold. *The Russian Marxists and the Origins of Bolshevism.* Boston: Beacon, 1955.

————. "The Parties and the State: The Evolution of Political Attitudes." In *The Structure of Russian History*, edited by Michael Cherniavsky, 309–341. New York: Random House, 1970.

————. "The Problem of Social Stability in Urban Russia, 1905–1917." In *The Structure of Russian History*, edited by Michael Cherniavsky, 341–381. New York: Random House, 1970.

————. *The Mensheviks.* Chicago: University of Chicago Press, 1974.

Harding, Neil. *Lenin's Political Thought.* Combined paperback edition of vols. 1 and 2. London: Macmillan, 1983.

Hasegawa, Tsuyoshi. *The February Revolution. Petrograd 1917.* Seattle: University of Washington Press, 1981.

Herzen, Alexander. *From the Other Shore* and *the Russian People and Socialism.* Oxford: Oxford University Press, 1979.

Hirschman, Albert. *The Strategy of Economic Development.* New Haven: Yale University Press, 1961.

————. "Obstacles to Development: A Classification and a Quasi-Vanishing Act." In *A Bias for Hope*, 312–328. New Haven: Yale University Press, 1971.

Hosking, Geoffrey. *The Russian Constitutional Experiment.* Cambridge: Cambridge University Press, 1973.

Huntington, Samuel. *Political Order in Changing Societies.* New Haven: Yale University Press, 1968.

Ivanov, Boris. *Zapiski Proshlogo. Povest' iz Vospominanii Detstva i Iunoshestva Rabochego-Sotsialista.* Moscow: Gosudarstvennoe Izdatel'stvo, 1919.

Ivanov, L. M. "Preemstvennost' Fabrichno-Zavodskogo Truda i Formirovanie Proletariata v Rossii." In *Rabochii Klass i Rabochee Dvizhenie v Rossii, 1861–1917,* edited by L. M. Ivanov, 58–140. Moscow: Nauka, 1966.

Ivanov, L. M. "Vozniknovenie Rabochego Klassa." In *Istoriia Rabochego Klassa Rossii, 1861–1900,* edited by L. M. Ivanov, 9–61. Moscow: Nauka, 1972.

Ivanov, L. M., B. S. Itenberg, and Iu. N. Shebaldin. "Nachalo Puti." In *Istoriia Rabochego Klassa Rossii, 1861–1900,* edited by L. M. Ivanov, 62–129. Moscow: Nauka, 1972.

Ivanov-Razumnik, R. V. *Istoriia Russkoi Obshchestvennoi Mysli.* Vol. 2, 3d ed. St. Petersburg: M. M. Stasiulevich, 1911.

Johnson, Robert. *Peasant and Proletarian.* New Brunswick, N. J.: Rutgers University Press, 1979.

Kanatachikov, S. *Iz Istorii Moego Bytiia.* Vol. 1. Moscow: Izdatel'stvo Staryi Bol'shevik, 1932. Vol. 2. Moscow: Moskovskoe Tovarishchestvo Pisatelei, 1934.

Karelina, V. "Na Zare Rabochego Dvizheniia v S-Peterburge." *Krasnaia Letopis',* no. 4 (1922): 12–20.

———. "Pis'mo Rabotnitsy o 9 Ianvare 1905 g." *Krasnaia Letopis',* no. 1 (1922): 124–125.

Kaiurov, V. "Oktiabr'skie Ocherki." *Proletarskaia Revoliutsiia,* no. 7, 42 (July 1925): 136–156.

———. "Rabochee Dvizhenie v Pitere (1914 God)." *Proletarskaia Revoliutsiia,* no. 9, 44 (September 1925): 185–195.

Katkov, George. *Russia 1917. The February Revolution.* New York: Harper & Row, 1967.

Keep, John. *The Russian Revolution—A Study in Mass Mobilization.* New York: Norton, 1976.

Kern, Fritz. *Kingship and Law in the Middle Ages.* New York: Harper Torchbooks, 1970.

Kerr, Clark, John Dunlop, Frederick Harbison, and Charles Myers. *Industrialism and Industrial Man.* New York: Oxford University Press, 1960.

Kimerling, Elise. *The Disintegration of the Tsarist Order:* The Worker Question, 1905–1912. Masters' thesis, Brandeis University, 1977.

Kir'ianov, Iu. I. *Rabochye Iuga Rossii. 1914–Fevral' 1917.* Moscow: Nauka, 1971.

Klaas, G. K. *Moi Pervye Shagi na Revoliutsionnom Puti.* Leningrad: Priboi, 1926.

Kleinbort, L. M. *Kak Skladyvalas' Rabochaia Intelligentsiia.* Moscow: Izdatel'stvo VTsSPS, 1925.

Kochan, Lionel. *Russia in Revolution 1890–1918.* London: Granada, 1970.

Koenker, Diane. *Moscow Workers and the 1917 Revolution.* Princeton: Princeton University Press, 1981.

Kokovtsov, V. N. *Out of My Past.* Edited by H. H. Fisher. Stanford: Stanford University Press, 1935.

Korelin, A. P. "Russkii 'Politseiskii Sotsializm' (Zubatovshchina)." *Voprosy Istorii* (October 1968): 41–58.

———. "Krakh Ideologii 'Politseiskogo Sotsializma' v Tsarskoi Rossii." In *Istoricheskie Zapiski* 92 (1973): 109–152.

Korkunov, N. M. *Russkoe Gosudarstvennoe Pravo.* Vol. 1. St. Petersburg: M. M. Stasiulevich, 1899.

Kornhauser, William. *The Politics of Mass Society.* New York: Free Press, 1959.

Korolev, G. K. *Ivanovo-Kineshemskie Tekstil'shchiki v 1917 Godu.* Moscow: VTsSPS, 1927.

Korolev, P. *V Podvale.* Moscow-Leningrad: Gosudarstvennoe Izdatel'stvo, 1926.

Krieger, Leonard. *The German Idea of Freedom.* Boston: Beacon, 1957.

Kubikov, I. N. *Rabochii Klass v Russkoi Literature.* 3d ed. Ivanovo-Voznesensk: Osnova, 1926.

Kungarov, P. "Zapiski Rabochego." *Proletarskaia Revoliutsiia*, no. 4 (1922): 245–60.

Lande, Leo. "The Mensheviks in 1917." In *The Mensheviks*, edited by Leopold Haimson, 1–93. Chicago: University of Chicago Press, 1974.

Landes, David. "Japan and Europe: Contrasts in Industrialization." In *The State and Economic Enterprise in Japan*, edited by William Lockwood, 93–183. Princeton: Princeton University Press, 1965.

Landsberger, Henry, and Tim McDaniel. "Hypermobilization in Chile, 1970–1973." *World Politics* XXVIII (July 1976): 504–542.

Laverychev, V. Ia. *Tsarizm i Rabochii Vopros v Rossii (1861–1917 gg.)* Moscow: Mysl', 1972.

Laverychev, V. Ia., ed. *Rabochii Klass Rossii. 1907–Fevral' 1917 g.* Moscow: Nauka, 1982.

Laverychev, V. Ia. "Vliianie Voiny na Chislennost', Sostav i Polozhenie Rabochego Klassa." In *Rabochii Klass Rossii. 1907–Fevral' 1917 g.*, edited by V. Ia. Layerychev, 234–281. Moscow: Nauka, 1982.

Leiberov, I. P., and O. I. Shkaratan. "K Voprosu o Sostave Petrogradskikh Promyshlennykh Rabochikh v 1917 Godu." *Voprosy Istorii* (January 1961): 42–59.

Lelevich, G. "Lenskii Rasstrel." *Proletarskaia Revoliutsiia*, no. 5 (1922): 12–23.

Lenin, V. I. *Collected Works*. 4th ed. Moscow: Progress Publishers, 1964.

————. *What Is to Be Done?* New York: International Publishers, 1969.

Lewin, Moshe. *The Making of the Soviet System*. New York: Pantheon, 1985.

Lidtke, Vernon. *The Outlawed Party. Social Democracy in Germany, 1878–1890*. Princeton: Princeton University Press, 1966.

Lockwood, William. "Asian Triangle: China, India, Japan." *Foreign Affairs* 52, no. 4 (1974): 818–839.

Lorwin, Val. *The French Labor Movement*. Cambridge: Harvard University Press, 1954.

Lozinskii, Evgenii. *Itogi i Perspektivy Rabochego Dvizheniia*. St. Petersburg: Tipografiia V. Bezobrazova, 1909.

Luhmann, Niklas. *Trust and Power*. Chichester, U.K.: John Wiley, 1979.

Luxemburg, Rosa. *Rosa Luxemburg Speaks*. Edited by Mary-Alice Waters. New York: Pathfinder Press, 1970.

Macpherson, C. B. *The Political Theory of Possessive Individualism*. London: Oxford University Press, 1962.

Malia, Martin. *Alexander Herzen and the Birth of Russian Socialism*. Cambridge: Harvard University Press, 1961.

Malloy, James. "Social Security Policy and the Working Class in Twentieth-Century Brazil." *Journal of Interamerican Studies and World Affairs* 19, no. 1 (February 1977): 35–60.

Mandel, David. *The Development of Revolutionary Consciousness among the Industrial Workers of Petrograd between February and November 1917*. Ph.D. diss., Columbia University, 1977.

————. *The Petrograd Workers and the Fall of the Old Regime*. London: Macmillan, 1983.

————. *The Petrograd Workers and the Soviet Seizure of Power*. London: Macmillan, 1984.

Mannheim, Karl. *Ideology and Utopia*. New York: Harvest Books, 1936.

Manning, Roberta. *The Crisis of the Old Order in Russia*. Princeton: Princeton University Press, 1982.

Martov, Iu. *Sovremennaia Rossiia*. Geneva: Tipografiia "Soiuza Russkikh Sotsial'demokratov," 1898.

————. *Sotsialisty-Revoliutsionery i Proletariat*. St. Petersburg: Zhizn', 1907.

————. *Razvitie Krupnoi Promyshlennosti i Rabochee Dvizhenie v*

Rossii. Petrograd-Moscow: Kniga, 1923.

———. *Zapiski Sotsial-Demokrata*. Cambridge: Oriental Research Partners, 1975 (reprint of 1922 Berlin edition).

———. *Proletarskaia Bor'ba v Rossii*. St. Petersburg: N. Glagolev, n.d.

Martynov-Piker, A. "Vospominaniia Revoliutsionera." *Proletarskaia Revoliutsiia* 11, no. 46 (November 1925): 262–283.

Marx, Karl. *The Eighteenth Brumaire of Louis Bonaparte*. New York: International Publishers, 1963.

Maura, J. Romero. "The Spanish Case." In *Anarchism Today*, edited by David Apter and James Joll, 71–97. Garden City, N.Y.: Doubleday, 1972.

McDaniel, Tim. "Class and Dependency in Latin America." *Berkeley Journal of Sociology* XXI (1976–1977): 51–88.

Meisner, Maurice. "Utopian Socialist Themes in Maoism." In *Peasant Rebellion and Communist Revolution in Asia*, edited by John Wilson Lewis, 207–252. Stanford: Stanford University Press, 1974.

Mendel, Arthur. "On Interpreting the Fate of Imperial Russia." In *Russia Under the Last Tsar*, edited by Theofanis Stavrou, 13–42. Minneapolis: University of Minnesota, 1969.

Menitskii, I. A. *Russkoe Rabochee Dvizhenie i RS-DRP Nakanune Voiny (1912–1914)*. Moscow: Editorial Krasnaia Nov', 1923.

Michels, Robert. *Political Parties*. New York: Dover, 1959.

Mikhailov, Iakov. *Iz Zhizni Rabochego. Vospominaniia Chlena Peterburgskogo Soveta Rabochikh Deputatov 1905 Goda*. Leningrad: Priboi, 1925.

Miliukov, Paul. *Russia and Its Crisis*. New York: Collier, 1962.

———. *Political Memoirs 1905–1917*. Edited by Arthur Mendel. Ann Arbor: University of Michigan Press, 1967.

Miller, Wright. *Russians as People*. London: Phoenix House, 1960.

Mironov, K. *Iz Vospominanii Rabochego*. Moscow: Izdatel'stvo Molodaia Rossiia, 1906.

Moiseenko, Petr. *Vospominaniia Starogo Revoliutsionera*. Moscow: Mysl', 1966.

Monas, Sidney. *The Third Section*. Cambridge: Harvard University Press, 1961.

Montesquieu. *The Spirit of Laws*. Berkeley, Los Angeles, London: University of California Press, 1977.

Moore, Barrington. *Social Origins of Dictatorship and Democracy*. Boston: Beacon, 1966.

———. *Injustice. The Social Bases of Obedience and Revolt*. White Plains, N.Y.: M. E. Sharpe, 1978.

Morgan, David. *The Socialist Left and the German Revolution*. Ithaca, N.Y.: Cornell University Press, 1975.

Naumov, I. K. *Zapiski Vyborzhtsa*. Leningrad: Lenoblizdat, 1933.

Nevskii, V. "Ianvarskie Dni v Peterburge v 1905 g." *Krasnaia Letopis'*, no. 1 (1922): 13–74.

Nove, Alec. *An Economic History of the U.S.S.R.* Harmondsworth, England: Penguin, 1976.

Orlov, Kirill. *Zhizn' Rabochego-Revoliutsionera ot 1905 k 1917 g.* Leningrad: Priboi, 1925.

Orlovsky, Daniel. *The Limits of Reform: The Ministry of Internal Affairs in Imperial Russia, 1802–1881*. Cambridge: Harvard University Press, 1981.

Owen, Thomas. *Capitalism and Politics in Russia*. Cambridge: Cambridge University Press, 1981.

Ozerov, I. Kh. *Politika po Rabochemu Voprosu v Rossii za Poslednie Gody*. Moscow: Izdatel'stvo Tovarishchestva I. D. Sytina, 1906.

Pankratova, A. *Fabzakomy Rossii v Bor'be za Sotsialisticheskuiu Fabriku*. Moscow: Krasnaia Nov', 1923.

Parsons, Talcott, and Neil Smelser. *Economy and Society*. New York: Free Press, 1956.

Pazhitnov, K. A. *Polozhenie Rabochego Klassa v Rossii*. Vol. 3 *(Revoliutsionnyi Period—s 1905 do 1923 g.)* Leningrad: Put' k Znaniiu, 1924.

Perlman, Selig. *A Theory of the Labor Movement*. New York: Augustus Kelley, 1949.

Perrot, Michelle. *Les Ouvriers en Grève, France 1871–1890*. Paris: Mouton, 1974. 2 vols.

Peshekhonov, A. V. *K Voprosu ob Intelligentsii*. St. Petersburg: Russkoe Bogatstvo, 1906.

Petrov, A. K. *Rabochii Bol'shevik v Podpol'e*. Moscow: Novaia Moskva, 1925.

Petukhov, I. "Moi Kratkie Otryvochnye Vospominaniia o Lichɪvkh Perezhivaniiakh i o Prokhozhdenii Surovoi Shkoly Zhizni." In Cheɪ..ɔ-mordik, ed. *Put' k Oktiabriu*, 51–77.

Plekhanov, G. V. *Russkii Rabochii v Revoliutsionnom Dvizhenii*. In *Sochineniia*, vol. 3, edited by D. Riazanov, 121–205.

———. *Sochineniia*. Edited by D. Riazanov. Moscow-Petrograd: Gosudarstvennoe Izdatel'stvo, 1923.

Pipes, Richard. *Russia under the Old Regime*. New York: Scribners, 1974.

Prokopovich, S. N. *K Rabochemu Voprosu v Rossii*. St. Petersburg: E. D. Kuskovoi, 1905.

Rabinowitch, Alexander. *Prelude to Revolution. The Petrograd Bolsheviks and the July 1917 Uprising*. Bloomington: Indiana University Press, 1968.

———. *The Bolsheviks Come to Power*. New York: Norton, 1976.

Rabochie o Partiinom Raskole. Published by the Central Committee of the Russian Social Democratic Party. Geneva: Partiia, 1905.

Raeff, Marc. *Plans for Political Reform in Imperial Russia, 1730–1905.* Englewood Cliffs, N.J.: Prentice-Hall, 1966.

Raeff, Marc, ed. *Russian Intellectual History. An Anthology*. New Jersey: Humanities Press, 1978.

Ridley, Frederick. *Revolutionary Syndicalism in France*. Cambridge: Cambridge University Press, 1970.

Rieber, Alfred. *Merchants and Entrepreneurs in Imperial Russia*. Chapel Hill: University of North Carolina Press, 1982.

Rigby, T. H. *Communist Party Membership in the USSR, 1917–1967.* Princeton: Princeton University Press, 1968.

———. *Lenin's Government: Sovnarkom 1917–1922.* Cambridge: Cambridge University Press, 1979.

Rimlinger, Gaston. "Autocracy and the Factory Order in Early Russian Industrialization." *Journal of Economic History* XX, no. 1 (March 1960): 67–92.

Rosenberg, William. *Liberals in the Russian Revolution*. Princeton: Princeton University Press, 1974.

———. "Workers and Workers' Control in the Russian Revolution." *History Workshop* 5 (1978): 89–97.

Roth, Guenther. *The Social Democrats in Imperial Germany*. Totowa, N.J.: Bedminster Press, 1963.

Rougle, Charles. "The Intelligentsia Debate in Russia 1917–1918." In *Art, Society, Revolution. Russia 1917–1921*, edited by Nils Nilsson, 54–106. Stockholm: Almquist & Wiksell, 1979.

Rozanov, M. *Vasilii Andreevich Shelgunov*. Leningrad: Lenizdat, 1976.

Rudé, George. *The Crowd in History*. New York: John Wiley & Sons, 1964.

Salisbury, Harrison. *Black Night, White Snow: Russia's Revolutions 1905–1917*. Garden City, N.Y.: Doubleday, 1978.

Sapir, Boris. "Notes and Reflections on the History of Menshevism." In *The Mensheviks*, edited by Leopold Haimson, 349–388. Chicago: University of Chicago Press, 1974.

Sapronov, T. *Iz Istorii Rabochego Dvizheniia*. Ed. Victoria Bonnell. Newtonville, Mass.: Oriental Research Partners, 1976. (Reprint of 1925 edition)

Schapiro, Leonard. "The Political Thought of the First Provisional Government." In *Revolutionary Russia*, edited by Richard Pipes, 123–145. New York: Anchor, 1969.

———. *The Communist Party of the Soviet Union*. 2d ed. New York: Vintage, 1971.

――――. *The Russian Revolutions of 1917*. New York: Basic Books, 1984.

Schmitter, Philippe. "Still the Century of Corporatism?" In *The New Corporatism*, edited by Frederick Pike and Thomas Stritch, 85–131. Notre Dame, Ind.: University of Notre Dame Press, 1974.

Schneiderman, Jeremiah. *Sergei Zubatov and Revolutionary Marxism. The Struggle for the Working Class in Tsarist Russia*. Ithaca, N.Y.: Cornell University Press, 1976.

Schorske, Carl. *German Social Democracy 1905–1917: The Development of the Great Schism*. New York: John Wiley & Sons, 1955.

Schumpeter, Joseph. *Capitalism, Socialism, and Democracy*. 3d ed. New York: Harper & Row, 1962.

Schwarz, Solomon. *The Russian Revolution of 1905*. Chicago: University of Chicago Press, 1967.

Selitskii, V. I. *Massy v Bor'be za Rabochii Kontrol'*. Moscow: Mysl', 1971.

Service, Robert. *The Bolshevik Party in Revolution*. London: Macmillan, 1979.

Shapovalov, A. I. *Po Doroge k Marksizmu. Vospominaniia Rabochego Revoliutsionera*. Moscow: Gosudarstvennoe Izdatel'stvo, 1922.

Sharyi, V. "Pravo Soiuzov." *Narodnoe Khoziaistvo* year 6, book 1 (January–February 1905): 84–100.

Shatilova, T. "Petrogradskii Soiuz Stroitel'nykh Rabochikh v 1917–18 g.g." In Anskii, *Professional'noe Dvizhenie v Petrograde v 1917 g.*, 175–190.

――――. "Petrogradskoe Obshchestvo Zavodchikov i Fabrikantov v Bor'be s Rabochim Dvizheniem v 1917 Godu." In Anskii, *Professional'noe Dvizhenie v Petrograde v 1917 g.*, 101–115.

Shchatsillo, K. F. "Rabochee Dvizhenie v Gody Pervoi Mirovoi Voiny." In *Rabochii Klass Rossii 1907–Fevral' 1917 g.*, edited by V. Ia. Layerychev, 281–337. Moscow: Nauka, 1982.

Shchatsillo, K. F. "Rabochii Klass v Fevral'skoi Revoliutsii." In *Rabochii Klass Rossii 1907–Fevral' 1917 g.*, edited by V. Ia. Layerychev, 337–374. Moscow: Nauka, 1982.

Sher, V. V. *Istoriia Professional'nogo Dvizheniia Pechatnogo Dela v Moskve*. Moscow: Nauka, 1911.

Shishkin, V. F. *Tak Skladyvalas' Revoliutsionnaia Moral'*. Moscow: Mysl', 1967.

Shliapnikov, Aleksandr. *Semnadtsatyi God*. Vol. 1. Moscow-Petrograd: Gosudarstvennoe Izdatel'stvo, 1923.

Shorter, Edward, and Charles Tilly. *Strikes in France*. Cambridge: Cambridge University Press, 1974.

Shotman, A. "Zapiski Starogo Bol'shevika." Part one: *Proletarskaia Rev-*

oliutsiia, no. 9 (1922): 138–153; Part two: no. 11 (1922): 91–116.

Siegelbaum, Lewis. "The Workers' Groups and the War-Industries Committees: Who Used Whom?" *The Russian Review* 39, no. 2 (April 1980): 150–180.

Sivtsov, A. "Profdvizhenie Sredi Rabochikh Kozhevnikov." In Anskii, *Professional'noe Dvizhenie v Petrograde v 1917 g.*, 131–150.

Skocpol, Theda. "Explaining Revolutions: In Quest of a Social-Structural Approach." In *The Uses of Controversy in Sociology*, edited by Lewis Coser and Otto Larsen, 155–175. New York: Free Press, 1976.

———. *States and Social Revolutions*. Cambridge: Cambridge University Press, 1979.

———. "Rentier State and Shi'a Islam in the Iranian Revolution." *Theory and Society* 11 (1982): 265–283.

Smith, M. G. "On Segmentary Lineage Systems." *Journal of the Royal Anthropological Institute* 86 (1956): 39–80.

Smith, Steven. *Red Petrograd*. Cambridge: Cambridge University Press, 1983.

Sobolev, G. L. *Revoliutsionnoe Soznanie Rabochikh i Soldat Petrograda v 1917 Godu*. Leningrad: Nauka, 1973.

Sombart, Werner. *Socialism and the Socialist Movement*. New York: Dutton, 1909.

Somov, S. I. "Iz Istorii Sotsialdemokraticheskogo Dvizheniia v Peterburge v 1905 Godu. (Lichnye Vospominaniia)." *Byloe*. Part one: 4, no. 16 (1907): 22–55; Part two: 5, no. 17 (1907): 152–178.

Squire, P. S. *The Third Department*. Cambridge: Cambridge University Press, 1968.

Stavrou, Theofanis, ed. *Russia under the Last Tsar*. Minneapolis: University of Minnesota Press, 1969.

Sukhanov, N. N. *The Russian Revolution 1917*. New York: Harper, 1962.

Sulimov. "Vospominaniia Obukhovtsa (1900–1903)." *Proletarskaia Revoliutsiia*, no. 12 (1922): 145–170.

Suny, Ronald. *The Baku Commune 1917–1918*. Princeton: Princeton University Press, 1972.

———. "Toward a Social History of the October Revolution." *American Historical Review* 88, no. 1 (1983): 31–52.

Surh, Gerald. "Petersburg Workers in 1905: Strikes, Workplace Democracy, and the Revolution." Ph.D. diss., University of California, Berkeley, 1979.

———. "Petersburg's First Mass Labor Organization: The Assembly of Russian Workers and Father Gapon." *Russian Review*. Part one: 40, no. 3 (July 1981): 241–262; Part two: 40, no. 4 (October 1981): 412–441.

Sviatlovskii, V. V. *Professional'noe Dvizhenie v Rossii*. St. Petersburg: Izdanie M. V. Pirozhkova, 1907.

Svirskii, A. I. *Zapiski Rabochego*. Moscow-Leningrad: Zemlia i Fabrika, 1925.

Szamuely, Tibor. *The Russian Tradition*. New York: McGraw-Hill, 1974.

Takhtarev, K. M. *Ocherk Peterburgskogo Rabochego Dvizheniia 90-x Godov*. 2d ed. St. Petersburg: Tipografiia V. Ia. Mil'shtein, 1906.

Tilly, Charles. "Reflections on the History of European Statemaking." In *The Formation of National States in Western Europe*, edited by Charles Tilly, 3–83. Princeton: Princeton University Press, 1975.

———. *From Mobilization to Revolution*. Reading, Mass.: Addison-Wesley, 1978.

Timofeev, P. *Chem Zhivet Zavodskii Rabochii*. St. Petersburg: N. N. Klobukov, 1905.

Tocqueville, Alexis de. *The Old Regime and the French Revolution*. Garden City, N.Y.: Doubleday/Anchor, 1955.

———. *The European Revolution*. Garden City, N.Y.: Doubleday/Anchor, 1959.

Touraine, Alain. *Vie et Mort du Chili Populaire*. Paris: Editions du Seuil, 1973.

———. *Les Sociétés Dépendantes: Essais sur l'Amérique Latine*. Paris: Gembloux, 1976.

Trotsky, Leon. *The History of the Russian Revolution*. 3 vols. London: Sphere Books, 1967.

———. *My Life*. New York: Pathfinder, 1970.

———. *1905*. New York: Random House, 1971.

Tugan-Baranovsky, M. I. *The Russian Factory in the Nineteenth Century*. Homewood, Ill.: The American Economic Association, 1970.

Turgenev, Ivan. *On the Eve*. Harmondsworth, England: Penguin, 1950.

Ulam, Adam. *The Unfinished Revolution*. New York: Vintage, 1960.

———. *The Bolsheviks*. New York: Collier, 1968.

———. *Russia's Failed Revolutions*. New York: Basic Books, 1981.

Valentinov, Nikolai. *The Early Years of Lenin*. Ann Arbor: University of Michigan Press, 1969.

Valk, S. "Materialy k Istorii Pervogo Maia v Rossii." *Krasnaia Letopis'*, no. 4 (1922): 250–288.

Varzar, V. E. *Statisticheskiia Svedeniia o Stachkakh Rabochikh na Fabrikakh i Zavodakh za Desiatiletie 1895–1904 Goda*. St. Petersburg: Tipografiia V. Kirshbaum, 1905.

Volobuev, P. V. *Proletariat i Burzhuaziia Rossii v 1917 g.* Moscow: Mysl', 1964.

Vol'shtein, Liza. "Zapiski Fabrichnoi Rabotnitsy." *Proletarskaia Revoliutsiia,* no. 9 (1922): 160–1181.

Von Laue, Theodore. "Factory Inspection under the 'Witte System': 1892–1903." *The American Slavic and East European Review* XIX (October 1960): 347–362.

———. "Russian Peasants in the Factory 1892–1904." *Journal of Economic History* XXI, no. 1 (March 1961): 61–81.

———. *Sergei Witte and the Industrialization of Russia.* New York: Atheneum, 1963.

Vovchik, A. F. *Politika Tsarizma po Rabochemu Voprosu v Predrevoliutsionnom Periode.* L'vov: Izdatel'stvo L'vovskogo Universiteta, 1964.

Waisman, Carlos. *Modernization and the Working Class.* Austin: University of Texas Press, 1982.

Walicki, Andrzej. *The Controversy over Capitalism.* Oxford: Oxford University Press, 1969.

———. *A History of Russian Thought from the Enlightenment to Marxism.* Stanford: Stanford University Press, 1979.

Walzer, Michael. *The Revolution of the Saints.* New York: Atheneum, 1968.

Weber, Max. *Economy and Society.* Edited by Guenther Roth and Claus Wittich. New York: Bedminster Press, 1968.

Weber, Max. *Istoricheskii Ocherk Osvoboditel'nogo Dvizheniia v Rossii i Polozhenie Burzhuaznoi Demokratii.* Kiev: Chokolov Press, 1906.

Weffort, Francisco. "State and Mass in Brazil." In *Masses in Latin America,* edited by Irving L. Horowitz, 385–407. New York: Oxford University Press, 1970.

Wildman, Allan. *The Making of a Workers' Revolution: Russian Social Democracy, 1891–1903.* Chicago: University of Chicago Press, 1967.

———. *The End of the Russian Imperial Army.* Princeton: Princeton University Press, 1980.

Wolfe, Bertram. *Three Who Made a Revolution.* New York: Delta, 1964.

Wolin, Sheldon. *Politics and Vision.* Boston: Little, Brown, 1960.

Woodside, Alexander. *Community and Revolution in Vietnam.* Boston: Houghton Mifflin, 1976.

Wortman, Richard. *The Development of a Russian Legal Consciousness.* Chicago: University of Chicago Press, 1976.

Yaney, George. *The Urge to Mobilize.* Urbana: University of Illinois Press, 1982.

Zaionchkovskii, P. A. *Rossiiskoe Samoderzhavie v Kontse XIX Stoletiia.* Moscow: Mysl', 1970.

Zelnik, Reginald. "Essay Review: Russian Workers and the Revolutionary Movement." *Journal of Social History* 6, no. 2, pp. 214–237.

———. *Labor and Society in Tsarist Russia. The Factory Workers of St. Petersburg, 1855–1870.* Stanford: Stanford University Press, 1971.

———. "The Peasant and the Factory." In *The Peasant in Nineteenth-Century Russia,* edited by Wayne Vucinich, 158–190. Stanford: Stanford University Press, 1968.

———. "Populists and Workers. The First Encounter Between Populist Students and Industrial Workers in St. Petersburg, 1871–74." *Soviet Studies* XXIV, no. 2 (October 1972): 251–269.

———. "Russian Bebels: An Introduction to the Memoirs of Semen Kanatchikov and Matvei Fisher." *The Russian Review.* Part one: 35, no. 3 (1976): 249–290; Part two: 35, no. 4 (1976): 417–448.

NEWSPAPERS

Delo Naroda
Golos Truda
Izvestiia Vserossiskogo Soiuza Obshchestv Zavodchikov i Fabrikantov
Metallist
Osvobozhdenie
Pechatnik
Pravda
Proletarii
Proletarskii Prizyv
Rabochaia Gazeta
Rabochaia Mysl'
Rabochii Put'
Rech'
Torgovlia-Promyshlennaia Gazeta
Vestnik Ministerstva Truda

Index

Designer: U.C. Press Staff
Compositor: Asco Trade Typesetting Ltd.
Text: 10/12 Sabon
Display: Sabon
Printer: Braun-Brumfield, Inc.
Binder: Braun-Brumfield, Inc.